ALCATRAZ

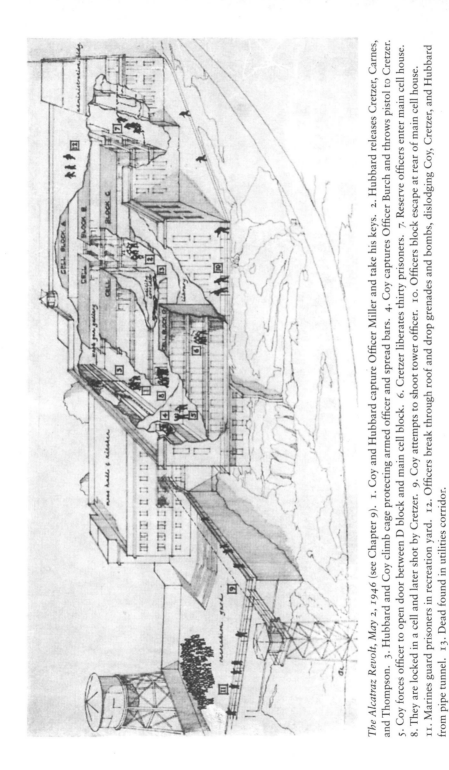

The Alcatraz Revolt, May 2, 1946 (see Chapter 9). 1. Coy and Hubbard capture Officer Miller and take his keys. 2. Hubbard releases Cretzer, Carnes, and Thompson. 3. Hubbard and Coy climb cage protecting armed officer and spread bars. 4. Coy captures Officer Burch and throws pistol to Cretzer. 5. Coy forces officer to open door between D block and main cell block. 6. Cretzer liberates thirty prisoners. 7. Reserve officers enter main cell house. 8. They are locked in a cell and later shot by Cretzer. 9. Coy attempts to shoot tower officer. 10. Officers block escape at rear of main cell house. 11. Marines guard prisoners in recreation yard. 12. Officers break through roof and drop grenades and bombs, dislodging Coy, Cretzer, and Hubbard from pipe tunnel. 13. Dead found in utilities corridor.

ALCATRAZ

THE GANGSTER YEARS

David Ward

WITH GENE KASSEBAUM

UNIVERSITY OF CALIFORNIA PRESS

BERKELEY   LOS ANGELES   LONDON

University of California Press, one of the most
distinguished university presses in the United States,
enriches lives around the world by advancing
scholarship in the humanities, social sciences, and
natural sciences. Its activities are supported by the
UC Press Foundation and by philanthropic contributions from individuals and institutions. For more
information, visit www.ucpress.edu.

University of California Press
Berkeley and Los Angeles, California

University of California Press, Ltd.
London, England

Library of Congress Cataloging-in-Publication Data

Ward, David A. –.
    Alcatraz : the gangster years / David A. Ward ;
with Gene G. Kassebaum.
      p. cm.
    Includes bibliographical references and index.
    ISBN 978-0-520-25607-1 (cloth : alk. paper)
    1. United States Penitentiary, Alcatraz Island,
California. 2. Prisons—California—Alcatraz
Island—History. 3. Alcatraz Island (Calif.)—
History. I. Kassebaum, Gene G. II. Title.
HV9474.A53A46 2008
365'.979461—dc22   2008021232

Manufactured in the United States of America

18 17 16 15 14 13 12 11 10 09
10 9 8 7 6 5 4 3 2 1

This book is printed on Natures Book, which contains
50% post-consumer waste and meets the minimum
requirements of ANSI/NISO Z39.48–1992 (R 1997)
(*Permanence of Paper*).

For Renée, Doug, and Andy

CONTENTS

PREFACE

My interest in Alcatraz—what it was like to do time there and how the experience affected prisoners in the long term—originated in the late 1950s, when I was interviewing prisoners and staff at the federal penitentiary at Terre Haute, Indiana, as part of a research team from the University of Illinois.[1] In the course of this study of five federal prisons, I also interviewed prisoners at Leavenworth, a long-established maximum-security penitentiary. There I met an inmate who had been at Alcatraz. Most staff and prisoners at Leavenworth viewed Alcatraz—still in operation at the time—as a kind of mystery prison, an island fortress where the most notorious, dangerous, and volatile prisoners from throughout the federal prison system were locked up under conditions of super-maximum custody.

Spiro Karabelas came to the interview from a disciplinary segregation cell. Having no better place to go, and enjoying the opportunity to smoke, he was quite expansive as he reviewed his experiences on "the Rock." Among many topics that came up, he explained how he had learned to pass hours and days in solitary confinement by "taking trips"—reliving in his mind, in infinite detail and minute by minute, those days and events in his life he savored most. This was the first description of various psychological mechanisms for coping with prolonged isolation that I would hear in talking with Alcatraz inmates. Karabelas seemed to be rather proud that he had not been "broken" by the regimen. This comment provided my first insight into the view that doing time on the Rock was considered the ultimate test of courage and inner strength for a certain class of convicts.

The idea that going to and toughing it out at Alcatraz might, for some convicted felons, represent an opportunity to show that a man could take the worst that the federal government could dish out was brought home by another event that occurred while I was at Leavenworth. As part of my own research for a doctoral dissertation on prison rule enforcement,

I attended a meeting of the disciplinary "court" chaired by the captain. Included in the committee's business were routine reviews of men who had been in "the hole" (disciplinary segregation or isolation) for a considerable time. In this case the inmate was brought from a dark solitary confinement cell into the hearing room, squinting his eyes in the bright light, a guard on either side. He raged from the moment he entered the room, announcing in a loud voice that he was not going to conform to prison rules, and yelled at the captain, "You might as well send me to the Rock!" The captain snapped back, "We're not gonna send you to the Rock, you're nothing but a kiddy-car bandit." The implication was clear: a transfer to Alcatraz was for some convicts a badge of honor, something to be achieved.

My next encounter with an Alcatraz inmate came during the postrelease phase of the University of Illinois study. I was stationed for a year in the federal probation office in St. Louis, Missouri, as part of the project's plan to find out what was happening to men we had interviewed in prison after they were released and back in what they called "the free world." One of these men, a Leavenworth parolee named Robert Robertson, had earned a long stint at Alcatraz by attempting to capture a crane being used for a construction project at Leavenworth in order to hoist himself and several other men over the prison's thirty-foot-high walls. In the course of my discussions with him, Robertson talked about his years at Alcatraz, focusing not on physical or psychological deprivation or punishment, but on how the prison affected his criminal career. He described a life, before Alcatraz, spent "running around," engaging in a rapid sequence of illegal activities interrupted only by occasional periods in jail or prison where the prospect of release in the not-too-distant future kept him oriented toward life and prospects on the streets. When he found himself at Alcatraz, Robertson realized that he wasn't going anywhere for a long time. And with time outside his cell limited to three twenty-minute meals, an eight-hour work assignment, and a few hours in the yard on weekends, he was faced with many hours of distraction-free time alone in his cell. This, he said, afforded him an opportunity to reflect, for the first time in his life, on the costs and benefits of his criminal career and consider a different course.

Robertson's response to doing time in a supermaximum setting—which could be summarized by the phrase "settling down"—was at variance with the then-current literature on the consequences of long-term confinement. Remembering what Karabelas had said about Alcatraz, and aware of the mystery and controversy surrounding the prison, I realized that Alcatraz was a very different kind of prison and that a study of its convict culture could provide valuable insights.

In the early 1960s, when I had moved to UCLA to work on a study of psychologically based treatment programs in California prisons, I wrote to the director of the Federal Bureau of Prisons, James V. Bennett, and asked if he would authorize a sociological study of Alcatraz. Familiar with my work on the University of Illinois project, Bennett approved a visit to the island for me and for my UCLA colleague Gene Kassebaum. In June 1962, with a letter from the director in hand, we traveled to San Francisco and boarded the prison launch for Alcatraz. It happened that our visit came immediately after the sensational escape by the Anglin brothers and Frank Morris, immortalized in the Clint Eastwood film *Escape from Alcatraz*. While the staff was preoccupied with the search for the missing prisoners and investigating the failures in the security system that made the escape possible, there was agreement that a study of inmates' adaptations to life on the island would begin once a research proposal had been developed and funding obtained. But that escape, and another the following December, provided the justification the Bureau of Prisons was looking for to cease operations. By the end of March 1963 Alcatraz was empty. The opportunity to study an unusual prison culture in operation had disappeared with the transfer of the prisoners and staff to federal penitentiaries across the country. The prison sat empty for ten years.

In fall 1973 Alcatraz Island was incorporated into the newly established Golden Gate National Recreation Area; it opened for public tours by the National Park Service.[2] For the first time, members of the public were allowed to see for themselves the prison that for more than thirty years had been the source of so much controversy and mystery. Lingering questions about the prison and the prisoners were given new life. Had some prisoners actually been chained to the bars of cells in "dungeons" located under the floor of the cell house? Had men been kept in isolation for months or years until they went insane? Had prisoners suffered physical abuse? And, the most frequent question, had the minds of all the prisoners been damaged by being locked up in a prison called "America's Devil's Island," a prison with no parole?

Since it began operations as a federal prison in 1934, Alcatraz had been kept under a shroud of secrecy. Prison employees had been strictly forbidden to talk with anyone about prisoners or events on the island; reporters had never been allowed to visit or talk to prisoners; nearly all communication between the island and the outside world had been effectively shut off. Even after the prison ceased operations, former members of the prison staff continued to assume they could not talk about Alcatraz to anyone outside the Bureau of Prisons. In addition, the Bureau had never undertaken any systematic documentation of policies, procedures, and events on the island prison. Due to the lack of official information, everything that was "known" about Alcatraz had come from the published stories of former inmates, media accounts based on terse government press releases, sensational testimony from prisoners on trial for murders that occurred on the island, rumors, and pure speculation.

Faced with the need to provide information about Alcatraz to the public—to "interpret" the island as a national historic landmark—park rangers had to rely on the stories offered by several ex-convicts who lived in the Bay Area, along with the mass of popular knowledge about the prison that had accumulated over the years. Much of this information, because of its origins, was biased, incomplete, and inaccurate. The crowds of U.S. citizens and foreign visitors who began touring the island left with the impression that Alcatraz had been a place of brutal punishment.[3]

James Bennett, director of the Bureau of Prisons from 1937 to 1964, believed strongly that the reality of confinement for most of the inmates had not been as horrific as it was portrayed by the former prisoners. In particular, he was personally acquainted with the cases of more than a few former Alcatraz inmates who had not only survived their time on the island with their mental health intact but had gone on to build law-abiding lives in the free world. Bennett suspected that a significant number of former Alcatraz cons fell into this category, but the Bureau had never assembled any data on what happened to the prisoners after they had served their sentences and were finally released from prison. No one, including the former director, knew how many former Alcatraz inmates had resumed their lives of crime on the outside and how many had managed to stay out of prison. Filling this gap in knowledge was an assumption held by most Bureau officials, professional penologists, university criminologists, and even Alcatraz staff and prisoners: that confinement on the Rock was unlikely to have helped change "habitual and incorrigible" offenders into law-abiding citizens.

Mr. Bennett remembered my original study proposal and urged me to revive the project, with the inclusion of an effort to find out what had happened to the inmates after they were paroled from their federal prison sentences. In September 1974 Bennett and I met with Norman A. Carlson, who had been appointed Bureau director in 1965; he agreed that a study to accurately determine what happened to the inmates in the Bureau's experiment with a maximum-custody, minimum-privilege penitentiary would be worthwhile. It would be one of only a handful of studies of American penitentiaries that systematically collected data on both the in-prison and postrelease experiences of the prisoners.

Norman Carlson began providing a high level of support and assistance that continued in many ways throughout the life of the project. He authorized Annesley K. Schmidt of the Bureau's central office to contact officials at every federal prison and at federal records centers across the country and ask them to locate the records of former Alcatraz inmates. A regional records center in the state of Washington received the Bureau's request just in time to save upward of four hundred sets of files that were sitting on a loading dock awaiting destruction.[4]

The inmate and administrative records, including those at Bureau headquarters in Washington, D.C., were shipped to the Archives Division of the University of Minnesota Library, where supervisor Maxine Clapp arranged for their storage in a private, secure room. Ms. Clapp advised me and other members of the research staff on the proper care of aging records. Rubber bands that were cutting into folders were removed; crumbling newspaper and magazine articles and torn pages were copied to avoid further handling of fragile paper. Records from the federal prisons in which the inmates served different parts of their sentences, in addition to their time at Alcatraz, were brought together and the entire collection was organized by Alcatraz commitment number. The total number of men committed to Alcatraz was 1,546, but commitment numbers totaled 1,576, because twenty-eight men were sent there twice and one (James Audett) had three commitments.

While the Alcatraz records were being sent to the University of Minnesota for use in the study, their final disposition became subject to an order to the Bureau of Prisons by the General Services Administration: destroy old files and reports in order to make room for new records. To assure the long-term preservation of the Alcatraz records, I solicited letters of support from prominent historians, sociologists, and legal scholars at major universities to make the case that these records had enough "historic value" to be saved. In addition, Norman Carlson instructed his staff to compile a list of other notable inmates whose files would also be preserved. The National Archives, which already housed a small number of administrative records in Washington, D.C., shortly thereafter classified the Alcatraz inmate and administrative records and Bureau files as having historic value and agreed to take custody of the collection when my research was completed; the collection was then placed in the Western Regional Office of the National Archives in San Bruno, California.

(Historians, criminologists, and other writers, including former inmates and employees and their family members, who have since been able to take advantage of this unique collection of records should know that inmate records and administrative files are not routinely rounded up from federal prisons and sent to the National Archives. If this project had not been funded by the National Institute of Justice and the case made for the preservation of the Alcatraz records, the collection at San Bruno would not exist.)[5]

Before we had received funds for the project from the National Institute of Justice (NIJ), Anne Schmidt of the Bureau's Research Division performed a preliminary analysis that produced surprising results: tabulating arrest, conviction, and return-to-prison records of 975 Alcatraz prisoners who had been out of prison for more than five years, she discovered that only 37 percent of these men officially labeled as "habitual and incorrigible" offenders had returned to prison and nearly two-thirds were still living in the free world. Of those who had not returned to prison, 27 percent had been arrested for minor offenses only, offenses that either did not result in imprisonment or resulted in sentences of less than one year in local jails, and 73 percent had no reported arrests.[6] These early surprising results motivated us to design a follow-up phase of the investigation that would focus on identifying the "successes" (men not returned to prison) and determining how they overcame the significant odds against them. We recognized, however, that locating the men who had not been returned to prison would not be easy; although the Bureau of Prisons knew exactly where all the "failures" were locked up, the only people who might know the whereabouts of the successes were dozens of federal probation officers, some retired, scattered over the country. (Federal probation officers supervise prisoners released on parole as well as offenders placed on probation.)

To be successful, the project required that additional information be obtained from the files of two federal agencies besides the Bureau of Prisons—the Federal Bureau of Investigation and the Administrative Office of U.S. Courts. At the outset of the project, the FBI agreed to Norman Carlson's request that the "rap sheets" (arrest and conviction records) of nearly all the 1,547 Alcatraz inmates be sent to BOP headquarters; the only records not available were those for eighteen ex-prisoners then over the age of eighty. The FBI provided additional information beginning in 1984, after Director Carlson, to test the new spirit of "interagency cooperation" offered by FBI Director William Webster in the post–J. Edgar Hoover era, asked the FBI to allow me access to investigative reports of "incidents" (murders, riots, escapes) that occurred at Alcatraz from 1934 to 1963, as well as the files of high-profile offenders sent to the island—Al Capone, George "Machine Gun" Kelly, Alvin Karpis, Arthur "Dock" Barker, and other "public enemies." Special Agent R. G. Schweickhardt provided valuable assistance as I examined these investigative files, explaining FBI procedures and the organization of files, and verifying J. Edgar Hoover's "H" signature and handwritten comments on certain records.[7]

The Administrative Office of U.S. Courts provided the third important group of records: the files of parolees and men released under conditional/ mandatory provisions.[8] Following authorization from Administrative Office headquarters, I sent lists of Alcatraz releasees to the federal probation offices in various judicial districts across the country, requesting what records and information they could provide for the men assigned to their jurisdictions. These probation offices forwarded the files of closed cases to the federal probation office in Minneapolis, where they were stored, organized, and temporarily made available to me and the University of Minnesota research staff. In addition to Garold Ray, other chief probation officers helped us establish contact with active and retired probation officers who had supervised Alcatraz parolees and conditional releasees. These agents provided important information about their clients' experiences, contacted men still under supervision, and, most important, called releasees who had successfully completed parole or conditional release to ask if they would agree to be interviewed. Their assistance was needed because we did not want to directly contact these ex-prisoners when we did not know what their work or family situations were, or whether they would be able to talk freely over the telephone with a stranger about scheduling an interview.

The cooperation and assistance of federal probation offices, particularly those in Boston, Washington, D.C., Dallas, Kansas City, San Diego, Los Angeles, Sacramento, San Francisco, and Portland, Oregon, was essential for a project that, unlike most prison studies, sought to identify men who never returned to prison. The complete, even enthusiastic, assistance provided by the probation officers, along with the personnel at the Bureau of Prisons and the FBI, allowed us to assemble a very large mass of hard data on which to base our conclusions.

In the fall of 1978 the National Institute of Justice awarded a study grant and I hired research assistants. My assistants and I turned to the challenge of systematically coding and analyzing the information from the 350 cartons of inmate files—the most complete set of records compiled for any American prison. This task, which involved integrating information drawn from three federal agencies, proved to be of such a massive scale that we soon realized that we could not complete it with the funds available from NIJ. Early experience determined that it took twelve hours or more to code the numerous items covering the personal life, criminal and prison careers, and postrelease experiences of one prisoner. Consequently, using every third file from the total of 1,546 files, we created a sample of 508 men whose records would be systematically coded. When it became clear that even a one-third sample could not be coded before the NIJ funds were exhausted, we selected 308 of the cases for coding on a lengthy form, leaving the remaining two hundred cases for coding on a shorter form on which we recorded only the most essential personal, offense, sentence, prison conduct, and postrelease data.[9]

With a group of well-trained, enthusiastic graduate research assistants working on the files, we began the process of locating former inmates, former employees, and BOP officials for interviews. To conduct interviews with former Alcatraz inmates who had returned to (or were still doing time in) federal prisons, we needed to know at which prisons they were housed; the Bureau of Prisons provided this information. If former employees were to provide any useful information during their interviews, they needed to know that the prohibition against talking to persons outside the Bureau could in this case be ignored. To this end, former director Bennett notified the Alcatraz Alumni Association, an organization founded by former employees, that the study had his approval and that, after many decades of silence, the officers, lieutenants, captains, and other members could finally describe their experiences and talk to me about events and personalities on the island.[10]

I interviewed prisoners never released or returned to prison as parole violators or with new sentences in federal penitentiaries in Atlanta, Georgia, Leavenworth, Kansas, Lompoc, California, and Marion, Illinois; at federal medical centers in Springfield, Missouri, and Rochester, Minnesota; at the Federal Correctional Institution in Butner, North Carolina, and the Metropolitan Correctional Center in San Diego, California; and at state penitentiaries in Jackson, Michigan, Stillwater, Minnesota, and Folsom, California. Because these men were always available and almost all turned out to be quite interested in talking about their experiences at Alcatraz and other prisons, some were interviewed several times.

Former prisoners on parole or who had completed postrelease supervision were in most cases interviewed in their homes or locations they selected—several chose Alcatraz as the setting. Interviews with almost all former employees took place in their homes; three were interviewed at Alcatraz. Lt. Isaac Faulk, Lt. Maurice Ordway, and Capt. Philip Bergen, all veterans of many years on the island, were each interviewed several times, as was former warden Olin Blackwell. For those inmates and employees interviewed on the island, that setting was very helpful in bringing back memories of events and the specific places where they occurred. Altogether, more than four hundred hours of interviews were conducted with fifty-four Alcatraz inmates and forty-six employees and Bureau of Prisons officials.

Because such a large proportion of the National Institute of Justice funds was expended on coding data from the inmate files, resources to underwrite much of the cost of travel to conduct interviews was provided by a series of grants from the University of Minnesota Graduate Research Office and the Hubert H. Humphrey Institute of Public Affairs. It became necessary, however, for me to use my own funds for travel expenses, particularly to meet with inmates and former employees for repeat interviews. Federal rules did not allow compensation for men in prison who participated in any research project, but Norman Carlson authorized the payment of a $50 honorarium from the Bureau of Prisons to retired Alcatraz employees to encourage their participation. (Although some declined payment, all former staff members interpreted the offer as support for the project by Bureau headquarters.)

While record clerks in various federal prisons sent us the files of the Alcatraz inmates they could locate, the records for a number of men are incomplete, most notably, those of men still serving time ("active" cases) during the period that records were being assembled for the University of Minnesota project. The postrelease records of inmates who were deported could not be located, nor could the complete files for several prominent prisoners, including Arthur "Dock" Barker and Al Capone. Former Director Bennett told me that file cabinet drawers of correspondence and other Capone materials may have been lost when the U.S. Navy took over the Terminal Island prison during World War II. (Prisoner files follow federal inmates from one prison to another, remaining at the final prison at the time of release.) In Bennett's opinion, "some day" files related to Capone will be found in a naval records center.

It should also be noted that prison staff did not assemble these institutional and inmate files for archival purposes. For example, some endnote citations from the files made available to us are not complete, such as the day, month, year, titles, or authors of some reports—particularly newspaper and magazine articles. To reduce "souvenir hunting" by staff even in Bureau headquarters, some administrative materials were sent to the University of Minnesota archive for safekeeping until the entire collection of Alcatraz records was returned to Washington, D.C. In 1972 James Bennett donated his personal files to the John F. Kennedy Library but because he had begun drafting chapters for his own book about Alcatraz he had assembled considerable materials that he kept in his home—some of which he made available to me during our visits. He noted in a July 26, 1974, letter to me the loss of one important set of records, "the monthly reports of the Warden and other information about operating problems I suspect have been destroyed. Indeed, after I left, no one [until Norman Carlson] was interested in preserving historical records." Mr. Bennett wrote to me again on September 7, 1976, that he was working on case histories of "prisoners I have known in my personal files"; two years later, October 3, 1978, he informed me, "I found Fred Wilkinson's detailed report on the escape (June, 1962 Anglin-Morris). I have put it in the folder I am saving on the official documents re Alcatraz." After his death the remaining Alcatraz materials were lost.

As the Bureau of Prisons became more bureaucratic after 1948, more information about inmates was compiled and records at Alcatraz were made in multiple copies. We were able to locate some missing inmate admission summaries, special progress reports, annual reviews, and other information in federal probation offices across the country. This collection of records for the University of Minnesota project is the most complete set of records compiled for any federal penitentiary but, for the reasons listed above, there are missing materials.

During or after their interviews, a number of former Alcatraz and Bureau employees gave or loaned me parts of inmate and administrative files, letters, reports of incidents, training manuals, San Francisco newspapers—many with front-page stories about escape attempts or killings on the island—cell house keys, photographs, and a wide variety of other Alcatraz memorabilia. By retaining these items as "souvenirs," their owners helped increase the breadth and comprehensiveness of our information about Alcatraz. Of particular note was a large collection of valuable records and photographs saved by acting warden Richard Willard after the prison was closed. (Several years later the island was occupied by protest groups and these items would likely have been lost, destroyed, or at least separated from the official records collection.) Three ex-prisoners gave me copies of books they were writing about their experiences in and out of prison.

While the interviews were being conducted, the coding of the inmate files was completed, and we were able to analyze the data. The results confirmed what had been indicated by the preliminary analysis: Alcatraz releasees had indeed succeeded in the free world at a much higher rate than anyone had thought they could. One-half of all the Alcatraz inmates—and nearly two-thirds of those who served time during the "gangster era," 1934–1948—could be considered successes in that they never came back to a state or federal prison.

At this point in the research we had put together a remarkably complete set of records for the most hidden and notorious prison in America, giving us access to a massive collection of memos, letters, official reports, and records that no one outside the federal agencies from which they came even knew existed. Through our interviews with the aging men who served time and worked at Alcatraz, we had extracted knowledge, facts, and experiences that would otherwise have died with the men who related them. Perhaps most important, we had produced results that contradicted both conventional wisdom and expert opinions about a prison that would subsequently become a model for how to deal with the most dangerous, escape-prone, and troublesome inmates in prisons across the country.

Given the interest of 1.4 million visitors to Alcatraz each year, it became clear that what we had learned about this unique penitentiary would be of interest to a wider audience than federal criminal justice officials and academic criminologists. Moreover, we had accumulated far more knowledge than could be conveyed in journal articles or research monographs. Thus I began laying plans for a book written for a general audience. Because the study had focused on documenting criminal careers both in and out of prison, the book would take a similar approach, including detail about the lives, experiences, and perspectives of inmates as a way of documenting the prison's history.[11]

Preparing a book about Alcatraz and the fates of its inmates led to years of additional research and writing. The prison had to be placed into an historical context, the rationale behind its creation explained, and the lives of many of its inmates—not just the "public enemies"—would have to be constructed from prison, parole, and FBI records, and from interviews.

After completing much of the writing, and following the advice of Jim Clark at UC Press, it was decided to limit this book's scope to the gangster era at Alcatraz. Broadly considered, this period corresponded to the years of James Johnston's tenure as warden—1934 to 1948—before Alcatraz took on more of the features of a standard penitentiary in terms of rules, programs, and population. The inmates imprisoned on Alcatraz during this period, compared with those who came after them, were the most successful in staying out of prison after release, lived under the most punitive conditions, included some of the most engaging personalities with the most interesting life stories, and most consistently followed the informal rules of conduct contained in the convict code. In other words, Alcatraz during the gangster years represents the "pure" version of the prison—the Alcatraz of legend, the Alcatraz with the most to teach us about the complex interplay between inmate personalities, conditions of imprisonment, and postrelease outcomes.

Finally it should be noted that the history of Alcatraz from 1949 to its close in March 1963 was quite different from its gangster years. During the 1950s, inmates found new ways to resist the regime, race relations became tense, and inmate-on-inmate violence increased. In 1962 two highly publicized escapes occurred. Those escapes and the growing criticism of "dead-end penology" (no effort to reform or rehabilitate prisoners) led the Bureau of Prisons to conclude that rather than concentrating troublemakers in one small prison, they should be dispersed through many prisons. That strategy, however, began to fail in the 1970s as violence related to prison gangs and drug trafficking increased. In October 1983, after two officers were killed on the same day at the federal penitentiary at Marion, Illinois, the Bureau's highest security prison, an Alcatraz-type regime called "indefinite administrative segregation" was reestablished, and the supermax was conceived.

A second book will describe the last half of Alcatraz history and the experiences of its inmates after they left the Rock, some to successfully return to life in the free world and others to end up at Marion—"the new Alcatraz."

ACKNOWLEDGMENTS

When James Clark signed this book up for the University of California Press he never anticipated the amount of time and the many revisions that lay ahead. After he became director emeritus Jim continued to exercise due diligence as the manuscript went through multiple revisions; he explained the university's rigorous review process and urged patience as more changes were requested. Jim Clark should be proud of the stature the University of California Press achieved during his years at the helm; we hope this book will add to that reputation.

Several years ago when this book was hundreds of pages longer than the final version, Jim expressed concern that the story of the prison was becoming lost among lengthy accounts of the criminal careers of the prisoners. To help in the painful process of cutting pages that had taken so many months to produce, I sought the assistance of my longtime colleague Gene Kassebaum. Gene and I first met at UCLA where we co-authored two books based on studies of California prisons. He accompanied me when I visited Alcatraz in June 1962 to discuss a study of that controversial prison. Years later he agreed to edit the current book to make sure that the focus stayed on the prison, not the prisoners' criminal exploits—exciting, daring, and outrageous as many of them were. He recast many sections to improve the organization and flow of material, applied his superior analytic and writing ability to basic themes in the story line, and reviewed multiple drafts. For a project in which a major problem has been how to extract the essential elements from an overabundance of data, documents, and first-person accounts, the value of a colleague knowledgeable about the topic but not emotionally attached to the various drafts cannot be overstated. The final version of this book reflects the encouragement and support Gene gave over the last four years along with pushing the "delete" button, adding chapter summaries and transition passages, and asking when he would receive "revised chapter X."

James V. Bennett, director of the Bureau of Prisons from 1938 to 1964, approved this project in 1962 and authorized our first visit to Alcatraz—we did not know that within nine months the prison would be closed. Twelve years later, after Alcatraz had become a National Park Service tourist attraction, Mr. Bennett approached me about restarting the study and suggested that we meet with his successor, Norman A. Carlson. James Bennett made this project a reality in many ways, not the least of which was notifying former staff members that after decades during which they were told not to discuss anything about Alcatraz with persons outside the Bureau, they could talk with me. During a series of interviews he shared his own recollections of major policy issues, problems and incidents on the island, his personal contact with several dozen prisoners, and the continuing debate over the role of Alcatraz within the Bureau of Prisons during the three decades when the prison was his responsibility. During meetings at his home, Mr. Bennett gave me documents, reports, and photographs—most of them marked "Directors Copy"—as well as several chapters he had drafted for a book he contemplated writing about Alcatraz. Before his death he had the satisfaction of learning that the records of many inmates provided evidence that serving time on the island did not preclude success after their release. He was, however, surprised to hear how many ex-prisoners expressed pride in having done time on the Rock.

As director, Norman Carlson first gave his approval for the Alcatraz project and then offered wide-ranging support and assistance that made possible a comprehensive and accurate history of this prison. After the study was under way Norm suggested that our work might be enhanced by my having access to FBI files and, to assure the collection of as much postrelease information on the prisoners as possible, he convinced the Administrative Office of United States Courts to give us access to the inmates' parole and conditional release records. Donald L. Chamlee, deputy chief of probation, paved the way for us to contact federal parole officers across the country and thus to interview former Alcatraz prisoners who had not been returned to prison. Norm Carlson also instructed Bureau personnel to locate Alcatraz inmates never released and those returned to federal prisons and facilitate visits and interviews with them.

Early in his career Norm had dealt with Alcatraz through his work at the Alcatraz desk at Bureau headquarters that approved transfers to and from the island. And he had every reason to presume that a study of this particular federal prison would not make the Bureau look good. With the authority of the director behind the request, all records required for this study were dispatched from federal prisons across the country to the

University of Minnesota. There is no comparable collection of records for any other federal prison.

The following persons who served as research assistants at the University of Minnesota did the work of abstracting and coding for statistical analysis essential information from the voluminous files stored in the university library, summarized prison, parole, and FBI reports, and in several cases conducted interviews with former prisoners and employees. Those who labored over the thousands of pages of federal files have gone on to their own successful careers, many as criminal justice professionals.

Before research funds became available and while Philip Bush was a law and sociology graduate student, he conducted interviews with former Alcatraz officers and prisoners at McNeil Island Penitentiary. After he completed his law degree and served as a public defender, Phil was appointed judge in the district court of Hennepin County (Minneapolis).

Anthony Calabrese, employee development manager at the Medical Center for Federal Prisoners, Rochester, Minnesota, worked longer and on more phases of this project than any other person. He coded hundreds of inmate files and established effective relations with a dozen former prisoners and employees that led to interviews in several cases. He also undertook an exhaustive photographic documentation of the prison; some of his photographs, particularly of the dungeon area, are reprinted in this book. Tony is a recognized expert on Alcatraz in Minnesota. His work for most of a year at minimum wage, paid by the author after federal funds were exhausted, was a measure of his commitment to this project.

Gretchen Gray Larson also worked for the author's low wage before she finished law school and became an assistant Hennepin County attorney. She transcribed hundreds of hours of taped interviews, read and cataloged thousands of pages of FBI investigations, inmate files, and Alcatraz and Bureau of Prisons records, and produced a definitive chronology of every significant event that took place at Alcatraz from 1934 through 1963. Gretchen also devised numerous special-purpose reports and listings (who was put in the dungeon cells, what were the offenses by the military prisoners, which inmates belonged to which gangs, and a catalog of love letters between George and Kathryn Kelly, etc.). Her summaries of information in FBI files and BOP reports became the basis of many sections in this book.

Mary Jo Ludvigson, lieutenant colonel, Judge Advocate General's Office, United States Air Force, reviewed and coded hundreds of files during her years on this study. Her good judgment is represented in the selection of many of the case studies, newspaper articles, and Alcatraz staff reports that appear in this book.

Others who coded inmate files were Nancy Heitzig, Dan McCarthy, Celeste Korbel, Jeffrey Stitt, and Herman Milligan. Constance Osterbaan-Milligan, director of research for the Hennepin County Attorney's office, also coded files but her most important contribution, assisted by Mary Ann Sheble and Karl Krohn, was managing the quantitative analysis of the statistical data abstracted by the coders from inmate files.

Kate Stuckert, Mary Drew, and Charlotte Lewis transcribed hundreds of hours of interviews and contributed valuable suggestions and comments on the pages of chapter drafts that passed through their hands. Alison Cox and Gwen Gmeinder also contributed to this project.

Maxine Clapp, Penelope Krosh, and Lois Hendrickson, supervisors of the Archives Division of the University of Minnesota (and horrified at the condition of inmate records when they arrived at the university library), gave expert advice on the measures we took to preserve this unique collection of prison records.

Bureau of Prisons staff who made important contributions in addition to those by Anne Schmidt already noted in the preface include John Galvin and Peter Chaplick. Anne has been a constant source of support. Former Assistant Director John Galvin provided me with several very useful preliminary (handwritten) compilations of the characteristics of Alcatraz inmates undertaken at his direction; the data on inmates' commitment offenses, race, age, transfers, and so on confirmed that our one-third sample of inmates accurately represented the entire population. Pete Chaplick, former medical staff member at Alcatraz, who later in his career became an administrator at the Western Regional Office of the Bureau of Prisons, helped us by locating and contacting former Alcatraz employees and assuring them that Directors Bennett and Carlson had encouraged them to talk with us. Pete's assistance allowed us to begin our series of interviews with the most senior staff and to record the views of employees who were on the island from the day the prison opened in summer 1934 to the day it closed in March 1963.

Former Alcatraz staff members who were of particular assistance because they agreed to more than one lengthy interview include Lt. Maurice Ordway, Capt. Phillip Bergen, Lt. Isaac Faulk, and Olin Blackwell, the last warden of Alcatraz. Lt. Ordway and several other veteran officers also provided important photographs, records, pamphlets, newspaper articles and other memorabilia collected during their years on the island. Associate Warden Richard Willard, the last associate warden who became custodian in charge of the island for several years after staff and inmates left, had the good sense—and the time—to salvage a large number of items from inmate files, prison records, reports, and photographs, which he made available to me.

Former gangster-era prisoners who were interviewed multiple times include James Quillen, Dale Stamphill, Charles Berta, and Willie Radkay. In addition to a daylong interview at his home, Harmon Waley continued to communicate with me by means of frequent telephone conversations and written correspondence; his was an especially important perspective since he spent twenty-two and a half years on the island and because he gave me a handwritten critique of every page in the book by Alvin Karpis, the only man who had done more time—twenty-five years—on the Rock. Willie Radkay's remarkable recall was put to good use during our five interviews, and through many letters, and dozens of telephone calls. Later, with the help of his niece, Patty Terry, Willie produced his own book, as did Jim Quillen. Jim, Floyd Harrell, and Floyd Hamilton also communicated ideas and information to me through correspondence.

Robert Kirby and Colleen Collins, supervisors of the National Park Service, both determined to give the visitors the most reliable information possible about the prison and the prisoners, helped me to explore every inch of Alcatraz Island. Working on the project with them as well as current ranger Lori Brosnan was a genuine pleasure.

Chuck Stucker, president of the Alcatraz Alumni Association (former Alcatraz employees, their children, grandchildren, or other relatives), and former officer George Devincenzi also provided important information.

Eric Engles's editorial work included a reorganization of chapters that would distinguish between the history of Alcatraz and the sociology of confinement there. Niels Hooper, history editor at UC Press, managed the process of obtaining evaluations of drafts from outside experts, guided the manuscript through the UC faculty review committees, and supervised the editing. A number of University of California Press staff members made contributions to the final draft of this book. Rachel Lockman attended to details regarding the photos that illustrate events and personalities. Kate Warne supervised the production process with sensitivity to the authors' concerns and assigned an outstanding copy editor to this project, Edith Gladstone, who identified endnotes that needed more detail, clarified confusing words and phrases, and provided valuable feedback about the narrative from a reader who was not in the criminology business and had no familiarity with Alcatraz or the federal prison system.

At the beginning and throughout this project, there were important legal issues related to my use of federal records and the need to protect the privacy of inmates' records and interviews with some staff and prisoners. The salience of these issues is evident by the fact that the National Institute of Justice approved funds for a legal adviser for this project. William Bennett Turner supplied expert judgment in regard to these matters. My access to the information in Department of Justice records required that I become an "unpaid consultant"; this appointment was authorized by Harriet Liebowitz, Peter Nacci, and other directors of the Research Division in the Bureau of Prisons. As this book neared completion, attorney Edwin T. Martin helped me understand the issues that involved reconciling the Freedom of Information Act with the Federal Privacy Act.

Two eminent academic colleagues reviewed an early draft of this manuscript for the University of California Press. Howard S. Becker from the University of Washington was already familiar with work by Ward and Kassebaum because our first book, a sociological study of a prison for women in California, was selected for a series he edited for Aldine Publishing Company. When another draft of this book was proposed by the University of California Press, Howie reviewed the manuscript a second time. James B. Jacobs, sociologist and law professor at New York University, whose own book on the history and sociology of Stateville Penitentiary in Illinois is a classic in the sociology of confinement, also offered helpful suggestions and criticisms.

My son, Doug Ward, academic administrator at the UCLA Animation Workshop in the Department of Film, Television, and Digital Media, digitized and significantly improved the quality of many of the book's photographs that were taken many decades ago and stored and handled casually. He also added identifying labels to important features of some photos. Joel Samaha, my colleague from the History Department at the University of Minnesota, provided a detailed critique of this book; his perspective as a legal scholar and historian was especially valuable to a sociologist writing history. Duncan McLaughlin, formerly of the Northern Ireland Prison Service, and more recently of Queens University in Belfast, Northern Ireland, reviewed chapters from the perspective of a man who knows all about resistance in prison. John Irwin, who has written the best accounts of doing time in California prisons, posed an important question for us after initial findings produced surprising results: "Does this study prove that punishment works?" Candace Kruttschnitt, my friend and colleague at the University of Minnesota, offered enthusiastic support for this project for many years—or was it decades? Professor Irving Tallman from Washington State University wrote hard-nosed reviews of our research findings and how they were presented, but this longtime friend's most important contribution, particularly after he and I retired to the Bay Area, was his persistent encouragement and his promise that this book would be published in my lifetime.

Most important, a few words about Renée Ward, my wife, editor, and secretary. All the people listed above made significant contributions to this project, but her assistance, judgment, and support were indispensable. Like a long-term convict she's seeking release after staying with this project (and with me) throughout the many years of its execution, manuscript preparation, and numerous revisions. She now deserves to do easier time.

RECONSTRUCTING THE LIFE
OF A PRISON

In the middle of San Francisco Bay there rises an island that looks like a battleship . . . and when it has not been armed as such, first by the Spaniards and then by the United States Army, it has been a prison of one kind or another. First it was a so-called disciplinary barracks for renegade Indian scouts. Then for captured Filipinos. And always for army traitors. The Spanish lieutenant who discovered it in 1775 might well have called it the Alcazar if he had not been struck by clouds of pelicans that floated around it. So he called it after the bird itself—Alcatraz.

This genial christening has long been forgotten; and since 1934, when it became a federal prison, Alcatraz—the mere name of the place—has sent a shiver through the tourists who come to peer at it from the shore. For the mile or more of intervening water separates them from the most atrocious murderers, the stoniest rapists, the subtlest jail breakers now extant in the United States. It is not, as the popular gossip has it, a prison for lifers. It is, the warden insists, a "corrective" prison for men who know how to organize sit-down strikes in state prisons; for incorrigibles; for the bred-in-the-bone mischief makers of the Republic; for the men who employ a life sentence as a lifelong challenge to discover how, with a twisted hairpin or a stolen razor blade, to break away from any prison they are put in.

A removal to Alcatraz is thus considered in the underworld as a kind of general's baton, the reward of distinguished field service that cannot be overlooked. And the guides on the steamers that ply through the riptides close to the island never fail to call off the roster of the incurable desperadoes who have battled the state prisons and landed here: "Limpy" Cleaver, Machine-Gun Kelly, Gene Colson, and Al Capone.

Alistair Cooke, radio broadcast, December 10, 1959[1]

Few periods in U.S. history have been without infamous criminals—those murderers, assassins, traitors, robbers, or outlaws whose unlawful acts, real or alleged, have inspired some combination of fear and outrage among Americans. While these lawbreakers often had sensational and well-publicized captures, trials, and executions, if they landed in prison they served their time along with more ordinary inmates in ordinary prisons—that is, until Alcatraz. When this federal penitentiary began operations in the summer of 1934 on a rocky island in the middle of San Francisco Bay, it opened a new chapter in American penal history as a prison explicitly designed to hold and punish the nation's criminal elite.

To federal criminal justice officials at the time, Alcatraz was needed to help the nation survive a crisis. In the half-decade or so preceding the opening of Alcatraz, a wave of sensational ransom kidnappings and daring train and bank robberies gripped the nation, and organized crime activity in large cities dramatically increased. These gangsters and outlaws—driving fast cars, armed with machine guns, and often able to elude capture for long periods of time—were branded "public enemies" because their exploits terrorized the citizenry and greatly eroded confidence in local and state law enforcement agencies. By 1933, with the arrest and successful prosecution of many of the most notorious lawbreakers, federal officials had achieved major victories in their campaign to show that they could deal with "the gangster element," but they faced a serious obstacle in winning back the public's confidence. The federal prisons then in existence were not prepared to hold such dangerous and important criminals. Corrupt and poorly managed, they were widely perceived as coddling influential felons by permitting special privileges and allowing them to continue involvement in criminal enterprises from behind bars, while flaws in their security systems offered them opportunities for escape.

Alcatraz was created to solve this problem. Surrounded by cold ocean currents, it was intended to hold the nation's "public enemies" to an iron regimen, reduce them to mere numbers, cut them off from the outside world, and keep them locked up securely for decades. With Alcatraz in business, the country would finally be safe from Al Capone, George "Machine Gun" Kelly, Dock Barker, Alvin Karpis, and their gangster cronies, and these notorious felons would finally get the punishment they deserved. Alcatraz was to became a monument to federal authority.

The extraordinary measures taken at this particular prison to control the behavior of its prisoners and to project the appropriate image of harsh punishment to the public made it starkly different from other American prisons, including other federal penitentiaries. For more than half a century, national leaders in penology had been moving away from the model of prisons as institutions designed mainly to punish and deter criminal behavior and toward a model that included the goal of reforming or "rehabilitating" prisoners. By the 1930s the Federal Bureau of Prisons had fully embraced the concept of imprisonment encapsulated in the term "corrections." When it opened, Alcatraz thus became a conspicuous anomaly in the progressive evolution of American penology.

The inconsistency between Alcatraz and other efforts by the Bureau of Prisons was noted by two prominent academic criminologists of the era, Harry Elmer Barnes and Negley K. Teeters, who wrote in the early 1940s:

> During the period between 1935 and the present we have witnessed amazing paradoxes in this area of the new penology—now referred to as corrections. We have seen the expansion of the efficient Federal Bureau of Prisons and the development of modern concepts of corrections in several of the states. But in the first instance we have witnessed the sorry career of that nullification of progressive penal treatment—Alcatraz, the super-maximum-security prison in San Francisco Bay, maintained by the same progressive Federal Bureau of Prisons.[2]

While officials in the Department of Justice believed that a maximum-custody, minimum-privilege regime at Alcatraz was necessary for practical reasons of security and to convince Americans that the "public enemies" were receiving their just deserts, they also recognized that the prison's deviation from the ideals of progressive penology could be controversial. In an effort to limit criticism of the prison, its methods and management—and because isolation of the prisoners from the outside world was a key part of the regime—they instituted a policy of secrecy, a deliberate effort to "create an air of mystery" surrounding the island.

Throughout Alcatraz's thirty-year service as a federal prison, news reporters were prohibited from interviewing inmates and staff other than the warden. Even after a bloody escape attempt by six convicts in 1946, reporters from the wire services and San Francisco newspapers were allowed only a brief and restricted tour of the damaged cell house conducted by the warden. They were not permitted to interview any prisoner or guard, including those who were injured or taken hostage.

For three decades, employees at Alcatraz followed the strict order laid down by four successive wardens: do not talk to reporters when you are on the mainland, and do not discuss events or personalities at the prison with family members or friends. The blood relatives and wives of prisoners given permission to visit the island for one hour a month could only look at their husbands, sons, brothers, or fathers through thick bulletproof glass and talk through a guard-monitored telephone. Visitors and the men behind the glass were warned that any conversation related to crime, prison life, or other prisoners would result in immediate termination of the visit. Written communications between inmates and their families and their lawyers were severely limited, censored, and retyped by guards to eliminate the possibility of secret messages being conveyed into or out of the prison.

The occasional official statements released over the years by Bureau of Prisons headquarters in Washington, D.C., and by Alcatraz wardens never satisfied the interest of the outside world in what was happening to Al Capone and Machine Gun Kelly, to Ma Barker's son Dock, to Alvin Karpis, Public Enemy no. 1, to kidnapper Thomas Robinson, to Floyd Hamilton, confederate of Bonnie Parker and Clyde Barrow, to the Fleisch brothers of Detroit's "Purple Gang," and to other prominent gangsters of the 1930s and 1940s, including Basil "The Owl" Banghart, John Paul Chase, partner of Baby Face Nelson, and confederates of John Dillinger, Charles "Pretty Boy" Floyd, and the Barker-Karpis mob. Bay Area reporters also wanted to hear about the well-known local bandit from Napa Valley, Roy Gardner, one of the country's last train robbers.

With only scant information about what was happening on the island, and able to observe directly only the occasional signs of trouble—escape sirens, sounds of gunfire, searchlight beams piercing the dark waters around the island, armed men on boats, stretchers being carried from the prison launch to waiting ambulances and to hearses—reporters relied on speculation and their imaginations in putting together the stories they knew the public craved. In addition to local newspaper accounts, articles about Alcatraz appeared in nearly every national magazine, from *Life* and the *Saturday Evening Post* to men's magazines such as *True* and *Saga*. These were predictably sensationalized and wholly or partially fictitious. Anthony Turano's 1938 article "America's Torture Chamber," for example, articulated a common theme—that punishment on the Rock, even for what the Bureau would call "the worst of the worst," had gone too far:

> The [prison's] immured tenants are constantly tantalized by the view of several alluring cities. On clear days they may even see the vehicular and pedestrian traffic in the closer sections of San Francisco. The barbarous effect is the same as chaining a starving man to a wall and spreading a feast beyond his reach. . . . One of the announced purposes of this regime of systematic cruelty was the general terrorization of the entire prison population of the federal government. The inferior convict who became unruly in such purgatories as Fort Leavenworth and Atlanta was threatened with a transfer to the full-fledged inferno of Alcatraz. Thus, the quality of the

rotten eggs in the general basket would be improved by picking out the most putrid ones for individual wrapping. . . . It may not be easy to wax sentimental about the tough hides of such personages as Al Capone and "Machine Gun" Kelly. . . . They must be securely segregated, of course, for the protection of the law-abiding population. [But] it is not easy to perceive the sociological wisdom of transforming convicted scoundrels into raving maniacs. Their summary execution would reflect more humanity and official dignity than the maintenance of a costly suite of torture chambers. . . . Alcatraz stands as a monument to human stupidity and pointless barbarity.[3]

With pronouncements such as Turano's setting the tenor of the public's response to Alcatraz, prison and Bureau officials found themselves with precisely the public relations problem they had tried to avoid. Ironically, the secrecy policy had allowed the media to create their own versions of the Alcatraz regime. That policy, however, remained in force, and the negative perception of the prison held by many newspaper reporters and citizens only worsened.

Since members of the press were prohibited from receiving any information directly from the staff or inmates, they eagerly sought accounts of life on the island from convicts after they were transferred to other prisons and then released on parole. These former inmates, pleased to have an opportunity to criticize the Bureau of Prisons and Alcatraz, clearly understood that the more sensational they made their accounts, the more attention they would receive. The stories they told of men going mad and suffering under miserable conditions like those on France's notorious Devil's Island were reported through the wire services to every part of the country.

One high-profile Alcatraz ex-convict, Roy Gardner, did more than most to add to the harsh image of the prison. In 1939, after he was released from Alcatraz via Leavenworth, he published a book he had written while on the island entitled *Hellcatraz: The Rock of Despair.*[4] San Francisco Bay Area reporters, residents, and tourists were finally provided with a dramatic, firsthand account of the struggle of the nation's "public enemies" to survive in a place Gardner called "the tomb of the living dead." He found other venues from which to tell his stories as well, appearing as an attraction at the Golden Gate International Exposition in 1939 on nearby Treasure Island, and then working as a guide on a tour boat that circled the island daily.

By the early 1940s, as a result of the stories written about Alcatraz, the American public had formed in its collective mind a vivid—and highly distorted—picture of life on the island. This powerful and harsh image lived on through the remainder of the prison's thirty-year history, fueled by more tell-all accounts from ex-prisoners, speculative journalism, and several real events that appeared to corroborate all the negative claims.

When the prison closed in 1963, the mythical Alcatraz portrayed by journalists did not fade away. Instead, Hollywood ensured that the Alcatraz myth would acquire more credibility. The tack that film producers and writers took in making movies about Alcatraz was to portray the convicts as heroes (or victims) and the guards and wardens as the villains. This was a time-tested formula for making films about prison inmates, reflecting the view in American culture that even though criminals are usually the "bad guys," we can also admire them for their individualism, cleverness, and courage.

In a string of movies made about real and imagined Alcatraz inmates, Hollywood made Alcatraz cons the protagonists—men who stood up to the inhumane conditions and the sadistic guards and wardens. Burt Lancaster played Robert Stroud, the wise, dignified *Birdman of Alcatraz* in the 1962 movie that followed the 1955 book of the same name; Clint Eastwood was Frank Morris, the cool and clever organizer of the famous 1962 escape in the 1979 film *Escape from Alcatraz*; Sean Connery starred as the imaginary former prisoner who saved San Francisco from a missile attack by right-wing fanatics in the 1996 film *The Rock*.

One of the more recent of the Alcatraz films, *Murder in the First,* is also one of the most inaccurate. Released in 1995, it purports to tell the true story of Henry Young, an Alcatraz prisoner put on trial for the murder of another prisoner. According to the *New York Times* review:

> *Murder in the First* is the semi-true story of Henry Young, who in March 1938 was placed in solitary confinement in an underground vault at Alcatraz and remained thus cruelly confined for more than three years. Released into the prison population and suffering the mind-altering effects of his ordeal, he killed a man he thought had wronged him. Was Henry Young responsible for his own actions after suffering such duress? Was he a murderer or a victim?[5]

This review followed a news story about the making of the film, which had appeared in the *Times* ten months earlier. In that article, the director related how the brutal treatment of Young "set off a chain of events that helped lead to the closing of the 'Rock,'" and actor Kevin Bacon reported: "To be honest, I almost went nuts playing this part . . . there's no light. It's wet. You're in shackles. You're naked. It's horribly cold. There are rats and bugs. It was a nightmare and I was in a controlled situation. I can't imagine living it."[6]

What *Times* readers and viewers of the film did not know is that the conditions described by Mr. Bacon were created for the movie and did not apply to Henry Young; Young was never confined in an underground vault; there were no rats in the cells at Alcatraz; and prisoners were not shackled, even in disciplinary segregation cells. Nor was Young tortured by "a sadistic warden" wielding a straight razor. A multitude of other events and claims in the film—including Young's suicide two years after the trial—were also false. This film, however, continued the standard media portrayal of Alcatraz prisoners and their keepers. That the film could claim it was based on a true story, and the most prestigious newspaper in the country could call it "semi-true," are indications of how deeply the Alcatraz myth has been ingrained in American culture.

More than a dozen movies have been made about Alcatraz since it opened and along with countless documentaries on cable television, the image of Alcatraz as "Hellcatraz" and "America's Devil's Island" has been sustained.[7] Not only has the prison retained its highly negative reputation, it has even become a symbol of harsh and inhumane punishment in other parts of the world. High-ranking American pilots in the Vietnam era who became prisoners of war, for example, used the label "Alcatraz" to describe a prison where "die-hard resisters" were subjected to particularly brutal conditions.[8] More recently, the *New York Times* reported that prisoners confined "at a notorious jail in Smrekovnica north of Kosovo's capital Pristina . . . were beaten, stripped of their identification cards and given little to eat. A sign there read: 'Welcome to Alcatraz.'"[9]

Behind the myths created and spread during its service as a federal prison and a tourist attraction is another Alcatraz. It is a place where prisoners deprived of the ability to make decisions about the most basic aspects of their lives nevertheless coped, adapted, and struggled to retain their sense of self; where men followed an ethical code, steadfastly refused to inform on their fellow inmates, and presented a common front against the government's attempts to exert maximum control over their behavior. It is also a place where a hard-nosed warden who survived a vicious attack in the mess hall made an exception to the rules to allow his attacker to receive the materials the man needed to continue his education in prison. In the real Alcatraz, inmate-on-inmate violence was relatively rare, especially compared to modern prisons, and guards did not employ corporal punishment. Although the inmates confronted an extraordinarily severe regimen, they were not pressed into chain gangs or subjected to the inhumane living conditions and physical abuse suffered by many of their counterparts in some state prisons of the time, and they had more freedom to move about and more congregate activities than those locked up in today's supermax prisons.

The main purpose of this book is to tell its story—or rather, the many stories that make up an authentic history of Alcatraz—as accurately and completely as possible. In relating this history based on hard facts and primary sources, the book tries to answer the most basic questions about America's most notorious prison and its effects on the men imprisoned there: How did the prisoners adapt to the isolation, deprivations, and restrictions they had to endure? Did they succumb psychologically or did they emerge with their minds and spirits intact? Did the isolation and time alone prompt them to review their lives, consider the costs and benefits of their criminal careers, and decide to lead more law-abiding lives, or did the strict controls and punitive conditions leave them bitter and more determined that ever to thwart government authority?

Many other books have been written about Alcatraz, some succeeding in accurately relating parts of the prison's history (see the bibliographic essay). This book differs from all others in several important respects. No other book draws on so many firsthand experiences—interviews with one hundred inmates and guards, almost all of whom are now deceased—or on the results of a federally funded sociological study that took many years to complete. No other author has been given such unrestricted access to the records of federal criminal justice agencies or received the assistance of federal probation offices—circumstances that combine to make this the only book about Alcatraz to document the long-term careers of Alcatraz inmates, from their criminal activities before confinement on the Rock to many years after their release.

Most important, no other book takes as its starting point the crucial fact revealed in the research and unknown to other authors: that a significant number of Alcatraz's habitual and incorrigible convicts proved the experts wrong and stayed out of prison after they were released. During the era of the "public enemies," Alcatraz confined the most desperate, dangerous, troublesome, and highly publicized inmates in the federal prison system—all of them shipped there precisely because no one held any hope of their being rehabilitated or reformed—and provided them absolutely nothing in the way of psychological counseling or remedial programs. Yet two-thirds of these men emerged from the experience to lead constructive, law-abiding lives. Explaining this unexpected, counterintuitive result is the key challenge that lies at the heart of this book.

Finally, this book does more than chronicle lives, describe events, and explain the culture of a famous prison—it raises questions relevant to the ongoing debate about the value and role of maximum-custody, minimum-privilege prisons. Alcatraz was this country's first supermax penitentiary, and since its closure it has become the prototype for similar prisons established over the past two decades in thirty-six states, and for the indefinite administrative segregation regimes established at its federal successors at Marion, Illinois, and Florence, Colorado. Like Alcatraz, these prisons have attracted controversy. The question today, as it was with Alcatraz, is whether a penal regime that attempts to control inmate behavior as completely as can be allowed under the prohibition in the U.S. Constitution against "cruel and unusual punishment" is justified and necessary, or whether it is too harsh even for the nation's most dangerous felons and most prolific prison hell-raisers. That doing time at Alcatraz did not cause significant, long-lasting mental health effects for most of its inmates or preclude their successful adjustment in other prisons and later in the free world, adds a new dimension to the debate: that a penal environment designed specifically for punishment, incapacitation, and deterrence does not negate the possibility of reform or rehabilitation even when the government does not expect or plan for that outcome.

PART I

ALCATRAZ FROM 1934 TO 1948

THE FEDERAL GOVERNMENT'S
WAR ON "PUBLIC ENEMIES"

Shortly after the First World War many Americans came to believe that rampant crime was a defining element of their society. Attention soon centered on the gangster, the paragon of modern criminality and eventually the subject of innumerable newspaper and magazine articles, scores of novels and plays, and more than a hundred Hollywood movies. The media gangster was an invention, much less an accurate reflection of reality than a projection created from various Americans' beliefs, concerns and ideas about what would sell. . . .

The rhetoric of crime gained a resonant new term in April 1930 when the Chicago Crime Commission released a list of the city's twenty-eight most dangerous "public enemies." Journalists across the country published the list, adopted the term, and dubbed the notorious Al Capone "Public Enemy Number One."[1]

On April 27, 1926, Illinois Assistant State's Attorney William H. McSwiggin was in a Cicero saloon drinking beer with five other men—a former police officer and four gangsters, one of them a man he had unsuccessfully prosecuted for murder a few months earlier. As McSwiggin and the others walked out of the bar, Al Capone and his men opened up with machine guns. Several members of the group jumped to safety behind an automobile but three men, including McSwiggin, were hit. As Capone and his henchmen roared away, the survivors placed the wounded men in an automobile and drove off; later in the evening, McSwiggin's body was dumped along a road outside of town.[2]

The murder and the suspicious associations of the assistant state's attorney created a sensation in the press. While state attorney Robert Crowe and other officials promised a relentless search for the killers, the *Chicago Tribune* concluded that the perpetrators of McSwiggin's murder would never be identified, citing a "conspiracy of silence among gangsters and intimidation of other witnesses after a murder has been committed." Concerning the latter factor, the paper claimed, "anyone who does aid the public officials by giving facts is very likely to be 'taken for a ride.'"[3]

In response to the *Tribune* story, Crowe announced that his office had established that Al Capone was not only responsible for the slaying of McSwiggin but had been behind the machine gun used in the assault. Capone and the survivors of the incident had disappeared, but Crowe ordered raids on Capone's speakeasies, clubs, and brothels. Gambling equipment and large quantities of liquor were destroyed, some prostitutes were arrested, and several ledgers were confiscated. Capone was charged with the murder, but when he appeared in court, an assistant state's attorney withdrew the charge due to lack of evidence. The judge then dismissed the case and Capone strolled out of the courtroom. Despite the impaneling of six grand juries, no other arrests were ever made and the case focused public attention on the inefficacy of local and state government.[4]

Chicago in 1926 was in the midst of what has been called "the lawless decade." The great national experiment, Prohibition, had given rise to the bootlegging business, creating an environment in which organized crime could thrive. Rival gangs ran prostitution, gambling, and extortion rackets along with their illegal liquor sales. These enterprises generated vast sums of money, and the gangs battled for control of distribution networks and territory.

At the same time, local government and law enforcement agencies were rife with corruption. Criminal entrepreneurs, emboldened by the presence of police officers, judges, and politicians on their payrolls, made little attempt to hide their activities, and violence spilled over into the streets for all to see. Gangs would abduct victims on the street and take them "for a ride" or drive past targets in their homes or businesses or while they were walking on the street, guns blazing from several cars.

Gang warfare in Chicago had been heightened by the arrival of Capone, a New York thug who took over the leadership of the Johnny Torrio organization and worked to expand its influence. Between 1922 and the end of 1925, gangsters killed 215 other gangsters in Chicago, and police killed 160. In the first ten months of 1926, 96 gangsters died in gang conflicts in and around Chicago, and police killed 60 more. Between 1927 and 1930 more gangsters died, "many of them on city streets."[5]

The public was alarmed by the rise in violence, and aware of widespread official corruption. However, as long as Chicago's gang members were gunning down mostly their own kind, public reaction remained muted.

The significance of the McSwiggin case was that it revealed a link between organized crime and law enforcement at the highest level in the state of Illinois. The public knew that Chicago mayor "Big Bill" Thompson was Al Capone's candidate, but corruption at the state level was more difficult to countenance. And Capone's seeming immunity made the public realize that both local and state government were powerless to prevent, control, or punish criminal wrongdoing.

McSwiggin's murder case represented a turning point in the fight against organized crime. It set into motion a series of events that would involve the federal government much more deeply in the anticrime effort and ultimately lead to the opening of the federal prison on Alcatraz island as a place to securely incarcerate the country's most dangerous felons.

Lawlessness, law enforcement's impotence, and the danger to public safety posed by gangsters and outlaws—both real and perceived—had to worsen, however, before the federal government began to respond with special measures.

AL CAPONE AND MOB VIOLENCE IN CHICAGO

During the remainder of 1926, gun battles between the Capone mob and Hymie Weiss and Bugs Moran continued. In August two incidents occurred in broad daylight on the crowded streets of downtown Chicago. In both cases, Capone mobsters fired at Weiss from speeding automobiles, smashing windows, and forcing passersby to run for cover. Incidents such as these prompted Charles "Lucky" Luciano, a dominant figure in organized crime in New York City, to remark after a visit to Chicago, "A real goddamn crazy place . . . nobody's safe in the streets."[6]

In 1927 Big Bill Thompson ran again for mayor despite condemnation of his candidacy in the press. One newspaper editorial claimed, "Thompson is a buffoon in a Tommyrot factory, but when his crowd gets loose in City Hall, Chicago has more need of Marines than any Nicaraguan town." The Capone organization worked hard for Thompson's election, contributing $260,000 and using every technique to assure a Thompson victory. (It was during this campaign that Capone was said to have advised the citizens of Chicago to "Vote early and vote often.")[7] When Thompson won the election, the last hope civic leaders had for controlling organized crime in the city vanished. Adding to the despair, the ability of gangsters to literally get away with murder was dramatically illustrated again a year later by one of the most notorious episodes of criminal violence in American history.

On February 14, 1929, seven men who worked for Bugs Moran were in a warehouse on North Clark Street in Chicago, waiting for some empty trucks to take to Detroit, where they were planning to pick up smuggled Canadian whiskey. A Cadillac touring car of the type used by detectives pulled up in front of the warehouse. Five men, three in police uniforms, got out and entered the warehouse with drawn guns. The seven occupants were told to line up facing a wall. When they complied they were cut down by machine gun fire. Neighbors, hearing what sounded like pneumatic drills, saw several men come out of the warehouse with their arms raised, followed by men in police uniforms holding guns on those in front of them. The "police" and their captives climbed into the automobile and drove off.

Inside the warehouse a dog owned by one of the victims began to howl. As the howling went on and on, one resident walked over to the warehouse to investigate. He looked inside and began yelling that everyone inside the garage was dead. He was not quite correct; Frank Gusenberg, who had been hit by fourteen machine gun bullets, was miraculously still alive. Rushed to a hospital, he was questioned by a detective with whom he had gone to school. "Frank, in God's name what happened? Who shot you?" "Nobody shot me," Gusenberg replied. The detective told him that his brother Pete was dead, that he was dying, and asked him to reveal the names of the killers. Gusenberg refused, uttering as his last words, "I ain't no copper."[8]

Chicagoans were horrified by the slaughter on North Clark Street. Headlines declared that the incident indicated a "Return to Frontier Lawlessness" and a "Complete Breakdown of Law and Order." One headline stated, "Police Unable to Cope with Mass Daylight Murder" and another asked, "Are We Under Gang Rule?"[9] The public was fascinated by the incident, which went down in American history as the St. Valentine's Day massacre. Newspapers printed close-ups of the corpses upside down "so that readers would not have to turn the page around to identify the victims."[10] The warehouse where the murders took place became a tourist attraction.

There was endless speculation about who was responsible for the killings. Rival gangster Bugs Moran commented, "Only Capone kills like that." The public and the press, who regarded the Chicago police as corrupt, did not seriously question the report that policemen had been involved. Frederick D. Silloway, the local Prohibition administrator, made this announcement:

> The murderers were not gangsters. They were Chicago policemen. I believe the killing was the aftermath to the hijacking of 500 cases of whiskey belonging to the Moran gang by five policemen six weeks ago. . . . I expect to have the names of these five policemen in a short time. It is my theory that in trying to recover the liquor the Moran gang threatened to expose the policemen and the massacre was to prevent the exposure.[11]

Al Capone had an unbeatable alibi as to his own direct involvement in the massacre—he was being questioned by agents of the Bureau of Internal Revenue's Intelligence Unit at the time of the killings. But Moran was out for revenge. To take the heat off, Capone arranged to have himself arrested in Philadelphia by a detective friend on a charge of carrying a concealed weapon. Taken before a judge with the understanding that if he pleaded guilty he would receive only three months in jail, Capone was surprised to get a sentence of one year and to be taken promptly to Philadelphia's Holmesburg County Prison. Three months later he was transferred to Eastern Penitentiary, where he received what is called "preferential treatment":

> Warden Herbert B. Smith made him more comfortable, giving him a cell to himself and letting him furnish it with rugs, pictures, a chest of drawers, desk, bookshelf, lamps and a $500 radio console. As his work assignment, he drew the untiring one of library file clerk. For ordinary inmates visiting hours were limited to Sundays, but Capone's friends and family could come any day. From the warden's office he was allowed to telephone whomever he chose, and he spoke often to his lawyers, his underworld colleagues and various politicians. . . .
>
> The reporters Capone was willing to talk to had little difficulty getting to him either and they filled column after column with the minutiae of his daily existence. CAPONE GAINS ELEVEN POUNDS . . . CAPONE DOESN'T GO TO CHURCH ON SUNDAYS . . . CAPONE PICKS CUBS TO WIN 1930 FLAG. . . . He bought $1,000 worth of arts and crafts produced by his fellow prisoners and mailed them to friends as Christmas gifts. He donated $1,200 to a foundering Philadelphia orphanage. Such Samaritan deeds, described at length by the press, aroused a good deal of sympathy for Capone. A civil engineer from Chicago, a total stranger to him, coming to Philadelphia on business, obtained permission to visit him, clasped his hand and told him, "Al, we're with you."[12]

Capone's outstanding behavior allowed the jailers to reduce his sentence by two months and on March 17, 1930, he was smuggled past reporters in the warden's car and driven to a nearby town where his own men picked him up and drove him back to Chicago.

HELP FROM THE FEDERAL GOVERNMENT

Capone's ability to evade arrest, let alone conviction, for any of the crimes he was believed to have committed, as well as his control of police officials, prosecutors, and city, county, and state judges, was growing along with his status as a benefactor of the poor. Thus community leaders began to look to the federal government for help in regaining control over their city. In 1929 Robert McCormick, publisher of the *Chicago Tribune,* went to Washington, D.C., to urge President Herbert Hoover to have Prohibition agents stop "victimizing ordinary drinkers and instead concentrate on the principal bootleggers who were the source of corruption in Chicago. For instance . . . Al Capone." McCormick was surprised that Hoover replied, "Who is Al Capone?" But after being briefed by McCormick and advised that Chicago police and courts had failed to bring Capone to justice, Hoover began asking his secretary of the treasury, "Have you got this fellow Capone yet. . . . I want that man in jail."[13] The *Chicago Daily News* publisher also led a delegation of civic leaders to Washington, D.C., to ask President Herbert Hoover to intervene. What the delegation wanted was an efficient, incorruptible criminal justice apparatus that would take over—and win—the battle against gangland in the nation's second largest city.

In spring 1930 Frank Loesch, the head of the Chicago Crime Commission, announced the establishment of a "public enemies" list:

> [It ranked] outstanding hoodlums, known murderers, murderers which you and I know but can't prove . . . and there were about 100 of them, and out of that list I selected 28 men. . . . I put Al Capone at the head . . . the purpose is to keep the light of publicity shining on Chicago's most prominent . . . and notorious gangsters to the end that they may be under constant observation by the law enforcing authorities and law-abiding citizens.

This list, as noted by Capone biographer Lawrence Bergreen, had significance "far beyond Chicago . . . it was reproduced in newspapers across the country . . . and continues to this day."[14] Becoming Public Enemy no. 1 made Al Capone the most notorious gangster in American history and brought to the nation's attention dozens of other hoodlums and out-laws who seemed to operate successfully outside the law.

The trips to the nation's capital by the newspaper publishers and other influential citizens of Chicago produced two federal initiatives. One, mounted by Eliot Ness and his Prohibition agents, was intended to break up Al Capone's bootlegging business under the provisions of the Volstead Act. The second involved an effort by Frank Wilson and Internal Revenue Service agents to charge and convict Capone—who had never filed an income tax return—of tax evasion.[15] It was the second strategy that finally brought him down.

IRS agents, operating under the assumption that they must produce evidence of income from illegal activities, had been unsuccessful in finding witnesses who were willing to testify against Capone before a grand jury. The break the government needed came when Agent Frank Wilson, working alone one evening, happened to open the drawer of an old file cabinet in a storeroom near the offices he and his men were using; inside he discovered a package wrapped in brown paper containing the three bound ledgers that had been picked up during the raid on one of Capone's establishments after the murder of McSwiggin. The books had not been examined at that time; they had been turned over to the IRS for safekeeping, placed in the file cabinet, and forgotten. As he examined the ledgers, Wilson realized that they constituted the financial record of an enormous gambling operation, along with many notations of payments to "Al." The IRS investigators immediately launched a search for the bookkeeper and by matching handwriting samples from bank deposit slips, voting registers, police records, and bail bond certificates to the penmanship in the ledgers they were able to identify the writer as one Leslie A. Shumway.

Shumway was located at one of Capone's businesses where he worked as a bookkeeper. Warned that failure to cooperate would force the investigators to send out word that he was being sought to testify, with the likely result that Capone would have him "bumped off," Shumway agreed to help the government in return for being hidden in California until the trial. With a key witness now able to link Capone to a source of income on which taxes had not been paid, the United States attorney, George E. Johnson, quickly assembled a grand jury and Capone was indicted for failing to pay $32,488.81 in taxes on an income of $123,102.89 in 1924. Twenty-two additional counts were then added, based on IRS calculations that Capone made at least $1,038,655.84 during the years 1925–1929 and should have paid $219,260.12 in taxes. The charges carried a sentence of up to thirty-four years in prison.[16]

To establish evidence of illegal income, the prosecution presented a parade of witnesses who described purchases Capone had made from them. The final witness, Fred Reis, a cashier in one of Capone's gambling houses, provided a critically important piece of evidence—a check endorsed by Capone. This check was the only piece of paper that government investigators had been able to find that bore the defendant's signature. In its closing argument the prosecution described Capone's lavish lifestyle, saying that he lived "like a bejeweled prince in a palatial home," bought "expensive motor cars" and "jewelry in vast amounts." "Does anybody think that this man did not have a huge income?" asked the prosecutor. "He had an income that called for his paying to the government a substantial income tax."[17]

Despite defense attempts to portray their client as a generous man who would not cheat on his income tax—"A tinhorn or a piker might try to defraud the government, but not Alphonse Capone"[18]—the jury returned a guilty verdict after less than a full day of deliberations. One week later, on October 24, 1931, Alphonse Gabriel Capone, alias Alphonse Brown, alias Al Brown, alias Scarface Brown, alias Scarface Capone, alias A. Costa, alias Scarface Al, returned to the courthouse for sentencing. Judge James Wilkerson imposed two consecutive five-year terms in federal prison, to be followed by one year in the county jail, fines amounting to $50,000, and $7,692.29 in court costs.

Capone was housed in Chicago's Cook County Jail, where his presence soon produced problems for federal authorities. Reports reached Judge Wilkerson that Capone was receiving special privileges and conducting business from the jail. The *Chicago Herald and Examiner* reported, "Capone Runs Underworld from Cell, U.S. Reveals: Al Living in Luxury." Capone, the newspaper contended, was living not in a cell but in a dormitory, "where he has the use of a comfortable hospital cot, a soft mattress, clean linen and a private shower."[19] There were allegations that alcohol was consumed in the jail, that a woman put on an "obscene" performance, and that his hoodlum pals were given free access to the jail after regular visiting hours. Despite an investigation that disputed most of these claims, the public again got the message that Capone's influence and money allowed him to receive special treatment.[20]

On May 2, 1932 the United States Supreme Court rejected an appeal of Capone's conviction and two days later he was hustled into a U.S. marshal's vehicle and, accompanied by fifteen police cars, driven to a railway station to board the Dixie Flyer to the federal penitentiary at Atlanta, Georgia. Bureau of Prisons officials had decided that Leavenworth

Penitentiary, closer by, was not a good choice for Capone's confinement because a number of his associates were already in that prison.[21]

Once Capone was in a federal prison many miles away from Chicago, the assumption was that his power and money would no longer bring him special privileges. But Atlanta's warden, the Bureau of Prisons, and the Justice Department soon faced the problem of conveying the right image about the consequences of criminal wrongdoing for the country's master criminal, even in one of the government's highest-security penitentiaries.

A WAVE OF CRIME ACROSS
THE COUNTRY'S MIDSECTION

While Chicagoans were preoccupied during the 1920s and early 1930s with the activities and antics of Al Capone and other Chicago-area gangsters, law enforcement agencies across the Midwest and the Southwest experienced a troubling wave of bank robberies, ransom kidnappings, and jail escapes. The exploits of John Dillinger, Pretty Boy Floyd, Clyde Barrow and Bonnie Parker, Baby Face Nelson, Machine Gun Kelly, Alvin Karpis, and Ma Barker and her sons Dock and Fred captured the attention of newspaper reporters and their readers across the country and supplied the basis for gangster legends and Hollywood movies for decades to come. And to a public increasingly concerned that crime in America was getting out of hand, these outlaws also provided compelling evidence of an extraordinary threat.[22] Criminals of this new class who used fast cars, carefully planned their crimes, and moved quickly and safely across state boundaries were not only difficult to capture but very likely to escape once in custody.

Robbery was the crime of choice for most of these outlaws—robbery of banks, trains, post offices, stores—whatever was nearby that held money. Pretty Boy Floyd and a number of different partners robbed numerous banks in small towns such as Paden, Castle, Sallisaw, and Henryetta in Oklahoma and the Citizens State Bank in Tupelo, Mississippi. Alvin Karpis, Fred and Dock Barker, accompanied on various jobs by Frank Nash, Harvey Bailey, Tom Holden, and others, robbed larger banks in Fort Scott and Concordia, Kansas, and in Minneapolis. The Barker-Karpis mob robbed the Swift Company payroll in St. Paul, Minnesota, a Federal Reserve mail truck in Chicago, the payroll at the Youngstown, Ohio, Sheet and Tube Company, and a mail train in Warren, Ohio. Clyde Barrow, Bonnie Parker, and their friends and relatives robbed banks, gas stations, and a food store in various Texas towns, and a bank in Orenogo, Missouri. John Dillinger and his confederates, including Baby Face Nelson, robbed banks in New Carlisle and Daleville and South Bend and Indianapolis and Greencastle, Indiana, in St. Mary's and Bluffton, Ohio, and in Racine, Wisconsin, Sioux Falls, South Dakota, and Mason City, Iowa. The Dillinger gang also broke into the police armory at Peru, Indiana, and stole machine guns and other weapons. While most of the bank robberies occurred in the Midwest and the Southwest, there were occasional forays into other parts of the country, such as the robbery of $100,000 from a U.S. mail train in Charlotte, North Carolina, by Basil "the Owl" Banghart, William Costner, and Dutch Louie Schmidt.[23]

In the course of committing these crimes, in the ensuing shoot-outs, and sometimes during attempts to break out of jail afterward many of these outlaws ended up killing or wounding police officers, sheriff's deputies, or other law enforcement officers. Pretty Boy Floyd kidnapped a sheriff and killed a police officer, an Oklahoma state investigator, and a Prohibition agent while robbing more than a dozen small banks.[24] In separate incidents, Bonnie Parker and Clyde Barrow gunned down a sheriff, a deputy sheriff, a town marshal, and a state police officer. John Dillinger killed a sheriff while escaping from jail in Lima, Ohio. Dock and Fred Barker and three associates killed a police officer in the course of robbing a Federal Reserve bank truck in Chicago. During a raid by federal agents on his hideout in Little Bohemia, Wisconsin, Baby Face Nelson killed an FBI agent. Some months after robbing banks in South Dakota and Iowa, Nelson, his wife, and a close associate, California bootlegger John Paul Chase, engaged FBI agents in a gun battle at a Dillinger hideout in Wisconsin. Fleeing the scene, Nelson and Chase became involved in a shoot-out that left two agents dead. Shortly thereafter, Nelson was located in Illinois and, after a high-speed chase and gun battle with federal agents, he was killed; his body was dumped on a highway by his wife and Chase.[25] After robbing a bank in Minneapolis, Alvin Karpis and Dock Barker shot and killed a police officer who was pursuing their getaway car.

A KIDNAPPING "EPIDEMIC" AND THE FEDERAL RESPONSE

While the high-profile robbers were busy, some began to engage in a different form of criminal enterprise—kidnapping the rich and holding them for ransom. Despite his success in removing large sums of money from financial institutions, Alvin Karpis complained that his chosen line of work was "becoming overcrowded":

> It seemed that every two-bit unemployed bum in the United States with the cash to dig himself up a pistol was taking a crack at the robbery business. . . . Crime was the last profession in America in the 1930s that still attracted crowds of applicants.[26]

(Alvin Karpis, Dock Barker, and Machine Gun Kelly too would jump on the kidnapping bandwagon in the early 1930s.)

The first ransom kidnapping cases occurred during the 1920s and involved children. The most notorious was the taking of fourteen-year-old Bobby Franks, who was subsequently murdered by Richard Loeb and Nathan Leopold. The sons of millionaires, Leopold and Loeb were defended in court by Clarence Darrow and received life sentences. Other cases followed, including the abduction, for $1,500, of twelve-year-old Marian Parker, the daughter of a Los Angeles banker. Seeing his daughter apparently asleep in a car, the father paid off the kidnapper, who left the victim wrapped in a blanket a short distance away. When the father lifted the blanket that covered the girl, he found she was dead. The chief suspect, a clerk in the father's bank, subsequently confessed. He was found guilty despite a plea that he was insane and, ten months after the crime, he was hanged at the California State Prison, San Quentin.[27]

The Midwest bank robbers considering kidnap prospects got the message—don't kidnap children. Businessmen seemed the ideal alternative target.[28] In December 1930 Nell Donnelly, a wealthy Kansas City clothing firm owner, was abducted with her chauffeur. Despite a threat to blind her with acid and kill the chauffeur, the $75,000 ransom was not paid and the victims were released unharmed thirty-four hours later. Earlier that year Charles Pershall, a Granite City, Illinois, banker, had been kidnapped, a $40,000 ransom was paid, and the kidnappers were never caught. Four months later a Monroe, Wisconsin, brewery owner, Fred Blumer, was taken and a large ransom paid, and his kidnappers were never found. In January 1932 a Colorado baking company executive, Benjamin Bower, was released after a $50,000 ransom was turned over to kidnappers, who also were never identified.

As other abductions were reported in Minnesota, Missouri, Colorado, Indiana, Arizona, and Illinois, prominent businessmen across the Midwest concluded that because of the repeal of Prohibition and the absence of jobs during the Depression, robbers who had learned to live off crime would be grabbing more of them as a source of income. What they wanted was federal legislation, law enforcement, and prosecution—and a federal death penalty. As the effort to lobby Congress was mounted, a survey by the police chief of St. Louis was released, reporting that 279 persons had been kidnapped in twenty-eight states during 1931.[29]

Congressional committees were arguing about the death penalty as a feature of the proposed legislation, and the expense of enforcing the new law, when on March 1, 1932, one of the great crimes of the twentieth century occurred—the abduction of twenty-month-old Charles A. Lindbergh, Jr. The shocked reaction of the nation was matched by that of President Herbert Hoover, who met immediately with William Mitchell, his attorney general. Mitchell announced on March 2 that every federal law enforcement agency, as well as the U.S. Coast Guard, the customs and immigration services, and the Washington, D.C., police would aid New Jersey authorities even though no specific federal law was known to have been violated.

Out of respect for Colonel Lindbergh, who was concerned that a law providing for the death penalty might prompt rash action by his son's kidnapper, the federal kidnapping bill did not move forward until his child's body was discovered on May 11.

When the bill passed and was signed into law by President Hoover on June 22, 1932, it required that the victim would have to be taken across state lines and did not provide for the death penalty as punishment. It did not seem to deter kidnapping—a week later the twenty-two-year-old son of St. Paul executive Haskell Bohn was abducted; he was released unharmed after a payment of $12,000. No arrests were made in this case, nor was there evidence that it was an interstate crime.[30]

Ransom kidnapping continued. Then on February 12, 1933, came the first case involving federal authorities under the new law. The wealthy broker Charles Boettcher II was abducted at gunpoint by two armed men as he and his wife got out of their automobile in the driveway of their home in Denver, Colorado. He was forced into the rear seat of the kidnappers' vehicle and his eyes bound shut with tape. Verne Sankey and Gordon Alcorn drove the victim to a ranch owned by Sankey's wife, near Kimball, South Dakota. The kidnappers demanded $60,000 for Boettcher's safe release. While Sankey conducted negotiations, Alcorn and a third confederate, Arthur Youngberg, guarded the victim.

Based on a tip from an informant, Sankey and Youngberg were arrested by federal agents and indicted on March 29 on kidnapping charges. Alcorn was able to avoid capture until he was arrested in Chicago a year later. He pleaded guilty to "conspiracy to kidnap" charges in federal court in South Dakota on February 8, a week after his arrest, and was promptly sentenced to a life term; two days later, Alcorn was in a cell at Leavenworth. His co-defendant, Sankey, who confessed that he was involved in the Bohn case, hanged himself in his cell while being held for trial.[31]

In May 1933 a group of kidnappers led by Walter McGee abducted Mary McElroy, the twenty-five-year-old daughter of the city manager of Kansas City, Missouri, and demanded a $60,000 ransom. The kidnappers accepted $30,000 and released the young woman, whom they had held in Kansas. Since state lines had been crossed, the FBI entered the case. When the kidnappers were caught, however, they were prosecuted in state court because Missouri had the death penalty. His associates received long prison terms, but McGee was given the death penalty even though the victim had been freed unharmed. Subsequently the victim asked that her abductor's life be spared; McGee's sentence was commuted to life in prison, where Mary McElroy visited him regularly.[32]

During the summer months and the remainder of 1933, a series of very high-profile kidnappings brought notoriety to Alvin Karpis, Dock Barker, and George Kelly, as well as fame to J. Edgar Hoover, the director of the newly reorganized Federal Bureau of Investigation. As a result of these cases, the press proclaimed that the nation was in the grip of a kidnapping "epidemic":

> Within a five-week period . . . six ransom kidnappings were reported, along with less publicized extortions and attempts. The impression was growing that state and federal legislative actions were not having the deterrent effect intended by their sponsors. The 1932 federal laws had enabled the Department of Justice enforcement and prosecuting forces to make significant contributions . . . but new cases kept occurring. The nationally publicized capital prosecution in Missouri, as a result of the McElroy kidnapping, likewise was perceived as exercising little deterrent effect.[33]

During the noon hour on June 15, 1933, William Hamm, president of the Hamm Brewery in St. Paul, Minnesota, left his office for his usual walk home for lunch. At an intersection a half block away, he encountered two men, one of whom asked, "You are Mr. Hamm, aren't you?" and extended his hand. Hamm replied "Yes" and took the man's hand. The second man quickly moved to the other side of Hamm, and the two of them, each firmly holding an arm, pushed Hamm toward the curb where a car had drawn up. They thrust him into the car and down to the floor of the vehicle behind the driver's seat and pulled a white sack over his head. The car drove off, and when it stopped some time later Hamm heard voices, and the sack was lifted. The kidnappers put four pieces of paper into his left hand and a fountain pen in his right, and one said, "I guess you know what this is all about." Hamm replied "Yes," and was told, "Well, then just sign these four slips of paper," which he did. The kidnappers pulled the hood back over his head and the vehicle drove off. Some time later, with the hood replaced by goggles, Hamm was able to glimpse a sign that said "Janesville and Beloit." Shortly thereafter the vehicle stopped and the men led Hamm into a house and to an upstairs room. They allowed him to sit down and gave him a pork sandwich, a glass of milk, and some water. Three days later, after a $100,000 ransom was paid, the kidnappers brought Hamm back to Minnesota and released him.[34]

While the search went on for Hamm's abductors, other prominent citizens fell victim: an Atlanta banker was taken in an unsuccessful effort to get $40,000 in ransom; John J. O'Connell, Jr., the twenty-four-year-old son and nephew of several New York politicians, was kidnapped and $250,000 demanded for his return; August Luer, an Alton, Illinois, banker, was abducted and then released without the $100,000 being paid. In response to the Luer kidnapping and others, forty Chicago millionaires were placed under twenty-four-hour police protection to prevent them from becoming kidnap victims as well.[35]

The fifth ransom kidnapping during this five-week period in the summer of 1933 attracted the attention of the entire nation and catapulted Machine Gun Kelly to a place in American popular culture. It also helped to establish the image of FBI agents as relentless, efficient, incorruptible gang busters—"G-men"—who would save the country from the outlaws, bank robbers, and ransom kidnappers who were outwitting, outgunning, outrunning, and corrupting local police and county sheriffs.

On a Saturday evening in July Charles F. Urschel, a wealthy oilman, was playing bridge with his wife and their friends, Mr. and Mrs. W. R. Jarrett, on the screened porch at the back of their home in Oklahoma City. At about 11:15 P.M., a Chevrolet sedan pulled into the driveway, and two men, one with a pistol, the other with a machine gun, got out and quickly stepped through the porch door demanding to know which man was Urschel. When no one responded one of the men said, "Well, we'll take them both." Urschel and Jarrett were forced out of the house at gunpoint and into the back seat of the sedan, which then sped away. Within five minutes Mrs. Urschel, recalling the instructions of J. Edgar

Hoover in a *Time* magazine article concerning the wave of kidnappings across the country, called the director's office to notify the bureau of the abduction of her husband and Jarrett.

With this latest in a string of ransom kidnappings, the pressure was on the FBI to demonstrate that it could bring the perpetrators to justice—not just for reasons of punishment and deterrence but also to showcase the effectiveness of the Department of Justice's campaign to subdue the "criminal element." In addition, Charles Urschel was not just a prominent citizen of Oklahoma City, he was a personal friend of President Franklin Delano Roosevelt. The special agents in charge of FBI offices in San Antonio and Dallas, additional agents from Dallas and El Paso, and all but one agent in the Oklahoma City office were ordered to work on the case.

On Wednesday July 26 an oilman and close friend of Urschel, E. E. Kirkpatrick, received a package from a Western Union messenger containing a letter written by Urschel asking that he act as intermediary with the kidnappers. The Urschel family paid a ransom of $200,000—a huge sum during the Depression—and at 10:30 P.M. on July 31 Charles Urschel walked in the door to his home, having taken a taxi from Norman, Oklahoma, where his captors had released him. He was interviewed briefly by federal agents and allowed to rest; the following day he made a detailed statement that provided many clues about the kidnappers and the places in which he had been kept during the nine days of his captivity.[36]

The investigation that followed brought two Fort Worth detectives to the home of Kathryn Kelly, an attractive woman known to consort with gangsters. They noticed in the yard a Cadillac registered to Kelly's mother, Ora Shannon, who lived on a farm in nearby Paradise, Texas. The detectives were well acquainted with Kathryn, who had a record of arrests for robbery, had been the chief suspect in the murder of her first husband, and had been linked to an ex-Leavenworth prisoner named George Kelly. The detectives notified federal agents that Kathryn and George should be considered suspects in the Urschel case and that Urschel may have been held captive at the Shannon farm. The FBI immediately put the farm under surveillance.

At 6 A.M., ten days after the victim had been released, fourteen men—four federal agents, four Dallas detectives, four Ft. Worth detectives, a deputy sheriff from Oklahoma City, and Charles Urschel himself—surrounded the farm of Ora Shannon and her husband, R. G "Boss." One of the men called out Kathryn's stepfather's name, and he came out of the house.

FBI Agent Dowd noticed a man sleeping on a bed in the yard and asked Shannon who he was. Shannon replied, "Bailey." Dowd realized that they had happened to come upon Harvey Bailey, one of the nation's most successful bank robbers and an escapee from the Kansas State Penitentiary. According to Dowd's report,

> Special Agent in Charge Jones rushed over with a machine gun and put it close to Bailey's head. . . . On the bed along side of Bailey was a fully loaded 331 Winchester Automatic Rifle and a Colts .45 Automatic Pistol. . . . Bailey had been sleeping in his BVDs [underwear] and his pants and shirt were at the foot of the bed. In Bailey's pants were found $1,200.00 in paper money, $700.00 of which consisted of $20.00 bills, being part of the ransom money paid by Charles F. Urschel.[37]

Bailey, Boss and Ora Shannon, and their son and his wife were taken to the Dallas office of the FBI where all but Bailey and Shannon's daughter-in-law quickly made statements admitting their participation in the detention of Charles Urschel. They placed the responsibility for the whole episode on the shoulders of George Kelly and Albert Bates, another man well known to federal authorities. Harvey Bailey, the elder Shannon claimed, had nothing to do with the kidnapping and had only appeared at his house the previous evening and asked to spend the night. The Shannons and Bailey were lodged in the Dallas County Jail, with Bailey booked in under a false name and placed in the solitary confinement section of the jail to avoid publicity about his arrest. Albert Bates was arrested in Denver a few days later on suspicion of passing stolen checks and was quickly transported to Dallas to stand trial for the kidnapping.

Harvey Bailey had robbed banks for more than a decade. He was movie-star handsome and was reputed to have nerves of steel. He liked robbing banks for the money, but he also enjoyed the sheer excitement of engaging in this highly dangerous activity—a trait he shared with many other bank robbers. He talked about the "kick" that accompanied bank robbery, particularly during the getaways that followed.[38] Bailey's careful planning and calm demeanor paid off not only in the money gained from robbing dozens of banks, but in the fact that he had carried on this dangerous trade for twelve years without making a serious mistake. His FBI rap sheet listed an arrest on March 23, 1920, for investigation of hijacking and burglary; the next entry on his arrest record did not appear until July 7, 1932, when he was finally charged and convicted of bank robbery and received a sentence of ten to fifty years in the Kansas State Penitentiary.

Less than one year later, Bailey had led a sensational escape from the prison, during which the warden and several guards were taken as hostages.[39] After the break from the Kansas penitentiary, Bailey had robbed a bank in Kingfisher, Oklahoma, and hidden out for several days in the Cookson Hills. He had then driven to the Shannon farm to return a machine gun he had borrowed from George Kelly. At the farm, Boss Shannon handed Bailey an envelope containing $1,000, which was Kelly's repayment of a loan Bailey had given Kelly two years earlier. Because he was tired from the long drive, Bailey had decided to stay the night at the farm but when he awoke the next morning, three FBI agents were standing over his bed, each with a machine gun pointing at him. The money the agents found in Bailey's possession included the $1,000 from Kelly, which had been taken from the Urschel ransom money.

Boss Shannon's protest that Bailey had nothing to do with the Urschel kidnapping was simply disregarded, since he was seen as a friend and confederate of kidnappers and bank robbers. The Justice Department and Hoover's FBI needed a big arrest since no one had been charged in the Union Station massacre that had occurred a month earlier in which Bailey had been identified as a suspect. In addition, the Urschel case was, up to that point, unsolved. Attorney General Homer S. Cummings sent his chief assistants to Oklahoma to prosecute the case. The problem, as they would discover, was that Bailey did not intend to wait for his trial to take leave of federal authorities.

Harvey Bailey was held in the Dallas County Jail, where he established extremely cordial relations with several guards and inmate trusties. On September 4, with their assistance, he escaped. The subsequent investigation revealed that a deputy sheriff had paid a jail employee to smuggle hacksaw blades and a gun into Bailey's cell, claiming that "Bailey is one of the finest men I ever met and he is just as innocent as he can be."[40] Bailey was soon recaptured by a local police chief, but the Department of Justice and FBI Director Hoover were outraged by the manner in which the county jailers had handled the federal government's notorious prisoner.

Once Bailey was back in custody at the Oklahoma County Jail in Oklahoma City, Hoover ordered that special precautions be taken to guard him and Albert Bates, who was already being held there along with the elder Shannons and their son. Since local jailers were regarded as "thoroughly unreliable," Hoover notified Attorney General Cummings that he had instructed his men to take complete control of the prisoners even though they were held in a county jail, not a federal facility. Hoover ordered that even attorneys were not to be allowed to visit Bailey, Bates, or the Shannons; if a federal court subsequently ordered otherwise, he instructed his agents to search any attorney visiting these prisoners, and their interviews would have to be conducted with an agent present.[41]

Bailey and Bates were restrained at all times in special handcuffs; their legs were shackled, and the chains were attached to the floor. They were clothed only in undershorts and were denied reading and writing materials along with physical exercise. An armed FBI agent was stationed in front of their cells twenty-four hours a day. On the lower floor of the two-story jail an FBI agent and a deputy sheriff armed with machine guns guarded the entrance to the jail. Three additional machine guns were strategically placed across the street from the entrance to the jail, and the whole area was lighted by floodlights. No other prisoners were allowed in the jail, and Bailey, Bates, the Shannons, and their cells were searched each day.[42]

With federal authorities during the 1930s determined to demonstrate to the country that swift and certain punishment was the consequence of serious criminal wrongdoing, the federal criminal justice process moved rapidly. In an era before suspects received Miranda warnings and public defender offices were established, prosecution could be expedited. Nor did thoughts of plea bargaining enter the minds of the 1930s bank robbers and kidnappers after they were apprehended; these men held to the fatalistic view that after committing a long string of robberies and getting away with them, your number just might come up. Thus, being awakened in the early morning hours at the Paradise farm and finding three gun barrels pointed in his direction, Harvey Bailey threw up his hands and said simply, "Boys, you've got me." In contrast to today's criminal subcultures, the Midwest gangsters during the 1930s were prepared to plead guilty to their own complicity in criminal activities, and they were not about to take friends, associates, or even foes down with them. The tradition of never cooperating with the police and never betraying any associates, manifest in the example of Frank Gusenberg's refusal, while he lay dying, to name his own killers, was firmly fixed in the tenets of the outlaw or convict code. And in this era of criminal justice, federal prosecutors and FBI investigators had not become sophisticated in the use of charge and sentence reductions or promises of concurrent rather than consecutive sentences, let alone witness protection, to break down the prohibition against informing that was deeply rooted in men like Harvey Bailey.

The most dramatic contrast to contemporary criminal justice processes was the speed with which events moved when federal agents wanted to prove how quickly they could catch, convict, and send crooks and desperadoes to prison. A little more than a week after the arrests of the Shannons, Bailey, and Bates, a federal grand jury in Oklahoma City returned kidnapping indictments against the four. Also indicted, although not yet apprehended, were George and Kathryn Kelly and seven underworld figures accused of laundering part of the ransom money. Three weeks later, while the search for the Kellys went on, the trial of the other principals began in Oklahoma City before Federal District Judge Edgar S. Vaught.

The kidnapping of Charles Urschel, the capture of Bailey and Bates, Bailey's escape from the Dallas County Jail, and the nationwide search under way for Machine Gun Kelly and his wife, Kathryn, attracted national attention. Newsmen poured into Oklahoma City from all over the country to cover the trial. Heavy security surrounded not only the defendants, but the jury, the judge, Assistant Attorney General Joseph Keenan (who had been sent out by Attorney General Cummings to manage the prosecution's case), and the local U.S. attorney. Bailey's reputation as an accomplished jailbreaker and Bates's record of escape from prison added an element of suspense that was enhanced by rumors that associates of both men had arrived in Oklahoma City with plans to liberate them.

George Kelly's true name was George Barnes. He was born in Chicago on July 17, 1895, to parents considered to be upstanding citizens; his father worked as an insurance agent. He attended the University of Mississippi, where he studied engineering and agriculture for three years. Despite a university education Kelly claimed that he never held a "legitimate" job in his entire life, although he operated cabarets for a number of years and had an interest in a cabaret in Chicago. Shortly after he met Kathryn Thorne, he was convicted of violating federal liquor laws and, on February 11, 1928, he was sent to Leavenworth Penitentiary to serve a three-year sentence. On his release from Leavenworth on July 3, 1930, Kelly traveled to Minnesota, sent word to Kathryn asking her to join him; they were married in Minneapolis but returned to Ft. Worth to live in Kathryn's house. From 1931 to 1933 Kelly, in the company of Albert Bates, Edward Bentz, and other gangsters, built his reputation by robbing banks in a number of localities, from Tupelo, Mississippi, and Colfax, Washington, to Blue Ridge and Sherman, Texas.[43]

While the government was prosecuting Bailey, Bates, and the Shannons in Oklahoma City, George and Kathryn Kelly had been moving rapidly from state to state, from city to city, changing cars, hotels, and the color of their hair. Finally, acting on a tip, FBI agents and local police raided a house in Memphis, Tennessee, and apprehended the Kellys.[44]

On October 7, 1933, a week after the Kellys had been brought to Oklahoma City for trial, U.S. District Court Judge Edgar Vaught sentenced Bailey, Bates, and Ora and Boss Shannon to life terms in prison; Shannon's son, who had cooperated with federal authorities, was given a ten-year sentence that was then suspended.[45] Two Minneapolis businessmen who had fenced the ransom money received five-year prison terms. With the nation's press already gathered in town for the trial of Bailey, Bates, and the Shannons, the Justice Department wasted no time putting the Kellys on trial. George refused to testify but after listening to the damaging testimony, Kathryn took the stand to tell her side of the story. The jury, however, had no difficulty finding the Kellys guilty, and on October 12, only two weeks after their arrest, Judge Vaught sentenced them to life imprisonment.

After the trial, the FBI's public relations campaign moved into high gear. The account of the capture of Machine Gun Kelly was embellished by the allegation that when he saw armed federal agents in the hallway of the house in Memphis, Kelly shouted, "Don't shoot, G-men." Yet not one report by the arresting agents to FBI headquarters, not one newspaper account at the time of Kelly's arrest, and not even the highly sensationalized account based on interviews with the special-agent-in-charge that was released through the magazine *Startling Detective Adventures* included this statement.[46]

The special security measures taken to guard Bailey, Bates, and Kelly reflected a lack of confidence by the Department of Justice and the FBI in the ability of any county jail or state prison to contain and control lawbreakers with such outstanding records of escape and risk taking. Furthermore these prisoners were just beginning life sentences and had plenty of gangland friends inside and outside of jails and prisons ready to help them obtain earlier releases than the law allowed. Homer Cummings, appointed attorney general by Franklin Roosevelt in 1932, and the new director of the FBI, J. Edgar Hoover, were determined that high-profile felons who survived gun battles with federal agents and received long sentences after highly publicized trials would not escape from the federal government's penitentiaries. But the matter of providing security confinement for Kelly, Bates, and Bailey in McNeil Island, Atlanta, and Leavenworth—the existing federal prisons—was complicated by an embarrassing history of escapes from these institutions in the late 1920s and early 1930s.

ESCAPES AND CONCERN ABOUT
SECURITY IN FEDERAL PRISONS

Prison escapes had become common by the late 1920s. Baby Face Nelson had escaped from the Illinois State Prison at Joliet; Harvey Bailey, James Clark, and three other prisoners had forced their way out of the Kansas State Penitentiary; and ten Dillinger gang members had broken out of the state prison at Michigan City, Indiana. The federal prisons at Atlanta, Leavenworth, and McNeil Island were supposed to be more secure, but even they proved incapable of holding the more daring and ingenious inmates.

On January 25, 1927, an Illinois gangster, Basil "the Owl" Banghart, and two other prisoners removed bolts from an interior ventilator window at the Atlanta Penitentiary, cut a bar in an outside window, climbed through an opening, and jumped to the ground ten feet below. A guard spotted the escapees as they ran from the building; he opened fire but failed to stop the three men, who disappeared into the nearby woods. Prisoner Joseph Urbaytis and another convict were found at the window ready to join the others but had been deterred by the sounds of gunfire. The five prisoners had been released from their cells by an inmate turnkey. Banghart remained free for almost a year and a half before he was apprehended by Bureau of Investigation agents (later Federal Bureau of Investigation).[47]

In July of the same year Atlanta prisoners Roy Gardner, Joe Urbaytis, and John Boyd succeeded in getting two pistols, one hundred cartridges, and a quantity of nitroglycerin smuggled into the prison. After determining that they could not blow a hole in the prison wall, the inmates built a ladder, took the captain and two guards as hostages, and went to the yard, where they tried to convince a tower guard to throw down his gun and allow them to climb up the ladder and escape over the wall. The tower guard refused to cooperate. Although the plot failed, it revealed serious flaws in the security: the success of convicts in obtaining weapons and smuggling explosives in from outside the prison represented the greatest breach of security in any penitentiary.[48]

The July escape attempt was only the latest by Roy Gardner, who had gained fame in California for escaping twice from U.S. marshals en route to federal prison. After he had been recaptured and federal authorities finally succeeded in placing him in McNeil Island Penitentiary, Gardner told the warden that he "would not be staying long." Five months later he escaped. Until he was recaptured two months later while robbing a train in Arizona, Gardner's ability to get away from government agents was a source of acute embarrassment, as one marshal complained in a letter to the attorney general:

> It seems to me that the government should exert every effort to recapture Roy Gardner, who escaped from McNeil Island Penitentiary on the fifth. The fact that he has escaped from federal officers so often had created a great deal of sympathy for him, generally the comment being that he was "so clever getting away that they ought to let him go," and talk along those lines; this from good citizens. On the other hand the fact that he is still at large gives considerable satisfaction to the criminally inclined.[49]

Like Atlanta and McNeil Island, the federal government's maximum-security penitentiary at Leavenworth, Kansas, experienced a series of embarrassing escapes in the early 1930s. At about ten o'clock on the morning of February 28, 1930, Thomas Holden and Francis Keating, serving twenty-five-year sentences for mail robbery with firearms, appeared at the south gate of the penitentiary carrying counterfeit trusty gate passes. They were stopped by guard Charles Miller, who allowed them to walk through the gate when they showed their passes, containing their physical descriptions and names and photos. Their escape was not discovered until three o'clock in the afternoon, when a guard noticed that Keating was absent from his job in the kitchen. At first the searchers assumed that the two men were hiding within the walls, but then the passes and prisoners' clothing were discovered outside the prison near an intersection, where the escapees had presumably been picked up by prior arrangement.

Subsequent investigation revealed that the trusty passes were relatively easy to obtain and had been produced in the prison print shop. In the months that followed, the identity of an inmate in the print shop who helped produce the bogus passes was rumored among the convict population to be George Kelly.[50]

Several months later, another well-known offender left Leavenworth Penitentiary before his official release date. Frank Nash had been in and out of prison since 1913 for crimes that included murder and burglary with explosives. He had been sent to Leavenworth to serve a twenty-five-year federal sentence for assaulting a mail custodian. After serving six years, he had been appointed trusty in the deputy warden's residence. On October 19, 1930, he simply walked away from the prison. At the time of his escape, Nash was a well-known outlaw who had formerly been connected with the Al Spencer gang, and he was known to have many contacts in the underworld.[51] His name, however, would go down in the annals of crime when in June 1933 he was killed during an effort to liberate him from federal authorities that came to be called the Union Station massacre.

While on escape status, Nash met up with Holden and Keating and the three were implicated in a number of bank robberies in the Midwest, as well as several murders. Among these was the October 1931 Kraft State Bank robbery at Menominee, Wisconsin, in which $10,000 in cash and $140,000 in securities were stolen; the vice president of the bank was shot and killed when he resisted the robbers.

Even though on the run, Frank Nash and a recent Leavenworth releasee, Harold Fontaine, carried out a plan to help some friends they had left behind the prison walls. According to Charles Berta, one of the participants in this plot, Nash had given Leavenworth inmates Stanley Brown, George Curtis, Will Green, Thomas Underwood, Grover Durrill, and Earl Thayer an escape plan before he walked away from the warden's house. The plan involved knowledge Nash had gleaned working outside the prison as a cook for the warden: fifty-two-gallon barrels of glue used in the prison shoe factory were left overnight on a loading dock at the railroad station in Leavenworth.

Nash and Fontaine, possibly with the financial assistance of Thomas Holden and Francis Keating, obtained a barrel similar to those used to transport glue. Inside the barrel they placed a formidable arsenal—a rifle, a sawed-off shotgun, five pistols, ammunition, and fifteen sticks of dynamite with caps and fuses. The weapons and dynamite were sealed inside cut-up rubber inner tubes used in tires and the rest of the barrel was filled with glue.

Knowing that the prison sent a truck to the railroad loading dock to pick up the glue barrels in the middle of the night, Nash and Fontaine added their barrel to the others. A note was sent to one of the prisoners to alert the group of the shipment: "Aunt Emma very ill, leaving St. Louis tonight." The barrel was trucked inside the prison and left in the shoe factory freight room where it was identified by the plotters.

Two weeks later, on December 11, 1931, five of the convicts used fake passes to make their way to the front entrance. There, they produced the weapons they had removed from the barrel and ordered the guard to open the gate. Guard Dempsey refused to follow the prisoners' demand, telling them that he was an old man and to go ahead and shoot. Meanwhile, the other two prisoners arrived at the front gate with Warden T. B. White and his office staff, who they had taken as hostages. The prisoners threatened to light a stick of dynamite and kill everyone. Warden White ordered the gate to be opened.

The prisoners, however, were without transportation. They had planned on securing Warden White's car but, as Charlie Berta related later, "T. B. White outfoxed us. He had the car key in his desk. When we came in he dumped it in the waste basket." The escapees, guns trained on their hostages, exited the front door of the prison as White told the tower guard not to shoot. The group made its way up the road to an intersection, where they stopped an approaching automobile. The vehicle contained five soldiers from Fort Leavenworth army base who were going rabbit hunting. The prisoners took possession of the vehicle and the soldiers' guns and piled into the car with the warden as a hostage. Berta drove down the country road and then onto a dirt road that was muddy after heavy rain the previous night. The car became stuck and the escapees split up. Berta, Brown, and Underwood left the other four men with Warden White. After the prisoners told him they were going to kill him, White tried to grab the gun away from Will Green, but one of the other prisoners hit him on the head and Green shot him. Leaving the warden for dead, the four convicts ran to a nearby farmhouse, which was soon surrounded by soldiers sent from Fort Leavenworth. Earl Thayer, dressed as a farmer, walked out the back door of the farmhouse and got away.[52]

What happened next is an example of convict thinking in the early 1930s. According to Berta the three men in the house took "'the Dutch route' [because] when you go out of the institution with firearms and anytime you take an official, like a Warden or Deputy Warden, out of an institution don't ever come back because if you do you are going to have a hard, hard time." Following this credo, one of the prisoners shot and killed the other two and then shot himself. Berta along with Brown and Underwood, soon surrounded by soldiers, made their own attempt at suicide:

> Brownie had six sticks of dynamite, he tried to set them off, but he couldn't light the fuse. If he had set it off that would have been it. But the funny part is that when we got back to the institution they never laid a hand on us. Warden White was a hell of a man, he left strict orders, "No hands on these people, leave them alone. Treat them just like the rest of the prisoners." All we got was Isolation. Otherwise we'd have got our heads broken in. We got a light sentence for escaping—five years. Of course, I lost good time on the 25 [his original sentence]. I'd have to do 25 flat and five on top of that. We were lucky. They had just organized the BOP and they didn't want no publicity. We went to court and pled guilty because they wanted to get it over quick.[53]

In the subsequent investigation by federal agents, three guards were identified as having assisted the prisoners: two committed suicide before they could be prosecuted and the third was tried and convicted. Although J. Edgar Hoover and Bureau of Prisons Director Sanford Bates defended White's handling of the escape attempt, Attorney General Mitchell was critical of White's leadership:

> The general tenor of the reports would suggest that he has been deficient in executive ability in the administration of the prison by the lack of training of his subordinates and failure to establish discipline and proper methods to detect and avoid trouble of this kind.[54]

After Warden White recovered from his injuries, Bates transferred him to a new federal penal farm and appointed a warden at Leavenworth who was to implement new training procedures.

The plan to aid their inmate associates having failed, Nash, Holden, and Keating were busy trying to elude federal agents. Through confidential sources in St. Paul, Minnesota, the FBI learned that Thomas Holden had been living with a paramour in a nearby suburb, and that he and the other escapees, Francis Keating and Frank Nash, frequented certain nightclubs and restaurants in St. Paul, sometimes with other Leavenworth convicts, including George Kelly. Nash was identified by a waitress, who reported that he appeared to be wearing a wig. Holden, Keating, and Harvey Bailey were said to have played golf frequently on a course in St. Paul.

This affinity for golf had prompted the FBI to begin watching golf courses throughout the Midwest and it was on the Old Mission Golf Course in Kansas City that Holden and Keating, unarmed and accompanied by another man and three women, were arrested; their male companion was subsequently identified as Harvey Bailey. Holden and Keating were taken back to Leavenworth on July 8, 1932; Bailey was sent back to the Kansas State Penitentiary (from which he would escape eleven months later).

The search for Nash focused on St. Paul, where he had been seen in the St. Paul Hotel and at the home of Harry Sawyer, a local racketeer well known in gangster circles and reputed to represent Capone interests in the Minneapolis–St. Paul area. In early June 1933 the FBI received a report from a confidential informant that Nash had been seen in Hot Springs, Arkansas, another hideout location favored by gangsters. On June 13, FBI agents Lackey and Smith, along with the chief of police from McAlester, Oklahoma, Otto Reed, went to a store identified by the informant, arrested Nash, and immediately left town.[55]

When the agents and their prisoner arrived in Fort Smith, Arkansas, Nash was locked up in the county jail while the agents asked for instructions from a supervisor. They were told to purchase tickets for a train to Kansas City, Missouri, where they would be met by other agents with a car; the group would then proceed directly to Leavenworth.

On Saturday morning, June 17, 1933, Frank Nash and agents Lackey and Smith were met at the Union Station by agents Caffrey and Vetterli, along with Kansas City detectives Hermanson and Grooms. The group walked out of the station to enter Agent Caffrey's car. Nash was placed in the middle of the front seat to allow three officers to watch him from behind. As Lackey was about to get in to the driver's seat he noticed two men, one with a machine gun and the other with a rifle or shotgun. The man with the machine gun pointed at Caffrey was alleged to have said, "Up, up, up!" or "Stick 'em up !" Realizing they were friends of Nash's, Lackey said, "Here they are." At that instant one of the men said, "Let them have it" and proceeded to fire on the officers and the car. Lackey reported that his gun was jammed, that Nash ducked, held up his hand-cuffed hands, and yelled, "My god, don't shoot me," but was shot almost immediately after the firing began. Agent Smith leaned over between the two front seats and crouched down while Lackey crouched down behind the driver's seat.

After Agent Lackey was hit by three bullets, he realized the persons who were shooting were very close to the car, so he lay perfectly still. When the shooting stopped, one of the gunmen approached the car, looked in the window, and said, "He is dead. They are all dead in here." After the gunmen left, police officers arrived to find agents Smith and Lackey still alive in the car. But both Vetterli and Nash were dead, and detectives Grooms and Hermanson were lying dead near the car. Caffrey, who had been shot through the head, died en route to the hospital.

In the weeks that followed the Union Station massacre, the FBI received many conflicting statements from witnesses as to the identity of the shooters. Some bystanders said they saw notorious gunmen Verne Miller and Wilber Underhill; others identified Pretty Boy Floyd and Harvey Bailey. In addition, Alvin Karpis and the Barker brothers were reputed to have wanted Nash killed after he refused to kill his own wife because she knew too much about their activities and could not be trusted. The search for the shooters never produced clear evidence of the actual identities of the gunmen, but it did result in a wide variety of theories.[56]

The investigation of the events at the Union Station resulted in charges being brought against several individuals who were not present at the

Union Station gun battle but were alleged to be friends of Verne Miller or Harvey Bailey or Frank Nash and were said to be responsible for trying to arrange Nash's liberation. Frank Mulloy, Richard Gallatas, and Herbert Farmer received two-year sentences. Despite their short terms they would end up at Alcatraz, "as a matter of public policy."[57]

Regardless of who was responsible for the massacre, the incident brought to national attention the consequences of inmates escaping from federal prisons. Once free, they could not only continue their criminal careers but also mount efforts to free friends and partners from jails, state prisons, and federal penitentiaries, causing death and mayhem in the process. As a result, Department of Justice officials became even more apprehensive about the safekeeping of high-profile federal offenders.

This general apprehension had a specific focus in the cases of George Kelly, Albert Bates, and Harvey Bailey, the principals in the Urschel kidnapping. After the three received life sentences, the problem that confronted Attorney General Cummings and FBI Director Hoover was how to make certain that Kelly, Bates, and Bailey—with their underworld connections, still hidden ransom money, and ability to ingratiate themselves with local law enforcement officers, county jail deputies, and prison guards—were actually delivered to federal penitentiaries and kept there. Hoover was not convinced that even the high-security prisons at Leavenworth and Atlanta could contain such desperadoes. He warned the Bureau of Prisons not to compromise the new image of federal criminal justice invincibility by letting any of the celebrity criminals captured by his agents escape from custody. He reminded Director Bates that Harvey Bailey and Albert Bates were "desperate and dangerous criminals" and that their associates Holden, Keating, and Nash had managed to escape from Leavenworth. Hoover identified members of "the Bailey gang" as among those responsible for the Union Station massacre and claimed that Kelly had "boasted that he could not be held in a penitentiary and that he will escape."

After they were sentenced, Bailey and Bates, surrounded by ten armed agents, were flown from the Oklahoma City jail to the military airfield at Fort Leavenworth, Kansas. They were loaded into an armored car and transported to the Fort Leavenworth Annex, a former U.S. Army disciplinary barracks adjacent to the federal penitentiary. Each man was placed in a solitary confinement cell to prevent any contact with other inmates. The importance of keeping the nation's most highly publicized kidnappers securely locked up was emphasized in a personal letter sent directly from the attorney general to Warden Robert Hudspeth at the Annex:

Because of the especially fine work of the Federal officers in capturing and prosecuting Harvey Bailey and [Albert] Bates, and the notoriety given to the case . . . I consider that it would be a shock to the country should either of these men escape. I shall expect, therefore, that you give personal attention to these men. I am informed that you have ample means to keep them in confinement. I shall hold you personally responsible for their safe-keeping.[58]

George Kelly was transported separately. Handcuffed and placed in leg irons, he was placed aboard a special railroad car fortified with bars and special bulletproof armor plating. Inside the car, eight agents armed with machine guns kept watch. When the train arrived at the Leavenworth station, Kelly was transported to the federal penitentiary, where he was said to have told a guard "I'll be out of here by Christmas," prompting the guard to retort, "What Christmas are you talking about, Kelly—1960?" [59] Director Bates clearly outlined to Warden Fred G. Zerbst the conditions under which Kelly was to be kept:

[He] should be held incommunicado and no messages or letters should be delivered to or from him. He should be permitted no visits, not even from lawyers, except with the special permission of the Attorney General. He may be seen by the Doctor or by the Chaplain if in your judgment that is wise and safe. I suggest that he be placed in one of the cells in the segregation building; that he be permitted under no circumstances to communicate with other prisoners or to mingle in the yard. He will, of course, be given exercise but in the small exercise yard connected with the segregation unit. He will have regular food, tobacco, books, and newspapers but no other privileges.[60]

The same rules applied to Bates and Bailey, except Bates's privileges were even more restricted due to his refusal to discuss the whereabouts of his share of the ransom money—he was not permitted access to the daily newspapers given to Bailey and Kelly.

Despite these extraordinary measures, J. Edgar Hoover reported to the Bureau of Prisons that his agents, after a visit to the Annex, were not particularly impressed with the security arrangements. Bates and Bailey had both been allowed to go to the hospital on the same date for the purpose of being fitted for eyeglasses, leading the director to comment, "I believe they were there for the sole purpose of looking over the situation and getting the lay of the ground. . . . I also ascertained that both Bailey and Bates, while confined in small cells in the prison, are given the opportunity to wander around the cell block." This interference by the

FBI in Bureau of Prisons matters prompted Sanford Bates to note on Hoover's memo, "These two men were in the hospital under three guards having their pictures taken and giving them routine prison exams like any other prisoners. Who's running this prison anyway?"[61]

On January 7, 1934, Albert Bates began a hunger strike to protest what he considered the brutal and unjust treatment he was receiving, which included being deprived of mail, visits, and other privileges ordinarily granted newly arrived prisoners.[62] A week after Bates began his protest, Harvey Bailey also refused to eat. Bailey said his intention was "to end his life by starvation," and that he was protesting for the same reasons as Bates, except that he also claimed he was innocent of any involvement in the Urschel kidnapping. When informed that the two prisoners were starving themselves to death over the restrictions of their confinement, Assistant Attorney General Keenan advised Director Sanford Bates that Albert Bates "should be kept in solitary until the ransom money is turned over to its rightful owner." Finally a U.S. Public Health Service physician at the Annex decided that Bates would have to be force-fed. A single bed was placed in the corridor outside his cell; the doctor requested that Bates come out for the purpose of being fed; he refused, and two guards were ordered to go into his cell and carry him out: "He made little resistance, quietly submitted to being placed on the bed and strapped down after which food was given him by nasal feeding . . . which consisted of eggs with milk." Another forced feeding was administered later in the day. The following day Bates experienced severe hunger pains when he was given no food and agreed to call off his protest. Bailey, when advised that Bates had stopped his hunger strike, also resumed eating.[63]

For more than a year Bailey, Kelly, and Bates remained isolated from each other and from other inmates in the two prisons at Leavenworth. They would next meet again on a prison train bound for Alcatraz.

CORRUPTION AND SCANDAL IN FEDERAL PRISONS

Preventing high-profile federal inmates such as Bates, Bailey, and Kelly from escaping was not the only concern of the Bureau of Prisons, the Department of Justice, and FBI Director Hoover. There was also the problem of notorious and influential inmates carrying on their lives in federal prisons much as they had outside its walls—receiving special privileges and wielding considerable power in the convict social hierarchy. Press reports of inmates' special treatment and revelations of alcohol and drug smuggling and bribes were bad publicity for a federal justice system trying to portray an image of competence and invincibility. Moreover, inmates' ability to communicate easily with associates in the outside world and with other inmates, to obtain smuggled contraband, and to influence prison staff raised anxiety about security.

The root causes of these problems were lax management and a system that tolerated—even encouraged—influence peddling, the buying of favors, and other improper relations among prisoners and guards. The potential for corruption and mismanagement in the federal prison system had been recognized for some time. During the late 1920s, the Bureau of Investigation sent undercover agents posing as inmates into all three federal prisons. Wardens were not informed of these agents' presence; they reported only to their own headquarters and were expected to spy on prison staff as well as prisoners. Warden Finch Archer at McNeil Island (already unhappy at what he saw as unwarranted meddling in his affairs by bureaucrats located thousands of miles away in Washington, D.C.) was furious when informed that the FBI had sent an agent disguised as an inmate to work undercover without his knowledge. It didn't help that the agent had discovered that the warden's trusted male secretary was the leader of a group of employees who, for payoffs, dealt drugs to and mailed letters for inmates and did other favors. Warden Archer was also criticized for some of his management techniques, such as administering physical beatings to inmates and handcuffing prisoners to the bars of their cells and then forcing castor oil down their throats.[64]

A series of articles in the *New York Times* in March 1929 exposed the undercover operation, called "Snoopervision." The publicity produced angry reactions from the three wardens and from new Bureau of Prisons Director Sanford Bates, who learned only through the *Times* series that the information gleaned by the agents had not been forwarded to his office. In the decades to come, the relationship between the FBI and the Bureau of Prisons (BOP) would be continually strained by similar FBI practices. FBI agents, investigating law violations on the grounds of federal prisons, would also collect information about management practices (which, in the agents' opinions, contributed to killings, riots, and escapes) and forward this information directly to J. Edgar Hoover, who referred it to various attorneys general without the knowledge of BOP administrators. Bates and his successors learned of these reports only in instances in which the attorney general's office asked for their response to criticisms of prison policies, practices, and personnel.

During the early 1930s, events occurred that highlighted staff corruption and incompetence at all three federal prisons. Allegations that employee collusion with certain prisoners was rampant at the Atlanta Penitentiary prompted Director Bates to send Assistant Director James Bennett, this time accompanied by an FBI agent, to the prison in June 1931 to conduct an investigation. Bennett reported "incontrovertable [sic] evidence that some of the inmates have been shaken down for as much as $300 or $400" for favors "such as assignments to preferred jobs, transfers to prison camps and assignment to cells with friends."[65] For example, an attorney who represented a former warden, and later a guard accused of rape, was permitted to take two federal law violators out to the prison after they were sentenced but before they were committed, to demonstrate his cordial relations with the captain and other employees. Impressed, each of the men gave the attorney $500 to use his influence to assure them of favorable job assignments. When they did not like the first jobs they were given, they complained to the attorney and the next day were moved to new work assignments. Bennett's investigation further revealed that the wife of one of these influential inmates stayed at the home of a guard when she came to Atlanta to visit her husband.[66]

Bennett reported that he personally compelled another guard to resign in the light of testimony that the guard had offered to do favors for influential inmates. He also suggested that when the Bureau of Investigation completed its investigation it should send a copy to the warden with a demand that he explain how these problems developed under his administration. Bennett concluded his report by noting the problems posed by high staff turnover and the use of inmates rather than civilians as secretaries, clerks, hospital attendants, and even as mail censors. He offered this explanation of the reasons for Atlanta's problems:

> An inmate who has always had to buy off some District Attorney, Prohibition Agent or other Government official is indeed surprised when he gets to the penitentiary and finds that there is at least one branch of the Government which is trying to be honestly run. It is no small wonder that he will think that it is necessary for him to depend upon the almighty dollar to ease the period of his confinement.[67]

A week after this report was submitted to Director Bates, another problem at the federal penitentiary in Atlanta became a headline in the *New York Daily News*: "Rich U.S. Convicts Buy Vacations; Probe Bares New Scandal in Prisons." The article included photographs of Leavenworth and Atlanta under the heading, "Prisons? Naw, Just Winter Quarters," and went on to describe the situation as "a federal prison scandal of national importance." The reporter explained how wealthy New York convicts, mainly "racketeers and bootleggers," paid bribes ranging from $800 to $1,000 to staff in exchange for summer transfers from "hot Atlanta and Leavenworth cells for more pleasant confinement in Army detention camps." Three Manhattan jewel thieves, he wrote, "were discovered enjoying the summer breezes of the harbor [at Fort Wadsworth on Staten Island] . . . when the federal prosecutor believed they were safe in Atlanta—to which he had heard them sentenced only a few weeks earlier." These illegal transactions, the paper claimed, had been traced to the deputy wardens, a prison chaplain, and other "minor prison officials who are considered merely the collectors for more important figures in the prison administration."[68]

The problems of special treatment and influence peddling were particularly troubling in the case of Al Capone, who had been sent to the federal penitentiary in Atlanta in May 1932. During these early days of the newly organized Bureau of Prisons, most of the Atlanta guards—working-class men of limited education hired at low wages—were accustomed to doing favors for convicts they liked and certainly for those who could pay. It should not have been a surprise to Bureau headquarters that many Atlanta employees were genuinely impressed by Capone's celebrity status. Their prisoner had been described in the press as a folk hero, a Robin Hood who donated money to soup kitchens and arranged jobs for the down-and-out. No less an authority than Damon Runyon had written, "It is impossible to talk to Capone without conceding that he has that intangible attribute known as personality, or, as we say in the world of sport, 'color.'"[69] Students at Chicago's Medill School of Journalism included Capone when asked to list the ten "outstanding personages of the world . . . the characters that actually made history." (The other finalists were Benito Mussolini, Charles A. Lindbergh, Admiral Richard E. Byrd, George Bernard Shaw, golfer Bobby Jones, President Herbert Hoover, Mahatma Gandhi, Albert Einstein, and Henry Ford.)[70]

Ordinary citizens tended not to pass moral judgment on Capone's activities. According to biographer John Kobler, they generally accepted his own claim that he was a "public benefactor" providing a service that had merely been labeled illegal:

> You can't cure thirst by law. They call Capone a bootlegger. Yes. It's bootleg while it's on the trucks, but when your host at the club, in the locker room or on the Gold Coast hands it to you on a silver platter, it's hospitality. What's Al done, then? He's supplied a legitimate demand. Some call it bootlegging. Some call it racketeering. I call it a business. They say I violate the prohibition law. Who doesn't?
>
> At the Charleston, Indiana, racetrack thousands stood and cheered Capone when he appeared with his bodyguards, waving his clasped hands above his head like a prizefighter entering the ring. U.S. Attorney Johnston was appalled during the American Derby at Washington Park to hear the band strike up "This Is a Lonesome Town When You're Not Around" as Capone, a sunburst in yellow suit and tie, took his seat and to see droves of race fans rush forward, eager to shake his hand.[71]

Between 1929 and 1931, seven books about Capone were published, a magazine titled *The Inside Story of Chicago's Master Criminal* sold 750,000 copies, and Howard Hughes began work on a movie about the life of Capone. The script called for the film to depict fifteen killings, including the St. Valentine's Day massacre.[72] The movie encouraged the press and the public's thirst for knowledge of how the "Big Boy" was doing as a prisoner—a thirst that proved to be too powerful for Atlanta officials to satisfy with terse, formal statements.

Eight months after his arrival at Atlanta, newspapers across the country carried an International News Service series authored by "Ex-Convict no. 35503," a man prepared to reveal all about Capone's life in the Atlanta penitentiary. The *Baltimore News* headline for January 23, 1933, read, "Capone Leads Soft Life in Atlanta" and the *Philadelphia Evening Bulletin* caption for the story was, "Capone Coddled in Atlanta Prison." According to the ex-convict writer, who claimed that he had worked with Capone in the Atlanta shoe shop, "the big shot" was able to get just about anything he wanted, had plenty of money, and wore silk underwear, suits tailored for him in the prison tailor shop, and special shoes. His work assignment in the shoe shop was described as "a joke," since it was limited to an hour or two in the morning, after which he left the industries area for visits, treatments in the hospital for his ailments, or to play tennis. The ex-prisoner reported that Capone spent many nights in the prison hospital where the beds were softer than the cell bunks and was allowed to purchase food from the commissary that was far better than the regular fare; in the prison hospital he was addressed as "Mr. Capone." As the series continued, it alleged that Capone was allowed a cell with a number of other "big shots," and that he was receiving abundant legal advice not only from his own lawyers but also from a cellmate who was a former judge serving federal time for using the mails to defraud.

Despite Capone's near-folk-hero status, the special treatment he was reported to be receiving at Atlanta did not reflect well on the federal prison system. Warden A. C. Aderhold tried to refute the charges; in a letter to Director Bates he denied that Capone was allowed to leave the prison at night (he had been out of the prison twice for daytime appearances in the U.S. district court), that he had special hours on the tennis court (he was allowed thirty minutes per day, the same as other inmates), and that Capone spent excessive time in the hospital (he had been hospitalized on only two occasions on doctor's orders), and he had not been issued silk underwear, tailor-made suits, or special shoes.[73]

Later in 1933 the *Washington D.C. Times* published an article under the headline, "Capone Becomes Fine Tennis Player," which reported that Public Enemy no. 1 was playing tennis for one and a half hours on weekdays and all afternoon on Saturdays and Sundays. FBI Director Hoover noted on a copy of this story, "This kind gets more recreation than we do. No wonder prison 'walls' fail to instill fear."[74]

The desire of the press for information about Capone led a deputy U.S. marshal to allow a newspaper reporter to pose as another deputy and accompany him while delivering prisoners to the penitentiary. Since U.S. marshals often asked for and received a tour when they delivered prisoners, the bogus deputy marshal was allowed to look around the prison and to ask questions about Capone. A guard, assuming he was chatting with a fellow employee of the Justice Department, commented to the reporter, "We would need to put Capone in a cage in front of the prison if we satisfied the curious visitors. . . . Three thousand persons asked to see him each week. Other prisoners still glare at him. Each new prisoner asks to be put near Capone."[75] Several weeks later a United Press news release described Capone's life in Atlanta, characterizing his eating habits as those of "a starved lion."

Bureau headquarters, worried about these claims of preferential treatment, sent Assistant Director Austin MacCormick to Atlanta to investigate Capone's living conditions. Without prior notice to the warden, MacCormick arrived at the prison during the noon meal and asked to be taken immediately to Capone's cell. In a 1979 interview, MacCormick described this visit:

[Capone] succeeded in getting into one of those eight-man cells with a bunch of big shots of the underworld. . . . [At that time] an inmate could order food from downtown and it would come into [the prison] in brown paper bags. . . . A guard told me that the inmates had been getting rotten food at the noon meal and night meal. He said it looked like a dog threw up . . . and so these eight big shots with money could order [food] . . . into their cell. . . . I saw a big chicken and pie on the table.[76]

Capone's conduct at the Atlanta Penitentiary inevitably became the subject of FBI investigations. In September 1934 a Federal Bureau of Investigation agent reported that an inmate at Atlanta had informed him that Capone was the head of an organization that smuggled drugs into the penitentiary through a member of the medical staff. That same month Warden Aderhold notified BOP headquarters that a particular guard was the subject of persistent rumors that he smuggled letters out of the prison for Capone. Three months later the guard was confronted with evidence that he was "living beyond his means," and his resignation was accepted "with prejudice."[77]

In late January 1933 Warden Aderhold wrote again to Bureau headquarters denying a newspaper story titled, "Santa Claus Capone," based on the report of an ex-Atlanta felon that on Christmas Day Al had donned whiskers and distributed boxes filled with candy, cake, and tobacco to his fellow convicts. The most that could have happened, said the warden, was for Capone to share some of the Christmas gift boxes that he, like all other inmates, was allowed to receive. A few days later, however, Aderhold received an angry letter from Director Bates, disputing his claim that Capone was being treated like all other prisoners:

I recently wrote you sending a newspaper clipping with reference to Al Capone being Santa Claus and you replied giving your explanation of the matter. I am now informed that at the time of the visit of Mr. Finch, our inspector, there was a large table in the cell piled high with boxes of candy, nuts and fruits; that the walls of the cell in which Capone lived were decorated with pictures and that he had monopolized the whole cell to the exclusion of the other inmates; that there were several padlocked boxes in the cell; and that it was quite obvious that special privileges had been granted in the matter of furnishing Capone's cell allowing him to keep goods which would be perhaps contraband with anyone else and also permitting him to lock boxes containing property. Mr. Finch did tell me that you knew nothing about this matter. It seems strange after the number of letters which we have written about his man. I don't know what more we can say to impress upon you the importance of this matter and the wishes of the Department. Certainly somebody in the institution must have known when this tremendous quantity of Christmas packages came in and must have realized that one man could not use them all. Please advise me whether or not you are prepared to give your personal and continuous attention to this matter from now on.[78]

Warden Aderhold responded that the best solution would be to put Capone in a single cell.

The experience of trying to manage Public Enemy no. 1 provided an important lesson for Sanford Bates and his associates at BOP headquarters. Sending celebrity criminals to the big penitentiaries at Atlanta and Leavenworth would inevitably afford opportunities for inmates and unsophisticated employees to do favors for these celebrities, whether it was for the sake of associating with notorious offenders, making a profit, or simply experiencing the excitement of conveying information to eager reporters. Even though most of the stories about Capone's soft life at Atlanta were not entirely accurate and many were misconstrued, his image as a big shot receiving preferential treatment, conducting business from behind prison walls, and manipulating gullible prison staff was not the picture of incorruptible federal justice that Homer Cummings and J. Edgar Hoover were trying to establish.

Federal officials had tried to reform the existing federal prisons, but the attempts to establish higher standards of employee conduct, hold wardens more accountable, enforce rules uniformly, and restrict press access to certain prisoners had met with only limited success, especially when it came to high-profile prisoners such as Capone, Bailey, and Kelly. In 1933 J. Edgar Hoover and officials in the attorney general's office came to the conclusion that the only way to effectively control and punish the nation's "public enemies" would be to establish a new federal prison where influence peddling, special privileges, and opportunities for escape would no longer be possible.

2

A NEW FORM OF IMPRISONMENT

On October 12, 1933, Americans listening to the Flag Association's radio series heard U.S. Attorney General Homer Cummings announce that the federal government was building a new prison on Alcatraz Island in San Francisco Bay for convicts with "advanced degrees in crime." The prison, he explained, would symbolize the federal government's determination to reestablish law and order in American society. "Here may be isolated the criminals of the vicious and irredeemable type," said Cummings, "so that their evil influence may not be extended to other prisoners who are disposed to rehabilitate themselves." Among the prison's first inmates, he promised, would be Machine Gun Kelly and Harvey Bailey, and Al Capone would soon follow.[1]

Cummings's address signaled the final phase of an executive branch plan to act decisively against the wave of crime that was widely perceived as a threat to American society. When the first inmates arrived on Alcatraz less than a year later and were locked up securely on the island fortress, the capstone of that overarching campaign would finally be in place.

The federal anticrime crusade had begun in 1929, more than four years before, instigated by newly elected president Herbert Hoover. Described as a "rational social engineer" by criminal justice history scholar James Calder, despite his notable lack of success in coping with the deepening Depression, President Hoover was predisposed to deal with the crime problem in new and different ways. When he came into office, J. Edgar Hoover had "cleaned out the Bureau's hacks, nuts, and incompetents," in his effort to reform a major component of the federal crime-fighting apparatus.[2] The president recognized, however, that much more had to be done, with people across the country concerned that gangsters and thugs were free to prey on the public. In his inaugural address, he proposed a major federal effort to fight crime—becoming the first president to mention crime in his initial speech to the nation.

A believer in the power of enlightened leadership, science, efficiency, and innovation, President Hoover realized that the federal government had a major role to play in meeting the transjurisdictional challenges posed by state- and locality-based law enforcement.[3] He recognized, too, that the federal criminal justice system, as it was then constituted, was not adequately filling this role.

The president checked off the first major item on his reform agenda in May 1929 when he appointed the National Law Observance and Enforcement Commission and charged it with investigating the scope and character of crime in America and the agencies arrayed to combat it. Chaired by George W. Wickersham, who had served as attorney general during the Taft administration, it became popularly known as the Wickersham commission. Although the commission's reports on Prohibition received the most attention, it made an impressively broad-based effort to examine crime and the criminal justice system in the United States, aiming, in the words of Calder, to "draw on intellectuals and practitioners and employ new social science information from the fields of criminology, law, political science, psychology, public administration and sociology."[4] The commission's report on federal prisons, released in 1931, would play an important role in shaping the regime established at Alcatraz two years later.

While the members of the Wickersham commission set about forming committees to examine the major issues in the administration of justice, President Hoover looked for a progressive penologist to expand and professionalize the federal prison system. He selected Sanford Bates, then Massachusetts commissioner of corrections, as the new superintendent of prisons. Bates had risen to national prominence as a result of his reforms in Massachusetts, which included creating the first special camps for male and female delinquents, enacting a wage bill for prisoners, and consolidating all jails and county houses of correction into a single agency.[5]

According to historian Paul Keve, Bates had turned down the position of superintendent when it was offered during the Coolidge administration; the salary was low, and his family did not want to move to Washington, D.C. More important, Bates was not assured that Coolidge and his chief advisors would advance the reforms he regarded as necessary. Three years later, Bates accepted the leadership of the federal prison system, convinced that prison reform was in fact a top priority for President Hoover and his attorney general, William D. Mitchell.[6]

After Sanford Bates was sworn in as superintendent on June 1, 1929, he began to assemble new headquarters staff. Austin H. MacCormick, president of the Osborne Association, a prison reform group, was appointed assistant superintendent, and Bates induced James V. Bennett to leave his post at the Federal Bureau of Efficiency to take on the responsibility for developing federal prison industries. Held over from the previous administration, William T. Hammack was charged with developing a career civil service system and a staff training program. Meanwhile, Bates prepared legislation to reorganize the office of the superintendent (subsequently changed to "director") of prisons into a new Bureau of Prisons (BOP).

Legislation formally creating the Federal Bureau of Prisons was approved by Congress and signed by President Hoover on May 14, 1930. The bill transferred to BOP jurisdiction a U.S. Public Health Service hospital located at Springfield, Missouri, to house federal prisoners needing medical or mental health treatment and authorized the construction of a new penitentiary at Lewisburg, Pennsylvania, several regional jails and minimum-security camps, and a facility for treating drug addicts. A women's prison and several youth reformatories were also incorporated into the new Bureau.

In 1930 the federal prison system consisted of three penitentiaries established in 1891 by the Three Prisons Act: two were big, walled, maximum-security penitentiaries that held several thousand inmates each—in Atlanta, Georgia, and Leavenworth, Kansas—while the smaller former territorial prison located on McNeil Island in Washington state housed medium-security inmates from the territories of Alaska and Hawaii and federal law violators from the western states. The wardens were appointed according to their connections to political patrons, particularly United States senators. Guards received relatively low pay, no uniform training program existed, and promotion was based on currying favor with higher-ups.

As a result of having only three regional prisons and no system in place for classifying inmates, the populations in each penitentiary included first offenders and career criminals, compliant prisoners and men whose bizarre conduct would in later years call for confinement in mental wards or—beginning in the mid-1930s—in the special federal prison hospital at Springfield. New federal criminal laws related to drug trafficking, interstate automobile thefts, and Prohibition violations, passed between 1910 and 1920, had produced serious overcrowding. But most problems in the three prisons reflected the presence of untrained, incompetent, corrupt, and poorly supervised personnel. The challenge for the new superintendent was to establish strong central control over these prisons and professionalize their staffs.

During the Hoover administration, penal policies and their underlying philosophies were fair game for reexamination, but various countervailing forces pushed in different directions. In general, there was a strong tendency to shape penal policy to better reflect the emerging literature in the social sciences that emphasized the importance of both rehabilitating offenders and deterring criminal behavior by "instilling respect and fear in the minds of those who have not the intelligence and moral instinct to obey the law as a matter of conscience." Bates was committed to the rehabilitation side of the equation, while others in the administration, sensitive to the public outcry over rampant crime, focused on deterrence and advocated a tougher stance. Anticipating the reasoning that would characterize penal policy in the next administration, President Hoover recognized that it might be necessary to "segregate degenerate minds where they can do no further harm."[7]

In a meeting with the president, Sanford Bates was asked which was more important: deterring members of the general population from engaging in crime, or reforming prisoners. His judicious reply was

> Why not do both, Mr. President? Why not so contrive the punishment of the 90,000 that it will be both deterrent and constructive? A prison need not be dirty, or lax in its discipline; or managed by grafting officials, or overrun with idle men, to exercise a deterrent effect. Men can be punished, and at the same time their bodies can be rid of disease and their minds cleansed of delusions. They can be kept busy at productive tasks, and they can be given opportunities for education and betterment without weakening the sanctions of the law.[8]

As the reorganization and expansion of Bureau facilities proceeded during the early 1930s, however, philosophy took a back seat to immediate, on-the-ground reform. The problems described in the previous chapter—escapes and incidents involving staff corruption and incompetence—embarrassed Bates and his associates and made it clear that better selection, training, and supervision of new employees were urgently needed. Poorly run federal prisons were inconsistent with the president's plan for the federal government to provide the states with a model of an efficient and professional prison system. The escapes in particular underscored the need for a prison to house the government's most disruptive prisoners and sophisticated offenders—a prison that would be more secure than any existing federal penitentiary.

THE DECISION TO ESTABLISH A "SUPER PRISON"

In early 1933, as Franklin Roosevelt began his first term as president, most Americans believed that in spite of all that President Hoover had done to fight crime and strengthen and reform the federal criminal justice system, the country was still under siege by organized criminal gangs. Violence, graft, and corruption plagued many urban areas, and bank robbery rates were at historic highs. But the problem was also perceptual. In the grip of the Depression, Americans had a psychological need to focus blame for their misery and anxiety on something they could visualize and understand, and that something was increasingly the "public enemy."

The despair felt across the country that gangsters and thugs were free to prey on the public, was recognized in Washington, D.C.:

> Oppressed by a sense that prohibition and the depression were draining American society of discipline and order, popular culture sought to explain the national plight as the work of a new breed of criminal. Once the image of the public enemy had been pieced together from the careers of the most famous criminals of the day, the myth took on a life of its own, persuading Americans that the authorities had neither the brains nor the courage to cope with what seemed to be a calculated rebellion against society.[9]

With the exploits of the gangsters and outlaws described in the previous chapters as real-life fodder, the press, Hollywood, and pulp-fiction authors constructed an image of a new breed of sophisticated criminal who preyed on law-abiding citizens. Because it undermined Americans' faith in the ability of the federal authorities to maintain order and protect them, the public-enemy myth (and its underlying reality) posed a serious problem for President Roosevelt, his new attorney general, Homer Cummings, and Director Bates. Americans increasingly saw the government as impotent, lacking the intelligence, courage, resolve, or competence to maintain the rule of law. Incidents such as the June 1933 Union Station massacre in Kansas City, in which three police officers and an FBI agent were killed and two agents were wounded, only solidified the sense of government weakness.

Roosevelt recognized this perception as a threat to the government's effort to restore the trust of citizens. According to historian Richard Powers, the president and Attorney General Cummings crafted a kind of public relations campaign with the explicit goal of promoting "a 'new psychology of confidence' in the law and in society's ability to defend itself."

As part of the campaign, Cummings wove into each big criminal case "a continuing Justice Department saga, an adventure cycle that demonstrated the solidarity of society, the strength of the law, and the potency of the government." While other federal agencies waged their battles against the Depression, the Justice Department under Homer Cummings "was giving the country a war against an even more dramatic villain, the public enemy."[10] With Cummings's encouragement, the media used martial metaphors when reporting on all the big cases, portraying each as a battle in an ongoing confrontation that the federal authorities, under the leadership of Attorney General Cummings, would ultimately win. One popular magazine explained the situation as understood by the typical citizen: "This is war time. The Roosevelt administration is fighting against fear, against depression, against moral decay. It is fighting against the octopus of crime."[11]

When the Urschel kidnappers were apprehended and put on trial, Cummings could claim a major victory in the federal war on crime. Cummings's assistant Joseph Keenan made certain that the jury in the Urschel case knew what was at stake in realizing this victory:

> We are here to find an answer to the question of whether we shall have a government of law and order or abdicate in favor of machine gun gangsters. If this government cannot protect its citizens, then we had frankly better turn it over to the Kellys, the Bates, and the Baileys . . . and the others of the underworld and pay tribute to them through taxes.[12]

While Cummings and J. Edgar Hoover could convincingly claim they were doing their part, they were skeptical about the ability of the other arm of the Justice Department—the Bureau of Prisons—to contain and control gangsters and hoodlums once they were apprehended and prosecuted. By early 1933, senior policy makers in the Roosevelt administration and FBI Director Hoover—but not Sanford Bates and his associates in the Bureau of Prisons—were convinced that the federal prison system needed a new type of penitentiary. According to Richard Powers, an

> idea that Cummings appropriated from popular culture was the "super prison" for the super criminals his "super police" were catching. Spectacular escapes like Frank Nash's from Leavenworth made a new maximum-security federal prison a sensible idea, but the proposal's chief attraction to Cummings was its publicity value. The public wanted proof that the government was getting tough, so adopting the popular notion of an Amer-

ican Devil's Island was a made-to-order way of giving the country what it wanted.[13]

CHOOSING ALCATRAZ ISLAND

In its search for a site for the new prison, the Department of Justice had to consider the public-relations impact of the location in addition to practical concerns. Islands were a focus at the very beginning because they dramatized isolation and conjured up a powerful image of real punishment in the minds of citizens. Testifying before a U.S. Senate subcommittee, New York's former police commissioner reflected the widespread sentiment that isolation on an island was indeed a good idea for the most dangerous felons:

> Exile the hardened criminal, isolate them. They could raise products for their keep: work outdoors in excellent climate—and they would not swim thousands of miles in an effort to escape. If prisons can be conducted humanely so could an exile base be conducted.[14]

The press was also supportive of an island prison. The same magazine writer who deplored the grip of the "crime octopus" called for

> a new form of punishment that will terrify all potential wrong-doers and take out of circulation those individuals who by the repeated perpetration of crime, have proved that they deserve no place in normal society. . . . America needs an isolated penal colony if it is ever to shake off the tentacles of the crime octopus.[15]

If an island site appealed to the citizenry, it also provided the federal government with ready solutions to the problems of secure incarceration. Cummings suggested to Assistant Attorney General Keenan that a special prison for racketeers, kidnappers, and gangsters be located "in a remote place—on an island, or in Alaska so that the persons incarcerated would not be in constant communication with friends outside."[16]

The government's quest was solved when the War Department offered the Department of Justice its prison on Alcatraz Island in the San Francisco Bay. Since the Civil War, this military prison had been a depository for assorted misfits and societal problems, including military offenders and deserters, "secessionists" and supporters of the Confederacy, Indians who made trouble for the government either in the Indian wars or on reservations, foreign stowaways found on American ships, and conscientious objectors during World War I. For a short time in April 1906, prisoners from San Francisco's Broadway Street jail had been removed to the island when the great earthquake struck the city but did not damage the Rock.[17]

Initially, Bates rejected the military prison as too small and too far from Southern California, from where he expected most of the commitments for a West Coast federal penitentiary to come. In addition, the island had no source of fresh water. But despite these drawbacks, Alcatraz offered several advantages. Since it was already being used as a prison, it could be retrofitted and opened relatively quickly. Its proximity to major cities and ports facilitated transport of prisoners. And it was an island, separated from San Francisco by 1.4 miles of cold, choppy water. Bates was forced to admit that it was a viable choice for the new federal prison, and on October 13, 1933, the secretary of war approved a permit for the Department of Justice "to occupy Alcatraz Island as a maximum security institution for hardened offenders, including racketeers and incorrigible recidivists."[18]

The attorney general saw in Alcatraz the potential for a dramatic and visible symbol of federal authority. Press releases and speeches issued from Cummings's office emphasized the extraordinary security measures that would be necessary to hold the nation's worst desperadoes, and how Alcatraz would fit the bill. According to Powers,

> the country was demanding that criminals be given new and more impressive punishments for their crimes. Setting up Alcatraz satisfied this demand, and gave American popular culture a new symbol of the ultimate penalty short of death.[19]

The choice of a small, rocky island for a new high-security prison was invested with powerful cultural connotations. In late 1933, the concept of an isolated island prison conjured up the image of France's infamous Devil's Island. One of several islands in the penal colony of French Guiana devoted to punishment, Devil's Island had become well known during the Dreyfus affair, in which it came to light in the mid-1890s that French Army Captain Alfred Dreyfus had been wrongfully convicted of treason and imprisoned on the island. It had become even more notorious in the United States in 1928, when American author Blair Niles published *Condemned to Devil's Island,* a novel based on a manuscript by an actual penal colony convict, René Belbenoit, who related its horrors—forced labor, starvation, dysentery, hookworm, malaria, "blistering sun, deluges of rain," and, for those who attempted to escape it, months of solitary confinement. The entry of Devil's Island into American popular culture was then assured when a "talkie" movie version of the novel, written by screenwriter Sidney Howard, appeared in November 1929 as *Condemned*.[20]

When the federal government announced the establishment of a special escape-proof prison for the country's worst felons on an island—a prison to be devoted only to punishment and incapacitation—the press and the public were quick to seize on the analogy to Devil's Island.[21] This harsh image had diverse implications. On the one hand, it dovetailed nicely with the Justice Department's effort to restore faith in the government's ability to protect its citizens and provide appropriate punishment for the country's worst lawbreakers. On the other hand, the connection planted itself so deeply in the popular consciousness that Alcatraz became enduringly associated with deprivation, severe punishment, strict discipline, and psychological torture. As a result, the Bureau of Prisons for decades would have to counter the popular view that its new penitentiary was an American version of Devil's Island.

While the country at large welcomed this new form of punishment, the same was not true of the prison's future neighbors. Attorney General Cummings's rhetoric produced cries of outrage in the city of San Francisco. Led by Police Chief William J. Quinn, dozens of civic groups and organizations protested the location of this new home for the "the criminal element" in San Francisco. They argued that the new Golden Gate Bridge, then under construction, would add thousands of citizens and visitors to those entering and leaving the Port of San Francisco. Those living on the hills surrounding the bay complained that the prison would dominate their views. To these segments of public opinion, this highly negative and frightening symbol of the Justice Department's determination to win the war against the gangsters was an unwelcome intrusion. (It is hard today to imagine how the little island of Alcatraz could "dominate" views of the bay, so it is likely that citizen concern was not about personal safety, but about real estate values and civic image.)

Chief Quinn claimed that federal inmates, unlike military prisoners, would be serving longer sentences and would thus have a greater incentive to escape. He noted that a seventeen-year-old girl had been able to swim from Alcatraz to the shore in forty-seven minutes, "arriving with long easy strokes, not even panting."[22] Quinn also speculated that confederates in small boats could pick up inmates who got off the island into the bay, that the island was too small for any industry, and that "there would be nothing for the prisoners to do but wander around in the sunlight in rather pleasant surroundings." Bay Area citizens, said Quinn, were of the view that "these gangster criminals do not give up their operations even though incarcerated. . . . They continue to keep in contact with their associates . . . who congregate in surrounding territories . . . and create a police problem."[23]

The *San Francisco Chronicle* printed editorials opposing the prison, pointing out that twenty-three military prisoners had escaped from Alcatraz over the years, many by stealing boats or swimming. In January 1934 the *Chronicle* suggested in an editorial that instead of a prison, a peace statue be erected on the island.[24]

To assuage the concerns of the citizens of San Francisco, a statement was issued assuring them that Alcatraz would "not be a Devil's Island" in their beautiful bay. It would be an integral part of the federal prison system, operated "in conformity with advanced ideas of penology." The prison, it promised, would "house but a mere handful of men," and would employ "all modern scientific devices . . . to insure the restraint of the inmates." It concluded that the establishment of the new federal prison would offer "a splendid opportunity for the citizens of San Francisco to cooperate in a patriotic and public-spirited manner in the Government's campaign against the criminal."[25] Despite these assurances, the citizens of San Francisco were not prepared to cooperate in the federal government's campaign, and they would complain about the prison until it closed thirty years later.

THE RATIONALE FOR THE PRISON-TO-BE

When top Department of Justice officials decided to open a new, high-security federal prison they had an explicit penological rationale in mind. They reasoned that if the small number of convicts in the federal prison system who could not be controlled by "ordinary discipline" were segregated in a special institution, the inmate population at large would benefit. The presence of these troublesome convicts at Leavenworth, Atlanta, and McNeil Island forced wardens to operate these prisons as though every inmate was trying to escape, operate a strong-arm gang, or engage in illegal activities. It followed that removing these inmates to a separate prison would

> permit the Federal Prison System to enter a period of rapid penological progress, unimpeded by the presence of inmates who would have forced its programs to remain geared to the lowest common denominator in terms of custody, privileges and regimentation.[26]

The Bureau of Prisons put forth this characterization of Alcatraz in its official communications, and the press accepted it readily. The *Saturday Evening Post*, for example, in a December 1933 editorial used all of the Bureau of Prison's arguments to praise the establishment of the new island prison:

> Unfortunately, in many prisons the treatment and discipline of [the] majority must be geared down to the small but worst element of stick-up men and killers. It is this element, rather than the majority of prisoners, which seeks to escape and which commits so many violent crimes after escaping. . . . To classify, segregate and isolate them not only narrows down the problem of preventing escapes, it makes more feasible the task of reformation of a great mass of potentially useful human material.[27]

This logic resonated with the public and criminal justice officials alike. It became so fixed as a commonsense principle that it would later be the leading justification for Alcatraz's supermax successors at Marion, Illinois, and Florence, Colorado.

The rationale for the establishment of Alcatraz in large part predetermined the prison's character. Since Alcatraz would hold America's most dangerous and prominent felons, biggest escape risks, and worst prison troublemakers, security and control had to be the highest priorities. Because the problems presented by these convicts arose in part from their reputation and influence in the underworld, they would have to be effectively isolated from the outside world and from other inmates. And perhaps most important, because the men to be incarcerated on Alcatraz were officially labeled "habitual and incorrigible," resources and staff time would not be wasted trying to rehabilitate them. Designed for "irreclaimable," "recidivistic," "irredeemable" offenders, the new prison would exist solely to punish, incapacitate, and deter others.

The deterrence aspect of Alcatraz was important to Department of Justice officials. The idea was that inmates at other federal prisons would look at the harsh, punitive regime on the island and think twice about landing there themselves by assaulting or threatening staff, attempting to escape, participating in strikes and protests, or refusing to follow rules and obey orders. Similarly, it was hoped that the general public would see in Alcatraz a lesson about the harsh consequences of engaging in criminal conduct. This reaction, the essence of deterrence theory, is what comparative literature scholar John Bender calls "imaginative sympathy" for the unfortunate souls in prison. Bender cites the eighteenth-century philosopher and economist Adam Smith to explain the deterrent effect of imprisonment:

By the imagination we place ourselves in [the prisoner's] situation, we conceive ourselves enduring all the same torments, we enter as it were into his body, and become in some measure the same person with him. . . . He must be made to repent and be sorry for this very action, that others, through fear of the like punishment, may be terrified from being guilty of the like offense. The natural gratification of this passion tends, of its own accord, to produce all the political ends of punishment; the correction of the criminal, and the example to the public.[28]

If the designers of Alcatraz considered "deterrence theory" open to question, these doubts were not evident in the regime they constructed for the new prison. With other federal penitentiaries seen by many as too lax, they were determined to make Alcatraz project an image of punishment that was certain, prolonged, and unpleasant.

Therefore, while the BOP worked to quell local opposition and moved ahead with plans to transform the former military disciplinary barracks into a facility suitable for its new mission, Bates and his assistants had to reconcile themselves to the fact that the prison envisioned by Homer Cummings and J. Edgar Hoover would be at odds with their progressive vision of penology.

This philosophy—based on the idea that criminal activity was rooted in social ills and that all criminals were redeemable—had deep roots. The first penitentiaries in the United States, Eastern State Penitentiary in Philadelphia and Auburn Prison in upstate New York, were created to improve on the existing congregate jails, in which all types of offenders were thrown together, and where disease and a wide range of illicit activities, including prostitution and alcohol consumption, proliferated.[29] The new penitentiaries isolated offenders from the idleness, drunkenness, and violence of their home communities as well as from other lawbreakers so that they could face the failure of their former lives, undergo remorse, learn self-discipline and good work habits, and in this way achieve a psychological rebirth that allowed them to emerge from years of solitary confinement industrious, sober, and compliant.[30]

In 1871 the landmark National Congress of Corrections moved further in this direction when it codified an emerging model of penal practice based on a conception of criminals as persons lacking certain social, educational, and work skills. These deficiencies, it was argued, should be remedied through education and remedial programs. An offender sentenced to prison for "correctional treatment" was to be subject to periodic assessments to determine when he was suitable for release. Education and application of the "medical model" of diagnosis, treatment, and cure made rehabilitation, rather than punishment and deterrence, the central purpose of imprisonment.

During the Progressive Era, various measures and reforms were instituted, all with the intention of substituting rehabilitation for punishment as the purpose of imprisonment. These included probation, parole, the classification of prisons and prisoners, the establishment of courts and penal institutions specifically designed for juvenile offenders, and efforts to reduce brutal treatment by guards and various forms of corporal punishment.[31]

Although none of these reforms and innovations had fully achieved its intended effect, support for the correctional treatment model was strong among federal prison administrators and academic criminologists during the 1930s. When the Department of Justice proposed a prison that would completely forsake the essential progressive idea of rehabilitation in favor of punishment and control, Sanford Bates believed that this concept was a step backward. In January 1933 he wrote to the attorney general, arguing that the goal of rehabilitation should not be abandoned at Alcatraz:

> Fundamentally I would object to putting too much emphasis upon the irreclaimability of the men who are to be sent to this institution. We should, of course, welcome an additional institution because of the opportunity for further classification that it gives us but our prison system is built upon the hope that every man has the germ of reform somewhere in him. . . . I confess, however, that I do look with misgivings upon the effect which the establishment of this institution, which is becoming notorious, will have upon our whole prison system. After all, there are but very few of the prisoners of the type of "Machine Gun" Kelly. Most of them are more of the reformable type and our work should really be judged by what we can do for these men and not have as its apex a penitentiary which is admittedly reserved for those whom we announce as hopeless and irreclaimable. I cannot predict what the effect would be upon the group of convicts who are sent there under this designation. It seems to me that we are unduly magnifying the difficulty and responsibility of the Warden every time we emphasize the danger of the men who are to be sent there. While we do have a group of desperate men, so does every State penitentiary and while I approve separation into institutions of maximum security for these men I cannot help recording my belief that this small number of men should not be brought into such prominence in the public imagination that the fear of them should blind people to the importance of the Federal prison work as an opportunity for rehabilitation.[32]

The following summer Bates inspected Alcatraz, assessing it as "a local prison to be used generally by prisoners on the Pacific coast." Bates told the attorney general that he had not carefully examined the prison for "its ultimate suitability for desperadoes alone." He allowed that the prison "gave the impression of strength. The fact that every prisoner is in a cell alone and that the whole institution is compact and easily guarded was noted."[33]

Having raised his objections, Bates reluctantly accepted the reality that the attorney general and J. Edgar Hoover were determined to establish the island prison as a place whose purpose was to punish and incapacitate a special population of inmates. In a book he wrote after leaving his post as Bureau director in 1937, Bates seemed to agree with the official justification for Alcatraz—accepting the idea that segregating "irredeemable" inmates in a maximum-security prison improved the likelihood of reform for inmates at other federal prisons:

> There were in the existing penitentiaries a small but dangerous group of prisoners, all guilty of serious crimes, who would not accommodate themselves to the ordinary discipline, and who made it difficult to apply the routine measures of education, rehabilitation, etc., to the larger proportion of inmates. Some prisoners just cannot get over the temptation to escape, and continually plot to accomplish this end. Others are known as agitators, "Big shots" and disturbers, and still others by an incurable disposition to disobey the rules and make frequent trips to the solitary. The Bureau of Prisons had for a long time felt the need of an institution with maximum security defenses where this group could be safely quartered.
>
> To Attorney General Cummings goes the credit which has been so freely accorded by press and public for the conception and establishment of the new federal Penitentiary on Alcatraz.[34]

If he had been less diplomatic, Bates might have used the word "blame" instead of "credit" in assigning to Attorney General Cummings the responsibility for Alcatraz. But this statement identified two generally separate groups of prisoners for whom Alcatraz was intended—a small number of notorious gangsters and offenders from the FBI's Most Wanted list, and a large number of troublemakers and escape risks not known to the public.

Although the purpose of the prison-to-be on Alcatraz was set down by the attorney general, aided and abetted by J. Edgar Hoover, Bureau of Prisons' officials had the authority to determine how that purpose would be realized. In shaping the general outlines of how the prison would operate, Bates and the assistant director, Austin MacCormick, had available to them the negative examples of existing federal penitentiaries and major state prisons. Acutely aware of the overcrowding, poor management, and inhumane treatment that characterized these institutions, they were careful to avoid replicating these problems at Alcatraz.

Bates and MacCormick were familiar with the state of the nation's prisons not only because they ran the federal prison system, but because they had both been members of the Wickersham commission that President Hoover established in 1929 to examine and then recommend improvements in penal policy and practice.

The commission's reports, submitted in 1931, had listed a wide range of problems with the penitentiaries of the day, beginning with the aging, often decrepit physical structures in which inmates were housed. Exacerbating the conditions of confinement were poor sanitation, lighting, and air circulation, extremes in temperature, and overcrowded living space. Large numbers of prisoners were housed in giant cell blocks comprised of cells as small as seven feet long, three feet three inches wide, and six feet seven inches high; most cells had solid doors that limited ventilation and outside light and did not contain sinks with running water or toilets. In many prisons inmates were doubled or even tripled up in cells intended for one man, with slop buckets containing human waste emptied only once every twenty-four hours. Many cells were drafty, encouraging physical ailments such as rheumatism. The practice of changing underclothing and sheets only once each week and allowing only one shower in the same period was widespread. Medical services and hospital facilities for prisoners who became ill or were injured were generally inadequate.

The commission had been even more critical of disciplinary measures. Along with an extensive set of rules that proscribed and prescribed inmates' behaviors to an excruciating degree were various policies and practices used to encourage or enforce compliance with these rules. When these inducements failed to produce obedience and maintain order, the rule breakers were disciplined, often in ways that, in the eyes of the commission, crossed the line from mere punishment into brutality. All prisons used some sort of solitary confinement to punish and isolate troublemakers, but this often meant locking them in a cramped, dark, unfurnished cell for indefinite periods on a diet of bread and water with no more than a pail for sanitation. In addition to this disciplinary segregation, many prisons employed other harsh, punitive measures. Some inmates were forced into a standing position for the work day, handcuffed to their cell bars, or locked standing in cages in which they could not move. In more extreme cases, chained or cuffed inmates were sprayed with streams of cold water, beaten with fists, clubs, or rubber hoses, or whipped with straps. These practices were often against official policies but tacitly condoned by prison management; the commission suspected that their extent and frequency were higher than what was acknowledged by wardens. A 1929 survey by the National Society on Penal Information—on which the commission relied heavily in its study—noted "the existence of barbarous methods of discipline that were unknown or denied."[35]

In addition, there were the management problems cited earlier. Many wardens and their chief assistants were political appointees, not trained to manage prisons or prisoners. Guards were often poorly trained and incompetent, and lax supervision allowed widespread corruption that included the sale of favors, smuggling, and black-marketing. In some state prisons, the general inmate population was largely managed by proxy: across the bay from Alcatraz, convict bosses at San Quentin ran the shops, offices, and cell blocks, keeping their fellow convicts subdued in exchange for special privileges such as single cells, tailored denims, meals from the guards' kitchen, and freedom from much of the usual prison routine.[36]

The Wickersham commission had concluded that penal confinement was for the most part transforming lawbreakers into hardened criminals rather than law-abiding citizens. If the mission of America's prisons was to protect society by reducing criminal behavior through reformation, the prisons were failing—and the harsh punishment so prevalent in the criminal justice system bore much of the blame.[37]

As members of the commission, Bates and MacCormick had supported this conclusion, and in their capacities as heads of the federal prison system they put their beliefs into practice. Both disapproved of inhumane and brutal physical punishment, and they demanded that it be eliminated where they encountered it. In the federal prison system generally they sought to phase out or limit traditional punitive measures such as solitary confinement, bread and water diets, and the practice of handcuffing prisoners to the bars of a cell in a standing position.

In the case of Alcatraz, Bates's and MacCormick's views prevailed in their effort to eliminate forms of corporal punishment they believed to be inhumane. The planners for the new federal prison agreed that physical abuse would not be part of the regime. Punishment at Alcatraz would not involve the gag, the powerful spray from cold-water hoses, the lash, the rubber hose, or beatings by club-wielding guards. No convict would be allowed to boss other inmates in return for favors from the staff. Nor would heating, sanitation, food, and medical care be withheld or manipulated as punitive measures. Instead, Bates and his associates sought to create a sophisticated regime that would punish the wills and the spirits, but not the bodies, of the prison's residents. The complaints of inmates who came to the new penitentiary over the next thirty years emphasized the psychological pains of imprisonment.[38]

ESTABLISHING A MAXIMUM-SECURITY, MINIMUM-PRIVILEGE REGIME

The directives from the Department of Justice were clear and unambiguous. Alcatraz was to have an unprecedented level of security, isolate its inmates from the outside world, and greatly restrict their opportunities for interaction even within the prison. All prisoners were to be treated the same, regardless of their notoriety or prestige among the inmate population. The Justice Department's requirements for Alcatraz were ambitious:

- Escape must be virtually impossible. Convicts who had tried to escape other prisons using force or violence, along with those who had contrived escapes using ingenuity and subterfuge, must find opportunities for escape completely eliminated.
- Inmates must be deprived of opportunities to foment riots, organize resistance to the regime, or perpetrate violence against other inmates or staff.
- The power and influence of big shot racketeers and gangsters must be eliminated, not just reduced. The message has to be clear—no inmate could be allowed to conduct business from prison or enjoy any special privilege while confined.
- The flow of information into and out of the prison must be strictly controlled to inhibit rumors and to deny not only to the inmates but also to the press any basis for stories that would further glamorize "the criminal element."
- The regime must represent real punishment. Inmates whose criminal activities earned them the "menace to society" label must finally be held accountable for their actions.

The Bureau of Prisons set down a variety of policies to accomplish these ends and create what it announced would be a "maximum-security, minimum-privilege" institution, a regime to be described in detail in the following chapter. Director Bates and his assistant directors realized that controlling personnel was vital in the control of prisoners. Thus, an important component of the Alcatraz regime would be the requirement that all administrative personnel live on the island: the warden, deputy warden, captain, lieutenants, the chief medical officer, the chief steward, industry supervisors, important maintenance staff such as plumbers and electricians, and most of the guard force. In spite of the social isolation that this policy entailed, the BOP expected no recruitment problems because federal employment in the early 1930s offered more security than most other jobs. In addition, working at Alcatraz would include inexpensive living quarters with great views of the bay.

Having staff members reside on the same small island where they worked made them available in the event of an emergency situation, but more important it allowed the warden to establish strict rules for employee conduct both off and on the job. When not working, employees would be prohibited from discussing any aspect of prison operations with any person outside the federal prison system; this prohibition was intended to apply in particular when employees took the prison boats over to San Francisco, where eager newspaper reporters might be waiting. Relatives and close friends could visit employees on the island, but each visit required permission to board the prison launch. By limiting the ability of employees to socialize with people in the outside the world, the rules would greatly reduce opportunities for establishing corrupting relations. On the job, guards were told to refrain from talking with prisoners, apart from issuing orders and directing routine activities. This rule was intended to eliminate opportunities for prisoners to try to corrupt or improperly influence employees.

It was important that all rank-and-file officers and industries staff receive close supervision, and this was made possible by the small cell house and the limited inmate work and recreation areas. Compared to their counterparts at the big Atlanta and Leavenworth penitentiaries, supervisors at Alcatraz would have an easier time keeping tabs on both employees and prisoners.

A key policy decision by Cummings and Bates was to permanently bar the press from the island. Once gangsters, high-profile kidnappers, and bank robbers had been sent off to prison, they should not be further "glorified" by news stories or reports pertaining to their prison experiences. Continued attention from the press would only bolster the egos and reputations of big shot offenders and possibly earn them sympathy from the public. Wary of negative press, federal officials assumed that if reporters had access to inmates, they would write articles critical of staff actions, administrative decisions, the prison regime, and probably all of the above. The only person authorized to release information or news about any person or event at Alcatraz would be the warden.[39] Bureau of Prisons headquarters in Washington, D.C., would issue statements only on those occasions when government policy needed clarification or the justification for the prison needed to be repeated.

With Alcatraz destined to house a relatively small number of troublesome convicts—less than 1 percent of the total federal prison population—special rules were established for transfer to and from the island prison. Offenders would not be committed directly to Alcatraz after conviction in federal courts. A convict would merit transfer to the island only after he had demonstrated his inability or unwillingness to adjust at other prisons, or because his stature in the convict subculture or as a "public enemy" gave him undue influence over other inmates or members of the staff. Transfer from Alcatraz was similarly constrained. A punitive measure at other penitentiaries, transfer to another prison would be a reward for good conduct on the island. Yet it would come only after four or five years of improved conduct. No man was to be paroled directly from Alcatraz island. (According to guard Robert Baker, this policy was to assure Bay Area residents that Alcatraz convicts would not be released directly to their communities.) The only other legitimate way for an inmate to leave Alcatraz was by dying, being deported, or serving every day of his sentence (going out "flat").

READYING ALCATRAZ FOR THE FIRST INMATES

In late 1933 the Bureau of Prisons turned to the task of refurbishing the military prison. James A. Johnston—former warden at two California state prisons, San Quentin and Folsom—was appointed warden in November, began supervising the refurbishing process on January 2, 1934, and moved into the warden's home on the island on April 5. Trained as a lawyer, Johnston was an influential businessman and banker who had important political connections to California's United States Senator Hiram Johnson. But Johnston was also known to Sanford Bates as a member of the Wickersham commission. While Johnston assembled a staff, he worked with Bates and BOP headquarters to outline the policies and procedures that would be in place for the first prisoners, who were expected to arrive during the following summer.

Instead of transferring experienced guards from other federal prisons to staff the new special-purpose penitentiary, Bates and Johnston decided that operations would begin with a large contingent of new officers. The advantage to this strategy was that new employees could be selected and trained as BOP administrators wished. The FBI was moving to establish higher standards for recruitment, training, and supervision of agents, and federal prison officials intended to move in the same direction. Another advantage of hiring guards with no prior experience was that they would not bring with them bad habits learned under other administrations or inappropriate relationships with any prisoners.

In addition to the custodial staff there were several stewards who managed kitchen operations, supervisors of inmate work crews at laundry, tailor, carpenter, and mat shops, two chaplains, a medical staff, including physicians who worked for the Public Health Service and orderlies (later called medical technical assistants), electricians, plumbers, painters, clerical workers, and a business manager.

To make the old military prison secure enough to control the federal prison system's most influential convicts and its most prolific escape artists, the Bureau of Prisons undertook major modifications of three of the existing cell blocks. The old, flat, soft steel grills and doors that covered the front of each cell on both sides of B and C blocks and the B side of A block were replaced with bars of tool-proof steel; two gun cages were erected at each end of the cell house. Three new guard towers, to be manned around the clock, were constructed to supplement the existing one, and a fifth tower was installed on the northeast side of the powerhouse for use in emergency situations.[40] Barbed wire fencing was strung between walls and buildings close to the sea and on the cliffs themselves. A new armory with tool-proof steel doors was constructed in the administration building outside, and immediately adjacent to, the main cell house. New steel detention sash windows were installed in the laundry and workshop buildings. Tear gas canisters were attached to the tops of columns in the center of the inmate dining room and above the main gate between the administrative offices and the cell house.

A "dead line" marked by orange buoys three hundred yards offshore ringed the island; outsiders who ventured within the dead line risked being fired on. Large warning signs painted on exterior walls and erected at other points on the island made the prohibition against coming too close clearly visible to vessels approaching Alcatraz from any direction. Employee housing—barracks for single men, apartments for families, and the houses for the warden, chief medical officer, and other senior staff— was remodeled and renovated. As the Bureau of Prisons completed its retooling and the army vacated Alcatraz Island on June 19, 1934, Warden Johnston announced that the prison was open for business.

Anticipating the arrival of the first inmates, the public and the press became intensely curious about the facilities, the convicts who would occupy them, and the regime those convicts would face. Reporters' desire for information, however, ran up against the policy decisions to bar the press from the island and limit the release of public information.

In July Warden Johnston informed Director Bates that wire service and newspaper reporters were very anxious to obtain information about certain features of the prison; for one thing, they wanted to know how the prisoners would be controlled and prevented from escaping. "They have heard about gun detectors, wooden gates, light beams, robot guards, and electric eyes," said Johnston, "and some of them seem to think that we have secret stuff that we are concealing." The press also wanted to know the names of the "public enemies" to be shipped to Alcatraz and the dates and details of their transfers. Most reporters were assuming that Capone, Kelly, Bailey, and Albert Bates would be included, along with the surviving associates of John Dillinger, Pretty Boy Floyd, and Baby Face Nelson, and (when apprehended) the leaders of the Barker-Karpis gang—in short, the most highly publicized criminals in the country. Johnston suggested that reporters be allowed to tour the prison before any inmates arrived "so as to be able to deny such requests immediately after we open."[41]

Director Bates gave his approval. But he advised Warden Johnston to make only the most general responses during the press tour and to deny specifics due to "security considerations." He recommended that Johnston purposely create "an air of mystery" about the measures that would safeguard the country from the prisoners.

On August 1, 1934, Attorney General Cummings and Director Bates officially activated Alcatraz as a federal penitentiary. Two weeks later, just before the arrival of the first inmates from Leavenworth and Atlanta, the members of the press were given a guided tour of the prison—on the occasion of an inspection of the island by Attorney General Cummings. Reporters' requests to learn the identities of the notorious group of desperadoes who would soon populate the island were not assuaged by the tour. From that day until the prison closed in March 1963, the "air of mystery" so carefully crafted by the Bureau of Prisons shrouded the lives of inmates and employees and every event that occurred on the island. Again and again, a lack of accurate information led to speculation, rumor, and fantasy.

SELECTING THE "WORST OF THE WORST"

It was one thing to design a new federal prison for the likes of Machine Gun Kelly and Harvey Bailey and another to fill the 270 cells on Alcatraz with inmates appropriate to the prison's mission. Bureau of Prisons officials knew from the beginning that once all the Kellys, Baileys, Capones, and other "public enemies" in the federal prison system—men federal officials many years later called the "worst of the worst"—were designated as Alcatraz transferees, there would still be room for a large number of prisoners of lesser notoriety. Therefore, in the autumn of 1933, about the same time the federal government announced the future opening of a prison on Alcatraz Island, the BOP set about determining who those other prisoners would be.

In October 1933 Director Bates asked each of the wardens at Leavenworth, the Ft. Leavenworth Annex, Atlanta, McNeil Island, and the new prison at Lewisburg, Pennsylvania, to nominate "not over fifty men who might be classified as desperate or difficult enough to be suitable for transfer to Alcatraz Island."[1] As Henry Hill, the warden at Lewisburg, understood it, Bates wanted the wardens to choose "unruly, antisocial, agitating characters" who were sources of "constant trouble," men known as "potential 'escapers'" and who by virtue of the terms of their sentence and the nature of their crimes would escape if possible," and men who "attract unto themselves numbers of prisoners through whom they might seek to control certain elements of the population."[2]

The opportunity to transfer a large number of troublemakers all at once to another prison came infrequently in the careers of federal prison administrators, so the wardens were no doubt enthusiastic about filling the director's request. Knowing that their performance was judged not on the success of their industrial or work programs, or on their prisons' recidivism rate, but on whether they could maintain order in their institutions, they were happy to remove from their responsibility the prisoners they believed were most likely to cause riots, escapes, deaths, and unrest.

At Bureau headquarters, Bates and his deputies reviewed the lists submitted by the wardens. They rejected many of the candidates proposed by the wardens of Atlanta and Leavenworth on the grounds that they were exhibiting evidence of mental health problems or had been selected only because they were nuisances. The Bureau officials sent the lists back to the penitentiaries with requests for revisions or further justifications. The wardens provided better arguments for the inclusion of certain prisoners and substituted the names of other candidates. By the time the refurbishing of Alcatraz neared completion in the early summer of 1934, upward of two hundred federal prisoners had been identified as Alcatraz transfers.

Each warden had to provide adequate justification for including an inmate on his list. Typically, the wardens cited such personality traits as "desperate," "constant troublemaking," "agitator," and "unruly." Here is a sampling of recommendations from the wardens at Atlanta, Leavenworth, and McNeil Island:

> a dangerous, mentally not normal, prisoner who has already stabbed one inmate with a pair of shears . . . claimed he was sorry that he did not kill the man [and] threatens when he comes out [of isolation] he will come out cutting.[3]

> was recently searched and shotgun shells together with a piece of pipe designed for a shotgun were found. He had planned a mass escape by shooting a tower guard and taking the power boat.[4]

> slippery as an eel, escaped three times from U.S. Marshals on way to prison. Was in plot for mass escape. Will make a break any time, a very dangerous man.[5]

> these men are all potential killers and have been actively engaged in a conspiracy, to smuggle guns into the institution for use in carrying out their plans of escaping.[6]

> this inmate is plotting right now . . . to seize our locomotive and escape by crashing through the east gate.[7]

Most of the prisoners selected for transfer to Alcatraz were indeed bona fide security risks, but other issues influenced wardens' choices. Wardens tried to take advantage of the transfer opportunity to get rid of prisoners whose behavior indirectly threatened order, including men (particularly if they were physically powerful) whose bizarre, unpredictable, or assaultive behavior jeopardized the physical well-being of staff or disturbed the peace and quiet of cell blocks. It was difficult to draw the line in some cases between custodial risks and those who were suffering genuine breakdowns in mental health. In any case, wardens and their subordinates were appreciative of the opportunity to put their problem inmates into the care of another warden.

Foremost among prisoners who made nuisances of themselves were the "writ writers." They annoyed wardens by filing briefs in federal court questioning elements of their arrest, conviction, or sentence, or they filed complaints about prison conditions and the actions of prison staff. These complaints brought the institution's business, the staff's behavior, and the warden's judgment into question before attorneys and judges, whom BOP staff regarded as ignorant and naive about prison management. Similar troublemakers sought to communicate their complaints about the treatment they were receiving to newspaper reporters, members of Congress, and even to Bureau of Prisons headquarters. Also in the nuisance category were a small number of "aggressive homosexuals" who needed to be controlled for the protection of younger or weaker inmates.

Finally, there were the big shots of organized crime or gangland, figures who could use their status, substantial financial resources, power of personality, and connections with associates on the outside to manipulate or seduce staff into providing favors or privileges not granted to the general inmate population. In most cases, the inclusion of these inmates on the transfer-to-Alcatraz lists was already a foregone conclusion.

Each federal warden had little trouble finding a place on his proposed transfer list for all the notorious gangsters, bank robbers, and kidnappers in his custody. But in each penitentiary such prisoners filled only a small percentage of the available slots. For the most part, therefore, the wardens offered up the names of convicts who were known only to other inmates and their own employees.

Press speculation about the identities of the prisoners to be transferred focused on the big-name offenders, and in some cases they were correct—Al Capone was included in the list of men to be shipped from Atlanta, Machine Gun Kelly headed the Leavenworth list, and Albert Bates and Harvey Bailey topped the list of transfers from the U.S. Penitentiary Annex at Fort Leavenworth.

THE ALCATRAZ EXPRESS

Wardens and Bureau officials debated about the best way to transport the chosen prisoners to Alcatraz. Some wanted them moved in small groups in prison cars that would be attached to trains on their normal runs; Assistant Director Hammack and others believed the prisoners should be sent in large groups on special prison trains. Hammack was worried about using regular trains because information about the trains' routes and stops would be too easily acquired by associates of the transported prisoners and by reporters. He compared the transport of prisoners in many small groups to "dropping our marbles all over the lot."

Hammack believed that transport by special train could be accomplished without publicity and in virtual secrecy: "I would be willing to guarantee the whole special train could move from Atlanta to Alcatraz with less publicity than you would be able to accomplish if you sent Al Capone on the same trip by regular service with any number of guards you chose to select."[8] The relative security of the special-train method hinged on the ability of the BOP to work with the railroad companies to control the conditions of transport. The final plan proposed by Hammack reflected extensive negotiations with the railroads:

> The railroad authorities have promised us there will be no publicity. They hope to get more business out of us and you could be sure they would live up to their agreement in that respect. Not only that, but the railroad authorities have agreed they will not stop the special train at regular stations, and, in fact, the only occasion for stopping the train would be to change the crew, take on water or fuel, or perform some regular service. This would be done in the yard or at some point distant from the regular passenger station. Nobody but the train crew would know where the stops were to be. To safeguard this phase the railroad companies have agreed they will have a sufficient number of special agents and detectives in the yard or at the service station to insure no unauthorized person even approaches the train. It would be impossible for anybody to know who was on the train unless the information was given out at Washington or at the institution from which the transfer originated. If the prisoners were selected before hand, the train placed in the prison yard, carefully searched, the prisoners moved in and properly shackled, then the entire party could move out without anybody knowing anything about it except the officers inside the institution.[9]

Director Bates approved Hammack's plan, and specifics were arranged with the rail companies. Although the trains would have to make stops at regular locations in order to take on water and ice, they would not stop in the passenger areas of stations, and no information would be issued beforehand about the location of stops for fuel and servicing. Instructions for the secure keeping of the prisoners called for sixteen guards to accompany each shipment. Prisoners would be shackled and handcuffed for the duration of the trip; two guards were to be stationed behind heavy wire enclosures installed at the ends of each car. One guard, armed with a pistol and submachine gun, was given the following instructions: "Each time it is necessary for a prisoner to go to a toilet or wash room, or whenever necessary to open the screen door between guards and prisoners, [the armed guard] must go out on the car platform and lock the door from the outside before the unarmed guard unlocks the inside screen door."[10] Both shifts of guards were to be at their posts whenever the train stopped; when meals were served, extra guards would carry out the actual serving of food; prisoners were to remain in their seats for the duration of the trip except when they needed to go, one man at a time, to the toilet; tear gas guns were to be stored in two cars, and no railroad employees would be allowed inside the cars that carried prisoners.

In early August, before the first special train was scheduled to leave from Atlanta, the Southern Pacific Railway carried fourteen men from McNeil Island Penitentiary in Washington State to Alcatraz in a prison car with barred windows. This first shipment of transfers arrived at Alcatraz on August 11 under the supervision of six guards, a lieutenant, and McNeil Island's warden. It was accomplished with no press or public notice. These prisoners were kept out of sight when Attorney General Cummings, with a contingent of reporters, toured the prison on August 18.

In the meantime, arrangements were made for the much larger Atlanta and Leavenworth shipments. The Bureau of Prisons asked that FBI Director Hoover have several of his agents accompany each shipment, but Hoover denied the request, asserting that his agents were "too busy with other duties." (In reality, Hoover was of the opinion that using his men as aides in a Bureau of Prisons operation was demeaning and would detract from the FBI's primary focus.) A medical officer with first-aid supplies was assigned to each train, and after a flurry of letters between Washington, D.C., and the prisons, four more guards per train were added, making a total of twenty on each train.

It was agreed that the arrangement of coaches containing the prisoners would call for them to be located between the sleeper cars (for off-duty staff) with the dining car to be situated in the middle of the train. The armed guards in the sleepers and in the dining car would thus be in positions to back up the armed officers stationed on the platform at each end of the prisoners' coaches and "provide an ideal disposition of officers for defense against outside interference. An attack from the outside can thus be met by a cross fire from front, rear and center of the train."[11]

Director Bates suggested that a pilot locomotive precede each train but this idea was discarded when Warden Zerbst noted that use of a pilot locomotive would "create wonder and gossip along the line of station agents." Zerbst assured Bates that the trains would be well protected against the most likely form of attack:

> Any organization attempting to liberate our prisoners would not use explosives, but will flag the train to stop and then attempt to attack it. We will be amply prepared to meet such an attempt. There will be two railroad special agents on the locomotive all the way and the Chief Special Agent will be on the train to see that his agents adequately protect the train at service stops.[12]

On August 19 at 6:00 A.M., the first prison train, traveling under the code name "Bamboo Cosmos," left the Atlanta Penitentiary. It also carried transfers from Lewisburg penitentiary in Pennsylvania, who had been moved by prison bus to Atlanta. Ruey Eaton, who traveled with Al Capone on this train, described the uneventful trip:

> On the way out, we sat in the same seats day and night. It was almost unbearably hot. You may remember that this was the year of the great drought in Texas and other Western states when so many cattle died of starvation and lack of water. On the trip out the guards were pretty good to us. We had food, and they changed our leg irons once. The train stopped in every city of any size along our route. . . . Everyone in the crowd wanted to see Al Capone and they would holler out "which one is Al?" Well, it happened that he was not in our car at all but in another one. But we would point out some guy in the crowd, and they were just as pleased as if they had seen Al.[13]

The trains were scheduled to arrive in the early morning in the Bay Area so that the transfer of inmates to the island could be completed in daylight. Despite the effort to keep all the arrangements secret, the train's movements had not escaped the notice of news reporters. Officers armed with rifles and submachine guns had been evident at every station on the train's route, so it was not difficult to track the train's progress. Reporters were waiting in large numbers when the train passed through stations in the Bay Area early on August 22. Even when the train was diverted from the logical terminal in the East Bay, Oakland's Southern Pacific Station, to a spur unused for twenty-six years on the west side of the bay, the press was waiting. As the train pulled into the small village of Tiburon, railway agents moved through the crowd of photographers and reporters, confiscating some sixty cameras. The agents and armed guards kept the crowd at a distance as the cars containing the convicts were shunted onto a large railroad barge. The barge was towed out into San Francisco Bay and escorted to Alcatraz by a Coast Guard cutter with armed sailors standing at its rails. Reporters and photographers had anticipated this move, and they crowded onto private boats and shot photos with telescopic lenses as the barge made its way to the island.

When the barge reached the island's wharf, the Coast Guard boat positioned itself to block the view of the photographers in their launches. Guards removed the leg irons from the prisoners, handcuffed them in pairs, and marched them along a heavily guarded route through the rear gate and into the yard. One by one, each pair was called into the cell building, where Atlanta Warden A. C. Aderhold and Alcatraz Deputy Warden C. J. Shuttleworth identified the men and assigned them identification numbers and cells. Each prisoner was escorted by a guard to the bathhouse, stripped of clothing, and his orifices examined by a doctor. After bathing, he was given a uniform stamped with his number and then taken to his assigned cell. That afternoon, Johnston wired Bates: "Fifty Three Crates Furniture From Atlanta Received In Good Condition. No Breakage. All Installed." In the early evening, the prisoners were taken to the mess hall and served their first meal on the Rock.[14]

Warden Johnston refused to answer any press inquiries until the day after the inmates arrived. With officers armed with rifles and submachine guns evident at every station on the train's route and with the Coast Guard boat and the prison launch providing armed escorts as the barge holding the prison cars made its way to Alcatraz Island, it was not surprising that reporters interpreted these sights and symbols as indicators of the dangerousness of the cargo. A *San Francisco Examiner* headline read "Bringing Sinister Cargo Here: Prison Train at Devil's Island" and *The San Francisco Call Bulletin* exclaimed, "Rush Capone and Enemy to Alcatraz 'Devil's Isle.'"[15]

In his statement to the press, Johnston, following a directive from Bureau headquarters in Washington, D.C., refused to identify a single rider on the prison train:

> No one is going to know the identity of the prisoners housed here, nor even the numbers they go by. . . . We are not even going to let the outside world know to which duties they have been assigned . . . [the inmates] . . . are not even going to have an opportunity to know what goes on outside. . . . Those men were sent here because the government wants to break their contacts with the underworld. That is going to be done.[16]

The press also sought to describe the experience of arriving at Alcatraz from the perspective of the inmates. The impact of seeing their new home, they reported, was powerful from the moment prisoners first viewed the "island fortress." With no firsthand information to support its contention, the *San Francisco Chronicle* printed a picture of Al Capone under the heading "Ex-Mogul of Underworld Cracks at Island Bastille" and went on to say,

> He couldn't take it—Al Capone, whose iron nerve he boasted would never break, cracked when he viewed the escape-proof ramparts of Alcatraz yesterday. . . . Sagging shoulders and listless eyes told only too plainly that [his] first view of the prison confirmed penitentiary grapevine reports that any attempt to flee Alcatraz would be worse than futile.[17]

In contrast, Ruey Eaton's account of his initial impression of Alcatraz provides a more accurate account of the inmates' first day on the island:

> Well, it was a relief to dock at Alcatraz and get off on the island. We were about as worn out a bunch as you could ever see. We could hardly recognize each other, we were so dusty and dirty. . . . I guess the women and children looking down from their apartments on the cliffs above the docks thought we were some kind of wild animals being unloaded on the island. We were marched into a small yard from which the guards would take us two at a time in the cell block for a bath, a number, and a cell. I thought I would freeze to death while I was waiting. That fine California weather the fellow had told me about was about to kill me. . . . Finally we all got inside. . . . We each had a separate cell, small but clean. I was pleased to have a cell by myself. When we went in for our first meal, we saw how tight security was. The kitchen was barred off from the mess hall and when we were inside the hall the great steel doors were locked. Guards were on catwalks outside the windows and another guard was in a gun cage over the door. We knew they had tommy guns. Ten men were seated at each table, five on each side. Gas cylinders hung from the ceilings above about every other table. In addition a guard was stationed at every second table. We were told that there would be no talking at the table except to ask that bread be passed. The meal was far better than any we had in Atlanta. But at Alcatraz there were no radios, no newspapers, no commissary where we might buy candy, toothpaste, or cigarettes. All of these we had at Atlanta. Already we felt lonely with nothing to hear but the sad sound of fog horns.[18]

Robert Baker, the first guard hired by Warden Johnston, described the arrival of the first large shipment of inmates:

> The Atlanta inmates came on a train from Tiburon, they brought these railcars over on a Southern Pacific Railroad barge, and they brought them all chained up. When they got to Alcatraz, the Coast Guard and the police boats and our boats, and we were lined up with machine guns, .45 au-

tomatics, and pistols. We walked the prisoners up the street and through that little round tunnel [in the back of the yard]. We walked them by the hill [guard] tower, and then down the road past what we call the road tower. Then they went up the steps into the yard; it was cold and windy and miserable and they were pooping their britches—they'd been on that railway car for five days. Then they went up the steps to the cell house. The warden was sitting right there, opposite Broadway [the corridor between B and C blocks] where you go into the kitchen. One guard was assigned to one convict—I guess they don't call them convicts now—but we call them convicts. The warden gave them a number and we took them down to the basement and they threw the coveralls away and we stood there and watched them take a shower. We gave them clothing, took them upstairs, put them in cells and locked the door.

Warden Johnston was sitting there and he asked the guys, "Who are you and what's your name?" Capone made a big splash about "You know who I am," and then he finally said, "I am Al Capone." The warden said, "Well, you're now number 85."[19]

Several days after the arrival of the inmates from Atlanta, Warden Johnston was notified that he would shortly receive eight additional prisoners. District of Columbia officials at Lorton Reformatory had asked that seven ringleaders of a food strike "and other trouble" be transferred to the Bureau of Prisons. Ordinarily troublemakers from a lower-security facility would have been sent to Atlanta or Leavenworth, but the Bureau was looking for candidates for its new prison and it had been decided to send these men, along with one inmate from the Washington, D.C., Asylum and Jail, directly to Alcatraz.[20]

Johnston was told to expect his largest shipment on September 4, 103 inmates from Leavenworth and the Leavenworth Annex. Experience with the Atlanta shipment indicated that because the ankles of some men had become swollen from the leg irons, a physician was needed on the train to make such adjustments as were necessary for medical reasons; it was also decided that drinking water could be provided by a pail and dipper circulated through the cars rather than having inmates leave their seats under restraints to go to a faucet. The Leavenworth prison train arrived on the scheduled day at 6:00 A.M. at Ferry Point in Richmond in the East Bay.[21] From here, the railroad barge, escorted by a Coast Guard cutter and the prison launch, transported the three coaches containing the prisoners to the island. Once again the warden sent a telegram to Bureau headquarters announcing that another 103 crates of furniture had arrived in good condition and had been unpacked. Alcatraz was in business.

A DIVERSE GROUP OF PRISONERS

By early September 1934, 210 prisoners comprised the population on the island. As Warden Johnston reviewed their records, he must have concluded that they were an odd assemblage. First of all, there were the thirty-two military prisoners (inmates nos. 1–32) who had remained imprisoned on Alcatraz when the War Department transferred the island to the Department of Justice. Ten of these men had been convicted of sodomy while in the military; another had killed his homosexual lover; two others had been convicted of rape; one had a prior sexual assault on a minor female; and another had assaulted his wife (and threatened to "make hamburger out of her" when he got out of prison). Fifteen of the military prisoners were serving time for robbery (all small-time compared to the bank, post office, and train robberies committed by the federal prisoners); and three other men had been convicted of larceny, counterfeiting, and forgery. One military prisoner had been convicted of shooting a Japanese merchant while stationed in Hawaii.[22] The records of the military prisoners hardly fit the description of the population intended for Alcatraz and several of these men would file protests of their detention in, as one prisoner's petition put it, "a penitentiary for habitual criminals and insidious menaces to society."[23]

The military prisoners had been very apprehensive about the arrival of the real convicts coming from Atlanta and Leavenworth. Those convicted of sodomy, rape, and sexual molestation were particularly fearful as they anticipated—correctly—that the gangsters, bank robbers, and prison escape artists soon to arrive would hold hostile views of homosexuals and men who sexually assaulted women and children. Warden Johnston recognized that these prisoners were out of place but took the position that he needed a core of nondangerous, compliant workers for the kitchen and the laundry, and to provide housekeeping and cooking services in his home. The military prisoners kept to themselves as much as possible when the federal prisoners arrived, and few posed disciplinary problems. About fourteen months after the trains arrived, nine were shipped off to McNeil Island; within three and a half years, all had been released or transferred.[24]

Similarly, the first contingent of fourteen McNeil Island prisoners (inmates nos. 33–46) did not contain any big-shot gangsters or notable prison management problems. Prior to the opening of Alcatraz, most of these men would have been sent to Leavenworth or Atlanta. Eleven, however, had plotted escapes or had actually tried to escape from McNeil Island or other jails or prisons. Most were described as "agitators" and "desperadoes," men who were "willing to do anything to gain freedom." They had sentences of ten years or longer in most cases, but two had only three-year terms. Their lack of even regional notoriety was evident in the ability of the Bureau of Prisons to effect their transfer to Alcatraz without the public noticing, and the inability of the press to identify any prisoner in the shipment after they had been "installed" on the island.

Nor did the troublemakers from the District of Columbia's Lorton Reformatory (inmates nos. 47–54) fit the criteria established for Alcatraz prisoners. Prior to August 1934 they would have been transferred to the penitentiaries at Lewisburg or Atlanta. Like the McNeil Island and military prisoners, they were sent to Alcatraz only to help fill out the population. The same was true of some of the transfers from Atlanta and Leavenworth who had nevertheless made it through the BOP's filtering process.

Rounding out the list of inmates who arguably did not fit the Alcatraz criteria were seven inmates from the Leavenworth Annex. One man, Roy Gardner, showing some naïveté about the regime awaiting him on the Rock, actually requested the transfer to Alcatraz. He was well known in California for his earlier exploits as a train robber and for three successful escapes from federal custody. Despite this history, he had posed "no trouble from a disciplinary or custodial standpoint" at the Annex. Indeed, the warden had praised him as "a conscientious workman" who taught other inmates in the electrical school and appeared "to be sincere in his desire to rehabilitate himself."[25] Gardner requested the move partly because he was offended not to be included on the original lists of America's most accomplished desperadoes and escape artists, but more important because his wife and other relatives lived close by in the Napa Valley. The other Annex volunteers included a trusty, the institution's head baker, a clerical worker whose only fault was described as an "insolent attitude and inclination toward conniving and possession of contraband," a man whose disciplinary record indicated that he had been found intoxicated "and would probably become so again if the opportunity presented itself," and two prisoners said to pose no disciplinary or custodial problems, but they had "long criminal records."[26]

It was customary for a prison—particularly a newly opened prison—to have a contingent of nonproblematic prisoners to take care of basic institutional maintenance tasks, such as working in the laundry and the kitchen and serving as janitors and hospital attendants. These men provided a bit of leavening in a larger population of prisoners who posed more serious custodial problems. But as Alcatraz opened, the proportion of inmates who did not meet the Bureau's own criteria of notoriety, dangerousness, and escape potential represented well over one-third of the Alcatraz population. Up to the time the prison ceased operations thirty years later, there would always be men whose confinement at Alcatraz violated the official criteria; most fell into the nuisance category and some during the last decade of the prison's operation were simply convenient commitments of men convicted on the West Coast. There never were anywhere near 250 men in the federal prison system at any one period from 1934 to 1963 whose criminal and prison records could match the imagery of the press or the official pronouncements of the Department of Justice.

THE ALL-STAR TEAM OF FEDERAL LAWBREAKERS

Despite the fact that some Alcatraz prisoners fell short of being notorious, desperate, escape-prone, or dangerous, most had records and reputations that justified these labels. The men collected together on the Rock in the autumn of 1934 made up the most complete assemblage of infamous outlaws, kidnappers, gangsters, murderers, and escape artists the country had ever seen. This became even more true in subsequent years, as more notorious criminals were captured and prosecuted or committed acts in other prisons that earned them a transfer to Alcatraz.

Al Capone and George Kelly were names well known to the press and the public, but the passengers on the first prison trains included a remarkable collection of lesser-known gang members who were the associates or partners of notorious bank robbers who couldn't be sent to prison themselves because they had fallen in gun battles with police, sheriffs, or G-men. From Chicago, in addition to Capone, came five members of the Roger Touhy gang and two members of Bugs Moran's organization. From New York, there were five members of Dutch Schultz's West Side gang. They were joined by ten members of the Barker-Karpis mob, three leaders and one member of Detroit's Purple Gang, seven associates of Harvey Bailey and Kelly, five members of the Irish O'Malley gang, and two partners each of John Dillinger, Baby Face Nelson, and Bonnie Parker and Clyde Barrow. Even several aging members of the old Frank Nash–Al Spencer gang settled down on the Rock with long sentences ahead of them. Gordon Alcorn, kidnapper of Charles Boettcher, and Frank Mulloy, Richard Gallatas, and Herbert Farmer—convicted of conspiring to free Frank Nash in the Union Station massacre—had seats on the first train from Leavenworth as well.

The federal prison system's most notable escapees were also among the first arrivals. They included Roy Gardner, Joe Urbaytis, and John Boyd, Atlanta Penitentiary escapees; James Clark, who with Harvey Bailey escaped from the Kansas State Penitentiary; Charles Berta, Tom Underwood, and Stanley Brown, who took the warden as a hostage in their escape from Leavenworth; and Thomas Holden and Francis Keating, who walked out the front door of Leavenworth.

In addition to the "public enemies" with nationwide reputations, there were other federal lawbreakers among the first crop of Alcatraz inmates whose notoriety was more ephemeral or limited to local newspaper coverage. In any prison other than Alcatraz they would have been the highest-profile prisoners because of their criminal or escape histories. Among them were John P. Carroll, who escaped from prison to aid his sick wife, and Charles "Limpy" Cleaver.

These luminaries and semiluminaries of the "underworld" were joined in later years by other notable Public Enemies. These included Dock Barker, Volney Davis, Alvin Karpis, John Paul Chase, Floyd Hamilton, Ted Walters, and Harmon Waley.

The criminal exploits of some of these robbers, kidnappers, and outlaws were described in chapter 1. The pre-Alcatraz lives of various others deserve brief mention here for two reasons: their crimes were representative of what it took to be sent to Alcatraz; several will be central characters in events described in subsequent chapters.

At age sixty-one, John P. Carroll was considerably older than most of his fellow passengers on the train from Leavenworth, but he had the type of record that called for a transfer to a prison for habitual incorrigibles. Carroll's record of incarceration had begun at age twenty when he was sent to the Wisconsin Industrial School for Boys after conviction on forgery charges. This sentence was followed by terms in the Wisconsin State Prison at Waupun for larceny, four separate periods of confinement in the state penitentiary at Joliet, Illinois, three years and one month in the state penitentiary at Sioux Falls, South Dakota, for assault with a dangerous weapon, and a year and three months in the state penitentiary at Stillwater, Minnesota, for burglary.

Carroll's federal trouble began when he and his wife, Mabel, stole seventy money order forms from a post office in Cartersville, Montana, and cashed them in a number of cities. When they were caught, Carroll received a seven-year federal sentence at Leavenworth, which he began serving on March 28, 1926. Mabel was convicted along with her husband and also received a seven-year term that—because a federal prison for women did not open at Alderson, West Virginia, until November 1938— she began serving in the Women's Reformatory at Leeds, Missouri.

In February 1927, while working in Leavenworth's new shoe factory, Carroll enlisted the aid of Charles Thompson, the assistant superintendent of the factory, who helped Carroll crawl inside a wooden box three feet long, three feet wide, and thirteen inches deep. The box was placed on the prison mail truck with other boxes and taken out of the prison; it next appeared on the sidewalk outside Thompson's rooming house in the town of Leavenworth. Thompson asked two young men if they would each like to make fifty cents by carrying the box up some stairs to his room. They did so, and Thompson then disappeared with Carroll in a rented car, leaving his own belongings in his apartment. Acquaintances of the assistant superintendent were mystified as to the reasons for his involvement with Carroll. Some three weeks later, Thompson was arrested in New Orleans, where he explained his actions by claiming that Carroll had bribed him by offering to split $100,000 that Carroll said he had buried in Tennessee. Thompson never received any money for his efforts but earned a sentence of one year in jail after pleading guilty to helping Carroll escape.

The primary motivation for Carroll's escape became apparent on July 7, 1927, when he succeeded in effecting his wife's escape from the Leeds reformatory. When he learned that Mabel had become seriously ill with tuberculosis, he made plans to deliver her from prison, take care of her, and see that if she did die, it would not be in prison. After freeing Mabel, Carroll robbed post offices and jewelry stores as necessary to support himself and Mabel, who passed away six months later on January 18, 1928. Carroll remained at large until June 12 of that year when he was arrested in Philadelphia.

Carroll's exploits in getting his dying wife out of prison were depicted in a 1928 movie that was accompanied by the following promotional statement:

> Shipped out of the penitentiary as a box of shoes, got his sick wife out of jail at risk of his life, hid her and robbed to make her last days comfortable, and now goes back to Leavenworth satisfied—a movie thriller in real life.[27]

In October 1928 Carroll received a two-year sentence for the escape, to run concurrently with his seven-year term. After a period in solitary confinement at Leavenworth (the real punishment, since the concurrent sentence did not extend his time in prison) Carroll was released into the general population. On July 1, 1929, guards noticed that his clothing was wet and on investigation they found that he and another prisoner had cut a hole eighteen inches deep into a sewer line. In a search of his cell, guards found that Carroll had hidden a 114-foot-long rope made of bed sheets; he was returned to isolation.

Some months later Carroll was charged with stealing money orders from a post office in Maryland while he was on escape status; he demanded a jury trial and was returned to Baltimore, where he agreed to plead guilty; this time he was sentenced to an eight-year term to run consecutively to his seven-year sentence and was transferred to the federal prison at Atlanta. He did not appreciate the transfer to Atlanta, as he made clear in a letter to the director of the Bureau of Prisons:

> Dear Sir: I want to be transferred back to Leavenworth. You transferred me here in the first place against my will and I don't like it a little bit. Besides the officials here are too cruel and hateful. No one would stay here if he could get away and you know it. Make it snappy and get me back to Leavenworth where civilized men run the prison.[28]

At Atlanta two mechanical bar spreaders were found concealed in the mattress in Carroll's cell. After seventeen days in isolation he was placed in the disciplinary segregation unit, where he remained until December 10, 1933, when he was transferred back to Leavenworth. In June 1934 Carroll was placed on the list for transfer to Alcatraz based on the following justification prepared by the staff at Leavenworth:

> He is an inveterate criminal and there is no hope he may be reclaimed. He has escaped from here. Since his return from escape he has constantly been plotting further escapes. He is a menace within and without a penal institution and always a menace to the public safety when at large. His transfer to Alcatraz is recommended.[29]

Charles "Limpy" Cleaver, regarded as "hardened and dangerous . . . a member of the Chicago underworld," earned a transfer to Alcatraz because he combined a sensational mail train robbery with a sensational escape from jail after he was apprehended. The postal robbery, as described in a report to a chief postal inspector, had the character of a Hollywood movie:

> At about 8:25 AM, February 25, 1928, Charles Cleaver and seven others held up a mail train near the outskirts of Chicago, Ill., and robbed it of

$135,000 in currency, which was being transported by registered mail from Chicago to Harvey, Ill. There were two clerks on duty in the mail car at the time the train reached the point where the hold-up took place and all of the car doors were locked. The bandits used dynamite to blow one of the doors off the car, after which they entered with drawn guns and revolvers, and forced the two clerks to surrender the registered mails. Not only were the lives of the two clerks placed in jeopardy by the dangerous weapons, but the manner in which the mail car door was dynamited indicated a total disregard for consequences to the occupants. Throughout the hold-up two of the bandits armed with machine guns were stationed at points of vantage, one on either side of the train, and doubtless they would have made deadly use of these weapons had this been necessary in effecting the robbery. Charles Cleaver was one of the leaders of the gang and took a prominent part in the preparation and in the execution of the crime.[30]

Cleaver was arrested and locked up in jail at Wheaton, Illinois. But on June 10, 1928, with four other prisoners, he overpowered a jailer and escaped. Four days later, police caught up with the men, and a gun battle ensued in which at least five hundred shots were fired. Cleaver received several bullet wounds and was recaptured.

He was committed to Atlanta in August 1928 and transferred to Alcatraz in August 1934 on the first prison train. At that time, at age sixty-two, Cleaver was described as a "wrinkled old man" who "seemed quite proud that with two exceptions he is the oldest man in the institution." By his own count, he had over the course of his criminal career sustained a total of twenty-seven bullet wounds, and many of the slugs were still lodged in his body.[31] He remained imprisoned on Alcatraz until 1944, when he was transferred to Leavenworth. There prison doctors began removing bullets he had been carrying in his shoulder since his capture in 1928.

Joe Urbaytis was mentioned briefly in chapter 1 because of his involvement in two separate escape attempts from the federal penitentiary in Atlanta. His place among the first Alcatraz inmates, however, was ensured by more than his determination to escape.

At 1:50 A.M. on February 17, 1921 a mail truck pulled up to the loading platform of the U.S. post office in Toledo, Ohio. When the driver and his partner walked around and unlocked the rear door of the truck, they were suddenly confronted by two armed men, who ordered them to lie face down on the ground. Two more men jumped out of an automobile parked nearby and began pulling pouches from the trucks and throwing them into a vehicle where Urbaytis sat at the wheel. After taking ten pouches, the four men jumped into their car and roared away. They had taken 173 pieces of registered mail that contained Liberty bonds, jewelry, commercial bonds, and stock certificates amounting in value to $915,961—one of the biggest hauls in the history of post office robberies. Urbaytis was arrested four days later. Some eighteen other principals and accomplices were rounded up and put on trial, and on June 24 Urbaytis was found guilty on seven counts of grand larceny. He was placed in the Lucas County Jail, but on September 5 he and two of his fellow bandits escaped; he remained at large for some two and a half years, until May 5, 1924.

After a gun fight with detectives in which he was shot, Urbaytis was captured, tried, and sentenced to two consecutive twenty-five-year terms in federal prison and transferred to the Atlanta Penitentiary. On his arrival at Atlanta, he noted that the police considered him a likely suspect in "every unsolved robbery in which $100 or more was stolen."[32] This claim was probably not far from the truth, since he had accumulated some fifteen prior arrests.

Urbaytis had been in Atlanta only for a few weeks when he was locked up in isolation for ten days as the result of a fight in the dining hall; during the next two years he was charged with attempted escape (fourteen more days in isolation) and "loafing on work detail" (four days isolation). As noted in chapter 1, Urbaytis, Roy Gardner, John Boyd, and two other inmates attempted to scale the thirty-foot-high walls of the penitentiary on July 19, 1928, after succeeding in getting two .25 caliber revolvers smuggled into the prison and taking the captain and two guards hostage. After the escape attempt failed, Urbaytis was locked up in "permanent" isolation on a restricted diet and lost all the statutory good time he had earned or could earn on his sentence—3,000 days, or more than eight years. He grew resentful when he learned that Roy Gardner, despite his central role in the escape, had been transferred to Leavenworth and that two other men involved in the plot had spent only six months in isolation.

After Urbaytis had been in isolation for thirty-one months, the prison psychiatrist, C. R. F. Beall, received a letter with a return address marked "Vault 10, The Wilcox Museum for the Living Dead," in which Urbaytis expressed the view that he might remain in isolation for the remainder of his fifty-year sentence. At the end of January 1931, however, he was finally released to general population, although a guard was to accompany him whenever he moved about the prison. The following April Dr. Beall reported that Joe was "pleasant, courteous, talkative and cheerful," expressing only the hope that he could be transferred from a job in the tailor shop to an outdoor assignment so that he could "get into the sunlight."[33]

In November of that same year, an inmate about to be released from Atlanta was questioned by the deputy warden regarding reports that a recently released prisoner was to obtain three guns and smuggle them into the penitentiary to aid an escape attempt; the inmate readily admitted his knowledge of this plan, stating that he agreed to help the conspirators out because he feared he "would be cut to pieces" if he refused. The informant identified Joe Urbaytis as one of the intended recipients of smuggled weapons.[34]

When the list of transfers to Alcatraz was made up at Atlanta, Joe Urbaytis's name was certain to be included. On November 16, 1934, he arrived on the island accompanied by this note in his file: "He is a gangster and bandit leader and exerts a bad influence . . . for this reason he is unsafe to mingle and mix with other prisoners."[35]

Albert Bates had an important role in the Urschel kidnapping (as described in chapter 1), but he never reached the level of national prominence attained by his rap partners, George and Kathryn Kelly and Harvey Bailey. For some reason, the press and the FBI's publicity machine gave him only passing attention. Since his criminal career was at least as interesting as those of his partners, it deserves additional space here.

Bates was the only rider on the prison trains from Leavenworth and Atlanta who knew about doing time at Alcatraz. He had spent fifteen months on the island—then known as the Pacific branch of the U.S. Army Disciplinary Barracks—as punishment for deserting from the U.S. Army, in which he had enlisted in 1911. Given the intense Kansas summer heat he experienced in the basement of the Leavenworth Annex, Bates was said to have been pleased when he learned that he was going back to the cold, windy island.

Bates came to Alcatraz in 1934 with considerably more prior experience in penitentiaries than either George Kelly or Harvey Bailey. He had served time in the Nevada State Prison on a burglary conviction, and two terms in the Utah State Prison for burglary. While serving his second Utah sentence, he had been placed on a road camp from which he escaped; after he was arrested in Nebraska on charges of safecracking, he was returned to the Utah State Prison for the third time; six months after his release from Utah he was convicted of burglary and larceny in Colorado and was sent to the state penitentiary in Canon City and then to the state reformatory, from which he escaped and to which he was returned in 1930. In 1931, he was sentenced to thirty-five days in jail in Michigan for driving while intoxicated, but he escaped from the jail and remained at large until he was arrested in Denver in connection with the Urschel kidnapping. After Bates had been installed in a cell in the Leavenworth Annex with a life sentence, various states lodged eight separate complaints against him for various forms of criminal conduct if he was ever released from federal custody.

John Paul Chase was the first inmate on the list of Alcatraz notables who arrived after the initial mass transfers in the latter half of 1934. Contrary to the official policy that inmates would be sent to Alcatraz only after their cases had been reviewed at other federal prisons, Chase was committed directly to Alcatraz in late March 1935 after having been convicted of murdering two FBI agents. When he arrived at Alcatraz two weeks later, he was the only inmate who had not previously served time in jail or prison.[36]

In the late 1920s and early 1930s, Chase was involved in bootlegging activities in the San Francisco Bay Area. In early 1932 he met Lester Gillis, alias Baby Face Nelson, who had escaped from the Illinois State Prison at Joliet in February and come to San Francisco.[37] The two became close friends, and Chase left his home in Sausalito to travel to Minnesota with Nelson and his wife, Helen. Chase and Nelson became the chief suspects in a murder in Minneapolis, prompting them to move to Reno, Nevada. Again they became suspects, this time in the murder of a witness who was to testify against several of their underworld friends. In mid-April 1934, while Chase was in Chicago purchasing a car, Nelson, John Dillinger, and other members of the Dillinger gang were hiding out at the Little Bohemia Lodge in Wisconsin when FBI agents raided the lodge and all the gangsters got away.

Following the escape from Little Bohemia, Nelson attempted a holdup in Koerner's Place, Wisconsin. FBI agents arrived on the scene and Nelson shot and killed one agent and wounded another. On June 30 a police officer was killed during a bank robbery in South Bend, Indiana; Nelson and Dillinger were identified and it was suspected that Chase was also involved. Chase continued to perform numerous services for Nelson, including purchasing automobiles, guns, ammunition, and bullet-proof vests.

The offense that assured Chase would end up in Alcatraz occurred on November 27, 1934. Nelson, his wife, and Chase were on a highway near Barrington, Illinois, when two FBI agents in a passing car recognized the license plate number on Nelson's vehicle. The agents turned their car around to follow but were surprised to see that Nelson had also reversed direction and was coming toward them. After the two cars passed, Nelson turned again so that both cars were traveling in the same direction. Nelson pulled even with the agents and, with Chase in the back seat pointing an "automatic monitor rifle" at the agents, ordered them to pull over. The agents accelerated and Chase fired five shots through their windshield; one of the agents returned fire, damaging the radiator in Nelson's car.

Two other FBI agents, Samuel Cowley and H. E. Hollis, who happened to be approaching, came on this gun battle. In the course of their pursuit, Nelson suddenly stopped his car and Cowley and Hollis passed it by several hundred feet. As the agents got out of their car, they fired at Nelson and Chase, who returned fire with "automatic rifles and a machine gun." In the exchange, Cowley, Hollis, and Nelson were all hit—the two FBI agents died but Nelson, although he was severely wounded by six bullets, was able to walk to the agents' car, drive it back to his disabled vehicle, and pick up their weapons, Chase, and his wife, who had been hiding in a nearby field. Chase drove Nelson to the home of a priest in Wilmette, Illinois, seeking help but was turned away. Nelson died that evening and his body was left on a country road the next day.[38]

Nelson's wife, Helen, was soon arrested and Chase fled to the West Coast. He was arrested in Mt. Shasta, California, on December 27. Admitting his participation in the murders of FBI agents Cowley and Hollis, he was found guilty and on March 25, 1935, the judge proclaimed that he would "be imprisoned at the USP Alcatraz for the term of his natural life."

Harmon Waley arrived on Alcatraz on July 17, 1935, after having spent only twenty-six days in the penitentiary at McNeil Island, Washington.

He would spend more than two decades at Alcatraz—longer than any other prisoner except Alvin Karpis—mostly because of his misconduct on the island.

After a commitment at age seventeen to the Washington State Training School, Waley joined the army, deserted six months later, and after a court martial was sentenced to hard labor for nine months. At age twenty he was committed to the Idaho State Penitentiary to serve five to fifteen years for burglary but was pardoned due to the efforts of his mother. Two months after his release, he was charged with another burglary and began a two- to fifteen-year sentence at the state penitentiary at Walla Walla, Washington. A year later this sentence was also suspended, because a judge believed that Waley had "learned his lesson." But Waley continued to disappoint those who interceded on his behalf—he was back in Walla Walla two months later with a new two- to five-year sentence for grand larceny. After a number of commitments to solitary confinement for rules violations, he was paroled in September 1933.

Waley had met William Dainard at the Idaho State Penitentiary. In the spring of 1935 the two met again and, with Waley's wife, decided to make some money by kidnapping and holding for ransom the son of J. P. Weyerhaeuser, president of a major lumber company. After observing the Weyerhaeuser children going to and from school, Waley and Dainard grabbed seven-year-old George, the youngest child, on May 24, 1935. They hid him, secured by heavy chains, in a hole they had dug in the woods near Issaquah, in western Washington. He remained there during the night of May 24, wearing only a sweater, a pair of corduroy knickers, and cotton stockings. He was forced to sign his name to a ransom note that demanded $200,000 for his safe return.

Fearful they had been seen, Waley and Dainard moved the boy to another hole they had dug near Kanaskat where he spent the next night shackled; they gave him two blankets for warmth. On May 26 they again became apprehensive that they would be located, so they placed George in the trunk of their car and drove to an area outside Spokane where they handcuffed the boy to a tree until approximately 7:00 P.M. the next day, when he was again placed in the trunk of the car and taken to a house Waley's wife had rented in Spokane. He spent the next four days in a closet.

On May 31, Margaret Waley and William Dainard collected the ransom in Seattle and returned to Spokane. That night they once again placed the boy in the trunk of their car and drove 375 miles to Issaquah. At about 3:00 A.M. they released George, who was shortly thereafter returned to his parents. Because the boy claimed one of his kidnappers was referred to as "Alvin," suspicion was cast on Alvin Karpis and his gang.[39]

After dividing the ransom money, the Waleys and Dainard parted company; the Waleys went to Salt Lake City, Utah, where Harmon cashed a number of the ransom bills. On June 8, 1935, while buying a birthday present for her father with some of the ransom money, Margaret was arrested. Harmon was taken into custody on the same day and turned over to the U.S. marshal. Charged with kidnapping, he pleaded guilty on June 13 and was sentenced to forty-five years on the kidnapping count and two years on a conspiracy count, both sentences to run concurrently. He was sent to McNeil Island Penitentiary but shortly thereafter transferred to Alcatraz for "safer custody, considering the nature of his offense and criminal record."[40]

William Dainard would also end up at Alcatraz, but not until several years after his partner Waley. It took authorities almost a year to arrest him after the Weyerhaeuser kidnapping, during which time he was designated Public Enemy no. 2 (at the time, Alvin Karpis held the top spot of Public Enemy no. 1). He was given a sentence of sixty years for "transporting a kidnapped person in Interstate Commerce" and committed to McNeil Island on May 8, 1936. He was subsequently transferred to Leavenworth, transferred again to the medical center at Springfield, Missouri, and then back to Leavenworth. Dainard was sent to Alcatraz in the summer of 1939 because he was "a dangerous hardened offender who because of long sentence and detainer [legal hold placed against a prisoner's release by another jurisdiction, usually a state] must be considered as a potential escape case."[41]

Arthur "Dock" Barker disembarked from the Alcatraz prison launch on October 26, 1935, with a life sentence for the ransom kidnapping of St. Paul banker Edward Bremer. He was the son of Ma Barker and brother of Fred, both of whom had been gunned down by FBI agents. Barker's criminal history (some of which was described in chapter 1) also included the killing of two Minneapolis police officers after a Minneapolis bank robbery, the robbery of a Swift Company payroll in St. Paul, and the robbery of a Federal Reserve bank truck in Chicago, in the course of which a police officer was killed. When Barker was arrested on a Chicago street by FBI agents he had no weapon, but in the apartment where he was staying agents found a machine gun taken from a St. Paul policeman.[42]

With his outstanding criminal record, prior commitment to the Oklahoma State Penitentiary for murder, and a new federal life sentence, five months after he was received at Leavenworth Arthur Barker was a definite candidate for Alcatraz.[43]

Volney Davis's criminal history was closely tied to that of Dock Barker, and the two joined the Alcatraz population at about the same time, in the autumn of 1935. Davis met Barker while serving a three-year sentence for robbery at the Oklahoma State Penitentiary. After their release from prison, Davis and Barker killed an elderly night watchman in the course of a robbery, for which each received a life sentence. Two years later, in February 1923, after his return to the penitentiary at McAlester, Oklahoma, Davis and several other convicts escaped over the prison walls using ropes and a ladder. After twelve days at large, Davis was captured and returned to McAlester, where he served time until November 1932, at which time he was granted a "leave of absence." According to Davis, Dock (who had remarkably been paroled) and Fred Barker provided the money for an attorney to "put in the fix" to allow his "leave" from McAlester.[44]

Davis, indebted to the Barkers, joined them in a series of robberies, thereby becoming a fugitive from the state of Oklahoma. His connection to the Barkers led to his association with Alvin Karpis, and subsequently to his involvement in the kidnapping of Edward Bremer. Captured by FBI agents in Kansas City on February 6, 1935, he was handcuffed, shackled, and put in a small plane guarded by two agents. En route to Chicago the pilot became lost and the plane made a forced landing in a cornfield in Illinois. Since the incident attracted nearby residents, the agents, "to prevent curiosity and publicity," removed Davis's leg irons so that he could walk to the car being loaned to the agents. When they arrived at a hotel, the agents removed Davis's handcuffs, again to "avoid publicity and curiosity." While one of the agents went to a telephone booth, Davis and the other agent ordered glasses of beer. Davis suddenly knocked the agent down, "leaped head-first through a window," and ran from the building. The agent who had been knocked to the floor ran to the window, fired twice, but missed the fleeing prisoner. Davis stole a car and got out of town.[45] But several months later he was captured in

Chicago and taken to St. Paul to face charges related to the Bremer kidnapping. Davis pleaded guilty and received a life sentence on June 7, 1935. He was initially committed to Leavenworth, but four months later he was on his way to Alcatraz.

Burton Phillips arrived on Alcatraz at about the same time—October 1935—as Barker and Davis. He had received a life sentence seven months before for robbing $2,090 from the Chandler Bank of Lyons, Kansas, then taking the cashier and the assistant cashier as hostages while he and an accomplice drove away in a stolen car. It was Phillips's second conviction in Kansas. He had robbed a bank before robbing banks became a federal offense; on this conviction he had served one and a half years in the Kansas State Reformatory before he was paroled.

After the federal robbery conviction, he was sent to Leavenworth, where the staff quickly concluded that although he was only twenty-two years old, he was "undoubtedly a dangerous major criminal." It didn't help that while in jail awaiting transport to Leavenworth he had planned an escape by seizing the sheriff and obtaining weapons. He then intended to hold up the same bank he had just been convicted of robbing. The U.S. attorney labeled him "a habitual criminal that can never be reformed."[46] His transfer to Alcatraz was recommended, but because of his age Bureau headquarters suggested that he first be given a try for a couple of months at Leavenworth. He failed the test and was sent to Alcatraz on October 26. Phillips arrived on the island angry and resentful and began to establish an impressive record of misconduct that would include a violent assault on Warden James A. Johnston.

Alvin Karpis had associated with so many of the era's notorious outlaws that his arrival on Alcatraz on August 7, 1936, was in many ways a reunion with old friends. He would need these friendships because he was destined to spend twenty-five years on the Rock.

One of the best-known outlaws of the day, Karpis's criminal exploits were highlighted in chapter 1. More biographical background is useful here because unlike the other Alcatraz big shots—Capone and Kelly—Karpis actively participated in some of the organized resistance to be chronicled in subsequent chapters.[47]

Karpis was a Canadian citizen whose early criminal conduct earned him a ten-year sentence for burglary at the Kansas State Reformatory. After a successful escape, he was captured one year later and was sent to the state prison at Lansing. Following his release, he began a series of armed robberies of banks, corporate payrolls, and even the Erie mail train. He was accompanied during various heists by Dock Barker, Fred Barker, Harvey Bailey, Frank Nash, Thomas Holden, Fred Hunter, Harry Campbell, and other confederates, most of whom would also end up on Alcatraz.

Karpis was most widely known for two sensationalized kidnappings described in chapter 1: the $100,000 ransom kidnapping of William Hamm in St. Paul, Minnesota, in June 1933, and the January 1934 kidnapping of St. Paul banker Edward Bremer for a $200,000 ransom. Branded Public Enemy no. 1, his criminal career received national attention when FBI Director J. Edgar Hoover claimed to have personally arrested him in New Orleans. Karpis's version was that Hoover "didn't lead the attack on me. He hid until I was safely covered by many guns. He waited until he was told the coast was clear. Then he came out to reap the glory. . . . I made Hoover's reputation as a fearless lawman. It's a reputation he doesn't deserve."[48]

After his arrest on May 1, 1936, Karpis was flown to St. Paul, where for five days he was kept in handcuffs and leg shackles locked to a radiator. Following his aggressive interrogation by FBI agents, Karpis pleaded guilty to kidnapping charges; several weeks later, on July 27, he was sentenced to a life term. The next day he was taken to Leavenworth by train but there was no question that as Hoover's prize catch he would be moving on to the Rock. The Leavenworth staff recommended his transfer because he was "a notorious prisoner . . . agitator, and possible escape risk."[49]

Floyd Hamilton and Ted Walters became part of the Alcatraz population in June 1940—well after the other prisoners described above but in plenty of time for each to be involved in an escape attempt as well as to be eyewitnesses to the most spectacular event in the island prison's history— the battle of Alcatraz in May 1946.

Both men grew up in poor, working-class families in West Dallas. In 1938 they began a string of robberies, burglaries, and automobile thefts. On one occasion they were arrested but broke out of a county jail by cutting the cell bars and outwitting the jailer. Two weeks later they stole a car and robbed the bank of Bradley, Texas, obtaining the modest sum of

$685. More auto thefts and grocery store robberies followed, as state and federal agents tried to track them down (they had been identified as the perpetrators of the bank robbery by a third man who had accompanied them and was subsequently arrested). Through these efforts Hamilton and Walters earned the titles of the state's Public Enemies nos. 1 and 2.

After three more automobile thefts in Indiana and Arkansas, they robbed the payroll of a Coca Cola plant in Nashville. While making their getaway they were confronted by Arkansas highway patrol officers; a gun battle ensued, but Walters and Hamilton succeeded in running from their vehicle and escaping in some nearby woods. Ten days later when they returned to their old haunts, they were captured by Dallas police officers. Five weeks later each received a twenty-five-year term to be served in the Texas prison system for robbery by assault. Hamilton received another five years for theft and Walters was sentenced to ninety-nine years for violation of the Texas Habitual Criminal Act. Texas authorities, however, turned them over to federal agents, who took them to Arkansas to face federal motor vehicle theft and bank robbery charges. Walters pleaded guilty, received a thirty-year federal prison term to go with his multiple state sentences, and was transported to Leavenworth where Hamilton arrived soon after.[50]

Personnel at Leavenworth took one look at their records and immediately asked Bureau of Prisons headquarters to authorize their transfers to Alcatraz. The report on Walters concluded:

> Subject's criminal record indicates that he is an habitual criminal, a hardened and dangerous offender and a menace to society. . . . May be expected to present some problem as to custody and also present some problem as to discipline of a serious nature. His behavior is entirely unpredictable. . . . Recommendation: Transfer Alcatraz Island [for the] benefit of inmate population at large. A confirmed and vicious criminal and a definite custodial risk.[51]

While awaiting a response to the transfer request, the Leavenworth staff asked that Hamilton be sent to the Atlanta Penitentiary, due to the inadvisability of confining in the same prison two such dangerous co-defendants. Bureau headquarters, however, decided that Walters and Hamilton should be given a trial period of six months to determine if they could "adjust." Within a few weeks, however, an inmate reported to the deputy warden that Walters and Hamilton had approached him because of his knowledge of chemistry. They had wanted to know about materials, such as sulfur and saltpeter, that could be used to construct bombs and shotgun shells. According to the inmate, Walters and Hamilton intended to construct a shotgun in the machine shop and they wanted him to make the shells as well as sixteen bombs that would be used to blow their way out the front gate and to destroy the guard tower in the front of the prison.

When further information was received in the warden's office that Walters and Hamilton were also casing the truck entrance to the prison, where they were planning another attempt to break out in which they would conceal themselves in a truck carrying sawdust out of the prison, the Leavenworth staff again appealed to Bureau headquarters for permission to transfer both men to Alcatraz. This time their request was approved.

Many more men imprisoned on Alcatraz during the period when lawbreakers were called "public enemies" and James Johnston ruled as warden had notable criminal or prison records. Including biographical sketches of all of them here would fill the remaining pages of this book. Once they were locked up together on the island in the San Francisco Bay, big questions faced Attorney General Homer Cummings, Bureau of Prisons Director Sanford Bates, and Warden James Johnston. How would this unique collection of prisoners react to a regime designed to tightly control them? How would these prisoners get along with each other? How would Alcatraz achieve the level of punishment for serious offenders that the public was demanding?

4

THE PROGRAM

Since Alcatraz opened to the public in 1973 as an attraction managed by the National Park Service, millions of visitors have walked through the cell house, looked into the small cells for a few moments, and viewed the mess hall and yard, all the while trying to imagine the experience of doing time on the Rock. Visiting the prison is one way to obtain some insight into what it was like to be an Alcatraz prisoner; another is to read the words of former Alcatraz inmates and guards as they describe life on the island. Although nearly all the inmates and employees from the gangster years are now deceased, transcripts of the author's interviews with some of these men provide first-person accounts. These commentaries, along with prison records, are the basis for the following description of daily life under one of the most restrictive regimes in American penal history.

On arrival at Alcatraz, inmates were told, "you are entitled to food, clothing, shelter, and medical attention. Anything else that you get is a privilege."[1] This statement meant that an inmate's basic needs would be met, and if he obeyed the simple rules, he could leave his cell to eat, work, and spend a few hours in the yard or attend chapel on weekends. He was allowed to write and receive a few letters and have one visit a month from his wife or blood relatives. Through it all he could try to establish a record of conduct good enough to earn a transfer back to Leavenworth or Atlanta or McNeil Island. In those prisons the comparative abundance of privileges and activities, and the openness of daily life, made transferees feel as if they were returning to the free world. At Alcatraz inmates were expected to "go along with the program"—that is, to obey all rules and refrain from making any trouble for the staff.

The strict regimen when the prison opened and throughout the 1930s was described by guard Robert Baker:

> We fed the inmates cafeteria style. They'd go in and put their food on a tray—you have to eat what you take, if you leave any, you don't eat the next meal. It's that simple. Then you go and sit ten to a table, five facing

five. The blacks sat together. They had about twenty minutes to eat. A guard stood at the end of every table. When the inmates got up the guard counted the silverware—a knife, fork, and spoon for every man and then they all went out. The officers ate the same food.

The yard was just dirt, later on we put in concrete steps where the inmates could sit. They played chess, handball, horseshoes, and bridge. They played bridge with dominoes because we wouldn't give them cards.

We were very very strict at first—their collars had to be buttoned up. At the beginning it was absolute silence and don't give them a thing—no cigarettes, no chocolate, no candy, no hot water, no radio, no nothing. We had nothing to do with them. There was no school and there was nothing after 5 P.M. It was utter silence. If they refused to work you put them in the hole [disciplinary segregation].[2]

ROUTINES OF DAILY LIFE

The regime at Alcatraz was designed to prevent anything unusual or unexpected from happening. Daily life, therefore, was routinized, controlled, and monotonous. Each day began with a wake-up call at 6:30 A.M. By 6:50 inmates were to have cleaned up their cells, to have washed, dressed, and to be ready for count; at 6:55 they proceeded to the dining hall. The process by which inmates were to make their way to the dining hall was scripted in fine detail:

> Prisoners will stand by door facing out and remain there until whistle signal, during which time lieutenants and cellhouse men of both shifts will make count. When count is found correct, lieutenant will order unlock of doors. Whistle signal will be given by Deputy Warden or Lieutenant. All inmates will step out of cell, stand erect facing mess hall. Upon second whistle signal all inmates on each tier will close up single file upon the head man.
>
> Whistle signal. Lower right tier of Block #3 and lower left tier of Block #2 will move forward to the mess hall, each line followed in turn by their second and third tiers, then by the lower tier on the opposite side of their block, followed by the second and third tiers from that side. Block #3 line will move into the mess hall, keeping to the left side of the center of the mess hall; Block #2 line will go forward at the same time, keeping to the right side of the center of the mess hall; both lines proceed to the serving table, right line served from the right and will occupy tables on the right, left line served from the left side and will occupy tables on the left side of the mess hall.[3]

In the dining hall, every aspect of the eating process was prescribed, from start time to posture:

As each man is served he will sit erect with hands at his side until the whistle signal will be given for the first detail to begin eating. Succeeding details will follow the same procedure except that the signal to start eating will be given by the detail guard as soon as the last man in his detail is seated.

Twenty minutes will be allowed for eating. Guards will remain in their designated positions until their details have finished eating. When prisoners have finished eating, they will place knives, forks, and spoons on their trays, knife on top of and at the left, fork in the center, and spoon on the right side of tray. They will then sit erect with hands down at side. After all in detail have finished eating, guard will walk to each table and see that all utensils are in proper place. He will then return to his position.[4]

Prisoners picked up a tray and walked by food containers, directing inmate servers as to what they wanted. There was no limit on the amount of food the men could take, but they were required to eat everything they took or risk losing the next meal.[5]

By 7:30 A.M. breakfast was over, and inside work crews proceeded to their assignments, while industry details lined up in the yard according to shop assignment. For a few minutes, workers could talk or smoke (roll your own cigarettes) until a whistle sounded, at which time they marched out through the yard gate in two ranks and proceeded down the steps to the shop areas. At 9:30 A.M. a rest period of eight minutes began during which inmates could smoke and go "one at a time" to toilets.

At 11:15 A.M. work stopped, inmates marched back up to the cell house and their cells for another count, after which a twenty-minute period for lunch was allowed; at 12:00 noon men reported to sick call or for interviews with the warden, deputy warden, mail clerk, or the chaplain; at 12:30 P.M. inmates marched back to work, where they stayed, with another eight-minute break, until the work day ended at 4:10. Inmates were back in their cells to be counted at 4:20, marched to supper at 4:25, and were back in their cells for a standing count at 4:50 P.M. For the next fourteen hours of each day they did not leave their cells. By the time the wakeup bell woke them up the next morning, inmates had been subjected to fourteen counts in the previous twenty-four hours:

6:30 A.M.	Wake-up call
6:50 A.M.	Count
6:55 A.M.	Line up for march to dining hall
7:00 A.M.	Breakfast
7:30 A.M.	Proceed to work assignments
9:30 A.M.	Eight-minute rest period

11:15 A.M.	Morning work period ends, followed by count
11:30 A.M.	Dinner
12:30 P.M.	Proceed to work assignments
2:50 P.M.	Eight-minute rest period
4:10 P.M.	Afternoon work period ends
4:20 P.M.	Count
4:25 P.M.	Supper
4:50 P.M.	Return to cell

Floyd Harrell provided an inmate's perspective on the daily routine:

On a weekday your day began about seven o'clock in the morning by the ringing of a bell. You were expected to get up, make up your bed, attend to your toilet, sweep up your cell. About fifteen or twenty minutes later another bell would ring and you were to stand at your door with your hands on the bars while the count was made. If the count was okayed, another bell would ring and you would wait for your particular cell block to be opened and you would proceed into the dining room for breakfast. After breakfast, if you were fortunate enough to have a job, you went out on the yard and lined up in certain places for the laundry, the tailor shop, and various other jobs, where you stayed until lunchtime. You went through the same procedure at lunch as at breakfast and then you went back to your job. You came back in for the evening meal with the same procedure. . . . After supper was over and the count was completed then you were free to do whatever you could do in your cell. That consisted primarily of reading.[6]

Every weekday was virtually identical to the others (see table 1). Showers, issue of clean clothing, and shaving were the only regular activities that did not occur every day. Harrell described the shaving routine:

Twice a week the same attendant [who delivered writing materials] came by your cell with a board with numbered cells on it; your razor blade was on this board; he left this blade on your cell door. You were given a short time to shave, with cold water, and then the attendant would come by and put your razor back on the board.[7]

Weekends offered slight variations on the weekday routine. On Saturdays inmates could go to the small concrete yard from 12:40 to 4:10 P.M. On Sundays, the resident Protestant chaplain and Catholic chaplains who came over from the mainland held religious services in the small auditorium; these were attended by a handful of prisoners. After services, prisoners could be in the yard from 8:40 to 11:10 A.M. In the yard, they played softball, handball, and horseshoes, and those inclined to less active recreation found partners for dominoes, chess, or checkers, or just walked the yard. Movies were shown in the auditorium on the seven legal holidays each year.[8] The policy regarding movies was that "they will not be used for entertainment but may be employed by the Warden for education and improvement of the inmates when he deems it advisable in the interest of good discipline."[9] Here is Harrell's view of weekends:

> The weekend days were somewhat different; after breakfast you had a few hours in the yard as well as after lunch. You had a choice of playing handball or softball or bridge or walking up and down in the yard or sitting and talking with your friends. . . . There was one guard in the guard house and one walking the catwalk around the yard; they were there to break up fights and they usually broke up fights by firing down on the yard.

Since a work assignment offered the only opportunity to be outside the cell for any significant period, it was a privilege that had to be earned. An inmate was first assigned a job that involved some routine maintenance task. Then, if his performance and behavior were "outstandingly good and of outstanding value to the institution," he could be awarded meritorious good time and/or pay in addition to statutory good time; he could also be transferred to a job in the prison's industries, which carried a small wage and extra good time, called "industrial good time." For men without a job assignment—and this included anyone locked up in the disciplinary segregation units—there was little to relieve the boredom. According to Harrell, "the only thing they could do is sleep, read, or walk the floor."

Few inmates' days on the island were interrupted by visits with attorneys; no caseworker or psychologist ever called them in to discuss their early childhood experiences, their criminal careers, their home life, or their problems with authority figures. Outside of FBI agents investigating crimes committed on the island and a very small number of official visitors approved to tour the cell house or work area, no outsider disturbed the daily routine. The activities that began in prisons during the 1960s and 1970s—attending class, going to meetings of Alcoholics Anonymous, the Toastmasters Club, or the black culture group, or attending individual or group counseling sessions—were never available on the Rock. No newspaper reporter or university criminologist called inmates out for interviews; the only conversations allowed with persons not employed by the federal prison system were with FBI agents or other legal authorities who wanted information, testimony, or confessions in other criminal cases.

Except for three twenty-minute meals each day and work activities, there was little to disturb the monotonous routine on the island. As Harrell commented, "any day in Alcatraz was twenty-four hours of pure boredom."

With so much cell time, reading became the most common means of passing the hours. The Alcatraz library contained some ten thousand books, most of them left by the army. Inmates were not allowed to go to the library, but according to Harrell, "every prisoner had a catalog listing the books that were supposed to be in the library"; books selected would be delivered to, and picked up from, his cell. Newspapers were prohibited, ostensibly to remove the means by which the prison's gang lords and notorious bandits could have their egos and reputations bolstered. Inmates could subscribe to certain magazines, such as *Popular Mechanics*, but because articles relating to crime were removed, the magazines were "often so mutilated by the censors they were practically useless." When correspondence courses from the University of California became available, a small number of men signed up for them.

EDUCATION AND RELIGION

Reports from Protestant chaplain Wayne Hunter describe the inmates' level of interest in correspondence courses and religious services offered on the island. In October 1936 forty-six men were listed as actively pursuing UC courses; another twenty were described as "enrolled but indifferent." Most enrollees were taking English grammar or "shop arithmetic"; among those completing courses were Albert Bates, Ralph Roe, and Harmon Waley. Two months later, the chaplain reported that 17 percent of the inmate population was involved in various courses including new offerings in the rudiments of music, harmony, advanced shop mechanics, and beginning algebra. Elementary French and Spanish were added in 1937 and one course was dropped because it never had a single enrollee—"training for citizenship."

Chaplain Hunter was also responsible for the institution orchestra, library, and recreational activities including the baseball league, horseshoes, and handball. Men interested in music had to choose between going to the yard on weekends or practicing on musical instruments; kitchen workers were allowed to practice during afternoons. According to the chaplain, thirty inmates were interested in "musical opportunities and of this number we have developed a 10 piece orchestra. The orchestra has played the three Sunday afternoon concerts thus far."

Hunter reported that the addition of a Catholic chaplain, Father

Joseph M. Clark, increased biweekly attendance at Catholic services—from 33 on October 4 to 62 two weeks later. Protestant services attracted only 12 inmates on October 11 and 25. An April 2, 1937, report to Warden Johnston indicated that six men had attended Jewish services on March 27. A report in the same month to the Federal Council Committee on prison chaplains included the results of a survey of inmate religious preferences as Roman Catholic, 132, Protestant 131, Jewish 15, and 22 were listed as "no preference."[10]

In the April 7, 1937, report on prison chaplains, Hunter reviewed the programs and activities available to inmates at Alcatraz concluding, "The library is the most important part of the educational and welfare program in as much as reading is the only occupation of the larger percentage of the men during the evening hours. The library circulation for last month was 2045 books and 812 magazines. According to these figures, each man draws on an average of about seven books and three magazines per month. This does not take into consideration the private magazine subscriptions and book purchases."

ENFORCING A MONASTIC REGIMEN

In addition to making the daily lives of inmates as predictable and routine as possible, the Alcatraz regime severely restricted the goods inmates were allowed to keep in their cells, their contact with the outside world, and their social interaction with each other. There were no evening programs or activities. Restrictions were intended to facilitate control of the inmate population and eliminate problems found in other prisons where association was allowed. Combined with the detailed scripting of daily life, serving time at Alcatraz was an experience that can be best described as monastic.

When inmates were locked up at 4:45 P.M. each day, to remain in their cells for the next fourteen hours, the cell house fell silent. The only sounds were those of a toilet being flushed, the cries of sea gulls, the moan of a foghorn, and the occasional sound of a ship's horn as it passed in or out of the Golden Gate. During these hours prisoners read books from the prison library; some painted (freehand or by numbers); many wrote brief letters to their approved correspondents, read again and again the letters they received from the same people, and sat on their bunks and thought. Alcatraz inmates did not come to the island of their own volition to pursue a calling, and during the long hours they spent alone they were more likely to relive the past and think about the future than they were to contemplate spiritual matters, but in other respects their lives were very much like those of monks. They ate at prescribed times, spoke infrequently, had little to do with the world outside the institution, were denied most sensual pleasures, possessed few worldly goods, and spent much of their time in contemplation.

The designers of the Alcatraz program placed a high priority on preventing the kind of underground economy that flourished in typical federal and state prisons of the 1930s and 1940s. All manner of goods, banned and allowed, were bought, sold, traded, and wagered there (as noted in chapter 2). In addition to creating a discipline problem and providing a means of obtaining items useful for escape attempts, black-marketing tended to reinforce a socioeconomic hierarchy, in which inmates with the most power and access to financial resources could significantly ease the hardship of doing time. At Alcatraz, a simple but effective measure— never establishing a commissary—meant the absence of goods above and beyond prison issue. Inmates could not buy so much as a stick of gum, a candy bar, or a tube of shaving cream. Since eliminating tobacco would have invited protest, it was made available—in unlimited quantity of small cloth bags of tobacco to negate its value as barter.

Inmates were allowed only a few items in their cells:

- 2 pieces of stationery
- 2 envelopes
- 3 pencils
- a sink stopper
- a 75-watt lightbulb
- a whisk broom
- one and one-half rolls of toilet paper
- a drinking cup
- an ashtray
- a cleaning rag
- a wastebasket
- a shaving cup
- a comb
- a bar of soap
- a toothbrush
- a can of tooth powder
- a shaving brush and a mirror—and not one item more

Contraband was defined broadly as "anything found on your person, or in your cell, or at your work place, which was not officially issued to you, or officially approved and purchased by you and officially listed on your property card."[11]

Isolation from normal society was an essential element in the conceptualization of Alcatraz. The island location clearly symbolized separation from the rest of the world, and to make this separation manifest, all means of communication with the free world—access to news media, visits, radio, or correspondence—were strictly limited.[12]

The rules regarding visitors were far more restrictive than those at other federal prisons. Visiting privileges had to be earned, and for a prisoner's first three months on the island none were allowed, not even with his lawyer. Thereafter, an inmate could visit with his wife or a blood relative once each month, with no more than two persons permitted to visit at the same time. Inmates and their visitors were separated on either side of the cell-house wall. They looked at each other through a thick, bulletproof window and—until telephones were installed in 1939—talked through a perforated voice box that required them to speak loudly enough to be heard on the other side of the partition. Inmates sat at the windows on chairs on the cell-house side of the wall with guards standing next to them to assure that the conversation did not stray to discussions of other inmates, to any aspect of prison life, to criminal activities, or to topics regarded by guards as "immoral."

Robert Baker was one of the guards who supervised visits. "When we started out it was six inches of concrete and three inches of glass between the inmate and his visitor. They had to talk to a little hole that was full of wire mesh like steel wool. You couldn't put nothing through the wire, you couldn't even blow cigarette smoke through it—there was no smoking anyway—but you couldn't put nothing through this hole. The first three or four months they had no visits and then eventually they got one visit. After about five years, we got telephones and inmates could still look through this glass, it was about six by eight inches, and talk over the telephone."

Warden Johnston's first drafts of rules forwarded to BOP headquarters proposed that no attorneys be allowed to visit their clients at Alcatraz, because any lawyer representing an Alcatraz convict was suspected of being a tool of the underworld or an unscrupulous character intent on making trouble. This prohibition was overruled on constitutional grounds in Washington, D.C., but the process by which an attorney could gain permission to meet with his client was made as slow and cumbersome as possible: the attorney was required to obtain written permission from the director of the Bureau of Prisons. In addition, verbal and written communications between inmates and their lawyers were not regarded as "privileged"; that condition, according to the Justice Department, pertained only to attorney-client communications before conviction. Prison administrators reserved the right to withhold any attorney-client correspondence if they deemed it was "being used for any social or business purpose or for any reason beyond legitimate and necessary legal communications."[13]

An inmate could order up to fifteen magazines from an approved list to be sent directly from the publisher, although all were screened by the mail censors for "objectionable articles."[14] In addition to prohibiting newspapers and radio and limiting visits, the third means of communication between a prisoner and the outside world—writing and receiving letters—was also tightly controlled. The rules severely limited the numbers and the content of letters to be exchanged by prisoners and their families. On arrival, each inmate filled out a correspondents list that could contain the names of up to five members of his immediate family. Other federal prisons allowed seven to ten correspondents and included friends as well as relatives, but at Alcatraz the only exception to the rule limiting correspondence to family members was for prisoners who had no relatives; they could request permission to write to a friend. The legal status of correspondents and their eligibility was to be investigated by federal probation officers in the cities or hometowns of the proposed visitors or writers. If it was determined that the person had no criminal record and did not have an "unsavory" reputation as far as local authorities were concerned, the Alcatraz staff was notified and that name could be entered on the approved correspondents list. Once the mail censor received verification of the accuracy of the relationship of correspondents, the inmate was issued three sheets of paper on which he could write, with a pencil, on one side only. Only one letter per week could be sent out. Harrell described the rules regarding letter writing:

> The cell block attendant would come by your cell and leave [writing] paper, an envelope and a pencil. . . . A short time later, the same attendant came by to pick up your letter and pen.

Letters to lawyers were routed to the deputy warden and, if approved, counted as the inmate's weekly letter. Inmates were warned, "Correspondence should be confined strictly to family and personal affairs or legal matters in connection with your own case, but shall not contain

criminal or objectionable material . . . use full names not initials or nicknames . . . letters addressed to General Delivery will not be allowed."[15]
Each outgoing letter was read and reviewed by the mail censor, who then
typed a copy for the correspondent and retained the original in the prison
files. (Retyping was deemed necessary, at least until 1940, to prevent secret messages from being passed in or out. Thereafter Baker, who served
as mail censor for fifteen years, began to test for hidden messages by
"putting it [the letter] through a blue light.") Incoming letters were also
read and retyped by prison staff, and any words, lines, or sections regarded as inappropriate or objectionable were deleted by Baker or the
guard acting as mail censor. "Objectionable" topics included "sex, crime
news as well as profanity, secret messages, and length of letter."[16] Neither inmates nor their correspondents were informed if any part of the
letters they sent or received had words, sentences, or whole paragraphs
deleted. (Baker told the author that after reading letters to inmates for
so many years, he realized that "the wives did not stick by their husbands.") Like other privileges, the ability to write and receive letters could
be removed for disciplinary reasons.

The principle of isolation extended to the world within the prison.
Compared to his counterparts at other prisons, an inmate on the Rock
had far fewer opportunities for social interaction. The primary isolative
feature was the use of one-man cells combined with short mealtimes, very
little yard time, and the assigning of work as a privilege.

When the prison opened, another important means of limiting social
interaction was the "silent system." Under this policy, silence was to prevail at meals, in the cell house, and on the job. Talking was permitted
during yard time on Saturday and Sunday, during the eight-minute rest
breaks that occurred each morning and afternoon for men working in
the industrial shops or other jobs, and when work crews were assembled
in the yard. Inmates could also engage in limited conversation when they
needed to ask each other for tools at their work assignments, and in the
dining room one man could ask another for utensils or condiments. Warden Johnston summarized the policy:

> We do not allow prisoners to ramble or loiter from cell tier to cell tier, cell
> block to cell block, or shop to shop. . . . [During weekend yard time] they
> are free to talk all that they want and as loud as they want in connection
> with their baseball games and horseshoe pitching . . . they can let off all
> the steam that they want and give vent to talking and shouting . . . any-
> thing short of trying to create a disturbance.[17]

The silent system at Alcatraz was not intended to be part of a redemptive process, as it had been in the early penitentiaries at Auburn, in New York, and Eastern State, in Pennsylvania. It was simply a punitive element whose main function was to help maintain order. Prison managers were always looking for ways to control unruly prisoners, and for a population defined by long records of misconduct, they employed all means that might be effective. Silence was supposed to reduce opportunities for prisoners to plot escapes, plan strikes, obtain forbidden items, and develop other forms of resistance. The silent system, however, proved to be unenforceable at Alcatraz. For a group of convicts with little or no hope of release, who had already lost almost all of its privileges available in standard penitentiaries, the threat of being disciplined for talking did not have much meaning. This vestige of the old penal philosophy was scrapped a year or so after the prison opened, when one day in the dining hall all the inmates began talking at once.

In addition to having comparatively fewer opportunities for engaging in the daily interaction with other prisoners that forged social bonds, built friendships, and sometimes produced conflict, inmates did not form relationships with guards—the people with whom they had the most contact or, in solitary confinement, the only contact. Harrell explained how inmates typically viewed the custodial staff and why their interactions were limited:

> Relationships between inmates and officers were cool—the majority of the inmates had very little to do with the officers. I didn't care for any of the guards and I certainly didn't want any kind of friendly relationship. The general climate at Alcatraz was not conducive to friendly relations between the guards and prisoners. That is not to say that the entire personnel was lacking compassion—there were a few guards that would give prisoners a fair shake but I arrived at Alcatraz believing that the personnel and prisoners were on different sides of the fence and I left feeling the same way.

Maurice Ordway, then a junior officer, had a remarkably similar view of "fraternizing" with prisoners:

> I do not believe in fraternizing with prisoners, when an officer does so, he has everything to lose and nothing at all to gain. He is subjecting himself to "suspicion" from his superiors, even though the object may be anything but what it appears to be. A man [guard] who fraternizes with the men [inmates] under him only brings contempt upon hisself [sic]. . . . All any officer has to do is remember that he is on one side of the fence

and the other man is on the other side, there can be nothing in common between the two. I believe in staying on my side and seeing that he stays on his.[18]

Predictably, the prison's enforced isolation, combined with the mind-numbing monotony of daily life, tended to exaggerate the importance of anything unusual—any event that broke the routine or offered the possibility of something different. All interviewees for this project remembered and enjoyed describing the extraordinary events that occurred during their time on the Rock: escape attempts, protests, demonstrations, and fights. These were dramatic events in any context, but they were particularly notable in a prison where so little else occurred, where staff were concerned primarily with preventing anything from happening that they had not planned. On four occasions during the prison's first fifteen years, larger-scale excitement was provided by the murder of one prisoner by another. Besides providing drama, these incidents allowed for unlimited speculation because the motives for the lethal violence were often obscure. In addition, the subsequent prosecution and trial of assailants continued the saga and sustained interest long after the actual event.

Even relatively mundane events could capture the attention of inmates as long as they were unusual or infrequent. The departure of a staff member or the arrival of a new "chain," or group of prisoners, was usually cause for lengthy discussion. (The latter event was cause for hopeful anticipation because it also signified the likely departure of a few of the Rock's residents who, until they were called out of their cells, did not know that they had been given transfers to other prisons.) Scuttlebutt spread among inmates and rank-and-file staff when an officer's job was terminated. When new employees arrived, particularly anyone at the middle and upper management levels, it prompted much speculation by prisoners and officers about the qualities and character of the replacement with whom they would be dealing. When a certain captain moved on to an assignment at another prison, a senior lieutenant wrote in the day's logbook, "X departed on a midnight boat—all staff were overjoyed at the blessed event."

Ripples of interest passed through the convict population when notable prisoners such as Al Capone, Harvey Bailey, George Kelly, John Paul Chase, and Alvin Karpis were transferred. Other events prompting weeks of talk among the prisoners were the construction of the new industries building and the remodeling of D block into a disciplinary unit. During World War II news about the war in Europe and against Japan was posted on a blackboard in the yard or the dining hall; these bulletins prompted speculation about Japanese air attacks in the San Francisco Bay Area given that antiaircraft guns had been mounted on the roof of the cell house. There were discussions of the occasional antics and outbursts of prisoners whose mental health problems led to their removal to the Springfield Medical Center and ongoing analyses by prisoners and staff of the personalities of prisoners and employees. And, there were always rumors that Alcatraz might be closed.

RULE ENFORCEMENT AND PUNITIVE MEASURES

Inmates who did not abide by the rules faced a number of possible punitive measures. The few privileges—a work assignment, a preferred cell location, the opportunity to go to the yard on weekends, the ability to visit and correspond with relatives—could be removed. More serious violations called for removal from B and C blocks, which housed the general inmate population, and confinement in disciplinary segregation, which meant being locked up in the old military cells in A and D blocks that faced the outside walls of the cell house.

If an inmate committed a particularly serious rule violation or continued to protest while in open-front (barred) cells in A or D block, he could be placed in a solitary confinement cell in those units. In those cells the last elements of normal living—food, water, clothing, verbal communication, and the light of day—could be taken away for extended periods. During the 1930s, solitary consisted of six retrofitted cells that faced the exterior wall on the third tier of A block and two more on the first tier of D block. The A block cells were constructed by simply pouring concrete into a wooden frame around the bars of the doors and the entire front of these cells, making them solid. However, in order not to turn these cells into concrete tombs a series of air holes were punched in the top of the concrete front and a heavy wire mesh screen was installed in the bottom quarter of the doors of the six cells. This opening allowed some air circulation and permitted the men locked inside to continue shouting to inmates in adjacent cells; although muffled, their voices could be heard even in the main cell house. On the opposite side of the cell house in D block, additional solitary confinement cells were created by constructing concrete vestibules around the grill fronts of two cells.

While the last amenities of daily living could be denied to men in these solitary confinement cells, occupants continued to yell and pound on their doors. The problem represented by these disruptive sounds was solved dur-

ing the first years of operation by removing the most intransigent prisoners to some barred alcoves in the basement of the cell house under cell blocks
A and D, called the "dungeons" by prisoners and "lower solitary" by staff.

THE SPANISH DUNGEONS

Alcatraz's reputation for harsh punishment was well established before
the Bureau of Prisons took custody of the island from the War Department. A report by the post surgeon in 1893 noted the use of dungeon
cells, "in one of the old howitzer casemates . . . these cells were so far
away from the ventilation openings as to be 'simply villainous.' The cells
in the dungeon were only about one quarter the size of the regular cells . . .
they must have been more like coffins." From 1907 to 1912, when the
old prison was demolished and the cell house that the Department of Justice inherited in 1934 was constructed, the basement of the citadel was
"preserved under the prison and used as punishment cells." During the
period the island served as an army prison, the harshness of confinement
was noted in news stories.[19]

In January 1934 James Johnston and Loring Mills, the administrative
manager, inspected the basement of the cell house and found two sets of
four alcoves with bars across the front of each alcove. Mills recalled, "Mr.
Johnston and I went down there before we opened the institution and
we decided that it should never be used. It was below ground, it was dark
and musty and damp, but they must have used it for disciplinary reasons."
(We can only speculate whether the omission of an updated disciplinary
segregation unit in the remodeling of the prison reflected Director Bates's
strong opposition to the common use of solitary confinement as a punitive measure.)[20]

It is difficult to understand why James Johnston, who had managed
two high-security penitentiaries—San Quentin and Folsom—did not anticipate the need for a separate disciplinary segregation unit and some
solitary confinement cells, particularly since Johnston was well aware that
he was charged with housing the federal prison system's most serious
and accomplished escape artists and troublemakers. Confounding this
operational problem was the warden's decision to confine protest leaders and other rule breakers in the two old military cell blocks that had
not been renovated by the Bureau and thus lacked tool-proof steel bars
for cell fronts or for windows in the outer walls. It led to precisely the
kind of publicity Sanford Bates and his successor, James V. Bennett,
wanted to avoid—evidence that the prison was not "escape-proof."

This deficiency became apparent with the first organized protest. Under a regime in which the rule of silence was to prevail, the problem for the warden and his staff was what to do with protesters who had been separated from the general population by locking them up in the old military-era cells in A and D blocks, where they continued to yell to each other and to prisoners in other cell blocks. As noted earlier only the hastily constructed solitary cells in A and D blocks provided some means of containing sounds of protest. Yet the task of dragging a resisting prisoner to the isolation cells on the third tier of A block, up several flights of the circular iron stairway with railings and bars the prisoner could grab, proved difficult and dangerous for both officers and inmates.

In October 1934 Deputy Warden C. J. Shuttleworth and other custodial administrators began placing the most obstreperous protesters in the alcove cells in the basement below the main cell house. Located in the outer walls of the foundation under A and D blocks, these cells were accessed through stairways located in the floors of these units.

The basement area extended from one side of the cell house to the other. Guards sometimes exploited this arrangement by taking a prisoner down the stairs from one block to one of the alcove cells, and days or weeks later bringing him back up to a first floor cell in the block on the opposite side of the cell house.

Officer Robert Baker described the cells and their use:

> When we took over in 1934 there were dungeons underneath the floor. A certain type of men are afraid of the dark. We had a big steel plate that covered the steps in the old Spanish dungeon. We'd take them down those steps in A block and put them in these cells with a bucket and turn the light off. Then we'd take them underneath [the cell house] and bring them up into the old D block and put them in cells over there. So when the prisoners saw them go down in A block they thought "they're down in the dungeon." Maybe they wouldn't see them for three or four weeks—all the time they were in D block. The cells under D block were also used. But the guys over in A didn't see them come out so they figured "Geez, they must have died or been swept out to sea." When [prisoners] were in there they got bread and water, the first six months we handcuffed them—there was a lot that went on down there.[21]

Constructed with brick walls, ceiling, and floor, the dungeon cells were fronted by a set of bars with a grill door in the middle that was secured by a chain and padlock. They contained no toilet, no running water, no light fixture, no mattress or furnishing of any kind. When they were first used, some prisoners were handcuffed in a standing position to the cross-bars in the front of the cell. The only light, when it was turned on, came from a dim bulb in the ceiling of the hallway in front of each set of alcoves. The prisoners were dependent on guards to allow them to take their waste buckets to be emptied in a hallway toilet. During 1934 and early 1935 the only sustenance was bread and water, but by 1936 regulations called for a meal to be provided every third day—at the discretion of guards and custodial officials. No exercise outside the cell was allowed, no reading materials were permitted, and once the hall light was turned off and steel doors over the stairways leading back to the main floor of the cell house were closed, sounds of protest could not be heard by the prisoners in the cell house.[22]

The first man to be sent down to what was variously cited in prison records as "basement solitary" and "lower solitary" was Leo McIntosh whose low number, 74, indicates that he was one of the first federal prisoners on the island. McIntosh was serving a relatively short sentence of five years for auto theft. He earned a trip to Alcatraz based on his escape from a Florida prison where he was serving a life sentence for murder and escapes twice more from chain gangs. Sent to Atlanta for transporting a stolen vehicle across state lines during his latest escape, he annoyed the staff by filing numerous complaints and thus was placed on the first train that took Atlanta convicts to Alcatraz. McIntosh arrived on August 8, 1934, and one month later, September 8, after his refusal to stop talking in the cell house, he was placed in D block isolation, where he continued yelling to other prisoners. He was then removed to a lower solitary cell under D block where he remained for nineteen days. McIntosh kept a record of his time by scratching a line for each day on the wall of the cell. His was not only the first but also the longest stay in lower solitary by any Alcatraz prisoner.[23]

On October 1, 1934, John Stadig was sent to lower solitary for two days as punishment for circulating a petition among the prisoners. On December 3, a group of prisoners were taken down to dungeon cells. One of them, Charlie Berta, was cited for "sending out defamatory comments, agitating and promoting trouble, making slanderous remarks about guards and hollering at officers on the wall." Berta described his experience in a lower solitary cell under D block:

> You came in at A block and you came out by D block. There was no beds, you slept on the bricks, but it was warm. I had a jumpsuit. You didn't need nothing. You got bread and water, but there was no running water. You had a shit bucket but after a couple of days you had no bowel movement because you didn't take nothing in. The light was a not very strong light

in the hall; no guards were stationed down there. When they'd come down you'd know it—there was a slight draft—you could feel it—and you knew somebody was coming down. They tried to sneak in on you. I was hand-cuffed to the door in daytime during working hours. You couldn't sit down or lay down. If you had to go to the bathroom, you just went. The dungeon was better than the cells in A block where all they done was pour some concrete over the bars because you'd get the fluctuation of the weather but in the dungeon the temperature was always the same.[24]

In the basement Berta had the company of several other prisoners. John Messamore was confined from December 2 to 14, 1934, for "writing a letter . . . inferring an escape plot." Clyde Hicks's brief stay, from December 3 to 4, 1934, came as a consequence of being caught conveying a note from one prisoner to another while working as a cell house orderly. After eleven days, Berta was brought back up to an A block isolation cell where he spent another nine days before he was returned to the general population.

Maurice Ordway, who started work as a guard in October 1934 and during his many years on the island was promoted to lieutenant, described the process by which a prisoner ended up in the basement:

> When we first opened up we used lower solitary—we never called it the dungeon. I'll tell you exactly how it worked. You'd have these characters raising hell—this would always happen at night—and Captain Miller would come in the cell house and sit down at his desk and say, "Bring that clown down here." A couple of officers would get the guy out of his cell and Miller would ask him, "What's going on?" And of course the guy would be cussing him out, so he'd say, "throw him downstairs." Nine times out of ten that guy never walked down those stairs; that guy would slide down those stairs and hit that steel door—then you'd open the door and lock him up.[25]

George Boatman, who also rose to the rank of lieutenant during his career at Alcatraz, remembered Berta's confinement in the dungeon.

> The dungeons were a kind of a cell. We had to put a padlock and chain [around the bars of the gate] to lock the door. They weren't very good security . . . there wasn't a thing inside—just a pail. When I first went there they handcuffed Charlie Berta to the bars . . . they had to stand up all day that way. The [solitary] cells on the third tier of A block had a toilet and washbasin in them. The [dungeon] cells had absolutely nothing. They were like the strip cell now in D block except they didn't even have a hole in the floor. They had a bucket [for a toilet in lower solitary]. You had to feed them a square meal every third day—bread and water was their reg-

ular ration. The doctor had to visit them . . . you had to call him if a prisoner said he was sick. It was dark down there. Unless the officer went
down there you turned the lights out. You let the inmate out to empty his
[slop] bucket and get some water. They had no mattress [compared to
solitary cells in A block]. . . . [Bureau of Prisons' assistant director] Bixby
was quite unhappy [about the use of the dungeons] because we had Charlie Berta chained up to the door when he came out. Washington didn't
like the use of them. I suppose Johnston authorized it but [deputy war-
den] Shuttleworth gave the orders to put the strike leaders down in the
dungeon.[26]

Boatman was right—BOP headquarters was concerned when word
reached Washington, D.C., that several prisoners had been chained up.
On a trip to McNeil Island Penitentiary in July 1931 after Director Bates
found a prisoner standing with his arms attached to an iron ring, he wrote
to the warden expressing his displeasure:

I don't know whether it was understood at the time I left your institution
but this letter will confirm my understanding that the iron ring formerly
used to secure men undergoing punishment in standing position is to be
removed. Please advise me when this is done.[27]

Thus when Bates's representative reported that during an inspection of
Alcatraz he "found two or three men in the 'dungeons' . . . in chains,"
the director immediately informed Warden Johnston:

The use of chains in this manner is specifically and definitely disapproved.
We have provided Alcatraz with every practicable scientific device to make
it secure, and I cannot bring myself to believe that it is necessary to resort
to the antiquated practice of chaining men.

I think it is very undesirable for us to use the old dungeons as punishment cells. If you feel that we have not provided sufficient or suitable isolation facilities, please submit at once estimates on the cost of remodeling
cells in the unused portions of the building in such a way as to adapt them
to fulfill the need which you are now meeting by use of the dungeons.[28]

Prison records and staff and inmate testimony provide evidence that handcuffing inmates in a standing position ceased after this order from headquarters but the use of the dungeon cells continued. Johnston told Bates
that he agreed that use of the dungeons was "undesirable" and that two
solitary cells separated from each other had been constructed in D block
(by extending the fronts of regular cells with concrete walls and ceiling)
"to give us a two-door instead of a one-door entrance."[29]

Bates's concern that his order might not be carried out was reflected in a follow-up letter to Johnston, asking for "your assurance that these cells will not be used except in rare cases; that when they are used a special report will be sent to this Bureau; and also that the use of the shackles has been discontinued."[30]

Understanding that these forms of punishment could lead to allegations of physical as well as psychological abuse, about two weeks later Bates asked Johnston for further assurance that

> there is no stringing up by the wrists or otherwise; they are using the old cells in the basement only as a last resort; that our most severe means of punishment is solitary confinement for short periods, meaning from three to 10 days; and that under the regular rules of the Prison Bureau, a doctor representing the United States Public Health Service visits twice a day all men in solitary and no reports of insanity resulting from disciplinary measures have been received . . . in your letter of April 3, you stated, "we are not using shackles in connection with confinement or punishment." Does the word "shackles" include leg irons, handcuffs and chains of all kinds? Do you make a careful discrimination in your punishments between those who have consciously and deliberately disobeyed the rules and those who have any suspicion of a mental aberration? We cannot afford to have it said that we are punishing men who are insane or mentally disturbed.[31]

These exchanges between the director, far away in Washington, D.C., and James Johnston reflect in very civil language the tension between Bureau headquarters trying to avoid negative publicity related to a very controversial penitentiary and a warden used to having almost complete autonomy in running a prison placed in his charge.

The most serious punishment that could be imposed upon an Alcatraz inmate was the removal of some or all of his good time. Most of the men on the Rock were quite accustomed to doing time in isolation or disciplinary segregation units, but the loss of months or years of good time substantially lengthened the actual time served. It also generally foreclosed the possibility of transfer from Alcatraz and thus weighed heavily against any consideration for parole. Through normal disciplinary proceedings, an inmate could lose days or weeks of the good time he had already accumulated, and he could lose months or years of accumulated good time—as well as good time yet to be earned—through a pseudo-due-process procedure carried out by a "good time forfeiture board" usually comprised of the deputy warden and the captain or a lieutenant. Such boards were constituted when an inmate committed a serious violation of prison rules, such as attempted escape or assault.

At these hearings, an inmate was not allowed to call other inmates as witnesses; he was not given advance notice of the charges lodged against him; and no appeals were permitted. Since inmates were asked insultingly, "Can you tell your own story or do you need someone to help you?" none asked for help. A verbatim transcript of the testimony was recorded, since the warden was required to submit a copy of good time forfeiture proceedings to the Bureau of Prisons' central office in Washington, D.C.

No decision at Alcatraz regarding loss of good time—which in some cases amounted to as much as ten years—was ever overruled by Bureau headquarters. Throughout the prison's thirty-year history, no inmate was ever given the right to a review of the reasons for his transfer to the island, officially informed of the reason(s) for denial of his request for a transfer from the island, or provided with the reasons for losing privileges or for being placed in disciplinary segregation or solitary confinement or for losing months or years of good time. Alcatraz convicts never had a law library; no lawyers from the civil rights division of the Justice Department, the American Civil Liberties Union, or any prisoner's legal aid group ever visited the island; and no congressional committee or federal judge ever ordered an inquiry into conditions for prisoners on the Rock.

INTERNAL CONTROL VS. EXTERNAL IMAGE

The restrictive regime at Alcatraz was intended to establish and maintain control of the prisoners. In this sense every rule, prohibition, and policy was a practical (though not necessarily effective) solution to the problem of managing a population of inmates defined by their unmanageability at other prisons. But there was also another reason for the tight controls on prison life—to project an image of severe punishment to deter criminal wrongdoing by the general public as well as to discourage escape and misconduct by federal inmates. This rationale, less apparent on the surface, was important to the Department of Justice and the Bureau of Prisons.

The dual nature of the regime at Alcatraz helps explain the changes that occurred in prison rules and policies over time. When the prison was designed, it was hoped that the program at Alcatraz would simultaneously serve the purposes of internal control and external deterrence. But it soon became apparent to prison administrators that the practical concerns of running the prison were not always well served by rules rooted in the need to project a harsh image. The silent system is a good example of a rule that helped create an appropriately harsh image of punishment but was almost impossible to enforce and thus did not contribute to inmate management.

The competing purposes of the control systems in place at Alcatraz also help explain the divergence and conflict that arose between Warden Johnston and the Bureau of Prisons headquarters around issues related to prison rules and practices. Johnston naturally made practical considerations of control a priority. When he felt that effective management required practices not in line with Bureau guidelines—for example, his use of the dungeons during the prison's first years—he was not afraid to put them into effect. The punishment that occurred in lower solitary was explicitly forbidden by Bureau headquarters, but for almost four years Warden Johnston insisted that it was absolutely necessary to have the dungeon cells available to deal with the most disruptive rule breakers.[32] Several cases in which confinement in dungeon cells involved handcuffing prisoners in a standing position to the bars in front of the cells were as close as Alcatraz got to physical punishment of prisoners.

It has been emphasized in this chapter that the solitary, almost monastic nature of existence at Alcatraz was intended to control inmates, not rehabilitate them. But is it possible that despite official intentions, keeping inmates isolated from the outside world, allowing them very few material goods, and requiring them to spend long hours alone had unforeseen positive consequences?

This possibility would not sound farfetched to the thinkers of the eighteenth century who considered the problem of the lawbreaker in society and put in place the foundations of the progressive penal philosophy that has shaped American penal policy for more than two centuries. In the early penitentiaries that arose from their theories, it was believed that solitary confinement, combined with religious instruction, would help produce self-reflection, guilt, and a determination to sin no more. In this way, imprisonment, while unpleasant and even painful, would be rehabilitative. Relating literature to prison reform in the late 1700s, John Bender points out the central importance of solitude and contemplation in this formulation and cites the classic popular novel *Robinson Crusoe* as an example. Crusoe was an idle, heavy-drinking hellrake who refused a place in his father's business and struck out on his own. After a series of adventures, including being a slave, he is shipwrecked and cast up alone on a desolate island— a kind of solitary confinement. Separated from normal existence, Crusoe thinks with clarity for the first time. Reviewing his entire life, he transforms the despair of solitude into remorse and then resolve. Bender explains how this story works to put incarceration in a positive light:

Prison, now equated with solitary reflection, is first viewed as negative, random, punitive, vengeful; but it slides into another thing entirely—something salubrious, beneficent, reformative, and productive of wealth and social integration.[33]

Bender sees the equation of incarceration with solitary reflection as the basis of a "mythology of reform," but when a prison is organized in such a way that austere solitude becomes a dominant feature—as it was at Alcatraz—it is difficult to completely disregard the possibly redemptive aspects of solitude and isolation.

The question of how the monastic mode of existence that prevailed on the Rock may have contributed to the unexpected "rehabilitation" of many gangster-era convicts will be explored in part 3. For now, it should be noted that the absence of visual and auditory stimuli on Alcatraz and the many hours spent in quiet contemplation were cited by many convict interviewees as important factors in their decisions to end their criminal and prison careers.

ORGANIZED RESISTANCE

A Regime Tested

THE FIRST STRIKES

The answer came early to the question of whether a large custodial force could control a small group of trouble-prone prisoners confined to single cells with every element of daily life carefully regulated. The first shipments of prisoners from Leavenworth and Atlanta arrived on the island at the end of August and in early September 1934; organized inmate resistance came less than one month later, on October 1.

The protest began in the laundry, where inmates complained about the limitations on their privileges, particularly the denial of radio, movies, and newspapers. Warden Johnston received word that "the agitators would slug any prisoners who held out and perhaps wreck the laundry."[1] Johnston ordered that four convicts identified by guards as fomenting the unrest be locked in their cells, but at the end of the eight-minute morning smoking break, other "agitators" refused to return to their work posts. All of the laundry workers were promptly rounded up, marched back up to the cell house, and locked up. After questioning the entire crew, guards took twenty-one men to isolation cells. The remaining workers were allowed to leave their cells for the noon meal, after which they were told to return to their jobs; nine men refused and were taken to A block to join the first group of protesters. Since there were not enough isolation cells in this unit to accommodate thirty men, the more vociferous strikers were put in the barred alcoves below the floor of the main cell house—lower solitary, or what the prisoners called the dungeons.

Over the next four years lower solitary was used to house prisoners too loud and too insolent to be kept in the A and D block isolation cells. In addition to Leo McIntosh, Charlie Berta, John Messamore, and Clyde Hicks cited earlier, other dungeon residents in late 1934 and early 1935 included Edward Wutke from December 27, 1934, to January 4, 1935, for refusing to work, insolence, and "profanity"; and Edgar Lewis from December 31, 1934, to January 14, 1935, for refusing to work, insolence, and "cursing guards and the deputy warden."

Charlie Berta was sent to lower solitary again on February 2, 1935, after being told by a guard to hurry his shower:

> Berta squared off as if he wanted to fight and said in a loud tone of voice, "God damn it, if you want to fight, come on and put up your hands." I marched the other inmates out of the bathroom and when they had gone, Berta again offered to fight not only myself but guards Faulk and Chandler. All the time this was taking place Berta was very insolent.[2]

No other dungeon cases were recorded during 1935, since no strikes were recorded during that year. But these cells came back into use in January 1936 when prisoners began another protest. Eight strikers, including those identified as ringleaders, were taken to the basement cells where they could talk to each other but could not communicate with the rest of the inmate population.

Harmon Waley, one of the Rock's most obstreperous prisoners during the more than two decades he spent on the island, earned two trips to dungeon cells. His first, after being confined in an A block isolation cell for refusing to work, followed his refusal to stop singing in a loud voice, "they'll hang Jim Johnston in a sour apple tree." The disciplinary action taken against Waley was reported to Bureau of Prisons headquarters:

> Waley was sent downstairs, that is to basement solitary . . . for insolence to the doctor . . . he would not work . . . and he was making noises to attract attention and disturb others in the cell house. It therefore became necessary to move him downstairs where he was kept until he promised to behave and was then moved back to regular solitary. [The entry in Waley's file recorded his movement "from lower solitary to upper solitary D block."][3]

Waley returned to the dungeon on September 27, 1937, and remained there for thirteen days; on this occasion his offenses involved participating in a work strike and "creating a disturbance in the isolation section of the cell house."

> They took me down the stairway through D block floor, and across to the cells under A block. There appeared to be four or five cells with the old-time flat bars, as was in A block itself. None of the cells had toilet, water, sink, bed, or anything save a slop bucket, which they did not empty. They gave us the three slices of bread each morning, then every fourth day we

got a small bowl of watery tomato soup, and I mean watery! There was no lights in the cells, and only one light, about 100 watts, in front of all four or five cells, it was pretty dark. The doctor came down every morning to see if there were complaints. Usually it was Hess or sometimes Beacher. Every morning and evening the guards gave us a drink of water. We wore slippers and coveralls, which we slept in since there were no blankets. The floors appeared to be rock or cement, the light was so bad it was hard to see for sure. We got fed up, and since they didn't dump the slop buckets we threw the contents out into the corridor and started to urinate through the bars. Because of the stench the doctor refused to come down into the dungeon. No guards were stationed in the dungeon. We were down there fourteen or fifteen days, then back into D block. The dungeon cells that previously were under D block evidently had their bars scrapped for I saw none going over to the A side. James V. Bennett, head of the U.S. prison system, lied about the dungeon "not being used" to newsmen at the close of the Henry Young trial![4]

Six other protesters in the work strike joined him in lower solitary (see table 2).

On September 11, 1937, Warden Johnston notified Bureau headquarters that J. Edgar Hoover had visited Alcatraz two days earlier with Clyde Tolson, Guy Hotte, and J. H. Rice (Hotte and Rice were FBI agents from San Francisco).

They arrived shortly after the prisoners had left the mess hall following the noon-day meal but in time to see the details lined up in the yard preparatory to going to their assignments in the work area. I then took them through the prison building, cell blocks, library, auditorium, kitchen, basement, bathhouse, hospital—in all of which they seemed to be interested.

Mr. Hoover seemed to be very keenly interested in our set-up, the routine, handling of prisoners and safety and protective measures. When they arrived, Mr. Rice had told me that they would like to go back on the boat leaving here at 3 PM and so I made that arrangement. . . . I was very glad indeed to have the opportunity of a visit from the group and Mr. Hoover expressed himself not only interested but pleased with all that he saw.[5]

According to Alcatraz records, inmate Jerry Cannon was in a basement cell at the time of Hoover's visit. Johnston's letter did not indicate whether Hoover's tour included the cells there.

From October 1937 to June 1938, since no strikes occurred, the basement cells were not needed. George Sink, however, had the distinction of being sent to the dungeon on four separate occasions between June

ALCATRAZ PRISONERS PLACED IN LOWER SOLITARY, 1934–38

Inmate	Dates of Confinement	Reason for Placement in Solitary
Leo McIntosh	9/8 to 9/28/34	For yelling to other inmates while in solitary
John Stadig	10/1 to 10/3/34	For circulating a petition
John Messamore	12/2 to 12/14/34	For "writing a letter . . . inferring an escape plot"
James Grove	12/3 to 12/14/34	Daring guard on wall to shoot him
Charlie Berta	12/3 to 12/15/34	For "sending out defamatory comments, agitating and promoting trouble, making slanderous remarks about guards and hollering at officers on the wall"
Clyde Hicks	12/3 to 12/4/34	For conveying a note from one prisoner to another
Edward Wutke	12/27/34 to 1/4/35	For refusing to work, insolence, and "profanity"
Edgar Lewis	12/31/34 to 1/14/35	For refusing to work, insolence, and "cursing guards and the deputy warden"
Charlie Berta	2/2 to 2/8/35	For insolence and challenging a guard to fight
Samuel Berlin	1/21 to 1/31/36	For "agitating" and participating in a strike
John H. Carroll	1/22 to 1/31/36	"He is one of the ring leaders in the strike and is a communist . . . while in solitary he kept hollering to other inmates . . . kept making insulting remarks to the guards and making personal challenges for them to come in and fight"
Lafayette Thomas	1/22 to 1/25/36	For "verbal attacks made to officers"
Jack Hensley	1/22 to 1/31/36	For "whistling, hollering, and creating unnecessary noise"
Frank McKee	1/22 to 1/31/36	"Due to personal verbal attacks made against officers"
Walter Beardon	1/22 to 1/30/36	In isolation, "he continued as one of the main agitators of the hunger strike, yelling at the top of his voice trying to get other prisoners to join in the strike"

ALCATRAZ PRISONERS PLACED IN LOWER SOLITARY, 1934–38

Inmate	Dates of Confinement	Reason for Placement in Solitary
Olin Stevens	1/22 to 1/30/36	"When he got down in the basement he said, 'I'm not going any further.' I put one hand on the seat of his pants and one hand on his collar and pushed him to his cell" [Lt. Miller]
John Donohue	1/24 to 1/30/36	"He was in D Block calling to someone in the dungeon in a very loud voice"
Harmon Waley	8/21 to 8/23/36	For singing in a loud voice
John Kulick	9/20 to 10/8/37	For being "a dangerous agitator . . . participating in strike . . . he urinated on the walkway outside his cell"
Walter Beardon	9/20 to 10/8/37	For "beating his pillow on the floor of his cell and yelling at the top of his voice trying to get other prisoners to join in the strike"
Jerry Kannon	9/20 to 10/2/37	For "agitating and creating a disturbance in the cell house . . . had his coveralls off and was beating the floor with them"
Richard Neumer	9/21 to 10/3/37	"At intervals of 45 minutes to an hour he would start clapping his hands, yelling, and whistling. This continued from midnight until 6 AM."
Ludwig Schmidt	9/23 to 10/4/37	For insolence and making threats
Charles Bequette	9/24 to 10/5/37	"He wanted all the privileges that other prisoners had in other institutions"
Harmon Waley	9/27 to 10/10/37	For participating in a strike and "creating a disturbance in the isolation section of the cell house"
John H. Carroll	9/28 to 10/8/37	For participating again in a strike and for "trying to remove his toilet bowl from a wall in a solitary dark cell"

Inmate	Dates of Confinement	Reason for Placement in Solitary
Bob Phillips	9/28 to 10/9/37	Agitating, yelling, creating a disturbance in isolation
George Sink	6/4 to 6/5/38 7/9 to 7/11/38 7/22 to 7/24/38 12/8 to 12/9/38	For various infractions
Frank Brownie	8 days [dates unknown]	"Agitating" [joining a work strike]

Source: Information abstracted from prisoner files.

and December 1938. His periods of confinement were brief: June 4 to 5, July 9–11, July 22–24, and December 8–9. His rule infractions included

> Continuous hollering and agitating;
>
> Causing commotion in the cell house by hollering and [for] his free use of obscene language directed at Warden Johnston. While being taken to lower solitary, Sink broke away from Lt. Starling and Jr. Officer Roberts as they entered through the basement door and ran about 20 feet. He picked up a window sash weight and threw it at Lt. Starling. Lt. Starling hit [Sink] with his gas billy [a heavy 9½-inch metal club with tear gas], which went off, the gas striking Sink in the face.
>
> Making so much noise the Associate Warden [usually, "deputy warden"] could hear it while at his house eating dinner.[6]

George Sink was the last prisoner to be sent to lower solitary; his misconduct represented that mixture of disciplinary and mental health issues that characterized a small number of Alcatraz prisoners. After he accumulated twenty-nine disciplinary reports during a two-year period on the island, a neuropsychiatric board diagnosed him as "paranoid" and "psychotic"; he was transferred shortly thereafter to the Federal Medical Center at Springfield, Missouri, for treatment.

In June 1938 Warden Johnston described the problem in dealing with Sink's disruptive behavior in a letter to Director James Bennett:

> when in Solitary, he became very noisy and made repeated efforts to disturb all other occupants of the cell house. After consultation of the Associate Warden and Chief Physician, Sink was removed to the Hospital, but there he

proved to be a disturbing factor, upsetting other patients and participating in two fights. Dr. Ritchey checked him out of the hospital and reported him as one who should be held to account and subject to disciplinary action.

The Associate Warden placed him in Open Cell, just for purposes of segregation, and gave him two meals a day. On the night of June 4, 1938, he began yelling and disturbing the occupants of other cells in the several cell blocks. . . . He was so resistant to all appeals to keep quiet that the Lieutenant of the Watch sent for the Associate Warden. Failing to get Sink to stop, he finally removed him to the Basement Solitary.

When you are here on your next visit I would like to show you the Basement and have your advice concerning what alterations are advisable in order to make occasional use of the basement cells for just such instances as I have named above.[7]

Four years after the Bureau of Prisons took custody of the island, Johnston was still informing Bureau headquarters of the existence of, and need for, "the basement cells."[8]

FROM LOWER SOLITARY TO
THE SPECIAL TREATMENT UNIT

Noise making was the primary offense that earned prisoners trips to lower solitary during the 1930s. No inmate involved in an escape plot or attempt or who assaulted or killed another prisoner or an officer was ever placed in the dungeon; even Burton Phillips, who attacked Warden Johnston in the dining room, was not confined to the most punitive accommodation on the island. The need for a newly designed disciplinary segregation unit separated by a solid concrete wall from the other cell blocks was answered by the remodeling of D block, which came after an attempted breakout in January 1939 by five prisoners. That escape plot clearly revealed the weakness in the A and D block isolation areas: the failure to install tool-proof bars to replace the old flat bars left over from the military occupation of the island had allowed prisoners to cut through the bars of their cells and the windows in D block and reach the waters of the bay.

On August 28, 1941, a new "special treatment unit" opened with three tiers of cells fronted by grills of tool-proof steel bars. Six cells on the main floor were constructed with steel floors and featured solid steel doors in addition to barred grill doors. Two of the six cells had "oriental toilets" (a hole in the floor). The new design allowed for isolation of rule breakers from the general population and solitary confinement cells for those who continued to make trouble even in a punishment unit. From that date forward Warden Johnston and Director Bennett could honestly deny that any prisoner on the Rock was locked up in the dungeon.

As the trial of an Alcatraz convict in 1941 demonstrated, the earlier use of the dungeons would continue to trouble Bureau of Prisons officials who did not want to be held responsible for having employed such a primitive means of punishment. The grills that covered the fronts of the basement cells were removed and discarded and their use as places of punishment appears to have been forgotten by Alcatraz wardens after James Johnston. Sanford Bates's successor, Bennett, denied these cells had been used when after his retirement he was asked if dungeon confinement had been an early feature of the Alcatraz regime. He contended that while he was aware that many prisoners had claimed that the dungeon was used, "If the Alcatraz staff had actually placed prisoners in these cells Bureau Headquarters would have known about it."[9] Despite correspondence reporting the use of lower solitary from Warden Johnston to Directors Bates and Bennett, and despite the numerous entries referring to these cells in prisoners' files and in other Alcatraz records, James Bennett's position remained as expressed in a letter to Supreme Court Justice Harlan after the Bureau had ceased operations on the island:

> I am personally much interested in the history of the island and the purposes it has served over the years. When we occupied the island there were frequently charges that we were utilizing some of the alleged dungeons under the institution for the punishment of prisoners committed to the island. Apparently there was a time when some of the caverns on the island were used but this was long discontinued before we ever took over the administration of the institution from the military.[10]

The tension between Bureau headquarters and James Johnston over the use of a form of punishment that lent credibility to charges that confinement at Alcatraz was brutal and inhumane was never clearer than in regard to the use of the lower solitary cells. Lieutenant Maurice Ordway summarized the disagreement between Alcatraz and Bureau administrators:

> Johnston and [his deputies] said, "We're going to run this thing and we're going to run it our way." They did. And they used those cells.[11]

A MORE SERIOUS CHALLENGE TO AUTHORITY

Toward the end of 1935, the initial mix of military, McNeil Island, Lorton (D.C.), Leavenworth Annex, and Lewisburg prisoners combined with the more sophisticated, long-term offenders from Atlanta and Leavenworth had changed markedly. Many of the relatively short-term, lesser offenders had been transferred, more real convicts from the two penitentiaries had arrived, and more of the big-time felons, such as Dock Barker, had been caught up in the government's dragnet and shipped to the island.

As the inmate population approached more the character originally envisioned by the Department of Justice, it was only a matter of time before prisoners organized another work strike. On December 25, 1935, and again on December 31, rumors about a strike were frequent and specific enough that the guard force was alerted to the possibility of trouble. Then again on the morning of January 20, 1936, all staff were advised that a strike was to begin that morning in the laundry. Extra guards armed with gas bombs were dispatched to the laundry and sent to the towers, gun galleries, and cell house.

The walkout began when six men left their work assignments, walked down the stairs to the door of the laundry, and clapped their hands. At this signal, sixty-eight other inmates left their work places, while twenty-four remained at their posts. The men proceeded to the door amidst shouts of "Let's get the guys that wouldn't quit work," but no action followed this threat. Other prisoners then walked off their jobs in the blacksmith shop, the mat shop, and the carpenter shop as well as the entire general labor crew—a total of 101 men.

Deputy Warden Shuttleworth found himself with a much larger number of angry strikers on his hands than he had had in the previous year's protest. Having stationed himself in the industries area in anticipation of trouble, he confronted the protesting inmates with a large group of guards. The strikers obeyed his instructions to march back up the steps to the cell house, where they were locked in their own cells. Shuttleworth reported to Warden Johnston that most of the "agitation" was due to five men he identified as "communists."

A precipitating factor in this strike was convicts' anger over the death of prisoner Jack Allen a few days earlier. After his transfer to Alcatraz, Allen was determined to have "active, moderately advanced pulmonary tuberculosis," and his transfer to the Springfield Medical Center had been recommended. But when an inmate in the hospital alleged that Allen had exchanged sputum cups with another prisoner in the ward, Allen was sent back to the general population.[12]

During the daytime sick call on January 13, 1936, Allen had complained of pain in his stomach and was examined by the Public Health

Service resident intern, who reported that he could find nothing wrong. During the evening of the same day, Allen called from his cell to the lieutenant on duty to complain that he was sick and experiencing pain and cramps in his stomach. The intern was called down from the hospital. After examining Allen, he determined again that the inmate

> did not appear to be critically ill in any way. . . . In fact, in view of the absence of any physical findings and having in mind his previous history of malingering . . . I was decidedly under the impression that the patient was putting on a show in order to get back into the hospital.[13]

The intern gave Allen some aspirin, told him to return in the morning for reexamination, and left orders with the custodial staff that he was not to be called again that night. Allen, however, continued to complain and his moans and groans prompted a warning from the lieutenant that if he kept making these sounds he would be placed in solitary. When Allen continued to moan and call out for the chief medical officer, guards removed him from his cell and put him in a D block isolation cell. When guards checked him the following morning, they saw that something was wrong and Allen was taken to the prison hospital, where it was determined that his stomach was badly swollen and he was running a high temperature. Several hours later he underwent exploratory surgery, which revealed a perforated gastric ulcer for which treatment was initiated. Two days later Allen developed a high temperature, began to cough, and experienced difficulty in breathing. At examination this time it was determined that he was suffering from pneumonia; treatment commenced, but his condition deteriorated rapidly and on the afternoon of January 17, Jack Allen became the first prisoner to die at Alcatraz.

Inmates' resentment ran high over what they regarded as callous treatment given to Allen by the medical staff. Combined with widespread frustration over the lack of privileges such as radios that were allowed at other federal prisons, it was enough to fuel the strike. After interviewing every strike participant, and receiving information from several informants, Shuttleworth was able to identify the leaders of the protest and ordered them placed in isolation cells. Convict Henry Young was among those selected for isolation because he admitted to dumping some four hundred pounds of prepared vegetables on the floor before he abandoned his job on the kitchen crew. Norman Whitaker was identified as one of the principal agitators because he had begun a hunger strike at breakfast on the morning of the twentieth, and another seven or eight inmates had joined in this form of protest over the next several days. John Paul Chase, Ralph Roe, James Lucas, and several other men were placed in isolation, not because they were identified as leaders of the strike but because they "lost their heads during the excitement."[14]

Fifteen men in isolation cells went on a hunger strike to protest their restricted diet of one full meal and two issues of bread and water per day. After they refused food for three days, the chief medical officer ordered that they be force-fed, at which point five men accepted the liquid mixture of milk, eggs, and sugar; ten others were fed through a tube forced down their throats. After several more days, all of the protesters stopped the hunger strike, but they were held in isolation to separate them from men in the general population who were by then reporting to their regular work assignments.

Warden Johnston, while assuring Bureau headquarters that everything on the island was peaceful and under control, reported that he had been required to move inmate ringleaders in and out of the solitary cells in A block and in the dungeons below the cell house. The basement cells were used to separate the leaders from the followers, in order to disrupt inmate solidarity. Johnston also reported that the unrenovated D block had been pressed into service as a separate disciplinary segregation unit. He complained that the lack of any wall or barrier between D block and the B and C blocks allowed the agitators to continue trying to influence other inmates by shouting threats from their D block cells. What was needed, said Johnston, was a separate disciplinary segregation unit. Approval from Washington, D.C., to remodel D block would not come, however, until a sensational escape several years later demonstrated the folly of placing the prison's most disruptive inmates in old cells that did not have new tool-proof steel bars like those in the other cell blocks.

Eleven men identified as the major instigators of the strike lost all the good time they had earned on their sentences up to the date of the strike. In addition, Warden Johnston asked but did not receive approval from Bureau headquarters to remove all the good time the strike leaders could ever earn in the future—a punitive measure amounting to many years of additional imprisonment.

Two months after the strike, eleven strikers remained locked up; four months later, five of them were still in isolation cells. Newspaper reporters heard rumors but as usual were unsuccessful in obtaining any firsthand information. Nevertheless, stories appeared even in the nation's capital with sensational headlines such as "Fox [Norman Whitaker] Headed

3 Days of Madness in Western Crime Fortress" and "Capone Now Cowers in Cell Fearing Death from Mutineers."[15]

THE PRESS TRIES TO SATISFY PUBLIC CURIOSITY

If Alcatraz had been located in a relatively unpopulated area and hidden from view, the public might have lost interest in it after the initial uproar over its creation. But the prison was in the middle of San Francisco Bay, in full view of more than a million Bay Area residents, and everyone knew it held a collection of newsworthy felons. Ferryboats transporting hundreds of commuters steamed past the island daily, plying their routes between Sausalito, Tiburon, Angel Island, and San Francisco. Sailboats and pleasure craft cruised around the island, sometimes coming as close as several hundred yards from the rocky cliffs. Telescopes mounted on piers at Fisherman's Wharf offered residents and tourists a close-up view of the prison's walls, buildings, barred windows, and gun towers. But no one was allowed to look behind the walls, and not one word about what was going on inside was issued by Alcatraz or BOP headquarters.

As time passed and officials remained silent about how the prison's remarkable assemblage of outlaws, desperadoes, gangsters, and prison troublemakers was getting along, curiosity only intensified. Newspaper reporters, editors, and representatives of the national wire services and every major newspaper and magazine in the country besieged Warden Johnston and his superiors in Washington, D.C., with requests to visit the prison and to interview staff and inmates. Every news organization promised to present to the public "the truth about Alcatraz" but what they all really wanted was to exploit the rumors of madness and torture and to obtain information about how Big Al, Kelly, and the rest of the Rock's star-studded cast were getting along with each other, and with Alcatraz.

After failing in repeated requests for its reporters to visit the island, a Bay Area newspaper attempted to force a response from the Bureau of Prisons and Warden Johnston to allegations of brutality. In fall 1935 the *San Francisco News* claimed that it had received information smuggled out of Alcatraz that conditions at the prison were so harsh and inhumane that three prisoners had been driven mad and four other men had tried to kill themselves. It printed a story under the headline "Note Says 3 Driven Insane at Alcatraz: Brutality and Torture Charged in Letter Smuggled from 'Devil's Isle.' Ridiculous says Warden. Prisoner Declares Inmates Beaten, Shot with Gas Guns, Starved."[16]

According to the story, the smuggled note claimed that inmate Edgar

Lewis had been "kept in a dungeon for a total of more than 6 weeks, starved, shot in face with gas gun, beat over head with clubs by three guards." Because of this punishment, Lewis "is now insane and is kept in a cage in the hospital." The note, it said, ended with a plea: "In the name of God, do something!"[17]

Bureau of Prisons headquarters regarded this article as an attempt by the press to force disclosure of information about specific inmates. Warden Johnston was reminded that the policy approved by Attorney General Cummings to neither affirm nor deny any news related to the prisoners at Alcatraz was still firmly in place:

> In no instance should we be put in the position of becoming a disputant with a prisoner, or be drawn into a publicity article in an attempt to answer any rumor or charge made to or through newspapers. Everything possible should be done to build up a tradition for complete stoppage of news relating to prisoners confined in Alcatraz. As far as the public is concerned, a veil of mystery should hang over the prison, and the prisoner in Alcatraz should lose his place in the public notice that attended his capture and trial.[18]

This initial instance of a sensationalized "news" report was a sign of what was to come. The press would always be able to glean bits of information—whether it was from "smuggled letters" of questionable authenticity, careless remarks by a small number of employees who lived on the mainland, the statements of released or transferred inmates, or terse press releases from the warden or the BOP—and transform them into sensational stories to feed the public's curiosity. And as long as the Bureau maintained its policy of not responding to the stories, readers in the outside world generally concluded that the reports must be true.

CRACKS IN THE "WALL OF SILENCE"

In early February, shortly after the January 1936 strike, a former Alcatraz inmate was released from Leavenworth, where he had been transferred a month earlier. Reporters were eager to talk with Al "Sailor" Loomis, and he was happy to answer their questions about the sixteen months he had spent imprisoned on the Rock. His comments were reported in newspapers across the country. The story printed in the *San Francisco Chronicle* under the headline "Just a Life of Hell—That's Felon's Alcatraz Story—Monotony Breaks Spirit" focused on the psychological elements of punishment:

Once again that wall of silence surrounding Alcatraz Island has been pierced and details learned of what is asserted happening to the Nation's no. 1 public enemies in the rocky Federal prison. Al (Sailor) Loomis, counterfeiter, recently released from prison, told his story in Kansas City yesterday. It is similar to other stories told by convicts who previously have been released from the island. "It's hell," said Loomis. "I don't know enough words to make a person realize just what the convicts have to endure on the island," he said. "The real truth has never been told." Loomis complained bitterly of mistreatment at Alcatraz, but indicated it was mental rather than physical. "Why a man can talk only six minutes a day in that place," he said. "Three minutes in the morning and three in the afternoon. It's the 'island of mistreated men.' Soon it will be the 'island of mad men.' Life gets so monotonous you feel like bucking the rules to break the monotony."

Loomis depicted the daily routine as unvarying and stupefying, with rules against everything. He made a point of mentioning lower solitary, which he called "the hole," characterizing it as "a dungeon where rule breakers are confined on diet of bread and water. There wasn't a day I spent on the island that there wasn't at least four in the hole for violating some regulation."[19]

The story of another former Alcatraz inmate also appeared in early 1936. Harry Johnson, a citizen of England and a first offender, had been in the federal prison system only because he had committed his crime in a U.S. territory (Alaska), and he had wound up at Alcatraz only because the Bureau of Prisons needed to fill up the new prison's cells. As a federal prisoner, Johnson developed into a prolific and accomplished writer of short stories and essays—and numerous requests for clemency.[20] His appeals for a reduction in his prison term paid off when President Franklin Roosevelt commuted his sentence. He was turned over to Immigration and Naturalization Service officers on October 21, 1935, transported to New York, and put on a ship for England. He never returned to the United States, but he did reflect on his thirteen months at Alcatraz in an article sent from England that appeared in U.S. newspapers under the title "Terrors and Tortures as the Background of the Riots on Uncle Sam's 'Devil's Island.'"

The eternal silence, the underground dungeons, complete severance from the world of free men, from newspapers and letters from relatives and friends, no comforts, not so much as a photo on a cell wall—a straightjacket, changeless routine under threat of Alcatraz "solitary" which is different from any I ever heard of, guards' clubs, guns and tear gas. Tear gas, why, there are vents in each cell from which if some jailer pressed the button, the stuff would pour out; in globes that would shatter from a finger-flick, it hangs from the dining and other hall ceilings, and a "screw" could bring them smashing down like rain with a button push.

Unlike Loomis, Johnson highlighted violent incidents, such as an inmate protest against the rule of silence and other restrictions:

> In the kitchen, at a signal, we began dropping pans, shouting and jumping about, beating the tables. The guards opened the doors and rushed in. That's what the planners of the strike, whoever they were, waited for. A convict named Walsh had a knife; he rushed at the first guard, a guy named Presshure [Officer Clarence Preshaw]. He stabbed him repeatedly, in frenzy, in the face, in the belly. Screaming like a pig, Presshure was a fountain of blood before the guards beat Walsh to the floor. . . . He was unconscious, blood oozing from wounds, trickling from the mouth . . . they put him in "the hole" that way.[21]

The themes established by Loomis and Johnson were reiterated and embellished many times in the coming years by newspaper reporters who interviewed Alcatraz releasees. Some stories appeared only in local papers as former Alcatraz inmates returned to their hometowns and answered reporters' questions, while others had broader circulation. Many releasees, not as articulate and literate as Harry Johnson, had their accounts inflated by reporters seeking to satisfy readers' demands for more dramatic tales from Devil's Island.

PUSHED OVER THE EDGE

After the January 1936 strike, no other organized protest was mounted for eighteen months. During this period, however, several inmates reacted to the Alcatraz regime in self-destructive ways. Their fellow prisoners—now largely comprised of Leavenworth and Atlanta graduates—saw these incidents as evidence of the negligence and callousness of the staff and of the harmful psychological impact that confinement at Alcatraz was having on some men.

The first incident occurred in April 1936. Warden Johnston defined it as the first escape attempt from Alcatraz, but the inmate population viewed it differently. Joseph Bowers had run afoul of the law one October day in 1931 when he and an acquaintance, each with a gun, robbed a post office in a small California town, took $16.63, and got away. They were soon apprehended and both drew twenty-five-year terms. After a year at McNeil Island, and another year at Leavenworth during which he was not a disciplinary problem, Bowers was nevertheless transferred to Alcatraz. Officially, he was transferred because he had a long sentence, was considered a "menace to society," and had a detainer lodged against him. The detainer had in fact been dropped, and the real reason for the transfer seems to have been that Leavenworth staff regarded Bowers's odd and brooding demeanor as threatening. His transfer was a classic example of a prison warden getting rid of a nuisance.

Joe Bowers had a difficult time settling down at Alcatraz, accumulating ten disciplinary reports during his first two years on the island. Most of his offenses were minor. Once he shouted, "Put me in the dungeon. I do not want to work," and the staff obliged. On two occasions, however, Bowers rushed up to guards with whom he had no prior contact or conversation and began "striking them blindly with his fists." In October 1934 the prison's consulting psychiatrist examined him and concluded that Bowers was an epileptic, but four months later the psychiatrist made another report:

> During his examination, while recounting the manner in which he has been persecuted and tormented both while in his cell at night and during the day when taking his bath, etc., tears are streaming down his face. There is a strong temptation to believe that this man is truly psychotic, but one must be on one's guard, as he has something to gain if he can induce us to believe that he is insane.[22]

A month later the psychiatrist concluded that Bowers was likely faking mental illness. In March 1935 Bowers tried to kill himself by cutting his throat with a piece of glass broken out of his eyeglasses and the following month he received treatment in the hospital after he repeatedly butted his head against his cell door. Two months later, he was reported again for butting his head, this time against a post and a clothes rack; he also suddenly attacked another inmate and then ran away.

That Bowers's conduct was seen as abnormal is evident: no disciplinary report was written regarding these actions, and three inmates helped guards subdue him in order to take him to the hospital area for treatment of wounds to his head. This time the chief medical officer diagnosed Bowers's condition as "dementia praecox" and he spent the next year in and out of the hospital, the isolation unit, and the main cell house.

On April 27, 1936, Bowers was assigned to an outside work detail where he could be kept under the surveillance of guards and at the same time be separated from other inmates. His job was to put rubbish into a large incinerator surrounded by a fence located on the cliffs on the Golden Gate side of the island. Officer E. F. Chandler, who was on duty that day in the road tower above the incinerator, reported at approximately 11:00 A.M. that Bowers had climbed to the top of the wire fence:

> [He was] attempting to go over, then I yelled at him several times to get down but he ignored my warning and continued to go over. I fired two shots low and waited a few seconds to see the results. He started down the far side of the fence and I fired one more shot, aiming at his legs. Bowers was hanging on the fence with his hands but his feet were pointing down toward the cement ledge. After my third shot I called the Armory and reported the matter. When I returned from phoning the body dropped into the Bay.[23]

Other guards reported that they looked toward the incinerator when they heard shots and saw Bowers on the fence. One reported that Bowers was "going over the fence," two reported that he was on top of the fence, a fourth said Bowers was on the ground outside the fence, and a fifth reported that he saw Bowers start to climb the fence from the outside,

> apparently trying to get back inside the yard. He succeeded in getting an arm and one leg over the top-most strands of barbed wire when a third shot sounded. His body stiffened and hung there for a few seconds, then he fell backwards out of my sight, over the cliff.[24]

Bowers's death had an ironic twist. Abandoned by his parents at birth somewhere in Europe and deported to the United States before the First World War, Bowers never knew his country of origin. He had always longed to know his true identity. The social services department at Leavenworth had continued an effort to establish Bowers's background even after his transfer to Alcatraz and, at some point before his death, had been informed by Austrian authorities that he was in fact an Austrian citizen. Alcatraz records do not indicate (and no surviving inmates or officers could recall) whether or not Joe Bowers was ever aware of the successful inquiry. Had he lived three days longer, he might have been released from Alcatraz to join a group of deportees being returned to western European countries.

Bowers's file is marked Died While Attempting to Escape, but most Alcatraz convicts regarded his death as murder by a guard who panicked when a mentally disturbed prisoner climbed a fence to retrieve some debris that had been blown outside the incinerator. Other prisoners claimed that Bowers—by attempting to climb over the fence at the edge of a seventy-five-foot cliff at midday under the eyes of the tower guard—had committed suicide. Under either interpretation, Bowers's death provided evidence to support critics' claims that the regime was so harsh that some prisoners would not survive their sentences on the Rock.

The death of inmate John Stadig five months later gave prisoners eager to condemn the prison additional evidence that Alcatraz was pushing emotionally disturbed prisoners over the edge of sanity. Stadig, convicted of counterfeiting, had been sentenced in March 1934 to McNeil Island Penitentiary for a term of six years. A month later Stadig and another convict commandeered a prison truck and ran it through one of the prison gates in an effort to break out. Unable to find a way to cross the waters from McNeil Island to the mainland, Stadig was captured the following day, put into a dark isolation cell, and had two years added to his sentence.

In August 1934 when McNeil authorities had the opportunity to get rid of problem cases (such as escape risks), Stadig became one of the first prisoners to be sent to Alcatraz. He was well educated compared to most other inmates, having completed two years of college, and his IQ was measured at 124. After his arrival on the island he filed for a retrial on his original conviction, and in December U.S. marshals escorted him back to the federal court in Portland, Oregon, for a hearing. He did not fare very well in this effort: stemming from his conviction on another charge of counterfeiting, the judge added another seven and a half years—for a total sentence of over fifteen years.

On his way back to Alcatraz, Stadig was seated in a private compartment on the Cascade Limited, guarded by two U.S. marshals. He was handcuffed throughout the journey, but as the train neared its destination the evening meal was brought to the compartment and Stadig's handcuffs were removed so that he could feed himself. Before the handcuffs were placed back on his wrists, he was given permission to use the toilet in the compartment. The train had stopped at Richmond. A few minutes later, when it began to move out of the station, Stadig emerged from the lavatory, suddenly bolted forward, and dove headfirst, "like a bullet," through the double windowpanes of the moving train. He landed near the tracks and disappeared. One week later he was recognized by a police officer in Concord, California, and arrested; a day later he was back at Alcatraz, where he lost 1,800 days of statutory good time.[25] During the next eight months he made several trips to disciplinary segregation for refusing to work and refusing to obey orders.

In September 1935 Stadig wrote a letter to his family—confiscated by the mail censor because it was judged to be "scurrilous, libelous, and defamatory"—that conveys this prisoner's frustration and sense of despair:

> Dear Mother, Brother and Sister . . . here's the situation: I will continue to write as long as I can, and then if and when it gets too rocky, I'll clip the silver thread and try the fourth dimension for a change—and, aye! a rest. All notions that I ever had of doing my time are no more: I'll do whatever is convenient, and the rest can hang. . . . So don't worry and don't blame anyone if I have chosen a hard road. It's my choice and my life—let 'er ramble.
>
> —With Love, /s/ John M. Stadig, no. 46

Four months after this letter was written, Stadig tried to commit suicide by cutting his forearm with a blade from a pencil sharpener. He was hospitalized and, according to a psychiatric evaluation, evidenced symptoms of paranoia. While in the hospital he was visited by Assistant Director Hammack, who noted that Stadig was "very discouraged and says he cannot serve his term. He feels he will die in the hospital."[26]

Two days after this meeting, Stadig attempted suicide again, this time by cutting himself with a fork that had been smuggled into his room. In June 1936 he left a suicide note addressed to his brother and made another attempt to take his own life, cutting his forearm in two places when razors were handed out so that he and other hospital patients could shave. In the operating room Stadig remarked, "I thought I got an artery, but I guess I didn't cut deep enough. Guess I didn't have the guts to do it. This proves to me a man can't be a coward and commit suicide. It takes guts."[27]

Discharged from the hospital but back in the cell house Stadig refused to work or to go to the mess hall for his meals and was placed in solitary confinement. In D block he succeeded in cutting his neck with a piece of copper from the light socket in his cell. Two days later, back in a hospital room, he climbed up the bars of the door, reached a light in the ceiling, broke the bulb, cut his wrist, and lost a pint of blood before an attendant noticed the cut.

Several weeks later he refused to eat and the consulting psychiatrist noted that he required constant surveillance, was "close to the border line of insanity," and should probably be sent "at once to Springfield."[28] During a visit to the island, the superintendent of the Springfield Medical Center interviewed Stadig and concluded that his "persistent suicidal tendencies" warranted transfer to his institution. A few days later the chief medical officer at Alcatraz wrote to his supervisor, the surgeon general, recommending Stadig's transfer to Springfield despite his view that the inmate was not really insane, that his suicide attempts were not "sincere," and that the patient was simply "an egotistical individual who cannot make up his mind to serve the sentence imposed on him."[29] When Warden Johnston concurred in the recommendation, Bureau of Prisons headquarters approved Stadig's transfer not to Springfield, but to Leavenworth, "for further mental examination."

On September 21 Stadig arrived at Leavenworth, where he was assigned to the mental annex in the prison hospital. A hospital report indicates that he appeared depressed and refused to talk with the ward surgeon, saying, "I want to forget it all and do not care to talk." Stadig spent the next several days reading magazines and newspapers, for which he was allowed to use his eyeglasses. On September 24, the inmate attendant on duty during the evening discovered that Stadig's bed had been moved against the door of his room to prohibit entry; the inmate called for the assistance of another inmate attendant and with some difficulty they pushed the door open. Stadig was lying on the bed bleeding heavily from two cuts in his arm and from a two-inch gash in his neck that had severed the jugular vein. He was pronounced dead ten minutes later. It was determined that he had used a broken lens from his eyeglasses to cut his throat—at last able to "clip the silver thread."[30]

Stadig's mental health represented the classic challenge for prison authorities to distinguish between prisoners with bona fide mental health problems and men the custodial staff regarded as "conniving," who simulated disturbed behaviors in order to obtain transfers to less restrictive prisons. In the following year another incident convinced many inmates that while they felt that they could manage their time at Alcatraz, some of their fellow prisoners could not—particularly the loners who did not have the friendship and emotional support of other convicts.

Working on the cleanup crew the afternoon of June 25, 1937, Rufe Persful walked into the garage area to sweep and pick up trash. Without saying a word to his co-worker or to the guard supervising them, Persful moved into a section of the building occupied by the fire truck, removed the ax that was attached to the side of the vehicle, placed his left hand on the engine hood, and chopped off four fingers. When the other inmate gave a shout, the guard ran into the garage and found Persful walking toward him with the ax in his right hand and his left hand bleeding profusely. The guard grabbed the ax, applied a handkerchief as a tourniquet to Persful's wrist, and then placed his own hand over the stumps of the fingers to try to stop the bleeding. The guard and the other prisoner rushed Persful to the trash truck and drove up the hill to the cell house, where he was taken to the hospital. As the medical staff tried to treat his wounds, Persful had to be forcibly restrained as he struggled to grab the razor that was being used to clean the stumps. When the deputy warden came into the hospital ward Persful told him that he would have cut off his other hand and his feet if he had found a way to do it.[31]

In the month after this event, Persful experienced delusions and hallucinations. He insisted that he be moved to get away from an alligator in his room, claimed that the warden had cut his hand off, and tried to make nooses out of sheets, towels, and an electric cord. The chief medical officer reported to Warden Johnston and to Bureau headquarters that an examining board had diagnosed Persful as suffering from "dementia praecox, hebephrenic type" and recommended that he be transferred to the Springfield Medical Center.

What the doctor did not report was that Rufe Persful had a very serious problem—his fellow convicts wanted him dead. In the course of his long criminal career, Persful had committed acts that made him a pariah in the eyes of other inmates. At the age of eighteen, he had been sentenced to fifteen years in the Arkansas State Penitentiary for killing and robbing an elderly man. Arkansas prisons had no walls, and convicts worked in fields and on farms under the supervision of inmate guards mounted on horseback and armed with high-powered rifles. When Persful arrived at the Tucker Prison Farm he was offered a job as a trusty guard, a "high power." The high power's job was to shoot any convict who tried to escape, and his reward for stopping an escape, apart from not having to labor in the fields, was that he could earn a quick parole. In the performance of these duties, Persful shot and killed a prisoner who was attempting to escape. His sentence was reduced from fifteen to nine years and he was almost immediately released on parole.

Some eighteen months later, Persful was indicted for shooting a woman in the back with a shotgun and his parole was revoked, but he was not apprehended for two years. When he was picked up and returned to prison, owing to the "congested condition of the [court] docket at that time," state authorities never tried him on the charge of attempting to kill the woman. Back at Tucker Prison Farm as a parole violator, Persful resumed his position as a high power, shot and killed another escaping prisoner, and was paroled again. Several months later he was arrested on a charge of robbery with firearms, for which he received a new sentence of five years. He returned to his position as trusty guard and once again halted an escape, killing one prisoner and wounding three other men so gravely that they were left "permanently crippled."[32] As usual, Persful was released on parole, but at the request of a circuit court judge, for reasons unknown, that parole was revoked and he was returned to the prison farm and his old job. In October 1933, for the fourth time, Persful shot and killed another convict attempting to escape, and eight months later received his fourth parole.

When Persful entered the Atlanta penitentiary in December 1934 to begin a twenty-year term for kidnapping, the initial staff evaluation concluded that he would not pose any unusual disciplinary problems.[33] But at the federal penitentiary Persful found himself in a prison world where a vastly different convict code prevailed, one that emphasized the importance of inmates sticking together and helping each other out and certainly not interfering with any man's attempt to escape. This code also condemned offenses committed against women and children.

Two other Tucker Prison Farm convicts had been sent to Atlanta with Persful. When they circulated word around the penitentiary that Persful had killed and maimed escaping prisoners, and that he had shot a woman in the back, the Atlanta inmates began threatening and beating him. Although the beatings were not officially reported, it came to the attention of Atlanta officials that Persful's life had been threatened and that he was being ostracized and periodically assaulted by other inmates. It was determined that he needed placement in a prison far removed from the deep South, one that afforded tighter controls over inmates while providing security appropriate for a man with a record of violence and a long sentence— namely the newly opened penitentiary at Alcatraz.

Once again Persful's record in Arkansas preceded him to the island, and when he arrived in December 1935 he found himself confronting more threats and violence from the Alcatraz convicts (alerted by others transferred from Atlanta). Shortly after his arrival, Persful was locked up in solitary confinement for fighting with longtime convict Francis Keating, who had called him "a shotgun son of a bitch" and attacked him in the yard. Persful had to be watched closely when he was in proximity to other inmates in the dining room and in the yard and could not be placed in any of the usual work assignments. For this reason he was assigned the job on the cleanup crew.

By September 1936 Persful had become so anxious over his safety that he wrote to Warden Johnston, appealing for a transfer to another prison, telling the warden that in the performance of his duty as a trusty guard he had killed and wounded a number of prisoners and, "as a result, it is only natural that many enemies were made among the criminal element." Several of these "enemies," he went on, tried to poison him in the Arkansas penitentiary and later, after committing federal offenses that resulted in their being sent to the Atlanta Penitentiary, they informed other inmates of his actions as a trusty guard. Persful claimed that he had tried to get away from these men by asking for a transfer to Alcatraz but then found out too late that they were going to arrive on the Rock before he did, and they had turned the Alcatraz inmates against him.[34] His request for a transfer to the penitentiary at McNeil Island was rejected; nine months later he used the ax to emphasize the seriousness of his problem.

The question for Alcatraz officials was whether Persful's self-mutilation was an attempt at suicide, the act of a deranged man, or a ruse to get off the island. The mental illness theory was supported by Persful's behavior in the prison hospital after he severed his fingers and this provided the rationale for his transfer in January 1938—first to the mental ward at Leavenworth and then to the Springfield Medical Center. His mental health rapidly improved, and in October 1940 Persful was transferred to McNeil Island. Three days after his arrival, however, word had spread among the McNeil prisoners about his actions in Arkansas and when he walked into the prison dining room he was greeted by loud and prolonged booing from the inmates. Subsequent to this incident he received his meals in his cell, was kept locked up when other inmates were moving about the cell block, and had to be seated by himself in the rear of the auditorium during movies. The McNeil staff were required to watch Persful closely at all times to prevent other prisoners from assaulting him; his job assignment was cleaning the cell house after the other inmates had left to work elsewhere in the prison.

In November 1941 the McNeil Island warden requested that Persful be sent elsewhere, and Director James Bennett asked Warden Johnston to consider taking him back and confining him to permanent isolation in D block. The chief medical officer on the island argued against this proposal based on his judgment that Persful would, under these circumstances, become psychotic again. Several months later, when the Mc-

Neil Island staff tried to place him in a group cell, Persful's cell mates warned him and the staff that if he was not moved they "would cut his fucking throat out." Persful was returned to a single cell and resumed his restricted contact routine. Nevertheless eighteen months later, when his cell door was opened for cleaning, he was attacked by another inmate who shouted, "I've been waiting for months to do this"; at this point, Persful appealed to the warden:

> Now I am asking you to do me a favor, for the rest of the time I'm here I want you to order my cell door padlocked, leave me where I am at, leave my radio and smoking tobacco in here and shoo everyone to hell away from me."[35]

In subsequent years Persful was attacked on two more occasions. In April 1948 he was conditionally released from his federal sentence and took up residence with a relative in Gary, Indiana. He never returned to the federal prison system, where for fourteen years he had suffered a unique form of punishment.

Bowers, Stadig, and Persful were all morose and solitary types. While their mental health problems could be attributed at least partly to the harsh Alcatraz regime and convict culture, they brought these problems with them to the island. This was not the case with another inmate.

Hayes Van Gorder had attended Luther College in Iowa and the University of Minnesota and taught school until he was convicted of murdering his father-in-law, for which he received an eight-year sentence in the Iowa State Penitentiary. He was released in 1924 but shortly thereafter came into federal custody with a twenty-eight-year term for forging government documents and using the mails to defraud. He soon developed a reputation as a writ writer, enhanced by his success in escaping from Atlanta through the use of a bogus habeas corpus order. He was captured a year later and a five-year term for escape was added to his sentence.

At Atlanta and Leavenworth Van Gorder was noted for his willingness to help other inmates with the legal briefs—activities that earned him a transfer to Alcatraz and high status among the convicts when he arrived on the island. But the men who knew him noticed that soon after his arrival he became very depressed and took up a largely solitary existence, spending most of his time reading. He lost weight, his memory for recent events became impaired, and during several outbursts he tore up his cell—and he stopped filing writs. Earlier psychiatric evaluations had noted evidence of "paranoid trends," but his growing difficulties at Alcatraz were diagnosed as resulting from "senile arteriosclerosis."[36] His fellow prisoners were not aware of this assessment, but they knew something was wrong; their interpretation was that the intellectual who was a good con in a less restrictive prison could not stand up to the pressure of doing time on the Rock.

Van Gorder was admitted for observation to the hospital ward in September 1936. In the months following he experienced hallucinations, as well as bad dreams that caused him to cry out at night. He expressed bitterness toward the judge who sentenced him to prison, not because he was innocent, but because the length of the term was so long. He argued that prison officials should not hold his escape attempts against him given the injustice of his sentence and he complained about the climate, the lack of privileges, and the "depressed atmosphere" on the island. In July 1937, after he was declared to be "of unsound mind," he was transferred to the Springfield Medical Center. He complained of stomach problems and was diagnosed with cancer; in April 1938 he died from the disease. Hayes Van Gorder was buried in Springfield with his wife in attendance— she had remained faithful to him through all the years of his prison terms, including the time he served for killing her father.[37]

The shooting of Bowers, Stadig's suicide, Persful's effort at self-mutilation, and the sharp decline in Van Gorder's mental health, all within a relatively short period, combined to plant firmly in the minds of inmates an image of Alcatraz as psychologically destructive for some of their fellow convicts.

ANOTHER STRIKE AND AN
ASSAULT ON THE WARDEN

On September 20, 1937, James Johnston assembled his officers and advised them to be alert for trouble. After the noon meal, when the bell was sounded for the inmates to return to their jobs, twenty-three men remained in their cells. Each protester was interviewed by Deputy Warden Edward J. Miller and offered the opportunity to return to work. All refused and they were removed to disciplinary segregation cells. The strikers said they were protesting because they did the same work as men at other penitentiaries and ought to have the same privileges. The following day, ten more inmates refused to report to their work details and they too were locked in segregation cells. That evening, the protesters began yelling and creating a disturbance. Four of "the most boisterous" strikers were sent down to lower solitary in an attempt to prevent the protest from spreading over the cell house.[38] The next day another twenty-four inmates joined the protest and they were placed in cells on the unused side of A block. By September 24, one hundred prisoners had joined the strike.

Warden Johnston agreed to meet with some of the protesters, including Burton Phillips. Having been locked up in solitary four times for refusing to work and refusing to obey orders, Phillips had several grievances. Before the strike, he had written to James Bennett, who had succeeded Sanford Bates as director of the federal prison system in 1937, complaining that the constitutional rights of Alcatraz prisoners were being violated:

> Is it not denying the prisoner access to due process of law by denying him access to the legal publications which would inform him what the law is and how the courts hold on legal questions in which he is vitally interested since his liberty is involved? . . . I'll grant you the point that there is nothing in the constitution to keep you from starving, torturing and mistreating me but it must be a regrettable oversight on your part to deny me full access to legal documents.

He asked to be allowed to subscribe to the *Federal Reporter* so that he could be informed of court decisions related to laws passed since 1932, one of which had been used to give him a life sentence; he also asked that the *Reporter* and copies of Supreme Court and Appellate Court decisions be made available to the inmates as a right. Without these materials, Phillips went on,

> I would be better off to slit my throat, or perhaps, someone else's and make you hang me, ending quickly and mercifully a life which would otherwise be carried on tortuously year after weary year without hope or possibilities of legal release.[39]

The denial of access to legal materials was only one restriction that bothered Phillips; he was also angered by the lack of sugar and sweets in the prison menu, writing to Warden Johnston in June and again in early September asking that more sugar, syrup, sweet rolls, and bread pudding be provided. After presenting his arguments for more privileges, Phillips agreed to return to work and was escorted back to his cell, where he waited for release for the noon meal. In the dining room he took his complaints to the warden in a way that impressed his fellow inmates.

In the dining hall Warden Johnston assumed his customary position— standing in the middle of the room facing the door to the cell house with his back to the two columns of inmates who passed by him on either side as they exited. Lieutenant R. O. Culver, the senior officer on duty in the dining hall, described what happened next:

> Everything seemed to be in order until prisoner no. 259, Phillips, reached a position directly in back of the Warden, whereupon he drew back his fist and without warning hit the Warden a terrific blow in the back of the head, knocking him to the floor unconscious. Inmate Phillips, with a determination to kill the Warden (as he stated to me later) kicked him in the side and in the face while he was prostrate. He also jumped on the Warden and continued to hammer him about the face and head until subdued by Officers Joe B. Steere, John F. Gilmore, and myself. After securing a firm hold Phillips continued to resist and would not let go of the Warden until struck a blow on the head [in fact, several blows] with a "Gas-Billy," which rendered him unconscious.

The warden and Phillips were taken to the prison hospital; the rest of the inmates scattered, trying to find cover behind columns and tables when an officer on the catwalk outside broke the windows of the dining hall to point the muzzle of his automatic rifle inside. The inmates were reassembled and marched back to their cells. About three hours after the assault, Lt. Culver questioned Phillips in the hospital, and Phillips told him, "I am sorry that I did not kill him, now it will all be to do over again."[40]

In later years, when Alvin Karpis recounted the incident, he noted that the three blows to the head of Phillips, administered in a "calm and cool manner" by Lieutenant Culver, involved the use of a club eight inches long that contained a tear gas shell in one end. Only lieutenants at Alcatraz were authorized to carry one of these gas billies or a sap, a leather-encased chunk of lead. Karpis also noted that the guard on the catwalk caused panic in the room when he thrust his rifle through the glass because the inmates recognized him as the same man who had shot Joe Bowers off the fence.[41] Harmon Waley told the author that when the unconscious Phillips was removed from the dining hall he "was dragged by the feet up the stairs to the hospital, Culver sapping him continuously and his head flopping on the stairs."[42]

After receiving first aid, Warden Johnston was treated for multiple contusions to his face and ear and for "slight shock." Phillips remained in the prison hospital for two weeks during which time he was examined by the psychiatrist, who noted that his patient was in "mechanical restraint [straps]." Shortly thereafter, Phillips was moved to a solitary confinement cell and put on a restricted diet (one meal per day, bread and water at other times) for seventeen days, after which he was moved to an open-front (barred) cell in the D block segregation unit with his food increased to two meals per day.

Johnston, anticipating a news release by Bureau headquarters about these events, authorized his clerk to release a brief statement noting that a strike was in progress and that he had been assaulted. The "vicious slugging" of the warden was reported by the press in the usual inflammatory style and was placed within the context of the "seething revolt" that had been under way for several days in "the Federal Government's Devil's Island."[43]

On September 30 Johnston felt well enough to dress and return to the main cell house. He went directly to the dining room, stood on the spot where he had been assaulted, and resumed his normal procedure of checking the lines in and out of the mess hall. "I deemed that to be the best way in which to resume my duties," he said in a report to the director. By October 14 the strike had essentially ended: of the 132 inmates who joined the strike all but 15 had returned to work and those 15 were locked up in solitary confinement. With the exception of Capone, most of the big names on the island—Kelly, Keating, Bates, Holden, Bailey, Barker, and Karpis—had participated in the protest and stayed out for a week or more. The holdouts included the leaders of the protest the year before, along with two recent arrivals—Henry (sometimes Henri) Young and Harmon Waley. In early November Johnston reported to Bureau of Prisons headquarters that Phillips was still "unrepentant" and that it was "probably best for all concerned that he be kept [in segregation] for a long time."[44] Burton Phillips remained in the D block disciplinary segregation unit until June 23, 1946—a period of almost nine years.

The strike produced no changes in the regime and generated little sympathy for the inmates in the outside world. Most newspaper editors across the country expressed the view that whatever the Alcatraz cons had to endure they had earned and that other prison administrators should emulate the "no-nonsense" policies in place on the Rock. Their editorials confirmed the government's success in creating an image of punishment appropriate for a group of master criminals.

The *Dallas Times-Herald* went further, suggesting that punishment on the Rock was not severe enough for this particular group of lawbreakers:

THE REBELLION IN ALCATRAZ PRISON

The authorities in Alcatraz prison have shown remarkable patience in dealing with the convict "sit down strikers," if reports from the place of confinement are true. Alcatraz is at least one prison that is not classifiable as a reformatory. Its inmates are persons who are so far gone in crime that very few can be regarded as prospects for rehabilitation. . . . Criminals of their type cannot be expected to respond to fair treatment. These inmates may resent the stern discipline of the prison, but many of them are killers and ruthless gangsters who were absolutely merciless while they were at large. They are more dangerous than wild beasts which must be held in cages. The situation in Alcatraz might be regarded as an argument for capital punishment. It hardly seems worthwhile to spare the life of a criminal who is so incorrigible that he must be confined in this stronghold.[45]

The *Rapid City Journal* took a similar position:

NO PITY FOR CONVICTS

America has had a lot of prison disturbances in recent years. On investigation a dismaying number of them proved to be society's fault. The prison was out of date, overcrowded, filthy; the management was lax, the guards were venal, the politicians had interfered too much. And so on. The newest outbreak, at Alcatraz, seems to stand in a class by itself. None of the above-mentioned defects applies there. Indeed, the trouble seems chiefly due to the fact that Alcatraz contains the toughest and most vicious thugs in America who don't like the way society has put them down for the count. Alcatraz is a hard-boiled place; it has to be.[46]

The *Spokane Spokesman-Review* joined in invoking France's Devil's Island as a model for American prisons:

PRISONS SHOULD BE GRIM

Men incarcerated behind bars cannot be dealt with as ordinary individuals. Most of them have depraved natures, or they would not be there in the first place. Yet too many sentimental persons are prone to contend that convicts should be pampered. They hold to the fallacy that penitentiaries are reform institutions instead of places of punishment. America might benefit by the experience of the French in dealing with criminals. A French penal institution is a place to be shunned by every one. Confinement in a French prison is punishment which most men of criminal tendency fear worse than death. If our prisons were a little more grim they might have fewer occupants. A prison should be a prison.[47]

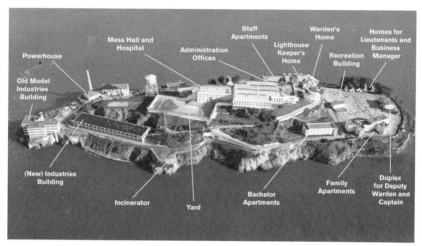

Alcatraz Island, federal penitentiary, 1934–1963; identifiers by Doug Ward.
(Bureau of Prisons.)

Alcatraz boat dock, employees' apartment building with warden's house and chief
medical officer's house above, dock guard tower, cell house roof tower. (Bureau of Prisons.)

Warden James A. Johnston and Deputy Warden C. J. Shuttleworth. (Bureau of Prisons.)

Warden Johnston supervising prison train cars being loaded on barge at Tiburon.
(Bureau of Prisons.)

Prisoners disembarking from train cars at Alcatraz, August 22, 1934. (Bureau of Prisons.)

Prisoners being escorted up to cell house. (Bureau of Prisons.)

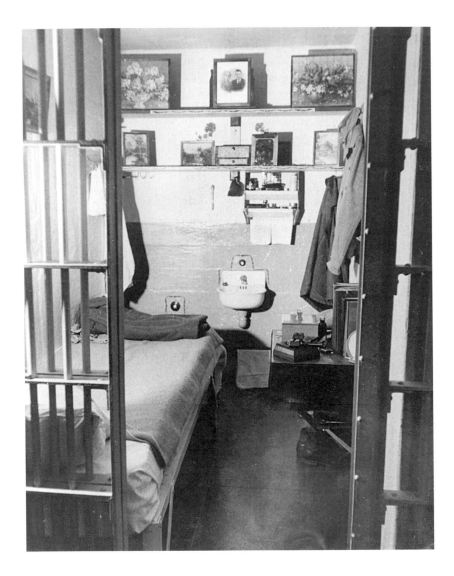

Interior of standard cell. (Bureau of Prisons.)

Prison yard: views of San Francisco Bay and Golden Gate from top steps.
(Bureau of Prisons.)

George "Machine Gun" Kelly, AZ-117, and William Radkay, AZ-666, watch convicts
playing bridge with dominoes marked like playing cards; identifiers by Doug Ward.
(Bureau of Prisons.)

On their way from yard to industries building, convicts pass through "snitch box" (metal detector). (Bureau of Prisons.)

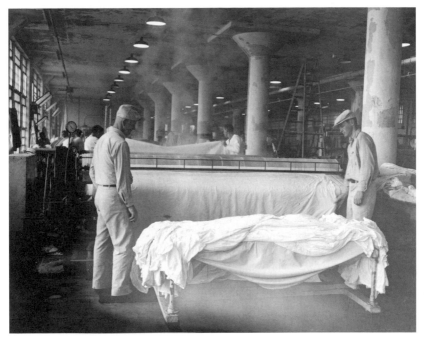

Convicts at work in the laundry. (Bureau of Prisons.)

Convicts making cargo nets for the navy; on left, Arthur Leigh, AZ-246.
(Bureau of Prisons.)

Spiral staircase in A block on left; entrance to steps down to lower solitary. (Anthony Calabrese.)

Spiral staircase in A block, up which prisoners were taken to solitary cells on the third tier. (Doug Ward.)

Solitary cells in A block, with ventilation areas at bottom of concrete doors.
(Anthony Calabrese.)

A dungeon cell, with grill removed. (Anthony Calabrese.)

Dungeon area below A block, cells on right. (Anthony Calabrese.)

The dungeon cell (under D block) with days marked by Leo McIntosh, AZ-74; his confinement began on September 8, 1934. (Anthony Calabrese.)

Leo McIntosh, AZ-74.
(Bureau of Prisons.)

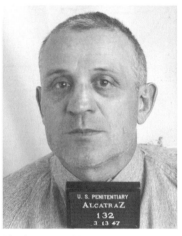

Charles Berta, AZ-132.
(Bureau of Prisons.)

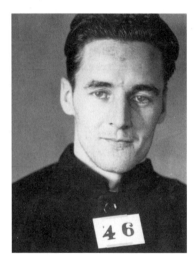

John Stadig, AZ-46.
(Bureau of Prisons.)

Burton Phillips, AZ-259.
(Bureau of Prisons.)

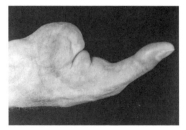

Left hand, minus fingers, of Rufe
Persful, AZ-284. (Bureau of Prisons.)

In general agreement with these views, the *Kansas City Star* accurately described the Department of Justice's intention to cut down the reputations of the "public enemies":

WHAT HAPPENED AT ALCATRAZ

The strike of 100 inmates at Alcatraz, followed by an attack on Warden James A. Johnston, probably constituted a protest against the government's policy in handling prisoners on the . . . island. It is an interesting circumstance, attested to by all criminological experts, that an inflated ego is a characteristic of the super-criminal. . . . But Alcatraz knows how to break down that self-esteem of theirs. It is not done by ill treatment. The prisoners are fed well, clothed well, kept busy, and given excellent medical care. But they undergo the experience, terrible to a supreme egoist, of becoming less than mere nonentities—of becoming in effect, nothing more than statistics. Their individualities are taken from them. Their reputations, no matter how formidable in the outside world, are left behind them at the prison doors. Men like Capone, Kelly, Waley and Bates, inside Alcatraz are mere numbers to the authorities, to the other prisoners, even to themselves. . . . When such men as now occupy Alcatraz are released at the expiration of their sentences, they may not have reformed. They are perhaps too hardened for that. But there is the hope that they will have been so impressed with the understanding that society is bigger than any of them that they will out of sheer respect for its power conform to its code.[48]

These editorials demonstrate that the press during the 1930s promulgated two seemingly contradictory views on Alcatraz. On the one hand, newspapers published rumor-based, sensationalized stories about incidents on the island that tended to cast a negative light on prison policies and management. On the other hand, many newspaper editors supported the federal government's "get tough on crime" policy, and Alcatraz as a central component and emblem of that policy. They expressed little surprise that a prison designed for the worst bad guys in the country had occasional disruptions, protests, assaults, and escape attempts.

FINDING A HOLE IN THE ROCK

The First Escape Attempts

The fog on the morning of December 16, 1937, was so heavy that the work crews were held in the yard for twenty minutes while the gun tower guards tried to determine how much visibility they had from their vantage points. The reports were negative and the inmates were sent back to their cells. After the noon meal, however, the fog appeared to thin out and the work crews were sent out to the industries area.

Ted Cole and Ralph Roe reported to their jobs in the model building (in full, the Model Industries Building; the first floor was called the "Model Shop"), on the north end of the island on the side facing the Golden Gate Bridge. Cole worked in the blacksmith shop as a janitor, Roe in the shop where used tires were converted into mats. Cole and Roe had carefully prepared for a day like this one. For weeks, perhaps even months, they had sawed away at the bars of one of the windows, cutting whenever the guard left their area. After finally severing the bars, they had temporarily reattached them with a mixture of paint scraps and putty.

Officer Joseph Steere made the 1:00 P.M. count of inmates and left the mat shop to check up on the inmates in other shops in the building. Roe and Cole dislodged the cut bars, crawled through the window, dropped about five feet to the ground, and walked quickly to a catwalk next to the ten-foot-high fence that ran around the bay side of the building. They knew from looking out shop windows that the fence was topped by five feet of barbed wire and had a locked gate, so they took with them a twenty-four-inch Stillson wrench from the machine shop, which was available for use by any inmate worker in the area. They used the wrench to twist off the padlock that secured the gate.

Once through the gate, they dropped some ten or twelve feet to the rocks at the bottom of the cliff, which were covered with pieces of automobile tires discarded from the mat shop. They waded out into the water and began swimming toward the mainland. No one saw them again.

Cole and Roe were the first inmates to seriously attempt an escape from Alcatraz. That no prisoners had tried to make a break before the end of 1937 is remarkable. Almost half of the men sent to the island had attempted to escape from one or more prisons before their transfer and many of those tries had been successful. Indeed, a history of plotting and attempting escapes was one of the main characteristics that wardens and Bureau officials were looking for in selecting candidates for transfer to Alcatraz.

Alcatraz's escape artists, however, confronted a custodial staff very intent on keeping them on the island. "The inmates' job is to get out," said a senior custodial officer; "our job is to keep them in." With Alcatraz labeled by the press and the popular media as escape-proof—a characterization not seriously denied by the Bureau of Prisons or the Department of Justice—many guards and their supervisors took it as a personal and professional challenge to thwart escapes. In an ongoing battle of wits, skills, and courage, they took it on themselves to keep escape-inclined prisoners from locating, as one convict put it, "the hole in the Rock."

Although many Alcatraz inmates were escape artists, planning a break was not for all prisoners. As in planning the robbery of a bank or monitoring the daily routine of a potential ransom kidnap prospect, plotting an escape required intelligence, skill, patience, and courage. Escape routes had to be carefully figured out, the patterns of guards monitored for long periods of time, the actions of escape partners closely coordinated, and clothing, ropes, flotation gear, and other paraphernalia constructed, prepared, and hidden. Such preparations occupied weeks and even months of time and involved activities that were risky in and of themselves. It is not surprising that most of the men who attempted to escape from Alcatraz had robbed banks or kidnapped someone, crimes involving considerable advance planning, a sense of timing, and the ability to think quickly and to act decisively while working under life-threatening circumstances—all the while maintaining emotional control, or what admiring confederates called "nerves."

The custodial staff at Alcatraz expected that the greatest collection of escape artists ever assembled in one prison would devise some sophisticated escape plots, and they were not disappointed. Several of the attempts involved planning, preparation, and execution of such a high order that they rank at the top of the list of the most ingenious and daring escapes in American penal history. They have been featured in such films as *Escape from Alcatraz* and *Six Against the Rock*, and even today they are reenacted on various "true crime" television series.

Escape attempts from the island were concentrated during the period from 1937 to 1946. After 1946, only two serious efforts to break out occurred, both in 1962, and they contributed to the closing of the prison in March 1963. Several of the breaks that occurred during the prison's thirty-year history came close to success—inmates were able to get out of their cells and the cell house or the industries building—but none of the escapees was able to overcome the last security barrier, the cold, fast currents of San Francisco Bay.

"LOST IN A FOG"

Theodore Cole, one of the first two men to test the Rock's security system, had all the credentials that justified a transfer to Alcatraz. He was sent to the Oklahoma State Training School for Boys at the age of fourteen. Shortly after his release, he was convicted on a burglary charge and sent to the Arkansas State Penitentiary; a short time later he was released to Oklahoma authorities so that he could be tried for the armed robbery of a Dr. Pepper bottling plant in Tulsa. Armed robbery was then a capital offense in Oklahoma and the judge, contending that "the boy is a potential killer," sentenced him, at age seventeen, to death in the electric chair. Subsequent protests by women's clubs and other organizations, however, were successful in convincing the appellate court to set aside the death penalty in favor of a sentence of fifteen years.

At the Oklahoma State Penitentiary Cole got into a dispute with his cell mate, pulled out a prison-made knife, and stabbed the other man twenty-seven times, killing him. As this murder charge was pending, Cole escaped by concealing himself in a bag that was thrown in the back of a laundry truck. The truck drove out of the prison and Cole jumped off, unseen by the driver. While on escape status, he approached a man who was preparing to get into his automobile and drive to Cushing, Oklahoma. He asked for a ride and the driver agreed, but a short distance outside of town.Cole produced a gun and forced the man to drive him to Springfield, Illinois. Cole was identified as the kidnapper by his victim, and because kidnapping had recently become a federal offense, state and local police were joined by the FBI in the effort to track him down.

On January 5, 1935, Cole was arrested in Dallas, Texas, and returned to Oklahoma City to be tried on federal kidnapping charges. In the Oklahoma City Jail he tried, unsuccessfully, to escape by concealing himself in a garbage can and by sawing the bars of his cell. On May 20, he pleaded guilty to kidnapping in U.S. district court and was sentenced to a term of fifty years; Oklahoma authorities filed detainers to hold him after service of his federal sentence for his escape from the state penitentiary and the murder he committed there. Cole was shipped off to Leavenworth on the same day that he was sentenced. His admission summary classified him, at age twenty-three, as a habitual criminal; an FBI report characterized him as "moronic, vicious and a killer." At Leavenworth Cole readily admitted to the staff that he had murdered his cell mate in the Oklahoma state prison and this statement, plus the length of his sentence and his record of escapes, provided the basis for the recommendation that he be transferred. Five months later he was on the Rock.

Ralph Roe was on the same train that brought Ted Cole to Alcatraz. Roe had also run away from home at the age of fourteen and had also compiled an impressive criminal record. After serving time in a youth prison in California for robbery, he traveled to Arkansas, where he was sent to prison on a grand larceny conviction; eighteen days after his release from Arkansas he was arrested for theft in Oklahoma and went off to the state reformatory at Granite City for two years; six months after his release from the reformatory he was sentenced to twelve years in the Oklahoma State Penitentiary for robbery with firearms. He served six years, but seven months after his release he was charged with harboring a fugitive and robbery with firearms, charges that were ultimately dropped; six months later he was arrested for auto theft and burglary. These charges were also dropped but two months later he was arrested for the robbery of the Farmer's National Bank at Sulfur, Oklahoma, and for kidnapping the cashier as he and an accomplice made their getaway. These charges were not dropped. On January 18, 1935, he received a ninety-nine-year sentence and was transported to Leavenworth. The Leavenworth medical staff determined that he was "acclimating himself to his very restricted life in an unusually excellent manner; despite his 99 year sentence he is facing his fate in an optimistic manner and has retained a cheerful personality." Despite this positive evaluation, he was put on the same train with his friend Ted Cole to help build the Alcatraz population.

Ralph Roe settled down to do his time quietly and soon won over the medical staff, who pronounced him "a likeable individual with good intelligence." Ted Cole was caught up in several protests, including the strike that began a few months after his arrival. When asked by the deputy warden why he was refusing to work, Cole replied that he did not know what the strike was about, but he "felt that he had to stick with the boys a few days as he had to live with them for many years."[1] Cole's only other disciplinary reports were for possession of contraband (some clothes stolen from the laundry and a piece of fudge smuggled from the kitchen).

Cole and Roe, like so many of the escape plotters, understood that a man could not engineer a break if he was not as free as possible to move about the kitchen, the hospital, and the industrial area to look for weaknesses in windows, doors, and fences. The two created no trouble, attracted little attention from staff or inmates, and served their time quietly, but they were determined to find a flaw in the security system.

Their jobs in the Model Shop afforded them this opportunity. They discovered that the bars in the windows were not tool-proof steel, and that for relatively long periods between head counts they were not under direct surveillance by guards. Although a guard was stationed on the flat roof of the building, he could not be looking on every side of the building at once, and fog reduced his visibility.

Cole and Roe correctly saw that heavy fog would be the key to their escape because it would obscure their movements, both on the island and in the water. When the fog remained thick and close to the water on the afternoon of December 16, 1937, they were ready.

Inmates who worked in the industries shops were counted every thirty minutes and the two were observed at their jobs at 1:00 P.M. by Officer Joseph Steere. After the count, Steere left the mat shop to check up on the inmates in other shops; when he returned to make the 1:30 count, Cole and Roe were gone. He called the deputy warden, heard the alarm siren go off, and began to look around the work area. He noticed that one of the windows was missing some bars. The officer assigned to routine patrol along the edge of the flat roof rushed to the bay side of the building but saw no sign of the men—even the fence gate through which they passed was closed in its normal position. He had not looked over the side of the building during the few minutes that the inmates were climbing out of the window, running to the fence, twisting off the padlock, and jumping down to the edge of the bay and swimming away from the island.

A massive search was launched, with Warden Johnston ordering several of his men to join San Francisco police officers in a search of every fishing boat that came in to dock at Fisherman's Wharf and other piers. (As an indication of the poor weather that day, the guards reported that they helped search only fifteen boats, when normally fifty or more would have gone out and come back.) Angel Island, the closest landmass to Al-

catraz, was carefully searched, as was Red Rock Island, a rocky out-
cropping located near Richmond some seven miles inland from the
Golden Gate Bridge. No sign of the fugitives was found on these islands
or along the shores of San Francisco, Sausalito, Tiburon, Richmond,
Berkeley, Oakland, or other communities ringing the bay.

On Alcatraz, guards looked in every corner in the shop buildings, the
docks, shrubbery, and sewers, and the caves along the shore at the northwest end of the island. The caves were searched with lights and the largest
cave was flooded, first with tear gas and then with a gas that produced
vomiting, and guards were assigned to watch the area around the en-
trances to the caves for any sign of life.

Prison officials hoped that the bay would offer up the bodies of the
two convicts as tangible evidence that the escape attempt had failed. Harbor officials and keepers of the eight lighthouses then operating were contacted to inquire whether they had observed any unusual sights or events
and urged to keep their eyes open for floating objects that might be related to the escape. The direction and rate of the flow of tides was calculated to plot the probable movements of bodies. Harbor officials reported that the afternoon ebb tide on December 16 was stronger than
the returning flood tide, which meant that a body carried ten miles out
with the ebb tide would return only six miles on the flood tide; bodies
carried out under the Golden Gate Bridge, they said, would likely be
returned to coastal shores rather than back into the bay.

Since Alcatraz represented the most visible symbol of the federal government's promise to keep the country's most desperate lawbreakers
securely locked up, the disappearance of Cole and Roe tarnished the image of the escape-proof fortress that the Justice Department had sought
to create. As the lead from the *San Francisco Examiner*'s full-page spread
the next day put it,

> Two desperate Alcatraz prisoners vanished from the American "Devil's Is-
> land" yesterday into the obscurity of one of this winter's heaviest fogs.
> Theodore Cole, 25, and Ralph Roe, 32, Oklahoma desperadoes with long
> careers of crime, apparently had escaped from the Federal Prison that was
> supposed to be escape proof.

The *Examiner* reported that the search for the two inmates was "one of
the greatest manhunts in Northern California experience." The paper offered a $500 reward for information leading to the arrest of the "des-
peradoes" and complained that when a boat hired by the newspaper approached Alcatraz, guards on the island fired warning shots across its

bow. The *Examiner* also ran a separate story in which the prison was labeled "a menace to San Francisco."

> When Attorney General Cummings and the Department of Justice decided to make Alcatraz an American Devil's Island, vehement protest arose from San Francisco and all the Bay Region. The Bay Cities bitterly resented conversion of a beautiful island on San Francisco Bay into a sinister repository of what were advertised by the Department of Justice as the most vicious Federal prisoners in captivity. Repeated efforts were made to convince Cummings that Alcatraz was not escape proof. The *Examiner* had a girl swim completely around the island and back to shore as proof that escape by swimming was no very difficult matter. The fogs of the Bay as cover for an escape were no secret. But someone seems to have been too much intrigued by the publicity value of Alcatraz. Here was the most effective possible dramatization of the G-Man. All the nation's Public Enemies on an island that loomed like a fortress under the windows of a million people. What a monument to the Department of Justice! Now the worst fears of this region may have been realized. If the two convicts that escaped yesterday have reached the mainland then two beasts have been turned loose upon these communities. If the men are as advertised, two of the nation's most desperate criminals, they will kill any man, woman or child who stands in their way of escape. Their past records include kidnapping and murder. Their future records may well include another murder or murders. Even if they are later found hiding on the island or if they are drowned, the stupidity and cynicism that underlie the whole Devil's Island scheme are apparent. Alcatraz was, and is, a bad choice, and it is a continual affront and menace to every city that borders on the Bay.[2]

A poem penned by an anonymous prisoner on the island summed up the convicts' view of the escape and the reaction of Deputy Warden Edward Miller, known to the prisoners as "Meat Head."

LOST IN A FOG

Twas a few days before Christmas,
With the fog like a sheet,
When over the fence two boys did leap,
With all the Bulls [guards] in the towers fast asleep,
With high powered rifles, tommy-guns and grenades,
They said, "Old Alcatraz" boys can never be made,
With thousands of dollars spent day by day,
I wonder now what the public will have to say,
Such tumultuous excitement we have never seen before,

All the Bulls in the joint were walking the floor,
As we marched in to supper, there stood,
"Ole Meat Head" with a puss that was ashen gray,
Though they called out the Army, Navy, Coast Guard, Marine Corps,
The boys kept right on swimming for the opposite shore,
Now dear public be very skeptical when you hear Edgar J. Hoover say,
We have the incorrigibles where they can't get away,
All night through we wished the boys luck,
While the screws in the joint were passing the buck.[3]

A couple of days passed, and the continued absence of bodies allowed for the possibility that Cole and Roe actually reached land. As the FBI launched a widespread search, along with an investigation into the circumstances surrounding the escape, the San Francisco field office was instructed by FBI headquarters to include interviews with the Alcatraz staff in the investigation, since in Director Hoover's view, "as far as we are concerned everyone over there is under suspicion."[4] Agents examined the backgrounds, family situations, and credit records of the thirteen guards and civilian employees who worked in the industries area and held long interviews with each man. In response to questions about the degree to which they conversed with inmates, the guards reported that they had been instructed not to talk with prisoners except to issue orders or instructions and therefore they had not talked with Cole or Roe and had not heard anything about the escape from other inmates.

The civilians who worked in the laundry and other shops had more informal, friendly relations with the prisoners under their supervision, but they also reported that they had heard nothing that aroused their suspicions or would provide any clue as to the plans or whereabouts of the escapees. One guard reported that some three to four weeks before the escape he personally had hammered the bars on the window from which Cole and Roe exited.

Close examination of the window through which the inmates crawled revealed that two of the bars had been cut and three small panes of glass removed, leaving an opening 8¾ × 18¾ inches. Since many of the Model Shop windows had been broken "for ventilation," the missing panes where the bars were cut had not attracted the attention of the guards or the civilian work crew supervisors. The bars showed evidence that small sections had been freshly cut while other sections showed signs of rust with putty smeared over the cuts to disguise them. The cuts were smooth, indicating that either a hacksaw or a first-class prisoner-made cutting blade had been used. A check of the equipment log indicated that no blades had been given to Cole or Roe. Other inmates had to have "loaned" the blades to the escapees and thus it was concluded that one or more men in the shops had knowledge of the escape.

During their interviews with FBI agents, several civilian employees emphasized the limited and restricted nature of communication between rank-and-file staff and inmates, one remarking that the regimen at Alcatraz was "so strict that a man must not even wear a smile or happy expression on his face." Another civilian worker, noting the absence of any conversation unrelated to work with inmates, recalled that an inmate had once asked him how things were in San Francisco. When he responded that he didn't know, the inmate replied, "Hell, you live over there don't you?" He also reported that an inmate once asked him about the weather in San Francisco, and he replied that it was probably the same as it was on Alcatraz.[5]

The officer directly responsible for supervising the inmates in the shop area also reported that he had not seen or heard anything suspicious. He told the agents that one inmate whom he regarded as reliable told him that other prisoners had seen Cole and Roe in the water, that Roe was "floundering and just about all in" and that Cole was staying close by Roe. The inmate also claimed that the escapees struck out from the island with nothing to keep them afloat. When asked if any of the inmates in the shop area might talk about the escape, the guard replied that one convict had made a sound like a drowning man, but "that is as much as he would say even if you cut his eyeballs out."[6] This officer also reported that at the time the escape was discovered, he was able to see three hundred yards offshore and that the bell buoy marker was visible, so that he would have seen any boat in the area. Asked by agents about the possibility that the inmates might try to grab onto one of the large ferries passing in the vicinity, he replied that the boats were propelled by large side wheels or screw propellers that created so much suction that anyone coming close to them would be pulled into the blades and "ground into mince meat." In addition, the distance from the surface of the water to the decks of the ferries was six feet, a distance too great to allow the escapees to jump out of the water and gain a hold on the boats.

Alcatraz staff and FBI agents, alerted to the possibility that one or more of the five-gallon oil cans stored in the machine shop could have been used to help keep the convicts afloat, checked the cans, found none missing, and concluded that the cans were too large to pass through the hole the inmates had made in the window. A check of lubricants and grease kept in the shops provided no evidence that any substance was missing that could have been used to ward off the effects of the cold water.

In the months that followed, Alcatraz inmates transferred to other federal prisons were questioned on their arrival by FBI agents. Two men shipped to Atlanta denied any knowledge of the escape and both stated that if they did have any information they would not "rat" on a fellow prisoner to the FBI or anyone else.[7] Agents even sought to identify the sender of a card, addressed to Warden Johnston and postmarked Denver, Colorado, which stated simply: "Tut tut goodbye, give my love to the boys.—T. Cole."

From time to time in later years, rumors of the escapees' whereabouts, or their fates in the cold waters of the bay, would appear in the press. In 1941 the *San Francisco Chronicle* reported that Roe and Cole were in South America, had "plenty of money," and were "living comfortably in their hideouts" in Peru and Chile.[8] A guard at Leavenworth said it was common knowledge among ex-Alcatraz guards and inmates that Cole and Roe were killed by Alcatraz guards while trying to escape and to avoid negative publicity their bodies had been dumped in the bay.

In 1958, some twenty-one years after the escape, there was a report that the escapees had finally surfaced and were playing banjo and guitar in a bar in North Bergen, New Jersey; the FBI took it seriously enough to launch an inquiry. Over the years the FBI continued talking with relatives and associates of Cole and Roe and followed up on reports and rumors. In September 1974, some thirty-seven years after the escape, the active investigation was discontinued. No firm evidence ever came to light indicating that Cole and Roe made it or died in the attempt.

A VIOLENT BREAKOUT
ATTEMPT AND MURDER TRIAL

After the Cole and Roe escape, Warden Johnston enhanced security at the model building. He posted a second guard on the roof whose assignment was continuous foot patrol around the perimeter of the building; the other guard was instructed to remain in the enclosed guard box. New tool-proof steel bars were placed in the shop windows. Despite these measures, men bent on escape understood that the model building, by virtue of its location immediately adjacent to the waters of the bay, was still the weakest spot in the prison's security perimeter. In May 1938, less than six months after Roe and Cole's break, three other men attempted to exploit this weakness. Their escape plan did not rely on stealth and cunning; it involved a direct assault on guards in the shops and on the roof of the model building.

The three convicts in on the break, Thomas Limerick, James Lucas, and Rufus "Whitey" Franklin, were typical of the general Alcatraz inmate population during its first decade. They had limited education and work skills and robbed banks because it seemed an obvious way to get money. Though well known in their local communities, they had not achieved the notoriety or celebrity status held by Alvin Karpis, Dock Barker, George Kelly, Harvey Bailey, John Paul Chase, and the other big shots on the island.

Limerick, who had been transferred from Leavenworth to serve a life sentence at Alcatraz, was characterized as a "habitual criminal of the more vicious type." Earlier in his life he had served time at the Iowa State Reformatory and the Nebraska State Penitentiary. At Alcatraz he joined in the January 1936 general work strike and was locked up in the D block segregation/isolation unit. Limerick received two additional disciplinary reports in this first year at Alcatraz, one for refusing to eat all of the hash on his tray and another for refusing to eat all of his beans. But, with only these minor infractions and an attitude that seemed to have improved, he was assigned a job in the Model Shop.[9]

James Lucas had escaped twice from the Texas State Reformatory and arrived at Leavenworth with federal terms totaling thirty years; the state of Texas wanted him on charges that totaled 128 years. He was one of those Alcatraz inmates who, as the staff put it, "did not go along with the program." By May 1938 his misconduct record included citations for disobeying orders, refusing to go to the mess hall, insolence, refusal to work, possession of contraband (a small amount of gunpowder in a cigarette paper), joining in a strike with other inmates, fighting with Capone (which cost him 3,600 days, or approximately ten years, of good time), and fighting with another inmate. But in May 1938 Lucas was also working in the Model Shop.[10]

Whitey Franklin was sent to reform school in Alabama at age fourteen; when he was sixteen he received a life sentence when his partner in a robbery shot and killed a store owner. Four years into his term at Kilby Prison, Franklin's mother died and he was given a fifteen-day furlough to attend her funeral and visit with family members. While on leave he and a confederate stole an automobile and robbed a bank, which earned him a thirty-year federal sentence. Committed to Atlanta, his escape from Kilby had made him a candidate for the Rock.

On May 23, 1938, Limerick, Lucas, and Franklin were at work in the Model Shop. They waited for the guard who supervised them, Royal C.

Cline, to go into his office to check his count sheet. They knew that he typically remained there fifteen minutes—plenty of time for them to put their plan into effect. Working quickly, they placed wooden boards against the ceiling and at the base of one of the shop windows that opened out from the top and swung inside the room. The boards held the bottom of the metal window frames at a horizontal angle so that a man could climb out the window, stand on the frame, and reach up to the roof of the building. The three could not, however, simply climb up over the edge of the roof because four strands of barbed wire on supporting bars stood out on all four sides of the roof. Lucas's plan was to cut the wire strands with pliers they had picked up in the workshop, but as Lucas and Limerick prepared to climb up on the outside frame of the window, Officer Cline unexpectedly walked out of his office back into the work area. Franklin ran to the surprised officer and hit him with a hammer in the head, again and again. Cline fell on the floor, with a widening pool of blood seeping out from under his body.

Their plan had called for the men to cut the barbed wire and climb over the edge of the roof at the moment the guard on patrol, Clifford Stewart, walked behind a concrete elevator shaft that kept him out of the sight of the guard box—and the escapees. But on this day Officer Stewart was delaying his walk at the far edge of the roof because he had been instructed to keep an eye on the civilian workers who were installing new tool-proof steel window guards on the bay side of the building following the escape of Cole and Roe. When Stewart moved out of sight, the three inmates climbed up onto the roof and ran toward Officer Harold Stites in the guard box.

But Stites heard noises behind him, turned around, and saw the inmates advancing in his direction. The three began throwing heavy iron bolts, a hammer, and wrenches at the windows in an effort to force him to seek cover before he could grab his rifle. One of the missiles thrown by the inmates crashed through a window and hit Stites, but he pulled out his pistol and felled Limerick with a bullet to the head. Franklin, still clutching the bloody hammer he'd used to subdue Officer Cline, was hit by bullets in both shoulders; he fell back over the edge of the roof onto some uncut strands of barbed wire. Lucas dove for cover next to the guard tower, where he quickly found himself lined up in the sights of a rifle held by Officer Stewart who, on hearing the shots, rushed from behind the elevator shaft to assist Stites.

At the sound of gunfire other guards quickly appeared on the scene. Officer Cline, who never regained consciousness, was taken by stretcher up to the prison hospital. The unconscious Thomas Limerick was also taken to the prison hospital. Whitey Franklin, to the disgust of his fellow convicts, was left lying wounded on the barbed wire strands for some thirty minutes before he was removed and taken to the prison hospital for treatment. James Lucas was escorted up the hill to the main cell house, where he told Deputy Warden Miller that if the three men had been successful in getting the guns from Stites and Stewart, they were going to make a run for the dock on the other side of the island and try to capture the prison launch to complete their escape.[11] Lucas was locked up in the D block isolation unit.

Warden Johnston—in San Francisco acting as an honorary pallbearer at the funeral of the former chief of police—was called and informed that there had been trouble on the island; shots had been fired, and an officer had been injured. He ordered the prison launch sent back to San Francisco to bring him back to the island.

Limerick never regained consciousness and died that evening. Officer Cline was transported to the U.S. Marine Hospital at the Presidio in San Francisco, where his condition deteriorated. He died the next afternoon.

At first the violent breakout attempt by Limerick, Lucas, and Franklin attracted only moderate press attention, even though one inmate had been killed and another seriously injured, and an officer had died in the line of duty. The decision to try the surviving prisoners in federal district court, however, brought the incident to the headlines of Bay Area newspapers and produced what was called "the trial of the year."

The press was particularly excited about the prospect of learning directly about life on the Rock from the two convicts on trial and from six others who had been present in the model building at the time of the escape and were listed as government witnesses. When the Alcatraz cons to be called as witnesses were identified to the press, the greatest interest focused on Harvey Bailey, whom a reporter labeled "the most dangerous convict at Alcatraz." The question was whether Bailey would "rat on fellow convicts, cast suspicion on himself, or defy the federal court by refusing to testify."[12] He was reported to have warned government prosecutors that he would be a poor witness because "he's spending the rest of his life here and he has to live with these people. He didn't see anything and doesn't know anything. Number 139 is not talking."[13]

The local dailies also saw the trial as an excellent opportunity to satisfy the public's desire for the lurid details of courtroom testimony. Even the process of selecting jurors was written up in dramatic imagery as the widow of the slain guard took a seat in the courtroom:

There's a place reserved for a woman, with a red dress and a red hat and a granite face and eyes that stare bitterly at Lucas and Franklin. She's Mrs. Royal C. Cline—widow of the Alcatraz guard who fell with bashed head under the hammers of his assailants on the day of the break attempt. Cline died a few hours later; he never recovered consciousness to say goodbye to his wife. She remembers that.[14]

Before the trial actually began, Lucas's attorney made an effort to stop the proceedings on the ground that his client had "gone mad," but after a court-appointed psychiatrist concluded that Lucas was malingering and "scared speechless," not insane, the judge rejected the motion.[15]

The question for the jury was not whether the two men had tried to escape—that they admitted; it was whether they had killed Cline. Franklin and Lucas claimed that other convicts in the shop had committed the murder because they did not like Cline.[16]

The trial began with the prosecution handing over for the inspection of the jurors close-up photographs of the battered head of Officer Cline and a white plastic death mask that had been formed by pouring a hot gelatinous substance over the dead guard's face. Mrs. Cline covered her eyes. The trial produced sensational reports of the "gruesome" death mask, the "ghastly" photographs, and the "death hammer." One story described the courtroom scene:

> Rows of spectators—and for the first time, most of them are women—shudder in delighted thrill as [Officer Harold] Stites tells of sending his bullet through a convict's skull, through another convict's back.[17]

Enhancing the *San Francisco Examiner* accounts of the trial was the commentary of former Alcatraz inmate P. F. Reed, who had been released several weeks earlier; Reed's remarks ran under the headline "Alcatraz Is Hell." Ex-Rock convict Roy Gardner showed up to watch the proceedings, and as author of a book entitled *Hellcatraz*, he pronounced Reed's characterization of the Rock accurate. Thus, behind the question of who committed the murder of Officer Cline was the debate over whether the long criminal records of Lucas and Franklin provided the explanation for their violent acts or whether the "grim discipline" of the prison provoked convicts' violence.

The two attorneys for Lucas and Franklin were unpaid and court appointed, but they mounted an aggressive defense to keep their clients out of the gas chamber. They attacked the government's case on the grounds that only circumstantial evidence tied their clients to the murder. They also sought to impugn the testimony of guard witnesses, drawing them into discussions of incidents of alleged brutality on the island.

In an effort to demonstrate that guard Otis Culver had "a motive to testify falsely against these defendants," attorney Faulkner made the following claim:

> I'll prove that in January of 1936, a convict named Jack Allen was yelling and screaming in his cell; that Culver slugged him to stop him. Despite the slugging, Allen continued to scream and yell. Then Allen was removed to solitary confinement, and died the next morning. . . . The next day, the convicts called a strike, in which Defendant James Lucas participated. Lucas was slugged by Culver or by another guard in Culver's presence; then he was kicked down an iron stairway, and the next day, had to be taken to the hospital.

According to the account in the *Examiner,* Faulkner's line of questioning went like this:

> *Faulkner:* Did you take Lucas to solitary confinement in January 1936?
> *Culver:* I don't remember.
> *Faulkner:* Do you remember one Jack Allen?
> *Culver:* I do not.
> *Faulkner:* Do you remember removing Allen to solitary confinement and next day Allen died?
> *Culver:* I do not.
> *Faulkner:* Do you remember the convicts going on strike over the Allen case?
> *Culver:* I do not.
> *Faulkner:* Do you remember fighting with Lucas?
> *Culver:* I do not.
> *Faulkner:* Do you remember escorting Lucas to solitary confinement; Lucas had no shoes on, but blankets on his feet, and you kicked him down an iron stairway?
> *Culver:* I do not.
> *Faulkner:* Do you remember slugging Lucas with a blackjack?
> *Culver:* I do not.
> *Judge Louderback to Culver:* Are Mr. Faulkner's statements true?
> *Culver:* Those statements are all untrue.[18]

By permitting this kind of questioning over the objections of U.S. Attorney Frank Hennessy, the judge enabled a defense strategy that put the staff on the defensive as they were interrogated about various incidents on the island in an effort to claim that a reign of terror existed on Alcatraz, that the prison was so brutal that it forced inmates into suicide, madness, and murder.

As the trial proceeded, the government produced only one inmate witness, a man already transferred to another prison, who testified that he saw Limerick, Lucas, and Franklin in the room shortly before Cline was killed, but the sensational testimony that had been expected did not materialize—the Alcatraz convicts weren't talking.

James Lucas and Whitey Franklin were convicted of the murder of Royal Cline, but the jury angered the Alcatraz staff by refusing to send them to the gas chamber. Franklin received another life sentence to go with the two already lodged against him and Lucas's new life sentence was added to his existing thirty-year term. The Alcatraz staff, having interpreted these sentences as constituting no additional punishment for convicts who had murdered one of their number, were determined to find their own means of administering justice on the island. Lucas and Franklin anticipated this reaction when they told reporters after they had been sentenced that they expected to spend "the rest of their lives" in isolation, which meant "continuous imprisonment in unlighted cells on one meal a day."[19] They were returned to Alcatraz and placed in D block. Lucas would remain there for the next six years; Franklin would not be released from disciplinary segregation until 1952—fourteen years later.

The trial demonstrated to Warden Johnston and Deputy Warden Miller that in any trial of Alcatraz prisoners, defense attorneys would seek to point the finger of ultimate culpability at the institution and its administration instead of the defendants. The experience discouraged them from prosecuting prisoners; instead, the prison would employ its own punitive measures, mainly taking away years of good time and locking inmates up in disciplinary segregation for months or years—decisions that required no due process proceeding or public scrutiny. The trial showed prisoners, however, that the press and Bay Area citizens were inclined to accept the argument that the prison was a genuine American version of Devil's Island. The government never responded to such allegations other than denying their accuracy—and future juries would be inclined to believe inmate claims that the regime on the Rock drove them to acts of violence.

FIVE REACH THE WATERS OF THE BAY

Attacking the armed guards on the roof of the model building was a desperate and very dangerous way of engineering an escape and, because it involved little ingenuity, had almost no hope of success. Only seven months after the attempt by Limerick, Franklin, and Lucas, five inmates devised a more clever and stealthy mode of escape. They succeeded in breaking through every level of the Alcatraz security system—they got out of their cells, out of the cell house, past the gun towers, and confronted San Francisco Bay as the final barrier to freedom.

Dale Stamphill, one of the leaders of the breakout, was well acquainted with prisons and how to get out of them. Sentenced on auto theft charges to the Oklahoma State Reformatory, Stamphill had whittled himself a wooden gun in an attempt to replicate John Dillinger's escape from jail at Crown Point, Indiana. He pointed his homemade gun at the guard in a tower, and the surprised man threw down his rifle—but not into the prison yard—and dove to the floor of the tower, where he set off the escape alarm that foiled Stamphill's plan. In solitary, Stamphill heard a commotion one day and to his surprise the door to his cell opened and an inmate poked his head in and said, "Come on, we're breaking out." Stamphill joined a group of some thirty convicts who, with several smuggled guns, took over the administration building and grabbed hostages from its visiting room. On their way out of the building, Stamphill and several escapees took the keys to the chief clerk's automobile, parked in front of the prison. Then they herded the hostages toward the main gate. The officer at the gate was armed with a shotgun but handed it over to Stamphill when he saw the crowd of hostages. One other obstacle, the front tower, remained. The tower guard was warned to throw down his gun but—with many inmates shouting instructions at the same time—he hesitated. Shots rang out from the ground below, the visitors scattered, screaming, and the guard fell, mortally wounded.

While the other inmates and all the visitors ran in many directions, Stamphill and seven other men raced to the vehicle, crowded in, and sped away from the prison. As they came to small towns, the escapees dropped off in groups of two or three. Stamphill and two men got out at the town of Seiling, where they promptly robbed the First National Bank, grabbed a local physician whose automobile was handy, and drove from Oklahoma to Texas. The bank robbery and kidnapping put federal agents on their trail, along with state and local police; the three were soon caught and returned to Oklahoma where they were tried, found guilty, and given life sentences for killing the prison guard.

Stamphill was sent to the Oklahoma State Penitentiary at McAlester and locked up in the disciplinary unit, where he remained for almost two years. After his release into the general population, he fell into a conversation with several older convicts in the yard, and one, a lifer named

Brown, told him, "I don't know your business but as someone who's done a lot of time, if you plan to escape, do it the first chance you get. Don't wait because you'll get institutionalized and you won't have the guts to do it."[20]

This advice registered with Stamphill, but it was not until he had been taken to federal court, convicted of kidnapping the doctor, and transferred to Leavenworth with another life sentence that he began to seriously consider Brown's advice. The guards in the disciplinary segregation unit there warned him, "We're going to send you to Alcatraz; you're not going to escape from us." Eighty days passed while the staff accumulated enough convicts to fill a railroad car for shipment to the Rock. While he was waiting, a guard allowed him to see a newspaper editorial that commented on Cole and Roe's escape attempt—and its apparent ending in the icy waters of the bay. The guard probably thought the editorial would send the message that it was futile to try to escape from Alcatraz. But the article made a different impression on Stamphill: "*They got out.* So, I started thinking toward escape."

Stamphill arrived at Alcatraz in December 1937, with escape foremost in his mind. He talked to prisoners who had been on the island for several years and learned about using a bar spreader. The idea intrigued him. "I looked at those curved bars over the windows in the dining room and thought, God damn, that's simple," Stamphill recalled years later. "I knew that D block was a weak place. The cells had flat metal bars just like A block. And it was used as a punishment unit." As the basic idea of a breakout plan formed in his mind, Stamphill sought out another convict he had known in the Oklahoma reformatory, a man who had a reputation for taking chances—Dock Barker. In Barker, Stamphill found someone already thinking about breaking out who was well connected with other convicts. Both men concluded that if their friend Ted Cole had escaped, "Hell, we can, too."

Barker convinced an inmate in the blacksmith shop to make some saw blades from an old wood saw to cut through the soft metal of the old flat bars still in place in the doors of the cells in D block. Then he had the inmate make a bar spreader or screw jack—a round metal rod about a half inch in diameter and four inches long, with a bolt on the screw and a groove on the bolt. When the bolt was turned with pliers or a wrench, tension was created that caused a bar to bend.

The next task was getting these tools into the cell house. It would be nearly impossible for inmates to smuggle them in, because they had to pass through a metal detector and pat-down frisks on their return from the industries area each day. When the staff asked an inmate machinist to build a device to sharpen the blades of safety razors, Barker saw the solution to this problem: he arranged with the machinist to hide the saw blades and bar spreader in the interior working parts of the razor-sharpening device. The machinist gave the finished device to an officer, who carried it up to the cell house, thereby bypassing the metal detector and body search. The sharpening machine was taken to A block and left for an inmate who would begin working on the worn blades.

Stamphill received saw blades and bar spreader on a day when, as part of his work as orderly, he was permitted to move around the cell house. He knew that a toilet in a cell on the second tier of D block had been removed for repairs, leaving a gaping hole in the back wall of the cell that was easily seen by inmates living across the corridor in C block. (The interior side of D block held no prisoners because like A block it had not been remodeled by the Bureau of Prisons.) Stamphill climbed up the stairs to the second tier and crawled through the hole into the utility corridor, the ventilation and plumbing area that divided the east and west sides of each cell block. He called out to Rufus McCain, who was locked up in one of the isolation cells on the other side of D block; when he responded, Stamphill crawled up pipes to the flat top of D block and down to the third tier on the other side in order to lower the tools through the railing. Then Stamphill reversed his journey, climbed back through the hole in the wall of the cell facing C block, and resumed his general housekeeping work around the main cell house. He told Barker, "Well, the stuff's over in D block. So he got into a fight and they locked him up in D block." Barker then recruited three inmates—Rufe McCain, Henry Young, and a black convict named William Martin—to participate in the break. According to Young, the four inmates began cutting the flat bars in front of their cells with Dock Barker humming, "I'll be home for Christmas."[21]

Three of the co-conspirators in D block had been allowed to move to cells near each other on the ground-floor level, which allowed them to easily communicate and exchange the tools. Furthermore, these particular cells were located on the far side of the two concrete vestibules that extended three and a half feet out from the row of cells to serve as solitary confinement cells; these obstructions blocked the view of the guard who looked down on their side of D block cells from the gun cage located on the north wall.

Using the tools provided by Stamphill, the four inmates began cutting the flat bars in front of their cells. The bottom of each bar in the lower section of each cell door was held to the frame by a rivet—so when the top was severed, the bar could be pushed to either side, leaving a hole some ten by sixteen inches through which a man could crawl. Once they were able to free themselves from their cells, the inmates could begin working on the bars of a window in the outer wall of the cell block. This was a riskier procedure because the window was not hidden from the view of the guard in the gun gallery.

By studying the movements of the gun gallery guards, the inmates had learned that the officer on duty left the D block side of the gallery at meal times to help supervise the general population prisoners in the dining room and the flow of inmates as they moved from the main cell blocks to and from the dining room. At meals the four men waited until the guard moved out of the D block side of the gallery. When he disappeared, Henry Young climbed up to the third tier of cells and took up his post as a lookout. The others took turns working on the interior set of bars covering the window. These bars constituted a serious obstacle since, unlike the cell bars, they were made of tool-proof steel and were resistant to the cutting blades. Here the bar spreader was essential. The men took turns laboring with the device, first pressing one of the curved bars to one side and then applying pressure to the other side of the bar, moving the bar ever so slightly in one direction and then in the other. When the guard was about to come back to his post, they returned to their cells and pulled the cut bars in the cells back into place, making them temporarily secure with a mixture of paint and floor wax.[22]

After days of work on the interior window bars, the inmates succeeded in snapping the bar at its weakest point—the section where it was welded to the frame. There now was an opening twelve inches wide and fourteen inches high—big enough for each man to squeeze through. The prisoners moved on to the next barrier, a set of old, soft, flat metal bars affixed to the outside of the window. These bars presented no more resistance than the flat bars of the cells, and they were soon cut. To resecure these bars the inmates used a puttylike substance comprised of tooth powder and the paint used in routine maintenance of the cell block.

In his account of this escape, Henry Young commented on the need for other convicts in D block who could see what was happening not only to keep quiet about the escape attempt but to make sure that their usual jawing and calling out to each other between cells did not fall off as they watched Barker and the others saw away on the two sets of bars in the window of the outer wall. Dale Stamphill explained this absence of leaks as follows: "You always worried [in prison] about somebody finding out about a thing like [an escape] and snitching on you. But Alcatraz was one place where every time that somebody'd become aware of somebody trying to escape, nobody would say a word. I guess they was afraid of what would happen to them."

While the four men in D block were working on the bars, Stamphill had to get himself locked up in disciplinary segregation or be left behind. This step proved to be more difficult than he expected. In late October he picked a fight with another inmate but found himself locked up not in D but in A block. Trying to get moved from A to D he raised a commotion, but that resulted only in his being moved into one of the solitary cells in A block; six days later he was returned to general population. His next effort involved smuggling a knife into his cell and making sure it would be discovered during a routine shakedown. He was locked up for possessing the knife, but again in A block. Finally in mid-December he was moved to D block, where his only task was to cut the bars in the lower front section of his own cell, all the other work on the outside wall window and grill having been completed by the other four men. But the saw blades, by the time Stamphill got them, were so worn down that he could not cut the inch-and-a-half-wide flat bar. To reduce the area to be cut he began working on the bars of the cell door rather than the bars that covered the front of the cell; the door bars were square rather than flat and were about one-half inch wide. He was able to cut through two of the bars but only at one point and he told the others that he would have to have their help in bending the bars down far enough to expose an opening wide enough for him to squeeze through.

When the bars on Stamphill's cell were cut, the prisoners dropped the cutting tools down their toilets and waited for a night when fog would provide cover for their escape. The tension they experienced is reflected in notes they passed among themselves; these notes, thrown down their toilets, were retrieved later by guards when they searched the cell block after the escape.

> —Henry how many rounds did the Bull make while I was trying to sleep? Give him time to git out good for he may walk right back. That was his second, he is staying out longer tonight than last night. . . . We are going to take it the next round. Take one of your sheets along, the best one—roll it up tight as we may need a rope to get down the cliff. It won't take but a minute to go out that hole so the bull in the cage would have to be mighty restless to wheel back so quick. No good yet, but ready to go anytime.
>
> —I hear someone moving—is that you? Doc wasn't asleep all night so he is getting some now. He said that if it gets good enough [to go] to punch

him awake as he got all his clothes on. I can't tell from where I am. I am leaving it up to Doc.

—There is nothing to it yet for I can see the Frisco light. We couldn't get a break on the time like this anyway.

—Yes things are lit up like Christmas but there is a lot [of fog] out there it may be here anytime. No breeze.

—Henry I have lost so much sleep I can't stay wake but have shoes on and clothes like fire man it will take just one minute so will sleep but if things get right, there looks like a lot of fog out there, if O.K. clear your throat.

—This stuff [fog] sure comes and goes fast. Now I can't see the lights in Frisco. Dale told me yesterday that he had a sure way of telling. Can you see the light out front?[23]

On the evening of January 12, 1939, the inmates got what they were waiting for: a heavy fog shrouded the prison. The Alcatraz lighthouse keeper noted in his log that continuous fog began to roll in beginning about 10:15 P.M. and that the visibility was "practically nil." The convicts in D block knew that there were three counts during the night: at midnight, at 3:00 A.M., and at 6:00 A.M. Shortly after the 3:00 A.M. count, the gun cage officer walked through the door in D block to provide coverage for a guard making counts in the other cell blocks. Barker, Young, Martin, and McCain dislodged the precut bars in their cell fronts, squeezed out into the corridor and crossed the sixteen-foot area to the outer wall. Martin walked quickly over to Stamphill's cell and pushed the door bars down by standing on them, allowing their confederate to join the group at the window.

The window bars were quickly dislodged, and with some boosting and shoving—particularly to get William Martin through, since he was a much larger man than the others—the five men climbed through the window, dropped eight feet to the ground below, and made their way toward the end of the island closest to San Francisco. They picked up pieces of wood and wooden lawn chairs as they crossed in back of the employee living quarters. When they reached the cliffs, the group split up.

Barker and Stamphill, with no flotation gear, found concrete steps leading down to the water's edge and immediately started out into the bay, hoping to catch an outgoing tide. "We got about twenty or thirty feet," Stamphill recalled, "and hit the tide, which just whipped us right around back to the shore." They decided to move toward an old dock, where they hoped to find some lumber they could tear off for flotation, thinking that they hadn't been gone long enough yet for their absence to have been detected. But the escape siren had already wailed, its sound obscured to the escapees by the many foghorns sounding around them, and guards both on and off duty had been mustered, armed, and sent to different parts of the island to search for the escapees.

Stamphill and Barker were unaware that Officer Clifford Ditmer, who had drawn a Thompson submachine gun from the armory, was standing on the cliffs above them. At first Ditmer could not see the water through the fog, but as he watched, a gust of wind blew some of the fog away from the cove at the base of the cliffs and he was just able to make out two white shapes moving from the shore into the water. Ditmer warned the men to stop and when they continued to move he opened up with the Thompson, firing a half dozen shots into the water in front of the forms; the forms continued moving, at which point he aimed directly at them and fired a longer burst. He saw both men go down in the shallow water. More shots were fired from the prison launch, which was now standing close offshore and shining its lights on the cove. Stamphill thought all the gunfire was coming from the launch: "This boat came around and they just opened fire—never said a word, just opened fire with a machine gun; they knocked us both down."

Both men were shot in the legs and fell in the shallow water. Barker, writhing in pain, raised up on his elbows to shift his weight, another fusillade sprayed in the water around him with one bullet hitting him in the head. He gasped to Stamphill, "Don't move, they're going to kill us."

In the meantime, Henry Young and Rufe McCain had descended the cliffs at a different location and frantically tried to make a raft out of rolled up bed sheets and the pieces of wood and chairs they had picked up on the way down to the shore.

Before they could launch the raft, they were discovered by Lt. Henry Weinhold, who with Lt. Isaac Faulk was near the road tower.

> We heard shots being fired whereupon we immediately ran down to the lower road to a point overlooking the cove on the beach immediately below the Road Tower and I began firing into the cove at some faintly white shadows, firing three to five shots to the best of my recollection. I then went . . . to the edge of the lower road overlooking the cove and instructed the officer in charge of the Road Tower to turn his light on the cove and after more light had been brought to bear on the water edge in the cove two pairs of legs could be distinguished.
>
> I then proceeded to the Sea Wall and as I arrived the Launch *McDowell* came around the northeast corner of the island throwing its searchlight along the beach. A makeshift raft was floating in the water near the end of the sea wall. I threw my flashlight along the beach toward the west side

of the Island and saw two men, one naked and the other clad in a pair of drawers. I called to them to surrender and they came around the ledge of the rock with their hands in the air. I then identified them as inmates Rufus McCain no. 267 and Henry Young no. 244.[24]

Left to himself, William Martin had made his way to the south end of the island, where he was trying to climb down a twenty-foot cliff. Lt. Faulk and Deputy Warden Miller walked along the beach past Young and McCain's raft and waded along the base of the cliffs with their flashlights shining among the rocks. According to Faulk, they had gone close to one hundred feet from the cove where McCain and Young had been captured when he caught a glimpse of movement above them. At that moment, Martin—naked except for a pair of socks—fell from the cliff, struck the bank, and fell into the water. He surrendered peacefully. Injured in his fall, he was taken to the prison hospital.[25]

In the hospital Stamphill was treated for shock and several bullet wounds. Martin was treated for exposure and the multiple bruises and abrasions suffered in his fall down the cliff. Barker had been shot through the left leg, and another bullet had entered his neck behind the right ear and emerged at the corner of his right eye. According to the medical report, there was bleeding from the right ear, indicating a fracture of the skull. Semiconscious, and complaining of pain in his leg and of feeling cold, he mumbled to Deputy Warden Miller, "I'm all shot to hell. I was a fool to try it." His wounds were dressed; he was treated for shock and given a sedative. Later in the morning he appeared to have periods of consciousness but uttered no words. During the afternoon he became more restless and his breathing more labored. At 5:30 P.M. his condition rapidly worsened and ten minutes later he stopped breathing.[26]

Since Henry Young and Rufe McCain had not been injured in the break, they were locked up in isolation. Deputy Warden Miller and an FBI agent came around two days later to talk to them, but Young said he had absolutely nothing to say to agents of the FBI or to any employees of the Bureau of Prisons. McCain refused to discuss the escape, only saying, when asked why he tried to escape, "I just wanted to go home."

Stamphill and Martin also declined to provide any information regarding the escape when questioned by Miller and several FBI agents. Earlier that morning, however, immediately after he had been brought up to the prison hospital, Martin had been interrogated by Miller and talked about the escape, with his statement recorded by the assistant chief clerk. Martin reported that the escape had been planned before he was

sent to D block, that cutting the bars took more than a month, that Stamphill had smuggled the files and the bar spreader into the isolation unit,
and that the five men had gone to the cliffs together but then separated
in order to find boards and other materials to make a raft.[27]

Stamphill, later reflecting on this and other attempts to break out of
Alcatraz, noted the preoccupation of so many escapees with getting out
of the buildings on the island, while giving so little thought to means of
surviving the cold currents of the bay and getting to the nearest land, a
mile and a quarter away: "The amazing thing to me is that in escapes all
you think about is beating the institution. . . . We never planned beyond
that. Escape from the institution—that's all we concentrated on . . . as
soon as the fog came in, off we went."

Five days after the escape, Director James Bennett wrote to Warden
Johnston. Noting that there were many "lessons" to be learned from the
incident, Bennett suggested a number of measures for improving security:

- Place an extra officer in the gun gallery during meals so that D block
  would not be left unsupervised.
- Discontinue use of the cells on the lower floor of D block, where
  the obstructions posed by the two solitary confinement cells allowed
  the escapees to saw away on the cell bars, hidden from the gun
  cage officer's line of sight.
- Remind guards of the need to vary their routines and to remember
  that their primary obligation is to the government, not covering up
  for fellow officers who had been derelict in their duties.
- Complete an inventory of all tools and materials on the island.
- Acquire improved outside lighting, police dogs to aid in searches,
  and flare guns to light up the island and the nearby waters in an
  emergency.
- Institute a policy of frequent cell changes for the most escape-prone
  inmates.
- Fingerprint all persons admitted onto the island, including workmen, friends, and relatives of the officers who live on the island,
  employees of the lighthouse, "and anyone else."
- Immediately prepare plans for constructing new segregation/
  isolation cells with tool-proof steel bars.[28]

Several of these suggestions, including the remodeling of D block, were
promptly accepted, but police dogs and flare guns were never acquired,
and the task of routinely processing fingerprints and undertaking crim-

inal record checks for everyone who came over to the island met resistance from both the FBI and employees.

The repercussions of the 1939 escape attempt, however, went far beyond matters internal to the Bureau of Prisons. Even though the Bureau could point to some positive elements in the response to the escape—the breakout was discovered within twenty-five minutes, and the escapees caught before they could get away from the island—the fact remained that the inmates had succeeded in breaking out from cells inside the most secure penitentiary in the federal prison system. For this reason, the FBI saw the attempted escape as evidence of defective security arrangements and poor management.

Always looking for incompetence, inefficiency, and evidence of corruption in lesser agencies, FBI Director Hoover made sure that the attorney general knew of the failure of the BOP to measure up to FBI standards and ordered an investigation into the escape. The investigation, conducted by the San Francisco field office, began on January 14, two days after the breakout attempt. By the end of the day, FBI agents had collected enough information to make a telephoned report to Director Hoover, who condensed it into a memo he sent to the attorney general.

This initial report was harshly critical of the management of Alcatraz. It identified a long list of defects in the security arrangements in place on the island, reported that some men in the kitchen crew were also planning an escape that involved taking wives and children of the staff as hostages, described the many knives and other forbidden objects discovered in inmates' cells, and noted hostile attitudes toward Warden Johnston on the part of inmates. The report recommended a number of rather obvious changes, including obtaining new and better metal detection devices, removing potential raft or flotation materials from the prison grounds, and, most important, overhauling the prison's security, calling for

an inspection of the windows, bars, and cells on Alcatraz at frequent intervals. In this case it is to be noted that these bars had been sawed and the bar at the window loosened and were in this condition for over a month, but were not at any time ascertained by any of the prison guards.

Some change should be made in the supervision and guarding of the isolation ward. In this case, it is to be noted that these five prisoners, in five separate cells at various times of the day and night sawed the bars from their cell doors and then crossed the hallway at least sixteen feet from the cells to a window from which they loosened a bar and then cut the framework of the window. The work that accomplished these results had extended over a period of many weeks, and yet no one noted these activities.[29]

On the same day, Hoover sent a supplemental memorandum to the attorney general based on interviews that his agents held with two guards. The guards identified several blind spots in D block, including the obstruction created by the concrete solitary cells, which had prevented the gun cage officer from seeing the doors of the five cells in which the escapees were housed. The memo outlined administrative problems that might be regarded as outside the range of an escape investigation but about which Hoover decided the attorney general should be informed; no copy of this report was sent to Bureau of Prisons Director Bennett.

Two days later, the San Francisco FBI office sent a fourteen-page "personal and confidential" report to Hoover titled, "Conditions at Alcatraz." This document conveyed information and impressions gained from interviews with rank-and-file guards who agreed to talk to the FBI investigators about general conditions apart from the escape. These officers "felt that there was a breakdown in the system at Alcatraz to such an extent that it would probably affect the entire system of the Bureau of Prisons," and "they just had to tell somebody of these situations."[30]

The agents noted that these guards and other line staff had given up reporting defects they observed in the security system because their comments or suggestions were regarded by Deputy Warden Miller as personal criticism of his ability, and Miller, in turn, was not about to make any suggestions to Warden Johnston. The officers complained of poor communication from supervisors to the line staff and cited instances in which their supervisors withheld information that the officers felt they needed to know in order to anticipate or control trouble in the cell blocks. They also resented the policy that prohibited line staff from reading the files kept on the prisoners whom they were supervising.

The practice, approved by Deputy Warden Miller, of allowing inmates to move to cells where and next to whom they wished in exchange for cooperation (namely for not creating disturbances), was also criticized. The placement of the five escapees in adjacent cells was a consequence of this policy, and members of various cliques and gangs gathering in cells close to each other was cited as another example of poor administrative decision making.

The guards complained that the light workload in the shops allowed inmates ample opportunities to fashion weapons and escape paraphernalia, and to "case" the industries area for escape routes. They also criticized the failure to install tool-proof steel bars in D block, where the prison's most serious troublemakers were kept.

Another guard provided the FBI agents with a memo he had written on January 9 to Warden Johnston, pointing out the structural defects that made D block the least secure unit in the prison and recommending that "at least two panels of grill screen be placed on and attached to the bars of both gun galleries" in order to protect the officer stationed there and prevent inmates from acquiring gas grenades, gas masks, and night sticks.[31] (If this recommendation had been approved and carried out, the serious and deadly breakout attempt that occurred in May 1946 would have been foiled.)

The FBI's critique of security measures also included a list of materials found in the shakedown of the entire prison after the escape attempt.[32] The final section of the report revealed that when the prison siren sounded, employees did not know whether it signified a fire or an escape. On the night of the break, three officers had left their living quarters and run to the fire truck; they were driving up the hill to the cell house when they were flagged down and informed that the alarm was sounded for an escape, not a fire.

The report concluded with a reminder and a caveat: the information obtained in the investigation had not been verified, and some of the officers' comments "might be prompted by personal prejudices or jealousies or personality." But the information should be sent to the director "for his interest."[33] On January 19 Hoover sent a copy of this report to the attorney general; five days later, he sent a copy to James V. Bennett. He requested that Bennett handle the information "in a most discreet manner"; it included the identity of employees who had made "confidential" statements to the FBI agents.[34]

The investigation into the escape from D block thus provided Bureau of Prisons headquarters and Warden Johnston with evidence that FBI agents called to Alcatraz to investigate violations of federal law by prisoners had also reported opinions from employees about management policies and practices. Relations between Hoover and Bennett would continue to be suspicious and tense throughout the history of Alcatraz.

If the FBI's criticism to the attorney general's office wasn't enough, within several months the prison's security arrangements came under attack from another source: criminal complaints were taken to mainland juries, U.S. attorneys, and federal courts. A coroner's jury investigating the death of Dock Barker came to the following conclusion:

The said Arthur Barker met his death attempting to escape from Alcatraz Prison from gunshot wounds inflicted by guards unknown. From the evidence at hand, we, the jury, believe this escape was made possible by the failure of the system for guarding prisoners now in use at Alcatraz Prison and we recommend a drastic improvement by those in authority. Further, that a more efficient system be adopted for illumination of shores and waters immediately surrounding the prison; that the citizens of San Francisco unite in an effort to have a more suitable location for imprisonment of the type of desperadoes at present housed at Alcatraz.[35]

Given the beating Alcatraz was taking in the press, and knowing that the FBI had advised the attorney general of "administrative problems" at the prison, neither the Bureau of Prisons nor the attorney general's office in Washington encouraged the U.S. attorney in San Francisco to initiate criminal proceedings against the four convicts who survived the escape attempt.

But Alcatraz had punitive measures of its own, and the escapees received all of them. Young and McCain were immediately locked up in isolation and when Martin's bruises healed, he was also taken to D block. Stamphill's injuries required him to be put in traction for eight weeks and then in a cast for two more weeks. On the day the cast on his leg was removed, he was able to limp from his hospital bed to the shower; the following morning he was escorted to D block isolation, where he remained for seventeen months.

The Bureau of Prisons then exercised its option to take away all the good time that the escapees had accumulated. Later in January at his good time forfeiture hearing, conducted by the deputy warden, the captain, and the chief medical officer, Henry Young could have given information that might have reduced his punishment; instead—in an indication of the power of the prohibition against incriminating fellow prisoners that prevailed in inmate society at the time—he stonewalled:

Deputy Warden Miller: You are charged with conspiracy and plotting to escape in company with William Martin AZ-370, Rufus R. McCain AZ-267, Dale Stamphill AZ-435, and Arthur Barker AZ-268, cutting the bars of cell number 529 "D" Block, cutting and breaking bar of window guard, escaping from the prison building no. 68, making way to the shoreline and attempting to escape from the Island, January 13, 1939. Is that correct?

Young: AZ, what's AZ?

Miller: That means Alcatraz.

Young: All right. No, not guilty.

> *Miller:* You were captured on the beach by two officers, and did
> not escape from the prison? You did not escape from
> your cell?
> *Young:* No.
> *Miller:* Your plea is "not guilty" to attempt to escape?
> *Young:* Yes, sir.[36]

Young ended up forfeiting 2,400 days, about six and a half years, of good
time.

At his hearing, Rufe McCain admitted that he was trying to escape but
refused to make any further statement. When Deputy Warden Miller recommended that he lose 11,880 days—almost thirty-three years—McCain
laughed and retorted, "I couldn't even do that much time." (The maximum sentence McCain could have received for escape in federal court
was five years.)

William Martin lost 3,000 days, or more than eight years. He also
paid a high price for a statement he had given to Deputy Warden Miller
after being captured and brought up to the prison hospital. The other inmates, as often happened, learned that he had given up information. Some
sixteen months later Martin, still in isolation, went on a hunger strike.
For several weeks he refused to explain why he would not eat, but one
day he told Miller that the other inmates were "hissing him," calling him
a rat, and threatening him; Martin thought that if he stopped eating the
inmates might stop calling him names. He asked to be moved out of D
block but Miller said that he knew of no place in the prison where Martin could get away from the other escapees, even though they were themselves in isolation cells. Several months later Martin's mental health problems resulted in a diagnosis of "paranoid" and he was recommended for
transfer to Springfield Medical Center. The transfer was not effected, however, and Martin assaulted several officers and got into fights with other
inmates while he was confined in disciplinary segregation. Finally, in May
1942, suffering from hallucinations and "bizarre delusions," he was
transferred to Springfield. By that time, he had been in D block for three
years and three months and had paid the usual price for being a rat.

Dale Stamphill settled down to do his time; he had a life sentence and
thus could not accrue any good time for the deputy warden to take away.
The friendship between Henry Young and Rufe McCain deteriorated as
they accused each other of cowardice for surrendering on the night of
the escape.

A year after the escape attempt, James Bennett sent a second letter to

Warden Johnston raising additional questions that came out of a review in Bureau headquarters of the institution's escape plan. The embarrassment caused by the near escape of such a prominent "public enemy" as Dock Barker was keenly felt by Bureau administrators, particularly in the light of the report sent to the attorney general by J. Edgar Hoover. The suggestions contained in Bennett's letter seem rather elementary for a warden of Johnston's experience and for a prison at the apex of the Bureau's security system. Bureau headquarters wanted to know, for example, what plans had been made for awakening officers in the houses and dormitories on the island in the event an escape occurred at night, why all officers reported to the armory when the emergency alarm sounded instead of having small groups of officers report to predesignated posts, whether new officers had received training in the escape procedures, and whether any escape drill had been conducted "recently."[37]

Several weeks later Johnston responded to the Bureau's suggestions. Concerning the proposal that prearranged locations be identified around the island to which officers would report when the escape signal sounded, Johnston demurred, arguing that flexibility was preferable to wasting manpower in locations away from the site of the escape. In regard to escape drills, the warden contended that having drills would put the administration "in the position of the boy in the fable who cried 'wolf.'" The warden allowed that "some" of the Bureau's suggestions were helpful but his response clearly indicated that he felt he knew best how to run Alcatraz.[38]

The escapes that occurred in 1937, 1938, and 1939 posed serious problems for Warden Johnston and Director Bennett—beyond the exposure of defects in the security system of an "escape-proof" prison—problems that came from having FBI agents and their suspicious and self-centered director, not to mention Alcatraz convicts and their defense attorneys, talk to the press and the public (or "confidentially," on the part of the FBI to the attorney general) about conditions and operations on the island, problems that put the Bureau of Prisons in a defensive posture. Bennett and Johnston did not suspect that the situation would only get worse.

ALCATRAZ ON TRIAL

ALCATRAZ AS "UNCLE SAM'S 'DEVIL'S ISLAND'"

Held out as the answer to one of the nation's major social problems, Alcatraz had quickly compiled a profoundly negative image. By the end of 1937 most Americans had read accounts of life on the Rock—"Uncle Sam's 'Devil's Island'"—from ex-prisoners Harry Johnson and Al "Sailor" Loomis, heard rumors about inmates being locked up in a dark dungeon, and seen stories about the desperate acts of Joe Bowers and Rufe Persful. On November 29 the *Philadelphia Inquirer* began a three-part series about Alcatraz that further reinforced the notion that the prison was psychologically brutalizing its inmates. Based on interviews with a local resident who had been transferred out of Alcatraz and then released, the serialized piece appeared under these headlines:

Alcatraz Horrors Doom Men, Ex-Convict Says

Alcatraz Silence "Breaks" Toughest Gangsters: Machine Gun Kelly Through Bragging; Karpis Is Cracking, Human Beings Can't Endure "the Rock"

Riots and Bloodshed Are Forecast at Alcatraz; Convicts Can't Win But Silence Is Worse than Machine Guns; The Rock a Barrel of Dynamite with Tough Warden Sitting on Lid[1]

In an editorial that accompanied the series, the *Inquirer* likened Alcatraz to "some dark chapter out of medieval lore [where] . . . the most hardened and desperate criminals in the country [are confined] under the most rigid system of discipline ever enforced in America." The question to be asked, said the *Inquirer,* "is whether the Alcatraz system serves a useful sound purpose, or whether it defeats its own end and turns the men who come within its clutch into even more hardened, more reckless and more desperate criminals." The *Inquirer*'s readers demonstrated their ambivalence about penal policy when several days later the paper reported that its articles on the prison produced "one of the most violent controversies Philadelphia has ever known" with "scores of letters . . . written at white heat" directed to the newspaper; the conclusion of the *Inquirer* after reviewing the response of readers was "Alcatraz Horrors Held Best System for Desperados: Majority of Readers Agree Criminals Deserve Rigors."[2] The paper had elevated the discussion to the conclusion that the Alcatraz regime was indeed brutal, but perhaps necessarily so.

A few weeks later, in January 1938, Roy Gardner met newspaper reporters after he was transferred from Alcatraz to Leavenworth and then released. Several other former Alcatraz convicts had made headlines with their accounts of life on the island, but reporters had been really waiting for the release of one of the big-name convicts. Their wish was fulfilled in the person of Gardner, who was widely known in California not only as the "Phantom Train Robber," but for his escapes from U.S. marshals.

As the date of his transfer to Leavenworth approached, Gardner finished the draft of a book on Alcatraz and its inmates and sent the manuscript to Director James Bennett for his review and approval. Gardner assured Bennett that he would delete anything found to be objectionable and would incorporate any suggestions from Bennett; he intended, he said, to dedicate the book to Warden Johnston. Asking the director of the Bureau of Prisons for editorial assistance was an unprecedented request but Gardner went even further, asking that he be sent copies of photographs and the case histories of Alcatraz's most notorious prisoners, an unheard-of request from a confined federal prisoner. Gardner also hoped Bennett would help him secure employment as an electrician at the Singer Sewing Machine Company in the Bay Area and thanked the director for becoming his friend.[3] On June 17, 1938, after almost seventeen years in prison, Roy Gardner walked out the front gate at Leavenworth Penitentiary and was transported to Kansas City, where he was greeted by a crowd of reporters. Reaching down to pat a puppy, Gardner remarked, "Boys, you miss dogs in prison."[4]

Gardner's comments to reporters focused on the "mental torture" experienced by Alcatraz inmates. While the stories that came from this interview made headlines, the book that Gardner published after his release entitled *Hellcatraz: The Rock of Despair* made a greater impact. Although Alcatraz inmates were absolutely prohibited from writing anything about the prison and other inmates, Gardner's story apparently carried out a theme that Bureau officials regarded as consistent with the image of Alcatraz they wished to project—a prison that could subdue the nation's toughest gangsters and most rebellious convicts. The book was not given an official Bureau of Prisons seal of approval, but Gardner was permitted to carry the manuscript from Alcatraz to Leavenworth and out to the free world.

In a brief earlier draft of *Hellcatraz* titled "The Rock of Remorse," Gardner's flight of rhetoric about Alcatraz as "the mausoleum of the living dead" exceeded even the dramatic imagery in the earlier descriptions of Loomis and Johnson:

> The easiest way to get a clear essential picture of Alcatraz is to imagine a large tomb situated on a small island and inhabited by corpses who still have the ability to walk and talk. In other words, a mausoleum holding the living dead. . . . The system on Alcatraz changes desperate public enemies into listless, lifeless automatons, walking around apparently waiting for death to release them and not caring how soon it comes. The breaking of desperate men on that rock is all mental. There is no brutality or physical violence practiced or permitted by the prison officials; however, the mental torture is much worse than any phyisical *[sic]* torture could possibly be. . . . The daylight hours on Alcatraz are not so bad because the prisoners have something to do to occupy their minds, but the hours between 5:00 P.M. and 7:00 A.M. are the hours that sear men's souls and break their spirits. 75% of the prisoners there know they will never again experience the rapture of a woman's kiss. They will never again shake the hand of a true friend. Never again enjoy an hour of freedom. During the first year of imprisonment they spend many sleepless hours looking at the ceiling and wonder who is kissing her now. Some of them go raving mad and awaken the entire cellblock with their insane screams. Others suffer in silence. . . . The fact that there is no escape leaves death as the only alternative for most of the inmates. Some of them realize that fact and go the suicide route. . . . Watching these hopeless men walking around and existing from day to day is a pitiful sight. Of course they are a menace to society and have to be restrained; however, it seems that that restraint could be made more endurable without losing any of its effectiveness. An indescribable something prevails on Alcatraz that is not felt in any other prison. It seems to be a mixture of hopelessness, hatred, self-pity and cowardice. Most of the long timers lose hope after about a year and begin feeling sorry for themselves. The next step is to become suspicious of his fellow prisoners, and then hatred develops. . . . There are plenty of prisoners at Alcatraz today who talk to themselves only. That condition does not readily develop in other prisons because they can see a ray of hope, maybe parole, maybe escape, but still a ray of hope. On Alcatraz that ray of hope does not exist, and the lack of it actually kills men's souls. Of course the men confined there can expect no sympathy from society because 95% of them are habitual criminals, and probably 50% are murderers. That type of prisoner has forfeited all claims to consideration by society, and theoretically

dug his own grave. He would have been much better off had he committed suicide, and let others dig his grave.[5]

Gardner described Alcatraz as "the toughest, hardest place in the world." *Hellcatraz* was published after his release, and there were, as usual, no disclaimers or denials from Alcatraz or Bureau of Prisons officials.[6]

Back in San Francisco Gardner found employment on a tour boat. As the boat cruised around Alcatraz, Gardner told stories about "the lifeless automatons" on the "rock of despair." (At the San Francisco exposition in 1939 he operated a booth at which he reiterated this same theme.)

While Gardner's *Hellcatraz* confirmed the prison's harsh image, events within Alcatraz supported the growing body of journalistic opinion that the federal government was treating prisoners so cruelly that they were ending up in insane wards, on suicide watches, or dying while trying to escape. Following Rufe Persful's self-mutilation and Roe and Cole's escape attempt in 1937 came the deadly escape attempted by Lucas, Limerick, and Franklin in May 1938 and ensuing trial for the murder of Officer Cline, the work strike and assault on Warden Johnston in September 1938, and the January 1939 breakout attempt led by Stamphill and Barker, which also had fatal results.

In addition, strikes and protests continued, and the press always seemed to catch wind of them. On February 26, 1939, seven men in disciplinary segregation began a hunger strike. Among the protesters were Henry Young, Rufus McCain, Whitey Franklin (who had killed Officer Cline), and Jack Hensley, the determined leader of the work strikes. According to Deputy Warden E. J. Miller, the inmates were protesting because they wanted to exercise in the yard and smoke and because "they didn't want an officer to be placed in isolation to watch them all the time."[7] The hunger strike lasted five days. In July, following several nights of protests during which the prisoners yelled, sang, and banged their bunks into the floor, another hunger strike began over the same issues. The leaders, Young, Franklin, Hensley, and Stamphill, were moved from D block to A block isolation cells; four days later all resumed eating.

One year later, on July 15, 1940, another protest began, this time involving more than one hundred inmates; they came into the dining room for meals but took only coffee and bread. This protest was not accompanied by any work stoppage or the usual booing and shouting at nonparticipants. No particular complaints were presented, except that the protesters wanted transfers to other prisons.

To Warden Johnston, "it was apparent" that the men "were acting in collusion according to an agreed plan." He explained to Director Bennett what he believed to be behind the prisoners' behavior:

> So far as I can judge at this moment, the men seem to be making their annual bid for attention and perhaps came to the conclusion that striking was not the way to do it but going without food, ala Mahatmi *[sic]* Gandhi, would be a better sort of protest. But, really I can find no foundation to the complaints about the food; I think it is merely used because they think that is a spot in which the public has interest.[8]

To support his contention that the quality of food was not the basis for the protest Johnston sent a copy of the week's menu to Bennett (see p. 186).[9]

Having learned that no event on the island could escape the attention of San Francisco newspapers, usually through information from civilian employees who worked in industries or maintenance jobs and lived in the city, James Johnston adopted a proactive posture by releasing news himself rather than waiting for rumors to reach the press. The problem with this protest was that like all other news about Alcatraz, it captured front-page attention. Johnston noted ruefully to Bennett, "*The Examiner* gave as much space to the food protest as was given to President Roosevelt and the Democratic Convention and more attention than [was given] to Hitler, Mussolini and the World War."[10] Bureau headquarters felt it necessary to send a memorandum to the attorney general suggesting that the purpose of the strike was to gain public sympathy for the prisoners' lot.[11]

Alcatraz had become a major public relations problem for the Bureau of Prisons. All that the prison was supposed to represent—federal resolve to punish "public enemies," a means of getting the worst troublemakers out of the other federal prisons, and setting a standard for state high-security prisons—became lost in the welter of denunciations directed at the Bureau for maintaining a penitentiary that seemed to contradict so many aspects of progressive penology.

No longer confident that the prison's benefits outweighed its liabilities, James Bennett proposed to Attorney General Frank Murphy (who had succeeded Homer Cummings earlier that year) that Alcatraz be converted into a facility to house the Bureau's "old and crippled prisoners," along with West Coast drug users, and that the Department of Justice seek funds from Congress to construct a new maximum-security insti-

BREAKFAST	DINNER	SUPPER
	Monday, July 15, 1940	
Stewed peaches	Navy bean soup	Steamed frankfurters
Wheat meal	Beef stew & vegetables	Lyonnaise potatoes
Milk & sugar	Steamed potatoes	Succotash
Minced bacon	Creamed peas	Lettuce salad
Scrambled eggs	Sour pickles	Rice custard pudding
Hot cornbread	Bread	
Bread, coffee	Coffee	Coffee
	Tuesday, July 16, 1940	
Fruit cocktail	Macodine [sic] soup	Southern hash
Rice Krispies	Baked link sausage	Steamed dumplings
Milk & sugar	Country gravy	Stewed tomatoes
Fruit pastry	Mashed potatoes	Beet & onion salad
Bread	Corn on cob	Mocha cake
Coffee	Bread, coffee	Bread, tea
	Wednesday, July 17, 1940	
Stewed apricots	Barley soup	Chili con carne
Oatmeal mush	American pot roast	Steamed rice
Milk & sugar	Brown gravy	Braised carrots
Cinnamon pastry	Cottage fried potatoes	Cottage cheese salad
Oleo [margarine]	Summer squash sauté	Watermelon
Bread, coffee	Hot biscuits, bread, coffee	Bread, coffee
	Thursday, July 18, 1940	
Applesauce	Vegetable soup	Fried beef liver
Corn flakes	Boiled short ribs	Onion gravy
Milk & sugar	Horseradish sauce	Hashed brown potatoes
Hot cakes	Baked macaroni	Mustard greens
Syrup	Buttered string beans	Bread & fruit Pudding
Bread, coffee	Bread, coffee	Bread, tea
	Friday, July 19, 1940	
Crushed pineapple	Potato chowder	Corn fritters
Hominy grits	Baked rock cod	Cream sauce
Milk & sugar	Spanish sauce	Sliced bacon
Bear claws	Boiled navy beans	Buttered peas
Bread	Cauliflower polonaise	Combination salad
Coffee	Bread, coffee	Ice cream, bread, coffee

BREAKFAST	DINNER	SUPPER
	Saturday, July 20, 1940	
Stewed prunes	Minestrone soup	Stuffed bell peppers
Bran flakes	Hamburg steak	Tomato sauce
Milk & sugar	Pan Gravy	Au gratin potatoes
Parker House rolls	Rissole potatoes	Peas & carrots
Oleo	Creamed corn	Bread & fruit pudding
Bread, coffee	Bread, coffee	Bread, tea
	Sunday, July 21, 1940	
One-half cantaloupe	Mulligatawny soup	Spaghetti italienne
Steel-cut oats	Fried beef steak	Sliced cheese
Milk & sugar	Pan gravy	Buttered spinach
Butterhorns	Baked potatoes	Blackberry pie
Bread	Stewed tomatoes	Bread
Coffee	Bread, coffee	Cocoa

tution in southeastern Iowa to replace Alcatraz.[12] In his memo to Murphy, Bennett acknowledged the importance of Alcatraz in the federal prison system, noting that it housed the inmates who disrupted operation in the other prisons, provided "deterrent punishment for the gangster, kidnapper and ruthless killer," and countered the claims of those who believed "prisons did not deter crime because they were all 'country clubs.'" But because Alcatraz had become "an extremely difficult institution to administer," and because its per capita operating cost was two and a half times that of any other federal penitentiary, Bennett concluded, it was perhaps best to end its brief career as a maximum-security prison for "famous criminal personalities."[13]

But Alcatraz still had powerful backers in the federal government and elsewhere. Former Attorney General Cummings, for example, responded to the criticism of Alcatraz with an article in *Colliers* magazine entitled "Why Alcatraz Is a Success." The idea of ending maximum-security operations at Alcatraz joined all the other rumors about ending operations that prisoners and staff would hear throughout the life of the prison.

More negative publicity was generated following the evening of January 10, 1940, in a dramatic gesture, when Roy Gardner underscored his own point that doing time at Alcatraz left inmates psychologically damaged. Gardner sat down in his room in the Hotel Governor in San Francisco and began writing notes. One note, addressed "to whom it may concern," provided instructions for the disposal of his body; a second asked newspapers not to mention his daughter's married name in reports of his death. After finishing these notes, Gardner wrote another that warned, "Do not open this door. Poison gas. Call police" and attached it to the outside of the door to his room. He then sealed the door from the inside, went into the bathroom, dropped some cyanide pellets into a glass of acid, placed a handkerchief over his head, and inhaled the rising fumes.

When the police entered his room, they found Gardner's belongings neatly packed; on each of the four suitcases containing his worldly belongings they found a fifty-cent tip for the porter and the maid. They also found a fourth note, addressed "to the newspaper reporters":

> Please let me down as light as possible boys. I have played ball with you all the way, and now you should pitch me a slow one and let me hit it. I am checking out simply because I am old and tired, and don't care to continue the struggle. There are no love affairs or disappointments of any kind connected with this in anyway, just tired that's all. I hold no malice toward any human being, and I hope those whom I have wronged will forgive me for it. If I had realized what the future held for me, I would have "checked out" in 1920 and saved my loved ones the disgrace and shame that they have had to endure these many years. Also I would have dodged plenty of grief that I endured unnecessarily. All men who have to serve more than 5 years in prison are doomed, but they don't realize it. They kid themselves into the belief that they can "come back," but they can't—there is a barrier between the ex-convict and society that cannot be leveled. . . . I did not decide to check out on the spur of the moment. In fact I bought the cyanide 2 months ago for this very purpose. I got it at a drug store on the north side of Market St. near Kearney. I don't remember what name I signed, but my address was given 1404 Post St. Good bye and good luck boys, and please grant my last request. Thanks. Sincerely yours, Roy Gardner[14]

Gardner's death by suicide was given wide publicity in the Bay Area. The United Press International news service sent a story across its wires, "The quiet end of a two-gun man," which characterized Gardner as "the last of the train robbers, a 20th-century Jesse James [who] cashed in his chips with neatness and dispatch, will malice towards none, and the hope of forgiveness in his heart."[15] At the inquest that followed, San Francisco coroner T. B. Leland wrote Roy Gardner's final epitaph: "This is the case of a man who was down and out, who was going blind, who could not make a comeback after his long criminal career. He did not want to be a burden on his family. That's all."[16]

After years of hearing Alcatraz characterized as this country's version of Devil's Island, the public and the press were predisposed to interpret acts of violence on the island as a product of a repressive regime that drove men mad. Thus when one prisoner killed another in December 1940, the ground was well prepared for Alcatraz and its officials to be questioned, along with the perpetrator, Henry Young, in the trial that followed.

THE MURDER TRIAL OF HENRY YOUNG

In the prison tailor shop on a Tuesday morning in early December 1940, Henry Young began walking briskly in the direction of Rufe McCain, attracting the attention of several other inmates. George Kelly noticed the intense expression on Young's face and, remembering that Young had attempted to stab McCain some months earlier, called out, "Rufe! Rufe!" McCain turned around, but not soon enough to defend himself; Young was already next to him and drove a prison-made knife deep into McCain's abdomen.

Senior officer Frank Mach was giving instructions to a new guard when he heard the commotion behind him. As he turned, he saw Young, knife in hand, standing over McCain, who was lying on the floor bleeding from the stomach. Mach ran over, grabbed Young's arm and pinned it to his side until the other guard wrested the weapon from Young's hand. The knife, a blade taken from a plane used in the prison's furniture shop, had been sharpened to a point at one end; tape was wrapped around the other end of the blade so that it could be held without cutting the user's hand. The officers searched Young and found a second knife stuck in a crude scabbard attached to his belt. As he was escorted out of the tailor shop, Young muttered to no one in particular, "I hope I killed the son of a bitch." McCain gasped, "I think he got me good." Other guards arrived with a stretcher and transported McCain up the hill to the prison hospital.

While McCain was on the operating table, Deputy Warden Ed Miller asked him what happened. McCain replied, "Looks like I got stabbed!" Miller asked, "Who did it?" to which McCain responded, "Why ask me? You know the son-of-a-bitch that did it; he did a fair job too." McCain refused to make any further statements.[17] The doctor on duty worked to close the gaping wound, but McCain lapsed into unconsciousness and died.

Deputy Warden Miller interrogated Henry Young as soon as he was brought up from the tailor shop to the cell house. Asked why he attacked McCain, Young replied, "They were fixing a trap to get me and I sprung the trap before they got me." He refused to identify the persons he referred to as "they," and after stating that he "found" the knives in the workshops, Young would answer no further questions. He was placed in solitary confinement.

Four and a half months later, on April 15, 1941, Henry Young's murder trial opened in the federal district court of Northern California. After the jury had been impaneled and the proceedings initiated, it became evident that something unusual was going to occur. Henry Young was in the dock, but because the judge had allowed a novel defense strategy, Alcatraz was going to be on trial as well.

Before the trial began, Judge Michael Roche asked Young if he had legal counsel; Young replied, "I have a preference in lawyers. The more youthful my lawyers are the better. I should like to have two attorneys of no established reputation."[18] When the newspapers reported Young's request, Judge Roche was said to have been deluged with offers from young lawyers asking to be assigned to the case. Roche selected Sol Abrams, a former assistant United States attorney in his early forties, and James MacInnis, twenty-seven, only four years out of Stanford Law School.

Abrams and MacInnis, after a short meeting with Young, announced that Young was going to plead not guilty. They also said they would offer no evidence to prove either self-defense or traditional insanity. What they would seek to prove was that Young was in a "psychological coma" when he stabbed McCain—a kind of temporary insanity brought on by his confinement in the toughest prison in the world. The issue in the case, Abrams and MacInnis asserted, would be the psychological consequences of being locked up at Alcatraz.[19] To provide evidence for this unusual defense, the attorneys asked the court to allow two dozen convicts to be brought over from the island to give testimony, even though none of them had witnessed the assault on McCain; they would be asked on the stand to describe life on the Rock.

The judge granted the request, setting the stage for one of this country's most sensational trials involving penitentiary life. Not only would the courtroom drama include a cast of notorious bank robbers, kidnappers, and escape artists, but for the first time the outside world would be able to hear about life on Alcatraz directly from the mouths of its inhabitants. The Bureau of Prisons was about to begin paying the price for its policy of denying the press any access to the prison and creating the "air of mystery" over the island.

When Judge Roche agreed to allow testimony from twenty-two convicts about conditions at Alcatraz, reporters covering the trial apparently assumed that testimony given in a court of law—even testimony from some of the country's most sophisticated and notorious lawbreakers—would be truthful. With this naive assumption in place, the trial began.

Warden Johnston was the first witness called by the prosecution. He was asked to explain the types of punitive measures used at the prison. He reported that the cells in the solitary confinement unit had no lights and no beds, but that mattresses were issued at night, and if the occupants behaved themselves, they received a single blanket. As to the diet, Johnston testified: "It's the usual rule now that men in solitary get three meals a day, but there was a time when they got only two, there was a time when they got only one a day, and there was a time when they got only one meal in three days."

Defense counsel MacInnis queried Johnston to establish the length of time Young had been in the isolation unit: "If I said he [Young] had never been taken out between September 1938 and November 1941, would you say I was correct?" Johnston replied, "I wouldn't dispute it" but later commented that he thought that Young had been removed from isolation for a period of "30 to 35 minutes" a year.[20]

Questioning witnesses about the use of lower solitary was, as the Bureau of Prisons should have expected, an important part of the effort by the defense to create in the jurors' minds a picture of a sadistic staff brutalizing prisoners for minor breaches of prison rules. On the witness stand, Warden Johnston stated that "the so-called dungeons" had not been used since early 1938. He did admit that "persons confined in the dungeons would not have any light" and that because the dungeon cells "were not equipped with the usual plumbing equipment," prisoners were "furnished with only a bucket." When he took his turn on the witness stand, Deputy Warden Miller denied knowledge of any "Spanish dungeons" but confirmed the use of the eight basement cells. Asked if it was true that the buckets used as toilets had not been emptied "for as long as nine days," Miller answered no but entered into the court record the fact that Henry Young had never been confined in these cells.[21]

The twenty-two convicts selected by Henry Young to rebut the testimony of Johnston, Miller, and other prison officials came from a much wider pool of men anxious to testify for the defense. A story in the *San*

Francisco Chronicle under the headline "Hard Rock Criminals to Attend Trial" framed the upcoming testimony in a way that supported the defense strategy:

> For the first time in the grim history of Alcatraz some of the most savage and brutish criminals behind bars will be taken off the Rock and brought into a federal courtroom here. Heavily guarded, bound with chains and manacles, they will be taken off one by one . . . and grilled by defense attorney James Martin MacInnis. Through them MacInnis will try to probe the sullen whirlpools of passion that, this time, blazed into murder, and the timeless attrition that frays the minds of men into madness on the Rock.[22]

Thus began a parade to the witness stand of Alcatraz cons, some grim and subdued, some smiling and confident. They all took the oath to tell the whole truth and nothing but the truth about their experiences and those of the other unfortunates confined on the Rock. With sentences of twenty-five years, fifty years, and life, these men were hardly fearful of a puny two- or three-year conviction on perjury charges. The opportunity to take the boat trip over to the city and testify in the trial was a welcome break from the prison routine and carried with it the added bonus of being able to crucify the prison staff. Abrams and MacInnis helped this process along by asking leading and provocative questions of their very willing witnesses. The prosecution registered strenuous objections and Judge Roche often ruled the questions out of order—but the jury and the reporters listened as the inmates answered them anyway.

An important witness for the defense was kidnapper and longtime troublemaker Harmon Waley. By the time of the Young trial, Waley had spent not days, weeks, or even months in the various isolation units at Alcatraz, he had been locked up for years. He had been sent to a dungeon cell and had been subjected to every other form of punishment, from isolation in total darkness on a diet of bread and water to being forcibly restrained in a straitjacket in the prison hospital while food was forced down his throat. On the stand Waley listened carefully to a series of leading questions by defense attorney MacInnis. U.S. Attorney Hennessy objected to each question, but before Judge Roche could rule on the admissibility of the questions, Waley provided the answers in a loud voice. "You wait until I rule on the question," admonished Roche, but Waley continued to answer the questions immediately, finally turning to the angry judge and asking "What can you do? I've already got forty-five years—are you going to slap my wrists or something?"[23]

The *San Francisco Examiner* described Waley's performance before a courtroom crowded to capacity with spectators who listened "wide-eyed to the first sizable chunks of Alcatraz local color."

> In every way the star of the day's courtroom performance was Waley, tall and not unhandsome 30-year-old convict who is "doing" 45 years. It is for some reason not discernible to lay observers, he was permitted to testify on matters that other witnesses have touched upon only through the "bootleg" method of answering above the objections of Frank Hennessy, United States Attorney. Waley made the most of his chance. From the very outset, when he announced he has been in isolation for the last nine months, to the finish, when he sneaked over a response indicating he expected to be punished for his testimony, he was of obvious comfort to defense counsel. At some length and with considerable enjoyment, he related that he had been confined to the Alcatraz dungeon twice. Once, he related, he "made" the dungeon because he was sick, and applied for medical treatment, and was told he would receive medicine later; he insisted on aspirin at once; he was told he'd get his medicine later. "So," he recounted, grinning in retrospect, "I told the doctor what to do with his aspirin and was thrown in the dungeon." Then his mood changed abruptly. He became grave and obviously bitter as he was asked if he was ever beaten; words rushed out in a torrent over the objection of Hennessy, and everybody heard his answer, "Yes, I was beaten and taken to the hospital and put in a straight jacket and was half crazy." The court ordered that answer stricken. He was grinning again, however, as Sol A. Abrams of defense counsel inquired if he had ever heard McCain discuss Young. . . .[He answered that] he saw McCain one day shortly after McCain was released from isolation, and congratulated him. . . . The witness testified "[McCain] said Young had snitched on their escape attempt. He was very angry and said he intended to kill Young just as soon as Young got out of isolation." With language admittedly supplied by Abrams, Waley also testified that McCain had spread word about the prison concerning alleged depravity involving him and Young.[24]

The ability of MacInnis and Abrams to lead their witnesses, combined with their witnesses' desire to be led, produced a string of highly sensational story lines in San Francisco newspapers, most of them favorable to the defense side:

> Secrets of the "Rock" Told Death Jury: Details of "Solitary" Revealed by Warden (*San Francisco Examiner,* April 17, 1941)

> Brutality at Rock Charged: Young Beaten by Alcatraz Guards, Witness Declares (*San Francisco News,* April 23, 1941)

Witnesses in Alcatraz Case Fear Reprisal (*San Francisco News,* April 24, 1941)

In making the case that confinement at Alcatraz was driving men to acts of desperation, the defense attorneys elicited testimony from the convict witnesses that guards had beaten inmates so severely that in one case a man's skull was fractured, that some prisoners lay for days in solitary without medical attention, and that others resorted to the ultimate escape— suicide. The will to endure crumbled for some inmates, according to inmate Samuel Berlin, who testified that he knew of thirty men who had been transferred to the federal prison hospital at Springfield, Missouri. These men had been driven insane at Alcatraz, said Berlin, due to a "fear psychosis" produced by the brutal beatings administered by guards and by Deputy Warden Miller. Although U.S. Attorney Hennessy objected to almost every question asked of Berlin—objections that were sustained by Judge Roche—the answers were heard clearly by the jury and reported by the press. Defense attorney Abrams led Berlin through a series of inflammatory questions about lower solitary:

Abrams: Do you know an inmate named Walter Beardon?

Berlin: He was in the dungeon with me. He's dead now.

Abrams: Was Beardon sick in the dungeon and after five days there without food he fainted and slumped to the floor?

Berlin: Yes.

Abrams: It was damp and cold and there was seepage of water?

Berlin: Yes.

Abrams: There was no toilet there and a bucket was not cleaned for five days?

Berlin: Nine days.

Abrams: Two blankets were thrown in at night?

Berlin: Yes.

Abrams: You got a cup of water?

Berlin: Twice a day.

Abrams: Beardon was spitting up blood?

Berlin: Yes.

Abrams: Beardon cried for hospitalization during the 12 days he was in the dungeon?

Berlin: Yes.

Abrams: And Dr. Hess, the prison physician, only peeked in the cell twice a day?

Berlin: Yes.

Abrams: What was he looking for—to see if you were dead yet?

Berlin: I guess so. Lots of men have died there.

Abrams: Did you have a bath in the 12 days?

Berlin: I was 19 days without a bath.

Abrams: Beardon had tuberculosis?

Berlin: He died of it.[25]

The next witness, James Grove, described by a *San Francisco News* reporter as a "breezy felon," testified that McCain had told him that he was "out to get Young" and went on to describe the beating of Young by Alcatraz guards. His testimony was summarized in a *San Francisco News* story:

> The beating of Young, Grove testified, took place during the hunger strike of 1939, when both he and Young were occupying the cells in solitary confinement. Four guards came in and took Young from his cell. . . . They threw Young down the corridor steps and [Deputy Warden] Miller jumped up and came down on his face. "That's why Young hasn't any teeth today." Prosecution attorney objected and succeeded in having the last sentence struck out. "I saw the guards bend over Young, hitting him with clubs," Grove went on. He said Young had not attacked the guards, and that their only provocation was his refusal to leave the cell. . . . He said prisoners had enough water, but were fed once every three days. Young, he said, was placed in solitary for 19 days without a break following the beating. Voluble and sure of himself Grove had to be cautioned several times to allow the prosecution time to enter objections.[26]

The defense contention that Young was "driven to slay McCain by an irresistible impulse" was supported by convict witnesses who testified that McCain had made numerous threats to kill Young and that Young, as described by prisoner Harry Kelly, had come out of solitary a changed man:

> I first knew Henri Young in 1935, when he came to the prison, as a well-educated, sane young fellow. He liked to play ball and he disappeared into solitary for more than three years. When he came out he was about crazy, mentally unbalanced. . . . It was on the first Sunday in December 1940 just before the killing, that McCain received a message saying he had lost 33 years good time. McCain was thoroughly enraged. The next day he told me that Young was the cause of his losing the time. He said Young had made a break unsuccessful. He told me if it was the last thing he ever did, he was going to kill Young. I saw Young on the morning of the killing. He didn't seem to have possession of his faculties.[27]

Another witness, Carl Hood, who had killed a prisoner at Leavenworth, told the court that he had been in the "hole" (disciplinary segregation) with Young, and that the two of them had "wondered why the people of the United States let a prison like Alcatraz stand."[28]

The ability of Abrams and MacInnis to elicit the testimony they wanted over the objections of the prosecution was clear in the following exchange involving the testimony of William Dunnock (as recorded in the Bureau's annotated transcript):

> *Q:* On February 22, you were sent to solitary and were subjected to physical violence? [Objection sustained.]
>
> *Q:* Taken to the hospital you were hit with a blackjack across the face and your nose was broken? [Objection sustained.][29]
>
> *Q:* In solitary you were on a cement floor with no bedding? [Objection sustained.]
>
> *Q:* Miller tore your garment from your body?
>
> Yes. [The witness answered before Hennessy had time to object. Dunnock plainly showed his resentment of the prosecution objections and the court's rulings, and thereafter he snapped out his answer before the judge had ruled.]
>
> *Q:* Your garment was torn off and you were struck and pushed into the hole?
>
> *Dunnock:* Yes. [Objection sustained. The judge then admonished Dunnock to refrain from answering until the court had ruled, but Dunnock continued to answer as quickly as possible, ignoring the judge's order. MacInnis then brought out that Abrams had tried to see Dunnock in solitary, that he was refused, that Dunnock was first moved to a cell "that had a bed."]
>
> *Q:* And you were lying on a cement floor without bedding? Dunnock: Yes. [Objection sustained.]
>
> *Q:* Do you expect to be physically punished for testifying in this case?
>
> *Dunnock:* I do.

After Waley, Berlin, Dunnock, and the other convict witnesses finished their testimony, Deputy Warden Miller was called to the stand to provide rebuttals. "His memory appeared to be poor regarding incidents at the prison," reported the papers, "and his favorite answer was, 'I don't recall.'" Miller's vague responses allowed the defense attorneys to repeat all the previous inflammatory allegations of brutality as they sought to refresh the deputy warden's memory.

Attorney Abrams's tactics included questioning prison officials about inmate Vito Giacalone. His fellow prisoners testified that Giacalone—

whom they described as mentally ill—had thrown a cup of coffee on a guard, and that the officer responded by beating Giacalone on the head so badly that he died while being transported to the Springfield hospital.[30] Prosecution objections to this line of questioning were sustained, but the jury and the press got the message.

The defense captured more headlines by charging that the inmate witnesses were being warned by their guards to "lay off Alcatraz on the witness stand." The court asked for the names of particular inmates who had been threatened, along with the identities of the Alcatraz officers who had issued the warnings. Attorney Abrams replied that, unfortunately, he could not reveal the names due to the inmates' fear of violent reprisals at the hands of the guards.[31]

Most of the testimony offered by Young's witnesses focused on events and conditions on the island that caused his "psychological coma." But testimony was also offered to prove that Young was only protecting himself when he knifed McCain. The victim, several prisoners reported, made threats to get Young and had called Young a stool pigeon and a homosexual. According to inmate Harold Brest, Young was only doing what any self-respecting Alcatraz convict would do if someone insulted his mother: "Young killed a man for making a rotten reference to his mother—that's what he done—and that's what I would've done."[32]

The sensational testimony offered by the prisoners was received with little skepticism by the press. After years of being denied any access to the island, reporters were apparently prepared to accept what the inmates said as accurate and consistent with the rumors they had heard and the allegations that had been voiced over the years by released prisoners. The government's attempt to prevent this testimony from being introduced was regarded as evidence that the Bureau of Prisons had much to cover up.

Henry Young's appearance on April 26 was the highlight of the trial. According to the *San Francisco Chronicle,* "The courtroom was like a theater and everybody came to hear Henri Young."[33] The defendant's performance on the witness stand was described as "spellbinding" by the *San Francisco News* and as "superb" by the *Examiner:*

> Henri Theodore Young, a prepossessing youth who looks and acts as if he belongs on a college campus, but who is actually a bank robber "doing" twenty years on Alcatraz, began explaining yesterday just why he had to kill his fellow convict, Rufus McCain. . . . He was a superb witness. He chose his words with care and strung them together with profound regard for the rules of grammar; he uttered them in a voice generally mild and modulated. . . . Almost at once, he had spectators on the edge of their seats,

listening in open-mouthed silence, and, as the saying is, "eating out of his hand." His attorney, Sol A. Abrams, gave him . . . a record showing why and how often he had been disciplined, reprimanded, placed in solitary confinement and deprived of his privileges for infractions of prison rules. And as he proceeded to talk about the bare entries on those records, Young not only rid himself of virtually all blame in such matters but succeeded in placing Alcatraz penitentiary and its rules, guards and officials entirely on the defensive. There was no doubt, whatsoever, where the sympathy of the crowded courtroom lay after Young drew this picture of solitary confinement as he found it July of 1935.[34]

Young described his first trip to solitary confinement, the result, he said, of refusing to do what he believed to be too much additional work in the prison laundry. His testimony was given in the same *Examiner* newspaper story:

"Its size was approximately that of a regular cell—9 feet by 5 feet by about 7 feet high. I could just touch the ceiling by stretching my arm. . . . You are stripped nude and pushed into the cell. Guards take your clothes and go over them minutely for what few grains of tobacco may have fallen into the cuffs or pockets. There is no soap. No tobacco. No toothbrush. The smell—well you can describe it only by the word 'stink.' It is like stepping into a sewer. It is nauseating. After they have searched your clothing, they throw it in to you. For bedding, you get two blankets, around 5 in the evening. You have no shoes, no bed, no mattress—nothing but the four damp walls and two blankets. The walls are painted black. Once a day I got three slices of bread—no—that is an error. Some days I got four slices. I got one meal in five days, and nothing but bread in between. In the entire thirteen days I was there, I got two meals." The witness described the air as "foul" and went on to tell the court of a particular cell inmates call the "Ice Box" because it is directly opposite a large vent through which "the winds off the Golden Gate blow continuously." In the cell, Young asserted, a prisoner cannot possibly keep warm. "Standing in your stocking feet on that concrete floor is not conducive to health," Young complained. "I tried to huddle in a corner, and took my coveralls off and used them to try to keep my shoulders warm. Then I shifted, and wrapped them around my legs to try to keep my legs warm. That went on day after day." Asked about bathing facilities for convicts in solitary confinement, he replied: "I have seen but one man get a bath in solitary confinement, in all the time that I have been there. That man had a bucket of cold water thrown over him." A man in solitary confinement, the witness asserted, can think of but one subject—his own misery. "He attempts," said Young, "to understand how it is possible that human beings can do that to human beings. Over and over, it ran through my mind that this was too great a price to pay for the—shall I say?—crime for which I was thrown into solitary."

Young went on to characterize the work stoppages and strikes on the island as desperate measures by the prisoners to obtain basic privileges such as newspapers, radio, movies, and more tobacco and letters, which were, he contended, mandated by Bureau of Prisons regulations. Young reported that when Deputy Warden Miller was confronted with a copy of the rulebook that indicated the Alcatraz rules were deviation from Bureau policy, Miller replied, "You don't run Alcatraz. I run Alcatraz. And Alcatraz is not a penitentiary. Alcatraz is Alcatraz." Even his request for a bible, said Young, produced an angry denial by Miller. Young concluded his first day of testimony by telling the jury that beatings at Alcatraz were "as regular as meals."

Young next testified about the events that led up to his assault on McCain. He said the animosity between the two had a long history, going back to January 13, 1939, when Young and McCain, along with Dock Barker and two other inmates, had broken out of the disciplinary segregation unit and made their way over the cliffs to the rocks below. Before they could construct makeshift rafts, the escape was discovered and the alarm sounded. Knowing their capture was only minutes away, McCain proposed leaving the beach, running up to the nearby employee residences and taking some of the guards' wives as hostages. But, said Henry Young, "I refused to go along with the plan; I reminded McCain that freedom isn't everything."

Then Young got to the day of the killing:

> That morning I went into breakfast. McCain was sitting across the room from me. He sneered at me and ran his finger across his throat. He meant he was going to cut my throat. I had a chill. It was like a cold, clammy snake had been put against my skin. When I went out, my head was burning. I went to my cell and got my coat and hat. At the foot of the steps I saw McCain. He made a filthy remark. I stopped and looked at him. . . . Everything seemed to go blank. I went away.

At this point, Abrams asked, "Do you know what happened from that moment on?" Young responded,

> Some officers told me I had killed McCain. Deputy Warden E. J. Miller came down to my cell and asked me why I had stabbed McCain. I told him I didn't know I had hurt McCain. I was taken to a solitary confine-

ment cell. Miller came again and said I had killed McCain. I said I wouldn't deny it, but neither would I admit it. I told him I didn't believe I had killed him.

Henry Young's trial ended on April 29, and on the following day the jury returned a verdict of guilty, not on the charge of murder in the first degree, but on the lesser charge of involuntary manslaughter. Young, delighted with the verdict, expressed his gratitude to the judge for appointing "youthful attorneys" to defend him.

The jury had performed its official duty, but it had not finished. After rendering its verdict on the accused prisoner, the jury foreman sent the following telegram to James V. Bennett, Congressmen Thomas Rolph and Richard J. Welch, Senator Hiram W. Johnson, and Justice Frank Murphy of the United States Supreme Court:[35]

> It is my duty to inform you, on behalf of the twelve jurors who found Henry Young, an inmate of Alcatraz Penitentiary, guilty of involuntary manslaughter after our deliberations tonight upon the conclusion of his two and one half week trial for murder of a fellow prisoner that it is our additional finding that conditions as concern treatment of prisoners at Alcatraz are unbelievably brutal and inhuman, and it is our respectful hope and our earnest petition that a proper and speedy investigation of Alcatraz be made so that justice and humanity may be served.[36]

Both Alcatraz and Henry Young had been found guilty.

Several days later, when Young was sentenced, Judge Roche spoke angrily from the bench:

> I've known Warden Johnston for 30 years. I've watched him work. He is a man most respected in this community. I've visited San Quentin and Folsom unannounced and found everything in order. . . . Warden Johnston's work is outstanding. He admits that he made a mistake by letting you out of isolation.

"That's a rather perverse attempt to rehabilitate, don't you think, Judge?" interrupted Young. According to the newspaper account of the exchange, Judge Roche at this point "almost rose out of his seat" but continued, "Some men deserve sympathy, but you're not one of those. You planned a cold, deliberate murder of an unfortunate human being." At this Young smiled and asked, "Does my sentence run concurrently, Judge?" The judge replied, "When you finish this term, you serve the other."[37]

DAMAGE CONTROL AFTER THE VERDICTS

The trial demonstrated more clearly than any previous event that the Justice Department's attempt to make Alcatraz a powerful symbol of punishment and deterrence had a serious down side. The policies and practices that incapacitated infamous gangsters demonstrated the serious consequences of criminal wrongdoing and allowed the successful operation of an institution packed with troublesome and dangerous inmates. But they also left the prison and its administration open to charges of brutality and inhumanity. It was, in many ways, a conundrum inherent in the very conception of Alcatraz, but Director Bennett and Warden Johnston treated it as a public-relations problem that arose from a large gap between perception and reality.

To defend the Bureau of Prisons and Alcatraz, Director Bennett distributed a statement to the wire services and to the San Francisco newspapers. It criticized the jury for believing Henry Young's testimony and for rendering a judgment with "no first hand information . . . as to the policies or methods followed in the management of the most difficult and desperate group of prisoners ever assembled."[38] The statement also noted that Alcatraz had been inspected by judges and members of Congress and had received a favorable report from the Osborne Association, a private prison reform group headquartered in New York City whose executive director was Austin MacCormick, a former assistant director of the Bureau of Prisons. Denying that the Bureau would tolerate corporal punishment in any form in any federal prison, Bennett promised a thorough investigation of the incidents cited during the Young trial. The director's statement, Warden Johnston reported a few days later, did not appear in any Bay Area newspaper.

Bennett also had to respond to a letter sent to the attorney general by Young's attorney, Sol Abrams, which cited trial testimony and the jury findings as reasons that changes in the regime in Alcatraz should be ordered. In his response to the attorney general, Director Bennett complained that Abrams's efforts had "prejudiced the jury and secured the release of one of the most vicious killers we have ever had in our institutions." He went on to claim that "upon Young's advice . . . the most psychopathic and unreliable of our inmates . . . shouted untruthful answers to [Abrams's] questions."

According to Bennett, the jury had voted eight to four on the first ballot to convict Young of first-degree murder but had been "worn down" by the foreman on subsequent ballots. The attorney general was invited to accompany the director on an inspection tour of Alcatraz.[39]

One of the most experienced troubleshooters in the Bureau of Prisons, A. H. Connor, was sent to San Francisco to prepare a report for the director on the trial and the jury findings. Based on the trial transcript, Connor constructed an eighty-page digest of testimony, insinuations, and innuendos reflecting on the management of the institution. Connor, of course, concluded that Judge Roche should not have allowed the defense attorneys to continually introduce testimony over the objections of U.S. Attorney Hennessy. Furthermore, he pointed out, "the prosecution contented itself with assuming that the jury would not believe convict witnesses and met this line of testimony merely with objections to its relevancy." What the prosecution should have done, wrote Connor, was to counter the defense strategy "with a full disclosure of just how Alcatraz is operated, and doing away with a lot of the mystery which has been built up around the conduct of the institution." Connor concluded that despite the negative publicity and the "unjust verdict," no further investigation of prison conditions, transfers to the Springfield Medical Center, or allegations of brutality were warranted: "My recommendation is to send the whole business to the files and forget about it."[40]

Bureau headquarters asked Warden Johnston to submit complete reports on the allegations of corporal punishment and the use of excessive force by staff, conditions in isolation and solitary confinement, the deaths of Joseph Bowers and Vito Giacalone, and the reasons for the transfers of prisoners to the Springfield Medical Center.

Johnston's detailed response included a denial that he had "authorized, sanctioned, or permitted corporal punishment to be inflicted on any prisoner as a matter of discipline." The only complaint he had ever received alleging the beating of a prisoner involved Harmon Waley; this complaint had not been written by Waley, but by another prisoner, Burton Phillips. In that case, wrote Johnston, "only necessary force had been used to drag Waley out of his cell in order to force feed him." All allegations of physical abuse by Henry Young and his attorneys involving Young, Waley, and Dunnock were false, said Johnston.[41]

In describing policies regarding isolation and solitary, Johnston reported that the chief medical officer made two visits each day to check on the physical condition of prisoners in these cells. As a result of the doctor's recommendations, the amount of food given to particular prisoners was increased "on a number of occasions." The warden described the policy regarding meals for men in solitary and isolation:

When we opened the institution and until the latter part of 1938, we followed the rule then in force of men in solitary receiving bread for the first days and then a full meal on the third day. . . . Following the strikes in January 1936 and September 1937 . . . we came to the conclusion that while two meals might be ample for a man who was in isolation and not working, we decided to give them all three meals a day.[42]

Johnston reviewed the circumstances surrounding the death of Joseph Bowers, which had been introduced at the trial to demonstrate that "an insane man was purposely shot by a guard while . . . trying to retrieve some cans that were at the top of the fence." The officer who fired at the prisoner had done his duty, said Johnston, and recalled the officer's claim that he had prevented an escape.[43] (The warden did not address the obvious question of how Bowers would have been able to reach the mainland in broad daylight with Alcatraz personnel fully alerted.}

Concerning the transfer of prisoners to Springfield Medical Center, Johnston noted that eleven of the thirty-one were "strictly medical cases," and that some of the twenty prisoners transferred for mental health reasons brought their problems with them to Alcatraz, presenting symptoms that were observed during their first days on the island.[44]

As Bureau officials studied the transcript of the Young trial along with the reports from Connor and Warden Johnston, concerns about the effects that the regime might be having on prisoners came to the forefront. In mid-May Assistant Director Howard Gill had written to Bennett:

> The issue has become the type of treatment accorded certain prisoners at Alcatraz. . . . If the system is so barren and hard as to leave justice without mercy, that too will cause men to crack and go berserk. These are the points at issue and James A. Johnston does not meet them.[45]

Several weeks later, Gill sent another memorandum to Director Bennett reiterating his view that Johnston's responses to the issues raised in the Young case indicated that the warden did not understand the need for more sensitive and innovative penal policy and practice in his very high-profile penitentiary:

> Unless we are to expect more of the same, I think the Bureau needs to have a man at Alcatraz supplementing Johnston who will represent individual treatment and stand as a guarantor of methods and treatments such as the Bureau endorses. Even if nothing is done to wipe out what has happened, this will put new hope in the lives of the prisoners and act as an agent toward calming troubled waters.[46]

Bureau headquarters did not send anyone from Washington, D.C., to help Johnston run Alcatraz, but Director Bennett increased the frequency and length of his visits to the island. The Bureau's concerns about the image of the regime it had created continued, but by late 1941 the public relations problems related to Alcatraz would vanish from the front pages of Bay Area newspapers as the United States entered World War II.[47]

As a corollary to a decline in the staff's use of gas billy clubs and saps after the Young trial, one Alcatraz inmate also attributed restraint on the use of force to the U.S. Public Health Service medical staff, who were not employees at Alcatraz but were called over to the island to treat any significant injuries the prisoners sustained. "Anytime a prison official beat up on an inmate," Arnold Kyle said, "the hospital people would be aware of that and make a report, so there wasn't too much brutality."

THE WAR YEARS

After the Henry Young trial, Alcatraz was more controversial than ever. The public, always schizophrenic about penal policy, perceived the regime at Alcatraz as both too harsh and just right for the nation's most notorious lawbreakers. The FBI and the attorney general considered the prison poorly (even incompetently) managed, and Bureau of Prisons headquarters openly questioned the warden's policies and procedures. Over the next four and a half years, five more escape attempts confirmed the accuracy of these views. But despite these accusations, criticisms, and FBI investigations, neither the prison's existence nor the jobs of its top administrators were seriously threatened—largely because both the public and the federal government focused their attention on the threats posed by the Axis powers in Europe and imperial Japan in the Pacific, and, after December 1941, on the prosecution of a war that spread across the globe.

ANOTHER ESCAPE TO THE BAY

Only weeks after the verdict in the Henry Young trial, a group of inmates took five employees hostage, escaped from the model building, and made it into the bay. Although the escape ultimately failed, it demonstrated that even with new security measures instituted after the breakout attempt by Stamphill, Barker, McCain, Young, and Martin eighteen months earlier, the prison still had vulnerabilities.

The idea for the escape was hatched by Floyd Hamilton, who had arrived at Alcatraz in June 1940. Listening to his fellow convicts talk about Cole and Roe's escape from the model building, Hamilton realized that this building still had exploitable weaknesses. Even though the soft iron bars in the building's windows had been replaced with tool-proof steel bars resistant to hacksaw blades, the building's location created blind spots for the tower guards, and the large number of rooms meant that continuous supervision by guards was not possible. The challenge would be to find a way to cut through the tool-proof bars of the windows, which constituted the only significant barrier between the convicts and the waters of the bay.

Hamilton also knew that opportunities for launching an escape from the old model building would soon be diminished. The escapes during the 1930s had revealed obvious weaknesses in and around the structure, and Bureau headquarters had authorized the construction of a new, two-story industries building to be placed dead against the rocky hillside below the prison yard. This location provided ample open space for two sets of fences between the building and the cliffs leading down to the water's edge. Guards in the gun tower on the roof of the old model building and in the road tower located at the base of steps leading down from the yard would have unobstructed views of the fences, the no-man's-land between the fences, and every door and window on the three sides of the new building that were not backed up against the hillside. Construction had begun in 1939, but in the spring of 1941 the new building was still unfinished. And inmates were still assigned to jobs in the old building.

Hamilton's first step in carrying out the escape was to request a job in the model building. Then he recruited two men to help plan and carry out the escape: Arnold "Pappy" Kyle and Joseph Paul Cretzer, both of whom had demonstrated the necessary patience, ingenuity, and courage in previous escape attempts.

At McNeil Island in April 1940 Arnold Kyle and his brother-in-law and crime partner, Joseph Cretzer, had begun serving twenty-five-year sentences for bank robbery. Then Kyle learned that he was going to be transferred to Leavenworth and Cretzer to Alcatraz.

> We figured that we had to do something right now. [Joe] figured we could grab one of those dump trucks, and then pull the bed up and have them go ahead and shoot at the back of the bed while we went over the hill. It was really a spur of the moment thing. Where Joe was working I could watch out the window of the tailor shop. He gave me a signal; I jumped up and went out. We grabbed the inmate driver and told him that we were taking the truck. He said "Go ahead" so we took the truck—it was half loaded with lumber.
>
> I drove. I laid down as far as I could on the seat and Joe scooted down on the floor and held the gas pedal down with his hand while I did the shifting. We hit the middle of the gate and dumped that lumber right in the gate area. I guess we were kind of lucky from what I heard because the

man in the tower got so excited that when he went to throw a shell into his rifle he pulled the whole bolt out, bullets and all. He didn't get a shot fired. We left the truck and hid out—that's a big island and it was four days before they found us.

Because they were regarded as such serious escape risks, Kyle and Cretzer were locked up in isolation cells until they were taken to Tacoma for trial on escape charges. They were held in a detention cell in the office of the U.S. marshal there. As Kyle told the author,

> While they were trying us for escape we seen a chance that we could get this marshal's gun and we might get away. So that's what we done—we grabbed this old marshal [Artis J. Chitty], but his gun was tied down a little better than we thought. One of the guards came in and tackled all three of us (Joe and I were handcuffed together). This marshal was elderly, he gets up and of course he was real excited. He turned around for a minute, then he dropped over. He died of a heart attack. So, they charged us with second-degree murder but that sentence didn't mean that much to us so we pleaded guilty.[1]

At the time of his sentencing, Joseph Cretzer told the judge he would rather be "a target for bullets" than be confined in prison. After he and Kyle got to Alcatraz and met Hamilton, he acted accordingly. The three men invited Lloyd Barkdoll—a physically powerful man with a reputation for taking chances—to join them and to take on the responsibility during the break of subduing guards and keeping hostages and uninvolved convicts under control.[2]

The escape plan devised by Hamilton, Kyle, and Cretzer (a far more sophisticated scheme than Warden Johnston and his officers knew) was to cut through the bars in the Model Shop, aided by two elements lacking in the earlier escape attempts—a special grinding wheel to cut the bars and a speedboat that would rush in close to the island when the escapees appeared and pick them out of the water. The first feature of the plan required that the plotters induce an employee to smuggle a special cutting wheel onto the island, and the second required that they communicate with a visitor who could make arrangements for a boat to stand by on the right day at the right time.[3]

To obtain the cutting wheel, the inmates prevailed upon a civilian worker who was not a member of the custodial force to help them (why he agreed to help them remains unclear). This employee brought the cutting device, a diamond-studded wheel, to the powerhouse, where he worked. It was then picked up by an inmate who brought it to the carpenter shop in the model building, where he turned it over to Kyle and Cretzer. The motor to which the cutting wheel was to be attached was the same motor used in the mat shop with an emery wheel to smooth down the jagged ends of the wires that held together the pieces of scrap rubber that made up mats for the navy. To hold the cutting wheel high enough up the wall to reach the bars of the windows through which they were to exit, the inmates rigged a rod two feet long to which the motor could be attached. Since they knew that an ordinary emery wheel could not cut through tool-proof steel quickly enough for them to climb out a window before they would be missed at a count, all hope rested on the special diamond-studded wheel.

A greater challenge would be to communicate the plan, including the date and precise time of the break, to a family member approved to visit. Mail was censored and guards closely watched visitors and monitored their conversations with inmates. A way around this obstacle was offered by Joe Cretzer, who informed the others that since his mother and father were both deaf mutes he had learned sign language as he grew up. Furthermore, his wife, Edna, had also learned sign language during a period when Joe's father lived with the couple. With only one visit allowed per month, it took several months for Cretzer to communicate to Edna the need for a fast motorboat to stand by, ready to move at the exact time the inmates would climb out of the model building window, clamber down the cliffs, and swim away from the island.

On May 21, 1941, the four men put their plan into action. Immediately after the 1:00 P.M. count, Barkdoll, Kyle, and Cretzer called to Officer Clyde Stoops, telling him that a machine was out of order. When the officer came over to investigate, the prisoners grabbed his arms, hustled him into a storage room, tied him up, and gagged him. Then they overpowered three other employees and took them hostage. Meanwhile Floyd Hamilton unbolted the grinding wheel and motor from the workshop table, attached it to the extension rod the men had devised, substituted the diamond-studded cutting grinder for the emery wheel, climbed up on a stool, turned on the machine, and began cutting the bars. When Captain Paul J. Madigan—a large man who the inmates thought might be hard to subdue—was seen making his way to the model building, the other inmates yelled to Hamilton to stop cutting and help them wrestle the captain down when he came through the door. But Madigan did not resist when he was suddenly grabbed and shoved into the room where the employee hostages (and several inmates) were being held. Luckily for Hamilton, Madigan had focused his attention on Barkdoll—who was standing in front of him, issuing orders and holding a hammer in case the captain tried to free himself—and did not look into Hamilton's face as Hamilton held onto one of Madigan's arms.

Barkdoll had been stationed as a lookout. Convicts working in the mat shop agreed to go into the storage room to be tied up so that they could support their claims later on that they were not involved in the break. Hamilton went back to cutting. Finally, one bar was severed, and Kyle and Cretzer, aware that a count was coming up, urged Hamilton to work faster. Hamilton responded by increasing the pressure of the cutting wheel on the next bar, at which point the wheel, as Kyle recalled, "broke into a thousand pieces."

> Then we didn't have anything except the regular emery wheel and we couldn't get through with that . . . time was running out on us. [The guy in the boat] got tired of waiting and he left . . . the count was about due, so we talked it over and decided that we better give up.

Captain Madigan was offering a deal, Kyle remembered: "if we gave up peaceably, they wouldn't come in and beat our heads off." The inmates agreed to the offer. "We gave our word and he gave his word," said Kyle, "and his word was good."[4]

After Cretzer and Barkdoll went to the captain and said "We give up," Cretzer, Barkdoll, and Kyle were marched up the hill to D block isolation. Another inmate, Samuel Shockley, was also taken to isolation, despite his loud protests that he had not been involved. Barkdoll and other inmates who had been "hostages" complained that Shockley was getting a bum rap. Madigan was asked if he remembered seeing Shockley tied up and after some reflection the captain allowed that perhaps he did remember seeing Shockley as a hostage. So Shockley was released from D block and returned to his cell. No disciplinary report, record, or notice of any kind was placed in Shockley's Alcatraz file to indicate that he had participated in any way in the Model Shop break.

Yet when Warden Johnston briefed the press that evening, and again the next day, he too identified Shockley as one of the "desperate plotters." Accordingly, every San Francisco newspaper listed Shockley as one of the principals in this escape. This was not only erroneous, it made little sense: with an IQ of 54, Sam Shockley was regarded by his fellow inmates at Alcatraz as slow, excitable, and lacking in judgment—traits not valued by escape plotters. Nevertheless, Johnston's statements forever connected Shockley with the escape: every book written about Alcatraz escapes has identified Shockley as one of the participants in the 1941 break.

In an ironic symmetry, Shockley's mistaken culpability matched Hamilton's evasion of it. The Alcatraz employees held as hostages had the strong impression that another man, in addition to Cretzer, Barkdoll, and Kyle, had been involved, but remarkably Floyd Hamilton's claim that he was one of the inmate hostages was never questioned, and the other inmates in the mat shop were not talking.[5] Hamilton thus avoided the others' prolonged confinement in the hole and the loss of good time. Moreover this experience did not change Hamilton's view that the model building was still the best place to break out of Alcatraz.

Although the escape attempt failed and resulted in no injuries, it was nonetheless an embarrassment for Warden Johnston. Since the escape attempt from D block, he had continued to assure Bureau headquarters that he had taken care of any defects in security on the island. To minimize the damage, Johnston sought to characterize the escape attempt as "foiled" by the tool-proof steel bars and, as one newspaper put it, "by the matching nerves of a resourceful guard captain."[6] According to the warden, the convicts had been unable to cut through a single bar and had been talked out of their "desperate" actions by Captain Madigan. The warden did not explain how the inmates had been able to take control of part of a prison building and hold five employees hostage, including the captain, for one and a half hours without attracting the attention of officers in the control room, the towers, or those working on other assignments in the industries area.

Johnston's reports to Bureau of Prisons headquarters so minimized the escape attempt that Director Bennett's memorandum on the incident to the attorney general consisted of only one typed page plus five lines on a second sheet, most of it a description of the four inmate participants, including Shockley; the one-paragraph account of the escape itself included the following:

> [The convicts] were unsuccessful in cutting the bars, and the Captain of the Guards, a Mr. Madigan, who had been seized and bound, managed to turn on the emergency alarm and obtained help. The incident was then suppressed without injury to any of the officers or prisoners.[7]

Official reports about this escape attempt, in contrast to previous plots, were limited because FBI agents had not been called to the island in connection with the case. Beyond an interview conducted with industries superintendent Manning at his home in San Francisco, none of the inmates or employees who were in the model building at the time of the attempted break were interviewed by the FBI. The "incident" had taken place between 1 P.M. and 3 P.M. but Warden Johnston did not notify the FBI field office in San Francisco until 9:50 that evening, and then only by telegram. The telegram arrived at the field office shortly after agents on duty had received a phone call from a reporter for the *San Francisco Examiner* asking if they could provide photographs of Barkdoll and Shockley.

Special-Agent-in-Charge Pieper of the San Francisco office called Johnston that same evening to ask whether an escape had been attempted. The warden replied that four convicts had attempted to break out of the mat shop, but when Captain Madigan entered, "he was able to sound the alarm and the subjects were immediately subdued by other guards who rushed in and placed the subjects in solitary confinement."[8] Pieper reported that Johnston "was very indefinite" as to when the escape had occurred, stating only that "it was in the afternoon." When asked why he had not immediately notified the San Francisco field office as prescribed by the policy, and reminded that possible federal law violations were supposed to be investigated by the FBI, the warden replied that his first priorities were to subdue the prisoners, place them in solitary, "restore order in the mat shop and elsewhere throughout the prison," and discuss the matter with the guards—and all this had taken time.

Pieper asked for the addresses of the employees who had been taken hostage. Captain Madigan and Officer Stoops were asleep on the island, Johnston stated, and he did not want them disturbed that night and, as far as interviewing the four inmate participants, he did not wish to take them out of solitary "for a while." Johnston provided the San Francisco address of one guard and the industries supervisor. FBI agents, in their effort to obtain statements as soon as possible after the event occurred, sought to contact the guard but could not verify his address; Manning, the industries supervisor, was located and interviewed. The investigating FBI agent who talked with Manning concluded his report with the statement that after discussion with FBI headquarters, "it is agreed that no further action would be taken in this matter due to the fact that this office had not been appropriately advised."[9]

By this time, the relationship between the Bureau of Prisons and the FBI was openly hostile. Both Warden Johnston and Bureau headquarters recognized the importance of handling incidents in a way that would minimize the chances of FBI agents interviewing inmates and employees and obtaining statements that would allow Director Hoover to complain to the attorney general about security defects and flaws in the management of Alcatraz. At the same time, James Bennett and other BOP officials had their own concerns about James Johnston's management of their highest-profile prison.

Three weeks after the abortive attempt to escape from the Model Shop, Assistant Director William T. Hammack wrote to Director Bennett expressing his frustration with Warden Johnston. The problem at Alcatraz, said Hammack, was Johnston's "insistence" that "everything be so systemized that probably everybody on the Island knows exactly what happens at any given time."[10] Hammack went on to complain that Johnston, in violation of Bureau policy, had allowed inmates to leave their area of the island to work in his house as servants or to work on the docks. And he had put convicts on cleanup details scattered all around the island, thus allowing them to learn about every aspect of the terrain, the buildings, and perimeter security arrangements. Hammack concluded his report with a warning that proved to be prophetic:

> Some time, some day, there will be a serious outbreak which will be possible because it is planned with full knowledge of all the Island's protective devices, including the routine involving use and storage of the launch and custodial routine in the prison area. I think that the Bureau should insist on establishment of a different procedure and . . . I would recommend we give positive orders that the Warden break up his own routine. At the present time the prisoners could almost bank on knowing where the Warden would be at any given time and it creates a ridiculous situation to have the principal officers of the institution taken into custody by the inmates.[11]

A few months later, in September, another escape attempt did take place, this time a one-man affair. John R. Bayless had begun his years in the federal prison system with a two-year sentence to the federal reformatory at El Reno, Oklahoma. After the staff received a report that he had become active in planning an escape, he was transferred to Leavenworth. Conditionally released in July 1937, he was soon back for a twenty-five-year term for robbing the Farmers and Merchants Bank of Mansfield, Missouri, of $606 and stealing an automobile at gunpoint from a garage attendant. After he was identified as plotting with three other Leavenworth inmates to secure knives, overpower the cell house guard, and take the associate warden hostage, he was shipped to Alcatraz at age twenty-two.

At Alcatraz, Bayless did quiet time and earned an assignment working with another inmate outside the walls. The two gathered refuse and garbage from various points around the island and, accompanied by an officer, trucked the debris to an incinerator. On September 15, 1941, a supervising officer noticed that when his crew and the inmate stevedores who worked on the dock lined up for a count, one man was missing. The control room was notified and the escape siren sounded. As one of the dock officers ran in the direction where the missing prisoner had last been seen, he encountered Bayless on the road dressed in his underwear, soaking wet, and bleeding from abrasions on his knee and feet. Bayless had simply walked away from the work area, climbed down, and stumbled over the slippery rocks until he reached the water's edge. Once in the bay he was so shocked by the frigid temperature of the water that he quickly concluded that he could not survive very long; he swam back to shore, climbed over the rocks, crawled up the hillside, and made his way to the road. Bayless was sent to isolation in the newly remodeled D block and tried by a good time forfeiture board. The board found him guilty of escape and took away 3,000 days of statutory good time.[12]

THE WAR COMES TO ALCATRAZ

The entry of the United States into World War II in December 1941 altered operations at Alcatraz in a variety of ways. On the day of the Pearl Harbor attack, Warden Johnston set up a blackboard in the yard to keep inmates informed about the war in the Pacific and in Europe. It relayed headlines from local newspapers, such as "Singapore in Grave Danger—Japs only 48 Miles Away and Striking Hard" and "RAF Smash at Axis and Slow Them in Their Drive in Libya."[13] A number of guards were called to military duty, and concerns were raised about the location of the prison near the entrance to one of the major harbors on the West Coast. A submarine net was installed to protect the entrance to the bay, and large numbers of Coast Guard vessels and navy ships from the nearby Treasure Island airbase began regular patrols in the waters around the island.

The inmates began to worry that Japanese planes might bomb the prison along with everything else in San Francisco Bay, and that in such an attack they would be left to die, locked up in their cells. In June 1942 four antiaircraft guns were brought to the island. One was mounted on the roof of the old model building, two were located on the cell house roof, and the fourth on the roof of the guards' apartment building. Locating these guns over their heads did little to assuage inmates' or employees' apprehensions about an air raid. The guns were removed in July 1944.

Like other federal prisons, Alcatraz took on war-related work, which included doing the laundry for many military posts throughout the Bay

Area and manufacturing rubber mats and cargo nets for naval vessels. In a report on the federal prisons' role in the war effort, the Bureau of Prisons noted, in an attempt to demonstrate the patriotism of even the most desperate and "unregenerate" federal prisoners, that Alcatraz convicts had purchased $3,250 in war bonds, donated blood, and "stepped up their industrial activities to meet the [laundry] needs of the many governmental agencies in the vicinity." In addition to describing Alcatraz's war contributions, the Bureau also demonstrated some defensiveness about the Rock:

> Contrary to popular misconceptions, Alcatraz is no "haven of the damned," no American Devil's Island. It is an institution with a necessarily strict regimen and discipline. It does house criminals whose past acts classify them as vicious and whose long sentences render them classifiable as desperate. But in all other ways and aside from the restraints necessary to the custodial security of such men, Alcatraz shares all of the benefits and amenities to be found in the other federal institutions. The food is good. The inmates receive humane and understanding treatment. There are opportunities for recreation and facilities for education and intellectual advancement. And practically any man on Alcatraz may earn his return, by good conduct and proper adjustment, to institutions where the strictures are less rigorous. . . . . Alcatraz exists not only as an incarceratorium for the vicious but it, no less than the other federal prisons, functions as a rehabilitative agency, for few men—even those regarded as "the worst"—are completely unregenerate, and, with increasing frequency, "corrected incorrigibles" are transferred from "the Rock" to be given new opportunities in the other prisons of the system.

The report also noted that in case of an attack on the Bay Area by Japanese planes, plans had been made to move the inmates into "virtually impregnable air raid shelters"—in other words, the cisterns and dungeons below the floor of the cell house. It concluded by observing that as war was unfortunately the best means of dealing with "international thuggery," Alcatraz was the best means available to deal with domestic thuggery.[14]

The presence of military personnel on the island and the flotilla of ships guarding the bay added an additional layer to the prison's security. While the Alcatraz staff was feeling more confident and most inmates were doing their part in the war effort, a handful of inmates made their plans to take advantage of the distractions of the war to take an early, unauthorized leave from the island.

The first of these escape attempts involved Rufus "Whitey" Franklin, a central figure in the failed 1938 model building breakout. Convicted of the murder of Officer Cline, Franklin had received a life sentence to go along with his original thirty-year term. He had lost 3,600 days of good time and was living on a permanent basis in D block disciplinary segregation, where his "adjustment" was not good. On one occasion, he had assaulted an officer who opened his cell door to retrieve a book, and on another occasion a brass plunger rod, sharpened at one end, was found in his cell. But by August 1942 Franklin was being allowed out of his cell to do cleanup jobs and to help serve meals to other inmates.[15] As he did so, he worked out an escape plan: cut several of the bars that enclosed the gun gallery (also called a gun cage), crawl inside it at the ground-floor level, climb the stairs to the second floor, and then surprise the armed guard who patrolled D block when that officer came back through a door after supervising inmate movements in the main cell house. The plan fell apart when an officer discovered him sawing away with a file on a gun-gallery bar.

Franklin's abortive attempt did not alert staff to this potential flaw in the cell house security system. No effort was made to cover the bars of the gallery on the floor level of D block with heavy wire mesh or metal plates to reduce the risk that an inmate could get inside the gun cage. And no change was made in the procedure that allowed the gun gallery guard to leave either the main cell house or D block unsupervised when he was on the other side of the door that separated the two units. (These weaknesses would prove deadly in May 1946.)

ONE MORE BREAKOUT

By 1943 the new industries building, set against the hillside on which the prison perched, housed almost all of the workshops. The old model building remained in place, however, with the guard tower in operation and the anti-aircraft gun emplacement manned by soldiers on the roof. The second and third floors of the building were no longer used, but several operations continued on the first floor. Three inmates worked in the carpenter shop; the paint shop employed two inmates; and in the old mat shop two men were assigned to make concrete blocks for use in building retaining walls at various points around the island.

The men assigned to make the concrete blocks were Floyd Hamilton, who had escaped detection as a participant in the May 1941 breakout attempt, and forty-three-year-old Fred Hunter, who was serving a twenty-five-year term. Hunter's hands were twisted from arthritis, and he weighed only 118 pounds. A staff report had stated that his body was "frail to almost childlike proportions" and that he would be unable to undertake "swimming or any strenuous exercise."[16] Despite his poor physical condition, Hunter joined Floyd Hamilton in plotting a breakout that would entail navigating the rough waters of San Francisco Bay.

The model building was still the best location from which to launch an escape. It remained as a large obstacle between the bay and the sight lines of the guard towers on the hill above and the road leading to the cell house, and it backed up to the edge of the cliffs. A daylight escape attempt from the building in the absence of heavy fog was considered too risky—not only was there the guard on the roof, but now there were soldiers with weapons and the entire harbor was filled with naval boats scurrying back and forth, and at night picket boats with floodlights illuminated the entire area along the submarine net. Escape would require a heavy cover of fog to have any chance of succeeding.

Two other men who worked in the Model Shop—Harold Brest and James Boarman—were let in on the carefully conceived plot to overcome all these obstacles. Brest was serving a life sentence for kidnapping, along with two concurrent twenty-five-year terms for interstate transportation of a stolen automobile.[17] The length of his sentence had been the reason for Harold Brest's transfer to Alcatraz and it was also the reason he was now ready to try to reach the bay.

James Boarman, serving twenty years for bank robbery, transportation of stolen securities, and interstate auto theft, was a volatile and aggressive prisoner. When sentenced in Owensboro, Kentucky, for his offenses, the U. S. marshal had stationed fifteen officers in the courtroom as a precaution; when his sentence was pronounced his mother started screaming and Boarman began fighting with court personnel in an attempt to reach a door fifteen feet away. Deputies grabbed him immediately but his brother rushed in to help him, and the two fought until they were subdued and dragged cursing and shouting from the courtroom. The U.S. marshal wrote to the attorney general to warn that Boarman was "the most desperate prisoner we have ever had in our custody" and that he intended after serving his time to "come back and kill everyone connected with the Federal Court."[18] At Leavenworth, Boarman was soon identified as a "leader of the younger radical element" and within a few months he was on his way west. When he arrived at Alcatraz he was twenty-one years old.

With Boarman providing energy and enthusiasm and Hamilton providing experience, the four men began their preparations for an early departure. Remembering that the drill had been too slow to cut the bars in his breakout attempt two years earlier, Hamilton looked for the parts of a better cutting device in a pile of burned out motors and other junk piled near the Model Shop. He found a motor "that looked like it was burned all to pieces" but took it back to the shop and succeeded in getting it to run. Hamilton and his fellow plotters then convinced an inmate in the machine shop to steal three "regular cutting wheels" that could "go through any kind of steel," and from an inmate in the paint shop they received "some paint and putty."[19]

The guard who supervised the men was gone during regular intervals each day, but he counted the inmates in the shop every thirty minutes. Between his rounds, the inmates worked on cutting the bars. To keep the guard and soldiers on the roof from noticing the noise, they would "get Harvey Bailey in the carpenter shop to run some lumber through the planer and that'd kill the noise." Knowing that swimming all the way to the mainland wasn't possible, they also began making flotation devices that Hamilton referred to as "surfboards." Using scrap lumber that Bailey planed down to a quarter of an inch in thickness, and watertight glue from the paint shop, they put together three surfboards with a three-inch air space in each, a twelve-foot board for Hamilton and Hunter, and a six-foot board each for Boarman and Brest. The plan was not to float on top of the boards, but to hang underneath them in "cradles" made of copper wire. A hole was bored in each board through which a rubber hose was inserted so they could breathe under water. Inside the board they stored army clothes and shoes. Finally they attached wooden paddles for rowing. Then they painted the boards blue to match the color of the water, using paint provided by an inmate in the paint shop.

Instead of trying to hide the boards from the guards, the would-be escapees camouflaged them by hanging them on the wall as shelves on which pieces of hardware were placed according to size and type. Recalled Hamilton, "Captain Weinhold came by one day and seen all them fittings and bolts and nuts and everything and the sizes and he complimented us on the neat job we were doing. And that was our sailboat home."

By April the bars were cut and the surfboards complete, but the inmates needed a thick fog. As they came to work on April 13, the conditions seemed right. "The foghorns were blowing and the Golden Gate Bridge was already covered up," remembered Hamilton, "and [it] looked like a thick, heavy fog [was] coming in." Hamilton and Hunter, however, were concerned that the typical spring pattern would prevail—the fog would roll in but then lift. Boarman disagreed and argued that this was the day. "He kind of considered this his break," recalled Hamilton, "and he went to arguing and cussing." With the fog continuing to move in, the four decided to go.

At approximately 9:45 A.M. Officer George Smith, who was in charge of the work detail, noticed that the pile of dirt the inmates were supposed to be spreading showed little sign of attention. As he walked into the old mat shop, Brest and Hamilton grabbed him, with Hamilton telling the officer, "We're going home, Mr. Smith." Smith struggled to free himself, and Hunter pointed a knife at this back, saying "Take it easy, Mr. Smith, we don't want to hurt you." But Smith continued to struggle, so Boarman punched him in the stomach. Smith fell to the floor and the inmates tied and gagged him. When Smith began to cough, Brest said "Wait, he can't breathe through his nose; you'll smother him and we don't want to hurt him unless we have to" and then used the guard's own handkerchief as a gag.[20]

While Hamilton began taking the surfboards down off the wall, the others watched for Captain Henry Weinhold, who was making his rounds. When Weinhold arrived, Boarman and Hunter seized him and ordered him to lie down on the floor. When he refused, they called to Hamilton for help. Hamilton came over, threw Weinhold down onto the floor, turned him over on his belly, and held him as Hunter tried to tie his hands. When he "kept jerking his hands loose," Brest came over with a hammer and began hitting him on the head. At that point Hamilton threw up his hands to catch the hammer blow. "I thought if we killed [an employee]," recalled Hamilton, "we would have a bad go."

With both guards subdued, Hamilton twisted off the precut bars, passed the twelve-foot surfboard out the window, and crawled out. Hunter followed and using "a kind-of blanket" to cover wires on the fence, they tied together two electrical cords about thirty feet long and threw them over the fence to climb down closer to the water's edge. Boarman and Brest removed their clothes and smeared grease on their bodies. As Boarman pulled a rubber hospital doughnut from its hiding place and began blowing it up, Smith heard him say, "This may get me to the beach." Then both men disappeared out the window.

Even though his hands were bound, Officer Smith was able to get his whistle out of his pocket, and Captain Weinhold was able to spit out the gag. Smith managed to get his whistle into the captain's mouth. But when Weinhold began to blow the whistle, the machines in the carpenter shop suddenly started up, drowning out the shouts of the officers and the sound of the whistle.[21]

Hunter tried to use the cords to lower himself down, but with his crippled hands he couldn't hold tightly enough and fell most of the way down to the rocks, injuring his ankle. Boarman and Brest followed Hunter over the fence but without their boards. According to Hamilton, Boarman and Brest "just dove off into the water and went swimming out toward that fog bank." Hunter got on top of the twelve-foot board and began paddling out into the bay, and Hamilton opted to swim for it. Fighting the surf, Hunter finally managed to get about a hundred feet away from the island but then became so fatigued that he decided to turn around and paddle back toward the island, to a cave he had heard about.

Up on top of the model building, Officer Frank Johnson became suspicious when he noted that Officer Smith and Captain Weinhold had been in the building for some time and that Smith hadn't answered his telephone call. After waiting a few minutes, Johnson leaned over the edge of the roof and called out for Smith and Weinhold. When there was no response he became concerned, called the control center, and told the officer in charge, "For Christ's sake, get someone down here right away." Johnson then left the tower and walked quickly to the back of the roof on the bay side. He saw two heads in the water some two hundred yards from shore and opened fire.

Hamilton—still in the water but not with Brest and Boarman—heard the shooting and then the prison siren. He swam underwater to the cave entrance, where Hunter had already paddled. The two men crawled into the cave and looked for hiding places under the scraps of rubber along the walls. Since Hunter's crippled hands prevented him from picking up large pieces, Hamilton scooped out a place against one wall, helped Hunter into the hole, and then covered him up. Urged on by the sound of men in boats, Hamilton crawled back to an area near the mouth of the cave where the floor was close to the roof. "I started digging out away from the wall," recalled Hamilton. "I dug and dug until I got them tires up in front of me. I got behind them and pulled others back over me."

On the roof, Officer Johnson continued to fire at the two men in the water. The guard on duty in the tower on top of the administration building also opened fire with his 30.06 rifle. One of the figures was hit and, according to Johnson, "the body seemed to raise out of the water." Other shots were fired by several guards, who on hearing the siren secured weapons from the armory and ran down the hill to the back of the model building. They heard Johnson firing from the roof and the soldiers on the roof yelled to them, "There are two in the bay." All of the officers later pointed out that the two figures in the water were so close to each other they made one target.

All firing from the island ceased when the prison launch came around the end of the island and moved between the men in the water and the shore. When the boat reached the northwest corner of the island, the boat guard saw two men in the water under heavy fire, but one was motionless with his head and feet under water, his midsection held out of the water by a small round rubber doughnut. The other man, recognized by the boat officer as Brest, signaled for assistance and swam toward the other man to help hold him up until the boat got closer to them. A boat hook was held out to Brest, who grabbed it shouting, "Pull us both up." Brest loosened his grip on the other man at the instruction of the boat crew; he was hauled onto the boat and told to lie on the deck while the guards turned toward the other man in the water.

William Knipscherr, the prison electrician—who had been working on the dock when word was sent to bring the launch around the island—leaned out of the launch, grabbed the belt of the man in the water, and tried to pull him out. As he raised the belt, James Boarman's face appeared and Knipscherr saw a hole over Boarman's right ear about the size of a quarter with what appeared to be brain tissue oozing out of the wound. As he tried to hoist the body out of the water, the belt broke and Boarman's body quickly sank out of sight. The men in the launch searched the area for ten minutes without sighting the body and returned to the dock to get Brest to the prison hospital. Brest, without realizing that the officers onshore and in the launch had seen only himself and Boarman, asked the boat officers, "Did you pick up the other two?"[22] Fred Hunter and Floyd Hamilton, however, were nowhere to be seen.

In the prison hospital, Harold Brest was treated for barbed wire cuts and a bullet wound to his right elbow. He was then interviewed by FBI agents, who this time had been promptly notified of the breakout attempt by Warden Johnston. Brest adhered to the convict code as best he could after inadvertently revealing to the officers on the boat that he and Boarman were not the only escapees. Brest did not know whose idea the escape was, he did not know whether it had a leader or not, he did not know how, when, or by whom the bars of the Model Shop windows were cut. He claimed that the four escapees had no plans as to what they would do if they made it to shore and he had no idea where Hunter and Hamilton might be.

The prison doctor, however, informed FBI agents that when the alarm sounded he had quickly moved to a vantage point where he could see the two men swimming away from the island with bullets spraying up the water around them. Dr. Ritchey reported that he had seen a third man, who he thought was Hamilton, swimming about a hundred yards from where Brest and Boarman were situated. He said that this man had been hit and that the body sank below the surface.

The search for Hunter and Hamilton went on under the direction of Deputy Warden Ed Miller, who was well aware of the cave at the northwest tip of the island. For several years during which the inmates made rubber doormats, prison staff had dumped pieces of scrap rubber and old tire casings into the cave. Miller was of the opinion that, if Hunter and Hamilton were alive, they would most likely have sought refuge in the cave, which ran some forty feet or more under the cliffs. A group of officers were sent twice to search the cave during the afternoon of the thirteenth; the first time they found no sign of the escapees but during the second search one guard noticed blood on a rock at the mouth of the cave. Miller, on receiving this information, decided that he would lead another search himself. Taking two officers in a small boat from the prison launch, Miller and his men entered the cave and began throwing tires and scrap rubber around. They worked their way to the back of the cave, wading through several feet of water and pieces of rubber, but they saw no sign of the missing men.

Just moments before they were ready to call off the search, Miller told FBI agents he suddenly saw something move under a pile of scraps. He turned his light on the area and saw "either the stomach or chest of a man or the white shirt covering the stomach of a man." Miller said loudly to the rest of the officers, "We might as well get out of here, there's no one here" and then backed up to the mouth of the cave. There, he quietly told his men that someone was hiding in the cave and that he was going to go after him. With his .45 automatic, he returned to the back of the cave and shouted, "Come out!" He fired one shot "and immediately Hunter's head appeared above the layers of rubber." Miller told Hunter to put his hands up; when he did not do so, Miller "fired a shot into the rock immediately above Hunter's head, whereupon Hunter promptly complied with the directions." Miller asked him where Hamilton was, and Hunter replied that he did not know.[23]

Hamilton later related a somewhat different version of Hunter's apprehension:

> I started digging out away from the wall. I dug and dug until I got them tires up in front of me. I got behind them and pulled others back over me. After just a little bit here come some people in there; they couldn't find

anything so after a while here comes the associate warden, Miller and two more lieutenants. When Miller came in he started cussing and fussing and digging around and finally he went to digging over where Fred was, and he jumped back and said, "Here's one of them sons-of-a-bitches" and boom, he shot right at him. Fred said some of them tires ricocheted the bullet and it went down behind him between him and the wall. So they made him crawl out where they told him to get in that little boat to go out to the big boat. [Miller] told Fred, "You make one crooked move and I'll kill you and these officers here will swear that you attacked me, won't you?"

The [officers] wouldn't give him no answer at all. So they went on out but directly here come Miller back in and he said, "If I find that other son-of-a-bitch I'll sure shoot him between the eyes." And he went to shooting—boom! boom! boom! He was shooting everywhere. He shot one bullet that came right where I was; it felt like a sledgehammer hitting me, it just knocked the wind out of me. [Miller] was cussing so loud I don't think he would have ever heard me if I'd hollered and he went on out.

Later on here comes Weinhold, the captain we'd tied up, sounded like he must have had about a dozen guards with him. And he says, "If that fellow's in here we'll catch him." I didn't know if he was looking for me, or Brest, or Boarman. So they kept moving tires 'til they come around to where I was. There was two guards out in front digging and one of them crawled right up to where I was and started throwing pieces of tires out; he was getting down so close to me it seemed like he was breathing right on my face. He talked about how tired he was getting, and directly he just stopped working and turned around and sat down on me. I says to myself, "Boy when he gets rested he's going to have to move just one or two more tires and he'll see me." But fortunately Weinhold says, "Tide's coming up, it's going to have this entrance covered up in a little bit, everybody out, we'll come back and finish the job when tide goes down." So everybody left.

With Hunter apprehended, Brest in custody, and Boarman presumed dead, Warden Johnston concluded that Dr. Ritchey had indeed seen Floyd Hamilton sinking under the waves, dead. Johnston notified the Bureau of Prisons that Hamilton had drowned and thus all the escapees were accounted for. The Coast Guard was notified to be on the lookout for the bodies of Boarman and Hamilton.[24]

Deputy Warden Miller, however, was not so certain that Hamilton had drowned, and the following day he told Captain Weinhold to take a squad of officers and conduct another search of the cave. The group moved dozens of rubber scraps around and searched with powerful lights, but they did not find Hamilton. Weinhold reported back to Miller that he was "pretty certain" Hamilton was not in the cave. No further searches of the cave were conducted on the fifteenth, but foot and boat patrols were instructed to keep an eye on the beach areas.

Warden Johnston, Dr. Ritchey, and the captain were wrong—Floyd Hamilton was alive and fighting fatigue and cold in the cave that had been searched four times. After Weinhold and his men left, Hamilton decided to move to a different hiding place closer to the mouth of the cave:

> I had to lay on a slant with my feet in the water. Them crabs would bite me when I first got there but pretty soon I couldn't feel them. The third night I didn't hear no noise. I figured well if I stay here another eight or ten hours I won't be able to move at all, so I crawled out and at first I couldn't get up. I started rubbing my arms and my hands and my legs.
>
> The moonlight was shining so bright I could see men walking on those submarine tenders and I figure they could see me if they looked that direction. I figured I'll get back [inside the Model Shop] through the same hole that I came out of and try to find something to float away on. I figured if I could get in that paint shop I could get some empty paint buckets or full ones and empty them. I got right up to the top of the bank but there was nothing to catch hold around. I finally found a rock sticking up a little ways. I put a lot of weight on it and threw my leg over it and the thing pulled out. I went backwards head over heels down the hill until I hit the water. The rocks cut my back all the way down and I lost a good bit of blood. I sat on the rocks and rested 'til I figured them people out on the boat may see me. But I figured I'll go back up that same way. I climbed back up to the top where this rock came out and left a hole. I got my hand in it and went on over [the edge of the cliff next to] a ten-foot fence with three strands of barbed wire. I got up on top of one of those fence posts and went over the fence down in between the buildings. When I stepped around the corner, the guard on the road tower was flashing the light on me, blinking it. I figured well I better not run—if I run he'll think something is wrong. So I looked at him and stuck up my hand and I waved and he turned the light off. He figured I was down there giving him signals that everything's all right.

Hamilton made his way to the model building but confronted a barbed-wire fence. In the bright moonlight, and with a guard two hundred feet away in the powerhouse able to see him if he did anything to attract attention, Hamilton found a piece of wood and used it to open a gap in the fence through which he could crawl. He next went over close to the old building where they'd broken out:

> There was the night patrolman sitting in the office in the carpenter shop— you could hear him clear his throat every once in a while. I guess he was reading too. So I went around and went back in the building through a

window into the old mat shop. Fortunately it wasn't locked—whoever closed the window never locked it and I pulled that window open and crawled back in and went through the two doors to the room next to where the guard was.

With dawn approaching, Hamilton took off his clothes and put them on a steam radiator to dry. When they were warm and dry he put them back on and squatted in a corner to rest. He tried to stay awake but ended up falling asleep. The next thing he knew, Captain Weinhold and a group of guards entered the room to search for the motor and cutting wheel the escapees had used to cut the bars. Seeing Hamilton in his corner, a guard "flattened up against the wall," looking at him "like he'd seen a ghost." "They must have been pretty surprised to see me," surmised Hamilton later, "because they had already reported me dead to the FBI."

Captain Weinhold ordered Hamilton to get up, but he was physically unable to comply. "My hands wouldn't move, my legs wouldn't move," recollected Hamilton. "I'd think about it, but they wouldn't obey." According to Hamilton, Weinhold walked over and struck him on the side of the head with his blackjack. "It didn't hurt then," said Hamilton later, "but after I got up to the hospital, got thawed out, and took a hot bath, then my head started hurting." In the hospital, Hamilton was treated for the more than four hundred separate cuts and bruises on his body. Then he was sent to D block isolation.

They stripped me down, they give me a little old pair of white shorts and they took me down to number 13 in the hole. It was a strip cell, it had a hole in the floor for a commode. If they wasn't real mad at you, they'd give you a mattress at night. But they didn't give me the mattress, they just give me a blanket or two, then they'd take them away from me the next morning. I was in that cell most of the time with just a pair of shorts on, walking back and forth. It was so dark that I couldn't see at first— I'd run into the wall because I couldn't see it and then finally I learned how to pace my steps. I'd take so many steps and turn, so many steps and turn. I got to where I could stay the same distance from the wall in the front or the back. They had two fans on the roof, one of them pumped air in and the other blew it out, and on the nights or the days that it was real foggy, that air would be so wet that the floor would get wet. It's pretty miserable with no clothes. I got one meal every three days. It would usually be just a little spoonful of each of whatever the menu was. It was never near enough. At other times you'd get two slices of bread. When twenty-one days was over, they tried me and took all my good time. When

I was coming out of the dark cell [Deputy Warden] Miller was over there supervising. He said to put me up in number 42 cell way up in the corner, and he says, "Don't let him have any privileges, don't let him write to anybody or receive any mail and don't let him have any clothes on but that pair of shorts. Give him an old mattress and two blankets—that's all he gets until I give further orders." I was there maybe about a month when they decided to come over and let me go down and take a shower. I'd occupied my time by walking back and forth, by cursing everything, and being mad at everybody. I think hate will bring you through; I was hating myself, I criticized myself an awful lot, which I do if I don't do something right and I mess up. I cursed myself because there was no way out on that breakout.

While Hamilton raged on in isolation, regretting that he had given in to Boarman's desperate urging that they make the attempt even though the fog was not heavy enough to provide cover, the search for Boarman's remains went on. A body washed ashore on Stinson Beach north of San Francisco Bay on June 17 and another was fished out of the water near the Point Bonita Lighthouse on June 19, but neither was that of James Boarman. Boarman's body, like those of Ted Cole and Ralph Roe, was never found.

The escape, combined with Hamilton's reappearance, was one more embarrassment to the Bureau of Prisons. Not only had four prisoners succeeded in cutting through bars and getting off the island using all kinds of paraphernalia, one of them eluded searchers for three days and had been able to climb back through the security perimeter into a prison building. While James Johnston's account (and other subsequent accounts) of this escape reported that Hamilton had reentered the Model Shop through the window he and the others had exited, he had in fact climbed over the fences and come into the building through another window that had been left unlocked. As FBI investigators soon reported to Director Hoover, Hamilton's success in breaking back into the prison was seen as one more example of careless and shoddy management on the island. When the FBI field office in San Francisco learned by telegram from Johnston that Hamilton had been found alive inside the prison, that office reported to FBI headquarters that the discovery of Hamilton was "indicative of the sloppy job they [the Alcatraz staff] did in searching." J. Edgar Hoover wrote on the report, "This prison outfit is certainly a mess."[25]

A month later, Hoover referred parts of an agent's report to Director Bennett at the Bureau of Prisons:

I am informed that the four subjects were permitted to spend considerable time without supervision in the Old Mat Shop which is located in the Model Building. This shop contains a number of large Stillson wrenches, pipe, cable benders, and other tools which could be utilized in effecting an escape. . . . Investigation has indicated that two outer cell bars wrenched off by the subjects had been partially cut sometime prior to the actual escape which would make it appear it is not the practice of the prison guards to examine the bars in this building.

The report went on to list the many items that the escapees "were able to acquire and use":

Map of San Francisco and Bay Area showing Alcatraz Island. Oilcloth bag containing an Army uniform, consisting of pants, shirt, tie, overseas cap, one pair of shorts, two handkerchiefs and a $5.00 bill. One gallon paint can containing a pair of Army style khaki trousers, a sun tan Army shirt and black Army tie. One and one half gallon paint can containing two cakes of soap and a pair of tan shoes. One and one half gallon paint can containing two black Army ties, one tan Army tie, three tan overseas caps, one tan Army shirt and a pair of Army trousers. One claw hammer, one doughnut shaped inflated rubber tube, one homemade life belt, four prison-made knives, one homemade wooden raft, two pair of pliers, one pair of scissors, one 50 foot coil of insulated wire, one 4" × 12" plank, 12 foot long, one section of canvas.[26]

Clearly losing patience with James Johnston, Bureau of Prisons headquarters called the warden to Washington, D.C., to discuss the lapses in security that allowed the inmates to escape and—if they had had better luck—traverse the waters of the bay and use the escape gear and military uniforms they took from the laundry to blend in with the large numbers of soldiers moving around San Francisco at the time.

With the Henry Young trial and the bad press it had brought the prison still fresh in everyone's minds, it was decided that trying the three surviving inmates for escape in federal court would only provide another forum for convicts to complain about conditions on the island. Furthermore, a trial would reveal the serious breaches of security that had occurred. In September 1943 the Bureau of Prisons notified the U.S. attorney in San Francisco that although Hamilton, Hunter, and Brest could be charged with assaulting federal officers, the officers had not been injured and thus the three could likely only be charged with attempting to escape. For this violation of prison rules, the Bureau had already ordered good time forfeiture hearings, and these had resulted in the removal of good time in amounts that exceeded the length of the escape sentences each man could have received if convicted in court. (For example, Hamilton lost 3,600 days, or nearly ten years, and Hunter 3,103 days.)

TWO SOLO ATTEMPTS AND A PLOT UNCOVERED

During the war the Alcatraz laundry facilitated two other escape attempts. Thousands of uniforms from large Bay Area military bases passed through the laundry, affording inmates the opportunity to rifle the pockets for money, identification papers, and other useful items. Entire uniforms could be stolen with relative ease. The military uniforms hidden away by Hamilton, Hunter, Brest, and Boarman for use if they reached the mainland or Angel Island were pilfered from the laundry. In the two years between July 1943 and July 1945, two inmates used uniforms as they tried to break out. Between these two attempts, custodial staff uncovered a sophisticated escape plot involving five inmates with previous escape experience.

Less than four months after Hamilton and his compatriots made their failed attempt, Huron "Terrible Ted" Walters—a longtime associate of Hamilton's—made his break in a U.S. Army uniform. Ted Walters arrived at Alcatraz in June 1940, to serve a thirty-year federal term for robberies. On the island he established himself as a man ready to protest the conditions of his confinement. In December 1940 he helped lead a brief strike by inmates working in the laundry, who complained there was too much work. Walters spent ten days in disciplinary segregation. After his return to the general population, he was written up for some minor rules violations; several months later he decided that he had had enough and it was time to leave Alcatraz.

Walters was assigned to work in the laundry in the new industries building. During work breaks, Walters noticed that on Saturdays when the road tower guard walked to the recreation-yard side of his tower to observe the yard, he could not see an area between the industries building and the perimeter fence, which would allow Walters to get from the laundry to the fence unobserved. Furthermore, Walters saw that there was a section of the fence that could not be easily observed by the road tower guard no matter where he was in the tower. The officer in the model building tower could see that section of fence—but on Saturdays no officer was stationed in the model building tower, even though (due to the heavy demand for military laundry services) the laundry crew worked on Saturday afternoons. Seeing an opportunity to get through the fence at relatively low risk, Walters stole and hid some wire cutters to cut through the fences. He also set aside some wooden boxes to stand on, several empty gallon buckets to keep him afloat, and a soldier's uniform to wear when he reached shore.

At about 2:00 P.M. on Saturday, July 7, 1943, Ted Walters made his break for freedom. He waited until the guard moved to the rec-yard side of the tower and then crossed the field from the laundry to the fences. The wire cutters proved not to be strong enough to sever the strands of the fence. By standing on the boxes and wearing gloves, however, he was able to climb through the barbed wire at the top of the fence, drop down into the no-man's-land between the two fences, and climb up the outer fence. But as he hurriedly crawled over the top of the second fence, he slipped and fell, injuring his back. Despite the pain from the fall, he made his way down a flight of steps to the area next to the water where an old wharf had once stood.

Walters had been gone for about fifteen minutes when he was missed by the shop foreman and the officer assigned to supervise the laundry crew. The alarm was sounded, and officers first searched the laundry itself to see if Walters was hiding inside the building. Warden Johnston, informed that a man was missing, came down from the administration building to lead the manhunt. Officers Edward Stucker and Robert Baker discovered Walter's wire cutters and a glove between the two fences, and with the warden they went through a nearby gate in the fence to begin searching the waterfront. While the warden walked in the direction of the Model Shop, the two officers went in the other direction. The warden described what happened next:

> I heard Stucker and Baker yelling that they had discovered Walters and I ran back where they were, and they saw Walters stripped down to his shorts and doing the best he could to conceal himself against the uneven ledges of rock in the little cove just beyond the end of the sea wall.[27]

By this time, Deputy Warden Miller had arrived on the scene, and he fired a shot in the air to convince the hesitant Walters to come out of his hiding place.

San Francisco newspapers carried brief notices of Walters's "capture by prison guards." At Bureau headquarters in Washington, James Bennett was furious at what he saw as carelessness by the guards on duty in the towers, who should have provided visual supervision of the laundry building and the fences. Bennett announced in a terse telegraph to Warden Johnston that he was sending one of his staff, Assistant Commissioner A. H. Connor, to Alcatraz to investigate the escape. To Connor, Bennett sent the following instructions:

> While at Alcatraz will you please check on escape of Ted Walters from laundry. Cannot understand how he could get over work area fence in plain daylight without being noticed by tower guards. Suggest you get Warden Johnston's version and also talk with officers on duty at that time. It seems to me that there must have been inattention to duty and that officer responsible ought to be placed on leave without pay for a reasonable time. Such incidents as this cannot be permitted to go without fixing responsibility and taking appropriate action.[28]

Connor reported to Bennett that the model building tower had had no guard assigned for four weeks—a situation he found inexcusable. He also noted what Ted Walters had observed: that the road tower guard could not see an area between the industries building and the fences when he was on the recreation-yard side of the tower. Connor reported that Warden Johnston had prepared notices of thirty-day suspensions for Lt. J. H. Simpson and Capt. Henry Weinhold.[29] Considering Johnston's action, Bureau headquarters recommended that because Simpson and Weinhold had "rendered meritorious and outstanding service over a period of years, no suspension should be made."[30] Johnston agreed.

Ted Walters was brought before a good time forfeiture board, where he pleaded guilty to trying to escape, saying that he had tried to swim away but that the pain in his back after his fall from the fence had forced him to return to the sea wall at the bottom of the cliffs. The board, comprised of the deputy warden, two lieutenants, and Dr. Ritchey, took away 3,100 days of Walters's statutory good time—in effect extending his term of imprisonment by approximately eight and a half years—three and a half years longer than the five-year term Walters would have received if he had been tried for escape and convicted in federal district court.

At some point after he was caught trying to cut the bars of the gun gallery in 1942, Whitey Franklin—still determined to escape from Alcatraz—

began plotting an escape with a group of at least four other inmates. They hit on the idea of gaining access to the utility corridor behind each block of cells, which contained air circulation ducts, plumbing, and electrical conduits, and then climbing up the pipes to the top of the cell house, where they would break through the roof.

The preliminary parts of this plan were already under way when, in May 1944, guards discovered a note in a magazine indicating an escape plot. The note was unsigned but matched Franklin's handwriting. When Franklin's cell was searched, a five-inch-long knife was found concealed under the linoleum floor in his cell. The subsequent investigation revealed other components of the escape plan and implicated other inmates, as described in a report to Warden Johnston by Deputy Warden Miller:

> A thorough search resulted in the finding of 2 small bits and a small piece of hack saw blade very cleverly concealed in one of the floor brooms. We removed the men and went around from cell to cell searching them while they were unoccupied. This led to the discovery that Franklin had used either the hack saw blade or the band saw blade, or knife blade, to attempt a cut in the ceiling of the cell in the process of attempting to make an opening to get into the attic. We also found two ¼ inch holes drilled through the metal ceiling in his cell. It was apparent that he could do this by standing on his bunk. In the cell occupied by Cretzer we found bored in the wall 20 holes making a line approximately 7 inches in length on the north wall of his cell which would be the south wall of the adjoining cell occupied by his brother-in-law, Kyle. The holes were under the bunk in Kyle's cell. The cuts made by Franklin in the ceiling of the cell were covered with soap and were not discernible until I had the ceiling of the cell washed and scraped.[31]

Miller concluded that in addition to Franklin, Joseph Cretzer, and Arnold Kyle, Ted Walters, and Floyd Hamilton were likely involved in the escape plan. This plot, involving five men who had all attempted to escape at least once before, demonstrated once again the determination of some prisoners to beat the government. It should also have informed the staff of deficiencies in the physical plant, patrolling practices, the habits of individual officers, and other weaknesses that provided inmates with escape opportunities. Deputy Warden Miller discounted the possibility of inmates getting inside the utility area behind the cells and climbing the pipes up to the top of the cell house for an escape, because he did not believe it was possible for inmates to get through the roof itself. Many years later another group of convicts would find a way to overcome this obstacle.

In July 1945, with the war in Europe over and Japan under attack, another Alcatraz prisoner attempted to escape on his own. Taking advantage of two aspects of the war effort—the availability of military uniforms coming to Alcatraz for laundering and the regular coming and going of military ferries—John K. Giles succeeded in getting off the island and making it as far as nearby Angel Island.

Giles, a train robber, arrived at Alcatraz with a twenty-five-year sentence. Several years later, in 1943, he filed a writ of habeas corpus in federal district court claiming that his robbery conviction should be voided because the law applied to successful robberies, not to failed attempts. He declined to apply for parole consideration, noting that "applications from Alcatraz are impracticable."[32] In 1945, at age fifty, having failed to gain his release through legal means, as he had at the Oregon State Prison a decade earlier, John Giles resolved to leave Alcatraz by escape.

At approximately 10:20 on the morning of July 31, 1945, the U.S. Army ferry *General Frank M. Coxe* was tied up at the dock on Alcatraz before continuing on to Fort McDowell on nearby Angel Island. Sergeant Sherman Casey on the *Coxe* noticed a man in a staff sergeant's uniform moving along a beam next to the boat but below the dock and apparently examining the beams with a flashlight. Casey then turned his attention to other matters. A few minutes later, however, a private informed Casey that an unidentified staff sergeant had jumped from the dock and piled into the freight hatch of the *Coxe*. As the boat left, Casey called out this information to Alcatraz guard Zenas Crowell who was standing on the dock. As the boat got under way, Casey instructed Corporal Paul Lorinez to locate the unidentified staff sergeant and ask where he was going. Lorinez found the man, asked his destination, and was told that he was a telephone lineman going to Fort McDowell to repair a cable. Sergeant Casey did not link the boarding of the unknown staff sergeant to an escape attempt because the week before the army had assigned several men to work on the telephone cables below the Alcatraz dock. The *Coxe* completed its fifteen-minute voyage, tied up to the pier at Angel Island, and prepared to allow its passengers to disembark.

Meanwhile, back on Alcatraz, the comment by Sergeant Casey to

Officer Crowell had prompted an immediate count of the crew of six inmates assigned to work as freight handlers. Crowell quickly determined that Giles, who had worked on the dock as a janitor and freight handler for nine years, was missing. Crowell notified the dock lieutenant, who called Warden Johnston with the news that Giles was missing. Johnston quickly telephoned Fort McDowell to ask that all passengers disembarking from the *Coxe* be screened; Deputy Warden Miller jumped into an army speed boat tied up at the dock and set out after the ferry boat as the siren sounded for an escape.

The officer of the day at Fort McDowell, Lieutenant Gordon Kilgore, received the news from Alcatraz that a prisoner, possibly dressed in an army uniform, had escaped. Taking a sergeant with him, Kilgore went on board the *Coxe*. Corporal Lorinez told him about the unidentified boarder and pointed to Giles, who was standing in the middle of a line of soldiers waiting to disembark. Kilgore approached Giles, asked him for his pass and dog tag, which were promptly produced and identified him as "George F. Todd." The only irregularity Lt. Kilgore noticed was that the pass had not been stamped as required at Fort Mason, the starting point for the ferry on the city side of the bay. Kilgore asked the staff sergeant to accompany him to the dock office where he was questioned as to his business at Fort McDowell, which he said was "to visit the Post photographer." Kilgore asked how long he had been in the army and the soldier replied, "off and on for about nine years." At this point Deputy Warden Miller arrived at the dock and was directed to the office where Kilgore was holding "Sergeant Todd." Miller walked into the office, took one look at the soldier, and placed handcuffs on his wrists. Giles was searched and handcuffed to the record clerk who had accompanied Miller in the boat. The party returned to Alcatraz, where after a physical examination Giles was locked up in solitary confinement on a restricted diet.

The San Francisco newspaper headlines reported "10 Years of Planning—Brief Moment of Freedom" and "Alcatraz Guest Nonchalantly Sails Away."[33] Warden Johnston asked U.S. Attorney Frank Hennessy to prosecute Giles for escape, not because the additional sentence would mean anything to Giles, but because the additional years for the attempt might deter other inmates. How the warden came to the conclusion that three- to five-year terms for escape attempts would deter men on Alcatraz who were already serving long sentences is not clear.

In subsequent interviews about his attempted escape, Giles reported only that he had picked up the various pieces of his uniform from the tons of laundry that were unloaded and loaded by the inmate freight handlers on the dock. He said that he had thought about trying to escape for nine years and that on 31 July he had decided "Today is the day." When asked why he did not board the *Coxe* when it was returning to San Francisco rather than en route to Angel Island, he replied that he thought moving in the latter, less expected direction would be more likely to succeed. Giles refused to disclose any further details when FBI agents sought to question him, saying only that no other person was involved in the attempt, that he had nothing to gain by supplying information, and that he was unconcerned about an additional prison sentence. He declined to disclose the place where he had hidden the uniform, or how he had obtained the substantial number of items found in his possession, including maps of the San Francisco Bay Area and of Marin County, two sets of enlisted men's passes, two sets of dog tags, seven associated U.S. Army shoulder patches, and other items.[34] Giles ended his interview with the FBI agents with a statement familiar to all Rock convicts and staff, "I'm a prisoner doing a long time. It's up to the prison officers to keep me and it's up to me to get away if I can. It is not in my book to tell anything because I don't want to injure the chances that another prisoner may have in escaping."[35]

Bureau of Prisons headquarters responded to Warden Johnston's report on the escape by asking how so many contraband items and uniform pieces could have been collected by Giles and remain hidden from the shakedowns conducted by the custodial staff.[36] Warden Johnston replied that all incoming laundry was first searched by an officer, item by item, but that the amount of laundry had become so large that some items in pockets possibly escaped detection.

Three and a half months after the escape attempt—after a good time forfeiture board had taken 3,000 days of his statutory good time—Giles was brought before federal judge Michael Roche in San Francisco and told the court that he did not wish to have an attorney represent him. A jury was impaneled with no objection from Giles, and the government proceeded to call six witnesses, primarily the military personnel on the *Coxe*, Lt. Kilgore from Fort McDowell, and Deputy Warden Miller. The government and the defendant concluded their arguments by 3:00 P.M. on the same day, with Giles asserting that he should not be charged with "attempted escape" because he had, in fact, escaped. The following morning the jury deliberated for eight minutes and rendered its verdict of "guilty." Giles was sentenced to three years to run consecutively at the end of his present twenty-five-year sentence; his only response to a reporter was: "I'll pay for what I get. But what I need is an undertaker, not an attorney."[37]

TUNNELING TOWARD FREEDOM

During the spring of 1946, as the nation recovered from the devastating world war, four prisoners assigned to work in the basement below the kitchen noticed a steel door in the floor that was secured with a padlock.[38] One of the men, number 1700, told the others that the steel plate covered the entrance to a tunnel through which the steam pipes that heated the prison passed. James Quillen—serving a forty-five-year federal term with a detainer against his release filed by the State of California—had heard stories from old-timers about Alcatraz being built "on top of the old Spanish prison." He theorized that if they could get access to the tunnel, they "should be able to go anywhere underneath the building" and find an "outlet somewhere."

To test the theory, 1700 picked the lock that held the door in place. When it was lifted a shallow tunnel three feet wide and three feet deep was revealed. Most of the space in the tunnel was taken up by a large steam pipe and two smaller pipes. Quillen crawled some distance into the tunnel to investigate. The plotters were encouraged when they saw that the walls of the tunnel were made of bricks, which unlike concrete could be dug out individually. In the yard, Quillen talked with "Ray," who worked in one of the industries shops (this was most likely Alvin Karpis, who was called Ray by his friends). Quillen convinced Ray that escape was feasible and that he could help by smuggling needed items from the shops. Quillen and 1700 removed another padlock from a cabinet in the basement that matched the lock securing the grate in the floor. This lock was smuggled to Ray, who removed all but one tumbler; the altered padlock was then used to replace the lock at the tunnel entrance. "That lock was real, the lock wasn't damaged, you couldn't tell it had ever been touched," said Quillen later. "Their keys worked in it, but anything we wanted to use would work in it."

Then the inmates obtained chisels and hammers from Ray, who smuggled them to the kitchen area using a system that involved hiding the items in garbage barrels. A flashlight was obtained from an inmate in the hospital. Quillen and 1700, along with Quillen's rap partner Jack Pepper and an inmate identified as "T," began working in the tunnel digging out bricks. The intense heat from the pipes was so debilitating that a man could be down in the tunnel for no longer than twenty minutes, and the workspace was so claustrophobic that no more than two men at a time could be in the tunnel. These efforts took place while the officer assigned to supervise the kitchen crew was stationed on the floor above during the serving of the evening meal. After working in the tunnel, the men had to be helped out, rushed to a nearby shower to cool down, and their soiled pants and shirts replaced by a clean set of clothes. The dirty clothes were placed in the laundry basket used by all kitchen workers.

While the digging proceeded, other kitchen crew inmates came down to the basement to use a toilet and on numerous occasions saw Quillen and the others climbing in and out of the hole in the floor. With members of the kitchen crew and other convicts in the shops aware of the plot, Quillen knew that even though none of these men would be likely to rat on them, someone might make comments to other convicts who might talk. Eventually, someone did.

One afternoon in mid-April as he returned to the cell house from the yard, Quillen was ordered to go to his cell instead of his job in the kitchen. A few minutes later, guards took him before a disciplinary court comprised of the deputy warden, the captain, a lieutenant, and the kitchen officer. He was charged with attempting to escape and told that the hammers and chisels, which were left each night in the tunnel, had been found wrapped in a sock that had Quillen's number on it. Quillen knew the claim was false. He told Deputy Warden Miller:

> I'm not so dumb that I would get into an escape plot and put something in a sock that had my number on it. . . . Damn, you've known me long enough to know that if I was doing that I sure as hell wouldn't put it in my sock.

Quillen and Pepper—the only ones of the four involved in the plot to be charged—suspected they had been "fingered" by an informant and that the sock story was just a way of hiding that fact.[39]

Alcatraz officers found an impressive number of contraband tools in the tunnel: two hammers, two chisels, two knives, two pieces of pipe each eighteen inches long, three homemade keys that were nearly finished and an eighteen-inch steel hook. Quillen and Pepper found it very strange that neither of them was questioned as to how all of this escape paraphernalia had been obtained.[40] Quillen was relieved, however, to learn that while he drew nineteen days in solitary confinement followed by indefinite segregation in D block, he did not lose any of his 5,400 days of good time.

Soon after they were locked up in D block, Quillen and Pepper became involved in a protest. This disruption was initiated by a man who had become well known at Leavenworth for killing a guard in the dining hall. During the years this prisoner had spent in disciplinary segregation, he had begun raising canaries and other birds and writing articles about their diseases. As bird fanciers learned of his studies, they began a campaign to lighten his punishment. The growing publicity and demands for his freedom from persons outside the prison became a major nuisance for the Bureau of Prisons, and in 1942 Robert F. Stroud, without his birds, was sent to Alcatraz. To continue his punishment for killing the officer, he was confined to D block.

On the evening of April 28, 1946, according to the account Quillen provided later, Stroud "started moaning and groaning and carrying on that he was sick" and asked to see a doctor. The guards called a medical technical assistant, who took Stroud's temperature and told him nothing was wrong. The other inmates in D block demanded that a doctor be sent. When a doctor failed to arrive, the inmates threatened to "tear this place up." With Stroud "egging" them on, the inmates made good on their threat:

> It was probably about midnight by the time we really got around to wrecking the place. You took paper and you wadded it all up in your toilet. You flushed it and pushed all the water out that you could . . . you could make it go over the top and then you dried the bowl out—you got all the water out. You took paper or magazines or whatever the hell you could get that would burn and you wadded it all up and lit with a match and then you flushed it. And when you did the toilet just went—bang! It just shattered. Then you took a big piece of that and broke the sink. Then you cut the mattress up—tore it up. You'd set fire to it and throw it off the tier. Then you'd take your clothes off and you throw them out. There's water running everywhere. Oh, everybody was freezing their ass off! I was buck naked. I didn't have nothing on. None of us did. Everything in the cell went.
>
> We thought everyone participated. With everybody saying, "What are you doing, Stroud?" "I'm ripping this to pieces." "How're you doing, so and so?" "Well, I'm tearing this place apart." So the next afternoon about two o'clock they come in. We hadn't had anything to eat. We are cold and we are miserable and by then all this gung-ho spirit is gone. I don't know why I took my clothes off and threw my shoes out. Anyhow, they came up and they take you down to court. Well, I had fifteen years good time and I lost half of it. I lost seven and a half years for that caper. I had 5,400 days and I lost 2,700 of them. And you know who didn't break his cell up? Stroud—the guy that was sick.[41]

The new (1941) industries building, the incinerator where Joseph Bowers worked, and the road tower from which he was shot; identifiers by Doug Ward. (Bureau of Prisons.)

Theodore Cole, AZ-258. (Bureau of Prisons.)

Ralph Roe, AZ-260. (Bureau of Prisons.)

Aerial photo of the old (model) industries building with guard tower on roof, site of three escape attempts because of its proximity to the bay. The new industries building is on the right, with the power plant at the top. (Bureau of Prisons.)

The Model Shop building guard tower, with open windows below, which provided a "step" to the roof. (Bureau of Prisons.)

Protruding isolation cells with cut bars in D block; identifiers by Doug Ward. (Bureau of Prisons.)

Cut bars of Henry Young's cell. (Bureau of Prisons.)

Original outer wall of D block, where ventilators and heat pipes provided support for an inmate to cut bars of the window. (Bureau of Prisons.)

Arthur "Dock" Barker, AZ-268.
(Bureau of Prisons.)

Dale Stamphill, AZ-435. (Bureau of Prisons.)

Escapees' flotation gear hastily constructed from furniture outside the employees' housing. (Bureau of Prisons.)

Escapees' clothing and outdoor furniture from employees' housing. (Bureau of Prisons.)

Escape route from D block to the beach where Barker and Stamphill were shot. (Bureau of Prisons.)

Barker Beach, named in memory of Dock Barker. (Bureau of Prisons.)

1935   **1948**

Roy Gardner, AZ-110.
(Bureau of Prisons.)

Henry Young, AZ-244.(Bureau of Prisons.)

Rufus McCain, AZ-267.
(Bureau of Prisons.)

John Bayless, AZ-466
(later commitment no.,
966).(Bureau of Prisons.)

Joseph Paul Cretzer,
AZ-548.(Bureau of Prisons.)

Arnold "Pappy" Kyle,
AZ-547. (Bureau of Prisons.)

Floyd Hamilton, AZ-523.
(Bureau of Prisons.)

Huron "Terrible Ted" Walters, AZ-536.
Shirt and tie allowed for holiday photos
for families. (Bureau of Prisons.)

John K. Giles, AZ-250. (Bureau of Prisons.)

Inmates' band included three men who tried to escape, James Quillen, AZ-586, Arnold
Kyle, AZ-547, and John Bayless, AZ-466; identifiers by Doug Ward. (Bureau of Prisons.)

The escape attempts that occurred during the war years—none of them successful or resulting in staff injuries—were nonetheless cause for concern in Bureau of Prisons headquarters. All of the attempts involved deficiencies in staff training, supervision, or security procedures, somewhat consistent with J. Edgar Hoover's comment, "This prison outfit is certainly a mess." Even though Warden Johnston had lost a number of his experienced officers to the military services and many of the wartime replacements were not regarded as equivalent, the senior administrators—Lieutenant Paul Madigan, Captain Henry Weinhold, Deputy Warden E. J. Miller, and some other senior officers—had continued working on the island through the war years. Responsibility for the security breakdown thus appeared to be located at the top of the staff hierarchy. But because none of the escapes had been successful and the nation's attention was on foreign, not domestic, issues, sufficient grounds for removing Warden Johnston did not present themselves until another breakout attempt in early May 1946.

THE BATTLE OF ALCATRAZ

On the afternoon of May 2, 1946, one of the most dramatic prison escape plots in American penal history began to unfold on Alcatraz Island. In this bold attempt, a group of prisoners planned to achieve what was said to be impossible: obtain guns behind prison walls, take guards hostage with the weapons, and capture the prison launch to get to the mainland. It was an ingenious but very dangerous plan, requiring precision, luck, daring—and, most of all, speed—if it was to succeed. Instead, the attempt triggered a two-day military siege of the island, with automatic weapons and grenades and military forces deployed against the prisoners. Before it was over, two officers had lost their lives, thirteen had been injured, and three inmates had died from gunshot wounds in the cell house. Two more were later executed in the gas chamber at San Quentin while Alcatraz officers watched.[1]

THE CONSPIRATORS

The escape was planned by four inmates, all serving long sentences: Joe Cretzer, Marvin Hubbard, Miran "Blackie" Thompson, and Bernard Paul Coy. Of these four, Cretzer, Hubbard, and Thompson were experienced escape artists. Coy, younger than the others, nevertheless seems to have been considered the group's leader. Like most Alcatraz escapees, Coy was not regarded as particularly troublesome or violent. Serving a twenty-six-year sentence for bank robbery, he had accumulated only two disciplinary reports over a nine-year period on the island, one for joining in the September 1935 strike, the other for fighting with another kitchen worker. Coy had served sentences in Wisconsin and Kentucky state prisons and earned a transfer to Alcatraz because the staff at the Atlanta penitentiary had concluded that "he is possessed of superior intelligence, is prison-wise, reckless, impulsive, and erratic . . . the possibility of any reconstructive therapy of a permanent nature is very remote."[2]

Joseph Paul Cretzer had been involved in a series of escapes since his federal sentence began in February 1940. In a breakout attempt with his brother-in-law and crime partner, Arnold Kyle, at McNeil Island (described in chapter 8), the two blasted through a prison gate in a dump truck. This was followed by the attempt to break out of a detention cell in the federal courthouse in Tacoma, which resulted in the death of U.S. Marshal A. J. Chitty. In May 1941 Cretzer had participated in the attempt to cut the bars in the model building. His only comment after being caught was "I had a lot of time to do and could not see how I could do it; I might just as well get bumped off attempting escape than stay here until I die." In May 1944 he had been caught in a conspiracy with Kyle and another prisoner to escape from the disciplinary segregation unit by boring holes in the back walls of their cells. In an interview with the author Kyle said of his partner's final, fatal attempt to escape: "Cretzer had a life sentence and not much hope of getting out. He was young and when you're young like that a few years ahead seems like a lifetime away."

Marvin F. Hubbard was thirty-four years old and illiterate when he arrived on the island in December 1944. The reason for the transfer was his involvement in an escape plot at the Atlanta penitentiary.[3] Two years after his arrival at Alcatraz, he was involved in another escape plan that was never put into effect because an inmate informed on Hubbard and another plotter. The plan had called for constructing a ladder to go over the wall and taking several yard guards as hostages. For his role in this plot, Hubbard forfeited 730 days of good time. A psychiatric evaluation concluded that with an IQ of 65, he was "definitely on the defective side of the scale" and that an impulsive nature caused him to give "little heed to the consequences of his misdeeds until it is too late to rectify them."

Before he arrived at Leavenworth in June 1945 to begin a ninety-nine-year sentence for kidnapping and motor vehicle theft, Miran "Blackie" Thompson had eight successful escapes on his record—five from a boys' reformatory, two from the Alabama state prison at Kilby, and one from a county jail. Thompson had also served a one-year sentence at Atlanta and a two-year term at the state prison in Huntsville, Texas. At Leavenworth, a psychiatric evaluation found that Thompson "has no insight into the seriousness of his aggressive criminal activity and sees himself as a victim of police and the law." The classification committee unanimously concluded that Thompson's transfer to Alcatraz "would appear to be justified" because of his "long sentence," his "record of eight escapes," and the psychiatrist's conclusion that he was "a desperate individual who would take any opportunity to try to escape."[4]

Clarence Victor Carnes, one of the first convicts to be released from his cell by the others, and Samuel Shockley, who was being held in isolation in D block, were also identified as being closely involved in this breakout attempt. At sixteen, Carnes had shot and killed an attendant during a gas station robbery. He received a life sentence and was sent first to the Oklahoma State Penitentiary and subsequently transferred to the state reformatory.[5] Carnes received a ninety-nine-year federal prison term for kidnapping and escaping from the custody of the U.S. marshal and arrived at Leavenworth on April 24, 1945, at age eighteen. The psychiatric evaluation described him as "a desperate, cruel, aggressive individual who would not stop at anything to gain his own end. It is believed that he will find it impossible to make a good adjustment here. . . . He knows that . . . [he will] have to spend all or most of his life in this prison and in the state prison and will remain a desperate man for years."

As noted in chapter 8, Samuel Shockley was erroneously identified as a participant in Cretzer, Kyle, and Barkdoll's May 1941 escape attempt, but in 1946 the staff still believed he had been involved. Because of his emotional and erratic behavior, combined with his "mentally deficient" IQ of 54, staff vacillated between regarding Shockley as mentally ill or as a troublesome and potentially dangerous malingerer. He was described by a fellow inmate as being "batty as a loon."[6] Four days before the break began on May 2, Shockley participated in the general disturbance in the disciplinary segregation unit described at the end of the previous chapter, in which fourteen inmates in D block trashed their cells. Shockley smashed the toilet and washbowl in his cell, set his bedding and clothing on fire, and tore the clothing hooks off the wall.

PHASE ONE

The plot to escape from Alcatraz was a long time in the making. Kyle, Cretzer's partner and brother-in-law, who was in the industries building when the breakout began, said he knew of the plan and so did many inmates. By the time the break occurred, the planning for it "had been going for at least eight to nine months," according to Kyle, and it was "supposed to have come off three or four different times" before. Kyle also identified Coy as the key figure in the plan, the man the others waited for to make the first move.

In advance, Coy had asked Floyd Hamilton to get him a bar spreader, which would be used to gain access to the gun gallery. The spreader was made up of "one piece of pipe, a bolt and a nut, you cut a notch in the pipe to where it'd fit on the bar and couldn't turn and you put a nut be-hind there and start pushing it out." Hamilton recruited one inmate to get the parts and another to help him smuggle them into the cell house. He devised a clever strategy to foil the infallible metal detectors—called "snitch boxes" by the inmates—by focusing on the fallible guards who manned them. Hamilton had been alert: he realized that when a prisoner trying to smuggle in something metallic was closely followed by another man with a piece of metal, the second man could bump into the lead man at exactly the time the lead man entered the snitch box and set off the alarm, causing the guard at the box to conclude that the second man had set off the machine. The guard would tell the lead man to go on through and then shake down the second man. After succeeding in a trial run, Hamilton and an accomplice tried this tactic with the bar spreader, and it worked.

On the afternoon of May 2, it was business as usual in the cell block. With the noon meal concluded, the inmates with work assignments had returned to their jobs in the industries area, and the others were locked in their cells. Inmate Floyd Harrell said he knew something was up when he talked to Hubbard after lunch on the fateful day:

> My first real knowledge of this escape attempt came shortly after lunch. . . . I remember distinctly asking [Hubbard] if he had planned on going on to the yard. After a short hesitation he looked at me and said, "You're look-ing at a man that's ready to go to hell." Instantly I knew what he was re-ferring to and not wanting to know any more about it, I made no remark whatsoever, I just stuck out my hand; he shook my hand and I walked out of the dining room. Something told me that the cell block would not be a very good place to be, so without a moment's hesitation, I asked the guard to make sick call, went on up to the hospital, feigned some sort of illness, and was confined to the hospital. This proved to be a very wise decision.

Coy was authorized by his job as an orderly to walk freely in the cell house so he could deliver magazines to various prisoners. The cell house officer, William Miller, was covered by another guard, Bert Burch, who was stationed in the gun gallery located on the north wall of the cell house. The prisoners knew that Burch's duties called for him to go through a door in the gun gallery to the adjacent disciplinary segregation unit, D block, where he would cover Officer Cecil Corwin while Corwin was re-leasing men one at a time for showers. During this period only one guard, Miller, was in the main cell house.

Once Burch entered D block, Hubbard—as a kitchen worker, he had finished with the noon meal—appeared at the door between the dining room and the cell house. Miller opened the door to let Hubbard pass through and then turned his back to relock the door. As he did, Hubbard jumped him with a knife and, aided by Coy, took his keys and forced him into a cell on the north end of C block.

Coy and Hubbard ran over to unlock the cell of Cretzer, who took up a post standing guard over Miller. Coy and Hubbard quickly climbed up the bars of the gun cage to the point where the bars curved over to join the wall. With the bar spreader—which had been hidden in the utility corridor between the rows of cells that stood back to back in C block—Coy and Hubbard pried the bars just far enough apart to allow Coy, a very slight man, to wriggle through to a walkway. He clambered down a flight of steps to the second-level walkway that guard Burch would use when he returned from D block. Hiding behind the door, Coy waited until the officer was about to come through, then pushed the door into Burch, and jumped him with fists flying. (It is not known why their struggle did not draw the attention of Officer Corwin in D block.) The two fought briefly, with Coy continuing to hit Burch until he lost consciousness. Then Coy removed the guard's uniform, tied him up, and grabbed his .45 pistol, 30.06 caliber rifle, and ammunition. He lowered the rifle to Hubbard on the cell house floor, dropped the pistol to Cretzer, ran back up to the top of the gun cage, squeezed back through the bars, and climbed down to join the others. Coy, Cretzer, and Hubbard had achieved what the Alcatraz staff had always planned to prevent: prisoners were loose in the cell house, they had guns, and they quickly began releasing other prisoners from their cells.

Their plan called for getting more hostages, then using rifle fire to pin down the guards in the gun towers while they exited the cell house and made their way through the yard with their hostages. They would go down the steps on the west, or Golden Gate, side of the prison to the paved walkway and then turn south to the employee housing area where they would add some women and children to their collection of hostages. The hostages were essential if the plan was to work, as they would prevent anyone from firing on the inmates. The escapees would proceed to the dock area where the tower guard, under the threat of injury to the women and children, would be ordered to lower the key to the prison launch, which would take them to the mainland. As Cretzer's partner, Kyle, later explained, "They had to get out quick; the thing had to work fast or else it wouldn't work at all."

Carnes was one of the first men released from his cell. As he grabbed a knife, he saw Officer Robert Bristow enter the cell house at the east end and begin walking down Broadway. Carnes ran up to the surprised officer and forced him into cell 403, where Miller had been placed. Coy released Thompson to join the group. As guards Ernest B. Lageson and Joseph Burdette (the latter is missing from some accounts) entered the cell house to go to their posts, they were quickly taken hostage and also put in cell 403.

In the meantime, Cretzer went to the window in the door between the cell house and D block. Pointing his gun at Officer Cecil Corwin, he signaled the guard to open the door. Corwin complied. (Corwin would later claim that he opened the door in response to a threat by inmate Louis Fleisch, who as an orderly was out in D block talking to the guard at the time. Fleisch, however, would claim that he "advised" Corwin to open the door to avoid being killed, and that Corwin "was afraid and shaking badly." The plan was to free the D block inmates, particularly Franklin, who had been in isolation since May 1938 for the escape attempt in which Officer Royal Cline was killed. The D block inmates on the second and third tiers were quickly released, but the first-tier cell doors were locked and unlocked not by the mechanical levers of a gear box, but by an electronic system controlled from inside the gun cage. Thus Franklin and the other men on the first floor were never released, which would prevent them from joining the break but also from seeking refuge in other cells during the gun battle that followed.

As the D block prisoners walked through their suddenly open cell doors and down to the main floor, Coy told them that a break was in progress. James Quillen, one of the occupants of D block at the time, said later,

> The first time we knew anything was going down was when we heard the commotion in the gun cage . . . and you could hear voices out there. The door to D block was opened and then our cells were racked open. Hell, everybody was curious about what was going on so we all went down [to the first floor]. When we got close down to the door [to the main cell house], somebody says, "They've taken over the armory." Hell, everybody wanted to go, everybody wanted a piece of the action then.

One D block prisoner, Shockley, grabbed a wrench and joined Coy, Hubbard, Cretzer, Carnes, and Thompson as they searched frantically for the key to the door to the recreation yard. But Officer Miller had hidden that key in the neck of the toilet bowl in cell 403 shortly after he was taken hostage. This would turn out to be the crucial act that foiled the escape plot. As Kyle pointed out afterward, "If they would have gone on with the key like they were supposed to, they would have been [able to go] around to the front office in the armory before anyone knew what happened. They would have had the island."

Back in the control room, Officer Clifford Fish was waiting for reports from the officers normally assigned to the cell house, or from the officers who had gone inside to investigate why a report had not been received. Fish informed Captain Henry Weinhold of the situation. When Weinhold entered the cell house, Coy and Carnes grabbed him. Weinhold was forced to remove his uniform and hand it over to Coy. Quillen, who had come out of his D block cell, recalled:

> A lot of guys came out of their cells, saw the guns, and went back, which was the smart thing to do. But, I had to stick my nose in it and go out there. I walked out and over to the door in the dining room and looked down Broadway and they had just gotten Weinhold and were taking him around the corner by the lever box. Shockley and Cretzer and Coy were there. Something was said between Shockley and Weinhold and Coy told them both to shut up and then Shockley took a swing at Weinhold. Weinhold was very upstanding, he didn't take any guff—he didn't take anything from anybody. He had lots of guts. He turned around and hit Shockley back. Then they pushed him into the cell.

At this point, the escape plotters knew their plan was in trouble. Quillen remembered the words he exchanged with Cretzer and Coy before he returned to his cell to wait things out:

> I said, "How's it going?" He said, "It's all fucked up—go on back in, it's no good. We blew it." So I walked over to Broadway and I saw Coy . . . running around with the rifle. And I said, "What's going on? What can we do? Can we go?" He says, "Go back, we blew it." So I said to Pep [friend and fellow convict], "Let's do what they said and get our asses back in there."

When Captain Weinhold failed to report back, Officer Fish called Robert Baker, who was on duty censoring mail in the administration building, to tell him there was some trouble in the cell house. Baker and Lieutenant Joseph Simpson walked into the cell house only to encounter a rifle and .45 automatic pointed at them, as well as several inmates wielding clubs and knives. They were forced into cell 402, adjacent to the other guards. Officer Carl Sundstrom came in next and was confronted by Cretzer armed with the .45. He was thrown in the cell with Baker and Simpson. Shockley struck him in the face three or four times and ordered him to remove his pants. "Sundstrom was there with just his shirt on, they'd taken his pants off. . . . He's mad as a hornet 'cuz they took his pants," Baker later recalled. "We're sitting there on the bed. And I'm looking out and taking the numbers down of any prisoners I see. I knew 'em all by name and number. So I'm writing on a little piece of paper."

While Cretzer, Coy, and the others were moving about the cell house and taking hostages, a group of prisoners who had finished getting haircuts in the prison's basement barbershop were released by supervising Officer Edward Stucker. As the inmates emerged into the cell house, they glimpsed the break taking place and quickly descended back into the barbershop, shaking their heads. Stucker went up to investigate:

> So I walked up the stairs and looked over at the end of C block and there was Cretzer working the levers with a .45 in his hand. I said, "Good God almighty." About that time he just happened to look over there and he seen me. He swung that gun over that a way and I got back down the stairs.

Stucker called the control center officer to report "trouble in the cell house." (He claimed later that he mentioned Cretzer's possession of a gun, but this was disputed by other custodial personnel.)

Finally, at about 2:30 P.M. Officer Fish called the warden, who came running over and ordered the alarm to be sounded. Pandemonium ensued. The siren alerted everyone on the island that trouble had broken out, and the response was swift but chaotic. Coy began firing at the guard towers with the rifle, first striking guard Elmus E. Besk. From the hospital ward, Harrell saw the guard go down:

> I'd been in the ward less than an hour when we heard rifle shots; they seemed to be coming from the cell block. Those of us in the ward immediately ran to the windows overlooking the yard and the tower. The first thing that caught my eyes was a guard that was assigned to the tower, he was lying on the catwalk face down on the outside of the tower itself. From all indications this man was dead.

Besk was not dead but lay unmoving for many hours. Officer James Comerford, in the dock tower, heard a bullet whiz by. He yelled down to Deputy Warden Miller that there was trouble, heard the glass window behind him smash, and dove to the floor. A guard in the employee apartment building yelled across to him to stay down and he did. "I had a dust pan for protection," he recalled. He remained in the tower until the next morning.

From the hospital window Harrell watched the response to the shots and the siren:

In just a few minutes after this rifle shot, the sirens started screaming and in just no time at all it seemed that there were boats of every description, some with heavy arms, circling the island and most became stationed with their guns trained on the island. In the yard itself, there was guards scurrying about in every direction, seemingly in a state of confusion. But I can assure you this confusion didn't last long. In just a short time, the guards were surrounding the cell blocks—I would estimate in about eight- to ten-foot intervals—most of them armed with rifles that fired rifle grenades. Shortly thereafter the guards started firing these rifle grenades into the cell block itself.

It was clear at this point that the escape plan had failed, and almost all of the inmates returned to their cells, with inmates in D block barricading themselves behind mattresses and law books for protection during the gun battle they expected would ensue. But Coy, Cretzer, and Hubbard were not about to give up. Hamilton remembered an exchange with Coy and Cretzer:

I went to Coy . . . and I said, "What are you people doing fooling around here so much?" He said, "Well, we can't get the key so we're going to try to go some other way." I told him, "If it's alright with you people, I'm just dropping out at this point and going back to my cell; you people are fooling around too long." I told him, "If you'd done something right quick, they wouldn't be bringing the Army and the police over here. You haven't got a chance. The best thing you can do is just give your guns back to these officers and call it quits and a bad deal. The only thing you do is lose your good time. . . . But Cretzer and Coy said, "No we're gonna go all the way, go on back to your cell."

Deputy Warden Ed Miller was the next staffer to enter the cell house. He came with a gas billy club in his hand but he stopped short when he saw Coy pointing the rifle at him. Miller tried to activate and throw the billy, but as he raised his arm, the billy hit the walkway above his head and exploded in his face. With Coy firing at him, he ran back up Broadway and escaped through the steel door into the administration building.

By this time, the escapees had acquired the all-important key 107, which opened the door to the yard, by beating Officer Miller until he surrendered it. But, in their haste to use the key, they jammed the lock. Now with the siren wailing, and the exit to the yard blocked, Shockley began screaming they should kill all the hostages.

Urged on by Shockley and Thompson, Cretzer walked to the front of cell 403 and fired point-blank at the officers backed up against the walls.

Captain Weinhold was hit in the chest and arm. Senior officer X had rushed back to the island from his day off in San Francisco after he heard from a newsboy, "They got a riot over at Alcatraz." He recalled the shooting:

> Weinhold was the first man that was shot in the cells; he was a strict disciplinarian, a good prison man. The convicts, a majority of them, respected him because he was pretty fair. He tried to talk to Cretzer before he was shot. He said, "Joe, you give me the gun, unlock the door, go back to your cell, they can't do anything more with you because you are doing life, plus twenty-five years anyway." Cretzer told him, "There's going to be a lot of SOBs killed today and you're going to be the first." Boom. He got him through one of the arms. It just slivered the bone and of course he fell down and then Joe started to shoot these others.

Corwin and Miller were shot. Cretzer moved to the next cell, 402, where Baker was hiding under the bed with Sundstrom behind him. Cretzer shot Baker in the leg, as well as Joseph Simpson. He began moving away from the cells but on second thought returned to cell 403, reloaded his .45, and aimed at Ernest Lageson. "Lageson was pretty well liked by several of the prisoners; in fact, by most of them he was considered a fair officer," recalled Officer X. After Shockley tried to persuade Cretzer to shoot Lageson, Cretzer replied "I'm not going to shoot Lagy, he's my friend." According to X, Shockley persisted:

> "But the SOB will get on the stand and swear your life away, so shoot him, or give me the knife, I'll cut his throat." That's one thing they wanted to do—open the door and go in with this French knife that they had and cut the throats of the officers but Joe Cretzer said, "No, I'm not going to." This fellow kept egging him on until he said to Lageson, "Lagy, I'm sorry." Boom. The bullet just grazed his face and of course Lagy just dropped right over.

With escape now impossible, Carnes and Thompson returned to their cells and pulled the doors shut. Shockley returned to D block where he joined inmates Butler, Pepper, Sharpe, and Quillen, who had barricaded themselves in a cell behind mattresses and books. Coy, Cretzer, and Hubbard, however, were determined to go down fighting. They made their way to the top of cell block C with their weapons, knowing that with so many officers and the captain shot (and some probably dead), they would likely end up in the gas chamber. The would-be escapees settled into an area where they could try to increase the number of guards who would die with them.

The guards in cells 402 and 403 had no choice but to lie on the cold concrete, bleeding, as the cell house was bombarded by gun fire, tear gas, and grenades from the outside hour after hour. Robert Baker remembered that at one point one of the prisoners suggested, "'Well, let's take 'em out and cut 'em up and use 'em as hostages like they did in the Ohio Prison' but they decided no."

THE BATTLE

The response from the prison staff was poorly organized. Deputy Warden Miller and Warden Johnston gave contradictory orders. Fearing negative publicity, Johnston wanted to avoid both unnecessary bloodshed and recourse to outside help. Because there was no organized plan and the warden was indecisive, the fight dragged on and many officers had to act on their own initiative. The Coast Guard sent boats to circle the island. A contingent of marines came with a demolition expert and grenades, although at first Johnston did not want to let them on the island. Guards from San Quentin arrived with tommy guns, ready to do battle.

Shots began to pour in the windows of D block from outside and ricochet around the cells. For the convicts in the first tier there was no escape. According to Officer Don Martin, "The most amazing part was that no one was hurt except for Jimmy Grove. He got a ricocheted bullet." From the outside it was assumed the armed inmates were in the D block, and if they were kept occupied with fire from outside, it would be possible to rescue the officers in the main cell block. The inmates in D block were infuriated by the gunfire, since they weren't participating in the fight. They yelled out the windows, "You damn bastards! There's no gun in here!"

Harrell, who watched from safety in the hospital, recounted the battle:

> It would be impossible to say how many rounds of ammunition was fired into that cell block on that particular day. . . . The cell block was being rocked as if a state of war had been declared. The shrapnel would sing as it would careen from wall to wall and in the midst of all these sounds of firing we could hear prisoners screaming, some shouting obscenities at the guards, demanding "You bastards blow us off the face of the earth," while others were begging, imploring the guards to stop the firing and not to be killed. This firing continued with no letup. I don't recall the length of time that it went on. But I know it was late evening before a different type of sound was heard. We could hear what appeared to be air hammers on the roof, which later turned out to be true. They were boring holes through the concrete roof of the cell house itself and hand grenades were being

dropped into the cell blocks. After, I would guess, twenty minutes of this constant bombardment, we could no longer hear the voices of the prisoners in the cell block. I felt, and I'm sure other prisoners around me did too, that those prisoners confined to the cell block were all dead. I remember thinking how lucky I had been in asking to be admitted to the hospital. . . . I was consumed with a pure, unadulterated hatred for everything connected with Alcatraz. I was convinced then, and I'm just as firmly convinced today, that it was a deliberate attempt by the guards at Alcatraz to kill every prisoner in that institution.

The firefight continued through the night with no one really clear where the shots were coming from. Lieutenant Philip Bergen and Officer Harry Cochrane wanted to take over the cell block by entering the west gun gallery, but Deputy Warden Miller would not give the go-ahead. They waited armed outside for all of the afternoon and into the night. Finally Miller gave the order for them to get a ladder and look through the windows to see if they could gather more information about the situation inside. It was a risky proposition but, lacking an alternative, they agreed. From outside, the cell house appeared vacant with no one moving about.

Lieutenant Bergen gave permission to a group of officers to enter the west gun gallery through a door that could be opened from outside the cell block. Accompanied by Officers Stites and Cochrane, Bergen entered the gallery.

My God, here you are in a steel cocoon, it's like being under a washtub and somebody beating on it with a hammer, and in addition to that you have all that cordite smoke and they'd already thrown a lot of tear gas in there and you had that too. It was complete pandemonium down there on the ground floor. I said to Cochrane, "Let's get the hell out of here and up those stairs." And so we turned from where we were and started up the stairs, Stites saw us and came after us and at that point in time the guns are still blazing and the ricochets are flying and Cochrane catches one in the arm; we gotta pull back from the stairs and push Cochrane out so he can get some medical care.

They climbed the stairs to the first tier of the gallery, moving quickly since they were in an exposed position. Officers Herschel Oldham and Stites headed off to the right, while Bergen, joined by Officer Fred Mahan, moved to the left. Nothing was moving in D block, so they decided to check the main cell house. Stites came around and started to pass in front of one of the exterior windows, when suddenly he dropped to the floor, calling out that he had been shot. While the others kept up a volley of shots into the cell block to provide covering fire, officers brought out a ladder to get Stites to safety. A minute later Oldham cried out that he had been hit too, and then on the lower tier Officer Fred Richberger caught a bullet in the leg from a ricocheted shot. The gunfire was coming in the windows from outside, but the officers inside still believed it was enemy fire coming from the inmates. Mahan recalled: "You didn't know where the guns were and nobody knew where the shots were coming from. They're firing all over around in there. It was confusing, you couldn't tell who was shooting at what."

It was not until Bergen noticed a line of bullets on the wall opposite one of the windows that it began to dawn on him that the shots might be coming from outside. Richberger suggested "an old Indian trick" to test the theory. He put Bergen's cap on the end of a rifle and moved it in front of the window. Immediately a shot was fired, knocking the cap from the rifle. Bergen called out to Deputy Warden Miller: "Ed, there's some crazy SOB that's shooting at us from the roof of the hospital and there's already four or five shots been fired through that window and if you don't get him stopped, he's gonna accidentally kill one of us." Miller did not believe him until Bergen and Richberger repeated the rifle trick, and he heard the resulting shot. Miller ordered the man on the roof to stop firing. According to Bergen, Miller shouted, "You crazy SOB up there, you fire one more shot and I'll blast you off that roof with a Thompson!"

Bergen later commented,

> They fired half a dozen shots out of the prison and about ten thousand from outside the prison into the prison. For what? What was accomplished? If they had any regard for human life at all, if it was just inmates in there, it would have been bad enough. But in addition to inmates, there was a half a dozen or so officers in there and yet they're firing all this crap into that prison. I said to Ed Miller, "What in the hell is going on here?" "Well," he said, "we told them if they were fired on, to fire back and I guess they were fired on." No such orders should have ever been issued. You never fire unless you got a target. And even then you gotta exercise a little discretion about whether you fire or not. What was called for in that particular case was encircling the prison and covering all the access areas. Having accomplished that, the next step is to man the gun gallery. They had done that. They manned the east gallery and got scared off at the west. The third step is to go in and do your job. That's go into the cell house and take it over. Well here's a couple of guys that were expert gunmen, Cochrane and myself, we found out what the situation was and it was deplorable, but nevertheless, we said, "Okay if you're not going to man the west gallery, let's take step three and go in and get 'em."

Mahan wanted to continue inside and take over the cell house, but the warden, having learned that Stites had died and other officers were wounded, still presuming the shots had come from the inmates inside, gave orders to wait. The officers were furious. But in the meantime they were able to rescue Officer Burch. They waited all through the afternoon until midnight, while the cell house was bombarded with rifle grenades.

Several officers went down into the basement under the cell house and tried to track the movement of the armed prisoners through the sounds in the floor. Guards from San Quentin, several of whom had worked on the Rock, aimed Thompson submachine guns into the C block corridor and let off rounds of fire. No one knew where the hostages were because they were all keeping very quiet, not wanting to attract any more attention from the armed prisoners.

Inmates who had been locked in the industries building when the fighting began were brought up into the yard where they spent a cold night without blankets watched over by marines patrolling the walls. According to senior officer George Boatman, "The inmates were cheering on Coy and Cretzer and cussing the Marines and cussing the guards, but by the time they spent a night out there in the cold, they weren't nearly so noisy." The prisoners took down a scoreboard and built a fire to keep warm.

As the siege raged on, thousands of Bay Area residents watched through binoculars as shells, puffs of smoke from explosions, tear gas, and grenades lighted the island. News reporters and photographers crowded onto police patrol boats and a navy landing craft, which brought them to within fifty yards of the island. Newspapers and radio news programs across the country carried reports of the dramatic events taking place in the bay. As the headlines blared "Marines Battle Convicts on Alcatraz," "Terror Revolt on the Rock," and "Alcatraz Gun Battle Raging in Major Riot," the nation's dailies and wire services offered photos of wounded officers on stretchers and hospital gurneys, officers' worried wives and sobbing children, shells bursting against D block, and armed marines on the walls standing guard over inmates in the yard. The accompanying stories emphasized the bravery of the guards and the desperation of the convicts.

The media had always sensationalized attempted escapes from Alcatraz, but in this case reporters moved beyond exaggeration into fabrication. An Associated Press release stated that Officer Harold Stites had been "kicked to death" by convicts who had "a long standing grudge" against him.[7] Another AP report quoted a warrant officer who was supporting the prison staff:

I watched from the visiting room while [guards] rescued other guards. They put down a covering fire so that none of the rebels could raise their heads to fire. Then two at a time, guards would dash into the cell block and carry out one of their buddies until all were safe.[8]

Early news stories identified inmate Louis Fleisch as one of the seven "mad dogs of Alcatraz" and reported that after Joseph Cretzer shot Officer Miller, he "crushed Miller's chest with his boots."[9] The same paper quoted a marine officer who estimated "from the strength of their fire that the convicts might have had 3,000 rounds of ammunition." The *New York Times* reported that the rioting inmates had a machine gun and were picking up tear gas bombs thrown through windows and throwing them back through the windows before they could explode. The *Times* also declared that according to reports from the warden, "most" of the prison's guards had been taken hostage.[10] Other news organizations reported that the marines went ashore at Alcatraz "ready to fight their way in with bayonets and trench knives."[11] Newspapers supplemented their photos and accounts of the battle by listing the identities and gangland affiliations of the prison's notorious offenders—none of whom participated in the "mutiny."[12] In a particularly dramatic account a *San Francisco Chronicle* reporter claimed, erroneously, that the prisoners were firing from inside the cell house at guards on the hillside.

I am the only reporter on this particular boat, and we are 200 yards closer to the fight than the next nearest launch, which is loaded down with heavily armed "Feds." Just above me, it seems, guards are lying on their bellies firing rifles. I watched them hit the dirt—army style—firing, advancing, taking cover. There's a tinge of powder smoke mixed with the salt smell of the cold sea air. The slow, deliberate rifle fire of the guards is being answered by the tommy-gun bursts of the convicts. Apparently they have plenty of ammunition. They are throwing five shots for every one they take.[13]

The next morning, marine demolition expert Charles Buckner was up on the roof of the cell house drilling a hole through which to drop TNT, but he was stopped by Deputy Warden Miller, who did not want the building destroyed. Fragmentation grenades were dropped instead, bursting water pipes and sending shrapnel flying in all directions. "Of course [the inmates] took an awful hammering from the concussion bombs and grenades that were dropped in there from the roof," said Officer Mahan later. "When one of those concussion bombs went off it just seemed like it'd raise you off the floor."

After what seemed to everyone like an interminable time, the firing from outside was halted and quiet prevailed. Warden Johnston gave the order to enter the cell block. Lieutenant Isaac Faulk led the way with Officer James Comerford behind him and a group of San Quentin officers carrying Thompson submachine guns. As they ran down the corridor between A and B blocks, they were fired on but chased Coy, Cretzer, and Hubbard into the utility corridor in C block.

Then the hostages were found. One of them, Robert Baker, remembered the rescue:

> About 1:00 A.M., as near as I can gather, we heard a lot of "sons-a-bitching." It was Miller, the deputy warden, Lt. Faulk, and the plumber, Severson. He was a colonel in the first war and he had a medal of honor, a Congressional Medal of Honor. He come in like old Matt Dillon, standing up shooting. Miller had a machine gun and Faulk had a .45; they was a-cussing and a-swearing and coming in shooting anything that moved. Finally Sundstrom stuck his hand out and found that the gate to the cell had been unlocked, so he opened it. . . . And he run out screaming and waved down the hallway at Faulk and Severson and Miller, so they come in and got us. Of course they took Simpson out first because he had two in the belly, then they brought me out and put me in the deputy warden's office on a stretcher and treated this hole in the lower part of my leg. Then they took us in a marine landing barge over to the Marine Hospital.

Officer Y, one of the men who retrieved the wounded hostages, recalled entering the first cell where the hostages were.

> I found [Officer] Miller; Captain [Weinhold] had been shot, and Simpson, the lieutenant, had been shot, and Corwin was sitting over where the toilet is on the opposite side there at the end of the block and his blood had coagulated. I didn't even recognize him. His head was twice its normal size. I said, "Hell don't bother with him, he's dead. Let's get these others out." At that time [Miller] breathed and a big bubble of blood came out. That's when we decided to get him out of there real quick. Miller was crying. I thought Well Jesus this big sissy, he ain't even hurt. I got a guilt complex after that because the man died very shortly thereafter. . . . Simpson could talk, but you could see he was in pain. The captain was typical German type, stoic as hell. He was hurting real bad—you could tell, he had been shot twice. We got him out and then we got Baker and of course Lageson wasn't hurt. He helped get the others out. So we got all the hostages out and we went back outside and then that's when Mr. Miller said, "They're on top of this cell block, we gotta get 'em."

The armed convicts were presumed still loose in the cell block, and no one knew whether they were still hiding in the utility corridor. The warden and his senior staff talked about what should be the next move. "Just don't do anything," Officer Y recalled the warden saying. "I don't want any more killing . . . just let it go for a minute. Maybe we can wait 'em out." The waiting went on for a long time. Finally, at about two o'clock in the morning, Officer Y spoke and offered a plan to flush Coy, Cretzer, and Hubbard out of the utility corridor: "Let us go in there and ease that door open, real easy. Let me get some shots off. We'll find out where they are." Y described what happened next:

> We got that door open as easy as we could and then fired down at floor level, and kept firing up and down. We emptied about fifteen shots. We didn't get no response. So he [Deputy Miller] said, "Close the door up again." So we closed that steel door and waited and waited and nothing happened.

After a while Y offered to go back into the utility corridor and investigate. Miller gave his assent, Y grabbed a powerful flashlight and opened the door, his .45 in his hand, the light held high in case shots were fired at it:

> So I started back in through that pipe chase [utility corridor]. There's recesses in the floor just like in foxholes, but I finally got where I could see 'em. I could see Coy, he was sitting there with that gun like this across his lap, but he wasn't pointing the gun at me. His eyes was wide open looking at me. I said, "Coy lay the gun down. We'll get you out of here, we won't hurt you. Just lay the gun down." No answer, no moving. You know, I think that was about as frightened as I ever was in my life though. I've heard of people having a peculiar taste in their mouths, it tastes like copper. When I first saw him looking at me, I had this copper fish taste in my mouth, boy I just knew I'd had it. Because there was no place to go, no place to duck. I figured if the man is not firing he's got to be in shock or he don't want to give up, or he's unconscious or something. I could see he had his eyes wide open, looking at me.
>
> Well, I called back to the people outside and I said, "I found Coy." Somebody yelled in there, "Shoot the son of a bitch." I didn't even try to argue with them, what the hell, shooting somebody, that's out. I got closer and I said, "The man's in shock or he's dead or something. But his eyes are wide open and the gun's pointing almost at me, but it's not right at me."
>
> I had the drop on him if he'd moved I could have got him. . . . I moved in a little closer and he still didn't move. By that time I could see Cretzer's head and part of it was gone, with the brains hanging out. So I knew he was no trouble. And then I got on up to where I could see Hubbard and he had one of these knives that had slid out of his hand, laying there right by his hand. And I knew he was out of commission.

The dead prisoners, already stiffening into rigor mortis, were dragged from the utility corridor, Coy first, then Cretzer, and Hubbard. They were laid out on the cell block aisle called Broadway. The key to the yard, number 107, was found on Coy's body. Lieutenant Bergen, who was put in charge of the bodies, described the scene:

> They brought these three guys out, laid 'em down on the concrete floor outside the east end of A block and started counting the holes and one thing or another. Coy and Cretzer were in rigor mortis when we brought 'em out, Hubbard who must've been the last to die was still in rigor. They all were gradually straightened out, kind of a gruesome sight. . . . I was in charge so I got some blankets and covered them up. Very official delegations came in to view them and "ooh and ahh" and poke and look and count. Finally they moved them the hell out of there over to the coroner in San Francisco.

From the basement, Officer Ed Stucker emerged with the twenty-one inmates who had been getting haircuts in the barbershop when the escape began. Stucker and his charges had spent the entire ordeal in what turned out to be the relative safety of the basement barbershop. According to Stucker, the two days he had spent there with the inmates were uneventful, except for his fear that Cretzer—who had seen him poke his head up from the basement when the escape began—would come down and kill him:

> I stayed in down there from that day until Saturday with those men. As far as the men down there with me, not one bit of trouble did they give me. A couple of them told me, "Mr. Stucker, we'll try to keep you from getting hurt if they come down here." I said, "Don't get yourself in a jam because if you do they might hurt you."[14]

The inmates who had been held in the yard were finally returned to the cell house. Because of damage to many of the cells, they were locked up two, three, and four to a cell and subjected to frequent searches. Tear gas clung to every available surface. Waley recalled the hail of bullets in D block:

> It was Meathead [Deputy Warden Miller] that shot through my writing board and through the stacked books I had in front of myself. My cell had 127 bullet holes in it. I had law books and a mattress piled up, and I was under the bunk, they weren't going to kill me. . . .
> After the guards finally came through the door at the end of D block they said, "Don't anybody move." They told us to stand up and I'm a lit-

tle leery about standing up because the day before they had said, "Okay, we aren't going to shoot in here anymore. You guys can stand up and get out of that water." Well, a lot of guys stood up, including me like a big idiot and they really blasted us. When they did come in I didn't know whether to get up. I heard them talking, so I stood up. Then Miller said, "Aren't you dead yet Waley?" . . . I told him a couple of years previous to the breakout, "If you don't stop the tension in the institution, you're going to have a bloodbath." Old Meathead said, "Oh, I like to wade knee-deep in blood."

The press got a brief opportunity to take photos inside the cell house during a tour in which Warden Johnston pointed out the bent bars of the gun gallery, the bloodstained, bullet-scarred hostage cells, and the utility corridor where the dead ringleaders were finally found. During the days immediately following the end of hostilities, the press kept up a continuing flow of articles. The funerals of the slain officers were covered. There was speculation about the future of seventy-two-year-old James Johnston, who said "I can't even think about quitting, I can't let down this splendid staff we've got over here."[15] Readers were provided descriptions of the bodies of Coy, Cretzer, and Hubbard at the morgue, and they read about the "morbid curiosity of the scores of men and women of all ages [who] asked permission to see the bodies."[16] They learned that Joe Cretzer was cremated, and that "his ex-wife, Kay Wallace Benedetti, notorious Bay Area brothel keeper at one time, wept at the brief service." And, they read, Marvin Hubbard's body had been shipped to relatives in Alabama, while Bernard Coy's body lay unclaimed because "nobody wanted him."[17]

THE FBI INVESTIGATION

The FBI field office in San Francisco first learned of trouble at Alcatraz on May 2 when a telephone call at 2:45 P.M. from the warden's secretary reported that an inmate with a "machine gun" was loose in the prison; no assistance was requested. Several calls followed, but after 5:00 P.M., agents got their information from local radio broadcasters who were watching the assault on the cell house from boats offshore. FBI headquarters in Washington, D.C., was informed, erroneously, that in addition to holding guards as hostages, "the prison doctors have been captured." The U.S. attorney's office notified the special agent in charge of the San Francisco office that one guard had been killed and that four others were wounded and had been transported to the Presidio's marine hospital. The federal prosecutor expressed his view that agents should attempt to interview the wounded officers, "in the event they had some information of value to disclose before they passed away." [18]

Clearly annoyed by what he saw as a pattern of federal prison officials not cooperating fully in FBI investigations, Director Hoover told the San Francisco office that the FBI would conduct an investigation at Alcatraz only if it were requested by the Prison Bureau—"and then only if the FBI is allowed to make it *unrestricted* and *unhampered*." [19] Assistant FBI director E. A. Tamm echoed this feeling in a memo to Hoover, citing the necessity of having "free [rein] to conduct our own investigation in the manner and under the conditions we deem appropriate." [20]

In the early afternoon of May 3, BOP director James Bennett called assistant director Tamm to request an "investigation of the facts in this case as soon as the prisoners were subdued." Bennett assured FBI headquarters that he had instructed Warden Johnston and his staff to cooperate in every way and that there would be no interference by the prison staff. To further reassure Hoover, Bennett said he was leaving for San Francisco himself to ensure that the Bureau "got what it wanted." Hoover was not persuaded, however, and instructed Tamm:

> See that our San Francisco office doesn't subjugate itself to either Bennett or Johnston and the same goes for our staff at Washington. I am getting 'fed up' with the 'palsey-walsey' attitude of our officials both here and in the field with individuals who are constantly knifing the Bureau. [21]

In the meantime, San Francisco field office agents went to the Presidio hospital to interview the wounded officers. A "dying declaration" was obtained from William Miller that he had been shot in "cold blood" by Joseph Cretzer. Other hospitalized officers named Coy, Hubbard, Thompson, Shockley, and Carnes as participants.

On May 4 seven agents under the supervision of Special-Agent-in-Charge Fletcher arrived on the island to begin interviewing suspects and witnesses and to gather evidence. The naked bodies of Coy, Cretzer, and Hubbard were examined and photographed, their clothing was packaged up, and the .45 pistol and Winchester 30.06 rifle found with them were sent to FBI headquarters for examination, although prison personnel had handled the weapons in the process of removing them from the utility corridor.

The agents reported back to Washington, D.C., that all prison personnel had "been most cooperative." When James Bennett sent a telegram to Hoover offering his "sincere thanks" for the help of the FBI and the agency's "splendid cooperation and efficient assistance," he also offered to discuss "the details of this amazing mass escape attempt."[22] Hoover, however, declined to respond to his fellow director in the Department of Justice, and he continued to complain about coverage of the role of the FBI in the investigation, noting that news reports about the activity of the assistant U.S. attorney described FBI agents as "accompanying him to Alcatraz." Memos and telephone calls went to Fletcher ordering him "not to serve as a 'flunky' or satellite to the assistant U.S. Attorney or to the U.S. Attorney for that matter."[23] Two federal officers had died, as many as a dozen more officers appeared to have been wounded, and the federal government's highest-security penitentiary was the site of a battle involving the army, the marines, the coast guard, and personnel from San Quentin and other federal prisons—but J. Edgar Hoover was more concerned with the image of his agency.

With this preliminary communication, the relationship between the FBI and the Bureau of Prisons fell into its predictable pattern. For more than a decade, Alcatraz and Bureau of Prisons officials had tried to hold the FBI at arm's length whenever serious problems arose, because FBI investigations tended to go beyond specific incidents to management issues, and because the resulting reports were often labeled Confidential and sent directly to the attorney general rather than to BOP officials. The Bureau of Prisons knew that in a major event such as the abortive escape attempt at Alcatraz, Hoover and his close associates could be counted on to make the most of what might be an outstanding opportunity to heap discredit on another agency, even one within the Department of Justice.

Following their interviews with prisoners and staff, FBI agents identified nine inmates as likely subjects for prosecution, adding Louis Fleisch, Floyd Hamilton, James Quillen, Edgar Cook, Jack Pepper, and Edwin Sharpe to the list that already included Carnes, Thompson, and Shockley. Ninety other prisoners were interviewed. The men who were in the cell house or in D block during the escape attempt and the hours of shooting and bombardment that followed were not reluctant to cooperate with the agents when they were questioned about Coy, Cretzer, and Hubbard. Knowing these men were dead, the inmates readily identified them as the planners of the break, and as the ones responsible for shooting the officers. But no one would admit to seeing any other prisoner do anything wrong. As convict Earl Egan told the agents, "I am not going to say anything about no live guys."

However, the inmates freely condemned the actions of Alcatraz personnel during interviews. Fleisch, for example, contradicted Officer Corwin's account of how Coy and Cretzer gained access to D block and released the prisoners in the second and third tiers, painted Corwin as slow to recognize what was going on, and said he did not know why Corwin, after it appeared that a break might be in progress, had not picked up the telephone and warned the armory what was happening.

Shockley refused to answer any questions from FBI agents, stating only "I have nothing to say and wish to return to my cell." Thompson, on the other hand, anticipating his identification by guards, had written out an explanation of his participation and handed it to Deputy Warden Miller.

Agents interviewed Carnes for the first time, with Deputy Warden Miller present, on the evening of May 4. Carnes claimed that he had never left his cell during the entire break; he refused to say anything else. The following morning he was interviewed again; this time, he said he didn't think he should say anything until he had seen a lawyer. The agents told him to ask prison officials for legal counsel. Carnes thought for a few minutes, then decided to make a statement. The interview concluded when Carnes was allowed to go back to his cell for lunch. When he was called back an hour later, he announced that he did not want to talk any further and refused to sign the statement based on the earlier interview, although he agreed that everything he had said was true. In San Francisco, Special-Agent-in-Charge Fletcher reported that the hostage officers corroborated Carnes's story but identified Thompson as a participant who urged Cretzer to shoot them.

On May 7 a San Francisco attorney, Ernest Spagnoli, sent a telegram to Warden Johnston claiming that he had been retained to defend Carnes, Thompson, and Shockley. The *San Francisco Examiner* reported that Spagnoli had been employed "by a friend," but Fletcher told FBI headquarters that the newspaper had hired Spagnoli and two of his associates. Thompson, Shockley, and Carnes later rejected Spagnoli's effort to represent them.

A call from FBI Assistant Director Tamm instructed Fletcher to confine his investigation "to potential criminal law violations, etc., and not to conduct any administrative investigations of the prison or the authorities."[24] Fletcher was further told to refrain from contact with the U.S. attorney and to submit his investigative reports to FBI headquarters before providing them to the U.S. attorney's office. Fletcher responded that he and his agents were receiving "101% cooperation" from Director Bennett and Warden Johnston. Even so, Bennett was not informed that Thompson had told agents that the director himself might have been taken as a hostage in one version of the escape plan. Fletcher was also told not to provide Bureau of Prisons officials with information on any new leads his agents might develop, since James Bennett was advising the attorney general of developments and was not giving credit to the FBI for the information. Hoover, not satisfied with the credit being given to his agency, noted in handwriting at the bottom of memo: "I am outraged at this. Fletcher is being swept off his feet by Bennett and the Warden. It must stop."[25]

The cases against Fleisch and other inmates named during the investigation were determined by the U.S. attorney to be so weak that prosecution would not be successful. On May 10, a coroner's jury in San Francisco returned a verdict of justifiable homicide regarding the deaths of Coy, Cretzer, and Hubbard. Meanwhile, the U.S. attorney prepared to put Thompson, Shockley, and Carnes on trial.

ASSIGNING BLAME

After the dust of the battle had settled, it was clear to the custodial staff that the escapees' plan had been abetted by serious lapses in basic security procedures. An inattentive guard had allowed the bar spreader to be smuggled into the cell house. The gun cage officer had apparently taken a postlunch nap on his post—a regular occurrence well known to observant inmates. And Coy had been allowed to wander freely in the cell house without supervision. In addition, numerous mistakes had been made in responding to the escape. One staff member after another was sent into the cell house, where the escapees easily took them captive. The alarm was not sounded immediately, not until the warden arrived at his office. Most serious, gunfire was directed from outside into the cell house, which contained not only uninvolved inmates cowering in their cells but prison staff trying to rescue the hostages and subdue the escapees. A high volume of indiscriminate firing killed one officer and wounded several others. San Quentin personnel and U.S. Marine units summoned to the island and prepared for an armed assault in the cell house found little coordinated authority.

In reflecting on the events of May 2 through 4, Alcatraz administrators and officers singled out several guards for criticism: Bert Burch, both for getting careless about his work habits and for not putting up a better struggle with Coy; Cecil Corwin for not calling the control room due to being intimidated by Fleisch; and some criticized Edward Stucker for not giving a clearer warning than "Trouble in the cell house!" after he emerged from the basement and saw Cretzer with a gun. Philip Bergen, a lieutenant at the time of the break who was appointed acting captain to replace the injured Henry Weinhold, described the various breakdowns in security:

> What had happened unbeknownst to all us smart guys out in the front office was that Burch and Bill Miller had cooked up a little cozy arrangement between them which rendered null and void all the damn precautions that had been taken in setting up the security procedures. Burch thought that he was entitled to that full thirty minutes in the sunshine and he may have been dozing, who knows. Convicts have told me they seen him dozing up there. . . . The problem was that Burch, in order to keep from being interrupted during his lunch hour or his siesta or whatever the hell you want to call it, had left in Bill Miller's hands two keys that Bill Miller should never have had, the key to the dining room gate and the key to the yard gate. So now, Bill Miller no longer has to interrupt Burch's lunch, he had the keys. He can go ahead and do it contrary to orders and in violation of all the security procedures. . . . Miller had violated another rule, which said that no inmate could be loose in the cell house unless Burch was up there in the gallery covering him. . . . [So] there's Burch, he's violating his orders and there's Miller, he's violating the orders. That's what made it all possible. Burch is over there in peaceful bliss, eating his lunch, or whatever, and when he finishes his lunch after a leisurely half hour or so, he comes strolling back into the other section of the gallery and gets clobbered.

Some staff members were critical of Warden Johnston's leadership before, during, and after the "battle." George Boatman, for example, commented:

> Shuttleworth [former Alcatraz deputy warden] ran that place for two or three days, as I recall. During this time, Johnston was resting. It was almost too much for the old man, but he was on the phone to [Director] Bennett every day telling him, "We got everything under control." . . . Warden Johnston wanted to retire without any troubles. That [escape] spoiled that.

According to Officer Y,

> Warden Johnston was nervous and frightened, but he was a humanitarian to the end. He wanted to spare lives as much as possible and he was determined to do that. Of course, some of the rest of us didn't quite feel that way about it, Mr. Miller especially wanted to go after 'em. He was restrained by the warden from going ahead and doing some of the things that might have ended this thing a little earlier. . . .
>
> When you see some of your own people shot up like I did, then you get an anger. . . . I'm not no hero, but you get a feeling that, "I wonder how long it's gonna be before I get hit." [At one point] I went down to get a

sandwich and come back up. As I was walking back up the roadway I was wondering to myself, if I get hit, what's gonna happen to my family. What are they gonna do with them? Kick them off the island? Things like that were going through my mind. It wasn't that I was wanting to be a hero or anything, I had a job to do and we wanted to get it done. And, we had a feeling in our own mind that we might be next. It's a hard thing to describe, but when you see your own people hurt and killed, boy, you want to get in there and really whack 'em. That must be what motivates people in battle. They're not particularly heroes, they are not particularly anxious to hurt anybody but they want to get the people that hurt their friends and that's the feeling that went through the officers. . . .

[Officer William Miller] was a real hero of the whole thing. He really prevented the exodus from that place where they could of got out and taken control of the road tower and got down and took the women and children in the boat. And they'd already expressed the fact if they got to the boat they would get what they wanted or they'd kill one kid, or woman, and throw 'em off the boat just to prove what they was gonna do. They had enough fuel in that boat, they could of went a long ways. That man was the real hero because he dropped that key in that toilet with all the rest of the stuff in there and of course the water was dirty, and they didn't fish around to get the key. He didn't tell them and the result was they tried to force it out of him and I think that's why he got shot because he wouldn't tell. If anybody deserved an accolade, that man did. Of course he's dead.

Officers and midlevel administrators complained among themselves that the need for screening on the gun cage had been recognized before the escape—it had even been purchased and stored on the island—but had not been installed because Warden Johnston was of the opinion that the wire would impair the gun gallery's appearance.

Many officers criticized the lengthy and indiscriminant firing of bullets and shells into the cell house during the siege and were clearly angered by the fact that this "friendly fire" had killed one officer and injured several others. Philip Bergen focused on staff carelessness:

We knew who killed Stites, and we thanked our lucky stars that he [guard on roof] didn't have his rifle leveled when we went through that same damn place that Stites got killed a few seconds later, he coulda got us too. What was supposed to have been a pushover turned out to be a pretty dangerous operation, although we didn't have sense to realize it was dangerous until it was about over. It was dangerous for all the wrong reasons. There was no gun in D block and no shots were fired from D block, not at that point. . . . The guys in the segregation block told me later that they chased

Coy out of there because every time he fired a shot they would get about a thousand shots coming back from the outside.

They were scared to death that they were going to get hit, they were all at the back of the cells behind as many mattresses as they could pile up in front of them. Actually nobody in that block was hit, nobody was injured in any way, shape or manner. It's incredible. . . .

All the precautions that they set up for keeping contraband out of the cell house are easily rendered null and void by some dumb or inattentive officer, and we had enough of them to fill a barrel. You ask how you do it? Well, you put a false bottom in the garbage can. You send a push broom down to the shop to be repaired and you hollow out a place in the top part of the push broom where it comes together and you put your contraband in there. There's as many different ways of smuggling contraband in and out as there is of identifying contraband. And no matter how carefully you indoctrinate these [officers], the incidence of people who don't give a damn or who are careless or indifferent or whatever, will always confound you and defeat you. So that's how contraband got into the cell house, piece by piece.

Robert Baker, one of the injured hostages, made similar points:

Everybody was shooting. There were guards that got buckshot in their rear ends—the convicts didn't have any shotguns, so how'd that happen? Stites was shot getting into the west gun gallery . . . it came from the roof. The direction of the bullet that went through him, was from the guy on the roof. . . . The same with the two men . . . that had [been hit by] the buckshot—that was caused from the roof shooting down into anything. . . . This fella Burch who was in the west gun gallery, I'd heard that he said he fought for his guns, he fought this Coy, who was a little bitty man. He said he fought for his life to keep the guns from going down into the cell house. So he come into visit me [in the hospital] and I was laying there with a cast from [my waist] down. They'd found that other bullet hole, patched me up, and I was in no pain. So I looked him up and down and I said, "Where's all the black eyes and busted nose if you fought for your guns?" He had fifty rounds of 30.06 and then he had forty rounds for the .45 automatic. I says, "Where's all your hits?"

And if Stucker had told Fish [in the control room] that the guy had a gun, that would have made a big difference. We would have tackled the whole thing from a different angle. We'd have gone outside and looked in instead of going in naked, with no gun.

Finally, officers observed that escapes would always be possible as long as ingenuity and careful observation on the part of inmates were combined with lax attitudes, regular routines, and carelessness on the part of the custodial staff. According to George Boatman,

[The inmates] spent all their time thinking of ways to escape . . . they never quit. They were always looking . . . they watched the guard if he switched his routine, if he had a little weakness, they would capitalize on it. That was the story in that breakout of the Model Shop when Cline was killed. They noticed the guard in the hill tower, the one that looked down [on the model building], every afternoon as soon as the inmates went in, he went to the toilet, and there was a curtain you could pull around so that you'd be hidden from view. [The inmates] noticed that.

Boatman went on to give grudging praise to the conspirators:

This escape was ingenious; the inmates looked and looked for one little weakness and took advantage of it. Coy found that somebody had the brilliant idea that those bars of the gun gallery ought to be dusted and he was the cell house orderly so they sent him up there to dust the bars and he found that place where they didn't join and then somebody observed that Burch went over to D block and visited every afternoon and that was the two things they needed.

Staff mistakes aside, the breakout attempt nevertheless demonstrated the difficulty of actually overcoming the entire range of security measures on the island. Although the prolonged military-style assault left two officers and three inmates dead, several officers seriously wounded, and the prison badly damaged, no prisoner had succeeded in getting off the island.

THE TRIAL OF SHOCKLEY, THOMPSON, AND CARNES

On June 19, 1946, a federal grand jury indicted Shockley, Thompson, and Carnes for "committing murder on a federal reservation," assaulting federal officers, and violating the federal Escape Act. The defendants pleaded not guilty in federal court in July; their cases were bound over for trial in the fall. The court appointed attorneys for Carnes and Shockley and finally allowed Ernest Spagnoli to defend Thompson. Spagnoli tried to meet with Carnes and Thompson but was rebuffed by the federal district court and by Warden Johnston. His request was referred to Director Bennett, who after consultation with the attorney general's office, denied Spagnoli permission to visit the island or to bring members of the press with him. On June 21, however, a district court judge ordered Warden Johnston to allow Spagnoli to visit Thompson.

Meanwhile, James Bennett asked the attorney general to designate a

special attorney to handle the prosecution because, in his opinion, the
U.S. attorney in San Francisco, Frank J. Hennessy, "has not been successful in the prosecution of Alcatraz cases." Bennett had not forgotten
the success of inmate Henry Young five years earlier in overturning the
government's case against him and putting the prison on trial instead.
BOP headquarters did not want to provide another opportunity to the
prisoners and critics of Alcatraz to provoke more calls to close down operations on the island.

As the date for the trial drew near, the *San Francisco Examiner* described the defense strategy. For the Bureau of Prisons it had a familiar
sound, but Attorney Hennessy went ahead with the prosecution.

ATTORNEYS PLAN PROBE OF ALCATRAZ BRUTALITY

DEFENSE COUNSEL FOR RIOT TRIO
SLATE EXPOSURE OF PENAL TREATMENT

Sam Shockley, the Alcatraz convict scheduled to go to trial November 20
with two fellow inmates on charges of murder, may never reach the prosecution stage. Defense counsel for the trio, convinced that the rigors of
confinement on the Rock have "washed out" Shockley's mind, plan to request that a court-appointed psychiatrist examine the Oklahoma kidnapper-
robber before the case goes to trial. . . . Meanwhile, court appointed Defense Lawyers Archer Zamloch (for Carnes), William A. Sullivan (for
Shockley), and Ernest Spagnoli and Aaron Vinkler (for Thompson), it was
learned, are prepared to probe the whole Alcatraz system "down to its
roots" once the trial begins. Tentative plans call for parading a virtual
"Who's Who" of the nation's onetime toughest criminals, including one
set of witnesses to "alibi" the roles of Thompson, Carnes, and Shockley
in the riot, and another set to testify to these defense allegations: 1. That
"psychological brutality" has left many inmates "stir crazy" and has plunged
others into actual insanity. One convict, going over a tentative witness list
for defense counsel, crossed off 60 percent of the names. "You can't use
these guys, they're insane," the convict, Ray Stevenson, told defense lawyers
Spagnoli and Vinkler. 2. Failure of a prison doctor to treat six inmates in
D block on the night of April 27, after they claimed to have become ill
from the food they were served, produced a demonstration in which fourteen block members wrecked their cells.[26]

Among those who would be called, the newspapers reported, would be
Floyd Hamilton, Thomas Robinson, and George Kelly, all former stars
on the FBI's list of "public enemies," along with the "Birdman," Robert
Stroud. Other witnesses for the convicts would include Whitey Franklin,
who had killed a guard himself, Harmon Waley, one of the prison's ma-

jor troublemakers, and Ted Walters, who had also tried to escape from the Rock. Even J. Edgar Hoover was impressed: "This will be some aggregation if it is ever assembled. See that we play no part in 'security.'"[27]

But the inmates, the press, and the critics of Alcatraz would be disappointed if they expected a replay of the defense strategy employed in the Henry Young trial. Judge Louis Goodman excused the jury from the courtroom and then warned the attorneys for the accused that convict witnesses would be allowed to testify only to issues in the case and not to "extraneous matters," such as discipline on the island, the management of the prison, or comparisons of Alcatraz to other penitentiaries.

The trial began on November 20, with rumors persisting that the defense would put witnesses on the stand who would provide alibis for the defendants and "expose the brutalities that caused the men to want to escape."[28] The prosecution began with testimony from guard Ernest Lageson, who explained how he had written the names of six convicts on the wall of the hostage cell, names that identified the defendants in addition to the dead ringleaders. Cecil Corwin and other officers ended their testimony by leaving the witness stand, walking over, and placing a finger on each of the defendants as participants in the revolt. Guard Joseph Burdette explained how the key to the yard had been hidden from Coy:

> When Miller walked into the cell [where Burdette had already been placed], his thumbs were tied together behind him. I asked Carnes, "Alright to untie Miller's hands?" Carnes said, "Yes" and I untied him. Mr. Miller then gave me key 107. That was the key to the outside yard. The seat in the cell had been let down against the side of the wall. I hid the key behind it.[29]

Lt. Joseph Simpson testified that Thompson, with the rifle, was the convict who took him hostage, and Burdette said that Carnes looked into the cell after Cretzer had fired at the hostages and said, "They're all dead—let's go."

Deputy Warden Edward Miller had a difficult time on the stand. Defense attorney Archer Zamloch asked him if he was "the most hated and feared man on Alcatraz" and if, "on the second day of the Alcatraz breakout, he and another guard had taken Carnes out of his cell, stripped him naked, and incarcerated him in a small storage room." Miller denied taking such action, but Zamloch demanded, "Didn't you, on the third tier of the cell block, mercilessly beat and kick Carnes, and isn't it a fact that you put this knife [Miller's pocket knife] against his throat and said, 'I'll put a scar on you here that you'll have the rest of your life'?" Miller replied angrily, "No, I treated Carnes just like any other prisoner." "Then the Lord help the prisoners," replied the attorney.[30]

Captain Henry Weinhold was brought to the courtroom from the hospital at the Presidio. The jury was told that he was being retired from the prison service as a result of having been shot through the chest. Weinhold testified that Cretzer had fired at him just after the prison siren sounded and that Shockley had yelled, "There goes the siren. Go ahead and kill them," after which Cretzer shot him.

The defense introduced Shockley's mental health into the proceedings. Seven inmates, including Henry Young, Louis Fleisch, and Whitey Franklin testified that they considered Shockley to be "stir crazy." Shockley took the stand and told the jury that he received "radio voices" that "stayed on all night" communicating "evil words," telling him that he had been born on another planet, and that he was subjected to mental control by false accusations.[31]

Spagnoli asked Thomas Robinson, a former Public Enemy no. 1, about the mental condition of prisoners, and Robinson began to reply that Alcatraz was so badly managed that men were being driven crazy. The judge, however, cut his testimony short, warning defense attorneys that if more attempts to introduce "extraneous matters" were made, no further inmate witnesses would be allowed.

Henry Young, identified by the defense as a man who had spent "nine years in isolation at Alcatraz reading and studying psychiatry," testified that he had been helping Shockley with his mental problems: "I told Sam the sadistic environment in the institution was the direct cause of insanity here."[32] The prosecution objected to this line of questioning, but Judge Goodman allowed it. Then attorney Spagnoli, co-counsel for Thompson, angered the judge by "demanding a court order that Warden James A. Johnston produce Alcatraz hospital records to show how many convicts had gone insane."[33]

Eight of Clarence Carnes's fellow prisoners tried to help him after he followed Thompson in the dock. James Audett told the jury that he was working in the kitchen area when Coy and Hubbard came in, and that as Coy began shooting through the windows at guard towers, he described Carnes, "as a puppy tailing the heels of the tough guys, who nevertheless pushed Hubbard when he tried to shoot the deputy warden as Miller ran back down the cell block main corridor." Audett claimed that

Hubbard was angry with Carnes but did nothing about it. He further testified that Carnes was with him in the kitchen when shots were fired at the hostage guards. Carnes took the stand himself, claiming that he didn't want to hurt anyone but did want to escape from the island through "walled-up tunnels of the ancient Spanish dungeons." He admitted that he saw Shockley strike several of the guards, but that Shockley was running around, talking to himself, and Hubbard told him, "That's Sam. He's crazy." Carnes concluded his testimony by asserting that he had told Officer Lageson to lie low, and that he saw other officers breathing— "some were groaning"—but told Coy, "They're all dead."[34]

The trial ended up with the prosecution arguing that as conspirators, Shockley, Thompson, and Carnes were as guilty of killing Officer Miller as the man who actually pulled the trigger of the gun. U.S. Attorney Hennessy, however, told the jury that Carnes was "one of the better witnesses for the government. . . . I believe he probably assisted in saving the life of guard Lageson" (although he also disputed the claims that Carnes had jostled Hubbard to spoil his aim at Miller and that Carnes was in the kitchen at the time shots were fired into the cell).[35] Judge Goodman instructed the jury that matters of discipline at Alcatraz, how the break was handled, or other matters related to the operation of the prison, were not their concerns.

On December 22, the jury returned verdicts of guilty for all three defendants but recommended life imprisonment for Carnes rather than the death penalty. Judge Goodman then imposed these sentences. As he was being escorted from the courtroom, Miran Thompson shouted at reporters, "It's just as well! I'd rather have it that way [the gas chamber] than go back to the Rock." In his cell in the county jail on Christmas, Thompson told the U.S. marshal that he wanted to donate his eyes to a blind war veteran.[36] Three days later, Thompson and Shockley were transported to San Quentin's death row.

Samuel Shockley's mental health continued to be an issue as he awaited execution. A medical review by the acting chief medical officer at San Quentin concluded that while Shockley had a "borderline defective, inadequate, psychoneurotic, psychopathic, inferior personality," he knew "fairly well the difference between right and wrong, what he did, and what he is to be punished for," and therefore should "be executed, despite his mental instability."[37]

Several months later, however, two psychiatrists and the prison doctor examined Shockley again, concluding: "He, in our opinion, does not know the nature and character of his offense, nor does he appreciate fully the sentence that is imposed on him. We feel that he is mentally unstable, and there is a large question in our minds, whether he is legally sane."[38]

The possibility that an insanity diagnosis might allow Shockley to escape the gas chamber troubled federal authorities. U.S. Attorney Frank Hennessy wrote to the attorney general questioning the "right" of San Quentin officials to conduct examinations into the mental health of Shockley or Thompson, who were federal prisoners. If any further psychiatric examinations were undertaken, argued Hennessy, they should be conducted by persons selected by the attorney general.[39]

In June Dr. George Johnson from the Stanford University Medical School, and Dr. Justin Fuller, federal medical officer, examined Shockley and concluded that he was attempting to simulate insanity. In July three San Quentin psychiatrists concluded that Shockley understood the nature of the proceedings against him, knew that an execution day had been scheduled, and therefore was sane.[40]

In the months that followed, Shockley's and Thompson's legal advisors proposed that their clients receive executive clemency, and the pardon attorney asked James Bennett to comment on their applications. Bennett argued against the assertion that neither man was in on the planning, citing Thompson's request for a "lay in" on the day of the escape, and noting (inaccurately) that Shockley, having been involved in an earlier escape attempt with Cretzer, was one of the first men released by Cretzer in D block. Bennett also dismissed Thompson's claim that conditions at Alcatraz drove him to take desperate action, pointing out that he had been on the Rock for less than seven months.

The matter of the death penalty did, however, give James Bennett cause for soulful reflection:

> I have long had grave doubts about the wisdom of capital punishment in any case. I do not think I could qualify to sit on a jury where the death penalty might be imposed. If, however, there are cases where extreme penalty is justified, it seems to me here is one. It is the cruel and wanton killing of Guard Miller and the ruthless shooting of a group of officers who were defenseless hostages that is involved here. This was no accidental shooting or killing under emotional stress. It is the sort of crime almost impossible to understand. How could these or any other men, for that matter, commit such atrocious acts and have so little regard for human life? Unless one feels there is no instance where the supreme penalty should be

exacted, there is little that even the most understanding can say for these two men. There is finally to consider whether commuting such sentences to life imprisonment would hamper the administration of our penal institutions. Setting aside my own feelings about the death penalty, and measuring such action only in the way I know our Wardens and officers feel about this case, I can say unhesitatingly that they would consider it a serious setback to the discipline and well-being of our own service if these men were to suffer in effect no penalty. Since both of them now have life sentences, anything less than the death penalty would be tantamount to excusing them entirely. The increasing number of desperate offenders, kidnappers, and killers who are being sent to our institutions greatly complicate our problems. For men who have little to lose anyway to get the impression they can attack and murder prison officers with impunity would all but destroy the morale of our service and set back tremendously our efforts to develop a rehabilitative program for those prisoners who are cooperative and anxious to regain their self-respect and become useful, law-abiding citizens.[41]

Miran Thompson's sentence was appealed to the Circuit Court of Appeals by attorney Melvin Belli, who had been hired by Thompson's family, but the conviction was upheld. At 10:00 A.M. on December 3, 1948, Samuel Shockley and Miran Thompson were escorted to the gas chamber. Alcatraz officers, including hostage Robert Baker, Lieutenant Frank Johnson, Officer Joseph Steere, and Captain Weinhold's replacement, Ralph Tahash, attended at the invitation of the U.S. marshal; Tahash submitted an account of the execution to James Johnston's successor, Edwin Swope:

Our wait for the proceedings to get under way was very brief. Promptly at 10:00 A.M. Shockley was led in by three guards. The officers immediately began adjusting the 10 straps, one across the chest, one across the stomach, two on each arm and two on each leg. Shockley's face was expressionless and uninterested until one of the officers began adjusting the strap across his chest. Shockley then turned his head and a terribly vicious expression came over his face and he spat directly in the face of the officer. His face again became expressionless and he dropped his head and appeared to be staring into his lap.

Thompson was then led in. He walked in very erect and smiled when they instructed him to sit down. He sat very quietly while they strapped him in with a half smile on his face. When the last strap was attached and the officers were leaving the chamber, he turned his face toward Shockley, smiled and spoke. It appeared he was bidding Shockley good-bye, but Shockley did not look up neither did he reply.

The sound of a lever being thrown, the falling of the pellets in a container of water and their gurgling as they contacted the water was quite audible. Thompson began to hold his breath at the first sound as if wanting to prolong his life as he had to take a breath.

The fumes did not hit Shockley as quickly as they did Thompson, but when they did, his reactions were the same as Thompson's, head and eyes rolling back. His head remained in a half back and half side position for about a minute and then fell forward. After his head fell forward it remained in that position with saliva running from the corners of his mouth—still in seeming defiance even in death. We left the chamber at 10:07.[42]

Robert Baker found the trip to San Quentin satisfying:

When we got [to the witness area], they lined us up around the circle and I got way over at one end so I could see their faces. You couldn't hear anything except that the guards came in and went through the motions, but you couldn't read their lips or anything. The only thing interesting was to me that they did tell 'em take a deep breath and not to hold their breath. We could hear that over a loudspeaker and then one guy did as he was told and he just went to sleep, just like that. . . . I made a statement right there, I said, "Well, it evens things out . . . two of us were killed and five of them."

Following the executions, the story circulated among the Alcatraz staff that one of the witnesses had given the middle finger salute to the men seated next to each other in the gas chamber. The officers at Alcatraz might have been pleased that justice had been done regarding Coy, Cretzer, Hubbard, Shockley, and Thompson, but they were angry that Carnes had not gone to the gas chamber. As senior officer X put it,

[The officers] were very, very bitter. Carnes was one of the instigators. He was a no good little Son of a Bitch all the way through and he caused nothing but trouble. He would have been executed if the prosecuting attorney had kept his mouth shut but after summing up the evidence, he said if there is anyone of the three that deserves any leniency it's this boy, he's only nineteen years old. But he didn't say this boy of nineteen years had killed two or three people already.

THE AFTERMATH AND THE END OF AN ERA

In many ways, the battle of Alcatraz marks the end of what this book has referred to as the gangster era. That era defined the purpose of the new federal prison at Alcatraz as a measure specifically intended to combat sensational bank robbers and organized crime figures that were the focus of much publicity in the Depression era that ended with World War II. The celebrity figures of Capone, Dillinger, Machine Gun Kelly, and Bonnie and Clyde faded from the front pages. As the data in this book show, locking up "public enemies" was the primary business of the prison only for a short period; other troublemaking prisoners in the federal system, particularly those with escape histories or extremely long sentences, constituted the bulk of the population transferred to Alcatraz. Moreover, the composition of the institutional population at Alcatraz (and U.S. prisons in general) was beginning to shift, adding larger numbers of black and other minority offenders to the prison census. Alcatraz would run another fifteen years but would take on a broader range of problems. By 1946 the entire country was moving into what would be a decade of great postwar social change on many levels. The prison world itself would move from the cliché of the "big house" penitentiary intent on control and deterrence to the concept of "correctional treatment," best embodied in the newly organized California Department of Corrections with the indeterminate sentence and the as yet untested assumption that a variety of psychological and educational programs would lead to the rehabilitation of convicts.

The battle of Alcatraz was not only the most deadly, dramatic, and costly event that had ever occurred in the prison's short history, it was also one of the most serious disturbances in American penal history. Until the deadly violence at Attica State Prison in New York twenty-five years later, no prison uprising so thoroughly captured the attention of the public, the media, and government officials. An event of such magnitude could not pass without serious consequences.

As the nation was caught up in analysis and disagreements about the prison, its prisoners, and the federal government's reason for its establishment, Alcatraz administrators made several changes to improve security. Immediately after the revolt was put down, the silent system was reimposed. Inmates accepted it for a few days, understanding the level of anger the staff felt over the deaths and injuries sustained by their fellow officers. Heavy wire mesh screening was placed over the gun gallery bars, cross bars were applied to the gun gallery so that a bar spreader could not separate the bars, and heavy steel plates were installed over the entire west end gun cage from floor to ceiling in D block. Two officers were assigned to the west gun gallery, one on the cell house side and one on the D unit side, and one man was placed in the east gun gallery (a practice that soon stopped). Portholes to allow gunfire from outside were punched through the walls of the cell house at various places. The barred enclosure that covered the entrance and stairway from the cell house to the basement was made solid with concrete. The hole in the roof through which satchel grenades had been lowered to blow the escapees out of C block was repaired, the interior of the cell house was painted, windows were replaced, and the landscaping improved. The gates and doors between the cell house and the administrative area were reinforced. A window was placed in the door in the gun gallery connected to D block so that officers could look through to the other side. The improved security in the physical plant did little to alleviate the custodial staff's anxiety, however, because they remembered the confusion that characterized the response of the warden and other administrators and they worried that one of them might become a hostage in the next escape attempt.

In Washington, D.C., and elsewhere across the nation, the May 1946 drama of armed conflict in the nation's most visible penitentiary revived the issues surrounding Alcatraz that were somewhat dormant during the war. Bureau of Prisons headquarters had to contend once again not just with questions about the value of a special regime for habitual and incorrigible prisoners, but also with harsh criticism of the prison's management. As had been the case before, the American Devil's Island image that had grown up around Alcatraz colored the debates and helped shape public opinion. And it did not help that reporting of the battle itself had been so inaccurate.

In the nation's newspapers, the bulk of editorial opinion seemed to come down on the side of condemning Alcatraz, its administrators, or some aspect of the American criminal justice system for which the prison could stand as a symbol. As might be expected, many editorials expressed concern about security arrangements and flaws in the training and supervision of guards that allowed inmates to obtain guns inside the cell house. A *Newark News* editorial commented on the prison's problems, "It must be an ironic reflection for the federal authorities that this lethal riot outdoes the wildest imagination of scenario writers in the most romantic concepts of the composers of radio scripts."[43] Another article, "The Barbarism of Alcatraz" in the *Cleveland Plain Dealer,* condemned "the queer, perverted sentimentality of jurors which makes them hesitate to condemn a man to death for the atrocious crimes, but does not prevent them from consigning a man to linger out his life in a living death, a slow, anguishing torture of interminable confinement in hopelessness and despair. [In the future, Alcatraz will be regarded] as a curious relic of medieval barbarity extended into modern times." The writer concluded however that, "two brave and innocent men who served as guards would not now be dead . . . if society had not been so 'merciful.'"[44]

The *Washington Post* published a commentary entitled "The Rock, a Monument to Society's Failure," which cited the crime wave of the early 1930s as the source of the "public hysteria, or vindictiveness" that produced the prison. Alcatraz was, in the writer's view, "a place of horror and blood . . . the logical pinnacle of the 'eye for an eye' penal system . . . last week the blood and horror found their way to the front pages again."[45]

The *Philadelphia Bulletin* asked, "What About Alcatraz? Is It America's Shameful Devil's Island?" Two prominent academic criminologists, Negley K. Teeters and Harry Elmer Barnes, added their voices to the tide of criticism. They reminded *Bulletin* readers that they had long been critical of the "lock psychosis" that they contended would negatively impact the prisoners. In Barnes's view, "sending a man to the island has the effect of building up his prestige in his own mind, and to his cronies. He believes he has to become a real desperado to live up to his reputation." According to Teeters, "Alcatraz represents sterile penology, it smacks of the 19th century." He was "chagrined that no humanitarian in this country has come out against the glorification of the Rock and studied brutality toward the convicts there. Guards and prisoners live in a vicious twilight state of mutual hate." The two penologists also criticized the cost of keeping a prisoner at Alcatraz—$3,127, compared to $500–700 a year at other federal prisons. They concluded, "Progressive prison men deplore the existence of Alcatraz. It persists, a horrible contrast to the otherwise humane and scientific philosophy that permeates the federal system."[46]

The title of an editorial in the *Milwaukee Journal* posed a similar question—"Is Alcatraz a Relic of Medievalism?"—and then indicated its view in its subhead: "The Island Rock, Where Worst of the Bad Men Are Confined for Punishment, Not Reform, Has Been Severely Criticized as Modern Torture Chamber." The jurors' call for an investigation following the Henry Young trial in 1941 was cited as evidence of harsh treatment, along with the claim that confinement in the dungeons on a diet of bread and water, shared with rats, was the punishment for rules violations.[47] To its critics, Alcatraz appeared to stand in opposition to the arguments for humane custody and the rehabilitative aims of a profession now calling itself "corrections."

As always, there was a contrary perspective advanced mainly by editors of newspapers in smaller cities and towns. The *Reno Gazette* claimed that "The Alcatraz affair—instead of showing the unsuitability of that prison—has effectively demonstrated that the institution is ideally located and well-equipped as a 'cage' for incorrigibles." Articles memorializing the deaths of officers Miller and Stites appeared in many newspapers, and one asserted that "just as surely as though they had worn GI uniforms, they died like soldiers in the defense of their country . . . the nation's enemies are both within and without."[48]

New Hampshire's *Manchester Union* warned that "the silly and dangerous chatter about coddling prisoners" should not lead to laxity in prison discipline for "men who regard reform as an evidence of weakness." According to the *Portland (Maine) Press Herald,* the guards and marines responding to the escape "had but one duty—to take the prisoners alive or dead at whatever cost; to kill them, if necessary, like rats in a cage." One big city paper, the *Detroit Free Press,* also took a hard line, editorially commenting: "It can only be hoped that when the escape attempt is finally subdued the score shows a large number of dead among the prisoners, for no man locked up at Alcatraz has any business being alive in the first place."[49]

In San Francisco, the battle rekindled objections to using the island for the nation's most notorious penitentiary. The *San Francisco Examiner* sent a telegram to U.S. Senator William F. Knowland urging "the elimination of Alcatraz . . . as [a] menace to [the] population in [the] light of recent riots."[50] The Civic League of Improvement Clubs and Associations wrote to its congressional representative, asking that the prison, "inhabited by the most desperate criminals in the United States, many of whom are murderers who should have been executed instead of being supported by the tax-paying community," be removed from the metropolitan area. The league further expressed concern that due to the prison's proximity to the mainland, a mass escape with consequent danger to the citizens was a distinct possibility. An editorial in the *Examiner* agreed.

> What can be more conducive to hatching an escape plot in the mind of an embittered felon, serving out virtually his life than the location of Alcatraz? He sees the city's skyline before him, continually. It is so near—the Freedom, Life, and Lights. Days, months, he lives with it. It looms up, a constant mirage before him. . . . A prison's chief purpose is to change criminals into useful men. But Alcatraz, with its history of bloody revolts, appears only to aggravate criminality into hopeless vengeful savagery. . . . The Alcatraz penal institution is a blot on the bay. By now federal authorities should realize this—and transfer it elsewhere.[51]

Four members of California's congressional delegation met with U.S. Attorney General Tom Clark to appeal for the removal of the penitentiary.

They characterized the May uprising as evidence that the prison constituted "a constant menace to Bay Area citizens."[52]

Despite the storm of criticism following the battle, the Bureau of Prisons did not seriously consider the possibility of closing Alcatraz (that would not happen until 1963). But the battle did produce one major change—the ending of the Johnston era. James Johnston had weathered many controversies at Alcatraz, but this time he could not evade responsibility. Most Alcatraz employees placed the blame for the decline in security at the prison, and for the confused handling of the attempted breakout, at Johnston's feet—and Bureau of Prisons headquarters shared this view.

Johnston resisted the assertion that there were problems at the prison. Trying to look on the bright side, he pointed out that the breakout had failed; that the inmates had been able to obtain only one rifle, one pistol, and seventy-one rounds of ammunition; and that Coy and Cretzer had been unable to release Whitey Franklin, the man they most wanted with them. Even while the break was in progress, Johnston resisted the idea that he or any of his staff was responsible:

> My preliminary investigation . . . indicates that there was not the slightest dereliction of duty, negligence, or lack of courage on the part of any officers . . . the capture of guns was one of those incomprehensible and diabolically clever plots that no one believes could possibly have been anticipated.[53]

Despite the warden's claims, Bureau of Prisons officials were unhappy with his management style. On the anniversary of the revolt, Director James Bennett wrote to Johnston, citing a report by a Bureau jail inspector that listed "organizational and personnel weaknesses" at Alcatraz:

1. When the Inspector, who was unknown to Alcatraz personnel, arrived on the island, no effort was made to establish his identity or examine his credentials.
2. Cells were full of "junk" such as guitar strings, medicines, and even a "pet mouse sleeping in a pencil box in a nest of cotton . . . bread and water had been provided and a home made run-around wheel."
3. Officers were "appeasing the inmates" by not reporting rules violations. Officers that did report prisoners found their laundry "not properly done or torn."
4. Officers were allowing inmates to go into the employees' residential area to do maintenance, plumbing, and electrical work—jobs that should only be undertaken by members of the staff.
5. No annual systematic reports on inmate progress or lack thereof were made. The absence of such basic information would leave no record for future administrators to use in making decisions such as transfers or to

measure the effectiveness of certain policies. The same point applied
· to personnel records.[54]

A few days later, Bennett received a lengthy report from C. J. Shuttleworth, who had been deputy warden when Alcatraz opened and, after
working at other federal prisons, had returned to the island in October
1946 to serve as acting deputy warden in relief of the injured E. J. Miller.
Shuttleworth informed Bennett that Alcatraz had become "quite loose."
All but one copy of the original sheet of rules for inmates written in 1934
had disappeared; no new rule book had been developed. There were no
written orders for the various officers' posts. There was no daily report
of admissions to or releases from either solitary confinement or disciplinary segregation, no record of prisoners admitted to or released from the
hospital, no reports by officers leaving their watch of "anything unusual"
happening to alert those coming on duty.

Shuttleworth noted that the prison had been unable to fill twenty-three
guard positions, which negatively affected operations. Officers were spending too much time on one post, such as the officer who had had the same
assignment for more than nine years. At roundtable meetings with the
warden, officers had stopped speaking up or making suggestions, "because there was too much of an effort on the part of administrators to
talk them down and not correct the situations."·

In regard to the inmates' practice of sabotaging the laundry of employees they did not like, Shuttleworth reported that his own laundry
had been torn up and nothing had been done to remedy the situation.
Sixteen or more prisoners were assigned as cell house orderlies with insufficient work, allowing them to "run loose around the building all day
doing as they pleased." Shuttleworth reduced the number of orderlies to
six and they were locked up as soon as they completed their work assignments. He said he found one prisoner who had never been assigned
or forced to work during the two years he had been on the island. When
the disciplinary committee removed privileges from inmates, Deputy Warden Miller allowed them to go to the yard and attend movies before their
period of punishment had expired. The tower next to the powerhouse
was of no use, Shuttleworth reported, but Warden Johnston would "not
stand for it being vacated."

Beds in cells were not neatly made up—the blankets were simply pulled
up covering many items that should not be in the cells. According to Shuttleworth, the cells contained so many "books, magazines, musical instruments, sheet music, drawing pads, easels, paint brushes and finished paint-

ings and other things for so-called study purposes" that it was "physically impossible for any of the officers to thoroughly search the cells."

This harshly critical report concluded with a list of dishonest, incompetent, and "burned out" employees who Shuttleworth felt should be removed, including "several employees who are not now nor ever have been fully qualified for such work." The prison doctor, he said, should be replaced by a psychiatrist. Most notable of the employees who had been at Alcatraz "too long," he said, was James Johnston:

> While Warden Johnston is still in apparent good health, still talks a good game and puts up a good front for a man going on 74 years of age, he is not the man he was in the early years of Alcatraz's existence. In fact, I know that he does not know by any means everything that is going on. Some effort was even made to keep him from knowing what is going on.[55]

In his usual polite manner, Johnston asserted that the director must be receiving faulty or incomplete information because the problems cited either did not exist or had been resolved despite the strain on personnel due to the presence of many workmen engaged in making structural changes within the cell house. Given the Bureau's critical assessment of his administrative ability, it was not surprising to anyone on the island that the Department of Justice found a way to remove Johnston as warden by means of a promotion to the United States Board of Parole. On April 30, 1948, almost two years to the day after the battle of Alcatraz began, James A. Johnston retired.[56]

In addition to replacing Warden Johnston (and assigning a new deputy warden and a new captain), Bureau headquarters decided it was advisable to modify the policy that had denied journalists access to Alcatraz since its opening. In August 1947 Willard Edwards of the *Chicago Daily Tribune* was allowed to "lift the steel curtain of secrecy which has concealed America's 'Devil Island.'" Claiming that he had been "allowed to mingle freely with the 248 inmates," and that Warden Johnston "kept nothing back," Edwards included not a single comment by a prisoner or employee in his series of eight articles published in the *Tribune*. After reading the articles, James Bennett and his associates must have wondered why they had kept the press away from the island for so many years. Edwards commended "the cool confidence" and "calm supervision" of the warden and he praised Alcatraz officers as "stronger, braver, smarter than the officers at other prisons" while dealing with "the nation's most vicious and degenerate." According to Edwards there was "no brutality, no stark existence leading to 'stir-craziness,' no cruel or unusual methods of punishment, no deprivation of food or clothing or exercise for those abiding by the rules . . . during long hours of touring the island and it's structures, the reporter witnessed only the most orderly functioning of a well rounded institution."[57]

Following this praise of the work of the Bureau of Prisons in keeping the meanest felons—or "human TNT," as Edwards described the inmates—away from the public, the Bureau received numerous requests (many stated as demands) that reporters from other news organizations be allowed to visit the island.

In June 1948 another journalist, Albert Deutsch, gained access to the prison but his articles were somewhat less charitable to the federal prison system. He was not allowed to talk with any inmate or employee, other than brief conversations with several senior administrators, including the new warden, Edwin Swope, who had been on the island for only a month. Like Edwards, Deutsch employed dramatic rhetoric to describe "the Dreaded Isle of Dead-Enders in Crime," but he brought a perspective different from that of the *Chicago Tribune* reporter. He contended that spending $6 per day for each prisoner (much higher than the average for other federal prisons) to run a prison with as many staff members as inmates (106 guards and 148 additional staff to supervise a population of 245) was putting too much money into the "wrong end" of the criminal justice system:

> The Rock, rising like a ghostly fortress out of the fog of San Francisco Bay, is a grim monument to our perverse genius for concentrating science at the wrong end of the criminal road. One is overwhelmed by the bewildering array of scientific gadgets—including the latest in electronic devices—mobilized for the single purpose of keeping some 245 human beings caged on a five acre island. . . . As you pass through the intricate maze of steel gates and cell blocks you can't help thinking how much more sense it would make if we expended as much time, money and brains in preventing delinquency as we do providing cages for the dead-end debris of adult crime. If we did that there would be no need of an Alcatraz to remind us of our social failures.

Deutsch also claimed that "years of highly restricted movement" at Alcatraz, and being "out of contact with the normal world," had reduced many convicts to "a peculiar condition resembling feeble-mindedness" that could be compared to "a sort of living death." He claimed that the chief medical officer, Dr. Richard Yokum, supported this conclusion and added that Dr. Yokum estimated that "about one out of every four Alcatraz inmates is suffering from psychoneurosis."

Based on his one-day visit, Deutsch accepted the warden's statement that the inmates were treated humanely: there were no "sadistic, brutalizing individual beatings and tortures found in many penal institutions." Although Deutsch reported that the prison provided a "splendid industrial program" and good food, he concluded, "Personally, I'd rather be dead than a longtime Alcatraz inmate."[58]

At that point in the prison's history, neither the Bureau of Prisons nor Alcatraz's wardens could respond with any evidence to counter claims about the effects Alcatraz was having on the prisoners' mental health— or address the related question of how inmates fared after they were transferred to other prisons or when they returned to the communities they left. Part 3 of this book deals with these matters, based on data that Alcatraz employees and inmates and federal officials never had. But first, part 2 examines more closely the daily lives of inmates, the ways in which they resisted and coped with the restrictions placed on them, and the details of the lives of inmates who were notable either for their celebrity or for their extraordinary responses to confinement on the island.

PART II

LIFE ON THE ROCK FOR RESISTERS AND PUBLIC ENEMIES

10

RESISTANCE AND ADAPTATION

The daily existence of Alcatraz inmates as it was designed for them by the Bureau of Prisons, and as it was managed and enforced by the prison administration and custodial staff was discussed in earlier chapters. Here we turn to the related topic of how inmates reacted to and coped with the regime that was intended to regulate every aspect of their lives. Given the actions of Alcatraz convicts in chapters 4 through 9, it is easy to come away with the impression that some of these men were desperate and violent, and a few, mentally unbalanced. But in fact most prisoners stolidly did their time. They held strong beliefs about right and wrong, and had the same needs for social interaction and faith in the future as law-abiding people on the outside. Although the purpose of the Alcatraz regime per se was not to deny these elements of humanity to the inmates, the control exercised over them did in large part have this effect.

As indicated by the title of this chapter, inmates' responses fell into two main categories—resistance and adaptation. *Resistance* involved denying or seeking to minimize compliance with the order imposed by the prison or trying to reduce the influence of the regime on daily conduct. *Active resistance* reflected some level of conscious conflict. *Adaptation* meant seeking to utilize or assimilate elements of the imposed order to a form acceptable to the self and converting resources available to make life there more comfortable. *Active adaptation* involved some form of conscious accommodation.

These categories are conceptually distinct but overlapping. Resistance was for many inmates an important part of adapting, or coping. But some forms of resistance had little to do directly with coping, and some modes of coping did not involve resistance. The inmates responded to their circumstances by working the system, resisting the controls, and rearranging their mental lives to find ways to meet their personal needs.

A UNIQUE POPULATION

Although they had much in common with prisoners anywhere, it was also true that the Alcatraz inmates differed from most of their counterparts in state and other federal prisons—and this fact had important implications for their prison society. Many had been the leaders of sophisticated criminal enterprises, or the leaders of escape plots in other prisons. Compared to the average felon, they were intelligent, strongwilled, and self-assured. Almost all of them had accumulated considerable experience doing "big time" in very tough prisons. The members of this unique population approached their years on the Rock with a mindset somewhat different from that of their counterparts at Leavenworth or San Quentin. They referred to themselves as "convicts," not as "inmates," a term that connoted subservience to authority.

Each of them had been specially selected for transfer to the Rock, which even before it opened was widely regarded as the toughest joint in the country. For those who appreciated or sought reputations as the best of the bad, a transfer to Alcatraz could be seen as an achievement—a measure of a man's status in the world of penitentiaries. Being sent to serve time with Al Capone, Dock Barker, Machine Gun Kelly, Alvin Karpis, and the country's most notorious "public enemies," tough guys, and escape artists was, for some of these men, akin to gaining admission to the most prestigious law school or graduate program in the nation. Many Alcatraz inmates had large egos and an enhanced sense of their own importance. Warden James Johnston recognized this quality in the men who arrived on the first trains from Atlanta and Leavenworth:

> They were supposed to be the worst men in the country. They were reported to be dangerous. It was apparent that some of them liked the idea of being rated tough and intended to live up to their reputations—to do what they were expected to do to qualify as "big shots."[1]

Alcatraz convicts were also more likely than other prisoners to highly value and express the macho characteristics of toughness and the ability to endure hardship. While American culture in general encourages seeing hardship and overcoming obstacles in a positive light, Alcatraz prisoners saw doing time in a prison called the Rock as a test of character. If being able to take anything that prison guards could dish out without showing fear or weakness was an important measure of strength for American convicts, then the challenge of surviving the experience of doing time in a prison designed to be the toughest of them all provided the supreme test of character. Those who rose to that challenge felt justifiably proud and earned respect from others.

The fact that the men imprisoned on the island were a select group sharing a very challenging experience also predisposed inmates to develop socially cohesive bonds of camaraderie and solidarity. In this sense, Alcatraz inmates were very much like the survivors of a natural disaster or the members of a military unit during combat, experiencing the unique bonds that only shared trauma or hardship can produce.

Finally, many of those imprisoned on the Rock were facing very long sentences, with an unknown amount of that time to be spent on the island. As noted several times in earlier chapters, this prospect produced in some a feeling of hopelessness that translated into a tendency to take extreme risks. As Warden Johnston noted, "they were in a mood to risk anything, not caring much whether they lived or died."[2]

For prison administrators, these characteristics posed serious challenges to the task of controlling inmate behavior. On the inmate side, the particular characteristics of the men sent to this island prison created a unique prison society. To this day the successors of the Alcatraz convicts locked up at Marion, Illinois, and later at Florence, Colorado—the federal government's supermax penitentiaries—still memorialize the men, the time, and the prison where prisoner solidarity under the convict code was a reality.

INMATE CULTURE AND THE CONVICT CODE

During the 1930s and 1940s, the informal norms and rules that governed convict life and social interaction at Alcatraz—and made up the fabric of its inmates' culture—bore some resemblance to what prevailed at other federal and state prisons of the day. But the prison culture at Alcatraz had many distinctive features—the product of placing a unique population of inmates, with their particular value systems and life experiences, in the context of such a restrictive regime.

The majority of Alcatraz convicts were white and from working-class backgrounds. They had grown up in rural areas in the Midwest and Southwest and had been raised with very traditional values in poor but generally law-abiding families. Key among these values were the assertions that a man had to stand up for his rights and his self-respect, remain loyal to his friends, and take care of his family. These values became the foundation of a convict culture that emphasized psychological strength, solidarity with other prisoners, and unwavering opposition to the staff.

The solidarity came in part from doing time with men they already knew. During their first days on the island, many prisoners recognized in the yard, dining room, or workshops former crime partners, friends from the streets, acquaintances from other federal prisons, and associates from state penitentiaries and reformatories where they had served time. In this era of prison history, before witness protection programs and incentives for informing were in place, very few crime partners testified against each other in exchange for reduced sentences (a practice common in today's prisons that has produced hostile and often lethal relations between once close criminal associates).[3]

In addition to loyalty among friends and partners, there was a strong sense among inmates of shared values and interests. Even if a fellow convict wasn't a close friend or associate, there was a certain responsibility to look out for his welfare and expect the same in return. In a world defined by the opposition between guards and convicts, this sense of shared interests and reciprocity developed into an unwritten set of rules for behavior that idealized the white, male, working-class values shared by most inmates during the 1930s and 1940s.

This set of rules was not unique to Alcatraz. Indeed, in the 1940s it was recognized as such a distinctive feature of American prison life that sociologists began to study it and give it a name: the "convict code."[4] The convict code—with its essential proposition that one should never provide information about, let alone testify against, any fellow inmate— was very similar to the code mentioned in chapter 1. It was, in essence, the outlaw code transplanted to the prison context. Although the convict code existed in other prisons, gangster-era inmates on the Rock exemplified it: they followed its tenets more strongly and more consistently than any other group of prisoners in federal history.

For this reason, understanding the convict code is essential in understanding inmate culture at Alcatraz during the years that so many "public enemies" and their criminal associates occupied cell space. The code was much more than a prohibition on giving staff or FBI agents information about fellow cons. As an expression of a coherent set of values, it had a fundamental role in shaping the inmate community. Its general effect—as expressed by George Kelly in a letter about life on the island— was to create "comradeship—a rough kindness of man to man."[5]

In their classic 1960 study, Sykes and Messinger described the elements of the code, showing how it was embodied in various maxims that could be grouped into five clusters.[6] Even though their analysis was not derived from studying social life at Alcatraz itself, it accurately represents the essential components of the convict code as it existed on the Rock.

The first cluster of maxims involved group identification and solidarity. These directed a convict to be loyal to his "class," namely himself and his fellow convicts. As Sykes and Messinger put it, "Prisoners must present a unified front against their guards no matter how much this may cost in terms of personal sacrifice." The most important rule in this category was the prohibition against betraying a fellow convict to institutional officials, summarized by the rule Never Rat on a Con. Related maxims included Don't Be Nosy; Don't Have a Loose Lip; Keep Off a Man's Back; Don't Put a Guy on the Spot. All these directives existed to protect inmate interests, which according to Sykes and Messinger consisted mainly of "serving the least possible time and enjoying the greatest possible number of pleasures and privileges while in prison."

The second set of maxims instructed convicts to "refrain from quarrels or arguments with fellow prisoners." They included Don't Lose Your Head, Play It Cool, and Do Your Own Time. Sykes and Messinger pointed out that these maxims emphasized the control of emotions (they used the term "curtailment of affect"). They also noted that these rules were subject to exceptions: if an inmate confronted a "legitimate provocation," the need to maintain self-respect might demand a response.

In the third category were maxims prohibiting inmates from taking advantage of one another "by means of force, fraud or chicanery." They included the following: Don't Break Your Word; Don't Steal from a Con; Don't Sell Favors; Don't Be a Racketeer; Don't Welsh on Debts. According to Sykes and Messinger, these prohibitions were all related to an ideal: "inmates should share scarce goods in a balanced reciprocity of 'gifts' or 'favors,' rather than sell to the highest bidder or selfishly monopolize any amenities."

The fourth cluster of maxims revolved around the theme of "the maintenance of self." These maxims, best summarized by Don't Weaken, indicated the high value placed on maintaining personal dignity and withstanding "frustration or threatening situations without complaining or resorting to subservience." The maxims in this category—such as Be Tough: Be a Man—emphasized courage and tenacity as essential elements of self. These values tended to trump the value placed on avoidance of conflict. As Sykes and Messinger put it, "Although starting a fight runs counter to the inmate code, retreating from a fight started by someone else is equally reprehensible."

Finally, the fifth category defined the inmates' value system in opposition to that of the world of the authorities. For Sykes and Messinger the maxims in this cluster "forbid according prestige or respect to the custodians or the world for which they stand." Best represented by the maxim Don't Be a Sucker, they express contempt for "the values of hard work and submission to duly constituted authority" and express the general attitude that "guards are *hacks* or *screws* and are to be treated with constant suspicion and distrust."

The events recounted in previous chapters provide examples of how strongly the convict code—particularly its prohibition against incriminating fellow convicts—affected the behavior of Alcatraz convicts. Inmates in various industries shops provided materials to the plotters preparing several escapes and had information about plans, including the takeover of the cell house in May 1946. When Hamilton, Cretzer, Barkdoll, and Kyle tried to escape from the model building in 1941, inmates who were witnesses never provided the information that would have implicated Hamilton in the plot, allowing him to avoid the punishments given the other plotters. Similarly, other prisoners in D block before the escapes of Barker, Stamphill, Young, McCain, and Martin were well aware that cell bars were being severed. It was especially obvious that something unusual was happening because the plotters emerged from their cells a number of times to work on cutting the bars covering the window. In none of these cases did any inmate try to gain a transfer or to increase his chances for a parole by giving information to the staff.

Like all value systems that spell out an ideal for conduct, the convict code was sometimes violated, even at Alcatraz. The degree to which inmates adhered to the code had implications for the complex of roles that comprised the structure of the inmate community. Those who strictly abided by all the code's tenets were "good cons," "right guys," or, as Sykes and Messinger put it, the "heroes of the inmate world." These men earned not only the respect of their fellow convicts but also in many cases the respect of the staff, since in being good cons inmates were expressing some of the same basic working-class values held by the staff. Alcatraz convicts who achieved this status in a population comprised almost entirely of high-status convicts from across the country, men like Harvey Bailey, Floyd Hamilton, Charlie Berta, and Arnold Kyle, were characterized by strong personalities and outstanding careers as bank robbers and as escape artists. Although they had an affinity for risk taking, they were smart in assessing the costs and benefits of various courses of action. As bank robbers they were accustomed to exercising caution and care in planning their activities. In their lives before Alcatraz, their intelligence, personal charisma, and fearlessness had led others to seek them out as partners in criminal enterprises.

The inmates who violated the rules of the convict code had decidedly different roles in the convict community. Those who provided information to the staff about other inmates—the informers or rats—earned the contempt of their fellow inmates (and to a certain extent that of the staff). The ostracism, threats, and physical abuse directed at Rufe Persful was an example of the consequences of betraying fellow prisoners. There was also a small group of prisoners who fought with their fellow inmates or with staff for no obvious reason—thus violating the maxims Don't Lose Your Head and Do Your Own Time. Some of these men were admired for their continual confrontations with the regime, but the actions of others were seen as serving no greater purpose for the population at large and only served to make the perpetrators' lives more difficult. The most notorious of these "outlaws" will be described in the next chapter. Finally, there were the "crazies" or "bugs," whose erratic actions demonstrated an inability to show toughness and courage and stand up to the challenge of doing big time.

It should be noted that during the gangster years there was also a small number of men who were regarded by the general inmate population as outsiders by virtue of the fact that they did not share the working-class backgrounds and values of their fellow convicts and were imprisoned on the island for different reasons. Included in this group were several spies and some military prisoners who could not be controlled in military prisons but had long sentences for sex offenses, primarily rape, and were sent to Alcatraz during and immediately following World War II. These men had not violated federal laws for financial reasons, and since the Alcatraz convicts endorsed the traditional value of patriotism, several of the Nazi "saboteurs" were threatened or attacked on the yard and sex offenders were always treated with contempt.

CONTROL AND RESISTANCE

As chapters 4 through 9 have made very clear, the Alcatraz convicts did not simply acquiesce to the rules and restrictions imposed on them by the prison regime. The work strikes, food strikes, organized protests, escape attempts, disturbances, and individual acts of defiance described in those chapters show that resistance in its varying forms was a defining feature of life on the Rock, and a major determinant of the prison's historical development.

Acts of disobedience began almost as soon as the first shipments of convicts from Leavenworth and Atlanta arrived on the island and continued in one form or another throughout the prison's thirty-year history. Many of these acts were purely individual—a particular inmate refusing to obey a certain rule, for example. And many were collective efforts in which groups of inmates acted together, planning, strategizing, and coordinating activities. Both individual and organized resistance constituted direct challenges to the authority of the staff and clearly communicated the determination of the inmates not to passively submit to the existence on the island the Bureau of Prisons planned for them.

Bureau officials and Warden Johnston, of course, should have expected that of all inmates in the federal prison system, those selected for placement at Alcatraz would be the least likely to accept the excruciating degree of control over their activities envisioned by the regime's designers. Placing these troublemaking, defiant, escape-prone inmates in a prison with the most restrictive set of rules established in any American prison of its day was an explosive combination. Seen in this light, what is perhaps most surprising about Alcatraz's history is not the fact of inmate resistance but the relative peacefulness that prevailed for long periods of time in between episodes of confrontation. Understanding how inmate resistance could be a defining feature of life at Alcatraz without continuous and pervasive overt conflict between inmates and guards requires a closer examination of the phenomenon of resistance.

All prisons, regardless of their ultimate goals, engage in a fundamental activity: they endeavor to control inmate conduct. How a prison organizes the means for this control determines, more than any other factor, how it differs from other prisons. Alcatraz was distinctive in that it had the authority to employ an exceptionally wide variety of coercive sanctions for the direct control of behavior. But direct observation of actual prison life makes it clear that *resistance* to control is another fundamental dimension along which prisons vary. No prison has achieved complete conformity, and theoretically no prison ever could. Inmate conformity to rules is variable. No silent system was really silent; contraband flourishes in all lockups; prison rules are routinely violated; overt resistance, escape attempts, and various forms of individual and group rebellion are as much a feature of prisons as is control.

Neither full control nor effective resistance can be assumed. In many prisons of this era dominant groups of inmates exploited other inmates;

in some prisons staff entered into cooperative arrangements with certain prisoners to obtain information or cooperation. Some guards were intimidated and even at Alcatraz several officers became involved with prisoners by smuggling contraband in and out of the prison for them.[7] In some state prisons administrators gave up control inside prison walls to powerful convicts.[8] There were no such leaders or bosses at Alcatraz— a fact that was demonstrated when Alvin Karpis stepped forward to represent the interests of his fellow food strikers; this effort at leadership was promptly rejected by the custodial staff who locked Karpis up in disciplinary segregation and by the other strikers who did not recognize any other prisoner as their boss.

The phenomenon of control in prisons has received much attention from philosophers and sociologists. Jeremy Bentham and, more recently, the French philosopher Michel Foucault have portrayed the prison as a machine capable of minutely controlling all aspects of prisoners' existence. An alternative to the notion of the prison as an omnipotent machine has been provided by sociologist Erving Goffman, whose conception of the "total institution" highlights how inmates work out particular arrangements through a variety of devices and thereby fashion a mode of prison life more in line with their own needs and interests. But Goffman does not concern himself with evasion of rules by inmates or with effective control of inmate resistance.[9] To achieve a more complete view of prison life, it is necessary to conceive of the dimensions of control and resistance to control as existing in opposition to one another, always in tension, each shaping and affecting the other.

The reality of prison life at Alcatraz fits this conception. The custodial staff was never completely successful in enforcing rules, and the inmates were never completely successful in developing structured resistance. Attempts to implement a high level of control were met with active inmate resistance; the result could be a softening of control or suppression of the active resistance with a reimposition of control. A good example of this dynamic that was resolved in favor of the inmates was the silent system, which was an attempt to impose an extreme level of control, but inmate resistance to it was so strong and took so many forms, most notably when every convict began talking in the mess hall, that the administration abandoned it as unenforceable.

The push-and-pull nature of the power struggle, however, was not always active and overt. The conflict between the forces of control and resistance found levels of equilibrium that were stable for relatively long periods of time, until new or different challenges arose. The fact that no overt struggle was taking place during these periods did not indicate any diminishment in the inherent, underlying conflict—nor in its power to shape social relations in the prison.

The convict code played an important role in modulating the conflict between inmates and staff. The element of convict culture represented by the maxim Do Your Own Time meant to staff that an inmate should stick to himself and refrain from becoming involved in any organized activities, protests, or plots. An inmate following this directive would not present a custodial problem, but the convicts' interpretation of this maxim was: do not interfere with any plot or activity involving another convict. In other words, mind your own business and don't screw anything up for another prisoner.

An aspect of the convict code that tended to reduce overt conflict was the tenet that directed inmates to be tough and courageous—to face stoically the deprivations of prison life. As long as circumstances allowed inmates to see prison life as a test of their manhood, as a challenge to which they could rise, the tendency to engage in active resistance or confrontation was somewhat mitigated.

Other components of the convict code, however, pushed in the opposite direction, encouraging resistance. Maintaining self-respect tended to call for resistance, as did identifying with others as members of a group whose interests were opposed to those of the staff and refusing to accept the values of the regime that legitimized the prison's existence. For Warden Johnston and the Bureau of Prisons, the explicit purpose of the Alcatraz regime was to counter these attitudes and prevent the misconduct they produced; but the history of Alcatraz is the history of efforts by the prisoners to deny that purpose.

What these differing tendencies in the convict code point to is not so much a fundamental contradiction in the code as the contingent, situation-specific way in which the convict code, and inmate culture generally, played into the interaction between the forces of control and resistance. During the battle of Alcatraz, for example, the code can be seen operating in both directions, depending on the context and the individuals. The shooting of the hostages demonstrates the strength of the feeling that guards were a separate class to be despised and beaten into submission, whereas the decision by inmates loose in the cell house not to participate in the uprising, along with those in the basement under the supervision of Officer Edward

Stucker, show the importance of both minding your own business and Being Smart by Not Doing Anything Stupid.

From the point of view of individual motivation, each Alcatraz inmate had a number of reasons for resisting the regime. Some of those motivations were fairly obvious. By engaging in organized resistance with an explicit goal—such as a food or work strike—inmates could collectively hope to extract some sort of concession from the administration that might lead to an easing of restrictions or an increase in the quality of daily life. Because Alcatraz had a long list of onerous restrictions unknown in other penitentiaries, inmates had plenty of targets for their protests, as well as ample motivation for taking the risks inherent in resisting. Taking part in organized resistance also allowed a prisoner to express the solidarity demanded by the convict code. By showing support for fellow convicts, an inmate not only conformed to expectations, he achieved higher social status and the psychological reward of acting according to his own convictions.

Less obvious were the motivations for resistance based on psychological needs. For most men, it was important to assume a posture that would allow them to maintain their integrity and self-respect—this generally meant taking a stand to show first and foremost to themselves, and secondarily to the staff and other inmates, that there were times when they could not, would not, submit to the rules and regulations that were intended to control every aspect of their lives. This response is well founded in the "locus of control" theory in psychology, which explains behavior in terms of the need to be in control of personal environment.[10] All penitentiary inmates experience this need, but at Alcatraz—where an inmate's working and sleeping hours, his meal schedule, his food allotment, when he could take a shower and shave and what clothing he could wear and how it was to be worn were part of a conscious effort to remove any freedom of choice—the need to exercise some degree of personal control over life was particularly strong. Successfully establishing some degree of control through acts of individual resistance was an essential element of psychological well-being for nearly every prisoner. When an inmate refused to obey a rule or an order, he exercised individual initiative and decision making, thus claiming some measure of control over his circumstances. Even prison officers interviewed for this project commented that if they had been prisoners, they would have violated some of the rules from time to time. The chapters ahead will make clear that resistance rather than acquiescence to the regime had important consequences for postrelease survival.

Inmates were also motivated to engage in resistance because it could liven up the extraordinarily dull routine of prison life. This too was a psychological need. The changes and events that provide interest and emotional and intellectual engagement for those in the outside world—war, recession and economic boom, scandals, politics, marriage, births, the sickness or death of a family member, new jobs, disasters of both natural and human origin, and so on—had a different meaning to the residents of Alcatraz. Worldly events were largely irrelevant, and personal and family matters tended to fade into the dim outside world. Men felt bad that a mother died, that a wife filed for divorce, or that a brother or a son was in some kind of trouble, but they knew that they could do nothing about any situation or problem away from the island. In their small world there were few events to look forward to, beyond occasional special meals, weekend recreation in the yard, and movies on holidays. Only strikes, disruptions, occasional fights, escape attempts, new arrivals, and perhaps a better job assignment or cell location could lighten the monotony of a daily routine that stretched ahead for endless months and years.

Resistance manifested itself in a variety of ways at Alcatraz. Some forms of organized resistance, such as strikes, protests, and escapes, have already been described in detail in chapters 4 through 9. The other category—individualized resistance—itself took many forms and varied along a continuum, ranging from small acts of disobedience to open rebellion, with lesser rule violations the most common form of resistance.

At Alcatraz, because there were many rules to disobey, there were ample opportunities for not conforming to the "letter of the law" while at the same time not engaging in the overt insolence or gross misconduct that might result in disciplinary action. Many inmates chose this route of resisting, bending the rules governing conversation, food, clothing, mail, or the authorized contents of a man's cell. By limiting resistance to small acts that remained under the guards' radar or could be tolerated by them, an inmate could satisfy the psychological need of maintaining his self-respect without landing in solitary or sacrificing days of good time. When inmates practiced this form of resistance en masse in regard to a particular rule or part of the regimen, it morphed into a kind of organized resistance that could be very powerful.

A relative minority of inmates practiced individual resistance that was not tolerated by the custodial staff. These men refused to work or eat, demanded medical treatment or access to law books or other restricted material, disobeyed direct orders, or insulted or threatened guards. These acts of rebellion and rule violations did not in themselves constitute serious threats to order and security in the penitentiary, but they did earn the perpetrators the enmity of the custodial force, as well as disciplinary sanctions that often meant time in solitary and loss of good time. Many individual protesters were among active participants in collective protests, but both individual and organized protesters were men who were very experienced in doing penitentiary time and were well integrated into the inmate community. These men were respected for standing up to all levels of authority and for their ability to endure, without flinching, the punishment that followed their protests. Even when these resisters ultimately gave up their hunger strikes, work strikes, and refusals to obey orders, they were accorded respect and admiration by the general population, most of whom had been unwilling to carry their own protests so far. The exceptions to these cases were a small number of inmates who were seen as fighting the regime for no good group or individual purpose; the most notable and persistent of these individual resisters, and their many and varied acts of resistance, are described in the next chapter.

MEANS OF COPING PSYCHOLOGICALLY

The prospect of spending an unknown number of years on the island, isolated from the outside world, with every detail of existence rigidly controlled by the regime, required inmates to develop coping strategies.[11] These strategies were numerous and as varied as the individual personalities of the inmates.

John Irwin, a sociologist and former prisoner, has written extensively about the experience of doing time and identified several different coping strategies, all of which were in evidence at Alcatraz.[12] One important strategy, especially among prisoners with long sentences, is to focus on maintaining personal integrity, often through self-improvement. Another common strategy is "doing time." "This form of adjustment," according to Irwin, "involves passing through the prison in the least amount of time, with the least amount of pain, and with the maximum amount of luxury. It often involves some subterfuge and rule-breaking, but these are done covertly." A third strategy—withdrawal—is for most prisoners the least effective, often leading to negative psychological consequences. Irwin also cites individual and group resistance.

At Alcatraz, resistance was an important element of many prisoners' coping strategies. Resisting the regime by participating in organized protests or refusing to obey all the rules satisfied the psychological need to maintain personal integrity and locus of control and thus contributed to inmates' psychological well-being. For many inmates, pushing the rules just far enough to derive this psychological benefit without drawing the disciplinary actions that would add to the psychological burdens of incarceration at Alcatraz was the preferred strategy.

After living the monastic existence of an Alcatraz inmate, many prisoners developed a coping strategy that involved focusing on the here and now. Because there were so few distractions, especially after men were locked up in their individual cells for the night at 4:45 P.M., there was plenty of time to sit and think about what a man was missing in the outside world. It was natural for an inmate to wonder what his wife or girlfriend was doing that night, and with whom; if his sick or dying mother could forgive her son's absence; if his children would remember their father. An inmate pictured his old friends living it up in their favorite bars and clubs and imagined what it would be like to drive the new cars, travel by airplane, and see real women dressed in the latest clothing styles he could see only in magazines. At the same time, limitations on visits and mail made it extremely difficult to maintain satisfying emotional connections with anyone in the outside world. At some point, many inmates recognized that focusing on the past and what one was missing in the present—called "doing hard time"—was too painful emotionally. They realized that serving time, especially big time, was easier if a man forgot about the free world, to limit or even cut off communication with his loved ones (few inmates wanted or expected visits) and focus instead on personalities, relationships, and small events on the island.

Tracking unusual events, such as escape plots, protests, strikes, changes in the staff, and the arrival of new prisoners as well as the immediate realities of prison social life helped create a feeling of intensity in daily activity that would otherwise be absent. For some men, this concentration of the senses on the here and now evolved in an introspective direction, leading to the solitary contemplation mentioned in chapter 4.

COPING BY PLOTTING ESCAPE

Planning an escape was for a certain group of Alcatraz convicts an important means of psychologically adjusting to the deprivations of maximum-security confinement, and the prospect that those deprivations would continue for many years. Escape plotters were less likely to be depressed or discouraged about the years of imprisonment ahead compared to their fellow convicts because they believed they would not be staying around that long. But escape plotting can also be seen as a form of resistance that, like other forms of resistance, provided the psychological benefit of sustaining self-respect. When an inmate took part in an escape scheme, he declared his determination not to succumb to the mind-deadening effects of long-term confinement. In addition, for those men who found it difficult to deal with the intense boredom of everyday prison life, plotting and participating in an escape attempt was certain to generate excitement and emotional intensity.

In view of the attention given to escape attempts in previous chapters, it is important to emphasize that plotting an escape was a special adaptation practiced by a small minority of Alcatraz inmates. To contemplate escaping from the island, an inmate had to have patience, iron nerves, a quick and decisive mind, and the ability to plan. Most important, he had to be willing to risk his life—or feel that he had nothing to lose.

The men committed to escape sought to attract as little attention from staff as possible. They worked at being quiet, courteous, and obeying the rules; they were careful not to attract attention to the contents of their cell or their workplaces because they did not want guards to shake them down and detect escape paraphernalia. With the exception of Dock Barker and Floyd Hamilton, the most successful escape attempts at Alcatraz were engineered by convicts who were not celebrities, were not the leaders of the work strikes or the food protests, and were not combative with other prisoners or staff; in short, they were regarded by guards as among those convicts who quietly "did their own time." A man could not be locating escape routes, sawing away on bars, or accumulating escape paraphernalia if he was locked up in the disciplinary segregation unit. Rebelling against prison rules or staff instructions meant that an inmate could not earn a work assignment that would routinely bring him down to the industries building next to the waters of the San Francisco Bay or to other locations on the island that eliminated the problem of getting out of a cell and the main cell house. Most of the men bent on escape, therefore, could not have been identified beforehand by scrutiny of their misconduct records.

Experienced officers at Alcatraz understood the inclination of prisoners to dwell on escape and, given their escape records at other prisons, expected some to study and then test the security system. Several groups of convicts who tried to escape were recipients of grudging admiration on the part of prison staff. That admiration, naturally denied to inmates who injured or killed employees in the course of an escape, was reserved

for those men whose breakout attempts demonstrated daring and ingenuity, coupled with painstaking long-term planning and organization.

REACTING WITH VIOLENCE

In any penitentiary setting, coping and adjustment are never complete or
constant, leaving room for violence to erupt. Violent behavior has many
social and psychological causes, but in a prison context it has a direct relation to the interplay between inmate personalities, convict culture, and
imposed confinement. Violence can be conceptualized as a consequence
of the failure to find other adaptations or coping mechanisms in cases of
inmate-on-inmate violence, or resistance carried to an extreme level, in
the case of assaults on guards.

Since there is violence in most cities and towns, it might be expected
to be epidemic in the closed world of a penitentiary that combined the
outstanding histories of violence of the Alcatraz prisoners with the most
punitive regime in the federal system. Yet this expectation was not realized during the gangster era, 1934 to 1948—there were only ten inmate-
on-inmate assaults. Apart from the officers who were assaulted and the
two killed by inmates during escape attempts, only four other prisoner
assaults on staff members were recorded. And, as reported by our inmate
interviewees, there were very few unprovoked assaults on prisoners by
guards.[13] Not included in these figures are fights such as that between Al
Capone and Harmon Waley that never came to the attention of the staff.

The relatively small number of assaults among inmates included James
Lucas's stabbing of Al Capone with a pair of scissors in the barbershop
and a handful of attacks in which the weapons were knives, a workshop
scraper, a two-pound horseshoe, and a baseball bat (the latter two in the
recreation yard). In another incident two prisoners attacked a third in the
shower room. But four conflicts had lethal results. One of these—the murder of Rufus McCain by Henry Young in December 1940—has already
been recounted because of the importance of the resulting trial. In the next
section we briefly describe the three other homicides.

DEATH AT THE HANDS OF FELLOW INMATES
Snow vs. Herring

On the morning of July 15, 1942, Cecil Snow and Maurice Herring began fighting in the shower room. According to Snow and the one inmate

witness, Herring, the more powerful of the two, attacked Snow, knocked him to the floor and, while straddling him, kept hitting him in the head. Snow struck back with a knife he had begun carrying in response to threats from Herring, hitting Herring in the chest and the thigh. The stab to the thigh turned out to be the fatal blow because it severed an artery. Herring rose and staggered away until he collapsed due to loss of blood; thirty minutes later he was pronounced dead in the prison hospital.[14]

Snow was tried in federal court for murder and pleaded self-defense. Several inmates testified that Herring was aggressive and hot-tempered, and that Herring had been heard calling out from his cell telling Snow that he intended to kill him the next morning. Snow was acquitted.

The jury may have excused Snow's conduct, but the custodial staff made its own judgment and assigned its own penalty. A good time forfeiture hearing was held, Snow lost 1,700 days (more than four years) and was locked up in disciplinary segregation for nearly three years. During that time he filed a series of writs claiming "cruel and inhuman treatment" to no avail. Snow accumulated thirty misconduct reports on the Rock and was conditionally released directly from the island. Due to the loss of good time he had served fourteen years of his fifteen-year sentence.[15]

Greene vs. Branch

Another killing occurred on November 14, 1945. On the previous evening Claude Branch and Ralph Greene, both District of Columbia prisoners, had a "verbal altercation" during which Greene "called Branch a 'rat.'"[16] The next day the two were admitted to an area in the barbershop next to the shower room under the main cell house to practice musical instruments. Branch was carrying a putty knife blade in anticipation of trouble but did not have an opportunity to use it before Greene grabbed a metal stand used to hold barber's clippers and struck Branch in the head. Greene ran up the stairs to the cell house door, where the officer allowed him to exit; he walked over to stand at the door to D block, knowing that was his next destination.

Branch was taken to the prison hospital, where he appeared to respond to treatment but two days later his condition deteriorated, and he died during the evening of November 16. During his periods of consciousness he refused to talk about the fight.[17]

Alcatraz officials supported the prosecution of Greene on a charge of murder. Several prisoners testified as defense witnesses that the deceased

(Branch) had threatened the defendant and "had a bad reputation." According to Jim Quillen, this murder was a result of homosexual pressure:

> Branch was a notorious homo and he was always trying to turn somebody out. He tried to turn Greene out; Greene was a real nice little kid. He had been after Greene for quite a while and Greene kept telling him, "Get off my back or I'm going to hurt you." Branch came down one day when Greene was working in the barbershop—either working in the barbershop or waiting for a haircut—and it started again. They used to have something like a tripod that they used to hang the clipper between the two chairs and Greene picked that thing up and just whaled Branch across side the head and he died. I didn't witness it, but I knew what had gone down before and I testified to what Branch did. Branch was a guy that hit on everybody. People used to tell him, "Someday somebody's going to kill you." Finally Ralph did.[18]

Greene claimed self-defense and once again a jury found an Alcatraz defendant "not guilty." Greene was locked up in D block and three days later he was taken before a good time forfeiture board. He protested that his action in defending himself had been found to be "justified" in federal court and thus he should not be punished and if he was, it was because he was "colored." Deputy Warden Miller responded that Greene was being charged with assault, not the murder of another prisoner. The prison court then took away 240 days of good time Greene had accumulated and sent him back to disciplinary segregation, where he remained for four and one-half years.[19]

Grove vs. McMiller

In the late afternoon of March 20, 1946, "several colored men were heard quarreling in the first galley in the cell house." James Grove was said to have been angered over the attempt of two other prisoners to place a floor polisher in a cell where he stored the supplies he was using to paint sections of the cell house. Grove and another prisoner were having "hot words" when Ben McMiller stepped in front of the other inmate. Grove stabbed McMiller in the abdomen with a seven-inch kitchen knife.[20]

An officer arrived on the scene and escorted McMiller to the hospital. Despite the captain's effort to get a statement about the altercation, McMiller, holding to the maxim during the gangster era that you never help the government, refused to name his own killer; he said only that he "just fell and hurt himself." His wound did not appear serious at first, but when he went into shock two doctors from the Marine Hospital were called to the island. Anticipating surgery, they brought blood and blood plasma, but McMiller died shortly after the surgery was completed.

These three cases did not assume the dramatic proportions of the Young case because the combatants were not prominent figures in the convict population who had been involved in a highly visible relationship and their trials did not involve efforts to try the regime.

No interracial elements complicated these confrontations, since all three murders involved victims and killers of the same race. In two of these cases, however, there were convict allegations of jealousy, deteriorating homosexual relationships, or violent resistance to a homosexual advance. These cases should not be construed as evidence that homosexuality was common at Alcatraz. Especially when compared to contemporary prisons, overt homosexual behavior, both consensual and forced, was very rare. Among the 508 inmate files reviewed for this project, only nine references to homosexual conduct during the years 1934 to 1948 were discovered—this despite the fact that explicit sexual activity was a violation of prison rules and that homosexuality, whether admitted, observed, rumored, or inferred, was always recorded in inmates' files. In addition, no Alcatraz or Bureau of Prisons document or any of the more than one hundred former prisoners and staff members interviewed for this project reported knowledge of a single incident of forcible homosexual rape.

It is not surprising that so few men were observed or reported for engaging in homosexual behavior, given the separation of prisoners in single cells, the limited time and number of places that allowed for congregate activity, and the high level of surveillance. But the most important factor was that homosexuality was regarded as weakness and "perversion" in the convict culture, and even a suggestion of homosexuality evoked contempt from most prisoners and all guards.

The four incidents of assaults on staff recorded during the prison's first fifteen years was an extraordinarily low number, given the characteristics of the inmate population and the tension that existed between prisoners and guards. In 1935, convict James Walsh stabbed Officer Clarence Preshaw with a pair of scissors in the nose, the cheek, the abdomen, and the chest while two other prisoners held Preshaw's arms from behind. Walsh said that he was upset because Preshaw was "picking on him."[21] As described earlier, Burton Phillips attacked Warden Johnston in the dining room in 1937.

The only other assaults involved one officer who was attacked on two separate occasions by two different prisoners. In a March 1939 incident, guards King and Amende were collecting library books from prisoners in D block when Rufus Franklin—locked up for the 1937 escape attempt in which Officer Cline was killed—challenged the officers to come into his cell to get his books. As they opened the cell door, Franklin struck Amende in the left eye, causing "a slight bruise." In response, "Officer Amende took a hold of Franklin . . . and then Officer King hit Franklin with his billy, rendering him unconscious."[22] In the other incident in November 1940, Officer Milton Amende was attacked, again, this time by William Martin, receiving multiple contusions to his face.

The explanation for such a low incidence of violence in a prison for violent offenders lies in part in the limited time inmates had to interact with others outside their cells combined with the constant surveillance of a large custodial staff. But this factor alone cannot explain the relative lack of violence between prisoners and between prisoners and staff. Compared to other prisons both then and now, the direct causes of the conflicts that typically lead to violent confrontations were largely absent at Alcatraz. At other prisons, gambling and "wheeling and dealing" in contraband were widespread, due to the existence of commissaries and the relative ease of smuggling contraband into and out of prison introduced goods and items not made available to all prisoners. Engaging in activities related to these items created an inmate economy and produced disputes over indebtedness and the theft or robbery of goods. At Alcatraz, the various high-security measures, the fact that no inmate was allowed to receive money from the outside, the absence of a commissary, strict rules about and frequent shakedowns of cells, and the provision of unlimited amounts of tobacco and food combined to eliminate gambling and economic activity and the arguments and fights they produced.

With convicts unable to accuse others of cheating, stealing, or failing to pay gambling debts, there were fewer reasons to get into fights. When arguments that precipitated violent confrontations did erupt, their causes were more likely to seem trivial: arguments over baseball or handball games, making too much noise in the evening, and not quieting down when asked. Some assaults occurred for reasons unknown to other prisoners, and several involved attacks by men regarded by both prisoners and staff as mentally ill; in one of these incidents inmates helped officers subdue Joe Bowers, who was acting "crazy." There were also occasional minor fist fights that reflected anger and resentment over the past actions of rap partners, former friends, or cellmates in other prisons.

Another important but subtle factor that contributed to the low level of violence was that after a few years on the Rock, most prisoners tended to "settle down." Convicts recognized that they were at the end of the line of penitentiaries and would be at Alcatraz for an unknown number of years. Their psychological and physical distance from life in the free world prompted them to live in the here and now and focus on earning or retaining the few privileges that allowed them to enjoy some of the positive aspects of prison life such as a good cell location, a good job, and yard activities.

We now turn to a form of resistance that took up a disproportionate amount of the prison staff's time, resources, and patience—actions by a small proportion of inmates who lived by their own code of conduct.

OUTLAWS AMONG OUTLAWS

INDIVIDUAL RESISTERS

An inmate at Alcatraz who acted alone, on his own initiative, to disobey rules or defy authority was an individual resister. While many inmates engaged in individual resistance at a low level to derive its psychological advantages without accruing the disciplinary costs, only a relative few resisted regardless of the costs. Still fewer practiced this kind of resistance over long periods of time. Here the focus is on these persistent individual resisters, a small group of men who carried on prolonged battles with the staff and against the regime. These prisoners accumulated twenty, thirty, forty, or more misconduct reports each and spent not weeks or months but years in disciplinary segregation and solitary confinement cells. They paid for their determination not to go along with the program with years added to their stay on the island because of lost good time and significant postponements, or any serious consideration, of parole or conditional release.

Their resistance took many forms—refusing to work and obey orders, fighting with other prisoners and with staff, and going on hunger strikes that if prolonged led to forced feeding. Many of these men drafted myriads of protest letters to federal judges, elected officials, and the U.S. attorney in San Francisco; they also filed writs to protest their convictions, their sentences, and the conditions of their confinement. For some of the most prominent convicts in this group, writing itself was a form of resistance that resulted in numerous articles, short stories, books, even poetry about life in prison and life in general.[1]

The names of the island's most famous gangsters are not among the persistent individual resisters. Al Capone, George Kelly, Harvey Bailey, John Paul Chase, Basil Banghart, and Floyd Hamilton did their time quietly, only participating in a strike or some short-lived protest to show solidarity with their fellow convicts.

Resisting individually was very different from participating in organized resistance in which organizers and key participants collaborated and encouraged each other. Joint planning helped counter the fear and trepidation that accompanied death-defying actions like escape. Organized resistance won the respect of most of the convict population because it showed both courage and solidarity and risked receiving the most severe punitive measures available. Individual resistance, in contrast, was a lonely path. Not only did most individual resisters lack support and encouragement, their actions often cost them the respect of other prisoners. Without collective statements that explained the motives for such conduct, their actions often remained a mystery to their fellow convicts as well as to the staff. Their conduct appeared to bring a lot of grief on themselves and made doing time much harder. Their lack of friends and the absence of goals such as changing the regime to benefit all prisoners led most of these men to be labeled "crazy" by fellow prisoners and "psychopaths" by the staff. They were, however, not looking to be liked, admired, or understood; they had their own agendas.

It is important to know what these men did, what they said about their actions, how they were treated in response, and how their behaviors changed during their time on the island in order to shed light on their motives and on the relation between the prison's policies and inmate behavior. The prison careers of individual resisters are relevant for another reason as well: looking at their lives *after* they were released provides an empirical test of theories about the relation between prison conduct and postrelease behavior. Such theories then, as now, were the basis of policies regarding transfers between different security levels and the criteria governing parole and conditional release.

Except for a few brief summaries, this chapter is not concerned with how individual resisters fared on their return to the free world. Chapter 13 will examine the postrelease lives of these men and the other inmates of the gangster years. But by looking at the prison careers of individual resisters, this chapter provides the foundation for understanding the significance of the findings examined in part 3.

James Grove

James Grove's sad but noteworthy life started out badly. Raised by foster parents until he ran away from home at age twelve, he was convicted of burglary two years later and was sentenced to three years in the Missouri State Reformatory. After his release he worked briefly as a dishwasher in a dining car, but at the age of nineteen he was convicted of robbery and sent to the Utah State Prison. He escaped from that institution, was apprehended, and then released after two years. Soon after his release he was picked up on another burglary conviction, for which he was sent to the state prison at Walla Walla, Washington.

Paroled after one year, he was allowed to join the army despite his three prison sentences. But he soon was in trouble; five months after his induction he was charged with attempting to rape the ten-year-old daughter of an army major. The girl reported that, finding her alone at home, Grove had forced her upstairs into her room; when she resisted and cried out as he tried to place her on the bed, he almost choked her and then fled. For the rest of his life, Grove denied he had attempted to rape the girl, but he was found guilty and sent to the Fort Leavenworth disciplinary barracks with a twenty-year sentence.

Four years later, he stabbed another black prisoner, which earned him a twenty-year term to follow his original sentence—and a transfer to the federal prison system. At Leavenworth he got into three fights with other prisoners and made several attempts at suicide, one by cutting his wrist, and another by trying to hang himself in his cell. A Leavenworth surgeon/psychiatrist estimated his mental age at twelve years and four months and made the following assessment: "This classifies him as a case of borderline intelligence (I.Q. 77). . . . In view of this man's history and his psychopathic instability . . . he should remain under observation in the mental ward."[2]

Despite this diagnosis, James Grove was placed on the first train bringing transfers to Alcatraz on September 4, 1934; his first disciplinary report came four days later. Within a year he had been written up seven times for offenses ranging from "loud talking in cell" to yelling at a guard on the wall, "Go ahead and shoot." Meanwhile, his mental health became a more serious issue. In the hospital ward he managed to cut the veins in both arms with a safety razor blade. When this attempt at suicide, his third, was reported to Bureau headquarters, Director Stanford Bates wrote to Warden Johnston expressing concern: "In the light of recent publicity it would be extremely unfortunate if the attempt at suicide of one of our inmates should prove to be successful."[3]

Grove's condition in the hospital ward was described by a consulting psychiatrist:

attempted suicide by striking head on bars of cell—immediately placed in bed put in restraining sheet—necessary to use arm and leg cuffs. . . . I saw him in a maniacal state, yelling and screaming at the top of his voice and throwing himself about the bed in which he was restrained. . . . I regard him as extremely dangerous both to himself and others.[4]

A year after his transfer to Alcatraz, Grove again became hysterical when a guard attendant was taking his temperature. He broke the thermometer into three pieces, threw his hands about, calling out, "Mother, mother." The chief medical officer requested that a psychiatric evaluation board be appointed, which was expected to approve Grove's transfer to the Springfield Medical Center; instead he was returned to Leavenworth in October 1935 as a "mental patient." At Leavenworth, Grove wrote poignantly to Attorney General Cummings about his experience at Alcatraz:

> It's worst than hell out there Sir, with the sea gulls and fog horns, and wind blowing fifty miles an hour and nothing but silence. . . . I can't begin to try to picture that place for you. Your own prison for humans—why out there Sir, we are all living dead men, just living life that means nothing.

He went on to write of his lack of hope for his future:

> I am not asking you for anything. . . . I just want to be where I can forget a lot of things. . . . You can never realize what hell is like until you live through it. . . . So I will live through the rest of my life a wreck, and try to believe that some day it will all end as God wills it.

And at the end of the letter, Grove alluded to racial discrimination as a reason for his wanting to commit suicide: "I wanted to die out there, and tried to make it so. But not because I was a coward. But because it was just too much hell for me and my face was black. I remain your prisoner of Devil's Island."[5]

Grove was transferred to the Springfield Medical Center about a year later, where the prognosis of his condition was bleak and unsympathetic: "Segregation is recommended. Not that it will help this individual inmate in any manner but that others may be protected from his depravations and evil influence."[6] He was returned to Leavenworth in February 1938, where he attacked and seriously injured another prisoner.

Grove requested a transfer to another prison, "even if it be Alcatraz." The Leavenworth staff agreed, noting that he was not likely to get along in any prison but "the close confinement and supervision available at Alcatraz appears necessary as a most effective solution of the behavior problem subject presents." However, they admitted, "He will probably be unable to make a satisfactory adjustment at Alcatraz."[7]

Several months later, in July 1939, James Grove was back on the Rock, where the prediction that he would not "adjust" proved to be correct. Six transfers in ten years shows the difficulty Bureau officials had in finding the appropriate setting for an inmate with Grove's combination of violent outbursts, suicide attempts, bizarre conduct, and problematic behavior, but no official diagnosis of psychosis. Over the next twenty years James Grove accumulated thirty-four misconduct reports. Many of his infractions were serious, and his troubles continued even after he was placed in D block; thirteen involved fights with other inmates and he twice assaulted officers. For these actions, Grove spent years in disciplinary segregation and isolation cells.

In June 1943, given an opportunity to shave in D block, he slashed his elbows and both legs with a safety razor. He forcibly resisted being taken to the hospital, and once there, his hands had to be restrained to the sides of the bed to prevent him from tampering with the wounds. But, as in previous evaluations, the medical report concluded, "I do not consider him psychotic but he is subject to deep emotional fluctuations."[8]

During the battle of Alcatraz in May 1946, Grove was wounded by a bullet in the arm that other convicts claimed was fired from a gun held by fellow convict Joseph Cretzer. Grove did not share this view. Two months later he wrote to the NAACP complaining that he was a victim of discriminatory treatment. His letter noted that although he had "the privilege of reading *The Crisis, Negro Digest,* and the *Ebony* magazines" and "enjoyed the right of reading about the great work my people are doing for the more unfortunate of this world," he felt he was the victim of job discrimination on the island. He also complained that during the May 1946 fire fight, he was "deliberately shot in the arm while confined in a cell *with the door locked.* I was the only person so badly shot out of 265 innocent inmates during the escape attempt of three insane men." Grove claimed that he received poor medical care, insufficient pain relief, and that Dr. Roucek held to "that old hatred prejudice and . . . discrimination of the negro."[9]

Several months later Grove sent a letter to the secretary of war complaining that the food served in D block was "not fit for human consumption," that military prisoners had been beaten for protesting this treatment, and that a deliberate attempt had been made on his life by a staff member during the 1946 battle: "I escaped with my life only because of poor marksmanship." He asked to be transferred and called for an investigation of Alcatraz by the inspector general.[10]

Grove's next misconduct was his most serious. During a quarrel with other inmates on March 20, 1946, he stabbed fellow inmate Ben McMiller in the abdomen with a seven-inch kitchen knife, and McMiller later died from the wound (as recounted in chapter 10). Grove was tried and convicted on a charge of second-degree murder, for which he received a fifteen-year sentence to be served following his current forty-year term. He was returned to D block, where he spent the next four years in and out of solitary confinement. He spent some of his time writing special purpose letters, sending nine during 1951 to "courts, attorneys, Father Divine, and a senator."[11]

By 1952 his misconduct had cost him all his good time credits—4,378 days, the equivalent of twelve years—but a report in February of that year noted that he was "a heavy reader of both fiction and nonfiction . . . maintains no social ties by correspondence or visiting [but shows] some emotional maturity, appears less inclined to explode over minor frustrations and heeds staff counseling to remain free of the involvements prevalent among the members of the colored cliques."[12] The positive change in his behavior resulted in the restoration of 365 days of good time, but nine months later he committed another serious violation of the rules by attacking two officers in the prison dining room. Lt. Isaac Faulk reported:

> Grove walked into the dining room at the end of the line, picked up a heavy serving spoon as if to serve himself. Instead, he swung the spoon with all of his strength at Officer Burlingame's head. This vicious blow struck [the officer] just in front of his right ear inflicting a serious cut and a large bruised area. Grove then assaulted me by hurling a stack of nested serving trays which struck me in the chest. He then threw trays of potatoes savagely at me and other officers until finally overpowered. It was necessary to carry him bodily from the dining room so furious was his resistance to lawful restraint.

In no location in any penitentiary does violence call for more serious punishment than when it occurs in the mess hall where a large number of prisoners are together. When mess hall violence was directed at a staff member, the level of seriousness increased. Grove's response to the charges brought against him was to tell the good time forfeiture board that Officer Burlingame "would not leave him alone . . . that he had killed before, was all washed up and had no fear of any consequences." According to a November 27, 1953, special progress report, Burlingame had incurred Grove's wrath by reporting him "for giving home brew to one of his homosexual friends." Grove lost 1,365 days of good time and was locked up in "a dark [closed front] cell in D block" for an "extended period" on "a restricted diet." It was noted in his file that he was "considered an extremely dangerous individual with aggressive homicidal and homosexual tendencies."[13]

For the next three years Grove continued to accumulate misconduct reports for offenses such as shouting and beating on his cell bars, using abusive language, and possessing and passing contraband items. In June 1953 he sent another letter to the NAACP complaining about conditions in Alcatraz as they related to "colored inmates":

> Dear Sir:
>
> This is not an appeal to secure my release but rather a letter explaining existing conditions in Alcatraz as they relate to colored inmates. . . .
> From May 1st to 13th I was subject to the most inhuman, brutal treatment ever thought up by prison officials. I had no bed, shoes, the windows were kept open, the heat turned off, and what food I had was not fit for a dog. . . . At this date I am still treated worse than any inmate, I do not have sheets for my bed . . . books or magazines to read, no smoking tobacco, for seven months I have had no sun or fresh air. . . . Congress approved these things, even for a colored man.

In regard to his attack on the officers in the mess hall, Grove wrote in the letter: "There is always two sides to every story. . . . I was out of my head at the time, and have felt mighty sorry about it sense [sic] (But being colored perhaps you understand)." He closed the letter by pleading with the NAACP to investigate the treatment he was receiving and to help him.[14]

By the end of 1953 James Grove had the dubious distinction of having the lowest number in the convict population, meaning he had been on the island longer than any other prisoner. He had received no letters, and during two decades on the island he had only one visitor—an attorney who came once in 1951. His activities in the D block unit were limited to reading; his earnings from prison labor up to that time amounted to $1.25. A special progress report in 1954 noted that although the officers regarded him as helpful and hardworking, they considered his motives devious:

> One of the most accomplished connivers in the institution. His ability to steal, hide and transport food from the food cart to restricted inmates in the Treatment Unit is efficient and effective beyond belief. On the other hand, he likes to work . . . so that he is, aside from his conniving, a valu-

able man as orderly in the unit . . . he helps the officers and in turn gains opportunities to assist inmates in illicit activities.[15]

After his return to general population, Grove spent his time quietly playing handball and reading a variety of magazines including *Argosy, Ebony, True Life,* and *Saturday Evening Post.* Due to his improved conduct, 295 days of good time were restored. His military sentences were considered completed by the Department of the Army and because "his emotional conflicts had become less with age and his adjustment to close custody and environment seem to have made progress," he was recommended for transfer.[16]

In April 1959, after almost twenty-one years on the Rock, Grove was moved to Leavenworth. He became eligible for parole on his civilian sentence in July 1960 and began an effort to hasten his conditional release by appealing for restoration of the last forfeited good time. In June 1961 he won back five hundred days of good time, his conditional release date was moved up to August 1962, and planning for his release got under way. With no living relatives to assist him, a place to live and a job in San Francisco were to be arranged with the help of a former Alcatraz Catholic chaplain. His release after almost forty years of military and federal imprisonment was finally in sight, but James Grove did not live to return to the free world.

On the morning of August 11, 1961, Officer C. J. Mitchell found Grove dead in his cell. In a letter addressed to James V. Bennett, the warden, and a lieutenant, Grove described the reasons for his action:

> Gentlemen: My life cannot continue under the pressure and strain now placed upon me. I have nothing but (my) life to take, my years in prison have taken any hope for a free clean life outside the Walls. I have no kinfolks, no one will cry over me but a few sincere inmate friends. . . . I have nothing to leave, only regrets that I am one colored man who will not shine a guards shoe. Rather than do that as I am being forced to do, I take my own life. It was not hard to smile, keep a civil tongue, and even take care of the officer's dirty and clean clothes. But the shine *one damn pair shoes* (No) Not Jimmy Groves. And the only way I can win is to taking my life. . . . My friends who know (but don't believe my sincerity) tell me how foolish I am not to take a couple officer's life along with mine. I even had several wanting to help me after they found out how I was being forced to shine shoes. And these were (white) *folks.* But no! I won't hurt any-one but myself: Even though they are right. Lt. Concannon said, "Why Jim colored people always shine shoes. Colored people always like to shine shoes." Very nice thinking

on his part. I am sure he will find the colored man who *likes* to shine shoes.

Given the limited options he believed were available to him, James Grove employed suicide as the ultimate form of individual resistance. There were moral considerations in this choice, such as his decision not to take the lives of one or more employees along with his own, and the need to take a stand that other black prisoners would avoid. Grove's final act of protest was driven by what sociologist John Irwin has described as the prisoner's need to maintain his "integrity"—to stand up and make a statement or take a position the prisoner believes is right, despite the cost. James Grove had been paying the costs of resisting in prison for thirty-seven years before he decided not to bend any longer to government authority.

Harmon Waley

Harmon Metz Waley spent twenty-two years at Alcatraz, the longest continuous period of incarceration on the island among all Alcatraz prisoners. (Alvin Karpis spent a total of twenty-five years, but his time on the Rock was broken by a transfer to and return from Leavenworth.) Waley's crime—the ransom kidnapping of the seven-year-old son of a wealthy lumber baron—provided a perfect match between the federal government's war on the "gangster element" and Alcatraz, the highly publicized repository for such offenders. Tried, convicted, and sentenced to forty-five years on June 21, 1935, Waley was sent to McNeil Island Penitentiary on the same day he was sentenced—but he did not stay for long. Less than four weeks later he was personally escorted to Alcatraz by E. B. Swope, then McNeil's warden. By the time he returned to McNeil Island more than two decades later, in February 1957, Waley's forty misconduct reports covered every means of resistance and protest save one—he did not try to escape.

For his first six months, Waley quietly did his time, encouraged, he said, by Swope to believe that if he "kept his nose clean" he would soon be returned to McNeil Island. When it became apparent that no such transfer was forthcoming, Waley began to direct his anger at Alcatraz and Bureau officials. "I told them 'you are a dirty bunch of sadists,'" he said. "I wrote a five-page letter to James V. Bennett and I told him 'You got us out here and you don't even want to give us any candy bars because you are afraid we will jump over the walls from the added energy. You sent us out here to get some publicity for yourselves.'"[17]

Another reason for the deterioration in Waley's behavior was the hostile reception he received from other prisoners because he had kidnapped a child. In the view of the staff, Waley's misconduct stemmed also from his inherent criminal nature. Captain Philip Bergen recalled,

> Waley was crazy as a bedbug. Too bad they didn't shoot him when they arrested him . . . he was not psychotic he was just an advanced criminal sociopath. He was always in trouble and he had a big mouth and illusions of grandeur. The inmates didn't like him because they knew he was the one that put his wife into the penitentiary on that Weyerhaeuser kidnap rap. They used to throw it up to him, "No good son of a bitch." She almost had a pass on that thing until he included her in. He didn't want somebody else having intercourse with her while he was doing time. Of course you're not supposed to do that. Your girlfriend in the criminal echelon is supposed to be out there making money for you while you are in prison. So he was looked down upon by the others.[18]

A prison doctor described him as "the loneliest man on Alcatraz."[19]

In order to gain some respect from other convicts, Waley joined striking kitchen workers, for which he was locked up in open solitary, A block. This was the first of a long series of confinements in disciplinary segregation that extended over the next fifteen years. Two weeks after his return to the general population he demanded admission to the hospital, complained that the doctor didn't know anything and that he was "getting tired of this god damn shit around here." He was promptly locked up in an isolation cell. A few months later he fought with another prisoner but after both agreed they were at fault and held no "ill feelings against the other," they received only reprimands.

Although it was never noted in prison records, Waley next got into a fight with Al Capone:

> I was fooling around with a saxophone down in the music room and he's got a mandolin in a case and somebody hits me in the back and it's him. He hit me with his mandolin case. He said, "You son of a bitch. I've been looking for you for a long time." I stood up and thought about hitting him with the saxophone but I didn't want to hurt the sax. . . . I said, "Well I'm here" and he walked on off.

Waley solicited the help of convicts McDonald and Conroy to get back at Capone, who he knew would be constantly guarded by at least "two or three spaghetti benders." The next time Capone came into the band room, Waley said,

> I walked over to him and said, "Okay Capone you got me." I knocked him on the jaw and knocked him a little silly. He grabbed me by the hair; first he tried to bite me. He's trying to pull me down and lifting his knee trying to get me. I got a good sock in his stomach. Conroy grabbed a spaghetti bender by the name of Delbano, but he let him get away and he ran across the band room and hit me on the jaw.

The brief skirmish ended with Capone fleeing the room, then five minutes later sending Delbano back, saying, "Al doesn't want any trouble with you." Waley told Delbano, "If you people don't bother me, I won't bother you." After the incident, according to Waley, "Capone didn't say anything to me for three months, then he said, 'Hi.'"

Shortly after this altercation, Waley was charged with "insolence" for telling a doctor to "stick it up his ass" when the doctor denied him treatment for a cold. Two days later he refused to work and was placed in solitary. The following day he was written up for singing very loudly "They'll hang Jim Johnston in a sour apple tree." Told he was disturbing the cell house Waley replied, "I can't get in any deeper, so why stop?" That proved not to be the case.

Four warnings later he was taken down the stairs in A block to lower solitary, where he remained for two days. In a memorandum to Bureau headquarters reporting that lower solitary was being used, Warden Johnston explained that Waley "became noisy . . . he persisted in deliberately whistling and hollering and making noise in an endeavor to attract attention and disturb others in the cell house. It therefore became necessary to move him downstairs . . . that is basement solitary . . . for one day and 21 hours . . . until he promised to behave."[20] A few weeks later Waley was in an A block solitary confinement for disobeying a direct order.

His hostility toward the FBI and the Bureau of Prisons was relentless throughout his many years at Alcatraz. Claiming to be the government's "favorite whipping boy," he filled his letters to his mother and his wife with tales of his persecution.

On September 27, 1937, after being placed in isolation for participating in a strike, Waley was charged with agitating and creating a disturbance. After repeated warnings to keep quiet he was forcibly removed for the second time down to lower solitary.

Lt. Culver, an ex-jar-head [marine], thought he was tough. He had a guard hold each one of my hands and he hit me in the stomach and in the cheek. But the next time I saw his hand coming, I stuck my head down so he hit my forehead and broke his thumb, or else he faked it.

This time he remained in a dungeon cell for thirteen days.[21] When he was moved upstairs to a D block isolation cell he was limited to one meal each day, with bread and water for the other meals. A month later he was charged with ripping up his bed sheet and promising more of the same until he received food. While in D block, Waley continued to protest:

> I said why don't you just take my mattress and all my bed clothes and clothes too. So I took them, threw them out there. That was one of the reasons they thought I was crazy.

Then Waley refused to eat. His lengthy hunger strike was graphically described by U.S. Public Health Service physician Milton Beacher, who worked on the island for several months in 1937 and 1938:

> [Waley] became listless, indifferent. Rebelling against the entire prison set-up, he bluntly announced he didn't care what happened to him, life was too miserable at Alcatraz. First he went on a hunger strike. For seventeen consecutive days he steadfastly refused to eat. We finally resorted to tube feeding.
> On the seventeenth day, I visited Waley. "How about eating, Waley?" I asked. "This isn't doing you any good. If you don't eat, we'll just have to give you the tube and pour it down."
> Waley grimaced weakly. "I don't care. You can hose me with that tube day and night. The tube going into my nose and down my stomach doesn't bother me like it does other guys. I'm not eating."
> I inserted the tube and poured down a pitcher of hot broth. Several times Waley paled and became nauseated and regurgitated. As the broth bubbled up, the guard holding the pitcher caught it and poured it down again, saying, "As many times as it come up, it will go down again."
> "I don't give a god dam. You can give it to me with vomit puke, snot and all. What the hell do I care? I'm not eating until I get what I want. If it takes forty years, too. I'll tell you what I want. I want out of this god damn stinking joint. I want to go back to McNeil—that's where I was sentenced. There was no damn reason to transfer me here. I'm tired of the agitation and persecution here and getting the glassy-eye." . . . In the midst of his hunger strike, Waley announced he positively would not budge from his bed. He made that clear to the guards one day when they approached him prior to another tube feeding.

"I'm not getting out of bed," he said firmly. "Carry me if you want. If you want me to shave, then you shave me. If you want me to take a bath, then you carry me down and bathe me. I'm not doing a damn thing by myself any more. Get it?"

"Get out of bed," a guard commanded. "Get out or we'll drag you out!"

"Not on your life. Not while there's so God damn much antagonism against me."

"You're asking for it, Waley—GET UP!" the guard thundered. Whereupon Waley was forcibly hauled out of bed, slammed down on the floor and tube fed. That afternoon, he walked voluntarily into the hospital.[22]

Waley's version of this extended protest highlighted his ability to get out of restraints and the constipation that followed his refusal to eat.

They took me up to the hospital, put me in a straight sheet on the bed and handcuffed me to the side of the bed and handcuffed my feet down. I got out of the restraints—I got out twice. They put you in bed, handcuff you to the bedrails and handcuff your feet to the bottom of the bed with leather cuffs. Then they put this canvas sheet over you and strap it down to the bed. They had openings so your hands and your feet were outside this canvas sheet. They had me in one of those contraptions but I kept getting out of it. The sheet they put over you is strapped down on the side of the bed and you can holler for a bed pan but they wouldn't give it to you—they let you lay in [your own bodily wastes].

So finally they took me out of that thing and put me over in the observation cells and my bowels hadn't moved yet. Finally I figured, geez, these people are going to let me die here if I don't raise some kind of objection and I told them that my bowels hadn't moved. They poured all that eggnog down me and it's sitting up just back of my tailbone like cement. . . . I been up here in the hospital fourteen days and my bowels hadn't moved before then because I hadn't had anything to eat. So they gave me an enema with salt water and mineral oil mixture of some kind. Boy, I had a hell of a time getting that down. I finally got all right but they tried to get me to say that I would go back to the cell house and wouldn't do anything. I told them I would eat, so they started to feed me and they kept me [in the hospital] three or four months.

Although he eventually agreed to eat again, Waley continued to protest through desperate, self-destructive actions. First he removed his clothes and flooded his cell. Dr. Beacher found him naked, wet, and shivering on the floor. Waley was placed in an empty cell, in which even the bed was removed along with the chains which held the bed suspended from the wall. He immediately announced he would use the blankets to hang himself, so they too were removed. When the warden was notified, he ordered Waley to be sent to the hospital, where he was placed in a restraint jacket. Since Waley was judged to be neither sick nor insane, he was put back in isolation again the next morning. Guards made sure the cell contained nothing with which Waley might harm himself, and according to Dr. Beacher, "Waley was let into it entirely nude except a pair of shoes from which the laces were extracted. Laces were potential nooses—great for strangulation." Nonetheless, "less than twenty minutes later," according to Dr. Beacher, "a passing guard saw Waley hacking at himself with a broken safety razor blade. He was bleeding from his arms and wrists and had smeared blood over his face. This gave him an eerie slaughterhouse look. The guard was aghast."[23]

After Waley cut himself, a search of his belongings revealed a razor blade hidden in the sole of his shoes. In a letter reporting this episode to Bureau headquarters, Waley was quoted as claiming, "I have got too much sense to hurt myself, but I will get out of this place, Alcatraz, head or feet first."[24]

A more serious suicide attempt followed in September 1938 when Waley was found in his cell face down breathing, but with difficulty. He had double-looped strips of blanket around his neck and tied them to the wash basin in an attempt to hang himself. After Dr. Ritchey removed the strips, Waley quickly recovered and tried to run out of the cell but a guard blocked his exit. He told Ritchey that he could not get along at Alcatraz because nobody would allow him to get along there. Ten days later he attempted to commit suicide again with another strip of blanket tied around his neck. Two weeks after that he wrote to his mother, explaining the suicide attempt:

> I am in the observation tank in the hospital again for hanging myself. I cut my wrists and the vein in my elbow with a razor blade before. . . . I told you and the G-Men that I would rather be hung than be here before I ever was sentenced at all, because the place was injustice personified. I meant it. I am through this time. . . . Although I'm watched pretty close in the hospital, sooner or later I'll get some broken glass or something. I'm either going to be transferred to McNeil so I can see you, and be given a shake, or I'm not going to do this time for them. . . . You know yourself that you would rather see me dead than a spiritless slobbering idiot, to which this environment leads. . . . 'Tis better to be transferred or die, than live like a dog here.[25]

When he was discharged from the hospital, Waley got along in general population until September 1939, when he was charged with fighting in the yard with Rudolph Brandt, a prisoner born in Germany. The two argued over the war, began cursing each other, and then resorted to fist fighting. Waley went to solitary again, where he extended his time by calling the mail censor "a cock sucker, bastard son of a bitch."[26]

Next he was charged for creating a disturbance in the cell house by hitting a cup on the bars, yelling, and bumping his bed on the floor of the cell. Told to stop he refused, and when ordered out of his cell, he broke a medicine bottle and charged to the front of his cell trying to strike Deputy Warden Miller with the jagged neck of the bottle. Waley complained in a letter to Director Bennett that he did not attempt such an attack and that he was beaten up by Miller and Lt. Simpson.[27] In his own report filed months after the incident in response to Waley's claims of being beaten, Simpson wrote, "Waley told Miller, 'I will kill you, you son of a bitch.' [Miller] threw up his hands, striking Waley on the side of the head."[28]

Like many other convicts Waley spent much of his time drawing up legal briefs. He began with a writ of habeas corpus contending that he had been denied counsel and the right to confront witnesses against him and that he should have been tried in the state of Idaho.[29] By May 1941 Waley had filed eight petitions in the federal district court in San Francisco, all of which were denied. Several months later an appeals court judge noted that the petition contained "a threat to commit murder in the penitentiary in the event of the denial of Petition."[30] By September 1945 he had filed twenty-nine petitions for habeas corpus, motions to vacate judgments, and appeals to the Circuit Court and the Supreme Court. He also sent letters of complaint to the U.S. attorney in San Francisco and to the attorney general in Washington, D.C.

No Alcatraz convict was more enthusiastic about helping Henry Young put the Rock on trial than Harmon Waley. As described in chapter 6, he was a featured witness at Young's murder trial. His handcuffs were removed before he entered the courtroom, nattily dressed in a suit, tie, and fedora. His picture appeared in the *San Francisco News* next to the headline "Brutality at the Rock Charged."[31] He was cited in the *San Francisco Examiner* as "in every way the star of the day's court room performance . . . at some length and with considerable enjoyment he related that he had been confined to the Alcatraz dungeon twice." He was allowed to testify "for reasons not discernable to lay observers" to a wide variety of matters that had been introduced by other convicts, through the "bootleg" method of answering defense attorney's loaded questions over the objections of the U.S. attorney.[32]

Waley's intent was not only to help Young but to expose the "damn lies" of James Bennett that the dungeons had never been used. Anticipating a negative reaction from the Alcatraz staff to his court appearance and testimony, Waley made sure that the judge and the jury were warned of this possibility as "he sneaked over a response indicating that he expected to be punished for his testimony."[33] For Harmon Waley this highly publicized opportunity to condemn the Bureau of Prisons and the regime at Alcatraz was truly satisfying.

Waley's animosity toward Deputy Warden Miller was especially vehement. In a memo describing his inspection of D block, Warden Johnston reported the following incident:

When I stopped at Waley's cell I remarked that he looked well and appeared to be putting on weight. He replied, "I'm alright, I'm not crazy and I haven't been killed." Looking at Mr. Miller and resuming the remarks he said, "He said that he would see to it that he either drove me crazy or killed me." Mr. Miller said, "Waley when did I ever say anything like that?" Waley said, "Let's see, I think it was a year ago last July about." Mr. Miller said, "Waley you know that what you say is a lie." Waley said, "No it ain't no fucking lie."

When Johnston returned to Waley's cell later, Waley told him he planned to kill Miller when he got a chance. Johnston said he would see to it that Waley never got the opportunity, to which Waley replied, "Oh well, I will get a chance."[34]

Two days later he threatened not only the lives of Alcatraz officers but the life of the warden as well:

If one of these things doesn't soon happen which I have named in paragraph one [release or a fair trial] I am going to kill you or one of your officers and put the whole case before a jury at a murder trial. . . . I have no use for potential dictators or tyrants, and I've been punished for something I didn't do long enough.[35]

Waley then reiterated his threats in a letter to the U.S. attorney general:

If any of your agents or yourself think I can do nothing because you have confined me to my cell you are very sadly mistaken. I assure you that I will splatter the brains of one of your agents all over the wall opposite my cell; and I think I can kill two or three more before you get me to a trial. . . . I am now giving you sixty days to release me from my false imprisonment without a fair trial, and God Damn you, you had better use this opportunity.[36]

But a few months later Waley informed Johnston that he had changed his mind, telling the warden, "You need have no fear about me killing you or any of your officers since it was never my intent to do so at any time; for I would not lower myself to the same level."[37]

But Waley was not through resisting. In June 1944 he built a fire in his toilet and then kicked it until it broke apart. The next day he tore the covering from the drain in the cell and used it as a hammer to break the protective glass cover over the light in the cell. During his disciplinary hearing, Waley said his action was intended to secure a cell change: "Yes, I plead guilty. I'll smash more toilets if you don't move me off the flats and back upstairs. I am guilty but I will smash many more. I got 45 years, take it all. . . . I am not going in a cell on the flats. I am going to tear up every god damn toilet in Alcatraz." For this action—and attitude—he forfeited 1,000 days of statutory good time.[38]

A month later Waley received a misconduct report for verbally abusing Officer Frank Johnson. The hostile relationship between Waley and this officer related to Johnson's shooting James Boarman through the head during the April 1943 escape attempt. According to Waley, a Coast Guard officer who had been within twenty feet of Boarman to pick him up, called the act "deliberate murder." Waley claimed he observed Johnson washing his hands "two, three times a day" and because he had read some psychology book, he believed he knew why:

> When they put Johnson over as the officer in D block I was in the segregation unit . . . one day I'm trying to study. I'm into logic then and I got mad and said, "Listen Johnson, you're washing three, four times every day and I say you're causing a big disturbance—you can't wash that kid's blood off your hands. Get that through your head. But some night he's going to climb in bed with you, soaking wet and he'll bleed all over you." Jesus, he was fit to be tied he was so mad at me.

Throughout his long career at Alcatraz, Waley never missed an opportunity to challenge the authority of prison officials and the Department of Justice and to condemn the actions of individual officers and administrators using every means at his disposal. For years, he produced short stories, articles and poems, often with a pen name, sending some to Bureau headquarters, and asking in one case that his article be forwarded to a publisher such as *Colliers Magazine*.

In a letter to his mother he claimed to have invented "a fuel system for internal combustion engines . . . [as well as] a gravity engine," asking her to seek patents and promising her half of the proceeds. He suggested that the gravity system be sold for $500,000 and the fuel system for $1,000,000.[39] The secretary of war received a message from Waley describing a method to prevent guns and cannons from recoiling and suggested the use of an herb he called *coyotilla* that he claimed could paralyze but not kill enemy soldiers.[40] In 1950 he submitted a parole release plan in which he claimed that he could support himself by applying the "Waley Method," a surefire means of attaining financial success when betting on race horses. As his correspondence related to various projects accumulated in Bureau headquarters, James Bennett wrote to Warden Johnston characterizing Waley's efforts as "indications of the development of a delusional system of ideas" and recommended that Johnston "continue frequent psychiatric interviews."[41]

Waley's hell-raising began to wind down about fifteen years into his sentence. A report in 1948 noted, "This man has paranoid interpretations and blames federal officers . . . for his troubles . . . [but] will probably become better adjusted as he grows older."[42] Another report a year later indicated that Waley was working in the basement, which gave him a chance to play a piano in his spare time. Waley wrote songs with such titles as "Don't You Trifle Me," "I'm Riding on a Sunbeam," "Just an Old Oak Tree," "Old Man Frog," and "Oh My Baby." Five hundred days of statutory good time were restored for his good behavior.[43]

Waley's adjustment continued to improve in the 1950s. A consulting psychiatrist noted that while Waley's attitude was "sarcastic, egotistical and truculent . . . no evidence of an overt psychotic reaction or organic deterioration was found."[44] However, a year later the calm was broken at a meeting of the classification committee when Waley "launched his verbal pyrotechnics [and] stalked from the room."[45] He was locked up in a closed-front cell. Two more incidents followed over the next two years, with his last trip in October 1953 to disciplinary segregation, as usual for refusing to obey an order.

In all, Harmon Waley spent seven of his twenty-two years at Alcatraz in disciplinary segregation or solitary confinement cells. He was written up twice for fights with other prisoners, three times for participating in a strike, six times for refusing to work or obey orders, five times for destroying government property, seven times for creating disturbances in the cell house or D block, eleven times for insolence or cursing or threatening officers and sundry other infractions such as attempting to attack an officer, possession of contraband, and violating mail regulations.

In October 1955 the classification committee, taking into account that he had "been at this institution for over twenty years, longer than any other Alcatraz inmate, and needs a new environment and opportunity for some of the privileges afforded at a larger, general custody-type institution," recommended Waley for a transfer.[46]

A few months later, 300 days of good time, the last of 1,000 days he had forfeited, were restored. On February 14, 1957, he was returned to McNeil Island Penitentiary, where he spent six uneventful years before his release on parole in June 1963. Harmon Waley's remarkable prison career was followed by a remarkable postrelease life (see chapter 13).

Richard Neumer

More than a few of the men sent to Alcatraz did not have the lawbreaker or prison troublemaker credentials that would seem to warrant a transfer to the nation's toughest prison. Richard A. Neumer was one of these run-of-the-mill felons. His criminal history began at age sixteen with a commitment to the Boys Industrial School in Topeka, Kansas, for "chicken stealing, divers thefts, incorrigibility." Two years after his release from Boys School, and after an attempt to enlist in the navy failed (due to flat feet), he was arrested on a robbery charge and ended up in a jail in Ripley, Mississippi. Noticing a hole in the ceiling of the small two-story jail, Neumer was able to climb up to the roof, drop to the ground, and get out of town. He made his way to Memphis, Tennessee, where he was again arrested and convicted on a robbery charge for which he received a term of five to six years.

After two years in the state penitentiary at Nashville, he was transferred to the Brushy Mountain Prison. One night, along with four other men, he escaped through a hole in the wall in the building in which they were housed. Neumer and two of the escapees stole a car but, at a gas station, his confederates drove off without him. A few days later when these men were captured and charged with bank robbery, and the gas station attendant identified him as being with them, Neumer was also arrested. He was charged with participating in the bank holdup and with violating the firearms act (a sawed-off shotgun was brandished in the bank) and the Motor Vehicle Theft Act. Although he claimed he was not present, Neumer nevertheless pleaded guilty to the bank robbery and auto theft charges because an FBI agent assured him he would receive a term of only ten years. He was shocked when he was given two terms of twenty-five and twenty years to run consecutively. When he tried to withdraw his guilty plea, the judge replied that he was not bound by any promise made by the FBI and that the forty-five-year sentence would stand.

The judge asked Neumer, "Can you swim?" Stunned, Neumer made no reply. "For if you can," continued the judge, "I'll give you a break and recommend you to Alcatraz."[47]

Neumer did not go directly to the Rock; he was committed to Atlanta in October 1935. Although he was "in a state of dejection," he found the prison to be clean, the food "wholesome," and the educational facilities and opportunities "good for a prison." Neumer joined classes in art and diesel engineering and appreciated the fact that there was no "brutal treatment." Although he adjusted well and did not break any rules, he was soon told that he was going to Alcatraz. According to Neumer, the Atlanta administrators were as dismayed by this news as he was: the deputy warden, wrote Neumer, "realized I was a model prisoner . . . and he would like to see me stay there, but there was nothing he could do. The transfer orders came from Washington."[48] Neumer arrived at Alcatraz on December 22, 1935. His conduct at Atlanta provided no justification for the transfer, and neither did his record—his escapes from the jail and the state prison had not involved force, weapons, or hostages; he had simply exploited weak or incompetent security arrangements. But his body was needed to fill space on the island. Nonetheless, Alcatraz authorities soon found that this inconsequential offender, this "model prisoner" from Atlanta, would be a major disruptive force for more than a decade.

Still convinced that his forty-five-year sentence was unfair, and angered by the baseless transfer, Neumer began resisting the regime soon after he stepped onto the island. Less than a month after his arrival he joined a work strike and was locked up in D block. Over the next several years he was written up for a variety of rule infractions including making contraband items, disrespect, wasting food ("left his cereal at morning meal claiming it was sour"), participating in another strike, and creating a disturbance in the cell house by yelling at other prisoners who were out on strike. For a period of three years after this he received no misconduct reports, but then he began to oppose staff authority again. He refused to obey orders, defaced government property, wasted food ("left parsnips on his tray"), wrote an obscene message ("fuck Officer Hanson"), was insolent, did his work in a "slovenly" manner during the 1945 laundry strike, destroyed government property in the April 1946 D block protest, and created another disturbance in the cell house (also recorded as "attempting to incite a riot"). He was also cited for writing a false statement about the prison's use of blankets, sheets, and towels sent by the army to the Alcatraz laundry and for trying to smuggle this statement outside the prison by giving it to James Grove, an army prisoner about to be interviewed by army agents. In January 1946 he was charged with conspiracy in a case in which a guard was given $25 for smuggling a letter out to Neumer's sister. His conduct improved after this point, with only one report in 1948 for having an extra shelf in his cell, and another in 1954 for arguing with an officer about a piece of wood at which Neumer "was looking with possessive eyes" (this incident was written up as "arrogance and disrespect for authority").[49]

Neumer's resistance went beyond eighteen misconduct reports, thirteen sojourns in solitary confinement or disciplinary segregation, and the loss of 3,000 days of statutory good time. He set the prison's record for complaints about his health: from 1936 through August 1945, he reported to sick call 849 times. During the same period he was hospitalized ten times for a total of 151 days for ailments ranging from common colds and neuralgia to a fractured finger. A hospital report noted: "complains of headaches about twice a week . . . insists he has sinus trouble . . . has received considerable dental attention and has been furnished with six pairs of eye glasses since 1938, none of which has suited him for very long. His main complaints have been pains in the head and gas pains in the abdomen."[50] The prison psychiatrist described Neumer as "a sinister looking individual, who would be capable of all sorts of things."[51] In addition to amassing this remarkable record of sick calls, Neumer began adding another form of protest to his repertoire—filing legal briefs.

He petitioned the courts with claims of inadequate medical attention and sent the complaints to Bureau of Prisons headquarters and to the attorney general. He also filed petitions in the federal district court in San Francisco. In one he asked the court to "intervene in the administration of the institution," and in another to "force the Warden to allow certain privileges, not granted under regulation, such as receipt of articles . . . sent by relatives." In a third he claimed that his painting materials and paintings had been "stolen" by prison officials.

A fourth petition concerned the warden's refusal to allow him to complete a University of California Extension course in English. For the course's first assignment, which was to describe reasons for taking the course, Neumer had written,

> I am preparing myself to write a book, upon my release from Alcatraz, in which I intend to expose the brutality of the administration. . . . My suffering and the suffering of my co-inmates has aroused in me a desire to expose the prevailing conditions of Alcatraz, and a desire to tell the public about the many men these vile conditions have driven insane and to in-

sane attempts to escape. I have been a victim of these conditions for nearly eleven years. I realize that I must learn good English before I can expect to write a book that the public would read through to the concluding plea at the end: "Please help those poor men I left in prison."[52]

Warden Johnston did not take kindly to this attempt to use a privilege for the explicit purpose of attacking the administration of the prison and ordered Neumer to be removed from the class. In response, Neumer contacted the American Civil Liberties Union of Northern California to enlist support for the writ of mandamus he filed in federal court in an effort to overrule the warden. In a letter to Johnston, the ACLU director agreed that while Neumer had no legal right to enroll in the course, he supported the request.[53]

Neumer took his case to U.S. Senators William Knowland and Alexander Wiley. In his letter to Wiley, who was the chairman of the Judiciary Committee, Neumer advised the senator that an Alcatraz inmate "does not throw away 3,000 days [of good time], more than eight years, in one moment of protest against the mistreatment of someone else and himself unless he has a very strong sense of social obligation and he does not write letters like this one unless he has some courage."[54]

It was standard practice with such letters for Warden Johnston to forward them to Bureau headquarters along with his version of the truth:

> The fact of the matter is, we would like him and other men to enroll for courses because we do our best to encourage every inclination towards self improvement, however, when Neumer enrolled and wrote out the first lesson which consists of statements why a student is taking the particular course, he made it the occasion for a diatribe against the prison and the Bureau; said he was taking the course in order to equip himself to expose the prison and its officials upon his release. It was such a misuse and abuse of privileges, such a manifest display of his desire to flaunt regulations and to flaunt his intention to continue his contumacious conduct that I told the Deputy Warden to turn back his enrollment and take him off the list until he got himself in a frame of mind to improve. Before he was in "D" Block, we did permit him to purchase some paints and art materials as we wanted to encourage him but after he led a disturbance in "D" Block, we decided he was not in the mood to continue art studies.[55]

Neumer's efforts to reverse the prohibition on taking the English course were unsuccessful, and a year later he was back fighting the administration in one of his earlier styles—between January 1, 1947, and February 10, 1948, he reported to sick call 258 times, prompting the chief medial officer to comment, "It is my opinion that this man is a rather severe psychoneurotic, but seems better adjusted now then in the past."[56]

Neumer maintained a clear conduct record, worked on various jobs and in December 1946, by court order, "won a reduction of his 45-year sentence to 25 years . . . as it was determined that the first count embraced the offense related to the second count." In May 1950, when a major protest erupted in the dining hall, he did not participate. With the prospect of release now on the horizon, Neumer asked for the restoration of the 3,000 days of good time he had lost as a result of the destruction of his D block cell during the battle of Alcatraz. The classification committee noted that others involved in similar protests—William Dainard, James Quillen, and Howard Butler—had had good time restored but that Neumer had received "a heavier forfeiture than the others because it appeared he was the instigator of the plot."[57] Part of Neumer's lost days were restored, but 1,427 days were still outstanding. Paul J. Madigan, who had been promoted to deputy warden, recommended that half of the remaining forfeited time be returned because of Neumer's good conduct and his prospects for a job and productive life after release. As Madigan put it, "it would seem at this time he has no desire to associate himself with characters of the underworld."[58] Three months later, restoration of the remainder of Neumer's lost good time was recommended. When the state of Tennessee canceled a detainer for his escape from Brushy Mountain Prison, his conditional release date was moved up to the following April. In approving the restoration of all Neumer's good time Director Bennett commented, "I never thought I'd live to see the day when we could do this. But let's give him his chance."[59]

The last obstacle to Neumer's conditional release came when he reimbursed the government for the destruction of fixtures in his D block cell from his earnings in the prison industries. He left Alcatraz on April 19, 1951, with $218; he was met in San Francisco by his sister and brother-in-law, who drove him to stay in their home in Los Angeles. Through the efforts of a cousin he got a job at a brewery loading beer cases on trucks—a job that had been approved by his probation officer. Later he worked as a carpenter and a cabinetmaker. He never came back to prison.[60]

Richard Neumer's case is a classic example of a "surly and defiant" prisoner who was a management problem for many years and then made what staff called a "marked transformation." As was true for many other Alcatraz prisoners, Neumer's "transformation" was in part recognition that his days in prison were coming to an end. Having a parole or conditional release date gave Neumer and other prisoners like him a realistic goal toward which to work.

Burton Phillips

As recounted in chapter 4, Burton Phillips committed one of the most serious transgressions of prison rules when on September 24, 1937, he slugged James Johnston in the head and then kicked the unconscious warden in the face while he lay on the dining hall floor. Phillips himself was rendered unconscious by a blow to his head from a lieutenant wielding a metal billy club. Phillips was taken to the prison hospital, where he remained for two weeks. He was then placed in a solitary confinement cell until October 26, when he was moved to a segregation cell. He did not leave the disciplinary segregation unit until June 24, 1946—almost nine years later. Phillips had never participated in any of the organized strikes or protests; his was the action of a solitary prisoner protesting the failure of the warden to respond to his demands.

During his first months in D block, Phillips was limited to one full meal each day supplemented by bread and water at other meal times. When he refused to eat the full meal, claiming that the absence of vegetables or milk caused him to get "bloated with gas" and would make his teeth "fall out," he was forcibly fed through a tube down his throat.[61]

Over the nine years he spent in D block, Phillips was written up for "agitating," creating disturbances, calling guards "God damn rotten cock suckers," singing loudly, destroying government property (tore a strip from a sheet to make shoe laces), being insolent ("called Mr. Kaufman 'a goddamn kike'"), and throwing an urn of hot coffee at inmate James Grove (after Grove threw coffee at him). Each of these infractions resulted in Phillips being locked up in a solitary confinement cell.

Phillips was allowed out of his cell twice each week for yard recreation and was permitted to take correspondence courses in physics, math, and chemistry. His devotion to the study of physics was given surprising support. It all began in October 1939, when James Bennett walked through the disciplinary segregation unit, stopped to talk with Phillips through the cell bars, and suggested that Phillips write to him and describe "how he felt about things."

Phillips's response covered sixty-six pages. He began the letter by advancing his theory that the horsepower of any internal combustion motor could be increased by 10 to 20 percent without an increase in the weight of the motor. Citing his experience in "souping-up" automobile engines, he asked Bennett to refer his letter to the National Inventors Council to which he could provide the reasoning behind his theory and obtain a patent. Phillips then began an account of his early years:

> Born in Kansas . . . of a fanatically Baptist mother and an aloof, agnostic father, I early acquired the habit of questioning theological beliefs. These pious bumpkins were . . . on the side of the angels and against the missing links of Darwin whose Theory of Evolution seemed to me to be the obvious truth.

Phillips went on to describe a happy childhood and, at age fourteen, reading books on biology, history, war and the works of H. G. Wells. He purchased a series, *The Boy Mechanic,* and decided to become an electrical engineer. After he graduated from high school, however, his parents' divorce cost him the opportunity to study engineering at the University of Michigan. He took a job as a dishwasher, delivered newspapers, and worked in a large bakery, all the while resenting society's failure to provide him with the means to pursue a university education and a career in engineering. In his long letter to Bennett, Phillips cited the work of Wells, H. L. Mencken, Aldous Huxley, John Dewey, and Bertrand Russell. He wrote approvingly of the Nazi effort to create a super race through selective breeding. Returning to his life story, he wrote that when withdrawal from difficulties became impossible only one course was left to him—aggression:

> In the last six or seven years a decreasing optimism about my own future has steadily exacerbated this tendency to aggression and only with difficulty have I kept my hands off my persecutors. . . . Exposed for five years to sadistic, cursing guards; petty, illegal, arbitrary repressive rules; continual, unnecessary slamming of steel doors; with no possibility for relaxation, solitude and the humanizing tendencies of interesting work, constructive companions, friendly visitors and soft music I have begun to feel the sadistic impulses . . . the desire to inflict harm, to retaliate for my own misery and sense of frustration. This is an almost complete reversal of my earlier habits—in five years Society has succeeded in pushing me 50,000 years backward to the traits of my savage ancestors. This is called justice.

In another part of this letter, Phillips emphasized his determination not to give in to the prison authorities:

> I have no feeling of penitence or guilt or anything except exasperation over my carelessness which has been used by my persecutors as an excuse to

vent their sadistic, jungle impulses upon one of their fellow men. . . . [I am] psychically unable, and by habit unwilling, to adopt the expected attitude of cringing obeisance before my plutocratic "herren-folk."[62]

Remarkably, Johnston—the recipient of Phillips's violent assault—had Phillips's lengthy letter typed and forwarded it to Bennett. Johnston even accompanied the manuscript with a note stating that Phillips had asked that his "theory of disintegrating atoms with subsequent release of energy under almost perfect control" be referred to Dr. Paul R. Heyl, a well-known physicist at the U.S. Bureau of Standards. After reading the letter and Johnston's note, Bennett contacted Heyl, who agreed to review Phillips's theory. Heyl responded by saying that the theory was limited by the prisoner's limited access to recent scientific literature, and that review of this literature would cause him to modify his theory. Bennett asked Johnston to convey Heyl's remarks to Phillips and to remind him that "The fact that a distinguished scientist has read his paper and commented on the extent of his knowledge should encourage him to continue with his studies."[63]

Phillips was encouraged by this response and wrote to Johnston a few days later asking permission to send the design for a new type of vacuum pump to Thomas McFarland, professor of electrical engineering at the University of California. This request was also approved and Professor Mc-Farland, surprised to receive such a request from one of Warden Johnston's "wards," sent back a detailed technical reply. In the meantime Bennett instructed his headquarters staff to locate in the Library of Congress some technical books requested by Phillips. Over the next several years, dozens of books on electromagnetism and applied and theoretical physics were sent to Alcatraz and returned to the Washington office.

This level of attentiveness to a prisoner's interests—a prisoner who was being held in disciplinary segregation for slugging a warden—would not occur in any of the penitentiaries that succeeded Alcatraz. The personal interest of the director of the federal prison system in the welfare of a single prisoner in disciplinary segregation and the forgiving nature of a warden who was the victim of an assault would be out of the question in contemporary prisons, where staff–inmate relations are almost completely depersonalized and confrontational.

In addition to his involvement in scientific subjects unfamiliar to most of the rest of the convict population, Phillips's years at Alcatraz featured frequent correspondence with, and monthly visits from, his mother, who moved to San Francisco to be close to her son. Mrs. Phillips was allowed to meet several times with Warden Johnston to discuss her son's situation. Phillips's justification for his attack on Johnston, as suggested in his letter to Bennett, appeared in a memorandum prepared by the chief medical officer. According to Dr. Ritchey, "Phillips felt that in no other way could he gain the attention which he deserved in securing certain educational privileges to which he thought he was entitled. He is quick to resent any effort in what he calls the 'breaking of his spirit'"[64] Ritchey recommended that Phillips and seventeen other convicts, including Harmon Waley, Jack Hensley, and Dale Stamphill, be considered for transfer to the Springfield Medical Center since they had been "clearly defined as Constitutional Psychopathic inferiority."

Even after he had spent eight years in disciplinary segregation and was characterized as being "very opinionated and paranoid in his interpretations of daily events," Phillips was acknowledged to have "superior intelligence."[65] Finally, in June 1946 Phillips was returned to general population. He continued his correspondence course study of physics, math, and engineering through the University of California and received good reports for his work in the laundry.

He sent an explanation of his attack on Johnston to a friend of his mother's, an official of the Internal Revenue Service, who asked Phillips about his "attitude toward the Warden." Phillips replied as follows:

> My attitude toward the Warden is somewhat better than neutral—no resentment for past actions; no ill will or desire for future trouble; a certain amount of admiration and respect because he has been big enough to have made no attempt to avenge himself for my trouble with him in the past.

Phillips explained that the warden was only the symbol of the forces that said to him, "You are an outcast, we have no tasks for you to perform, no use for your brains and ability, no intention of helping you develop your skill. . . . You are serving a life sentence in an institution from which no one is ever to be paroled and the only thing left for you is to die."

He expressed his gratitude to the warden for being allowed to carry on his studies and concluded: "I have seen enough of prisons to realize that I cannot wear them out and I have no further desire to do so."[66]

Phillips's record of good conduct (after eighteen misconduct reports) and work continued. A report five years later noted, "He never complains or enters into any alliances with anyone. He tends strictly to his own business. . . . This inmate has made a complete reversal of form and is doing very well."[67]

In November 1950 Phillips was transferred from Alcatraz. At Leavenworth his continued "good attitude" led to his release on parole on January 12, 1952. When he came out of prison, he began working as a welder's helper in a blacksmith shop for $4 a day plus room and board—a job his mother had arranged for him. Several months later he took on a job in a print shop and six months after release he had saved enough money to buy the shop and go into business for himself. In the meantime, Phillips and his mother invested in oil wells—his father had been in the oil lease business—and they soon began receiving royalties.

In 1957 Phillips sold the print shop and became a full-time oil lease operator, a job at which he became very successful. By 1963 he was reporting monthly income in excess of $6,000. Phillips did not marry, maintained a rather solitary existence, and rigorously conformed to the conditions of parole. He had close and friendly relationships with his parole officers, but a report by one parole officer characterized him as "mad at society" and said that he was "very bitter toward the institution at Alcatraz and all of the persons and things connected with it ... especially ... certain wardens and Mr. Bennett in particular."[68] (When a copy of this report reached the Bureau of Prisons, James Bennett wrote to the parole officer expressing his surprise that Phillips continued "to bear animosity toward me because I, as much as anybody else, was responsible for his eventual parole, having, among other things, transferred him to Leavenworth despite his unprovoked attack on Warden Johnston.")[69]

In July 1965 another letter to the parole board described the importance of Phillips's relationship with his parole supervisors:

> Mr. Phillips and I have excellent rapport. He reports that I am the only one with whom he can sit down and discuss any of his problems not of a business nature. He confided that he certainly forgets his predicament when he is involved in the everyday struggle of business and earning a living, but he cannot forget the years that he spent at Alcatraz. He reports that he does not discuss these indignities with anyone else ... and that it relieves him a good deal when he can discuss some of his activities within the society at Alcatraz.[70]

Phillips's reporting requirements were reduced over the years from monthly to one report a year, and on July 15, 1976, at age sixty-four, his parole was terminated. He served his years at Alcatraz and, after his return to the free world by himself, did not associate with other ex-convicts, even to talk about the Rock, and he never had another arrest. But Burton Phillips never got over his anger and frustration at BOP and Alcatraz officials, including those who took extraordinary steps to help him, and his years on the island left memories and psychological scars that never healed.

Urbaytis, Hensley, and Butler

Three more inmates—Joe Urbaytis, Jack Hensley, and Howard Butler— deserve mention here because of their records of persistent individual resistance. In all three cases, their behavior improved over time, as the possibility of release became more real.

Joe Urbaytis accumulated a series of minor rules violations: for passing an article (a book of matches) between cells, wasting food ("left a large portion of dessert on his plate"), loafing, insolence, and speaking with profanity to an officer. When the January 1936 strike began, Urbaytis was one of the first men to walk off his job and was quickly identified as a ringleader, promoting the strike to other inmates. For these actions he was placed in solitary confinement and then sent to an isolation block cell, where he remained for the next seven months. When he was finally returned to the general population, Urbaytis continued to resist the regime with a series of infractions ranging from disobedience, refusing to work, insubordination, and insolence to participating in a strike, fighting with an inmate, and creating a disturbance. Each time he was placed in solitary confinement on a restricted diet and forfeited all privileges.[71]

Urbaytis's conduct changed for the better after these violations—not as a consequence of months in the hole but as a result of a significant change in the length of his sentence. In October 1941 his fifty-year sentence was ruled invalid and his time was cut in half. With fifty years ahead of him when he arrived at Alcatraz, Urbaytis had little incentive to conform to the rules, but when his sentence was suddenly halved and he calculated the good time he could accumulate and deducted it from the new parole eligibility date for his remaining twenty-five-year term, a return to the free world suddenly appeared on the horizon and provided a powerful incentive for improved conduct. As Urbaytis's experience illustrates, staff at Alcatraz used good time earned or yet to be earned in amounts that could add or detract years from a convict's sentence as a powerful punitive sanction for infractions and equally powerful incentive for good behavior. Two months after his sentence was cut in half, a portion of the good time he had forfeited was returned because his conduct improved; the remainder of the good time he had lost was restored a year later, which advanced his release date to February 13, 1943. At the end of February he was transferred to Leavenworth to spend a year in a standard prison environment before his release.

In 1946, following his release from Leavenworth, Joe Urbaytis was gunned down at an unlicensed after-hours supper club he operated. A newspaper account of this incident, titled "Joe Urbaytis, Gangland Desperado, Is Murdered," ended with the statement "There were no witnesses to the shooting and Urbaytis died within a short time of wounds in the shoulder and chest, stubbornly refusing to name his slayer."[72]

Jack Hensley arrived at Alcatraz from Atlanta on October 5, 1935, for the usual reasons—"the nature of the crime, duration of sentence, former prison record, and conduct of inmate in institution."[73] He had served previous sentences in the Tennessee State Penitentiary and at Tucker Prison Farm in Arkansas. With a confederate he had escaped from Tucker and kidnapped a taxi driver, who drove them to a town where they forced the postmaster and her husband to open the post office safe. Hensley and his associate took $27.89, bound and gagged the couple, and escaped in their car. Hensley lived off the proceeds of highway robberies for a year until he was apprehended, tried, and sentenced to twenty-five years for the post office robbery and assault. A psychiatric examination pronounced Hensley "correctly orientated in all spheres" but concluded that with an IQ of 77 he had "border-line efficiency . . . without psychosis."[74] After Hensley attacked another prisoner in the dining room and then "defaced" his isolation cell while continuing to "sing, whistle, and talk," he made his way onto the list of prisoners who were being designated to populate the new prison at Alcatraz.

Hensley's trouble on the Rock began two months after his arrival and continued for years. By December 1948, after his conduct finally improved and he was transferred back to Leavenworth, he had accumulated fifty-one misconduct reports, mostly for causing disturbances by talking too loudly or fighting with other prisoners. He was also cited for being a "mean leader and a dangerous agitator" in two strikes, for which he spent eleven days in lower solitary and twenty days in closed-front isolation cells on the third tier in A block. He resided for many months in D block isolation and solitary confinement cells as well as in the isolation cells in A block for insolence, possession of contraband, disobeying orders, refusing to work, creating disturbances, and assorted offenses ranging from smoking violations and wasting food to refusing to clean his cell and entering the cell of another inmate. A 1945 special progress report commented that though Hensley's misconduct reports were "not serious in nature," their frequency made him a "great nuisance . . . and reflected his 'maladjustment.'"[75]

The Alcatraz staff attributed Hensley's misconduct to a feeling of hopelessness related to a detainer that required he be returned to the Tucker Prison Farm after he had served his federal sentence. Tucker Prison Farm was noted for its brutality and for forcing prisoners to work as indentured slaves for private contractors.[76] In addition, a psychiatric assessment by Dr. Ritchey, the chief medical officer, diagnosed Hensley as having a "Constitutional Psychopathic Inferiority, Paranoid Personality."[77] In 1940, when Bureau headquarters was concerned about the possibility that mental health issues were becoming a problem on the island, Dr. Ritchey was asked to produce a list of prisoners suffering from "clearly defined constitutional psychopathic inferiority" to be considered for transfer to the Springfield Medical Center. Jack Hensley's name appeared on a list of eighteen, but like almost all of the others he was never transferred to Springfield.[78]

Hensley was also an active litigant. His first action in federal court, on November 21, 1934, shortly after he arrived, challenged the legality of his imprisonment. In October 1941 he filed a writ of habeas corpus arguing that his convictions and sentences should be voided because he did not have the assistance of legal counsel, that he did not voluntarily waive the right to the assistance of counsel, and that the U.S. attorney denied him assistance of counsel. He also contended that he was deceived and coerced into pleading guilty by the U.S. attorney, who threatened him with a sentence of thirty-five years and told Hensley that if he pleaded guilty he would get a term of only ten years—which was not the sentence he was awarded. In October 1943 he applied for executive clemency; he wrote letters to Congress and continued to file appeals and writs until 1946.

In September 1948, with his conditional release scheduled for June 1950, Hensley was transferred first to Leavenworth and then to Atlanta. He maintained clear conduct records in both institutions. A new test raised his IQ from 77 to 100 and he was regarded as a reliable worker. In April 1950 Hensley was conditionally released from Atlanta and taken into custody by Arkansas authorities. After serving only a short time in Arkansas, he was conditionally released to Memphis, Tennessee.[79]

From the beginning of his federal sentence in 1934, Hensley had maintained correspondence with Willie May Tanner, reported in probation documents to have "a good reputation in her community." Hensley's release plan called for him to marry Tanner as soon as possible after his release. (She had written to the warden in Atlanta pleading for his release: "he is awful dear to me and I am living and praying for the day when he can return to me . . . will you please do this for a woman that has loved and waited for 20 years for her one and only love?")

Hensley married Tanner and remained with her for three years until, as he put it in a letter to James Bennett, "things just drifted from bad to worse and now my wife and I have separated."[80] Hensley moved in with his aged mother and went to work for a company that manufactured furniture for churches. He informed Bennett that he had learned about machinery and woodworking at Alcatraz and had become the supervisor of eighteen men working under him. His postrelease arrest record, during eight years on conditional release, listed one arrest for selling heroin to undercover officers in Washington, D.C. The circumstances of this offense are unclear since no jail or prison time followed and he continued under conditional release supervision to its termination in 1959. Jack Hensley had accumulated more disciplinary reports at Alcatraz—fifty-one—than his fellow prisoners, but that record did not stop him from building a successful life in the free world, or from sending a Christmas card every year to his principal captor, James Bennett.

Howard Butler's criminal career, like Richard Neumer's, was unremarkable and would normally have qualified him only for confinement in a standard medium-security prison. He served some jail time for minor offenses and an eight-month sentence in an industrial school. Then Butler and a co-defendant robbed four gas stations in Washington, D.C., taking $35 and a radio in one case, $40 in another, $10.80 in a third, and $47.40 in the fourth. He received what appears to be a rather stiff sentence of twelve to twenty-two years for these robberies, and he was committed to the District of Columbia's Lorton Reformatory. There, he combined consistent insolence to staff and refusal to obey prison rules with assaultive behavior toward other prisoners.

After compiling eleven misconduct reports, he was committed to St. Elizabeth's Hospital for a psychiatric evaluation. He was diagnosed as a "constitutional psychopath" and returned to Lorton, but because he could not get along in a dormitory setting, D.C. authorities received permission to transfer him to the Bureau of Prisons. Butler was sent to the Atlanta penitentiary, but living in a cell did not improve his conduct.

Within a year, he had been locked up in solitary confinement on three occasions, twice for being disorderly and once for using profanity. After another psychiatric evaluation confirmed the earlier diagnosis, the Atlanta staff concluded that Butler would continue to be a problem "due to his inability to learn by experience" and predicted that he would "continue to agitate and resist . . . properly constituted authority." They asked Alcatraz to take their problem.[81]

Butler arrived at the island in June 1940, where a neuropsychiatric examination agreed with the "constitutional psychopath" diagnosis but added that the prisoner had a "paranoid personality." (Butler told Dr. Ritchey he had asked to be placed in isolation at Atlanta so that he could avoid the "nagging of officers.")

Howard Butler might have been an inconsequential felon, but the staff and inmates at Alcatraz came to know him well over the next ten years due to his continued inability to submit to "properly constituted authority." He was written up thirty-seven times, including nine times for fighting (each with a different inmate), fourteen times for infractions in the dining hall (ranging from loud talking and wasting food to causing confusion), and on many occasions for insolence, making threats to officers, and refusing to work (his usual response to guards was "fuck yourself"). In addition to refusing to obey orders and fighting with his fellow prisoners, he was caught on two occasions on his knees "committing an act of degeneracy," which made life with his fellow prisoners even more difficult. Altogether he lost 2,640 days of good time and spent many months in D block because he was labeled "a sex pervert and a troublemaker."

But by 1948, Butler was eleven years older than when his term began, and following a familiar pattern for prisoners at all penitentiaries, including Alcatraz, his conduct improved. He completed a course in English, read books of fiction, subscribed to five magazines, and gradually saw his good time restored. Although black, he tried not to associate with other black prisoners, particularly those who had been sentenced for offenses committed while they were in the military.[82]

Staff reported favorably on the turnaround of Butler's conduct even though he had occasional fights with other prisoners, interpreting these events as the consequence of his being provoked by other prisoners about his homosexuality, and because "his courtesy and affability with staff does not enhance his popularity." Large segments of his good time were restored, and in June 1952 he was conditionally released from Alcatraz to the District of Columbia with $195.

In 1954 Butler's freedom was threatened when he was arrested for having "carnal knowledge" and committing sodomy on two girls, one age thirteen and the other age fourteen, at the residence where they all lived. Subsequently, several of the charges were dropped and a trial on the other charges resulted in a hung jury. The assistant U.S. attorney then advised the court that all charges should be dropped because "the two girls were not truthful and both had bad reputations." Butler's supervision in the community was continued; he returned to his job as a steamfitter and continued working toward reconciliation with a woman he had married before his imprisonment.[83]

In these cases of persistent individual resistance the actions, irrational as they may have seemed to others, stemmed from the prisoners' unique psychological needs and personal histories. Some believed they were victims of injustice and acted out of anger and even a sense of moral outrage; others, perhaps with a stronger than usual drive to preserve their individual integrity and not bow to the humiliating demands of the regime, found that acting self-destructively was the only available way to assert their individuality. And most of these men seem to have been caught up in a self-reinforcing cycle in which their resistance brought on sanctions that only increased the anger, despair, and hopelessness that motivated the resistance in the first place.

These cases also cast doubt on assumptions about the relation between prison behavior and postrelease success. Interviews with staff revealed their uniform judgment that persistent rule breakers were highly unlikely to stay out of prison after release. In fact, this view was reflected in the rationale for the creation of Alcatraz. However, as intimated in this chapter and described more fully in chapter 13—and despite prodigious records of rule violations at Alcatraz—Howard Butler, Jack Hensley, Richard Neumer, Burton Phillips, and Harmon Waley all had productive lives after they were finally released and never returned to prison.[84] These cases raise important questions about the assertion that troublemaking in prison leads to troublemaking after release. This proposition will be discussed further in part 3, where the postprison experiences of all the men released during the gangster era are examined. Contrary to both conventional and penological wisdom, more than half of the Alcatraz convicts, including the rule breakers, decided in prison that they had served enough penitentiary time and that the remainder of their lives should be spent in the free world.

CELEBRITY PRISONERS

Of the 1,547 felons sent to Alcatraz during its thirty-year existence, three names stand out above all others: Al Capone, George Kelly, and Alvin Karpis.[1] Every television documentary, every article and book written about the prison and its inmates has featured these men. Their status in American criminal history and in popular folklore, however, is based on their exploits before they went off to federal prison, not on what happened during their years on the Rock. Hollywood movies about them, including *Machine Gun Kelly, The Alvin Karpis Story,* and several about Capone, centered entirely on their criminal careers.

When they arrived at Alcatraz, these men—along with the slightly less notorious "public enemies" Harvey Bailey, John Paul Chase, and Albert Bates—essentially disappeared from public view, a result of the deliberate attempt by the Department of Justice to diminish the reputations of the country's leading gangsters once they were incarcerated. The dearth of real information about their lives in prison stands in stark contrast to the publicity surrounding their apprehension, which was in large part engineered by J. Edgar Hoover and the FBI's public relations machine and intended to enhance the director's reputation. Even after Capone, Kelly, and Karpis were locked up on Alcatraz, Hoover made sure that selected columnists and authors, notably Courtney Ryley Cooper, continued to have material to publish dramatic accounts of how the FBI brought these men to justice.[2]

With the exception of Alvin Karpis, the Rock's best-known "public enemies" participated only half-heartedly, if at all, in the strikes and organized protests that occurred during their years on the island and (with the exception of Dock Barker) did not take part in any escape plots. They were accustomed to giving, not taking, directions from others, but more important they knew that the government would use any misconduct to deny their transfers to prisons where they could be considered for parole. For the most part, they kept to a small group of trusted friends, trying, as George Kelly put it, to "drift along" on "the tide of time." Nevertheless, other prisoners respected them as "stand-up convicts." Harvey Bailey and John Paul Chase, by virtue of the strength of their personalities and their unquestionable loyalty to the convict code, were held in very high esteem by their fellow prisoners. George Kelly was regarded as a good con, but somewhat full of himself. Albert Bates was a quiet convict whose status came not from his own reputation but from his association with Kelly. Al Capone was greatly admired as a genuine outlaw, but as his mental health deteriorated he began to become an object of derision.

An accurate account of the lives of these men after they disappeared behind prison walls is important because the ultimate villainy they symbolized served to justify the severity of punishment at Alcatraz. What will become evident in the pages ahead, however, is how unremarkable were their prison careers compared to their criminal careers. Readers will have already noted that at no place in the preceding chapters have Capone, Kelly, Bates, or Karpis featured in the descriptions of significant events on the island. They did not attempt to escape, and while Capone, Bates, and Karpis were involved in several fights, none had lethal consequences. None were identified as ringleaders during strikes (until that charge was levied against Alvin Karpis in the early 1950s). Each man acquired a handful of disciplinary reports, but none came even close to engaging in the kind of unrelenting resistance best represented by the record of the slightly less high-profile offender Harmon Waley.

AL CAPONE

Before arriving on the Rock in August 1934, Capone had spent ten months in Pennsylvania prisons, seven months in Illinois's Cook County Jail, and twenty-seven months at Atlanta, and in all three places he had received preferential treatment. At Alcatraz, Capone discovered that life was to be considerably different for him. There were no more special privileges, as Alcatraz staff wanted to make certain the press had no reason to report that Capone was being treated differently than any other prisoner. Whereas in his previous incarcerations he had enjoyed frequent communication with his family and friends by mail, telephone, and through visits, at Alcatraz these contacts were largely severed, although his mother and his wife, Mae, continued to visit and correspond with him. Nor could he make use of the influence and prestige he had commanded at the other prisons. Because of their own high-profile criminal or prison exploits, few convicts at Alcatraz were as impressed by Capone's persona and reputation as the inmates had been in Atlanta, the Cook County Jail, or the Pennsylvania prison.

Alvin Karpis, who later succeeded Capone as Public Enemy no. 1, compared the man he saw on the Rock to the gang lord he knew in Chicago:

> During the depression Capone dispensed life and death at a whim yet hundreds hailed him as a saint as they joined his "soup lines." His personal armored car was always flanked fore and aft by other vehicles loaded with machine guns and bodyguards.
>
> In Alcatraz, he's a fish out of water, he knows nothing of prison life. For example, he is allowed to subscribe to various magazines and like any prisoner he is permitted to send the magazines to other inmates after he reads them. Ironically, Capone, who gave orders to eliminate hundreds of lives, is now confined to rubbing out names on his magazine list when he becomes displeased or annoyed with fellow cons. It's kind of sad.[3]

With a sentence that was short compared to those of other convicts on the Rock, Capone kept his focus on his release, rather than on how he might make himself more accepted by the other convicts. He wanted to serve his sentence as easily and quickly as possible. That meant avoiding activities that would cause him to lose good time or be denied parole. His celebrity status, however, made it difficult for him to keep a low profile. He was involved in several altercations with other inmates who wanted him to finance their escape plots and other schemes, or who wanted to enhance their reputations by trying to intimidate the biggest name on the island.

Capone's troubles began shortly after his arrival on the Rock. The desire to keep his record clean in order to shorten his sentence with good-time deductions caused him to decide not to join in several strikes that happened not long after the trains from Leavenworth and Atlanta deposited their cargos on the island. His failure to support an effort to improve conditions for all inmates, coupled with the widespread belief that he controlled enormous financial resources and had minions awaiting his instructions for the distribution of those resources, made him an object of contempt and the subject of extortion rumors.

Even with Capone securely locked up in a single cell at Alcatraz, the FBI continued to investigate rumors and allegations that he had used his money and influence to gain favors at Atlanta, or alternately, that he had been the victim of extortion there. In February 1933 an Alcatraz inmate told FBI agents that Capone had been threatened with death or bodily harm by several inmates at Atlanta who connived with three guards to force him to provide money for drugs. Capone, the informant reported, had been threatened with a knife to his throat and told to deliver $1,800 to a small hotel in Atlanta where guards were to pick it up. The guards in turn were said to have used part of the money to purchase morphine, which they brought into the penitentiary and delivered to an inmate. Two of these Atlanta guards and the inmate receiving the drugs had subsequently been transferred to Alcatraz, as had the informant. The informant also stated that he had been told that Capone had paid off a prison doctor by sending him a Shetland pony.[4]

When apprised of these charges, Atlanta Warden Aderhold informed Bureau of Prisons headquarters that he had heard all these allegations before the informant had left for Alcatraz. Aderhold stated that there had been no other negative reports about the guards who were alleged to be involved in the extortion plot. As for the doctor, who lived on the federal reservation with other senior staff, no pony had ever been observed.[5]

Capone worried about the effect the rumors might have on his reputation and prison influence, and the treatment he would receive as a result. During his first year at Alcatraz, he applied for parole, concluding his application with this plea:

> I am 36 years old and all my life I have always tried to be a man, I have always keep my word, at no time did I ever steal or force anyone to give me any thing by force, I have keep up all of my family all the time, and the good Lord knows, I have, and intend to keep on doing so all my life. I have made mistakes, all of us have . . . I sure owe my dear son, wife, mother and the rest of my family for the grief I have caused them. . . . I was indicted for 27 counts, was found guilty of 2, got 5 years each, to run consecutively and 1 year for failure to file. . . . I realize that I broke the Laws, and should be punished, but not to the extent of 11 years, I realize also that I am notorious and make good copy for the Press, and used by every politician for Smoke screens in order to be elected. . . . So I would sure appreciate a new deal for Capone. Please try.[6]

In August two members of the board came to the island to listen to Capone argue his own case for parole, but on October 11, 1935, the full board rejected his application.

In May 1936 Capone's brother, Ralph, received a letter from a recently released Alcatraz prisoner named Charles Mangiere. In the letter, Mangiere alleged that a group of inmates known as the Touhy gang had approached Capone for $5,000 to be used to hire a gunboat for an escape attempt. According to the letter, they had threatened to kill Capone if he refused. Mangiere also claimed that the same group of inmates had planted a table knife under Capone's seat in the dining room, which "would have caused him to go to the hole and maybe lose his good time" had the deputy warden not decided that "Al could not have done it." Mangiere also described how Harmon Waley, who worked in the kitchen and was allied with the Touhy gang, had been trying to poison Capone with food and contraband candy, and that as a result, "Al is afraid to eat the food and his health is failing him." In addition, the group had been "burning his clothes week after week from the laundry." Mangiere explained that these attacks on Capone were the result of his refusal to join the strikes and his determination to be a model prisoner. He concluded his letter with this plea:

> I beg of you as his brother to make these facts known or have me brought before the proper officials at Washington and confronted with the Deputy Warden of Alcatraz. I am sure and feel that Atty. General would not stand to see Al killed in cold blood when he has proven himself a model prisoner and helped to better himself in music.

Mangiere's revelations had already been discounted by the staff at Alcatraz, but Ralph Capone, accompanied by an attorney, visited Bureau of Prisons headquarters, where he identified Alcatraz inmates most likely plotting against his brother. The names included Charles Berta, who was said to be behind the plan to dynamite a path out of the prison and escape on a speedboat, a scheme for which Capone had refused to provide financial backing.

Basil Banghart and other members of the Touhy organization on the island did have reason to hold a grudge against Capone. Convicted on charges that they kidnapped Jake "the Barber" Factor, they were said to believe that their convictions could have been avoided if Capone had prevailed on Factor, a longtime friend, to drop the charges against them.

Capone had a fight with William Coyler of the Touhy gang, an incident he described as follows:

> I was working in the laundry and this fellow tried to start an argument . . . and he picked up some towels and threw them at me; Well, I don't do nothing but he called me a dirty cock sucker and I said, "Why you dirty son of a bitch, I don't take that from no one" and hit him and he starts to hit me with a club handle he had and I picked up the bench and hit him in the arm. . . . I don't bother nobody if they just leave me alone.

In June the Associated Press asked Warden Johnston to verify a report that Capone was being provided a special guard due to threats on his life and that he had been knocked out in a fight with Waley. Johnston, as usual, refused to confirm or deny the story, but in Waley's recollection of the incident (see chapter 11), it was Capone who acted first, hitting him in the back when they were both in the music room one day, and saying "You son of a bitch, I've been looking for you for a long time."

As news of these incidents leaked to the outside world, Capone's family became fearful for his safety. His wife, Mae, wrote to Director Bates pleading with him to transfer her husband: "We love him, he is our life, our everything to us, he is in danger. Who can blame us for feeling otherwise?" Capone's attorney petitioned Bureau headquarters for a transfer for his client claiming, "it is common knowledge that when certain of your guards are off duty in San Francisco they have repeatedly stated, 'Al will never get out of there.'"

An encounter on the morning of June 23, 1936, appeared to justify the family's fears. Capone was at work, cleaning the shower area in the basement of the main cell block. At 9:45 A.M. he walked into the clothing supply room next to the showers and began looking at a mandolin that had been left on the counter. James Lucas, who had been issued a pass to get a haircut in the barbershop in the basement, came into the supply room at that moment. Moving quickly, Lucas stabbed Capone in the lower back with a barber's scissors. Capone whirled around, began wrestling with his assailant, and succeeded in striking Lucas in the face with his fist and the mandolin. The two men were then separated by guard Thomas J. Sanders, who had pulled out his billy club as the altercation began. Sanders pushed Capone behind him and demanded that Lucas surrender the scissors, which he did. Capone was taken upstairs to the prison hospital while Lucas was hustled off to solitary. Questioned as to the reason for the fight, Lucas said he blamed Capone for snitching on him, causing him and a friend to lose their jobs. But Capone reported that the attack was for the usual reason—Lucas had asked him for money that he had declined to provide. Capone suffered a wound in his back, a quarter inch deep and a half inch long, as well as superficial cuts on his hand and arm.

Warden Johnston notified Bureau of Prisons headquarters fifteen minutes after the attack, but he did not notify the FBI; the warden and the Bureau regarded the attack as an internal matter for the prison administration. In a rare deviation from policy, anticipating the flood of rumors that would reach the press due to Capone's celebrity status, a news release about the incident was prepared and distributed. The news stories that followed increased the concerns of Capone's brother, mother, wife, and other family members about his safety. Capone's mother wrote to Director Bates, saying, "I am sick in bed from the shock of hearing how he was stabbed." But their requests to visit him and have the family doctor examine him were denied.

The United States attorney, upon being notified that an assault on a government reservation had occurred, declined prosecution on the grounds that bringing Capone and Lucas over to federal court on the mainland would involve escape risks, and that the amount of good time Lucas could lose through normal prison procedures would be longer than any new sentence he could receive for the assault. On June 26, a good time forfeiture board chaired by Deputy Warden Shuttleworth was convened at Alcatraz. After listening to Lucas's revised explanation for the assault—that Capone had ordered his murder—the board concluded that if Capone had indeed made such a threat, it came after the assault in the clothing supply room, not before. Lucas was penalized by the loss of 3,600 days of good time, in effect adding ten years to his sentence.

Capone had no serious problems with other inmates during the next eighteen months, although he refrained from going to the yard as his health began to rapidly deteriorate. On February 5, 1938, the cell house officer reported he was confused as to the right clothes to wear to work, and he was unable to find his own cell after returning from the dining room. Guards directed him to his cell, where he was held until he could be questioned by Deputy Warden E. J. Miller. Capone's responses to questions were described by Miller as "indistinct, incoherent mumblings. Approximately one hour later, Miller was called back to the cell house after a guard reported that Capone had vomited in his cell and was having "a hysterical fit of some sort." The chief medical officer was called and after a brief examination ordered that Capone be taken to the prison hospital. A convict friend told the doctor that Capone's personality seemed to have changed and that Al was frequently wrong about dates.

An interview with a psychiatrist was scheduled; during it Capone was unable to recall short sentences or telephone numbers. He had been treated for syphilis since his commitment to Atlanta, but now the consulting psychiatrist concluded that the syphilis had "invaded his central nervous system as indicated by . . . changes in memory and personality."

He added, "the two convulsive seizures speak strongly for [a diagnosis of] general paresis."[7]

Warden Johnston feared the news of Capone's behavior would encourage widespread rumors and allegations that imprisonment at Alcatraz was driving inmates crazy. He promptly wrote to Bureau headquarters suggesting that since the expiration of Capone's two five-year sentences was coming up in less than a year, transfer to another prison for treatment before release be considered. To forestall press reports that Capone's mental problems were a result of doing time on the Rock, Johnston released a brief statement announcing that the prisoner was ill but receiving excellent medical care. Within hours, the Capone family was on the telephone to Alcatraz demanding to know the truth of press reports that Al was "raving mad, violent, and being restrained in a straitjacket."

Capone had never permitted the doctors at Atlanta to do a spinal tap to determine the presence of disease but now, confronted with the deterioration of both his mental and physical health, he agreed to the tests; they confirmed the diagnosis of paresis. The medical staff informed Warden Johnston that any patient in Capone's condition might, at certain times, require restraints to keep him from injuring himself or others. Capone, in the meantime, fearing that he had done something wrong that could affect his good conduct record, asked Deputy Warden Miller to come to the hospital so he could explain that "he did not know what had happened, that it was just like a curtain down over him that day . . . if he had done anything wrong, he did not mean to."[8]

Capone continued to have seizures and became incontinent at times. On some occasions he arose many times during the night to make his bed over and over. He sometimes made childish remarks to guard attendants, became noisy and started singing, and occasionally became violent. For one eighteen-hour period restraints were used to confine him to a bed. Hospital records describe the patient's deterioration. From February through May 1938, the records report that on various occasions Capone was "yelling at top of his voice and threw himself under the bed," that he persisted in strange repetitive behaviors including "arranging and rearranging his magazines, making his bed over and over," and dressing and undressing, and that he had also been found "lying in bed, tears running down his eyes." On May 18, the report stated that Capone yelled something about "crazy men" being put in his room and then "threw his bed pan full of fecal matters through his glass transom."

In August of that same year, Capone had an altercation with inmate Ryan:

Capone had been turned into ward "A" by the Guard on duty in the Hospital, to empty his bed-pan. He was in the toilet cleaning it perhaps with a towel which the Ward [Patients] used to clean the table in Ward "A." Ryan who was mopping in front of the toilet, asked him not to use it. Capone flew into a rage and struck Ryan in the temple with the bed-pan inflicting a small laceration. Ryan then struck Capone over the head with the mop. Capone grabbed the mop out of Ryan's hands and when the Guard, Mr. Comerford and Mr. Sabin arrived on the scene Capone was fighting off all of the Pts. in the Ward, but no other injuries resulted.

In September Capone had an epileptic seizure. The declining health of their best-known prisoner posed management and public relations problems for the Justice Department: should he be removed to the Medical Center for Federal Prisoners at Springfield, Missouri, with the likely flood of stories about preferential treatment that such actions would produce? Or should treatment of his medical condition be the decisive factor? The Bureau of Prisons asked Warden Johnston to begin providing daily reports of Capone's condition. The attorney general's office notified Bureau headquarters that Capone was to remain at Alcatraz, regardless of his mental status, until one or two months before his release date. Meanwhile, Capone wrote to his wife and son to assure them that he was feeling fine:

> So you see dearest, there is nothing for any of you to worry about. Smile and keep that smile until your dear dad comes home, and then sweet, watch me strut my stuff, and all my love, and I mean sweet, for you alone, and with heart and soul, and forever and ever.

Despite strenuous efforts by the Bureau to control information coming out of Alcatraz, *Time Magazine* published a story about Capone's behavior in the hospital. "Having finished 6 and ½ years of an 11 year term (almost four of them at Alcatraz)," said the story, "Chicago's no. 1 gangster, Al 'Scarface' Capone was reported to have gone berserk on leaving the dining hall, to have been carried to the infirmary where he spent day after day foolishly making and unmaking his bed."[9] The view of one citizen about what to do with Capone was contained on a postcard sent to Warden Johnston:

> Why fool with that rat Capone. He's only playing possum. Hit him in the head with an ax and dump his rotten carcus [sic] over the wall to the sharks in the ocean. Then keep it up with the rest of his ilk until you rid the country of them. Why should we pay taxes to keep them?

Capone was kept in the hospital but was allowed to go to the yard three mornings a week to do cleanup jobs while other inmates were working, but his days of association with the general population in the cell house, the dining hall, and the yard were over. In August the chief medical officer reported that Capone had suffered a strong negative reaction to the treatment he was receiving: "Temperature 104 degrees, muscle pains . . . became confused, tore up his prayer book . . . serious convulsive movement." At the end of September the medical staff decided to administer a new type of treatment, though they had some concerns about the effects this might have on Capone.[10]

Debates within the Department of Justice went on and on. In October, Bureau headquarters made an inquiry about medical facilities at the Cook County Jail but concluded that Capone would not be likely to receive the medical treatment he needed there. The Department of Justice tried to decide whether Capone, on completion of his two five-year terms, should serve the additional one-year term in the Cook County Jail or remain in the federal prison system, and if he remained a federal prisoner, in what facility. When asked by Warden Johnston as to his own preference, Capone replied that he had been fairly treated and had received good medical care at Alcatraz but preferred to end his sentence in the Cook County Jail because that location would allow much more frequent contact with his family. In December, however, James V. Bennett recommended to the attorney general that Capone be kept in federal custody:

> Capone has a serious case of paresis which seems to be growing progressively more acute. . . . The Cook County Jail has no facilities for treatment and to preclude accusations that Capone was driven insane at Alcatraz and also to do everything possible to prevent discharging Capone in such a condition that he would be more of a public menace than is already the case, I believe our correctional institution or jail at Terminal Island, L.A., ought to be designated for the service of the remainder of his sentence.[11]

The attorney general agreed to this plan, and the warden at the Terminal Island Federal Correctional Institution in Los Angeles harbor was instructed to prepare a special cell in the prison hospital for Capone. He was also told to allow a few other inmates in the area so that Capone "would not feel he is being kept in solitary confinement." While these preparations were under way, Capone was still anticipating a transfer to the Cook County Jail. He wrote to his wife on December 18, 1938, clearly expecting to see his family soon:

I hope to see you and Sonny again before I leave here next January the 18th. I have quite a number of songs written for him to sing them to you and I will play them on the piano and mandola. . . . Tell him [Sonny] to continue with his golf playing as I intend to play with him every day and night and the three of us will see either a movie or a show or go to one of our own nightclubs and dance our troubles away.

On January 4, 1939, Capone's attorney paid $37,000 of his $50,000 fine and court costs in preparation for his client's transfer to Chicago. On January 7 Capone, dressed in a prisoner's blue suit, covered by an overcoat, and wearing a fedora hat and leg irons, was accompanied by three Alcatraz guards to the Lark, a train which traveled due south to Los Angeles. The party got off at Glendale, a stop before the main Los Angeles station. Capone was placed in a car and driven to Terminal Island, where he was locked up in his second island prison. His confusion as to where he was and what was happening to him was evident in the first letter he wrote to his wife from Terminal Island: "If I am not out by the 19th, you will know there is something wrong." Terminal Island Warden Lloyd, given the letter by his staff, went to Capone and informed him that he would be at Terminal Island for a year. After this conversation, Capone, still anxious not to displease the federal government, agreed to rewrite his letter and inform his wife that he preferred to serve the one-year sentence where he was rather than at the Cook County Jail.

The departure of America's most prominent gangster from what had become the country's most prominent penitentiary brought forth expressions of relief in San Francisco. An article in the *San Francisco News* said it this way:

> One reputation San Francisco does not cherish, namely that here is situated the depository of the nation's No. 1 enemies. Al Capone was the symbol of that frightful era of gangsterism created by prohibition, an era we want to forget. As long as he was here his name was identified in the public mind with the name of San Francisco. At least we can do a better job of forgetting now that he is no longer with us. So we're glad he's gone.[12]

But expectations that the departure of Al Capone would diminish the Rock's reputation did not turn out to be realistic.

Capone's months at Terminal Island were marked by continued deterioration of his mental faculties. Upon arrival he was reported to be "confused, indifferent, somewhat depressed, [to have] periods of irritability but he was at all times the cooperative person as always."[13] In March his propensity for grandiose ideas was evident when he promised some Mexican inmates he would provide them all jobs at $100 per week and assured them that he would help them with their problems. He frequently became confused as to the location of his cell and his place in the dining room. When he became irritated, he threw items around his cell, broke windows, threw bottles, and threatened other inmates. He focused his hostility at one point on the inmate in the next cell, pounding on his door and threatening to kill him because he flushed his toilet (Capone claimed the inmate flushed his toilet to annoy him). On another occasion, he hit another patient for no apparent reason while they were finishing a game of dominoes. The medical staff recommended that Capone be transferred to the Medical Center for Federal Prisoners at Springfield, Missouri, but Bureau headquarters again turned down the request.

In May Director Bennett made an exception to the rule prohibiting ex-convicts from visiting prisoners and gave permission for Ralph Capone to visit his brother, mainly so that Ralph could see Al's mental condition for himself. After another experiment in which he was allowed to live in a dormitory, Capone got into a fight with several other prisoners and was returned to his room in the hospital. In August he went back to his job cleaning up the prison yard but was removed again after he became agitated during a wrestling match when he thought that one man was biting the other. On September 2, after seeing one inmate knock another down and start to go after him with a fork, Al intervened, striking the aggressor in the face with his fist and throwing him up against a table.

Five days later, he assaulted an inmate attendant in the hospital with no apparent provocation. When the attendant tried to rise from the floor while asking what was wrong, Capone struck him several more times, knocking him down again. When the staff told Capone that he was going to punitive segregation for this assault, he became enraged and shouted that they did not want him to go home and he might as well commit suicide. He then picked up a comb from his bed and scratched both sides of his throat. He forcibly resisted being taken to disciplinary segregation; after he was placed in a cell, he struck his head against the wall and threatened to gouge out his eyes. He was then stripped and given a blanket for warmth. After raving for some fifteen minutes, he finally quieted down and allowed the medical staff to swab his neck wounds.

The investigation into his conduct in the hospital revealed yet another incident ten days before his attack on the attendant. On the evening of September 8, a cardiac patient under strict bed rest in the hospital had reportedly asked Capone to get him a slice of bread when he saw Capone passing by his room. According to the patient, Al responded by telling him, "Go fuck yourself" and then spit in his face. But the following day Capone came into the cardiac patient's room and began tickling his toes. When the patient told him to stop and reminded Capone of how he behaved just the previous night, Capone allegedly "slapped him [in] the face and hit him a severe blow in the abdomen, causing him to vomit up his supper." The patient confided that he had been afraid to give this information as long as Capone was still on the ward but was willing to talk once he knew Al had been sent to isolation.[14]

In punitive segregation, Capone had an altercation with the inmate in an adjoining isolation cell over the noise each man created by flushing his toilet; both men tried to throw water from their toilets into the other's cell, and Capone tried to strike the other man's arms. After thirteen days, Capone promised to behave himself and to stay out of fights and arguments and was returned to his room in the hospital. He agreed to eat his meals in his room and come out only for general yard recreation each day from 1 to 3 P.M. He was not, however, able to stay in his room, so his door was locked except for the exercise period.

As the days passed and the November 16 release date drew closer, Capone became more and more cheerful, often holding forth at length with stories of how he had been poisoned at Alcatraz by inmate James Audett and how his present illness was related to the poisoning of his food. When the prison doctors urged him to seek hospitalization after his release, Capone denied that anything was wrong with him. He stated that Chicago was "too hot" for him and that he planned to live at his Palm Island estate in Florida.

In September 1939 the Bureau of Prisons contacted members of Capone's family, advising them to seek treatment for him on release. When Al's wife, Mae, and brother John visited him that month, they were alarmed at his appearance because he had some twenty cuts on his face that had been painted with mercurochrome. Warden Lloyd admitted to Bureau headquarters that Al did "look kind of wild at the time of the visit" but pointed out that the cuts and nicks were due to Capone's using a razor improperly when he tried to shave himself before the visit.

John Capone, anticipating the crush of newspaper reporters who would want to interview his brother on his release, suggested that Al and the family should stay for several weeks in the Los Angeles area to get the press coverage out of the way before they went on to Florida. The Bureau of Prisons, having no difficulty in imagining what Al would have to say about his unfair treatment in the courts, his troubles at Atlanta, the attempts on his life at Alcatraz, and the treatment applied to a disease he claimed not to have, intended to avoid any such scenario.

During the onset of his illness, FBI agents sought at various times to question Capone about both his own and the criminal activities of others, perhaps hoping that his impaired mental faculties might induce revelations that would not have come forth under normal conditions. For example, shortly before his release from Terminal Island, an agent visited Capone to seek information about certain individuals involved with the Chicago Motion Picture Operators Union and the escape from Alcatraz of Ralph Roe and Theodore Cole. Capone was described by the agent as "in high spirits during the course of the interview." When questioned about one individual in the union, he responded that the man had been one of his [Capone's] men but "got out of line and subsequently was killed in an automobile accident, giving agent a confidential wink of his left eye while making the statement." Capone went on to tell the agent that he had tried to keep Johnny Torrio from becoming involved in the prostitution racket. He admitted that he had made $10,000,000 during Prohibition, but he had never been interested in any of the rackets pertaining to vice. He expressed his contempt for newspaperman Randolph Hearst; he described a visit he had made with Jack Dempsey to Hearst's beach home in Santa Monica, California, where he claimed "to have witnessed various sexual activities which disgusted him." Capone then rambled on, periodically asking the agent, "What are we talking about?"

When asked what happened to Roe and Cole, Capone replied that in his opinion Roe had successfully escaped but not Cole, although he could not explain why one man made it and the other did not. Capone advised the agent that on his release he was going to establish four furniture and automobile factories in Florida that would provide employment for thousands of people. At the end of the interview Capone claimed that he was in charge of recreation at the Terminal Island Prison. This interview convinced federal agents that the accuracy of any revelations offered by the Big Boy could never again be known and that he would never make a credible witness in a courtroom.[15]

In October Ralph Capone notified Bureau of Prisons headquarters that he accepted the Bureau's strong recommendation that his brother be hospitalized on his release; he reported that he had arranged to have his brother admitted to Johns Hopkins Hospital to be treated by Dr. Joseph Moore, a specialist in the treatment of general paresis.[16] Director Bennett then instructed Warden Lloyd to transfer Capone to the penitentiary at Lewisburg, Pennsylvania, just before his release from federal custody.

Capone arrived at Lewisburg on November 16. He was picked up by Mae and his brother Ralph, driven to Baltimore, and placed in the care of Dr. Moore. The medical staff at Terminal Island was pessimistic about Capone's future:

> This patient has been given every opportunity to adjust to this institution and has remained poorly cooperative and viciously assaultive. He presents neurological, psychological, and psychiatric evidence of general paresis, expansive-grandiose type. He is in need of continued hospitalization and treatment upon the termination of his present sentence, and such is recommended. The prognosis is poor.[17]

In spring 1940 Capone was taken to his home in Palm Island, Florida. The Capone family compound consisted of some fifteen to eighteen rooms surrounded by high concrete walls on three sides and open to a canal on the fourth side. There Al and Mae had dinner several nights a week with their son Albert "Sonny," who was married and lived a completely law-abiding life. Al was said to be a doting grandfather to Sonny's two children. Five years later, when Al's youngest brother, Matthew Capone, was wanted for "unlawful flight to avoid prosecution for murder," the Palm Island residence was put under continuous surveillance.

This intense coverage was the basis of an "information" report to FBI headquarters that described daily life for the Big Boy and his family. Neighbors interviewed by federal agents could not recall a single instance of a disturbance or any suspicious activity involving the Capone residence since Al's release five years earlier. He had been seen making trips to grocery stores, to a dentist's office, and to visit his son who lived in Hollywood, Florida. Mae Capone was a regular churchgoer, but the local priest's only contact with Al was one visit to their home during the previous summer. Capone told the priest that he did not attend Mass because he felt his presence would arouse curiosity and be disruptive to the priest and regular members of the congregation.

Because Capone was said to be nervous about his safety and that of the family, no automobiles other than Al's and Sonny's were ever allowed to drive through the heavy gates into the compound. Also living in the house were Mae's sister and her husband, a former female friend of Mae's, and Mae's brother and his wife. The family employed two black servants; one was a houseman who did some of the cooking and most of the shopping, and the other was a housekeeper; both were present only during daytime hours.

The entire household worked around Al's fitful sleeping schedule, which called for going to bed at 10:00 P.M. and getting up at 3:00 A.M. The family spent considerable time sitting around the swimming pool, Al dressed in pajamas and a dressing gown. They watched movies on their own projector and screen. Visitors to the home, said to be limited by Ralph and John Capone, included a small number of old-time Chicago friends, including Jake Guzik. Al eagerly looked forward to these visits, and to playing gin rummy and pinochle with family members and old friends. Income for the family was reported to be provided in the form of weekly checks sent by Ralph, who had become the de facto head of the family. Al's main function became telling stories about "the good old days."[18] According to Capone biographer John Kobler, Guzik had been asked after Al's release from prison if his old boss was likely to return to Chicago to take charge of the rackets; Guzik had replied in the negative, noting "Al is nutty as a fruitcake."[19]

Capone was treated by Dr. Moore with antibiotics, which became available during World War II, but they could not reverse the damage already done. His speech became slurred, and on January 19, 1947, he suffered a brain hemorrhage. Last rites were administered; he rallied but then developed bronchial pneumonia. On January 25, with his mother, his wife, his son, his brothers, and his sisters at his side, Alphonse Capone was pronounced dead; he was forty-eight. His family refused to allow the attending physician to conduct an autopsy on his brain. He was the Big Boy, the Big Shot, and Big Al on the streets of Chicago, Cicero, and other cities, but at Alcatraz he was just convict no. 85.

GEORGE KELLY

For George "Machine Gun" Kelly, the transfer to Alcatraz represented a marked improvement over the conditions under which he had been held at Leavenworth. On the island he was back in the general population, where he could talk to Bailey, Bates, and other friends and bank-robbing partners; he began to play bridge during yard periods. Compared to his quarters in the Memphis and Oklahoma City jails and at Leavenworth, he had some freedom of movement at Alcatraz despite the limited confines of the cell house, yard, and work area. The prison surgeon/psychiatrist observed that Kelly adapted well to his situation and accepted his circumstances:

> He accepts the blame for his actions . . . has good insight . . . realized the risks involved in his manner of living . . . is not resentful . . . shows a fairly

normal reaction to a difficult situation . . . does not appear to worry too much . . . and [is] not considered psychotic in any way.[20]

Kelly received only minor disciplinary reports (talking in the dining hall and improper use of clothing) until he participated in the general strike in January 1936. He told the associate warden that he was not sure what the protest was all about but felt he should "stick with the boys a few days." He was placed in an open-front (barred) cell in A block, used during the 1930s as a disciplinary segregation unit. On the second day of his lockup, Kelly yelled to the other strikers that he was through with them, was ready to return to work, and that from that point on he would "do his own time." He was released from A block and returned to work with no loss of privileges.

In September 1937, however, his own frustrations with the regimen on the island prompted Kelly to join another work strike. He told the associate warden: "I just want some different tobacco, shows, and some diversions. I do not go in the yard because it is so inconvenient and uncomfortable. Also Mr. Bixby [assistant director] promised me that I would be able to correspond with my wife and he has not yet kept his promise." He was locked up in isolation on a restricted diet (one full meal every three days, bread and water on the other days) and remained there for eight days.

Over the years, Kelly was characterized in staff evaluations as having a "big shot complex," but it was also noted that "he does not become involved in any conniving or scheming and tries to hold himself aloof from the general population. He has only a few friends with whom he associates, he spends time playing dominoes and bridge." Kelly, whose IQ measured 118 on the Stanford–Binet test, enrolled in several correspondence courses available through the University of California, all of which he completed successfully. Like many other inmates, he spent most of his cell time reading. In February 1936 he wrote to the attorney general, offering to stay at one of the remote locations owned by the U.S. government in the Pacific, Alaska, or the South Pole to "make a meteorology survey" that "would be of benefit to science and the government":

> I could be taken from here secretly, placed on a boat in the Bay and transported with what supplies I would need. This could be managed in such a way that the crew need never know who I was or even that I was a prisoner from Alcatraz. Some kind of arrangements could be made for a boat to stop say every year or two, leave supplies, and take back what data I had accumulated. By this method I would be doing some useful work, serving

my sentence and I believe by the time I was eligible for parole I would be shown some consideration.

His proposal was denied on the grounds that it was too radical, but his writing indicated a high level of literacy, which became more and more evident in his letters as the years rolled by.

The most acute problem for George Kelly in adjusting to life at Alcatraz was the pain of missing his wife, Kathryn. Unlike Bates and Bailey and most of the rest of the Alcatraz convicts, who had severed any connections they had to the women in their lives, Kelly remained deeply attached to Kathryn. He was acutely aware of her anguish over the consequences her mother and stepfather had to suffer for their minor involvement in the detention of Charles Urschel. Before his transfer to Alcatraz, Kelly had written a letter to Kathryn (which was not delivered but forwarded instead to the Bureau of Prisons headquarters and then to the FBI) in which he disavowed any involvement by Ora and R. G. "Boss" Shannon in kidnapping Urschel.

When George arrived at Alcatraz in 1934, he was informed that for the first three months, he could have no mail contact with Kathryn. After that he would be allowed to send her only two letters a year, written on one side each of three sheets of paper, and subject to censorship. When asked by Warden Johnston to accept this special arrangement, Kelly refused, objecting on the grounds that this restriction was not imposed on any other Alcatraz inmates. Johnston and Bureau headquarters did not ease the restriction until November 1935, when the director authorized the four men at Alcatraz whose wives were serving time in federal prison (Kelly, Waley, and Dillinger associates Arthur Cherrington and Welton Spark) to write to their wives and receive letters from them every two months. A year later, this privilege was increased to one letter a month, and two years later the men were allowed to write and receive two letters per month. In 1939 Kelly was allowed to increase the amount of space available in each letter—he was permitted to write on both sides of two of the three sheets of paper allowed.

In July 1940 Kelly wrote to Ora Shannon explaining that he would no longer be writing to her because his letters had been reduced by the mail censor to "senseless drivel." He noted that he would try to continue writing to Kathryn, although the letters would consist of "some kind of foolishness just so we can keep in touch." But a week later, when Kelly had two of the letters he wrote returned to him by the censor, he decided that the interference in his correspondence with Kathryn had become intolerable; he wrote to her, proposing that they discontinue writing. "To me, writing has become an aggravation instead of a pleasure, and I firmly believe that when anything becomes a burden it is time to discontinue the practice." Though he worried about hurting Kathryn's feelings and hastened to assure her, "I love you entirely too much for that," he admitted that when parts of the letters were deleted he "was mad at everyone for days." He also complained that there was so little to tell from one letter to the next. He suggested: "Suppose we discontinue our correspondence until we can write under more favorable conditions; or until you get out and can visit me and we can talk things over. Of course that may be years and then again it may be a matter of only eighteen months or so." He then went into a reverie about their earlier correspondence:

> Do you remember the twelve and fourteen page letters you used to write me daily when I was serving that other "bit." I even recall one that was twenty pages long, and every page as sweet as you are.

Kelly closed the letter saying that if he did not receive a reply, he will know that she agreed. And then he wrote of his love for Kathryn:

> It is almost needless for me to repeat how much I love you. To me you are the grandest girl in the world, and I will love and adore you if I live to be a hundred. I hope you get transferred this month and have a pleasant trip. Give Ora my love and don't forget the one who worships you. All my heart will always be yours angel. Lots of hugs and kisses. As ever, your very own, Geo.

Kathryn responded several weeks later, chastising George for not accepting the reality of prison life, obviously disappointed that her letters had not done more to cheer him:

> I have thought in vain of how to word a reply to you that would express exactly how I feel about "us." And I find that it is most difficult to do. Your letter touched my heart. In fact I cried when I read it as I expected quite a different wording. I shrink from hurting you. That is the farthest desire of my heart. . . . I suppose the best thing I can do is to simply speak plainly and exactly how I feel. First, please understand that I am not "cracking up"; neither is prison getting me down, and in dismissing the love angle, which I admit is hard to do, I feel like this: that to help you in any manner I would gladly give my life, but I can't feel that I have added to you, in any manner, by consistently trying to encourage you, by writing you the long cheerful letters that I have, these years. I tried my level best to help you in doing your time; but it seems I failed miserably. Don't think

that I even considered you less strong than myself. I haven't—but I always feel that if either of us needed encouragement, I should attempt to give it to you because my surroundings have no doubt been more pleasing than yours. I longed for you to avoid trouble, to stand on your own feet for what you know is right and minutely be the man you really are. Well it seems to me you fell down on the job.

She then threatened divorce, stating that she was done with the criminal life, and blamed her marriage to George for getting her in such trouble:

Unless you have changed a lot darling, even if we two were free tomorrow we should be forced to say goodbye. Why? Well, because I'm happy to say that I know I shall never place myself nor permit myself to be placed in a position to ever re-enter prison. I shall be just a "little fish" so to speak if I am fortunate enough to get that one chance and like it. No more "big dough" for me in any place. In other words I find that I am completely cured of any craving for un-legitimate luxuries and my sincere hopes and plans for the future are of a sane, balanced mode in living. I'll never change that viewpoint. I have gone through hell and still am plainly speaking, seeing mother as a daily reminder of my own mistake. The mistake was in my love, and marriage to you. Not that I censure you, I don't. I blame myself. However, I "woke up." I hoped you would but I'm not sure of what goes on in your mind. As you know I like to finish things immediately and I feel if our goodbye is to come, why not now. The hurt will at least be dimmed in the years of incarceration yet ahead of both of us.

But then Kathryn exhorted Kelly to give up his criminal identity:

What you need to do is forget "Machine Gun" Kelly and what he stood for and interest yourself in being plain, kind George, who is just another "con" like myself . . . and if it's impossible for you to make yourself into a man who "thinks straight"—who will go straight when the opportunity presents itself, then I don't want you for a companion.

Having heard about a food strike at Alcatraz, Kathryn stated, "I'm fed up with worries, and god knows I have plenty of my own, so I do think I'd perhaps be happier, in placing you in the background and coasting along with just my own problems." But then she seemed to change her mind and closed the letter as follows:

Let's do this bit of time with the best grace and cheerfully . . . if you really love me as you say, you should be able to keep smiling with me and keep your mind free to a degree of prison non-essentials, and small annoyances, and instead look forward to at some future date, creating with me, the life together that I desire. I do love you, you know mister. . . . Wish I could see you, I do, I do. . . . Now settle down and be happy heart of my heart. Devotedly, your Katrinka

Despite her recriminations and threats of divorce in early September, Kathryn's appeal succeeded at encouraging George to resume their correspondence, although there were periodic misunderstandings when letters were returned to the sender by new or substitute mail censors, who were confused by the changing rules governing their communication. Since letters to and from Alcatraz inmates were censored and retyped, inmates and their correspondents could only guess at what had been removed from sentences that did not end logically or make sense. Both Kellys were well aware that they were also writing for the Bureau of Prisons, FBI officials, and especially the U.S. Parole Board.

During a spring 1940 visit to Alcatraz, Director James Bennett stopped on his walk through the prison to chat with Kelly. He commented that he had had occasion to talk with Charles Urschel (Kelly's kidnap victim) and that Urschel did not seem "hostile" toward Kelly. Bennett then asked Kelly if he had ever thought about writing to Urschel. In this suggestion was implied an extraordinary exception to the prohibition on prisoners corresponding with anyone in the free world other than family members—especially kidnap victims.

Several months later, acting on this suggestion, Kelly sent through Bennett's office a letter to Urschel. From that point on, the Bureau of Prisons allowed Kelly (and his rap partner, Bates) to write to and receive letters from their kidnap victim, Charles Urschel, and E. E. Kirkpatrick, the man who had conveyed the ransom money from the victim's family to them. This extraordinary deviation from a rule that was vigorously applied to other prisoners produced letters that were models of civility by all parties.

Kelly's first letter to Urschel is one of the most sophisticated and artfully expressed descriptions of the pains of imprisonment written by any inmate at any prison. It began with the explanation that he was writing at Bennett's suggestion. He asked Urschel to determine for him the truth of reports that oil had been struck in the vicinity of the Shannon property in Paradise, Texas, where Kelly still held title to a farm. Kelly hoped that Urschel was not feeling "too vindictive" about the threats made against him and explained that he had gotten caught up in "the Department of Justice's love of the dramatic and the public's desire for a good

free show." The remarkable soliloquy that followed was Kelly's answer
to a question he thought might be in Urschel's mind:

> I feel that at times you wonder how I am standing up under my penal servi-
> tude, and what is my attitude of mind? It is natural that you should be in-
> finitely curious. Incidentally, let me say that you've missed something in
> not having had the experience for yourself. No letter, no amount of talk,
> and no literary description in second-rate books—and books on crime can-
> not but be second rate—could ever give you the faintest idea of reality.
>
> No one can know what it's like to suffer from the sort of intellectual at-
> rophy, the pernicious mental scurvy, that comes of long privation of all the
> things that make life real; because even the analogy of thirst can't possi-
> bly give you an inkling of what it's like to be tortured by the absence of
> everything that makes life worth living. . . .
>
> Maybe you have asked yourself, "how can a man of even ordinary in-
> telligence put up with this kind of life, day in, day out, week after week,
> month after month, year after year?" To put it more mildly still, what is
> this life of mine like, you might wonder, and whence do I draw sufficient
> courage to endure it. To begin with, these five words seem written in fire
> on the walls of my cell: "Nothing can be worth this—the kind of life I am
> leading."
>
> What helps me to carry on? Perhaps the thought that I might be worse
> off. You may laugh, but it's probably true. I might be in a worse place where
> there is brutality or even bestiality. I might go blind. I might even be dead.
>
> I feel splendid and am in perfect physical trim. My one obsession is the
> climate of the Island. I am constantly bothered with colds. My cell, made
> of steel and concrete, is always a trifle chilly; but I've even come to believe
> that man is so made that the presence of a small superficial irritation, pro-
> vided the sensation is acute without being symptomatic of any serious trou-
> ble, is a definite aid to his mental equilibrium and serves to keep occupied
> the restless margin of his consciousness. He regards it too, as a sort of ring
> of Polycrates, for I suspect that there is in all of us, always, an obscure
> sense of fate, inherited from numberless ancestral misfortunes, which whis-
> pers: "We are not sent into this world to live too happily. Where there's
> nothing to worry us, it's not natural, it's a bad sign." A little misfortune
> gives us the assurance that we are paying our "residence tax" so far as this
> world is concerned—not much to be sure, but enough to ensure us against
> the jealousy and thunderbolts of Heaven.
>
> I have found the secret of how to "do" easy time. I just let myself drift
> along; the tide of time picks me up and carries me with it. It will leave me
> high and dry precisely where it chooses and when it chooses; consequently,
> I have nothing to worry about.
>
> But I must be fair. Being in prison has brought me one positive advan-

tage. It could hardly do less. It's name is comradeship—a rough kindness of man to man; unselfishness, an absence, or a diminution, of the tendency to look ahead, at least very far ahead; a carelessness, though it is bred of despair; a clinging to life and the possible happiness it may offer at some future date.

A person in prison can't keep from being haunted by a vision of life as it used to be, when it was real and lovely. At such times I pay, with a sense of delicious, overwhelming melancholy, my tribute to life as it once was. I don't really believe it can ever be like that again.[21]

No direct response to this letter was received from Charles Urschel; Urschel did respond in a letter to Albert Bates that no oil had been discovered near Kelly's farm. Bates received the reply because of the relentless search for his part of the ransom that had never been recovered.

In late February 1941 Kelly began an effort to obtain a transfer. He wrote to Warden Johnston arguing that as a long-termer he wanted to be sent to a prison where there would be more opportunities for recreation, diversion, and earning money:

> While not meaning to be flippant, I would say 7 years in this climate could not be considered a bagatelle judged by either the Gregorian or by the Julian calendar.

He complained of the high winds, lack of sunshine and cramped space in the yard, and expressed his desire to be able earn enough to provide a "few trifles," such as newspapers, makeup, and cigarettes, for his wife, to ease her time. He ended the letter: "I am writing to you before [asking for an interview] so that the audacity of my asking for a transfer will not come as too much of a shock."

In response, Johnston advised Kelly that he needed a longer period with "an excellent record." In fall 1944, before a transfer could be considered, Kathryn and George wrote to the attorney general requesting that George be considered for a transfer since it was their understanding that such a decision was to be made in his office, not by the Bureau of Prisons. Kelly noted that he was one of only eight or ten men still left on the Rock who had come on the first prison trains and referred to himself as "one of the original homesteaders of Alcatraz." The climate on the island he described as "murderous," and the cause of his continuing sinus trouble. He wanted to be in a prison where he could read a newspaper, listen to the radio, and receive visits from his sons. Kathryn asked that George be transferred to Leavenworth because she was concerned about both his mental and physical health. The following April Kelly wrote to Bennett:

I realize all the men who originally opened up Alcatraz were sort of guinea-pigs. No doubt some of us were kept here to justify the expenditure. After 11 years the place doesn't need justifying—it is here to stay; consequently I feel the Department could spare me from the Rock quite easily.

He pleaded that it was embarrassing for his sons to receive letters from him with "a big ALCATRAZ" on the envelope, and admitted, "I realize I should have thought of this 12 years ago when I put Mr. Urschel in the basement but that is neither here nor there."

In 1948, after James Johnston's departure, Kelly again applied for a transfer, hoping that the new warden would have a different view of the matter; Edwin Swope did not.

Please be advised that, in my opinion, he has earned the privilege of consideration for transfer by his general conduct, but on the other hand, it is my personal opinion that it would be ill-advised to transfer him at the present time taking into consideration all of the mitigating circumstances which brought about his commitment to this institution . . . we must take into consideration the fact that he not only was convicted of a serious crime, but that through his braggadocio attitude there were some very pronounced threats made with reference to taking the lives of the trial judge, as well as others, which in my opinion would revive the publicity that this subject craves if he were transferred at this time.[22]

Throughout the 1940s, Kelly kept up his correspondence with Kathryn, the connection—despite its difficulties—being essential to his emotional well-being. In 1949, however, their correspondence came to an abrupt halt when Kelly's son commented during a visit to the island that Kathryn was writing to a man in Texas. This news plunged Kelly into a deep depression, and he stopped writing to her. The change in Kelly's demeanor after this small event was so significant that Warden Swope felt called upon to report Kelly's morose condition to Bureau headquarters. Director Bennett, in response, ordered that an inquiry be made of the warden at the women's prison at Alderson, West Virginia. Bennett was informed that Kathryn's only correspondence to "a man in Texas" was to her stepfather, R. G. Shannon, who had been paroled. This information was relayed back to Warden Swope with the suggestion that it be "subtly communicated" to Kelly to ease his fear that Kathryn cared for another man.

In October 1950 Kelly again pleaded for a transfer in a letter to James Bennett: "I am the only man left who originally opened this place in 1934 . . . you transferred Bailey years ago." Not only did Kelly wish to be in a prison with normal privileges, he had become disgusted with the change in the character of the population at Alcatraz as the bank robbers and ransom kidnappers of the gangster era left the island. As he looked around the yard, he commented to his friend William Radkay, "Just look at this joint and tell me how many thieves [real professional criminals] you got in here . . . no more than twenty-five out of more than two hundred inmates!"[23]

Director Bennett noted that Kelly's request for transfer posed a problem: since his prison conduct was completely law abiding, the transfer denials raised a question as to whether there really was a reward for good conduct at Alcatraz. Bennett also conceded in an internal Bureau memo that Kelly was being made to "suffer because of his reputation and build up to a far greater extent than any others who had ever been to Alcatraz."[24] When Bennett finally approved a transfer in fall 1950, it was rescinded after Warden Swope again objected on the grounds of Kelly's "big shot complex."

An example of how this "complex" expressed itself occurred in September 1949. Kelly had complained that there were ants in his cell and asked to use a spray gun that was stored in an empty cell in A block. Accompanied by a guard, Kelly passed by the area where inmates sat on stools looking through windows at their visitors seated on the other side of a partition. As Kelly and his escort walked by, an inmate who was having a visit turned around and spoke to him. Kelly replied, waved, and remarked that the inmate had a "good looking wife." After retrieving the spray gun and walking back past the visiting area again, the same inmate called for Kelly to come over. Before the officer could stop him, Kelly covered the short distance to the visiting area and said "hello" to the visitor. When the guard came over to stop the communication, Kelly said he did not think there was anything wrong with trying to speak to the inmate's wife; the guard informed him that there was. Kelly's "big shot complex," said one of his supervisors, "is so ingrained in him that we just take it as a matter of course."[25] But the Alcatraz wardens and Bureau headquarters were also aware of the symbolic value to the continued operation of the prison in housing one of the country's best-known "public enemies."

In May 1951 James Bennett finally decided that after eighteen years, Kelly should be transferred to Leavenworth. The Bureau was correct in anticipating that moving the island's most famous occupant would not go unnoticed. Before he arrived at Leavenworth, word of Kelly's transfer was leaked to the press, prompting speculation that once free of Alcatraz, he would be considered for parole. The county attorney from Fannin County, Texas, immediately wrote to the U.S. Parole Board urging that Kelly not be released "to further prey on the innocent citizens of this country. Never again do we want to see the terrible destruction that was wreaked on this nation by the gangsters of Kelly's ilk." The county attorney reminded the board that Kelly had robbed the Farmers and Merchants Bank in Ladonia, Texas, and during the course of the robbery, "he machine gunned the town, leaving bullet holes which have not been erased."[26]

The FBI agent who supervised the Urschel investigation, and who had subsequently left the Bureau to go to work for the victim, Charles Urschel, wrote to the parole board requesting that he be allowed to appear if Kelly was considered for parole. The sheriff of Oklahoma City, Oklahoma, filed two detainers against Kelly for a robbery on the night of July 22, 1933, charges that related to taking wallets from Charles Urschel and Walter R. Jarrett after Kelly and Bates abducted them. Kelly protested that this was a phony charge, only filed as a threat to get him to plead guilty to federal charges, since a charge of robbery in the state of Oklahoma carried a possible death sentence. Kelly expressed his anger at the vindictiveness of Urschel, who he believed was behind this action and promptly petitioned the Oklahoma County Superior Court to have the detainers removed on the grounds that the time that had elapsed violated state statutes that assured a speedy trial on criminal charges; he also pointed out that the detainer acted as a barrier to his consideration for parole, and posed "a distressing mental health problem to the petitioner."

On June 1, 1951, Kelly and several other prisoners were taken from a prison railroad car at the Union Station in Kansas City and brought to Leavenworth. Two years later the Bureau of Prisons authorized Kelly's release to Oklahoma authorities for trial on the 1933 charges. Meanwhile, letters continued to come in to the Bureau asking if he was being considered for parole. Although eligible to file for parole consideration in 1948, Kelly had never applied because he understood the futility of such a request. (His wife and mother-in-law had failed in their effort to obtain paroles.)

What Kelly may have suspected was that the FBI had a standing order with the Bureau of Prisons stating that J. Edgar Hoover wished to be notified if Kelly applied for parole. The FBI's powerful opposition to any consideration of parole was evident in memoranda circulated within, and sent out from, Bureau headquarters. One note from Hoover to the attorney general asserted that both Kellys were seeking parole when in fact

George had not filed for consideration; both Kellys were also blamed for being uncooperative in the recovery of Bates's share of the ransom money. Hoover inaccurately reported that Kelly had previously applied for a parole and had been turned down by the parole board; he made reference to recent negative press comments about the parole board's decisions to release several associates of Al Capone. The letter concluded with a statement of Hoover's strong personal opposition to parole consideration for the Kellys, referring to their crime "as one of the most heinous against society."[27]

The Alcatraz Catholic chaplain, Father Joseph Clark, who was said to be championing the release of George Kelly and John Paul Chase, met with the FBI director in Washington, D.C. Hoover jotted a note on a memorandum summarizing the substance of the meeting: "Watch closely and endeavor to thwart efforts of this priest who should be attending to his own business instead of trying to turn loose on society such mad dogs."[28]

Back at Leavenworth, Kelly encountered the downside of a transfer from a small prison comprised of only single cells to a big penitentiary with large cells housing multiple occupants. He complained to the staff that after eighteen years living by himself he would "flip his cookie" if he was forced to live in a six-man cell. The Leavenworth staff understood the problems for long-term Alcatraz inmates who had to adjust to life in a standard penitentiary and share a six-man cell. Two months after his arrival, Kelly was transferred to a single cell. Six months later he asked to be moved to a cell being vacated by another inmate because it had a view of the countryside outside the prison, noting, "The cells I have had for the past 18 years have had nothing but a blank wall opposite." This request was denied on the ground that despite eighteen years on the Rock he could not be passed ahead of the others on the long list of Leavenworth inmates who had signed up for the cells with a view.

Kelly received no visits at Leavenworth, but he continued to correspond with one of his sons, his daughter-in-law, the Shannons, and Kathryn. His job as a clerk in the industries program allowed him to increase the amount of money for commissary items (sometimes up to $100 every two months) that he had been sending to Kathryn from the date he began earning small wages at Alcatraz. George and Kathryn were allowed to exchange photos of each other every few years, and George was allowed to write longer letters to her three or four times a month.

From Leavenworth, with more than a thousand inmates and the full range of prison activities as well as rumor and gossip, there was much more news to write about. In addition there was access to radio broadcasts and uncensored newspapers. Even for a correspondent as literate, insightful, and devoted as George Kelly was, writing from Alcatraz had posed challenges; inmates were permitted no news from the outside world and were constrained in their ability to mention anything about persons or events in the prison. Given these limitations and the slow turnover in the inmate population, there was very little to write about.

On July 16, 1954, Kelly was admitted to the prison hospital complaining of pain in his chest and shortness of breath; he was given a shot of morphine and oxygen. By midnight he was described as feeling cheerful and comfortable but shortly thereafter he began to vomit and complained of greatly increased pain and shortness of breath. At 12:20 A.M. he was pronounced dead. The cause of death was recorded as "hypertensive cardiovascular disease, arteriosclerosis of the coronary arteries, and terminal myocardial infarction."

Leavenworth Warden Chester Looney called Kathryn at the women's prison in Alderson, West Virginia, to inform her of her husband's death. The Bureau of Prisons approved her request to have her husband's body shipped to her stepfather, R. G. Shannon, in Paradise, Texas. Three days after receiving the word of George's death, which, it was said, she took very calmly, Kathryn stated that she never intended to go back to him anyway and did not intend to request permission to attend his funeral.

The Federal Bureau of Investigation and the principal players in the Urschel case in Oklahoma City were unmoved by Kathryn's effort to lay the responsibility for her troubles and those of her in-laws on George; the prevailing view was that Kathryn was the "brains" behind the kidnapping and the driving force behind a man named George Barnes, who took on the nickname Machine Gun Kelly and thereafter became a famous figure in American popular culture.[29]

ALBERT BATES

Because the prison career of Albert Bates was inextricably bound up with that of his rap partner, George Kelly, Bates's experience on the island is noted in this chapter along with Kelly's. During the 1930s, the press and J. Edgar Hoover always linked Bates with Kelly and Bailey, but his notoriety disappeared after he went to prison. His life on Alcatraz was exceptional only because along with Kelly he was allowed to correspond with his kidnap victim, Charles Urschel, and with Kirkpatrick, Urschel's brother-in-law and intermediary for the family.

Albert Bates, who scored 112 on a Bureau IQ test, was considered by his friends to be highly intelligent. A 1938 education progress report indicated that his scholastic work was "probably the best submitted at this institution thus far" and that he received high grades for the correspondence courses he took in English grammar and composition. Library records indicated that Bates read an average of three nonfiction books each week. A 1938 progress report characterized him as follows: "He admits his guilt, has sense of humor, and a marked feeling of loyalty to his partners in crime."[30] A psychiatric evaluation concluded that he was "not considered psychotic in any way. He is not resentful against his sentence, freely admits that he gambled everything on one chance to secure easy money and lost." The normalcy of all indicators did not, however, keep the examining physician from labeling him as "a constitutional psychopath."[31] Like so many of his contemporaries at Alcatraz, Bates was philosophical about his situation, holding to the convict credo If You Can't Do the Time, Don't Do the Crime.

During his first years on the island, representatives from various law enforcement agencies requested permission to interview Bates in order to determine the extent to which he had been involved in various criminal activities across the country before his arrest in the Urschel case. These requests became an annoyance for Warden Johnston, as expressed in a letter to Director Bennett in June 1939: "Since Bates has been here he has been interviewed several times by FBI agents, all of whom reported to me that Bates is noncommunicative and they have not been able to secure his interest or cooperation in any of the cases concerning which they have interviewed him."

For his part Bates, like other Alcatraz inmates, became anxious and uncomfortable when he was called out of work or his cell to be interviewed by FBI agents; he shared the convict view that "if they're talking with you, maybe you're talking to them." His method of dealing with this matter was to request that Harvey Bailey, a man of absolutely unquestioned integrity, be present during any interview as a guarantor that Bates did not supply any information to federal agents.

During the summer of 1942 Bates, with Bureau director Bennett's approval, joined George Kelly in corresponding with their victim, Charles Urschel. This correspondence was allowed with the hope that he might shed light on the location of his share of the ransom money, which was still missing. Bates's motivation in writing to Urschel was most likely to help Ora Shannon, Kathryn Kelly's mother, who was paying a high price in terms of prison years for her minor involvement in the kidnapping. Bates was, however, writing out of friendship with George, not for Kathryn.

In September 1946 Bates wrote to Warden Johnston asking that he be considered for transfer to another prison; his request emphasized the particular problems faced by a prisoner associated with one of J. Edgar Hoover's biggest successes:

> Over 12 years have elapsed since my arrival here. Needless to say, most of those years were exceedingly unpleasant, that is, compared with confinement in other institutions. I cannot believe that the purpose of Alcatraz was ever intended primarily to break men mentally, morally, and physically, consequently I have tried hard to weather the storm. . . . In the past year I developed a cardiac ailment which requires daily medication. I am getting up in years now and feel that my time on earth is a short duration. I would like to correspond with my relatives and perhaps even visit with them. I just cannot bring myself to write to them from Alcatraz. I know that my being here not only grieves them but shames them. . . . I just feel that after all these years and being one of the three remaining of the original transfer that I would ask you to consider my application for a change, that is, a transfer to some other institution.

Johnston and Bennett debated Bates's request but before any transfer could be scheduled, his health began to rapidly deteriorate and it was decided that a transfer to Springfield Medical Center was more in order. On March 24, 1948, however, before the transfer could be effected, Bates was admitted to the hospital at Alcatraz with a diagnosis of "coronary occlusion." The first attack was considered mild but, when it was followed by another two days later, his condition was determined to be grave. James Johnston's successor, Edwin Swope, was advised by the chief medical officer that there was no hope for Bates's recovery, due to the seriousness of his heart condition, and "it is only a matter of time until he dies." The doctor asked the warden to notify Bates's relatives, but Bates countermanded the request, making clear that he wanted no one to be contacted.

In June as his disease progressed, Bates pleaded with Swope to do something about the pain he was experiencing. "I do not believe you want me to suffer this pain if you can possibly prevent it, which I know you have the power to do." A memo from the warden, for the record, stated that it was extremely hazardous to give Bates any more than a limited amount of narcotics although it was noted at the same time that Bates "was not expected to live."

Bates died on the morning of July 4, 1948. The record of his death stated, "Patient expired while sleeping. Man awoke about 3:30 and smoked cigarette according to attendants. Man in no particular pain.

Found dead in bed 4:29. Pronounced dead 5 A.M. . . . met his demise . . . as a result of chronic cardiac decompensation."

During Bates's last days, George Kelly was allowed to visit him for extended periods—on one occasion, for an entire night. Kelly and Bates, friends when they arrived at Alcatraz, had had a falling out. Now his old rap partner was at the end of his life, and Kelly was allowed to sit by the bedside of his dying friend on the chance that Bates would finally reveal the location of the missing ransom money. A note in Bates's file stated:

> Bates, Reg. no. 137 died. There was apparently an effort on the part of Kelly, Reg. no. 117, to secure information from Bates as to where he had hidden the ransom that was paid in the kidnapping case, however, we feel that Bates talked to no one about the matter.[32]

A newspaper headline reporting his death at age fifty-seven provided Bates's epitaph: "Urschel Kidnapper Takes Ransom Secret to Grave."

ALVIN KARPIS

Alvin Karpis began his life sentence at Leavenworth on July 29, 1936, but remained only long enough to tell the deputy warden that he would "just as soon, and maybe rather, be confined at Alcatraz." With a special railroad car already scheduled to take eighteen prisoners to the island three days after Karpis's arrival, Bureau headquarters authorized his transfer, providing a psychiatric examination did not identify "any significant pre-psychotic tendencies."[33] He arrived at Alcatraz on August 6.

During his first years, Karpis ended up in solitary on three occasions for fighting with other prisoners, including two other noted gangsters, Volney Davis and Albert Bates. Other rules violations included hiding a small knife in his mattress, telling an officer who told him to stop talking in the mess hall "Aw, fuck yourself," and suspicion on two occasions of being "under the influence of some concoction of an inebrious nature." In April 1942 he refused to work and was placed in solitary confinement with loss of all privileges. While in D block he was allowed to write his sister to explain why family members would not be hearing from him for some time:

> On April 20, I was informed that the mat shop, where I was working would be closed due to lack of material, etc., and that would I have to go to the laundry to work which was agreeable, provided I wasn't put in a certain Dept. as things were rather unsettled there. It was insisted upon that I work

in that Dept. "or else." I chose the "or else" and when the "or else" was over with, on or about May the 7th, I was put in the cell without any privileges except to take a bath once a week, a shave three times a week, and a hair cut once a month and all other privileges taken until I knuckle under and do as I am told. Naturally my mail privileges were taken right along with my exercise, sunshine, fresh air, reading material, tobacco, personal property, etc., so I had no way of answering your letter. . . . I just have no way of knowing when I will be able to write again for I have no intention of going to work down there in view of the fact that I have already paid for my refusal with "or else" . . . so pay it no mind if you don't hear from me for a few years.

In January 1943 Karpis—who had been a baker before his criminal activities became his occupation—was sent to work in the kitchen. This assignment allowed him to make homebrew, bake special items for himself and other friends on the kitchen crew, and generally enjoy a vastly superior diet compared to that on the main line. In March 1945 he was written up again for "staggering around the yard and cell house this P.M. apparently from drinking some homemade brew."

Early in his sentence Karpis repeatedly tried to persuade Bureau authorities to allow him the privilege of corresponding with his common-law wife, Delores Delaney, who was serving time at Milan, Michigan, for harboring Karpis and with whom Karpis had his only son. In August 1937 Delaney requested correspondence privileges with Karpis, stating, "Although our union was never legalized by civil or church service, I have always considered myself his wife. He is the only man with whom I have ever had marriage relations and he is the father of my child." In September 1937 Karpis and Delaney were allowed to write due to the fact that Delaney had provided valuable information about the actions of the Karpis gang. Karpis's mother and father took care of his child.

Reports that in May 1936 J. Edgar Hoover had got out from behind his desk in Washington, D.C., traveled to New Orleans, and personally arrested Karpis, then Public Enemy no. 1, enhanced Hoover's reputation as a crime fighter (see chapter 3). As Richard Powers put it, Hoover had done "what the public expected of an action detective hero—to meet a criminal that popular culture had turned into a symbol of all crime in hand-to-hand, one-on-one combat."[34] The numerous versions of his capture had built up Karpis's notoriety as a gangster, and the continued exploitation of Karpis as a trophy catch for the FBI was evident in the 1936 publication of a magazine article by Courtney Ryley Cooper on Karpis's "Love Affair" with Dolores Delaney, who was serving time for "harboring" him. Cooper based this article on letters exchanged by the two prisoners, which had been given to him by the FBI. (Sanford Bates expressed his displeasure about publication of the letters, which the superintendent of the Federal Correctional Institution at Milan, Michigan, where Delaney was confined, had handed over to the FBI.)

Karpis settled into an easy routine, but he was preoccupied with a pending detainer that involved the murder of Sheriff Kelly in West Plains, Missouri, on December 19, 1931. Karpis claimed that he was ill in bed at the Barkers' home at the time; nevertheless, he said this event was a turning point in his life because it forced to him to become a fugitive.

Like other Alcatraz convicts during the gangster era, Karpis refused to discuss any criminal matters with federal law enforcement officers. Four postal inspectors called him out for an interview in August 1938 that lasted for five minutes. Meetings with FBI agents in July and in August 1946 lasted only ten and seven minutes respectively. These efforts may have been encouraged by the fact that in January 1937 Karpis had agreed to talk with three attorneys from Wisconsin and Minnesota in the presence of a court reporter and an Alcatraz guard. This interview concerned the robbery of the Kraft State Bank at Menominee, Wisconsin. Karpis was asked if he knew Lawrence DeVol and if DeVol had told him that he had robbed the bank; Karpis replied in the affirmative and identified three other participants, two of whom were shot and killed during the getaway; the third, Verne Miller, had later been killed. When asked why he gave up these names when he had previously denied any knowledge of the robbery, Karpis stated, "I would not make this statement at this time if DeVol were not dead. He is dead now and I can't hurt him." Karpis's cooperation was acceptable to other convicts because it consisted of identifying only dead men and denying that other suspects confined at Alcatraz—Tom Holden and Frank Keating—were participants.

A December 1948 report noted that while Karpis was a "good and a rapid worker, he is considered an evil influence on the other inmates in the kitchen. He is an organizer and agitator, giving instructions to new inmates coming into the kitchen. He is frequently close to the line in getting reported for insolence." Later that year, however, Karpis was given credit for foiling an attempt by disgruntled kitchen workers to sabotage a Christmas fruitcake.

In December 1950 the classification committee considered awarding him some meritorious good time but did not forward this proposal because good time could not shorten a life sentence. At the midpoint of his prison career Karpis was described as "a leader among the inmates and has their respect." Two years later, another report claimed that he was "unpopular among other inmates, but is treated with some measure of respect. The appellation 'creepy' is commonly used—but behind his back, for many of the younger prisoners still are prone to be awed by him, obviously impressed by his background."

While other inmates interviewed by the author described Alvin Karpis as "a nice guy in his later years," he had little communication with Kelly, the other famous gangster. Both spent their out-of-cell time with different small circles of friends. In an apparent clash of egos, Karpis disparaged the greeting he received from Kelly when he arrived on the Rock.

> Machine Gun Kelly is one member of a committee of the better-known criminals in Alcatraz who meets me on the yard one day shortly after my arrival and attempts to caution me about being too friendly with the "common" criminals on the island. I tell him bluntly, "Go fuck yourself! I'll talk to whoever I want. There's only one way you spell 'Big Shot' in my dictionary, 's-h-i-t'!"
>
> Ironically, Kelly spends most of his time down in the laundry entertaining new arrivals at Alcatraz with stories of his past adventures. This lasts until the new cons grow bored and begin avoiding him. But there are always new sets of ears arriving from outside who listen eagerly, awhile.[35]

Apart from his work as a baker and cook, Karpis spent time practicing his guitar and playing with the band; he corresponded with his mother and sister. He purchased several books seldom ordered by prisoners—a dictionary and world atlas; he subscribed to *Newsweek* and *U.S. News & World Report* and played bridge in the yard.

Karpis's quiet existence was disrupted in April 1949 when a warrant was issued charging him with the murder of the sheriff in Missouri—a charge that had been hanging over his head for the thirteen years since he arrived at Alcatraz. The warrant not only raised the prospect that he might have to do state time after his federal sentence, but its filing precluded his consideration for parole and his deportation to Canada.[36] This turn of events, according to a February 1952 staff report, "caused a fulminatory reaction which threatened the fairly satisfactory adjustment Karpavicz had developed during the recent years." Karpis accused the Alcatraz record clerk of "conspiracy" because the clerk had sent a letter of inquiry to the sheriff in Missouri asking whether a detainer was to be filed in view of Karpis's eligibility for federal parole. When United States Senator William Langer of North Dakota visited Alcatraz, Karpis was allowed to meet with him to complain about what Karpis referred to as the actions of "petty and small time [federal] bureaucrats," which gave Missouri authorities the opportunity to make trouble for him.

In March 1952 complaints from inmates about the quality of their meals prompted a Bureau of Prisons investigation that resulted in the replacement of the food steward and new rules that greatly limited the freedom of the kitchen crew. They could no longer make special items for themselves or function somewhat independently of the employees assigned to the kitchen. The inmate crew members were apprised of the new rules and asked if they would return to work under the new conditions. Karpis reacted with anger, claiming mass punishment was being applied to all workers "because of a few screw balls that messed up the detail." It was reported that Karpis "has had enough of the culinary unit and would not go back to work. . . . Karpis is undoubtedly one of the ring leaders in opposition to orderly rules."

Karpis was locked up in D block for refusing to work. About a month later a lieutenant reported that he was still "very indignant," would not go to work in the kitchen "under any circumstances," and was "satisfied to stay in [D block] for a year or more." In May, while still in disciplinary segregation, Karpis was charged with "Mutinous Participation in Group Resistance to Duly Constituted Authority" for continuing to refuse to return to work in the kitchen.

The following October Karpis received good news. Howell County, Missouri, authorities had dropped the murder detainer, making him eligible for parole consideration. He declined to apply, however, knowing that an application from someone locked up in disciplinary segregation was unlikely to be regarded favorably. Despite the removal of the detainer, he was described in March 1953 as "bitter," "cynical," and "sullen," an agitator who was looked on as a hero and leader by many inmates. "He has a 'Big Shot' complex," concluded a report. "His adjustment of several years ago . . . has deteriorated."

In May 1953, after the inmates in the shops began a work strike, Karpis stopped acting captain Emil Rychner in the cell house, told him he was acting as the inmates' spokesperson, and offered to put an end to the strike if "some assurance was given that no good time would be taken" and if "the inmates in the Treatment Unit [D block] were returned to the regular population." Rychner reported this proposal to the assistant warden, who advised the warden: "This is the first concrete indication of leadership since the work stoppage began. This inmate should be reported and punished."[37]

Alcatraz on the day the battle began; in the background is Angel Island, with its Welcome Home banner for returning military personnel. (May 2, 1946, Associated Press.)

Gun cage, first stage of breakout attempt; identifiers by Doug Ward. (May 5, 1946, Associated Press.)

Rifle grenades exploding on D block side of cell house; identifier by Doug Ward. (May 3, 1946, Associated Press.)

Wounded deputy warden, Edward J. Miller. (May 5, 1946, Associated Press.)

Robert Stroud, AZ-594.
(Bureau of Prisons.)

Samuel Shockley, AZ-462.
(Bureau of Prisons.)

Utility corridor,
ventilation and
plumbing area in
middle of C block,
where three ring-
leaders died.
(May 4, 1946, Acme.)

Warden James Johnston points to one of the cells where hostage guards were shot. (May 5, 1946, Associated Press.)

Bureau of Prisons Director James V. Bennett and Warden Johnston examine a bar spreader used in the gun gallery. (May 4, 1946, Acme.)

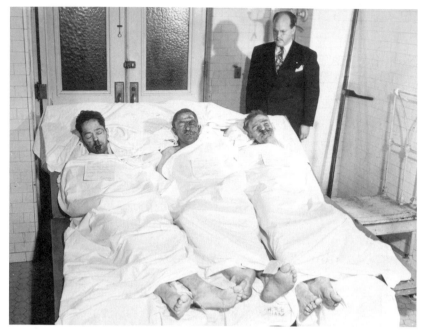

San Francisco coroner James Leonard with the bodies of Joseph Cretzer, AZ-548, Marvin Hubbard, AZ-645, and Bernard Coy, AZ-415. From a newspaper photo originally accompanied by the caption "Morgue Slab Claims Alcatraz Rioters" (May 5, 1946, Associated Press.)

New D block disciplinary segregation unit, opened June 1941; solid doors indicate solitary cells, and metal plate in foreground replaced the original opening to dungeon cells below this unit. (Bureau of Prisons.)

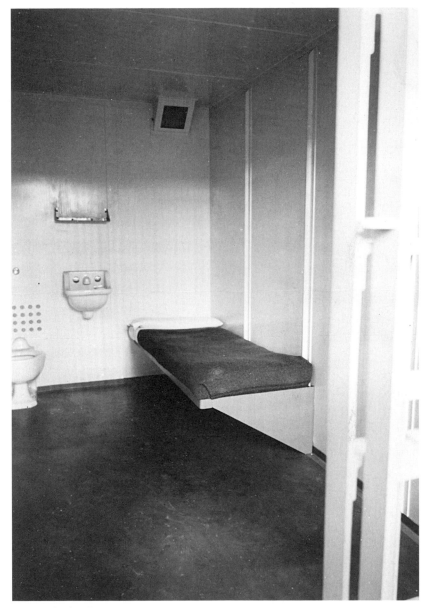

New D block cell. (Bureau of Prisons.)

James Grove, AZ-158.
(Bureau of Prisons.)

Harmon Waley, AZ-248.
(Bureau of Prisons.)

Richard A. Neumer, AZ-286.
(Bureau of Prisons.)

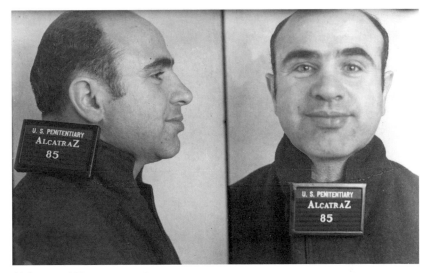

Al Capone, AZ-85. (Bureau of Prisons.)

Albert Bates, AZ-137. (Bureau of Prisons.)

Alvin Karpis, AZ-325.
(Bureau of Prisons.)

John Paul Chase, AZ-238.
(Bureau of Prisons.)

Harvey Bailey, AZ-139.
(Bureau of Prisons.)

Theodore "Blackie" Audett, AZ-208;
later, 551 and 1217. (Bureau of Prisons.)

Volney Davis, AZ-271.
(Bureau of Prisons.)

Rufus "Whitey" Franklin, AZ-335.
(Bureau of Prisons.)

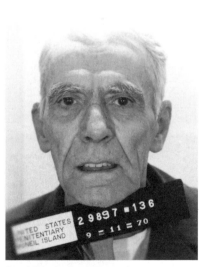

Gerald Peabody, AZ-701; later, 1264.
(Bureau of Prisons.)

Thomas Holden, AZ-138.
(Bureau of Prisons.)

Prior to 1973, telescopes offered the only way for the public to see Alcatraz. (David Ward.)

Alcatraz today. (Gene Kassebaum.)

The administration's reaction to Karpis's offer to act as a mediator was described by a senior officer:

> We had a strike and one day Captain Rychner and I were standing in the back of the cell house B and Karpis came over to us. He said, "You know, I've got a lot of influence with these inmates that are out on strike. If you'd give me the chance I'll go around and talk to all these inmates and I'll use my influence and I think I can get 'em to come back to work—provided that certain things are taken care of in regard to their work." Rychner and I thanked him and we turned around and walked out and got a hold of Associate Warden Delmore and Warden Swope and told them that we'd been propositioned. Delmore said "Write out a misconduct report on Karpis and throw him in segregation. So we wrote out the misconduct, walked back, and told Karpis, 'Say Karpis, we're sorry we can't take you up on the proposal, but we will put you over in the segregation unit for an extended period.' He was over there for two years."[38]

Karpis described this episode rather differently. In his version, he encountered a lieutenant who said, "You're pretty well known around here, Karpis. Everyone knows you aren't afraid of the hole. You're well respected. Why don't you find out if there are any suggestions as to how we can square this thing. What do you guys want?" Karpis then talked with Arnold Kyle and several other "influential" convicts in the yard who argued that some men in D block not involved in the strike should be released. Karpis told the lieutenant he would give him a list of these men, but before it could be delivered he was brought before the disciplinary committee.[39]

Whether Karpis's proposal was solicited by the staff or not, it was clear to inmates that Karpis had made a mistake. Morton Sobell, newly arrived at the time but quick to understand how the Bureau of Prisons operated, put it this way:

> He pulled a stunt . . . he tried to play the big shot guy to the captain. "I think we can get this thing settled." The Bureau of Prisons doesn't like an inmate who thinks he has power to settle things. You would think they might welcome the chance to get the thing over with, but they were afraid of somebody establishing himself as a leader. . . . I was surprised—he had been in there so long and he should have known that he couldn't do that . . . the other inmates laughed [at Karpis's effort].[40]

The Alcatraz convicts themselves did not support any attempt by any prisoner to establish himself as their leader or spokesman; there were no convict bosses in this penitentiary.

Karpis was locked up in a closed-front cell, but he was allowed to send a letter to his sister, written, he said, while "lying on the floor flat on my stomach." He told his sister: "Don't worry I have no intention of throwing in the sponge. I am just as determined as I ever was. Don't think for a minute that a day of reckoning isn't going to come over all this stuff. . . . [The Republicans may be] like the Democrats . . . just don't give a damn what happens in this place. To tell you the truth I don't much care myself anymore."

During his many months in D block, Karpis was allowed to work as a painter. In March 1954, when several prisoners began a hunger strike to protest the absence of full meals, desserts, and cigarettes, Karpis told them, "I told you the other night how I stood. I don't want anymore f——ing around. It's not worth it. I'm not getting into any more strikes. I'm not going to ruin my health for a piece of pie and a cigarette." Karpis received little credit for refusing to join this strike because he was still "considered extremely dangerous" and was believed to exert "continued influence on a certain group of impressionable inmates."[41]

In August 1954 Karpis was returned to the general population and assigned to work picking up and delivering library books. Six months later, a classification committee report noted that he was "serving his time with greater ease . . . and he has indicated a marked improvement in attitude and behavior." The committee recommended his transfer to Leavenworth—a proposal that would not be approved by the Bureau for another three years. In the meantime, Karpis continued his good work record, wrote to his sister, played his guitar, and read many fiction and nonfiction books and magazines.

In February 1958 Karpis was transferred to Leavenworth, where he remained for only seven months before Bureau headquarters received an "urgent" request from Warden Chester Looney that he be returned to Alcatraz "as soon as possible." Looney complained that soon after Karpis's arrival at Leavenworth, complaints about the food began to be heard and it was suspected that Karpis was "an instigator." Looney went on to characterize Karpis as a bad influence:

> Karpavicz had an unusual interest in an escape plot that was uncovered here. He has always been able to control other inmates and cause them to create problems while he drops into the background. He had a tailor-made organization when he arrived here through the large number of inmates who have previously served time at Alcatraz . . . he is a menace in the population here.[42]

Warden Paul J. Madigan (a former lieutenant and captain at Alcatraz) talked to Karpis a few weeks after his return to the Rock to determine his attitude.

> Strangely he does not seem bitter but he did say it was wonderful to be . . . where he could move around freely and go out to the big recreation yard. He also said he availed himself of the commissary and gorged himself on candy. . . . Karpis probably will fall into our routine again and get along well.[43]

Karpis went back to work in the library, then moved on to other work assignments in the industries office and in the clothing factory, quietly doing his time. He began corresponding with the director of the Catholic Rehabilitation Service in Montreal, Canada—the country to which he would be deported after his release from federal custody. Over the next several years, classification committees recommended that he either be returned to Leavenworth or be sent to Atlanta because he had an arthritic condition that might be less problematic in a warmer climate. In June 1961 the chairman of the U.S. Board of Parole met with Karpis, reviewed the positive reports of his conduct, and recommended that he be transferred to another prison "with the idea that he will perhaps be ready for parole after another two or three years."[44]

Karpis's complete conversion to law-abiding prisoner was noted in a September 1961 report that described him as having a "steadying influence" on other prisoners. Karpis was said to be

> cooperative, quiet, and trying to do his time in such a manner as to make it easy on the supervisor as well as other inmates assigned to the shop. The Lieutenant in charge of quarters comments that he wished he had 246 inmates like him. He gets along well with all the inmates and none at the present time treat him as a "big shot."

In February 1962, the director of the Catholic Rehabilitation Service, with whom Karpis had been working to develop a release plan to present to the parole board, informed newspaper reporters that former Public Enemy no. 1 might be coming out of prison. This information produced headlines across the country such as "Ex-Mob King Seeks Parole," "Widow to Fight Karpis' Release From Alcatraz," and "'Hood' Karpis Eyes Parole."[45] The last article described Karpis as a "pal" of John Dillinger and Baby Face Nelson and listed a number of crimes, other than the Bremer kidnapping, for which he was said to be wanted, including the Kansas City Union Station massacre and the murder of a Kansas City politician.

When a copy of this article was circulated in FBI headquarters, J. Edgar Hoover penned a comment, "They will parole this rat." The director had already written to the attorney general to oppose Karpis's release:

> In view of the ruthless crimes perpetrated by Karpis, I wanted to let you know of the alleged efforts to get him released from prison. By reason of his notorious background, Karpis is certainly not entitled to any consideration.[46]

Hoover sent a copy of this letter to James Bennett, asking that the FBI be informed of any efforts to release Karpis, and of any transfer within the Bureau of Prisons.

Hoover was not alone in his opposition to the release of the former Public Enemy. An article in the *Washington Star* summed up the editorial position of many newspapers: "His good behavior in prison hardly atones for the atrocious crimes which he and his colleagues committed when they were terrorizing the whole Midwest some thirty years ago."[47]

Karpis thus encountered the problem faced by many high-profile lawbreakers: records of good conduct in prison, no matter for how many years, had no bearing on their chances for parole. Prison officials understood this reality to mean that celebrity offenders who obeyed prison rules would become frustrated when they realized that records of good conduct would not give them credit for "having changed."

With the director of the FBI expressing his considerable opposition, Karpis's release to Canada would not come for many more years after his transformation from "a menace" to a "model prisoner." Yet in the end Karpis would have an opportunity to even the score with J. Edgar Hoover.

In April 1962 Karpis was transferred to McNeil Island—Leavenworth officials had rejected a proposal that he be given another try in their prison. While he maintained correspondence with a sister and his son, he worked closely with Frank Roberts of the Catholic Rehabilitation Service, who visited him at McNeil to discuss his employment as a cook or baker following release. He was assigned to work in the recreation department and for the first time was allowed to watch television and began attending a "self-improvement" group. He moved to a job with more responsibility—inmate payroll clerk—where his supervisor characterized his work as "exceptional." His housing unit officer called his attitude "outstanding," stating that Karpis exhibited "the biggest change he had ever observed in a man."

Several years later Karpis, now in his midfifties, moved into a residence for "model prisoners" outside the prison walls, where he became head of the resident council and occasionally acted as a tour guide for visitors. When arthritis forced him to give up general office work he took a job in the hospital records office. In 1965 the staff recommended him for parole, noting that his "reckless, anti-social tendencies are as defunct as the conditions that surrounded him in the Prohibition Days."

That parole board staff and members were sensitive to the objections of J. Edgar Hoover, however, was evident in the minutes of a September 1966 board meeting. Unfortunately for Karpis, a visitor to McNeil who had heard Karpis was going to a parole hearing notified a local newspaper, which led to an Associated Press story headed "He and Ma Barker's Boy: Ex-Public Enemy No. 1 Now a Model Prisoner," which once again triggered protests opposing his release. One parole board member noted that Karpis was fifty-eight years old and "is not a vegetable," that he had made an excellent adjustment at McNeil Island and had a "well worked out" parole release plan, and that the prison staff recommended his parole. She summed up the difficult situation facing the board:

> There is the continuing concern of J. Edgar Hoover and no doubt that the FBI, at least in the person of its Director is irrevocably determined to bring about all the pressure that is possible to prevent his release at any time . . . the Board must choose between coming to a decision according to our own rules and judgment, or accepting Mr. Hoover's attitude.[48]

Charlotte P. Reese, the parole board member who wrote this summary, rejected Hoover's position and recommended Karpis's parole "for deportation only."

Two years later Karpis, still at McNeil Island, was advised by an attorney for the parole board to obtain letters from former wardens and other prison personnel that would support his release, obtain assurance from the Catholic Rehabilitation Service that they would accept responsibility for him, and send a letter to the parole executive stating the following: "that you realize your early career was both wrong and stupid . . . [that] you regret it and are willing to go out, keep your nose clean and fit into society without indulging in any further controversy or illegal, immoral or wrong behavior."[49] Karpis dutifully asked for and received a strong letter of support from former Alcatraz and McNeil Island warden Paul J. Madigan, who commented that "a number of Karpis's old associates are now enjoying parole supervision and no doubt succeeding."[50] Retired Alcatraz and McNeil Island Officer Raymond May wrote to the parole board, arguing

> That if correction is to have any meaning [Karpis should be released, otherwise] from this point on the enthusiasm and the ardor that has been developed for a better life "if and when" which has sustained him the many years will gradually dim and we merely serve as a warehouse.[51]

The parole board still wanted Karpis to jump through a few more hoops before parole would be granted. The chairman, Walter Dunbar, met with Karpis and asked him to write a letter describing "The kind of person you were in 1936; How do you now view your criminal activities of the 1930s; How prison has changed you in the last 30 years; Your activities and behavior while in prison; How do you view yourself now; and What are your future plans."[52]

Karpis responded with the expected answers to these inane questions, concluding with a plea for a definite yes or no on his release. The yes came seven months later, on November 27, 1968; the Department of Justice announced that after thirty-two years in prison Karpis would be paroled, "for deportation only."

On January 11, 1969, Alvin Karpis was turned over to Canadian immigration officials and taken to Montreal, where at age sixty he began the rest of his life. He was a celebrity in the minds of those old enough to remember the Roaring Twenties and gangster days. He knew he had a story to tell, and he began to work on it with a writer while answering questions from various reporters. Interviewed when he arrived in Montreal, Karpis talked about his plans "to become a respectable citizen" and said that he wanted to see the movie about two people he knew—"Bonnie and Clyde." If his release job did not work out and he had to wash dishes, he stated confidently, "I guarantee you I'll be washing dishes in the best place in town within six months."

He declined, however, to answer the big question: Was it true that after a year on the run he had been personally arrested by J. Edgar Hoover? He responded as would any wise prisoner just released on parole: "I believe it would be bad taste for me to . . . say anything in the absence of Mr. Hoover. . . . Mr. Hoover has performed a credible job for his country."[53] Karpis knew that the account of his capture by Hoover, as written by Hoover, had been a major contributor to the FBI director's reputation; he also knew that his own version of this event would create publicity for the book on which he was working. In a feature article in the *St. Paul Pioneer Press,* he described how after thirty-two years in prison, he marveled at the expense of riding in a jet plane, seeing girls in mini-skirts, and going on a "simple dinner date . . . taking a woman to a restaurant, helping her into a chair, taking her coat, lighting her cigarette." Noting that he enjoyed such simple activities as "hailing a cab, riding on a bus, buying a tie, calling a friend on the telephone," he reflected: "you forget so much in prison. . . . I can't take freedom for granted the way other people do."[54]

In March 1971 Karpis's campaign to cut J. Edgar Hoover down to size began with an article in the *Weekend Magazine,* "I Made Hoover's Reputation," excerpted from his forthcoming book. Karpis described his arrest, along with that of Fred Hunter in New Orleans, after the two had climbed into their automobile:

I put the key in the ignition and turned it. I started to push the starter with my foot and, at that exact moment, a car cut sharply in front of our car and stopped at the curb. Five men climbed out very quickly. . . . I heard a voice at my window.

"All right, Karpis," the voice said, "just keep your hands on that wheel." I turned my head slight to the left and my temple bumped into the barrel of a gun. It was a 351 automatic rifle. . . . I held my head steady, looking straight out the window. I had no choice. Two men were leaning over the hood of the car that had cut in front of us. Each of them was aiming a machine gun at my head. Three other men were crouched in the street. They had pistols, drawn and ready. . . .

"Okay, Karpis," he said, "get out of the car and be damn careful where you put your hands." I slid out of the seat keeping my hands in plain sight. I stood up on the street. . . . It was bedlam.

I turned slightly and I was facing a man holding a Thompson machine gun. . . . [He] spoke to me in a calm assured voice. "Karpis, do you have a gun with you?" "No." . . . By that time, the action had attracted a huge crowd. There were a couple of dozen FBI agents and at least a hundred spectators. The commotion was terrific. But I could see that some of the men with the guns had turned their attention to another chore. They were looking over toward the corner of the building and they were waving their arms.

I heard one guy shouting, "We've got him. We've got him. It's all clear, Chief." A couple of others shouted the same thing. I turned my head in the direction they were looking. Two men came out from behind the apartment. They'd apparently been waiting in the shelter of the building, out of sight, while the guys with the guns had been leveling at Freddie and me.

They began to walk across the lawn and sidewalk toward the crowd. One was slight and blond. The other was heavy-set, with a dark complexion. Both were wearing suits and blue shirts and neat ties. They walked closer, and I recognized the dark heavy man. I'd seen pictures of him. Anyone would have known him. He was J. Edgar Hoover.

Noting that visiting "U.S. Attorney Generals, Senators, Congressmen, and prison officials" had all asked him during his years in prison if Hoover had personally arrested him, Karpis announced it was time "to set the record straight."

> The FBI story of my arrest is totally false. . . . [Hoover] didn't lead the attack on me. He hid until I was safely covered by many guns. He waited until he was told the coast was clear. Then he came out to reap the glory . . . that May day in 1936, I made Hoover's reputation as a fearless lawman. It's a reputation he doesn't deserve. I have nothing but contempt for J. Edgar Hoover.[55]

Hoover's angry response to the extensive publicity given to Karpis's magazine article and an appearance on an NBC television program was evident in the director's handwritten comments on a script NBC had sent to the FBI. After several of Karpis's remarks, Hoover wrote "He is a liar" and "A lie." FBI officials contended that the true account of Karpis's arrest had been written by the director himself in *Persons in Hiding* and that Karpis's claim was "a bid for public attention . . . at a time when he reportedly has a book of his memoirs pending publication." In response to Karpis's challenge to Hoover, at the end of his NBC interview, "to prove me a liar," Hoover initiated a search within the FBI to locate the eighteen agents who comprised the May 1936 raiding party in New Orleans. Since it was not likely that his agents would deny the director's central role, this effort may have been mounted to head off views to the contrary should any of the nine agents still living be interviewed. On the FBI's internal review of *The Alvin Karpis Story* Hoover wrote, "Karpis or/and his writer must be on dope."[56]

While Karpis could only imagine the effect of his campaign to disparage the reputation of his nemesis, the man who had so effectively blocked his release from prison, he could take satisfaction forever from knowing that he had raised questions about J. Edgar Hoover's credibility.[57]

Karpis disappeared from view after the publication of *The Alvin Karpis Story*. He moved to Torremolinos, Spain, on the Costa del Sol in 1973 and lived alone. In 1978 he received a visit from former FBI agent Thomas McDade, who had been in the raiding party that resulted in the deaths of Ma Barker and her son Fred. The two discussed doing a TV program together, but in August 1979, at age seventy-one, Karpis was found dead, "apparently of an accidental overdose of sleeping pills."[58]

Alvin Karpis is not as well known today as his fellow prisoners Al Capone and George Kelly, but his photo is still on the wall of the cell house and tourists are still buying his book about all those years he spent on the Rock.[59]

PART III

ALCATRAZ AS AN EXPERIMENT IN PENAL POLICY

RETURN TO THE FREE WORLD

While Alcatraz was not intended to rehabilitate its hardcore offenders, neither was it meant to hold them forever. Over the three-decade span of Alcatraz history, prisoners remained on the Rock for an average of four to five years before the staff and Bureau headquarters considered them ready to be transferred to Leavenworth, Atlanta, or McNeil Island. At these prisons, they served an average of two years before being released to civil society.

What happened to Alcatraz inmates after they left the Rock? That is the question the longtime Bureau of Prisons director James V. Bennett urged me to answer after the prison closed. The effort to find the answer led to the comprehensive study described in the preface and lies at the heart of this book. What it revealed about Alcatraz releasees—and through them, the prison itself—forms the basis for this chapter and the next. This chapter focuses on presenting the findings from the study that most directly answer Director Bennett's question about the fates of inmates after they left Alcatraz (see table, p. 386).

CONFOUNDING EXPECTATIONS

No one had high expectations for Alcatraz prisoners, as previous chapters made clear. They were labeled "habitual and incorrigible"—men for whom rehabilitation was thought to be impossible. No one anticipated that the veteran hardcore prisoners imprisoned at Alcatraz would emerge from their years on the island with improved behavior and reasonable chances for success as law-abiding citizens. In fact, many people predicted that, if anything, incarceration at Alcatraz would have the opposite effect. Members of the press, academic criminologists, and some corrections professionals assumed that these "career criminals" would return to their old ways or, perhaps more likely, that their mental health would be so damaged they would have trouble adjusting to imprisonment in

METHOD OF RELEASE FOR ENTIRE POPULATION, 1934–63

Transferred to other prisons	75%
Discharged directly under conditional release	12%
Discharged upon completion of sentence	4%
Released to state detainer	4%
Other	5% (including 3 transferred to San Quentin and 1 to Texas for execution)
Parole	0%

Source: Based on data from internal Bureau of Prisons audit, 1962 (conducted under the direction of the assistant bureau director, John Galvin; no authors were identified)

other penitentiaries, much less to life in the free world. These assertions, beliefs, and speculations surfaced when the prison opened in 1934 and remained part of conventional and popular wisdom for the prison's entire history, contributing to the decision to close Alcatraz in 1963. They have survived essentially unchallenged to this day.

Several members of the BOP headquarters' staff, including assistant directors Austin McCormick and Frank Loveland, were among those who expected only dire consequences for the Alcatraz prisoners. Their concerns were behind the Bureau's efforts to periodically monitor the incidence of psychosis among the prisoners. Director James Bennett, however, remained skeptical of such generalizations, an attitude that was influenced by the personal relationships he developed with some Alcatraz inmates.[1]

Members of the Alcatraz custodial staff and even the inmates themselves also had a gloomy prognosis for inmates after their release into the free world, and they carried this view with them after they left the prison. When the one hundred former Alcatraz prisoners, rank-and-file custodial officers, and Alcatraz and Bureau of Prisons officials interviewed for the University of Minnesota study were asked, "What do you think happened to the prisoners when they finally returned to the free world?" almost every respondent expressed doubt that many of the men succeeded. These knowledgeable groups of men had direct experience with what was happening in the prison and knew that only a small percentage of inmates had shown evidence of serious mental health problems—unlike the reporters, outside experts, and pundits who insisted that Alcatraz drove prisoners toward psychosis—and yet they still believed that most inmates had failed after they got out. The prevailing view was that the prisoners had probably drifted back to their careers as lawbreakers due to a lack of work skills and experience in legitimate employment coupled with their advanced ages and limited resources at release.

Another assumption was that they would have little or no family support: parents had died and wives had left them. Most interviewees cited anecdotal evidence of failures they knew or heard or read about, and the survivors explained how they themselves had succeeded. Nevertheless these men still held negative expectations about their fellow releasees, believing them not to be as determined, as smart, or as lucky as they were. Part of the reason for this view was the ready evidence of failure—the constant reaffirmation of seeing some former prisoners return—combined with the relative absence of evidence of success since those who succeeded were never seen again. In addition there was the well-known difficulty for all prisoners of staying out of prison. This tendency for negative examples to assume disproportionate importance in shaping expectations and views of outcomes underlines the need to systematically trace the actual lives of released prisoners.

Examining the Alcatraz inmates' experiences after they left the Rock requires some understanding of the adjustments they made to life in the standard penitentiaries where three-quarters of them spent several years before they were released. Since many convicts had been sent to Alcatraz in the first place because of failure to conform, satisfactory adjustment at these other prisons (meaning no return to Alcatraz) was considered by Bureau staff to be an important measure of the effect of doing time on the Rock.

The federal penitentiaries at Atlanta, Leavenworth, and McNeil Island, Washington, were very different from Alcatraz. Used to the restrictions and deprivations of life on the Rock, the Alcatraz convicts appreciated, as other prisoners could not, the diverse recreation programs, the room to move around in large yards, the availability of candy, ice cream, cigarettes, and other "luxury" items, and the ability to listen to multiple radio stations and read newspapers and uncensored magazines. Following his transfer after twenty years at Alcatraz on October 27, 1954, John Paul Chase described his reaction to life at Leavenworth in a letter to former Alcatraz chaplain Joseph Clark:

> Hello Father! Now that I am more or less settled down from my bewilderment, I feel somewhat safe in writing you without sounding like a complete idiot. I left Alcatraz on the 21st of September, and I saw for the first time in 19 years stars in the sky (and they were beautiful!) while passing through Wyoming. From the train window, my other "firsts" were cows in the fields, chickens, and even dogs. The big trucks and trailers high-balling

along the highways! Then at night-time, all the lights that light up the towns we passed. Then after arriving here, it was at midnight, the city of Kansas was a glittering with lights of many colors. My head was going around on my neck like an owl's trying to see everything on both sides of the streets at once. The day after my arrival (ours I should say) we were showered with candy, cigars, cigarettes, soap, razor blades, toilet articles, cookies, and newspapers from the Alcatraz alumni who are sojourning here. I don't know how I can express my reaction to the receiving of all those goodies. But as I look back now, there I was, right in the centre of all those luxuries I so often dreamed about and undecided just what or where to start making a glutton of myself!

And wonders of wonders, I'll soon go to the store and select those articles and goodies I am able to pay for. We are permitted to purchase $12 worth each month. Oh yes, Father, the longest walk I have ever taken in 20 years was when I went to the yard and walked around the path that encircles the field. There was something about that walk that I can't explain. Maybe because it was unhampered. Anyway, I can still feel my legs stretching out each step, just as free as free can be, inside these walls. . . .

I was first placed in an 8-man cell and it was quite an experience after 19 years in a single cell. I am now in a single cell and grateful for it. In my own cell I can move around and do those things a person gets into the habit of doing over the years, and without disturbing or imposing upon others.

Some more wonders! I have hot water in my cell, a set of ear phones. I can listen to the radio up 'til 10:15 each night, and Saturday and Sunday 11 P.M. I have a chair, a real chair, to sit upon, a large writing board that is attached to, and folds against the wall, out of the way when not in use. I have a large closet built into the wall over the sink (which is large). There is an iron form unit that consists of two bunks, one over the other. They have springs and a large drawer fitted to each bunk. On the wall there is a row of hooks upon which I have a light coat and a heavy naval pea coat. While I am writing this, I am chewing up a bag of peanuts coated with candy called Boston Baked Beans, and there is 5 newspapers from different cities waiting for me to read 'em. In short, Father, I guess I'm really living compared to what I left.

As this leaves me, I have gained nine pounds since leaving Alcatraz and feel pretty darn good mentally, physically, and morally—what more can a man ask?[2]

Another positive feature of life in these prisons was the good—sometimes preferential—treatment Alcatraz transferees received from former Alcatraz guards, and even from staff who had never worked at Alcatraz but nevertheless accorded the Alcatraz arrivals respect because of what they had endured. When Willie Radkay went back to Leavenworth after six

and a half years on the Rock, he appreciated the reception he received
from former Alcatraz officers:

> I was first worried about the rules, but Nova Stucker—used to be the cap-
> tain at Alcatraz—told me, "Listen, you don't have to worry about rules.
> Those rules are for them young punks who are getting out of line. . . . You
> won't have no troubles." And he was right. They wouldn't bother the old-
> timers and they treated the guys from Alcatraz well—"Hey, I want a sin-
> gle cell." You got a single cell.[3]

In Jim Quillen's view, Alcatraz convicts received special treatment and
respect from prisoners and staff at McNeil Island:

> I don't know if it's esteem or sympathy. Guys figure you've been deprived
> of something for a long time; they were sympathetic to the fact you've been
> under those conditions so they were willing to do more things for you.
> Guards were the same way—they figured that you've done a lot of hard
> time and now you worked your way back, you are entitled to a break from
> here on out as long as you stay within boundaries.[4]

Although inmates appreciated the good features of prison life they had
been missing at Alcatraz, they discovered that transfer had its drawbacks.
Most inmates, at least initially, had to share a cell with up to seven other
men with diverse personal habits and personality traits, which spelled the
end of years of privacy, quiet, and the ability to do what they wanted in
their cells. In addition, the more open environment, increased congregate
activities, and living in larger populations exposed transferees to more situations that could get them into trouble. In their interviews, inmates
frequently cited the increased likelihood of encountering "assholes"—
particularly aggressive, boisterous, younger inmates—with whom they
could have confrontations.

   As part of its 1962 audit of Alcatraz releasees, Bureau of Prisons staff
examined prisoners' "special progress reports" to determine how they
behaved at the prisons to which they had been transferred. The audit concluded that 85 percent of the transfers had adjusted "satisfactorily," 7.6
percent "erratically," and only 6.1 percent "poorly." The University of
Minnesota study, which was able to draw from more complete records
than Bureau headquarters, found that 47 percent of transfers did not receive any misconduct reports after they left the island, and another 31
percent received only one or two reports. After Alcatraz, the mean number of misconduct reports per inmate dropped to 1.6, compared to 4.5
reports during the prisoners' pre-Alcatraz and Alcatraz periods of confine-

ment. A tabulation of placements in disciplinary segregation units as a measure of the seriousness of post-Alcatraz misconduct indicated that 70 percent of the transferees spent no time in these punishment units, and approximately 20 percent were locked up only once or twice. Clearly, most inmates "adjusted satisfactorily" after their transfer to other prisons.

The decline in misconduct after Alcatraz was related in part to the aging and "calming down" of the prisoners, half of whom were age forty or older at the time of their transfers from the island. Also, as release from their sentences grew closer, the Alcatraz convicts, like other long-term prisoners, appear to have become more circumspect, and their behavior more restrained. They did not want to jeopardize their placement in more open, far less restrictive regimes, and they definitely did not want to jeopardize their release dates—the end of their aggravation and frustration with daily life in all the federal prisons in which they served their time was now coming into view.

For old hands at doing time, moving between penitentiaries only meant adapting to a different set of restrictions, annoyances, and risks. Leaving prison life altogether was a greater challenge for the Alcatraz population. Most releasees had been behind prison walls for a large part of their lives, out of touch with technological advancements and a rapidly changing world. Many were well into middle age, with few work skills. For a large number, the wives, girlfriends, family members, friends, and associates who could have given them support had given up on them, moved away, or lost touch. And few people—including parole officers, the FBI, and local law enforcement officials—believed them capable of staying out of trouble with the law.

As has been noted earlier, a surprising number of convicts who served time at Alcatraz met these challenges successfully. The University of Minnesota study found that virtually half (49.7 percent) of the inmates imprisoned at Alcatraz from 1934 to 1963 stayed out of prison after being released. These men, for reasons outlined below, can be considered "successes." Of those in the success category, 44.5 percent had no arrest record and 55.5 percent had only minor problems with the law—arrests or short-term jail confinement not serious enough to call for a violation of parole and return to prison. When this 50 percent success rate was determined during the course of the study, it surprised every participant, including former director Bennett and his successor, Norman Carlson. Contrary to all predictions, a large number of these habitual and incorrigible offenders had been able to overcome the odds and stay out of prison.

RECIDIVISM RATES FOR ALCATRAZ INMATES, 1934–63

Decade of Operation	Successful Release*	Returned to Prison
1934–1943	63.2% (46.5/53.5)	36.8%
1944–1953	39.5% (36.7/63.3)	60.5%
1954–1963	47.7% (48.6/51.4)	52.3%

*Numbers in parentheses indicate the percentage of these releasees who had no arrests and of those who had only minor problems with the law; percentages based on 430 cases.

Not only did the Alcatraz inmates, as a group, fail to behave as expected after release, they also upset official predictions for who was most likely to fail and succeed. After each man had been sentenced, federal prosecutors had sent a "report of convicted prisoner" to the Bureau of Prisons that placed him in one of four categories based on the seriousness of the crime and his criminal record. Analysis of these reports showed that offenders with the lowest expectations—those classified as a "menace to society" or a "habitual criminal"—succeeded at a much higher rate (57 percent of these categories) than those considered to be only "occasional offenders" or "victims of temptation" (22 percent of those in both categories combined).

The recidivism numbers are most surprising for the subgroup of inmates on which this book focuses—those imprisoned at Alcatraz during the gangster era. Dividing the sample population into three separate groups, or cohorts, based on the ten-year period during which the inmate was sent to Alcatraz, allows the fates of the gangster-era inmates to come into focus. A clear majority of the inmates in the first-decade cohort—more than 63 percent—managed to stay out of prison after they were released, making them by far the most successful of the three cohorts (see table, above).[5] Their success rate almost exactly matched the rate of 63 percent that we calculated for inmates who had served their time at Leavenworth, a standard federal penitentiary during the same period Alcatraz was in operation.[6]

The men in the first-decade cohort were those who lived under the conditions described in the preceding chapters, during James Johnston's tenure as warden and before the prison population and the regime changed substantially after World War II. Included in this cohort were the men whose years on the Rock were served while the silent system was in place, the dungeons were used, no payment was given for work, and fewer privileges and harsher restrictions on outside contacts were allowed than in subsequent decades. In short, Alcatraz convicts as a whole succeeded well beyond expectations, and those who succeeded at the highest rate after release were those who spent time at Alcatraz when the conditions of confinement were most punitive.

The study's findings deserve a closer look, to address questions that readers may have formed in their minds. Since arrest records reflect only officially reported criminal law violations, did some former Alcatraz inmates from the first-decade cohort commit major prison-worthy crimes after release for which they were never arrested? This is possible, but highly unlikely. Ex-convicts in the first group were under the supervision of parole agents who expected them to get into trouble and watched them closely. Further, it was standard practice for BOP officials to notify local police and FBI offices when a former "public enemy" or local bank robber returned to town. (Several interviewees reported that they were picked up by local police who wanted to obtain an up-to-date "mug shot," or because they were regarded as obvious suspects for a robbery that had occurred in the vicinity.) It is therefore reasonable to assume that because of their outstanding criminal and prison records, this particular group of ex-cons received a higher level of attention from parole and law enforcement officers than men who had done time only in standard penitentiaries. The sensitivity to their actions, and the initial low level of expectations for success by their parole officers, if anything, put these men at greater risk than most ex-prisoners of violating the terms of parole and conditional release and being returned to prison.

Another possible objection is that measuring success and failure based on whether a releasee stayed out of prison does not adequately reflect the degree to which he is reintegrated into the community as a productive citizen. For example, how successful was he in finding and keeping a job? What was the quality of the relationships he established with family members, wife, or live-in partner? Did he abuse drugs or alcohol? What was the state of his physical health and psychological well-being?[7] Of course, the answers to these questions vary—and these types of data were in fact collected for many former inmates in the sample. But for the purpose of establishing a quantifiable, broad-brush measure of success, staying out of prison is the fundamental outcome for a population of incorrigible convicts. As far as law enforcement agencies and the officials at the Bureau of Prisons were concerned, the overriding question related to the postrelease adjustment of these men was not whether they found work, got married, or felt discouraged or were content with their lives after release, but whether they committed new felonies.

How did the gangster-era inmates manage to succeed at a rate so far beyond anyone's expectations? What explained the ability of so many of them to return to the free world as law-abiding citizens? How much of their high rate of success was attributable to their unique characteristics as an inmate population and how much to the conditions of their imprisonment? These important questions, all with policy implications, are not easy to answer. Many factors influence success or failure after release, from the circumstances and personalities of individual prisoners to the penal environment in which they lived.

To form answers to these questions, it is necessary to start with the inmates themselves. Sorting out all the possible influences on the postrelease behavior of this group of lawbreakers, to determine which were most important and most predictive of success or failure, requires going beyond the statistics for the population as a whole and learning about each inmate's life before, during, and after imprisonment on a case-by-case basis. It means gaining an understanding of how each man understood the factors that shaped his behaviors, decisions, and outcome.

As noted in the preface, these data were obtained by conducting interviews with more than fifty former Alcatraz inmates. Armed with the knowledge that a surprising number of gangster-era inmates had returned successfully to civil society, we oriented our questions toward the experience of confinement on America's Devil's Island and adjustment to life in the free world.

The interviews made it clear that the kinds of causal factors that inmates ascribed to their fates after release—personal resolve to change, support from a wife, old or new, or from family members, and lucky breaks such as an understanding employer or parole officer—often had little to do with the time spent at Alcatraz. Once the influences of personality and individual circumstances were understood, they could be separated from the social factors—most notably, the conditions of confinement at Alcatraz—that applied to all inmates during the years 1934 to 1948.

Because they provide some insight, descriptions of the postrelease lives of fourteen Alcatraz convicts are profiled below. Half of these case studies are based on interview information. All utilize prison and parole record information. Divided into "successes" and "failures," they lead toward generalizations about resources and factors that helped determine postrelease success for this group. These generalizations provide a foundation for chapter 14's discussion of the findings related to the effects of confinement on Alcatraz.

SUCCESSES

Ten former gangster-era inmates make up the list of successful releasees profiled below. They do not represent all of the inmates in this category. Several of the Alcatraz convicts mentioned in earlier chapters who can be considered successful because they did not return to prison are not included. They include Joe Urbaytis, who remained in the free world for several years, arrest-free, before meeting a violent death; Al Capone, who lived his last years under close FBI surveillance and never returned to the rackets he helped establish; and Roy Gardner, who several years after his release took his own life. Many of the men profiled here were released during the second or third decades of Alcatraz's operation, but as convicts who served time during the gangster years, they typify the "public enemies" of the time who were deemed beyond reform.

Harvey Bailey

When Harvey Bailey arrived at Alcatraz on September 4, 1934, and looked around the mess hall, he saw some old friends. There were Tom Holden and Francis Keating, his golfing partners, and George Kelly and Albert Bates, against whom he bore no ill will, although Kelly often expressed frustration that Bailey was not doing more to fight the bum rap he received in the Urschel case. Bailey was philosophical about his situation, according to E. E. Kirkpatrick, Urschel's brother-in-law, who had been the intermediary between the kidnappers and the Urschel family:

> I sat beside Bailey during the Urschel kidnapping trial in the Federal Court Room in Oklahoma City and I became quite interested in him. He was immaculately dressed, a handsome fellow, and his conduct was conspicuously gentlemanly as compared to the other defendants—"Machine Gun" Kelly, Bates and others. Harvey and I talked quite a lot during the trial and his sense of humor was good. I asked him if he wasn't going to offer any testimony in defense of his case and he said, "Hell Kirk, I have a thousand years coming already, a 100 more won't make any difference."[8]

Bailey spent twelve largely uneventful years at Alcatraz. His only misconduct report came in September 1937 as a result of his participation in a work strike. When Deputy Warden E. J. Miller asked him why he refused to work, Bailey replied "that he had a long time to stay in prison and that he had to get along with the rest of the prisoners. Said that he realized he was not going to get anything, but he had to go in with the others for this was his home for the rest of his life."[9]

After two days in isolation, Bailey agreed to return to his work assignment. During his years on the Rock he worked in the prison carpenter shop, received no visits from his wife, who had became involved with another man and filed for divorce in 1947. He was well liked by the staff and respected by other inmates for his quiet, dignified manner—and his outstanding career as a bank robber, plus his escape from the Kansas state prison. On September 9, 1946, after twelve years at Alcatraz, Bailey was transferred back to Leavenworth. There he accumulated several minor misconducts, the most serious being "rattling the bars of his cell" and shouting at an inmate nearby who was snoring loudly and keeping Bailey from sleeping.

In April 1953 Kirkpatrick sent a letter to Warden C. H. Looney requesting permission to visit Bailey at Leavenworth. Efforts to obtain a parole for Bailey began in January 1956 when James Bennett wrote to Warden Looney suggesting transferring Bailey to the Kansas State Penitentiary at Lansing so he could serve his federal and state sentences concurrently. But, the Kansas Parole Board replied, since it was asking the governor to recommend a commutation of Bailey's sentence, he should stay at Leavenworth in the event it was granted, which would make it unnecessary for him to return to Lansing.

Meanwhile Kirkpatrick was allowed to visit Bailey in October 1957, ostensibly to help establish a parole plan for him. But Kirkpatrick really wanted Bailey to help him write a book about Bailey's career. This proposal was rejected by James Bennett, who noted,

> It's too risky a business. . . . We couldn't permit him to grant Mr. Kirkpatrick endless interviews to write the story of his life without an exception in his case to our general rules about permitting magazine writers, reporters, and free lance people to interview a prisoner while in our custody.[10]

After the sentences of Kathryn Kelly and her mother, Ora Shannon, were set aside, Bailey filed an affidavit in the U.S. District Court for the Western District of Oklahoma claiming that his constitutional rights had been violated during his trial for the Urschel kidnapping: his lawyer had not been given enough time to prepare his defense, he had not had an opportunity to confer privately with his counsel, and his lawyer was being investigated and interrogated at the same time by agents of the FBI. (Bailey's attorney was, in fact, indicted for receiving some of the ransom money as payment for his services and was sent to prison himself.) Bailey also contended that the constant popping of flash bulbs and the clicking of newsreel cameras distracted from the orderly course of the trial, that machine guns were stationed at every entrance of the courtroom, and that he was brought into the courtroom in handcuffs and leg irons.[11] This appeal was unsuccessful.

In July 1958 Kirkpatrick wrote a letter to the U.S. Board of Parole advising that he had talked with the FBI agents who arrested Bailey in the Urschel case, Edgar Vaught, the presiding judge at the trial, and Charles Urschel, who all agreed to recommend parole for Bailey.[12] Despite this promise of support, Bailey formally withdrew his application from the parole board in September:

> Much has appeared in the public press as to the likelihood of a parole in my case. This is to inform you that a hearing on my part will be unnecessary, as I will reject parole. Therefore limiting my case from your considerations for the reasons set forth in the following—I am not guilty of this offense. I had nothing to do with the kidnapping. I was merely an innocent person at the scene. I was a victim of hysteria and prejudice. The man who was kidnapped was a wealthy man and wielded great influence in the state of Oklahoma and elsewhere. He has boasted that he will spend $1 million to keep everyone in prison. By accepting parole, I would be admitting guilt and my future activities would be restricted. In view of all this I wish to advise you that I will reject parole and ask that you no longer consider my case.[13]

Over his fourteen years at Leavenworth Bailey continued quietly doing time, minding his own business, working in a furniture factory for eleven years and then in the industrial maintenance shops. During the 1950s his son visited him, but these visits fell off in the late 1950s. Although his son lived nearby in Kansas City, for reasons not indicated in prison records Bailey advised him not to write to him because "it might be detrimental to his [son's] welfare." Bailey did receive "occasional visits from a niece and a brother."[14]

In March 1960 Bailey was transferred to the Federal Correctional Institution at Seagoville, Texas; a few months after his arrival he wrote to Warden John C. Taylor at Leavenworth thanking him for facilitating his transfer:

> The relaxation and beautiful surroundings of this place has opened new horizons of thinking for me, which I did not think existed. . . . Last night

I sat in the comfortable visiting room, at a Personality Development Group and participated in the discussions. Then, we listen to a very good speaker, who illustrated his talk with colored slides. This group is sponsored by the Dallas Human Relations Group—a nationally known organization. After the meeting, we strolled out to the Compound under a full moon and shining stars. Can you imagine what this means to a man who has been locked up at night in D-Block at Alcatraz?[15]

He also thanked the warden for securing a reopening of his case before the parole board. With a new application for parole consideration, Bailey attached letters written by Kirkpatrick and the presiding judge at his trial in which both recommended his parole. This effort was unsuccessful, but in March 1962, two years later, Warden Gollaher of Seagoville wrote to the parole board concerning Bailey's case:

I have talked with the Board members individually about this case and have repeatedly expressed my concern about the length of time that this man has served. On several occasions I have talked to Mr. Bennett and we had agreed that this is the time that Bailey should be given an opportunity on parole. Bailey is getting older and if he is incarcerated for a much longer period of time, his health will preclude any chance whatsoever he has for gaining employment. . . . I am of the opinion that serving any additional time will only be to his serious disadvantage. In summary, we are slowly reaching a point of "diminishing returns" in this case and will have to say that the treatment and training goals that Bailey has reached since being at Seagoville have our wholehearted approval. I believe that this is the optimum time to release him to the community.[16]

But there were those who did not agree with the warden. When asked by the chief of classification and parole at Seagoville about the local employment market, the chief U.S. probation officer for the Southern District of Texas replied:

I felt all along that it would be just a matter of time when something suitable could be found [for Bailey], however, a chance meeting with Judge Allen B. Hannay, until recently our Chief Judge, throws an entirely different light on the whole situation. Judge Hannay has a large picture in his office of a courtroom scene in Oklahoma City when Kathryn and George "Machine Gun" Kelly received a life sentence from Judge Edgar S. Vaught. He got to talking about the greatest crime of the century, and I happened to mention your recent correspondence about the above name. The reaction was immediate, and he directed me to have nothing to do with that man [Bailey]. I then was given a couple of books written by E. E. Kirkpatrick, who was the payoff man in the famous Urschel kidnapping case. I have since read both books which were extremely interesting and have come to the conclusion that perhaps the Judge is right about Bailey. According to Mr. Kirkpatrick, his career in crime was without parallel in American History since the days of Jesse James. He was a strong suspect in the St. Valentine's Day slaughter in Chicago, Kansas City Union Station massacre, and many other crimes. He is described as a very smart and persuasive individual who had been one of America's most elusive criminals and a man said to be capable of conning himself out of hell. . . . I do believe, however, that it would be impossible for any district to receive Bailey without the word eventually getting out to the newspapers. This could be not only embarrassing, but possibly very dangerous and, as Judge Hannay said, "He is not worth the risk."[17]

Warden Gollaher anticipated this problem when he wrote another strong letter to the parole board. The issue for the wardens who argued for Bailey's parole was their concern that a prisoner who had a decades-long record of good conduct and cooperation with staff should reasonably expect that these good efforts would earn a parole—otherwise why go along with the program? In Bailey's case, however, along with those of other notorious offenders whose arrests helped build the reputation of the FBI and its director, the opposition of Hoover was a serious consideration for the board of parole. In this letter the warden directly confronted the matter of Hoover's intervention in the parole process:

> We have been advised that Mr. J. Edgar Hoover, Director of the FBI, is interested in sitting in on the review [of Bailey's parole]. . . . Bailey, as you are well aware, will soon begin serving his thirtieth year on his LIFE sentence. In the past we have pointed out with regularity the fact that although Bailey is 75 years old, he is a very exuberant individual, is in good health, and enjoys a very good outlook on life. We cannot stress too strongly the fact that his healthy outlook, good physical condition and faithful disposition is certainly based partially on the hope that he has of leaving prison before he dies. . . . We note that during the late thirties, many books were written using Bailey and his modus operandi as a theme. We can recall one book entitled, "Farewell Mr. Gangster" which devoted an entire chapter to Bailey and which states, "If Bailey was not the best bank robber in the United States, he certainly perfected the method of casing a bank." We realize that in his earlier life Bailey was no doubt a very, very serious threat to the community welfare. On the other hand, that information, along with other information that the Federal Bureau of Investigation has, is now thirty years old and we firmly believe that the material has little bearing on the current issue at hand. . . . If the law enforcement agency which seems to

have an interest in this case is allowed to color the decision of the Board, we are sure that Bailey will be convinced that his efforts during the past 30 years have been to no avail. . . . Our Classification Committee . . . can see no reason whatsoever why he should be retained in custody any longer.[18]

Regardless of the fact that Kansas parole authorities had indicated in 1956 they would recommend a commutation of Bailey's state sentence, Warden Gollaher was notified that Kansas was intending to exercise the detainer for his escape in 1933. This information prompted Gollaher to write to the director of Penal Institutions of Kansas, arguing that since Bailey should be released to the community, returning him to the penitentiary at Lansing would serve no useful purpose. But Kansas authorities insisted Bailey be returned to serve the time remaining on his detainer, stating they were unwilling to grant concurrent parole.[19]

Finally on November 15, 1962, Bailey was paroled from Seagoville to his state detainer and returned to the Kansas state prison from which he had escaped thirty years earlier. He served two and a half years before his sentence was commuted and he immediately became eligible for parole. He was released on March 31, 1965, at age seventy-six, under the joint supervision of federal and Missouri parole authorities (since he was to live and work in Joplin, Missouri). Bailey's release by Kansas authorities was effected due in large part to the efforts of the new chairman of the Kansas Board of Probation and Parole, the former warden of Leavenworth, Chester Looney, who ten years earlier had supported Bailey's transfer to the Kansas state prison so that he could finish his federal and state sentences at the same time, rather than consecutively.

Upon his release, Bailey was greeted by his son and granddaughter. He was employed at a construction company as a cabinetmaker using the skills he had developed at Alcatraz and Leavenworth. He got married, retired in 1973, worked with a writer to produce a book about his career as a bank robber and was terminated from parole in 1976. He died three years later at the age of ninety-one. Harvey Bailey expected to pay a very high price for being the nation's best bank robber. But he paid an even higher price for a kidnapping in which he did not participate—despite the strong support for parole he received from several federal prison wardens—because the press and J. Edgar Hoover made him one of the nation's most prominent "public enemies."

The book about Bailey's life devoted only six pages to his years at Alcatraz but did reveal his philosophy for doing time: "Once you learn to live with yourself, then you have learned to live with your fellow man.

This is caused by meditation. The question you have to resolve; four walls and no place to go. A lot of men don't ever learn what that is like; to have to sit down and meditate that *this is me*. I learned! . . . The main lesson is that crime don't pay. You have to pay for it."[20]

John Paul Chase

In prison, John Paul Chase, whose exploits with Baby Face Nelson (one of the country's leading bad guys) were mentioned in chapter 1, was another "stand-up" convict, a "good con" who took his punishment without complaining. He was friendly and respectful to his work crew supervisors but communicated little with the custodial staff. A progress report written near the end of his stay at Alcatraz noted the following: "In the cell house his conduct is very quiet and orderly. It is reported that one wouldn't know he was there. He spends his time reading or painting."[21]

After his transfer to Leavenworth in September 1954, Chase began working on his release. In this effort he would be frustrated for many years, encountering the classic problem of a prisoner who committed a very serious offense but thereafter accumulated many years of good work and good conduct reports. While misconduct reports could result in the loss of privileges and provide a justification for parole denials, good conduct could not earn him a release. Chase had been convicted of killing an FBI agent, and during this era no federal offense was more serious—especially when it had occurred during a nationally publicized gun battle between J. Edgar Hoover's G-men and "the gangster element." Linked with Baby Face Nelson in every verbal and written report, Chase found himself in that category of convicts who could not earn a parole no matter how good their behavior. If the parole committees he petitioned over and over had been frank and truthful, they would have had to reply, "You are not getting out because you are John Paul Chase and J. Edgar Hoover won't allow it."

Even a letter of support from one of the FBI agents who participated in the gun battle that resulted in the murder of agents Cowley and Hollis did not influence parole authorities. Thomas McDade wrote to Father Clark in 1952, giving his version of Chase's participation in the "affray":

> For my own part as one of the participants in the battle which cost Cowley, Hollis and Gillis their lives, I feel, and I felt then, that Chase's part was slight except for the moral support which he lent Gillis. Perhaps I should speak only for myself and not for other agents who, at the time of Chase's

apprehension, talked with him and formed an opinion about his character in general and the part which he played on that day. I can say, however, that I was not alone in the belief that he was a completely different type of individual than Lester Gillis and was perhaps led into the situation by that man. Considering Chase's general character up till the time of that episode, and in view of the opinions which you yourself have expressed, as well as those of the warden and deputy warden at Alcatraz Prison, I would think that Chase would be a good subject for parole. . . . It is eighteen years since the event which put Chase in prison, and all things considered, I think that the risk of releasing him at this time is one which we can well run.[22]

As the years rolled by, Chase continued to take a variety of self-study courses, including human relations, Spanish, sociology, trigonometry, public relations, and the Dale Carnegie course. He also compiled a long list of assessments that his work in the shoe factory was outstanding.

In July 1961, in a petition for executive clemency, he asked for a commutation of his sentence to thirty years:

My conduct in prison has been an exemplary one. This prison can be likened to a community of like size population on the outside. In it there is committed every crime that is committed on the outside. In prison there is an environment for every hate, for every respect accorded to man, for every frustration, and for every achievement; and they are comparable to those desires and aspirations of the people who live in the free world. . . .

And we have ourselves and our time to do what we will with them. We are free . . . to earn the contempt and hatred of our fellow man, or to earn their respect and their compliments.

Man makes his own environment from how he thinks, his every act being the blossom of his thoughts. My record will show that my behavior and my thinking for these past 26 years is comparable to that of the behavior and conduct of successful businessmen in like-size communities on the outside . . . in a truly rehabilitative sense the officials of this institution . . . have achieved their goal.[23]

Chase ended by listing persons who could describe his "character" and confirm his "rehabilitation." This list included sixteen Alcatraz and Leavenworth wardens, captains, lieutenants, officers, and work crew supervisors. And Director James Bennett headed it. Despite all this, his appeal was denied. Five years later another classification committee concluded unanimously that "there is little further purpose in confining Chase at Leavenworth."[24]

Finally, on October 31, 1966, after thirty-one years at Alcatraz and

Leavenworth, John Chase was released on parole to San Francisco. He had $500 in savings and $7,000 in savings bonds that he had sent to his brother, a retired San Francisco police officer. Chase, then almost sixty-five years old, took up residence and went to work as a custodian at St. Joseph's College, a Catholic seminary in the nearby town of Mountain View. Most of his free time was spent at his brother's home.

During his first few years under parole supervision, Chase was kept under close watch by his parole officer, who noted,

> I do not consider Mr. Chase a dangerous individual. He is perhaps not the most rational individual at all times but this is understandable in view of the facts and circumstances of the past 30 years. I do not think Mr. Chase could have survived from Leavenworth to a free society. . . . He went from Leavenworth into a seminary where he has a good deal of freedom but yet security, but it is still an institution and I think we can appreciate Mr. Chase's negative yet realistic attitudes towards institutions. Mr. Chase has done well on parole; he keeps to himself. He basically has a good attitude toward authority. . . . I think Mr. Chase is now reaching the point where he might be able to move away from an institution into a freer society without damaging himself or the society. As pointed out earlier, subject wants Presidential Clemency. He is not ready for this but it gives him something to do, namely fighting the system.[25]

Within two years, Chase was promoted to foreman of the janitorial crew at the seminary. His work ethic, however, was not shared by some of the other ex-convict workers, who complained to supervisors that he was too demanding. When these negative comments were referred to the San Francisco parole office, Chase was summoned to a meeting to discuss them; he reacted angrily, contending that the parole office wanted to send him back to prison. A strongly supportive letter from his work supervisor to the parole office and a letter of apology from the U.S. probation office for implying that his parole status was in jeopardy calmed the situation. Chase's statement to the probation office that he just wanted to be treated as "an ordinary Joe" elicited this response:

> Due to your past Mr. Chase, it is unrealistic that you expect all to be forgiven and forgotten and to be looked on as just any other "joe" passing by on the street. You will live the rest of your life with others doubting that you have completely rehabilitated yourself and are totally without a propensity for violence.[26]

Probation office contacts with Chase, who was under lifetime parole supervision, were reduced from monthly to quarterly reports and he continued his quiet existence at St. Joseph's until September 17, 1973, when he was admitted to the Stanford University hospital. During exploratory surgery, doctors found terminal cancer. Chase revived briefly but then lapsed into a coma and died on October 5.

After his death, the business manager at the seminary sent this commentary to Chase's parole officer:

> It was very sad to close the books on a man such as John Chase. His transformation from a celebrated underworld figure to that of a near-legend as a gentleman of our community was, well, an inspiration. In 4 years that I have known this man I have admired him, respected him, and am confident that he died as a man who has done his utmost to square his accounts in this life. Even with his death, I would request that this letter be included with his file to reflect the above sentiments of myself and many others. John was a good man.[27]

John Paul Chase, in prison and out, was a man who commanded respect, but he never achieved his last goal—a presidential commutation of his sentence. He died a parolee. But the supervisor in the San Francisco federal probation office closed the file on Chase with this note to the parole board: "Mr. Chase was always a gentleman and extremely cooperative. This is not a eulogy or an epitaph on the passing of a one time public enemy, but . . . I think one can conclude that John Paul Chase did become a legend in his own lifetime."[28]

Harmon Waley

In 1956 Harmon Waley, who spent seven years at Alcatraz in the disciplinary segregation unit, was recommended for transfer to McNeil Island Penitentiary. It had been almost ten years since he made his last trip to the hole, and Alcatraz authorities concluded that Waley's conduct had improved dramatically. The classification committee noted, "Although he is far from docile at the present time, he has become much more cooperative and he is an excellent worker."[29] The committee recommended the restoration of 300 days of lost good time and said that a transfer to McNeil Island would allow Waley to receive visits from his aged mother and benefit from "the increased privileges, especially in regard to music and library facilities." Bureau headquarters expressed concern that Waley's transfer could provoke "a public relations problem" but agreed to his transfer.[30] On February 15, 1957, he finally left Alcatraz after twenty-two years and six months on the island.

Waley adjusted easily to life at McNeil; a year after his arrival he was placed in minimum custody. He worked in the motor pool as a driver of a heavy tractor-trailer truck used to haul construction equipment, and when needed, he drove the island bus. Despite his good behavior, prison authorities noted that Waley's attitude was not always perfect. "At times [Waley] is rather surly," prison authorities noted in a special progress report, "and he criticizes governmental agencies due to his feelings that he should have been released sooner."[31] In particular, Waley was upset that his co-defendant, who had received a longer sentence, had already been released. (Waley never agreed that his extraordinary record of misconduct had played a role in extending his prison sentence.) Waley's time at McNeil was mostly trouble-free, except for a conflict with an officer who wanted to destroy a cat that hung around the motor pool. Waley hid the animal to keep it from being killed and as a result lost his job and his minimum-security housing assignment for six months.

At a parole hearing in March 1963, Waley's role in preventing his accomplice, William Dainard, from killing the Weyerhaeuser boy was acknowledged, and his release was ordered for June 3, 1963. A Tacoma newspaper reported his release with a story headlined "Waley, Weyerhaeuser Kidnapper, Goes Free," and noted that Waley, then age fifty-two, had spent twenty-eight years in prison for "the celebrated crime that rocked Tacoma and the nation in the '30s."[32]

What was not revealed in the news story was the importance of the communication that had been under way for three years between a friend of Waley, Waley himself, and his kidnap victim, George Weyerhaeuser, by that time a very prominent businessman. If Weyerhaeuser opposed his parole, Waley knew, it would definitely influence the parole board. But contact with the former victim revealed that he did not oppose Waley's release. From McNeil Island Waley wrote to Weyerhaeuser:

> I have been beginning to wonder if, or not, someone has been trying to curry favor with the Weyerhaeuser fortune by knocking me to the Parole Board, for I have served practically a quarter of a century for attempting to separate your father from $200,000 dollars, where your life nor any other's was placed in jeopardy. Yet, I have seen a number paroled in 17–18 years for first degree murder or raping some 9–10 year old girl or serving life sentences. . . . I am pretty sure that you and your kin do not think it justice either, because I know you are pretty much all "home folks." So far as I am concerned we are friends as we always were, and I was and am glad to hear that you are interested and think of me kindly.[33]

Waley was paroled to Portland, Oregon. The choice of this location was based on concerns that Waley might do violence to the operator of a nursing home in Tacoma, Washington, in which his mother had died. During his interview for this project Waley explained that when he had viewed his mother's body at her funeral, its condition led him to believe that she had been "starved to death" and he became so angry at the nursing home operator who remarked "Doesn't she look good?" that the guards who escorted him to the funeral had to restrain him. "I was ready to punch him," said Waley. "They figured that I was likely to kill him."[34] In Portland, Waley went to the offices of the Teamsters Union, signed up as a member, got a room at a nearby YMCA, and bought a wristwatch and an alarm clock. The Teamsters provided enough work that he could support himself for a year and a half, but in January 1964 he decided to return to the state of Washington without waiting for an official transfer of his parole supervision in order to explore the possibility of going to work for his former victim:

> I went up to the Weyerhaeuser Building and I told the secretary, "I'm here to see George Weyerhaeuser." She says, "Who shall I say is calling?" "Tell him Harmon Metz Waley is calling." She called on the phone and she said, "He said, go in." So I went in and he met me half way with his hand out for a handshake. So I went to work for Weyerhaeuser. . . . He said, "They gave you an awful way to go." He didn't appreciate it. His father said if it wasn't for the Depression, this wouldn't have occurred.[35]

Waley worked as a truck driver for the Weyerhaeuser Company for four years. During this time, Waley's probation officer wrote to the pardon attorney on his behalf. The letter began with an attempt to explain the improvement over Waley's earlier confrontational attitude toward all governmental authority:

> Presently, Waley can stand considerable more warp and frustration of his ego needs. To say that he has developed more tolerance, more insight, would, I believe, be pure conjecture on anyone's part. To say that the emotional and intellectual engine that is Harmon Waley is running down might be more accurate. He is considerably less violent in his emotional denunciations of things past and present, although he still denounces with fervor. His reaction now to the rather firm redirection of logic by the supervisor concerning Waley's bland pronouncements is an abrupt change of subject whereas in the past punctuation during the interview was accomplished by hard looks, a red face and abrupt departure from the interview

situation. The sharp edges are being dulled. . . . He is certainly a different being now than the 24-year-old obstreperous deviant sentenced for kidnapping in 1935. Thus, if pardon in this case would mean a remission of penalty, I would recommend it.[36]

No pardon followed this recommendation, however.

In January 1968 Waley took a job as an engineer for the Washington state ferry. After June 1972, when he was no longer able to work due to angina and resulting heart surgery, he lived on disability payments and social security.

In 1975 Waley's probation officer in the state of Washington appealed to the parole board to end his reporting requirements, citing a letter from George Weyerhaeuser that read, in part:

> I have been generally familiar with Mr. Waley's circumstances and conduct as a parolee for many years during which he worked for the Weyerhaeuser Company, and subsequently with the State of Washington Ferry System, and it is my conviction that he has acted in a responsible manner as an employee and subsequent to employment as a retiree. . . . In light of the fact that it has now been 40 years since he committed the crime for which he is still on parole, and inasmuch as his conduct subsequent to his prison term has proven him to be responsible, it seems to me entirely in order that he be relieved of the onus of reporting frequently. . . . I am sure that anyone looking over his long-term records would come to the conclusion that he has fully paid his debt to society.[37]

On July 23, 1976, Harmon Waley was discharged from parole. When interviewed by the author in 1980, he was living in a small town in Washington. He commented that he had never been "hassled" by police officers or FBI agents, expressed appreciation for the tolerance and understanding of his probation officers, and described George Weyerhaeuser as "a pretty nice guy," who provided employment and invited him to "stop by whenever you're in town." On several occasions Waley met with other ex-Alcatraz releasees who lived in Washington, to "cut up the Rock"— tell stories and recall incidents and personalities of the prisoners and personnel. He continued to voice complaints about American prisons and noted the lack of safety on the streets (he had been mugged one night in Tacoma).

Due to his "obnoxious attitude," as one Alcatraz staff member described it, his confrontational style, and his "colossal ego," none of the inmates or employees who knew Waley on the Rock expected that he would successfully complete parole. What they did not take into account was Waley's determination to continue trying to control events in his life and maintain his self-respect, whether that meant years of fighting the regime at Alcatraz or being bold enough to walk into the office of his kidnap victim to ask for help in finding a job.[38]

Charles Berta

Each time he walked through the yard gate at Alcatraz and down the steps to the industries area, Berta looked out on the city where he had lived as a free citizen. He came to Alcatraz with considerable experience doing hard time, having suffered through twenty lashes with a cat-o'-nine-tails at the British Columbia Penitentiary, and having spent many months in disciplinary segregation at Leavenworth after he and six other men took Warden White as a hostage and broke out of the prison.

On the Rock, Berta's defiance of authority and his attempt to assault an officer earned him two trips to lower solitary, the dungeon cells described in chapter 4. He accumulated nine additional misconduct reports, two for fighting with other prisoners, and one for "intimidating an officer." As the years went by, Berta's conduct improved, due in part, according to Alcatraz personnel, to visits he received from his mother during a ten-year period that ended with her death in 1945. Several months before his release, however, he received two more misconduct reports for "defiance and disrespect of authority."

Toward the end of 1948 Berta had 3,600 days of good time restored, most of it time lost at Leavenworth. His work at Alcatraz as an institutional blacksmith and welder was so highly regarded that he also earned industrial good time that further advanced his release date. On August 10, 1949, at the age of forty-seven, Berta was released "flat," at the expiration of his sentence with no requirement to report to a parole officer. One day before he left the island the chief medical officer's psychiatric report provided a poor prognosis for his release:

> This man has a long criminal record, and has been an aggressive, quick tempered and paranoid individual who has not been able to get along too well in prison. He does however have a good work record, and has developed a more tolerant attitude in the past few years of his incarceration. It is my opinion that his chances for civil adjustment are poor.[39]

When Berta stepped off the prison boat in San Francisco and into the free world, his wife, with whom he had been living before his arrest for train robbery, was waiting—this despite that fact that Berta had corresponded with her only occasionally during his eighteen years at Alcatraz and had received no visits from her. They would stay together for the rest of his life.

An old friend also greeted him on the dock. "They met me and we all had a nice big dinner at his house," said Berta during his interview. "I had these friends from the old days to take care of me. . . . I went to work as a plumber's helper."[40] He and his wife took up residence in Brisbane, a small town outside San Francisco. In a letter to James Bennett several years later, he described his return to the Bay Area and a job he had taken as a bartender—employment that would likely not have been approved if he had been on parole:

> I did a lot of walking around the hills and also along the beaches and just laid around for about three months. Work was hard to get . . . so I took a job as a plumber's helper that a friend got for me. A friend of mine had a half interest in a bar and wanted me to work for him. I didn't care for that kind of work but being in need of work I took it and have been there ever since—three years this month—haven't missed a day or been late. Things would have been much harder if it wasn't for people I knew helping me . . . my mother left me a little money and we put it down on a house, so between my job and working around the house I'm pretty busy. That is the score as of now. The bar I work in is across from the main post office. The next time you are in the city give me a ring as I would like to talk to you.[41]

Berta had three more encounters with law enforcement agencies. In August 1952 he was given a thirty-day sentence for contempt of court for refusing to answer questions before a federal grand jury investigating New York gangster Waxey Gordon's narcotics business. While out on bail, Berta filed an appeal, and the sentence was vacated. In May 1954 Berta and another man were arrested by San Francisco police on suspicion of burglary and grand vagrancy. In the town of San Anselmo in Marin County, a police lieutenant observed Berta and a friend driving around and arrested them, thinking they were there "to case taverns, motels, and some of the homes." The two men were released on writs of habeas corpus several hours later after they argued, apparently successfully, that they were "merely putting some mileage on a new motor car."[42]

As a result of this arrest and the subsequent newspaper article, Berta's criminal record became public, and he offered to quit his bartending job to avoid embarrassing the owner; his offer was rejected. Several years later when a man attempted to hold up the bar, Berta took the gun away from the robber and called the police.

In the mid 1970s, after Alcatraz became a tourist attraction and criticism of the prison was again heard, Berta was irritated:

> Those criticisms of Alcatraz –that's bullshit, they want to make a big thing of cruel and unusual punishment. Alcatraz was a good place to do time, in my opinion. At Leavenworth, man, in the summertime, you was roasting in that cell, you'd have to be stripped naked and the humidity was so bad, everything was all wet. They had to come around and give you ice cold water to cool you off. Alcatraz was terrific; you had to use a blanket every night, the weather was beautiful. When you were out in that yard, you could look around, the good fresh air; you could see the sunset, Sausalito, the boats coming in, the aircraft carriers coming in, the battleships coming in. You couldn't see that up in Leavenworth or McNeil Island. That place—Leavenworth—stunk. There were cockroaches and bedbugs. . . . The mess hall was filthy. Leavenworth was wide open for marijuana, cocaine, you name it, it was there—not at Alcatraz. And no queers; the homosexuals couldn't run around loose in the cell block. That's one of the worst things in prison, it causes all the killings; none of that was going on at Alcatraz, supervision was too tough.[43]

James Quillen

When he left Alcatraz, Quillen had accumulated eighteen misconduct reports—eight were for contraband; others were for disobeying orders—two for insolence and four for refusal to work (characterized as the leader of a strike in two refusals). He forfeited 1,113 days of good time for destroying property in his cell in disciplinary segregation. He also had one misconduct report for "uncleanness—while cooking hot cakes for officers, he dropped the hot cakes on the floor and picked them up, put them on the plates, and sent them in for the officers to eat. He said officers are no fucking better than the inmates on the main line."[44]

Before, during, and after the May 1946 battle of Alcatraz, James Quillen spent several months in D block for misconduct. The isolation, he noted later in an account of these years, gave him "considerable time to think" about his future. "The total weight of your time there," he said during one of his interviews for this project, "really brought your mind to the futility of the whole thing. It's like you took this much of your life and totally threw it away." After being released back to the general population, Quillen began a remarkable transformation.

He signed up for three University of California correspondence courses and asked to meet with James Bennett on the director's next visit to the institution. He told Bennett he planned to finish high school and earn back the good time he had lost, and the director responded favorably. "He assured me," said Quillen, "that if I would work and study for two years, he would recommend that at least five years of my forfeited good time be restored. It was a challenge that I accepted."[45]

A change in behavior accompanied this resolution. In addition to spending time studying, Quillen played music and began attending Mass. The changes in his conduct were noted in special progress reports. Whereas a report on Oct. 24, 1947, described him as "headstrong, impulsive and aggressive and capable of violence" and concluded that he had made "a poor adjustment to date," a report less than a year later, on July 16, 1948, said Quillen was "better adjusted at present" and mentioned as positive signs his new interest in music and attendance at religious services.

As a result of his attending Mass, Quillen began to associate with the Catholic chaplain at Alcatraz, Joseph Clark, who counseled him as they walked around the yard. When Clark's altar assistant was transferred, Quillen assumed his position. Thinking that family support might help improve Quillen's often-troubled frame of mind, Clark and another interim priest tried to locate members of his family. Clark learned that Quillen's mother had died, but he was able to contact and meet his stepfather. One day Quillen was very surprised to receive a visit from his stepfather and stepmother, and then another with his stepsister and her husband, at that time an Oakland police officer. In his interviews, Quillen identified this reunification with family members as a major turning point. He finally had "someone in the outside world to communicate and share with." With this support, said Quillen, "I resolved to turn my life around."

A progress report in 1952 corroborated the importance of his contacts with his stepfather and stepsister: "Their influence and encouragement contribute to his increasing stability and determination to avail himself of the institution's educational opportunities." The report went on to note an admirable commitment to his scholastic work. "This inmate, a brash and defiant malcontent earlier in his incarceration here," concluded the report, "has responded remarkably to the counseling offered by relatives formerly wholly uninterested in his welfare."[46]

Two years after their meeting, James Bennett fulfilled his promise and restored five years of Quillen's good time. Continuing to receive monthly visits from his family, Quillen applied for an assignment to a job as an orderly in the hospital. To his surprise, Warden Johnston approved the assignment and he was allowed to live in the hospital. After he showed strong interest in the work, the resident physician and medical technical assistants taught him how to conduct tests and perform other procedures. Soon he was giving injections, preparing surgical packs, and taking X-rays. Ten years and one day after his arrival at Alcatraz, and with the remainder of his lost good time restored, Quillen was told that he was being transferred to McNeil Island.

At McNeil, Quillen was allowed to continue working in the prison hospital. He was soon placed in charge of the tuberculosis unit and then moved into surgery as an assistant. During these years he had meetings with a psychiatrist whom he described in interviews for this project as helping him control feelings of anger and revenge:

> I met a psychiatrist, a guy named Garvey, who was fresh out of medical school. I thought well, this is a golden opportunity. I'll use this guy a little bit to get a good recommendation because I'm going up for parole. I was playing a game with Garvey, except that Garvey wasn't playing my game and I didn't know it. I was going to go in there and really slick-talk this guy, but I got to where I was going in there and really letting my hair down but I didn't realize it. Finally, this guy made me see a whole lot about carrying all this bitterness. I wanted that guy that almost killed me in the jail, but talking to Garvey it didn't make no difference anymore—it just kind of lost its importance.

Also at McNeil, Quillen had the opportunity to take a vocational nursing program that would give him a license and enable him to gain more experience as an X-ray technician.

At this point everything seemed to be going his way, but he still had a state detainer hanging over his head. He asked James Bennett for help in convincing the parole board to allow him to return to California so he could complete his state sentence and then become eligible for federal parole. Bennett suggested that a member of Quillen's family contact the victims of his crime; this was accomplished and one of the kidnap victims wrote to the parole board stating that Quillen had been punished enough and that he had no objection to his release. Bennett wrote to the head of the California Adult Authority to determine if Quillen could be released under "joint supervision" if he was granted a federal parole.[47]

After several years at McNeil Island, James Quillen was transferred to San Quentin to resume serving the California sentence from which he had escaped. When he was released from San Quentin in 1958 on federal parole, he moved in with his sister and brother-in-law, a police officer who lived in Ukiah, California. The couple agreed to provide a home and maintain him until he was able to find work. His own financial resources consisted of $150 he had earned fighting fires at a California Department of Corrections Forestry Camp and a $200 loan from his stepfather. In his interview he described his efforts to find work:

> I applied at the state hospital first as a psychiatric technician. I passed all the tests but they weren't hiring. I needed a job. So I went to work breaking up concrete—pick and shovel work. When I first came home I went down to the employment office and got all these papers and I was going to fill them out, but I got to draft status and all that garbage; hell, I didn't know how to handle it. So I took them back to the employment office and told the guy, "Hell, I can't fill these papers out." He says, "Why?" I told him "I just got out of prison; I don't know how to fill out all this garbage." This guy was really nice and he said, "Come on in and I'll help you." So we sat down and filled out these papers. I said I had done quite a bit of hospital work; I had of lot experience in surgery, some experience in X-ray, and I had a LPN license. I got a call the following week to go up to Hillside Hospital. I went up there and the radiologist was a super guy. I laid out everything on the line with him and the administrator—that I was an ex-con, but I needed a job, but I didn't know if I could hack it. They took me right in and I worked there for eight years.

Quillen married, divorced, remarried, and had a daughter. With the encouragement of the chief of radiology, he studied for and passed an examination to become a member of the American Society of Radiological Technologists. In 1967 he began work at a hospital in Marysville, California; two years later he was promoted to chief radiologist and radiology supervisor. In 1971 Quillen's active parole supervision was terminated. In 1976, U.S. Probation Officer William A. Barrett wrote to the board of parole to seek an early termination of Quillen's parole:

> He has been employed at the Rideout Community Hospital in Marysville for the past ten years and is now director of the X-ray department. . . . Mr. Quillen has been married to a registered nurse for the past ten years. . . . He has a nine-year-old daughter. He owns his own home and is obviously a respected member of the community. One cannot help but be impressed by the complete rehabilitation of this man . . . not only has Mr. Quillen functioned as a law abiding citizen for the past 18 years but he has also, through hard work and despite many obstacles, risen to a highly professional level. If there is any way that Mr. Quillen can receive an early discharge or termination without the necessity of a hearing, I think it would be very appropriate in this case and completely justified. Mr. Quillen did not request that I write this letter to you.[48]

The early termination was granted. Quillen then petitioned for a presidential pardon, and this was granted in December 1980.

In two interviews for this project, Jim Quillen reflected at length on the reasons for the abrupt change in his behavior at Alcatraz and his success after release. At first he discounted the suggestion that Alcatraz itself played some role in his transformation and instead cited all the positive influences mentioned above: the opportunity to work in the hospital, support from his formerly estranged family members, the ability to complete and continue his education, and help and counseling from various people such as Father Clark, the McNeil psychiatrist, Director Bennett, and Warden Johnston.

In his second interview, however, Quillen acknowledged that the quiet and isolation of Alcatraz played some part in his resolving to turn his life around, but he pointed out that his change in thinking could have happened at any prison: "Sure, I started changing while I was at Alcatraz, but it was because I was tired of loneliness and tension and frustration . . . you could have had those anywhere."

James Quillen was more fortunate than many of his fellow gangster-era releasees: he found meaningful vocational preparation, and there were many persons, in prison and out, who decided to help him. Other Alcatraz releasees were successful without the level of preparation and support Quillen received, but in almost all of the cases of success what seemed to make the difference was having someone—a parent, a brother, a sister, a wife, or friend—who provided acceptance, support, and encouragement.

Floyd Hamilton

After the failed escape attempt in April 1943—during which he spent several nights hiding in a cave at the northwest end of the island—Floyd Hamilton spent ten days in the prison hospital being treated for injuries, and then twelve more locked up in solitary confinement, much of it spent taking three steps in one direction, then turning to take three steps back for something to do. This gave Hamilton plenty of time for contemplation:

> It was so dark that I couldn't see at first, I had run into a wall because I couldn't see it but finally I learned how to pace my steps—I got to where I could stay the same distance from the walls. I got one meal every three days—it was usually just a little spoonful of whatever the menu was. It was never near enough; other times you'd get two slices of bread.
>
> When my time in solitary confinement was over, they tried me and took all my good time. [Deputy Warden] Miller said [to a guard] "Put him up

in a cell next to the corner of the third tier and don't let him have any privileges, don't let him write to anybody or receive any mail and don't let him
have any clothes on but that pair of shorts. And give him an old mattress
and two blankets—that's all he gets until I give further orders."[49]

Hamilton was allowed out of his cell to take a shower. During a shakedown of his cell on one of these occasions, his attempt to cut through
the ceiling with razor blades was detected. (Years before Hamilton had
cut his way out of a county jail using gem razors that had a blade on one
side.) After the search he was placed in a second-tier cell:

> [Deputy Warden] Miller came around a cussing and a swearing he said
> "Don't let him have nothing, don't let him write to his kinfolk, and no li-
> brary privilege." I stayed a whole year with just a pair of shorts on under
> those conditions. Then he gave me permission to receive mail from my
> mother and write to her and they gave me an old pair of shoes, a pair of
> pants, and a shirt and library privileges.

The months in solitary confinement gave Hamilton plenty of time for
contemplation. After much introspection, he began thinking about God:

> My first concept of God was sitting on a big, white throne. He had a long
> white beard and he had Jesus interceding for me. Others over on the other
> side were playing harps and singing to keep him in good humor. And I
> thought maybe if I catch him in a good humor I'd get out—that was my
> idea and that's the way a lot of inmates think they'll accept Christ as their
> savior if he'll help them right then.

With his privileges finally renewed after more than a year, Hamilton, still
in D block, began receiving mail from his mother and daughter and a
Baptist preacher:

> They wanted me to change my way of living—let God solve my problems.
> They would quote scriptures to me. Of course I didn't have no bible; I didn't
> have anything in that cell. I asked the chaplain to bring me over a bible.
> He sat down in front of my cell and went to instructing me where to find
> this and that.

Thinking that the preacher was just another employee of the government
he couldn't trust, Hamilton sent him away, but a seed had been sown.

After the inmate in the neighboring cell in D block died from a bleeding ulcer, Hamilton became very concerned about his own health because
he believed that he too had a bleeding ulcer. Pushed in a spiritual direc-

tion by his mother and daughter, he began to pray and underwent what he later called a religious conversion:

> One day I read the bible and I finally became aware that there is, was, a spiritual being in me. I never told anybody and I never talked to anybody about it but anyway I felt I had a guardian angel who had been protecting me all my life. And you know, one day it seemed like a heavy load just lifted off of me and I felt real good. I had a feeling that everything would be alright, I don't have to do more worrying and I was going to get out and be a respectable citizen. I told Bob Stroud next door and he was kind of an atheist and he made fun of me. I told him wait and see, I'm going to get out.

Floyd Hamilton's conclusion that "a guardian angel" was looking out for him came as he reviewed incidents during which he narrowly escaped death in encounters with law enforcement officers. In one such incident, a Dallas police officer shot at him with a riot gun through a window during a bank robbery attempt, and despite being less than five feet away, missed. Hamilton also noted that his guardian angel must have been present while he was lying under discarded rubber tires in the cave at the end of the island while Deputy Warden Miller and other officers fired bullets into the tires.

During his three years in D block, Hamilton began focusing more on getting out of prison through legitimate means rather than by escaping. He saw an opportunity to escape during the May 1946 battle of Alcatraz but decided against it. After being released back to the general population, he won back the good time he had lost and received good work reports. With only one minor misconduct report he was transferred in August 1952 to Leavenworth, where he appreciated the treatment he received from the warden, former Alcatraz deputy warden E. J. Miller. "He gave all the guys from Alcatraz breaks," said Hamilton. "He gave them preference in jobs and everything else."

At Leavenworth, Hamilton continued on the path he had begun at Alcatraz, taking up an active study of religion. "When I got to Leavenworth, I went to studying the life of Christ and his teachings, the Old and New Testaments, comparative religion, and I took two courses in human relations," said Hamilton. In 1956 his daughter, who had been a faithful correspondent, was indicted for poisoning her husband. With funds earned from his work in the shoe factory, he sent money to support his two grandchildren. He also hired an attorney to contest the computation of his sentence and his impending release to Texas authorities.

In December 1956 Hamilton was conditionally released from Leavenworth but then turned over to Texas state prison authorities—to whom he owed twenty-five years. He was taken to the state prison at Huntsville and locked up in a dark cell in disciplinary segregation with no reason given. He was soon transferred out of isolation—but into a regular segregation cell.[50] After months in segregation, *Dallas News* crime reporter Harry McCormick learned of his whereabouts from Hamilton's sister and began working to get him transferred to the general population. McCormick was apparently interested in Hamilton as a celebrated desperado from the Bonnie Parker and Clyde Barrow era.[51]

McCormick eventually succeeded in getting Hamilton moved out of segregation and into a work assignment in the electrical department. He received outstanding work reports and one year later was paroled—but only because of the efforts on his behalf by three men. One of these men was reporter McCormick; another was Ted Hinton, a former deputy sheriff who had helped gun down Bonnie and Clyde. Speaking of Hinton's role in getting him released from prison, Hamilton wrote later: "I feel that God was working through Ted Hinton to try to help me. He used Ted Hinton because Ted was in a position to help me more than anyone else, because anyone, and at least the parole board, would listen to him."[52]

The third person prepared to help Hamilton was William O. Bankston, an automobile dealer who had twice been allowed to visit him in the Dallas jail. McCormick, Hinton, and Bankston appeared on Hamilton's behalf before the Texas Parole Board and his release shortly thereafter confirmed the considerable influence they had with the board.

After his release from prison Hamilton met with Hinton and Bankston. Hinton gave him $10; Bankston loaned him $150 and offered him a job, which he accepted. He worked for Bankston for sixteen years before retiring. During his interview with the author, Hamilton claimed that Bankston helped him "because my guardian angel was directing him."

Hamilton and his ex-wife remarried shortly after his release, and they raised his daughter's two children. In the years that followed, Hamilton helped establish a nonprofit organization, ConAid, to help ex-convicts and was invited to talk to numerous church groups about his new spiritual life. He encountered Chaplain Ray Hostra, head of the International Prison Ministry, and at Chaplain Ray's request, Hamilton made a series of tapes describing his life of crime and his conversion into a law-abiding citizen. The International Prison Ministry broadcast the tapes, and parts were reproduced in a booklet for prisoners.[53] During this time, Floyd Hamilton had the unusual experience of returning to prison as a guest speaker—at Attica State Prison in New York, the federal prison at El Reno, Oklahoma, California Men's Colony, and other penal institutions.

In August 1963 President John Kennedy commuted Hamilton's sentence, "To expire at once." Two years later, Hamilton applied for a presidential pardon, which was granted by President Lyndon Johnson in December 1966. Governor John Connally awarded him a pardon from the state of Texas in April 1967.

Hamilton's association with notorious outlaws Bonnie Parker and Clyde Barrow, and his one-time status as "public enemy no. 1," followed him during all his years in the free world, and even into death. When he died in 1984, the news release from the Associated Press noted: "Floyd Garland Hamilton, 76, considered Public Enemy No.1 in the late 1930s and a close friend of Bonnie Parker and Clyde Barrow, has died after a lengthy illness."[54] Floyd Hamilton's success after release can be attributed to a religious conversion at Alcatraz, to his wife, and to the assistance he received from a number of helpful citizens. Ironically, his benefactors consisted of men who helped him precisely because he had been a notorious Public Enemy.

Volney Davis

Volney Davis was one of seven men sent to Alcatraz for their participation in the Bremer kidnapping case. From January 1936 through April 1939 he received nine misconduct reports, four for fighting with other prisoners. He engaged in a fistfight with Henry Young over a decision made by the umpire in a ball game, and he fought with two other men not connected with the Bremer case. In one of these altercations, "he untied [the other inmate's] apron and when Wells shook his penis at him saying, 'If you want it ask for it,' it made [Davis] mad and he hit Wells with his fist [stating that] he was 37 years old and didn't play anything like that [homosexual games]."[55] One of these fights may have been related to reported tensions among Davis and his rap partners—it involved an attack on Alvin Karpis in which Davis was described as the aggressor. After three of these fights, Davis was locked up in disciplinary confinement for three days each time. He made D block on two occasions for participating in strikes; in one case: "He is not in sympathy with the strikers . . . but he thought he would stick with them for a couple of days to make a showing and then return to work."[56] Three other misconducts during this period were for minor violations.

During his remaining years at Alcatraz, Davis curbed his tendency toward violence. Although he was written up fourteen more times for misconduct, the offenses consisted of such minor transgressions as "eating unauthorized food" and stealing "a large corned beef sandwich." On one occasion in 1942, an officer noticed that Davis was intoxicated: "Davis looked sheepish and was unsteady on his feet. Although I did not see him drinking, there is no doubt in my mind that he was under the influence of some concoction of an inebriaious [sic] nature."[57]

Davis was transferred to Leavenworth on April 2, 1947. There he continued to earn money working in the prison industry and was able to send a total of $1,400 to his elderly parents. He registered for courses in advanced arithmetic and industrial safety and received average work reports.

Preparing for a parole hearing in April 1950, he wrote to J. Edgar Hoover asking the director to support his application. In the letter, he referred to promises of help he had received from Hoover in exchange for information he had provided, as well as promises of a shorter sentence from FBI agents.[58] Davis informed Hoover that he had "taken a lot of abuse from inmates" and was determined to have no further contact with any of them outside prison. "Life even in prison can be pleasant if one can obtain peace of mind," wrote Davis. "That is man's greatest asset in this troubled old world. For with peace of mind the days pass one by one and you think of the past as little as possible." Asking Hoover for help was remarkably naive for a veteran criminal; Hoover had no intention of supporting Davis's parole request (when Davis was granted parole nine years later, Hoover would write on an internal memorandum: "this certainly is an instance of gross abuse of parole in the federal area").[59]

As the years went by at Leavenworth, Volney Davis maintained good conduct and work records. He filed legal actions regarding his sentence, including a claim that he was not represented by counsel, was never apprised of his constitutional rights, was "held incommunicado in a distant city in chains and in secrecy," and "was led to believe that if he entered a plea of guilty he would be given a [shorter] term." All of his appeals and several other legal actions were denied. In 1956 he wrote to his kidnap victim, Edward Bremer, apologizing "for the sordid crime that was committed against you" and contending that he "had no part in the preparation and the commitment of the crime." He asked that Bremer not oppose his release on federal parole to the state of Oklahoma where a life sentence was waiting for him.[60]

Davis's efforts to finesse his involvement in the kidnapping injured his chances for federal parole. After he claimed in a habeas corpus writ that he had "nothing to do with the Bremer kidnapping," the United States attorney reacted with the following: "Positive evidence was introduced by the Government that he was handling the Bremer kidnapping money with full knowledge as to what it was. He was thus found, in effect, to have committed perjury." The U.S. attorney also informed the parole board, "Mr. Bremer expressed to me that he thought [Davis] should stay in prison."[61]

Davis continued to send his industry earnings to support his elderly mother and kept in touch with family members through correspondence and visits with his mother, his sister, and several nieces and nephews. He participated in the Alcoholics Anonymous group for twelve years, was a regular attendee at chapel, and when his mother died in January 1959, he was allowed to make a funeral trip from Leavenworth in the company of a lieutenant for her burial. The governor of Oklahoma granted him a parole from his life sentence, to be effective on the date Davis received his federal parole.

In August 1959, after twenty-four years in federal prison, Volney Davis left Leavenworth with $390.90 in release money and traveled to his sister's home in California. His "pleasant, cooperative" attitude led his probation officer to note two months after Davis's first office visit: "it seems safe to expect that this will be a no-problem type of case." Using skills picked up at Leavenworth, Davis found steady work as a printer. He also became active in an Alcoholics Anonymous program. There he met a woman sixteen years younger; they got married, and he moved into her home. His main difficulties were learning to drive a car, and "lacking self-confidence" on the jobs he held. In 1961 he received a letter from James Bennett inviting him to visit the federal prison at Lompoc, where a printing shop was to be established. Because travel funds were not provided, he was unable to accept this invitation; his probation officer told him, however, that this request "was quite a tribute to the director's confidence in him."

Davis and his wife moved to Guerneville, California, where they bought a home within which they operated a gift shop featuring items made by Mrs. Davis. His probation officer worried about this venture but wrote: "Volney by this time has proved himself to be a pretty solid citizen and has demonstrated that both he and his wife are sober, industrious and honest persons." Success with the gift shop business was uneven and Davis was often unemployed, "not because of laziness on his part, but principally because of his age [sixty-two]." He polished cars for one period and then took a factory job at $1.25 per hour. In June 1964 his obligation to report to the probation office was reduced from monthly to semiannually.

In July Davis appealed to James Bennett for assistance in obtaining his release from parole because that status had prevented him from taking a job as an orderly at a nearby state hospital. (He couldn't even qualify as caretaker at a county dump.) Bennett responded that the parole board did not have the authority to discharge life sentence prisoners from parole; he advised Davis to apply to the president of the United States for a commutation of his sentence. Bennett asked the pardon attorney to send the appropriate forms to Davis, and to list him as recommending approval; he also asked the Bureau's employment placement officer to contact Davis to offer assistance.[62] The chief probation officer for the Northern District of California also supported commutation of his sentence.[63] Davis continued to take odd jobs and live quietly with his wife; two years later on June 9, 1966, President Lyndon Johnson commuted his sentence, to "expire at once."

Number 1600

Most Alcatraz convicts were determined to prevail in their adversarial relationships with federal authorities, and to walk away from the Rock with a sense of pride at having done the hardest time the government could deliver. But doing time on that island was not a walk in the park for every convict. The travails of several men who had severe emotional disturbances at Alcatraz have been described in chapter 4; the following account illustrates the difficult postrelease adjustment some of them experienced.[64]

Number 1600 (a fictitious identification number assigned by the author) came to the island in the mid-1940s to serve a twenty-year sentence for kidnapping. According to a special progress report, he was transferred to Alcatraz from another federal penitentiary for "conniving, distributing and dealing in Benzedrine," for "selling contraband food," and because he was "regarded by many prisoners as being dangerous and vicious." The report also noted that he had "revealed psycho-neurotic tendencies and was hospitalized 49 days under observation for this condition."

On the island 1600 had "extreme difficulties in adjustment" and was "checked into the hospital frequently for short periods to relieve his extreme tension." A report concluded that "he undoubtedly does have a serious nervous condition which governs his conduct much more definitely than in many other cases." During his time on the Rock, number 1600 received nineteen misconduct reports: four for fighting with other prisoners, and others for refusing to obey orders, insolence, creating a disturbance, mutilating himself, destroying government property, refusing to work, "mutinous participation in group resistance to duly constituted authority," and "agitation." He was locked up in the disciplinary segregation unit eight times—in one instance, only after four guards physically subdued him. In a letter to his sister, he wrote: "I still have the headaches constantly and am definitely a candidate for a nervous breakdown"[65]

One incident in particular reflects this man's inner and outward conflicts. He asked a lieutenant to admit him to the hospital but was told "there was no damn way" that was going to happen. Then, in front of the lieutenant, 1600 swallowed a dozen Nembutals, stating, "I'm going to the hospital one way or another." When he collapsed, he was taken to the hospital in a coma where he remembered the medical technical assistant (nurse) saying, "'his pulse is very weak.' I have to give credit to Dr. Yokum and the nurse for saving my life. Did I really want to die? My feeling at that time was—what difference would that make?"

After nine years on the Rock, 1600 was transferred to another federal prison. In October 1954 he was conditionally released with $7. Because conditional release, unlike parole plans, did not require a prearranged job, this man arrived at his sister's home with no money and no employment. While she provided room and board he looked for work, being rejected by many when he indicated he had been in prison. Returning to life in the free world was not easy after so many years in prison:

> Going back to my hometown meant entering the new world that I was totally unprepared to cope with—with $7, the clothes on my back, and no job. There were thousands of little frustrations, things everyone else took for granted. It meant not understanding little things, like trying to get a Coke from a machine—and failing. It meant people not willing to give me a job because of my past. It meant seeing an old friend cross the street to keep from passing you on the sidewalk. It meant meeting a deacon of the church meeting me on the street before services began, calling me off to the side to talk to me. He said, "I want to talk to you and I want you to know that I am talking to you as a friend." I replied, "Sure, go ahead." I'll never forget his words. He began, "You know, most of the people here know of your past, and I think you would be happier if you went to another church, so as to keep you from getting your feelings hurt."[66]

Thirty days after his release he found work at an iron company that paid 65 cents an hour. Three months later, when that company went out of business, his brother-in-law referred him to a job as a laborer on construction projects. During this period he met a woman and risked a parole violation for her sake:

> Three things you were not supposed to do—own an automobile, get married, and leave the state—I broke all three rules at one time. My wife and I went to Mississippi and got married; I told my parole officer, but he knew my wife was "a very nice person" and he was very lenient with me.

Because the construction job did not pay enough to satisfy the new couple's needs, number 1600 took the advice of his boss that he gain experience in a specific area of construction. He decided to concentrate on brick and concrete masonry, spending a year watching and learning on the job. A year later he went to work on his own, developed his skills, and eventually became successful. "My wife and I own our own home; we have two late-model automobiles and a savings account adequate for the remainder of our lives. I feel quite proud of what I have accomplished under the handicap of a prisoner released from Alcatraz at age forty-two."

But despite his successful marriage and work career following his release this man was deeply troubled as a result of his experience at Alcatraz—experience he said he was unwilling, or unable, to discuss with his wife during four decades of marriage. For twenty years following his release he had to contend with recurring nightmares and anxiety attacks. He saw numerous therapists and psychiatrists and spent several years receiving treatment from the state mental health department. He finally met a doctor who told him that his problems were due to "chemical imbalance"; with medication, his problems went away.

The difficulty this man expressed at many points while talking into a tape recorder to answer questions from our interview guide suggested that he suffered from a condition analogous to post-traumatic stress disorder. A particular cause of his trauma appears to have been his experiences during the 1946 battle of Alcatraz:

> Some thirty-seven years have passed since that terrifying and tension-filled day in May of 1946. Seldom does a week pass without my sleep being disturbed by the most frightening nightmares imaginable. In most instances I find myself sitting upright in bed drenched in a cold and clammy sweat, my heart pounding furiously in a desperate attempt to escape the confines of my body. Sometimes I have found it necessary to walk the floor for as much as an hour before I am able to convince myself that I am only reliving long hours of terror that occurred so long ago. During these nightmares

I usually find myself in a desolate, isolated area—nowhere in sight can I find a human being, a tree, a rat, or a building—not a thing one might refuge behind. Bullets are screaming around my head and bombs are exploding all around me, throwing dirt and debris over my face and body. I have no recollection of the actual time the bombardment of Alcatraz lasted—my best guess is twenty-four hours. This episode of man's inhumanity to man is what will live in my mind for as long as I live.

The case of number 1600 is one of the more remarkable stories of a successful life after Alcatraz. He had to overcome all the standard obstacles and conquer his own demons as well. His prison record indicates that his psychological problems predated his transfer to Alcatraz and were likely exacerbated by the strict maximum-security, minimum-privilege regime he encountered on the island.

> After my release I realized that Alcatraz was the worst thing the government had to offer if I did get into trouble. . . . I had no contact after release with any Alcatraz inmates. Their rate of success after release must have been minute. I like to think that I was one of the few who was successful. I was able to overcome problems and I am quite proud of what I have accomplished.
>
> [After my release] I didn't know whether I was glad or sad. I can only say that I felt hatred! I wanted revenge! I believed in no one except myself, and then only to the extent that I was a survivor—they couldn't destroy me. . . . All the wrongs I have committed over my lifetime hasn't been sufficient to warrant me serving [nine] years at Alcatraz, a place comparable to what might have existed during the Spanish Inquisition, a place that denied its occupants all contact with the outside world . . . the philosophy of Alcatraz seemed to me to be the breaking of the spirit of the prisoners.

Considering the profound effects it had on him, 1600 was justifiably proud that he made a successful life for himself after surviving the battle of Alcatraz and nine years on the Rock. He attributed his accomplishments to "my desire to make something out of my life"—a desire that "meant more to me than any fear of Alcatraz."

Henry Young

Henry Young's murder of Rufe McCain in the Alcatraz dining hall in December 1940 made him one of the most storied Alcatraz inmates. Not only did the murder and subsequent trial receive extensive news coverage at the time, but in 1995 Hollywood revived the Young story with a film, *Murder in the First*, that was purported to be based on the facts of Young's Alcatraz experiences. As noted in the introduction, however, the film got most of the essential facts of Young's life and incarceration completely wrong—he did not, for example, commit suicide two years after the trial—thus helping perpetuate the "Hellcatraz" image of the prison in the bay. The true story of Young's life after the murder trial may be less dramatic than the film version, but it contains many intriguing mysteries.

After the trial Young was returned to the disciplinary segregation unit at Alcatraz. By February 2, 1942, according to medical and psychiatric assessments, Young was spending most of his time in his D block cell reading, writing numerous writs, and exercising. His only complaint was that he was experiencing "dizzy spells," but there were no neurological signs or physical evidence to suggest that this was a serious problem. He petitioned the federal court in San Francisco for one hour of recreation every day and for his "rights" to send uncensored mail to a priest, his sister, and others, and to go to work.

He accumulated additional misconduct reports in D block, for such things as possessing a brass dagger fashioned from a toilet plunger, setting fires in his cell, ripping the cover off his mattress, flooding his cell with water from the toilet bowl, and fighting with another inmate during yard recreation. In 1944, while in D block (for reasons not recorded in Alcatraz or Bureau of Prisons records or known to any staff member or inmate interviewed for this project), Young decided to confess to a murder that had occurred many years before in the state of Washington. He sent the details to the prosecutor in Everett, who found that they matched an unsolved crime. Young was transported back to the state of Washington in November, pleaded guilty, received a life sentence, and was returned to Alcatraz to finish his federal term.

As the years went by he read many nonfiction books, wrote a book about hobos, and began another about his own life. A 1948 special progress report characterized him as "egotistical," a person "with homicidal trends" who "cannot be trusted." He remained in the disciplinary segregation unit from December 3, 1940, until he was transferred to Springfield on September 13, 1948, for "psychiatric observation." The reasons were outlined in a report filed after his arrival at the medical center:

> This inmate was transferred from Alcatraz with a diagnosis of schizophrenia, catatonic type, made by the psychiatric consultant. For a period of about two months he had appeared to be mute, disinterested, regressed, out of contact. He refused clothing, burned bedding, stood for long periods of time in strange postures.

The staff at Springfield suspected that Young had feigned mental illness in order to be transferred out of Alcatraz, and that he continued to do so—complete with a "superficial" attempt at suicide—to ensure that he would remain at the hospital. Deferring their diagnosis, the doctors decided Young needed "further psychiatric observation":

> Clinically he does not fit the usual picture of a catatonic schizophrenia and his symptoms just don't "ring true." Both psychiatric and psychological studies will be continued in an effort to arrive at a correct diagnosis so that appropriate therapy could be instituted. In the meantime in view of his desperate behavior at other institutions it will be necessary to keep him under maximum custody.[67]

Several months later, whether malingering or truly mentally ill, Young got his wish to remain at Springfield. After tests with sodium pentothal, he was declared psychotic.

> He says that all of psychiatric text books and knowledge is false due to the fact that all psychiatrists are merely Jesuits in plain clothes, that they have been indoctrinated by the followers of St. Ignatius (whom Young knows to have been a woman) as part of a grand scale attempt to subjugate the human race to their own purposes. . . . We now look on his superficial catatonic symptoms as a pathological defense against these primarily grandiose and paranoid delusions.[68]

Young spent his time in a locked ward reading and sleeping, although the staff psychiatrist reported that this quiet demeanor might cover "some plan of escape or revenge."[69] Young's psychotic status continued and in 1951, when his condition improved, he was assigned to work as an orderly. He did not associate with other patients, did not participate in educational, recreational, or religious programs, and did not correspond with anyone.

In 1954 Young became eligible for a conditional release from his original sentence. He still had a three-year term to serve for the involuntary manslaughter of Rufe McCain in 1941 but was turned over to Washington State authorities, who transported him to the state penitentiary to begin a life sentence for the murder he had voluntarily confessed to ten years earlier. Young arrived at Walla Walla on December 9, 1954, where an admissions summary reported the remarks of the prosecutor in his 1944 murder case: "It is my personal opinion that the defendant cannot ever be rehabilitated and he should never be allowed to be loose in society under any circumstances." The record clerk at Alcatraz stated,

"*Young had one of the worst records of any prisoner at Alcatraz and is considered the most cold blooded one of all*" [original emphasis]. The admission report concluded by stating the expectation that Young would "rapidly become a custodial problem" because he was "still capable of yielding considerable influence over the worst element of the prison population."[70]

At Walla Walla, Young at first refused work assignments and spent his time in his cell reading, but he maintained a clear conduct record. Over time, the diagnosis at Springfield of "schizophrenic reaction of a paranoid type" faded into the background. He began work in the institution cannery, received excellent evaluations, moved to an inside construction detail, began to attend Mass, and participated in yard activities.

By 1965 Young's good conduct record had resulted in a reduction of his custody classification to medium security. He completed the second year of high school, was a spectator at institution sporting events, and continued to receive good work reports and evaluations. Nevertheless, a counselor in 1966 concluded, "In my opinion, this is a hardened criminal who would not hesitate to again commit a serious crime when subjected to moderate stress."[71]

On June 8, 1967, assigned to a minimum-security building, Henry Young escaped from Walla Walla. What he did to survive during seven months in the free world is not reported in the prison records made available to the author. But after he was apprehended in Missouri on January 8, 1968, and returned to Walla Walla, he spent twenty days in isolation and six months in "special segregation." When he appeared before the Adjustment Committee, he "pled guilty stating that he didn't think he was going to get out so he took off."[72]

As time passed, Young was asked to develop a parole plan. He declined, saying he would develop a plan when he received a parole date. Told that he would not get a date until he had a plan, he refused to think about release. A 1969 progress report concluded, "This inmate is completely dependent on the institution as he apparently has no desire to formulate realistic plans or to do any positive thinking for himself that might someday prove helpful and constructive." In 1971 he was again classified as minimum custody. He had become active in the Lifers Club and finally proposed a release on parole to an Alcoholics Anonymous ranch where he would work as a maintenance man in exchange for room and board. The manager of the ranch was a former prisoner from Walla Walla well known to Young.

On March 17, 1972, after almost forty years in state and federal prisons, Henry Young at the age of sixty-one was released on parole. Two weeks later, on March 31, he "absconded." There is no record to indicate that he ever came back to prison; the life he led after he left the AA ranch remains one of many mysteries associated with this man. For the postrelease study, Henry Young falls into the "not known to be dead" category, and, in the absence of evidence that he was returned to any prison, he was classified as a "success" after release.

Unless Henry Young, or others who knew him after March 1972, are still alive, the truth will never be known about the reasons for his murder of McCain; why at the time he was suing federal prison officials over the conditions of his confinement he chose to confess to a murder committed many years earlier; whether he experienced genuine mental health problems or pulled off a clever ruse to get a transfer to the Springfield Medical Center; how he survived on the streets for seven months following his escape from Walla Walla; and most important, what happened to him after he walked away from parole supervision.

Rufus Franklin

Rufus "Whitey" Franklin spent thirteen years in D block disciplinary segregation following his conviction for the murder of officer Royal Cline during the May 1938 escape attempt from the old industries building; he now had another life sentence to go with the life sentence he had earlier received in Alabama for murder during a robbery. During his years in D block Franklin amassed thirty misconduct reports, included tearing up his cell, assaulting James Grove with a horseshoe when segregation inmates were allowed to go to the yard, stabbing Henry Young on the yard with a sharpened table knife, fighting with other inmates, striking an officer, and violating almost every other rule. He was force-fed three times as a consequence of the hunger strikes. In the late 1940s, however, his attitude changed and his conduct improved. In 1951 he was returned to general population and given a work assignment on the kitchen crew. In April 1952 for seventeen days he joined other members of the work crew on strike. When offered a chance to return to work and be quartered in the hospital, Franklin and four other inmates decided to return to work. For the next three years he had to endure threats, sneers, catcalls from other inmates, and an assault with a heavy steel pitcher wielded by a prisoner in the dining hall.

In a 1975 letter to the U.S. Board of Parole, Franklin described his violation of the convict code:

I think I should define for you the term "Prison Code." It is really an unspoken thing and actually only a way of thinking. Roughly it can be defined thus: the traditional inmate's attitude toward all people connected with law enforcement, which includes policemen, judges, prison personnel, and anyone else connected with the enforcing of laws, is that all these people are enemies and any inmate who aids or abets in any way, or attempts to be friendly with any of these enemies, is a rat and a renegade and is to be considered an enemy too.

The Alcatraz administrator in charge of food services described the consequences for Franklin and the other strike breakers of joining "these enemies":

> They were repeatedly threatened and subjected to ridicule and derision by the other inmates. It was necessary, for their safety, to arrange permanent quarters for them in the Alcatraz hospital. They could not go into the recreation yard, or participate in any kind of group inmate activities. It was necessary to extend supervisory protection to them at all times and in all their movements. . . . Franklin remained in this protection status in the Alcatraz hospital for some five years. To the best of my knowledge the other inmates there never forgave him for coming to work and helping to put down the strike. . . . It should be borne in mind that Franklin was no "stool pigeon"; he simply did what he thought was right, and did it in the face of considerable personal hazard.[73]

While living in the hospital, Franklin became interested in becoming an orderly and was given that assignment in 1955. Due to his outstanding work, in July 1958 he was transferred to Leavenworth, where he worked as a hospital orderly, took a training course in nursing, and was promoted first to hospital nurse and then to operating room nurse. In January 1963 he was turned over to State of Alabama authorities to begin concurrently serving his state and federal sentences. In 1969 he was awarded a state parole, but when he learned that he would be returned to federal custody he escaped from Gilby prison. After four days of freedom he was apprehended and sent to the Atlanta Penitentiary. In 1974 Franklin's situation was assessed by the U.S. Parole Board:

> For more than 20 years he has been cooperative and appears completely institutionalized. . . . Has never participated in formal counseling during the 41 years of his incarceration. . . . It is doubtful that he would become fully accustomed to community life and he still reacts criminally as evidenced by his recent (1969) escape. The examiner recommends parole effective June 19, 1974.[74]

Franklin completed a parole plan that called for his sister in Dayton, Ohio, to provide a room for him in her home; no job was assured but the sister was told by a local hospital that Franklin could apply for work based on his experience as an X-ray technician. He was released from a federal prison camp on October 29, 1974, and given the funds in his federal prison account—$34.07. He had only a short time to experience freedom—in January 1975 he was diagnosed with lung cancer and died at age sixty on May 17, 1975. However, he had achieved the hope of almost every long-term convict: he did not die in prison.

In an insightful and thoughtful letter to the parole board Franklin described his transformation from one of Alcatraz's most dangerous and dedicated troublemakers to a man who made a conscious decision to violate the inmate code and become a completely conforming prisoner. In his case, as in those of Floyd Hamilton, Jim Quillen, and Harmon Waley, "the light went on" when he was in a disciplinary segregation cell:

> There comes a time in the lives of most men who are incarcerated when the light of reform flickers on in their minds. It comes seemingly out of nowhere and without any conscious volition of the inmate. Where it comes from and why I do not know. Perhaps it comes from a feeling of shame and remorse; or from the sudden realization that he has wasted a good part of his life behind bars; or perhaps it is the inherent decency, which is common to all men, striving to be heard; or it might be the longing for a loved one that lights the light; or perhaps a combination of these things or something else; but whatever it is, please believe me, it exists. . . .
>
> Unfortunately, in most, this flicker is lost and dies out in a short time; but in a few it is nurtured and grows slowly into a steady flame. When this happens, the man is reformed. . . . I have known many thousands of men since I have been locked up and I have seen this amazing transformation many times and I have never known one man who has undergone this change to return to prison. I wish I could tell you how to recognize it, but I don't think I can for it is something you sense through close association and personal knowledge of the man in question. I can only explain my own case, which I shall do shortly. The outward symptoms are: where the man has been rebellious and perhaps arrogant he becomes strangely silent and withdrawn. This continues for a time and you see a different light in his eyes. Where before you have a cynical and reckless light there is a softer more kindly light. He seems to be more relaxed and his interest slowly begins to turn outward and he becomes more concerned with the problems of others around him and less concerned about his own troubles.
>
> The light flicked on in my mind in 1944. I was in the dark hole in Al-

catraz, having just been detected and foiled in my last escape attempt. I was pacing up and down in the dark when it occurred to me just what an utter idiot I had been all my life. I reviewed my entire life and found little of which I could be proud. The shambles I had made of my life was a sorry spectacle to view, and when I thought of the pain and heartache I had caused my family, I writhed with shame. These sordid thoughts caused me to consider committing suicide, but then I realized this was the coward's way out and I knew this would only add to the grievous wounds I had already inflicted upon my family.

So my thoughts gradually veered around to the positive side, and I considered what I could do that was constructive. I thought of trying for parole but that seemed long in the future and I shuddered at the thought. But I could not think of anything better. I realize this was the only way out. I knew I would never try to escape again; for, there in the dark, the full realization of just what would happen should I be successful in escaping dawned upon me. The thought struck me with the force of a powerful blow in the back of the head, that as an escaped convict I would not be free. I would be hunted and hounded like a wild animal. I would not be able to return to my family, and the only end I could hope for would be death or back to a prison cell.

This bud of reform lodged and stuck in my mind, but it did not grow easily. It took many months before I could erase all the bitterness and despair from my heart. But fortunately it did stick and grow into full-blown. . . . During the months that followed my release from the dark hole, I gradually turned to reading and studying more. I had always liked to read but had for the most part neglected doing so until this time. But now I did turn to books for companionship. We had a good library stocked with all the better authors and it was to these I turned. . . . I started to rebuild my life. . . . The turmoil that had seethed in my brain for so long was still and my thoughts became clearer and I felt calm and peaceful. . . . If I were to pick out any particular assistance that helped me most in this struggle, I should have to choose the thoughts expressed in the *Book of Job,* the gentle teachings of Jesus in his first instructions to his disciples, and Kipling's *If.*[75]

Because Whitey Franklin lived only a few months in the free world after his parole he did not have much time to test his resolve to "rebuild his life." But his decision many years earlier at Alcatraz to reject the inmate code and side with "these enemies" was likely a much more severe test of his own transformation then any obstacles he would have encountered after his release.

Another reason for including the Franklin story in this book is that this man took on the difficult task of trying to explain to others the circumstances, emotions, thoughts, and considerations—the rational cal-culation of costs and benefits—that brought about such a dramatic change in his life. He did not mention another factor that might have in-fluenced his decision. Confinement at Alcatraz was in many ways a monastic experience, but isolation in a dark cell in disciplinary segrega-tion unit was extreme; there were no distractions of any kind to inter-rupt Franklin's reminiscences of life in the free world or, as George Kelly put it, "all the things that make life worthwhile."

FAILURES

Those Alcatraz inmates who were returned to prison failed in different ways. Some, like James Audett and Gerard Peabody, represent a very small number of the genuine habitual incorrigibles who were sent to Alcatraz. Their criminal and prison careers lasted for their lifetimes; they stayed out of prison only at the end of their lives when they were old and in-firm and released to die outside prison walls. Others, like Tom Holden, were able to stay out of trouble with the law for only a short time be-fore committing serious crimes. The majority—represented below by Dale Stamphill—made serious attempts at living law-abiding lives but drifted back to crime and had to spend more time behind bars before finally suc-ceeding late in life.

James Audett

James "Blackie" Audett was one of the Rock's most outstanding failures. He had the distinction of being the only man with three Alcatraz com-mitment numbers. Audett, the prototypical career criminal, led a life of crime and imprisonment matched by few others sent to the island. His first arrest took place in Canada in 1921 at age nineteen, and his last oc-curred in 1974 when he was seventy-two years old. He served time in Alberta and in the Saskatchewan Penitentiary before violating laws across the border. He was committed to McNeil Island Penitentiary for auto theft, violated parole, was returned, and then escaped from a train that was taking him to St. Elizabeth's Hospital in Washington, D.C. Recap-tured, he was sent to St. Elizabeth's, where a psychiatric evaluation con-cluded that his mental illness was feigned and represented only an oppor-tunity for him to escape, an opportunity of which he had taken advantage. He was returned to Leavenworth and released from that institution in July 1933.

Six months later, back at McNeil on a new auto theft charge, he escaped again. When he was apprehended in July 1934, he was shipped to Leavenworth but only long enough to join the first trainload of convicts being sent to Alcatraz, where he was assigned number 209. He was released in May 1940 but was rearrested in August for bank burglary. For this crime he received a ten-year sentence that earned him a trip back to Alcatraz, and a new number—551. Seven years later he was conditionally released, but after six months he was charged with possession of stolen money and returned to McNeil Island as a conditional release violator. In September 1950 he was released once again, but two months later he was back in prison—this time in the Oregon State Penitentiary to serve seven and a half years (later reduced to five).

He was paroled in September 1952 to federal authorities, who wanted him for violating his conditional release. Audett went back to McNeil Island, finished time on his ten-year bank robbery sentence, and was released in April 1953. But by December of that year, he was back in the Oregon State Penitentiary for violating his state parole. Released from that prison in October 1955, he was arrested on a charge of bank robbery in January 1956. For this new conviction he was sent back to Alcatraz, this time as number 1217, to begin a twenty-year term. In March 1963 he was transferred to McNeil Island, where he served time until his mandatory release in January 1968. Six months later, in June, he was arrested in Portland, Oregon, for attempting to break into a food store, which resulted in one year in a county jail. A conviction for attempted burglary violated his federal release contract, and in May 1969 he was back, for the fifth time, at McNeil Island.

In February 1974, after another conditional release, Audett was instructed to report to the State of Oregon authorities, which he failed to do. A federal warrant was issued, but when he reported to the Seattle, Washington, federal probation office in April, the warrant was held in abeyance. Two months later, on June 5, 1974, he was arrested, along with ex-Alcatraz convict Gerard Peabody and two other men, all of whom were armed and masked when they robbed $17,500 from the Ballard Bank of Washington in Seattle. The driver of the getaway car was identified, apprehended, and soon gave up the names of his accomplices. Audett and Peabody were arrested the following day. Audett was subsequently indicted on a second charge that he had robbed another Seattle-area bank of $32,000 on May 8; he was also suspected of driving the getaway car in a third bank robbery.

Prior to sentencing, Audett provided a statement to the court, explaining that his long list of law violations was motivated by a "dreadful disease" fed by "hate and bitterness," and pleaded for "one break in life."[76] The judge, however, was unmoved and gave him a sentence of fifteen years. Audett was remanded to the Bureau of Prisons, which sent him to Leavenworth. There he settled back into the prison life he knew so well—had Alcatraz remained open, he might have earned a fourth commitment number.

As his health problems increased, Audett was transferred first to the Springfield Medical Center and then to the extended care unit at the Federal Correctional Institution in Lexington, Kentucky. As his health deteriorated due to heart disease, federal officials advanced his release date to allow him to return one more time to the free world. His case manager stated: "It cannot be overlooked that the instant offense was committed when Mr. Audett was seventy-two years of age. We do believe that he has 'burned out' due to the combination of age and ill health."[77] When given a form to fill out that asked who should be notified in the event of his death, Audett responded, "No one."

Part of Audett's remarkable criminal and prison career was documented in his book, *Rap Sheet: My Life Story*, and in a book-length article, "My Forty Years Outside the Law," in *True: The Man's Magazine*. These publications led to an offer from Jay Robert Nash (author of many true crime books) to assist Audett if he could be released to Chicago where Nash was located.[78] With Nash as his sponsor, Audett was released from Lexington on July 23, 1979, telling staff members he was proud to have lived through so many years of "turmoil" in state and federal prisons.

Blackie Audett overcame the convict's greatest concern—he did not die in prison (the date and cause of his death were not recorded in the records available to this project, however). He married twice during his brief periods of freedom. He never intended to "go straight"—he was proud of his gangster days, that his body was marked by seventeen bullet holes, and that he had been sent to the Rock more times than any other man. He was also proud to have known most of the noted gangsters of the 1920s and 1930s—John Dillinger, "Pretty Boy" Floyd, Lester Gillis (alias Baby Face Nelson), Frank Nash, and Wilber Underhill—men he called "big leaguers." He left an epitaph of sorts in the last paragraph of his article for *True:*

> If a heister [robber] gets along toward sundown and is still alive, it's time for him to throw away his gun. Maybe he should have throwed it away when he first picked it up. But if he didn't, like I didn't, and it's getting

along toward sundown for him, he better pitch it then. He can't win single handed, even if he thought he could back there when he was young. There's too many other guns. And all of them are aimed at him.[79]

Gerard Peabody

Another notable Alcatraz failure, Gerard Peabody was coincidentally Audett's rap partner in the 1974 bank robbery in Seattle. After serving eighteen months in the state reformatory in Rahway, New Jersey, and eight years of a fifteen-year sentence in the state prison in Baltimore, Maryland, for robbery with a deadly weapon, Peabody and several associates robbed four banks in Maryland—one of them twice, in order to "come back to get the money they missed in the first robbery." In all four robberies, cashiers, bookkeepers, and customers were locked in the banks' vaults "at the point of a gun."[80] Peabody was committed to the federal prison in Atlanta in March 1940 to serve a twenty-two-year term.

In 1944, with only one misconduct report, Peabody was described as "a shrewd, intelligent, prison-wise individual with a deep-seated antipathy toward institutional control" and recommended for transfer to Alcatraz because he "associated himself with the more violent, dangerous and troublemaking type prisoner and has required extremely close supervision on this account."[81] (A more important factor in Peabody's transfer recommendation may have been his appeals to federal court regarding his sentence and treatment while in prison.) In July 1945 he was transferred to Alcatraz—Atlanta got rid of a minor troublemaker and Alcatraz filled an empty cell.

Peabody adjusted smoothly to the regime on the Rock. His family made complete restitution of the money taken in the bank robbery for which he had been convicted (but had not admitted to). By the date of his transfer to McNeil Island three years later, in November 1948, no misconduct reports had been filed against him; he was described by officers as "friendly and cheerful." Except for two minor violations that resulted in no action, his good conduct and work records continued at McNeil. The State of Maryland dropped a detainer that charged him with a parole violation, and he received monthly visits from his two daughters. He was reported to have inherited considerable financial resources from his parents' estate before he was conditionally released in November 1953.

Three years later, on November 19, 1956, despite significant financial resources and a recent marriage (his third), Peabody and an accomplice robbed the People's National Bank of Washington in Seattle of $42,800. He was arrested the next day and a jury found him guilty the following April. Peabody and his co-defendant were sent to Alcatraz. The reasons for committing a fifty-seven-year-old prisoner with no record of escape, violence, or serious institutional misconduct to Alcatraz, and for keeping him there for six years, were not specified in institution records. At his annual review meetings, Peabody either asked to be excused or remained "absolutely mute throughout the interview."[82] He had six brothers, two ex-wives, two daughters, and a son but did not correspond with or receive visits from any of them. He continued to avoid misconduct reports, received good work reports, and was described as "popular" with other prisoners. His health problems and "nervousness" increased, however.

Dispersal of the prisoners before the end of operations at Alcatraz in March 1963 resulted in Peabody's transfer back to McNeil Island in December 1962. He reestablished relationships with his daughters and his adjustment continued to be satisfactory until July 1965, when he was reported to be assisting other inmates "in plotting and planning escapes." His motivation for helping others to escape was attributed to his belief "that he will not outlive his present sentence. . . . He is a highly sophisticated, criminalistic man who has devoted his life to outwitting the law."[83] The staff sought to have him transferred to a high-security penitentiary; a few months later, in September 1965, he was transferred to Atlanta, where he continued the convict lifestyle he knew so well, occupying his time working as a cell house orderly and reading. Like other Alcatraz transferees used to having their own cells, his most serious adjustment problem was in learning to live in a cell with up to eight other prisoners.

In October 1966 Peabody was returned to McNeil Island, where his daughters resumed visiting him. He spent many hours making leather goods in the hobby shop, maintained "an excellent attitude," but had "resigned himself to dying in prison." He became eligible for parole in 1957 but declined to apply due to the fact that "it will be necessary for him to admit his guilt to the current offense and that he is definitely not [going to do]."[84]

In June 1972 Peabody wrote in an application for parole, "I am 74 years of age and have only a few years to live. . . . I am old, infirmed, ill and am unable to be a threat to anyone . . . at my age there is little left in life except a few years of quiet living with my children and grandchildren." On March 1, 1973, Peabody was released on parole from McNeil Island. Despite his claim that he just wanted time with his family, it turned out that he had not just one, but three more bank robberies in him. He was arrested after a few months and, along with his Alcatraz partner Blackie Audett and another confederate, was convicted of robbing the Bank of Washington of $17,509. He was sentenced to fifteen years and sent back to McNeil Island.

In April 1978 Peabody was transferred to the Federal Medical Center in Springfield, Missouri, for treatment of cataracts in both eyes and cancer. Preparations were initiated for a release plan, but by this time he was a "bed-to-wheelchair invalid," and none of his family members would agree to provide housing for him. One of his daughters notified prison officials that she "could not take Mr. Peabody in her home as one of her own children threatened to leave if he were to live there."[85] The medical staff recommended that Peabody be paroled to a nursing home with costs to be covered by his social security payments, and on August 6, 1980, he was moved by charter plane from Springfield to a senior center in Seattle. Four months later, on December 23, he died of heart disease and cancer, outside the walls of prisons where he had resided for almost fifty years.

Audett and Peabody broke very few prison rules (except for possessing contraband), none involving serious confrontations with staff. Their good work records and congenial relationships with guards and work crew supervisors gave them senior citizen status at McNeil Island, where each spent so many years. They were men for whom prison had no deterrent effect; in his interview for this project, Peabody said he much preferred doing time at Alcatraz to putting up with the ever-changing rules at McNeil Island and living in cells with seven or eight other men at Atlanta. While they were on the streets for brief periods, Audett and Peabody enjoyed a series of marriages that were quickly dissolved once they returned to prison. Audett's charm was evident even into his seventies when a former female inmate at Lexington offered to take him into her home should he be released; this arrangement was not approved by parole officials.

Blackie Audett and Gerard Peabody might not appear to be candidates for confinement in a prison for "public enemies" and prison hell-raisers but Alcatraz always needed to fill beds; there were never enough gangsters and troublemakers in the federal system to maintain its population.

Ted Walters

Ted Walters, Floyd Hamilton's rap partner, came to Alcatraz with a sentence of thirty years for bank robbery and transporting a stolen automobile across state lines. He tried to escape in 1943 by climbing over a fence in the industries area, but the escape attempt failed when he fell on the rocks below, injuring his back. This action cost him 3,100 days of good time. He accumulated fifteen additional rule violations, several of which involved fights with other prisoners. In one of these Walters attacked Medley, a black prisoner, following an argument about the war:

> The Japanese [were] fighting in the Philippines and Walters stated that the Japs would rape all the white women, whereupon Medley said that if he were with the Japs he would probably be doing the same thing. . . . Walters stated he took offense at this . . . and started slashing [Medley] with a knife.[86]

Walters forfeited another 500 days of statutory good time for cutting Medley about the face and neck. He was also cited for refusing to work—in one case being identified as the ringleader of a strike—and for insolence, hiding a knife in an empty cell, hiding a sixteen-inch hacksaw blade under the linoleum in front of his D block cell, refusing to obey orders, and using profanity. He corresponded with six family members. When he wasn't segregated in D block, he worked in the laundry and the kitchen.

In 1951, after a two-year period of clear conduct, and what the staff regarded as better control of his temper, he became discouraged when none of his lost good time was restored. According to a January special progress report, "evidence of increase in depression and bitterness is becoming more apparent and subject now attends sick-call [almost] daily. He appears to view his present situation as hopeless." The classification committee, however, took Walters's improved "attitude" into account when it recommended his transfer to Leavenworth, which was accomplished on August 23, 1952.

Walters went to work in the shoe factory at Leavenworth. After visiting him, two of his brothers requested that he be released to the State of Texas, which held three detainers against him, one for violating the state's habitual criminal act for which he had received a sentence of ninety-nine years. He expressed confidence that if he was returned to Texas he could clear up these old charges. He received a conditional release in May 1957, was taken into custody by Texas officials, and soon succeeded in clearing up his three Texas detainers. He was released in November 1959, under joint state and federal supervision. In February 1962 he was returned to the Texas State Prison at Huntsville for assaulting a family member. He was released again from the Texas Department of Corrections in October 1968; this time he returned to Leavenworth as a conditional release violator. In 1970 Floyd Hamilton appeared before the U.S. Board of Parole to urge the release of his old friend, and Walters left the confines of prison one last time.

The final hours of Walters's life after he left Leavenworth were recorded by Hamilton, who had tried his best to counsel Walters:

> Now fifty-eight years old, he was still Terrible Ted. In October 1971 Walters held up a Dallas liquor store with a shotgun. He nearly got away with it. Fleeing the robbery, his car was stopped by a police officer only when he made an illegal right turn. As the officer approached him, Walters began firing his shotgun. The officer returned the fire, wounding him in the shoulder. Walters fled on foot to a nearby house, where he took Mr. and Mrs. Hoyt Houston and their five-year-old daughter as hostages.
>
> Police quickly surrounded the house. Walters emerged with his three prisoners. He held his shotgun to Mr. Houston's head. Officers stood by helplessly as Walters and his prisoners drove off in the Houston car. But Walters ran into a 150-man police blockade several miles out of town.
>
> The police talked to Walters for twenty minutes. The officers tried to bargain with him. If he would release his hostages unharmed, they would let him drive off. As Walters thought it over, he relaxed, moving his gun away from Mr. Houston's head. A sharp shooting Texas Ranger, Tom Arnold, saw his chance. Fired from a powerful rifle from a distance of one hundred yards, Ranger Arnold's bullet hit Walters in the head. Instantaneously, the other officers raced up to the car and fired three more shots into Walters' body. The Houston family was unharmed. . . .
>
> "The officers tried their best. They tried to convince him to throw down that shotgun and surrender. But Ted said he'd rather be gunned to death like a mad dog than go back to prison. And that's what happened. I don't know what Ted was thinking. He was just mixed up."[87]

Thomas Holden

Tom Holden and his rap partner, Francis Keating, arrived at Alcatraz on September 7, 1934, on the first train from Leavenworth Penitentiary. They had robbed banks and mail trains, associated with most of the major Midwest gangsters (including Frank Nash, George Kelly, Harvey Bailey, Alvin Karpis, and Fred Barker), and with forged passes they had been able to walk out the front gates of Leavenworth (see chapter 1). After Holden had been captured and returned to Leavenworth, a classification committee characterized him as "a constant menace to the public safety and would be again if at large" and said that he was an escape risk and "a serious hindrance within the institution to the employment of reclamation methods."[88]

At Alcatraz, Holden and Keating settled down to do their time quietly, surrounded by many old friends. Holden received just one misconduct report, for participating in a 1937 strike. His quiet manner and "good attitude" resulted in the restoration of 185 day of lost good time, advancing his release date to June 1950. His only visitor at Alcatraz—in January 1943—was his son, a private in the army.

On March 25, 1944, Holden was transferred to Leavenworth. A year later he experienced one of the painful consequences of being locked up in prison when he received a telegram from his mother informing him that his son was dying and asking to see him. Four days later another telegram arrived: "Tommy Passed Away, Thursday At 5 P.M."[89] More of his lost good time was restored. Holden was paroled to Chicago in 1947, where his wife was waiting for him.

At a family gathering in 1949, Holden exchanged angry words with his wife, drew a gun, and shot her dead. When her brothers tried to come to her defense, Holden shot and killed them and fled. He managed to avoid capture, and when the FBI created a list of the 10 Most Wanted fugitives in March 1950, Holden headed the list. Bureau officials described him as: "a menace to every man, woman and child in America." He remained at large until June 23, 1951, when federal agents arrested him in Beaverton, Oregon, after receiving a tip from a citizen who recognized Holden's mug shot among the Top 10 fugitives in the local newspaper. Holden was convicted of murder in Chicago and was sent to the Illinois State Prison, where he died two years later.[90]

Because they were not living when this study was conducted and because records of their postrelease experiences did not provide sufficient information, it was not possible to identify the reasons that Ted Walters was "mixed up," or why Tom Holden shot and killed the woman who had waited so many years for him to get out of prison.

Dale Stamphill

Dale Stamphill deviated from the usual pattern of survival on parole. He lived a law-abiding life for ten years in the free world after Alcatraz. Then he drifted back into crime.[91]

Stamphill received five misconduct reports during his first year at Alcatraz; four resulted in confinement in disciplinary segregation. In January 1939 he was wounded while trying to escape from D block with

Dock Barker, Henry Young, Rufe McCain, and William Martin. After three months in the prison hospital, he spent the next fifteen months in D block, where he incurred another misconduct report for creating a disturbance. A few months after his return to the general population, contraband was found in his cell—a knife, two razor blades, and a package of gum. He was locked up again in D block.

His conduct record improved over the next decade, and in December 1950 Stamphill was transferred to Leavenworth, where he compiled a good work record, received only one misconduct report (for "possession of brew"), took courses in advanced accounting and industrial safety, and received frequent visits from family members. State of Oklahoma authorities had identified him as a "habitual criminal of the vicious type" and placed two detainers against him for not completing his life sentence for murder and a twenty-year sentence for robbery with firearms. However, based on a recommendation for clemency by the state pardon and parole board, the governor of Oklahoma granted Stamphill a state parole to become effective when he was granted a federal parole, with state and federal parole officers sharing joint supervision. On April 22, 1956, at age forty-four, he was released from Leavenworth to reside with his brother and sister-in-law. He went to work for a paving company as a laborer at $40 a week.

Within six months of his release, he moved from the position of laborer to the foreman of a work crew. He married and began part-time work as a tax consultant for H&R Block during periods when the paving company had no work. In 1958 he went into business for himself selling insurance, providing bookkeeping services for several small businesses and also offering tax services. Marital problems developed but were characterized in his probation officer's report as being "entirely the wife's fault" due to her excessive drinking; divorce followed.[92]

Stamphill married for the third time and continued working as an accountant while his wife worked as a nurse. In 1965 his reporting obligation was reduced from monthly to quarterly. Then in late February 1966, after ten years of successful living in the free world, Stamphill and a minor felon were caught in the act of trying to open a safe in a Wichita Postal Credit Unit; they were charged with burglary. When questioned by federal probation officers, Stamphill described mounting financial obligations related to the purchase of a home and a car loan that had become his responsibility when his wife left him. Despite working two jobs, he was falling behind on his payments and receiving threatening letters from creditors. "I was tired, wore out, and didn't know where to turn," he said, "and it was affecting my work on both the night job and the day job."[93]

In an interview with the author, Stamphill attributed his return to prison to problems with alcohol.

> During my incarceration before I left Leavenworth I used to get loaded. I didn't always get reported for it but I used to drink that brew—I always had a drinking problem. When I made parole one of the guys talked to me and said [drinking] was just like a sword hanging over my head. If I started drinking again, I'll be back and there wouldn't be any chance of ever getting out again. So sure enough these three marriages went down the drain because of drinking. I started drinking and it was just a short time and I was back [in prison] with a violation.

Stamphill's parole was revoked; he was taken into custody and returned to Leavenworth. The State of Kansas sentenced him to twenty-five years for the burglary, to begin after he served his federal sentence. Determined to deal with his alcohol problem, Stamphill began attending Alcoholics Anonymous meetings, taught a course on taxes, and quietly served time while the Leavenworth staff urged the U.S. Board of Parole to parole him to Kansas so that he could begin his state term. (Oklahoma declined any further interest in returning him to serve more time on the two sentences he owed that state.)

In December 1970 Stamphill was paroled from Leavenworth again; he was transported to the Kansas State Penitentiary at Lansing. Due to his age and continuing good conduct he was soon placed in a minimum-custody dormitory, where he was assigned to work as a clerk typist in the prison store outside the prison walls. In June 1975, at age sixty-three, he was paroled from Lansing with instructions to report to the federal probation office in Kansas City, Missouri, to resume his federal parole.

In Kansas City, Stamphill went directly to an AA meeting to meet his AA sponsor. He took up a temporary residence at a diagnostic and treatment center, began work at Goodwill Industries, and was soon able to rent an apartment. His probation officer reported that Stamphill visited his office "accompanied by a frolicking redheaded woman whom he introduced as his intended." Stamphill got married for the fourth time. He continued his active involvement in AA and began making weekly trips to Leavenworth to offer AA classes. During the years he spent under supervision, he took a job as a maintenance man in a Kansas City park and worked as a volunteer with juvenile offenders. In 1978 he was appointed to the Board of Directors of the Kansas Council on Crime and Delinquency and his federal probation officer began asking him to counsel other parolees coming out of prison who had histories of alcohol abuse. In late November 1979 he was released from parole.[94]

When we asked him whether his prison experience, participating in prison programs, or just getting older were factors related to his success after his second release, Stamphill commented:

> All the time I was in Alcatraz, Leavenworth or any other prison they made no effort to change my attitude or correct my way of doing things. In fact, everything I would try to do I was running into opposition with the officials. I had to do it on my own. . . . Prisons are geared for one thing—when a man is convicted, they have to keep him in prison. . . . They're not geared to releasing the man. So what a man does, he has to do on his own.

Dale Stamphill's postrelease problems were like those that were cited by many returnees—the pressure that came from not having enough work or money combined with alcohol abuse. The surprising aspect of his career was that he attempted a high-risk burglary when he was fifty-four years old after a decade of quite successful adjustment in the free world. In several interviews with the author, Stamphill expressed embarrassment about his return to prison based on such a poorly conceived attempt to get a large amount of money quickly. But he was justifiably proud that he had succeeded in staying out of prison after his second release.

FACTORS DETERMINING SUCCESS AND FAILURE

Considering the successes described in this chapter, one important factor stands out: the assistance, encouragement, and trust from people in a position to make a difference in the prisoner's life, both during and after confinement. Clear contributions came from family members—often sisters, parents (usually a mother), new wives, or wives who waited—but of equal or, in some cases, greater importance were employment counselors, parole officers, even the director of the federal prison system, and, in a few cases, a prison chaplain. Significantly, in almost every case an employer who did not ask questions or was ready to offer a second chance contributed to success on the streets.

James Quillen is a good example of an inmate who received support at many critical junctures. While he was in prison, his family members, Father Clark, Director Bennett, Warden Johnston, the hospital staffs at Alcatraz and McNeil Island, the psychiatrist at McNeil, and San Quentin

Deputy Warden Louis Nelson (who had been a guard at Alcatraz earlier in his career) all assumed a role in ensuring that Quillen would be released with the determination to "make it."

One measure of Quillen's determination to succeed is his willingness to take any job to support himself until he could find work in a hospital. Knowing that few questions would be asked if he sought work as a manual laborer, he took a job at $2 an hour breaking up concrete driveways with a sledgehammer. After his release, emotional and practical support were no less important. He survived a dangerous period of excessive drinking and a bad first marriage with help from his stepfather, stepsister, and brother-in-law; he was able to get the hospital position he had studied and trained for at Alcatraz and McNeil Island through the acceptance and help he received from the employment office counselor and the administrator and chief of radiology at the hospital. Finally, strong support for his new life came from his second wife, and from the birth of a daughter.

Many people at critical times during Quillen's years in federal prison and the years he was under parole supervision made important, even critical, contributions to his postrelease success. But he had already decided to change the course of his life during the months he spent in a disciplinary segregation cell at Alcatraz. As Quillen himself said, a decision to stay out of prison might have come at Leavenworth or another prison, but key staff at Alcatraz, and James Bennett, took steps to encourage his transformation.

In most cases the resources, encouragement, and support from important people in the inmates' lives were necessary for success, but they were not sufficient. They mattered only to men who had clearly determined while in prison that the costs of their criminal careers outweighed the benefits. Yet the prison environment creates the conditions under which this psychological change is more (or less) likely to occur. Doing time at Alcatraz was endlessly boring, almost always frustrating, sometimes dangerous, and many men during our interviews asked us—and themselves—"Why would I want to spend the rest of my life surrounded by this bunch of assholes?"

Those inmates who failed generally lacked one or both of these measures of success. In some cases, as with Blackie Audett and Gerard Peabody, the determination to succeed was entirely lacking—apparently replaced with a determination to continue living outside the law. Among other cases, there was a desire to stay out of prison, but factors difficult to ascertain stood in the way. These men, in interviews, tended to attribute their returns to such causes as being "stupid" or "careless," falling back in with old friends, abusing alcohol, or "bad luck."

A resolve to turn their lives around and support from others helped many Alcatraz inmates become productive and law-abiding citizens after release; but these same factors have been important for men and women who have served time in other federal penitentiaries and state prisons. The next chapter's focal point—the stories of success and failure, with the other findings from this study—applies to Alcatraz specifically.

LESSONS FROM ALCATRAZ
FOR SUPERMAX PRISONS

During the three decades Alcatraz served as a federal penitentiary, and in the years following its closing, many claims have been made about the effects of the harsh regime on the men imprisoned there. Since operations ceased in 1963, most of these ideas have remained unquestioned, becoming part of the conventional wisdom about this special American prison. Many critics and even some BOP officials expected that the restrictive conditions would psychologically damage many of the inmates, leaving them incapable of functioning in civil society. Yet, prison and parole officials also insisted, the violation of these restrictions—misconduct—was an important indicator of character flaws and criminal tendencies that would land ex-convicts in prison again if they were ever released. As readers will remember, Alcatraz was specifically intended to confine "habitual and incorrigible offenders," a group of such hardened criminals that no reform or rehabilitative programs were to be wasted on them.

The foregoing chapters, and the study underlying them, have raised serious questions about the accuracy of these assumptions. As documented in the previous chapter, the label "habitual and incorrigible" was inaccurate for two-thirds of the gangster-era convicts. The statistical data, case studies, and anecdotal evidence we have described cast doubt on the claims that confinement at Alcatraz caused such serious psychological damage as to make postrelease adjustment unlikely and that misconduct was a predictor of postrelease failure. (On the careers of the prison's major hell-raisers, for example, see chapter 11.) This chapter expands these findings and then considers possible explanations for the remarkable success of the island's gangster-era convicts.

PRISON CONDUCT AND POSTRELEASE SUCCESS

During his twenty-two years at Alcatraz, Harmon Waley fought with other prisoners, refused to eat and work, threatened to kill the associate warden, cursed guards, and destroyed the contents of his cell. Yet, as the previous chapter reveals, he led a productive, law-abiding life after his release from prison. Conversely, Gerard Peabody caused little trouble while imprisoned at Alcatraz and McNeil Island but continued to commit bank robberies during several different periods of freedom, a pattern that continued until he reached the age of seventy-five.

The contrasting cases of Waley and Peabody were not unusual. The postrelease successes reviewed in chapter 13 make it clear that bad conduct in prison did not preclude good conduct after release, and the several examples of postrelease failure support the finding that good conduct in prison was not a reliable predictor of good conduct in civil society.

These points are supported by statistics collected during the University of Minnesota study. Data for the Alcatraz population from 1934 to 1963 show that 53.4 percent of the prisoners who received no misconduct reports at Alcatraz came back to prison after release, while prisoners with ten or more misconduct reports returned to prison at the slightly lower rate of 49 percent. Counting only serious misconduct—measured by the number of times a prisoner was locked up in disciplinary segregation at Alcatraz—we found that 54 percent who never went to D block failed after being released, compared to 37 percent of men who were locked up eight or more times in the disciplinary segregation unit. As a whole, these findings suggest an *inverse* relationship between serious misconduct at Alcatraz and post-release success.

Did the penal environment at Alcatraz have anything to do with this finding? Our data show a very sharp drop in the number of misconduct reports for inmates in post-Alcatraz penitentiaries. While this decrease might be explained in part by the aging process, another likely factor was the growing proximity to release and the inmate's appreciation of less restrictive regimes and greater privileges.

More significant is the pattern that emerged when we compared the misconduct rate during each phase of an inmate's sentence with his eventual postrelease outcome.[1] For the periods of pre-Alcatraz and post-Alcatraz incarceration, the results were consistent with the conventional wisdom—an inmate with many misconduct reports had lower rates of clear (without incidents) postrelease success, and recidivism was highest for men who got into disciplinary trouble most often. However, for the Alcatraz phase of these same prisoners' terms, the relationship was in a negative direction: inmates who accumulated many misconduct reports while imprisoned on the island returned to prison at a lower rate than those who had no, or very few, disciplinary reports.[2] In other words, success defined as no-return-to-prison was highest for men who were repeatedly cited for misconduct while serving time on the Rock.

Finally, a comparison of these results with our Leavenworth sample showed that the Alcatraz prisoners differed from their counterparts at this standard penitentiary. As predicted by custody staff, parole boards, and conventional wisdom, Leavenworth inmates who accumulated a large number of misconduct reports were less successful after release than were those with no or only a few misconduct reports.

Why were the men at Alcatraz who broke the rules most often somewhat more likely than their more conforming peers to lead crime-free lives after release? What was it about Alcatraz that made misconduct there a predictor of postrelease success?

To find the answer to this question we need to place the meaning of misconduct in a somewhat different light. For many Alcatraz inmates, misconduct was an expression of resistance, and resistance in that punitive environment was a healthy and adaptive response. A tendency to defy the regime reflected a level of personal strength and determination to maintain their integrity that is necessary to succeed in the free world.

Resistance in prison has generally been portrayed in films and in prison literature as a matter of heroic convicts standing up to brutal regimes, sadistic wardens, or cruel guards. For the Alcatraz convicts, however, resistance was not a response to physical punishment or inhumane living conditions—it was, as described in chapter 10, evidence of prisoners striving to maintain their personal integrity. By trying to maintain some control over decision making in their lives, they gained psychological benefits, even though they paid a high price, both immediate and deferred (in terms of transfer and parole).[3]

Alcatraz was unusual among prisons because most of the time it successfully limited traditional types of prison misconduct while simultaneously creating the conditions under which many inmates found it necessary to engage in resistance-related misconduct. The "traditional" types of rule-breaking—attacks on other inmates, drug use, possession of contraband as noted earlier—were limited relative to other prisons. Due to the strong prohibition in the convict code against homosexual relations, fights tended to be the result of personality clashes. With few personal items available there was little to steal, and no basis for gambling or strong-arming. These activities—the underlying cause of most violence and misconduct in most prisons before the early 1960s—were further limited by the severe restrictions on physical movement and out-of-cell-time, and the presence of a large custodial staff supervising prisoners confined in a small physical area. In this sense, the Alcatraz regime was largely successful in promoting conforming behavior.

For a significant number of Alcatraz inmates, however, conformity had its limits. They were not willing to do everything the regime demanded, that is, relinquish all control over individual decision making. To continue managing some elements of their own existence, they resisted in ways large and small, cryptic and overt, individual and organized. They refused to obey orders, bent the rules, gave insolent replies, exploited their work assignments for contraband and organized work strikes and other protests. Even the most innocuous of these acts brought disciplinary action, which explains why the most frequently occurring violations at Alcatraz were for "creating a disturbance," "insolence," and "refusing to work or to obey orders." A man who refused to obey an order was quickly written up to assure that the first hint of resistance to staff authority brought punitive consequences. Thus, even moderate resistance might over time result in a relatively long misconduct record. For some prisoners—Harmon Waley is a good example—incidents of more serious misconduct often began with a relatively minor attempt to resist; for this prisoner and others like him, being written up for refusing to obey a direct order could lead to rage, physically aggressive behavior, or a self-destructive act, as in the case of James Grove's suicide.

Both prisoners and guards were aware, even if just in the back of their minds, of the psychological and institutional significance of resistance-related misconduct and treated it accordingly. Many of the officers we interviewed commented that if they had been prisoners there would have been occasions when they would have been insolent or refused to obey orders. Flaring up and telling an officer, a work supervisor, or even the captain or deputy warden "where to go" was seen as a normal response for men who could not, would not, "put up with the bullshit" any longer. Staff and prisoners thus drew a line between insolence, disrespect, and even fights among convicts (considered normal due to the obnoxious or provocative personality characteristics of some prisoners) and more serious acts of rebellion such as assaulting an officer, leading a riot, or attempting to escape. Incidents in the latter category not only involved implicit threats to physically injure personnel who tried to block escape paths to freedom but also threatened the reputation of Alcatraz as an escape-proof penitentiary. Although rule violations in the former category were not ignored, they tended to be treated very differently from acts of rebellion, for which the full weight of the institution sanctions were usually brought to bear.[4]

Prisoners who occasionally made decisions not to go along with the program were more likely than conforming prisoners to maintain their psychological well-being and not lose their essential selves to the institution. Inmate and staff interviewees alike agreed that prisoners who resisted the regime were more likely to succeed. Their judgment was that a man who never protested the ever-present, overbearing regimen on the island was someone who would have difficulty functioning in the free world where many decisions had to be made every day.

With rule breaking often related to resistance, Alcatraz inmates with long records of misconduct were not only different from their more conforming peers on the Rock, but they also differed from inmates who accumulated many misconduct reports at standard federal penitentiaries. Our finding that Leavenworth inmates with the worst records of misconduct were more likely to return to prison after their release than those with better records bears out this point.[5] While the unique character of the population sent to Alcatraz and the unique character of the prison itself must be taken into account, there are nonetheless clear implications from these findings for supermax prisons.

PSYCHOLOGICAL EFFECTS OF MAXIMUM-SECURITY CONFINEMENT

No more pervasive criticism was directed toward Alcatraz throughout its thirty-year history than the assertion that the prisoners—among them the toughest prisoners in the federal system—were psychologically damaged by their confinement on the island. Allegations of insanity were numerous. The article that appeared in a San Francisco newspaper a year after the first prisoners arrived, cited in chapter 5, was an example of the kind of hyperbolic sensationalism directed at Alcatraz; it repeated allegations from an Alcatraz convict, supposedly "smuggled" in a note to the mainland, that three prisoners had been driven mad by the harsh conditions of confinement, one had committed suicide, and several others had tried to take their own lives but failed.[6] These reactions were said to be the consequence of doing time under a regime with no privileges, almost complete absence of contact with family members or anyone else in the free world, the inability to earn a parole, and the sense of hopelessness that went with the prospect of serving very long sentences.

These claims of psychological damage have survived to the present. They owe their staying power to their congruence with the media image of Alcatraz, and the possibility of negative psychological effects due to long-term confinement in contemporary supermax prisons has remained an issue for prisoner advocates and some mental health professionals. Critics of long sentences employ terms such as "prison psychosis," "deterioration," and "degeneration" to describe negative psychological effects, while academic researchers refer to the "institutionalization," "colonization," or "prisonization" of inmates. The latter term has been defined by MacKenzie and Goodstein:

> a process involving the following: losing interest in the outside world, viewing the prison as home, losing the ability to make independent decisions, and, in general, defining oneself totally within the institutional context . . . this constellation of reactions is assumed to be traumatic to the individual's personality and sense of self and to be a particular source of difficulty when the individual is ready to leave the institution.[7]

This project made an effort to gather data to test the accuracy of the complaint that Alcatraz caused psychological deterioration. Our task was complicated by the fact that the psychological assessments in inmate records from the 1930s and 1940s must be treated with skepticism, because they were made by the chief medical officer, who was trained as a surgeon, not a psychiatrist. (No social worker or psychologist was ever employed at Alcatraz.) Even more unreliable are descriptions of behavior in inmate files that seem psychological on their face—"antisocial personality," "psychopath," "emotionally unstable," "impulsive," "easily provoked," and so on—but came from custodial personnel and work supervisors trying to make sense of behavior they regarded as puzzling, irrational, or threatening. Lieutenants and captains, like guards, took the position that only they "really knew" the prisoners; in their view the consulting psychiatrists from the Public Health Service who were called to the island to decide whether a prisoner was psychotic were subject to the guile and manipulation of men who are experts at "conning" the naive.

With only rudimentary social history and no standard psychological test data available, we focused on cases in which there was a diagnosis reported by a mental health professional. These judgments occurred when the custodial staff was convinced that an inmate's behavior was so bizarre that genuine mental illness might be present and called for psychiatric consultation. Thus, the empirical basis for testing the claim that the Alcatraz regime was psychologically destructive was limited to cases in which the staff asked for psychiatric evaluations, along with a few judgments of what seemed objectively to be bizarre behavior made by the prison's chief medical officer. Confirmed diagnoses of serious disorders generally resulted in confinement in the mental health ward in the prison hospital, followed by transfer to the Medical Center for Federal Prisoners at Springfield, Missouri.

Despite numerous allegations that confinement at Alcatraz constituted "cruel and unusual" psychological punishment, we found that only a very small number of men experienced serious mental health problems during their confinement on the island. Of the 508 men whose records in prisons before, at, and after Alcatraz were included in our study, forty-one (8 percent) were diagnosed as psychotic during their confinement at Alcatraz. This figure has to stand on its own, because we do not know what proportion of prisoners in a standard penitentiary during this era displayed symptoms of serious mental health problems, and we do not know whether the psychological problems experienced by these Alcatraz prisoners would have appeared in any other prison in which they were housed.

It is likely that at least some of these forty-one men brought their psychological conditions with them to the island—in other words, their mental illness cannot be attributed solely to the effects of the Alcatraz regime. Of the twenty cases for which relevant information was available, five had a prior history of psychotic episodes or had been previously certified psychotic. In addition, there is the possibility that in some cases Leavenworth or Atlanta staff mistook genuine pathological behavior for rationally calculated misconduct or feigned mental illness and transferred to Alcatraz an inmate who should have gone to Springfield. Such may have been the case for nine prisoners in the study sample, who were diagnosed as psychotic by consulting psychiatrists within their first six months on the island—possibly too early for Alcatraz to have caused their mental declines.

To evaluate the reliability of these diagnoses, we reviewed transfers to the Springfield Medical Center and the records of those inmates who spent time in the mental ward at Alcatraz. The choice of these two indicators is based on the assumption that inmates who had been diagnosed as psychotic or seriously mentally ill would have been hospitalized in at least one of these two settings. Seventeen of the forty-one inmates were placed in Alcatraz mental wards one or more times and twenty-five were transferred to Springfield.

The dilemma posed by prisoners who had been diagnosed as mentally ill but assaultive at other prisons emerges clearly from the example of number 1800. He began a seventeen-year sentence for bank robbery at the Atlanta penitentiary in March 1942 and was soon involved in assaults on other inmates. After being diagnosed as suffering from "Dementia Praecox, Catatonic and Paranoid Features," he was transferred to the Springfield Medical Center in November. He and two other inmates attempted to escape through the front gate by taking hostages, including the warden and his secretary. He threatened staff with a knife and had to be forcibly subdued, and the Springfield neuropsychiatric staff supported 1800's transfer to Alcatraz.

He arrived on the island in March 1944 and soon accumulated fourteen misconduct reports, including destroying the toilet, sink, bedding, and light fixtures in his isolation cell, as well as trying to stab inmate Henry Young. In June 1944 senior officer Frank Johnson reported being attacked by the prisoner: "While being questioned by Deputy Warden Miller, [no. 1800] became enraged and struck at me. I warded off the blow and hit him over the head with my billy."[8]

In November 1947 number 1800 was checked into the prison hospital, where he told the chief medical officer that he had three hummingbirds in his cell. The doctor and a guard searched his cell "but found no birds [and 1800] then stated that someone had stolen his birds. He did not eat his supper, breakfast or dinner [because] he wanted his hummingbirds. . . . He knew that the Deputy Warden had put these birds in the stew and he did not want to eat his little birds."

In February 1948 he was back in the prison hospital, as the surgeon–chief medical officer reported to the warden,

> [admitted] with another attack of catatonic excitement . . . a type of schizophrenia in which the patient is very violent, often needs restraints, and is often a very difficult nursing problem. This patient is very untidy and filthy in behavior. He is completely unable to care for himself. It has become a daily routine to clean his cell of feces and feed him. . . . It has been necessary to restrain him in order to prevent him from killing himself. It has been necessary to administer large doses of sedatives to quiet him. . . . It is advisable to transfer this man to the Medical Center as soon as possible.

On April 13, 1948, number 1800 was transferred to Springfield, where the staff determined that his fear of being killed by another inmate (Henry Young) was the cause of his "catatonic excitement" evident at Alcatraz and that, having been removed from the island, "he had a remission of this condition." His transfer to Leavenworth was recommended by Bureau headquarters, with a proviso, "If he causes trouble, consideration could then be given [to a return] to Alcatraz." Determining the extent to which confinement at Alcatraz, in and of itself, provoked serious mental health problems appears impossibly complex in cases like this.

Other studies of psychological disorders associated with long-term confinement have reported a positive relation between the onset of these disorders and length of confinement.[9] More specifically, they found that as the amount of time served increased, the severity of psychological problems experienced by the inmates also increased. This line of research led to the expectation that the onset of these problems would occur after the inmates had spent a substantial amount of time at Alcatraz. The data from our study, however, did not support this prediction. Of the forty-one inmates diagnosed as psychotic at Alcatraz, sixteen received these diagnoses within the first year of their confinement; only ten inmates had been at Alcatraz five years or longer.

The preceding analysis suggests that if the conditions of incarceration at Alcatraz promoted the onset of psychosis, they did so only for a very small number of inmates. This conclusion was supported by almost all of the one hundred former prisoners and employees we interviewed. They identified the same handful of inmates as "crazy"—generally defined by the prisoners as not being able to "stand up" to the rigors of doing big time. Only three of fifty-four inmate interviewees reported that their own mental health had been seriously affected by confinement at Alcatraz; however, two of these men maintained that they had not been so negatively affected that hospitalization, psychotropic medication, or psychotherapy was required; no. 1600 was the exception (see chapter 13).

How were the majority of Alcatraz inmates able to withstand the psychological challenges that were an acknowledged part of serving time on the island? The inmates themselves had a clear idea of who was "crazy" and who was not; they made an important distinction between genuine mental illness and feelings of depression, frustration, anger, and hopelessness that almost every man experienced at one time or another. The majority of Alcatraz inmates—those not in the "crazy" category—were simply better equipped to stand up to the challenging conditions; after all they were old hands at doing time, including considerable time in tough state prisons. They understood that spending some years behind bars was an inherent risk of the life of a bank robber or ransom kidnapper, and they brought to Alcatraz ways of adapting to, and coping with, harsh prison conditions.

This conclusion is consistent with the very limited amount of research that has been done on the effects of long-term confinement. In their study of men in Illinois, Connecticut, and Minnesota state prisons, MacKenzie and Goodstein noted that different prisoners react to the experience of confinement in different ways. While those who were new to prison but faced long sentences reported a high level of "stress," inmates "who had received long sentences and had already served a lengthy time in prison appeared to have developed a method of coping with the experience."[10] Sociologist John Irwin makes a similar point, focusing on the importance of what he calls "pre-prison orientations." "Many offenders," he writes, "have considerable foreknowledge of prison and are relatively well prepared for what will happen to them during their confinement." Irwin cites a study of prisoners in a long-term facility in England by Taylor and Cohen that concluded, "those persons who were involved in systematic crime before their sentences acted very differently than . . . 'situational' criminals." Applying this idea to inmates in this country, Irwin states, "The old-style thieves, who were numerous in American prisons, learned about prison as they learned other aspects of a thief's life and took prison in their stride."[11] Most of the inmates at Alcatraz certainly fit into this category.

The point here is that for more than 90 percent of the gangster-era prisoners, confinement at Alcatraz did not produce such serious mental health problems that they could not function effectively in other prisons after transfer or in the free world after release. That very few inmates were diagnosed as psychotic and were transferred to the Springfield Medical Center does not mean that doing time on the Rock had no emotional impact or more subtle influence on inmates' post-Alcatraz adjustment. Every inmate we interviewed talked about the boredom, loneliness, and what George Kelly called "the absence of everything that makes life worth living." What we have tried to make clear is that the great majority of men in this particular prison population brought to the island with them values, associations, and lots of experience in doing hard time in other prisons that made it possible for them to adjust to and endure the Alcatraz regime.

Finding an answer to the question of which factor, or combination of factors, related to the experience of imprisonment affects a prisoner's postrelease adjustment is one of the great challenges in criminology. Speaking to this point, criminologist Donald R. Cressey has cautioned that it is inaccurate to talk about offenders "ending up" in prison since sooner or later, almost all of them—even "public enemies"—get out:

These prisoners, and thousands who preceded them to confinement, were forcibly removed from social relations in which they were participating and were locked behind walls of concrete and steel where, we are prone to say, they "served their time," "paid their debt to society," and, perhaps, "learned their lesson." But they did more than pay, and serve, and learn in their prisons. They *lived* in them. Each participated in a very complex set of social relations, including a wide variety of social contacts, associations, bonds, alliances, compromises, and conflicts between hundreds of prisoners, guards, administrators, teachers, tradesmen, and professional personnel like social workers, psychologists, and physicians. These social relations are really what make up any individual convict's prison, but the fact is that we know very little about them.

Perhaps it is for this reason that we are inclined to speak of the effects of prison life in generalities. We say prisons reform men. We say prisons are schools of crime. We say locking men in cages creates emotional problems. We say prisons make timid souls into "confirmed," or "hardened" criminals. Some of us even say . . . that only rarely does the prison have any appreciable effect on either the subsequent criminality or the subsequent non criminality of the men it cages.

The prison, as such, does not do anything at all. It just sits there upstate, across the bay, or on the edge of town ugly, menacing. What counts in the subtle specifics of each prisoner's participation is prison *life*."[12]

Below we relate some of the "subtle specifics" of Alcatraz inmates' lives on the Rock to their lives after their release from prison.

WHAT WORKED ON THE ROCK DURING THE GANGSTER ERA

Nearly two-thirds of the men who served time at Alcatraz during the gangster era did what no one expected them to do: they succeeded in building productive lives in the free world after years of imprisonment under the harshest conditions the federal government could devise. How did this prison achieve this result when none of the standard rehabilitation programs or personnel were ever present on the island? How could hundreds of prisoners labeled "menaces to society" emerge from Alcatraz and become law-abiding, even respectable citizens.

We cannot answer the legitimate question of whether the decisions of Alcatraz inmates to change their lives would have occurred if they had been confined in a standard penitentiary. Almost all the Alcatraz inmates had spent considerable time in other prisons but for most of them, their years at Alcatraz constituted the longest single stretch of time served and was the defining element of their prison careers. Therefore, it is toward Alcatraz that we must look if we hope to understand the basis of what criminologists call "desistance"—the absence of criminal conduct compared to earlier stages of an offender's life.

Clearly, something worked at Alcatraz from 1934 to 1948—and just as surely that something was not any single factor or characteristic, but a complex of factors working in concert. Some of these have been identified in preceding chapters. Here we bring together elements that were likely to contribute to the prison's unintentional rehabilitation of so many habitual and incorrigible offenders from the gangster era.

- The *inmates simply got older,* and by the ends of their relatively long terms they had settled down and were ready to abandon their criminal careers.—Criminological studies for decades have found that getting older has always been the most powerful influence on desistance in crime. The criminal activities of most felons eventually come to an end and, as indicated by the case studies in chapter 13, this was true even for the most notorious gangsters in the country.

- The Alcatraz inmates *followed a convict code that provided a basis for inmate solidarity,* a set of principles for coping with long-term confinement, and guidelines for getting along with other inmates and for dealing with the staff.—Adhering to this code helped prisoners maintain their psychological well-being through years of very difficult imprisonment. It elevated the needs of the group above self-interest, encouraged integrity and perseverance in resisting an oppressive regime, promoted loyalty and trust among inmates, and thereby helped defuse conflict.

- Most Alcatraz inmates *had the psychological support of friends and associates* during their criminal careers.—The presence of rap partners and old friends created a prison environment with less conflict and more congenial relations among prisoners. This support in turn helped inmates cope with the prospect of long terms and to maintain a positive psychological orientation that was essential for survival both at Alcatraz and after release. These friendships also encouraged an ethic of mutual assistance that resulted in, among other things, many inmates' receiving legal help and advice from a small number of writ writers and self-trained jailhouse lawyers knowledgeable about the law and legal procedure. Filing writs related to their convictions and sentences and constructing grievances against prison authorities was a satisfying—and legitimate—form of resistance. In the pursuit of this end, the Alcatraz convicts

had basic legal resources and plenty of time with few distractions
to develop their complaints.

- The population at Alcatraz during its first fifteen years was exceptional; its members *were well equipped in terms of intellect, skills,
and character to cope with imprisonment* and to succeed as law-
abiding citizens after release, if they resolved to do so.—Compared
to the populations of other penitentiaries then and now, the
gangster-era convicts were not typical prisoners. They included
prominent gangsters, thieves, bank robbers, leaders and key participants in escape plots, and men instrumental in organizing protests and strikes. They were more likely to possess intelligence,
ambition, leadership ability, self-confidence, and determination.
They attributed imprisonment to their own wrong decisions, not
to being poor or a victim of racial discrimination (80 percent of
the population was white), or to having psychological problems
or parents who were negligent, abusive, or absent. They understood if you did the crime, you will probably have to do the time.
These factors helped this particular population of prisoners psychologically survive their years on the Rock and succeed in the free
world after release.

- The *absence of an underground economy* in money, luxury goods,
drugs, and gambling virtually eliminated theft and strong arming
among prisoners. Nor was there a social hierarchy headed by
convict bosses that forced its will on other prisoners by intimidation and physical coercion.—Today's convicts can only imagine
what it was like to do time when prisoners were not trying to kill
and exploit each other and instead presented a unified front to the
staff.

- Compared to state prisoners, the federal offenders at Alcatraz
*lacked certain characteristics that might have increased their
chances of reoffending.* First, only a very few—5 percent of the
entire population—had been convicted for sex offenses, most of
them military offenders who had raped adult females and ended
up at Alcatraz as a consequence of subsequent misconduct at other
prisons. At state prisons, sex offenders often constitute a significant
segment of the population, but Alcatraz never held a prisoner who
had molested a minor child or committed incest. All sex offenders
were regarded by the Alcatraz convicts as "perverts," and the few
rapists who showed up made every effort to hide their commitment
offenses. Alcatraz convicts therefore did not leave prison with the
extra burden of trying to live down crimes that even their fellow
prisoners regarded as abhorrent and that made them subject to extra

surveillance by police and parole authorities. Second, and more important, the epidemic of drug use and abuse in free society, and especially in prisons, was yet to come. None of the gangster-era convicts returned to the free world with a record of drug addiction; and, because they had been in prison for an average of ten years, they had learned to live without alcohol. Only a few men, like Dale Stamphill, blamed excessive use of alcohol as a precipitating factor in their failure after release.

- The island's *monastic regimen encouraged self-reflection* and provided an opportunity for reevaluating values and priorities in life.—We know from our interviews that during their years at Alcatraz many men decided that they had done enough crime—and enough time. The many distractions present at standard prisons (frequent association with large numbers of other inmates, a variety of educational and recreational programs, movies, radio, newspapers, and other privileges) were absent on the Rock. This spartan existence left many hours for inmates to contemplate their lives up to that point—to think about the mother or father—or both—who died while they were in prison, the wife or girlfriend who was sleeping with other men, the children with whom they had no contact, and their inability to celebrate holidays, family occasions, and weekends on the town. As the aging process exerted its influence, the inmates knew from the departure of other prisoners that they too would eventually be transferred and released. During long hours of quiet isolation, interviewees recalled that they began to objectively weigh the costs and benefits of their criminal careers and, in many cases, resolved to take a different path for the remainder of their lives.

- Another factor absent from today's massive prison systems and mega penitentiaries is *the attention that Director Bennett, several wardens, and other prison and parole officers gave Alcatraz inmates during and after their imprisonment.*—As detailed in preceding chapters, these efforts provided some of our interviewees with the extra motivation or practical assistance they needed as they tried to turn their rebellious lives around. James Bennett made frequent trips to Alcatraz, set up an "office" in the old military cell block, and gave a considerable number of prisoners practical help along with the impression that he cared how the inmates would conduct their lives after release, and that they could change their ways. It should be noted, however, that Bennett's help and that of other prison and parole officials was important for those men who were at a point in their lives when they were ready to try giving up their criminal careers.

- A final feature that made the Alcatraz convicts unusual, compared to state and other federal prisoners, is *how they felt about their prison experience:* making it to the Rock, they knew, carried high status.—By the time we were able to interview them, Alcatraz's reputation as this country's toughest prison had been enhanced by such Hollywood films as *Birdman of Alcatraz* and *Escape from Alcatraz.* Beginning in the mid-1970s Alcatraz became a major tourist attraction as documentaries about the prison, famous escapes, the battle of Alcatraz, and notable prisoners began to appear on cable television channels. During our interviews, almost all the ex-prisoners expressed not regret, but pride, at having served time on the Rock. Instead of hiding their criminal and prison backgrounds, they found that their relatives, friends, neighbors, Park Service rangers, documentary filmmakers (and crowds of tourists when they visited the island) wanted to hear all about "what it was like" to serve time in this famous prison.

The results of this study call into question past and present assumptions about the effects of long-term confinement in what are now called supermax penitentiaries, notably,

- The label "habitual and incorrigible" was inaccurate for two-thirds of the gangster-era convicts and for half of the entire population of Alcatraz inmates when they were released from federal prison.
- A record of misconduct in the prison did not preclude success after release.
- A record of none or very few (one or two) reports of prison rule violations—being a conforming "model prisoner"—related to post-release failure, not success.
- The great majority of prisoners did not suffer serious psychological damage from their confinement on America's Devil's Island.

These findings emphasize the importance of conducting rigorous empirical evaluations of established penal policies and questioning the accuracy of conventional wisdom (generally comprised of "common sense" and "experience") and the judgments of experts. Almost everyone presumed that negative consequences would accompany and follow confinement at Alcatraz. Adherents to this view included several senior officials of the Bureau of Prisons, other workers in the field of corrections, mental health professionals, university criminologists—and even the Alcatraz convicts themselves.

The significance of Alcatraz has not faded with time. Contemporary supermax penitentiaries, based on the Alcatraz model—isolating a prison system's most serious troublemakers in a maximum-custody, minimum-privilege institution—now house thousands of prisoners. The evidence gathered for this study of America's first supermax suggests the need to evaluate beliefs and assumptions about the effects of confinement and the postrelease prospects for men serving time in the Rock's successors.[13]

EPILOGUE

World War II initiated a period of enormous social change in America. A rush of new developments from the war experience along with the economic and demographic shifts resulting from the return of millions of demobilized military personnel and the conversion of industries to peacetime production infused virtually every intellectual current in the society.

Along with many other aspects of government policy, established thinking about imprisonment and criminal sentencing came in for reconsideration and alteration. The policies embodied in the big house penitentiary with its focus on deterrence and control, of which Alcatraz was the prime example, began to be influenced by the concept of correctional treatment, which rested on the as-yet-untested assumption that a variety of psychological and educational programs would allow convicts to become rehabilitated during their imprisonment.

This effort to apply elements of the rehabilitation philosophy at Alcatraz was evident in changes in policies related to inmate reviews, transfers, and parole. After Edwin Swope replaced James Johnston as warden, Bureau headquarters instructed Swope to assign a staff member to prepare "special progress reports" on all prisoners, initiate annual reviews of each inmate, and form a "classification committee."[1] As inmates appeared before the new committee, staff began to provide the first written reports of each man's work, housing, educational and medical needs; his family problems; and his disciplinary record, including the loss and restoration of good time. These reports were prepared by the island's first classification and parole officer. This position, filled by a succession of officers, was as close as Alcatraz ever got to having a staff member assigned to a noncustodial social service function.

The classification committee began reviewing the status of veteran convicts, including Alvin Karpis, Harmon Waley, William Dainard, and Whitey Franklin. For the first time, terms like "adjustment" and "rehabilitation" appeared in written reports. The times were changing, but the skepticism of the custodial staff toward this new function was duly noted in this statement by the classification and parole officer:

> The custodial officer who has devoted most of his career to "guard duty"—and concerned himself primarily with that responsibility—is oft-times cynical and inclined to decry the efforts and mission of the classification group. Initially, we encountered difficulty with the described type [of custodial officer], and listened to volunteered criticism and suggestions, some of which seemed premised on the one-time theory of "Lock 'em up and forget 'em—that's the treatment they deserve and expect!"[2]

Accompanying changes in the field of corrections was a fundamental shift in the purpose of Alcatraz. As the need for a high-profile depository for the nation's leading gangsters faded in significance, the prison became a convenient place to put serious offenders convicted in federal courts on the West Coast; in previous years these prisoners would have been sent to McNeil Island or to Leavenworth. James Bennett described the need for this change in the prison's purpose to Assistant Director Frank Loveland after an inspection tour of Alcatraz in 1950:

> If we are going to keep this institution in operation, I think we have to change our policies somewhat about committing long-termers to this institution. Apparently, there are at present so few flagrant violations of our regulations that we are not going to be able to get enough prisoners to maintain the population in the neighborhood of 300, which I think is necessary to keep operating costs and other factors at a reasonable figure. While this, of course, is a point to be kept in mind, the most important consideration is whether the institution could not be more effective in serving as a deterrent to violent crime. As you well know, I am not a very strong believer in punitive measures as a crime deterrent, but, on the other hand, there is no doubt that fear of a strict prison regime has its effect on certain mentalities. If we receive an inmate who has a long previous record of violent crime, escapes and the like and whose most recent offense evoked a long sentence, I am inclined to think we ought to send him rather promptly to Alcatraz. This is especially true in those cases where there is little hope of parole. In such cases we should, of course, be more liberal in transferring them out of Alcatraz to other institutions. After the individual has had a taste, so to speak, of Alcatraz, he can be removed elsewhere if his record could justify it. As I indicated previously, I think too we have got to establish the principle that Alcatraz will be used for West Coast maximum custody offenders more frequently than for eastern offenders. Alcatraz will be a sort of Leavenworth or Atlanta for West Coast offenders.[3]

This redefinition of the function of Alcatraz was one of the major factors behind the third change—the types of prisoners sent to the island. The inmate population had already begun to change during the war years, when military offenders, many of whom were black but had caused problems in other prisons, joined the previously largely white population. During the 1950s, racial and ethnic diversity increased and interpersonal conflicts produced more prisoner-on-prisoner assaults. A small number of new types of high-profile federal offenders—"subversives," spies, saboteurs, and organized crime figures—took the place of the 1930s "public enemies." Combined with changes in the character of the inmate population, these modifications of the program made the experience of doing time on the Rock rather different from what it had been during the height of the gangster era. The prisoners who came to the island after the gangster era still conformed to most tenets of the convict code, but not as faithfully, and they employed new forms of resistance, notably filing numerous complaints in federal court about the conditions of their confinement at Alcatraz.

Throughout the 1950s and early 1960s, the image of Alcatraz as barbarous and outmoded continued to plague prison and BOP officials. Robert Stroud's sentence of life in solitary confinement became a cause célèbre with the publication of *Birdman of Alcatraz* and the movie that followed it. In June 1962 the sensational escape attempt by Frank Morris and the Anglin brothers, followed by another nearly successful attempt by John Paul Scott that December, gave the Bureau of Prisons the excuse it was looking for to close the prison, and operations ceased in March 1963.

When Alcatraz closed, it was widely considered a relic of an outdated penal philosophy. But the principle this prison represented—isolating the nation's highest-profile federal lawbreakers and the federal prison system's worst troublemakers and most assaultive inmates in a super high-security environment—began to take on new life in the 1970s. In an effort to cope with the rising violence related to the increased influence of prison gangs and the drug trade, a "control unit" was established in 1973 at the federal penitentiary in Marion, Illinois. During the late 1970s and early 1980s Marion became the depository not only for the federal system's most serious management problems but also for inmates who could not be controlled in the prisons in many states. As the trend toward higher security at the prison continued, the Bureau of Prisons, which had levels of security rated one through five, designated Marion in 1979 as its only Level 6 penitentiary. After the murder of two guards in October

1983, Director Norman Carlson ordered the Marion staff to terminate congregate activities and placed the entire prison on an "indefinite administrative segregation" regime, popularly called a "lockdown." This change in the function of Marion represented the rebirth of the Alcatraz model. In subsequent years, the high-security regime at Marion has been replicated at thirty-six state prisons, including Pelican Bay and Corcoran in California, Southport in New York, and Tamms in Illinois.

Was Alcatraz the toughest prison in America? In some respects it was. Rules for conduct were highly specific and even small infractions drew penalties that in the 1930s included confinement in underground dungeon cells. During its thirty years as a federal prison there was no television and no radio until headsets were introduced in the 1950s. No newspapers were allowed and the prison never had a commissary. Extreme controls were imposed on written communications and visits with family. No psychologists, social workers, teachers, or vocational training instructors were employed so no rehabilitation programs were ever offered. Boredom and isolation from the outside world were the burden of doing time on the Rock.

Yet it can be argued that Alcatraz was not the worst place to do time even under the silent system in its early days. Interviews with one hundred prisoners and staff members revealed there were no sanctioned corporal punishments and no incidents of deliberate physical abuse of convicts. Brutal treatment and inhumane living conditions that characterized southern chain gangs, the convict lease system in the turpentine camps and prison farms, or the electric volts of the "telephone" at the Tucker Farm in Arkansas were not features of confinement in the federal prison system. The absence of polarized, politicized racial-ethnic gangs at Alcatraz was not the result of deliberate prison policy but of the prevailing social conditions of the time. Without gangs and with solidarity due to a strong commitment to the convict code, inmate-on-inmate violence at Alcatraz was relatively rare and seldom fatal as compared to the day-to-day tension and simmering violence characteristic of life in today's prisons.

Nor did confinement on the island approach the twenty-three-hour daily lockdown of the contemporary supermax. Television surveillance, electronically controlled gates, and individual barred and concrete exercise pens would not appear until the 1970s and 1980s. At Alcatraz convicts could get frequent direct exposure to the outdoors, cold and foggy as the Bay Area climate frequently was, when they walked from the yard to the industries area. The silent, air conditioned, wrap-around solitary confinement in cells with solid front doors that is characteristic of supermax prisons was limited at Alcatraz to a half dozen cells in the disciplinary segregation unit. There was frequent daily contact between convicts and guards, often with large groups of prisoners going to or from the dining hall and work assignments. This close physical proximity is a far cry from staff-inmate contact in the modern supermax, where inmates only exit cells in shackles to shuffle down corridors between escorting officers armed with riot batons.

The possibility of escape from Alcatraz was minimized by not only the staff-convict ratio and custodial policies, but by the physical features of a prison holding only 260 men on a very small island. Nonetheless the possibility of escape was always present and some of the best-known escape attempts in American penal history were planned and executed there. In the Alcatraz era a prisoner could look at nearby San Francisco and plot an escape. The electronic motion detectors, coils of razor ribbon, and hardened exterior of supermax institutions have essentially removed escape from consideration by contemporary prisoners.

The means by which today's supermax prisons control inmates is different from Alcatraz. Along with the demise of convict solidarity, modern technology makes isolation and surveillance complete around the clock. One result has been the concentration of inmates' energy on aggression toward others in their immediate environment. Alcatraz convicts dreamed of going over the walls, floating along in the cold waters of the bay, and reaching the mainland and freedom. Most supermax inmates spend their time plotting how to counter "disrespect" and threats from other prisoners or how to get back at an officer who represents the controls imposed on them. The focus of the supermax fantasies is the closed world of the prison, not the outside world.

But if Alcatraz was not the worst of prisons and was not a true lockdown penitentiary, it was by intent and in fact a severe imposition of deprivation of personal mobility and individual choices. Security and control were the paramount concerns at Alcatraz as they are in today's supermax penitentiaries The objective was to keep disruptive convicts in compliance with a rigid set of conduct restrictions. Control was an end in itself. Alcatraz anticipated the aim of an institution devoted to the total control of prisoners and was therefore the precursor of the supermax that has become such a controversial aspect of American criminal justice.

Finally, it should be recognized that since the 1930s the federal government, in contrast to state prison systems, has sought to put the nation's highest-profile lawbreakers in a prison setting that symbolized harsh punishment for serious crime. As Alcatraz held Al Capone and Machine Gun Kelly, and as Marion, Illinois, has held Mafia boss John Gotti, drug-king Carlos Lehder, and assorted spies and traitors, Administrative Maximum (ADX) at Florence, Colorado, has been the preferred penitentiary for Timothy McVeigh (until his execution); Theodore Kaczynski, the "Unabomber"; Richard Reed, the "Shoe-bomber"; Sheik Omar Abdel-Rahman and Ramzi Yousef, convicted in the first World Trade Center bombing; and most recently, Zacharias Moussawi, found guilty of conspiracy in the 2001 World Trade Center bombing. The feminine names of the towns in which these prisons are located—Marion and Florence— do not connote a harsh and menacing penal setting, but federal officials have had their intention confirmed by the nicknames attached to these prisons by newspaper and television reporters, inmate lawyers, and prisoners' rights groups—Marion as "the new Alcatraz" and Florence as "Alcatraz of the Rockies." Decades after it ceased operation, the word Alcatraz still conveys the dramatic image of a tough prison where bad guys get the punishment they deserve.[4]

NOTES

PREFACE

1. This work was part of a Ford Foundation–funded study of federal prisons by a research team from the University of Illinois. For an account of this unusually comprehensive study see Daniel Glaser, *The Effectiveness of a Prison and Parole System* (Indianapolis: Bobbs-Merrill, 1964).

2. For more information about the GGNRA and its inclusion of Alcatraz, see Amy Meyer, *New Guardians for the Golden Gate: How America Got a Great National Park* (Berkeley: University of California Press, 2006).

3. After the original startup of tours, Robert Kirby, site supervisor for the National Park Service, improved the accuracy of rangers' presentations by inviting former guards, lieutenants, and captains who lived in the Bay Area to return to the island to provide information and answer questions.

4. These files included those of men who died of natural or unnatural causes at Alcatraz; were deported or released to state prisons; served their entire sentence and thus came out of Alcatraz "flat"; or were conditionally released directly from Alcatraz.

5. The only other set of federal prison records marked for historic preservation during Norman Carlson's term as director came from the Federal Women's Prison at Alderson, West Virginia.

6. See David A. Ward and Annesley K. Schmidt, "Last-Resort Prisons for Habitual and Dangerous Offenders: Some Second Thoughts about Alcatraz," in *Confinement in Maximum Custody: New Last Resort Prisons in the United States and Western Europe*, ed. David A. Ward and Kenneth E. Schoen (Lexington, MA: Lexington Books/D. C. Heath, 1981), 61–68.

7. In the chapters ahead, individual FBI agents who authored reports to the director are identified by name; during the Hoover administration such individual recognition was not agency policy.

8. "Conditional release" (later called "mandatory release") is release from prison when good time earned (every day without misconduct reports) is subtracted from the statutory maximum of a sentence. Conditional releasees were subject to supervision by federal probation officers and to rules and conditions similar to parole; violations constituted grounds for revocation and return to prison.

9. The following circumstances reduced the sample of 508 to 439 cases: the inmates' postrelease history was unknown (twenty-eight cases, mainly due to in-

complete FBI arrest records); they were deported (nine cases); or they died prior to release or during their first year after release (thirty-five cases).

10. Most former employees, having been told to keep their thoughts about or experiences on Alcatraz within the Bureau of Prisons "family," were initially hesitant about expressing candid opinions—particularly about the management of the prison by Warden James Johnston and other administrators and the influence of Bureau headquarters. They were advised that their comments would not be attributed to them by name, but as interviews progressed (and as they learned that their colleagues were also telling their stories), they agreed during the interviews to be identified with their remarks. As former employees got over their reluctance to talk, a number of wives who were at home during the interviews told me, "I've never heard him talk about his work like that."

Few former inmates expressed any concern about keeping their identities anonymous when they talked about the prison. For privacy and other reasons, three prisoners are identified by fictitious numbers: 1600, 1700, and 1800. Two senior officers are identified in this book only as "X" and "Y," one because many years following his retirement from the Bureau he was still concerned about the candor of some of his remarks; the other by the request of his former caregivers that they be asked to review any excerpts from his interview before agreeing to identify him as the source.

For both employees and prisoners, as Alcatraz became a major tourist attraction and more movies, books, and television documentaries appeared, everyone felt free to describe their experiences and more than a few started thinking that they should write their own books about Alcatraz.

11. Focusing on careers helps avoid the false dichotomy of explaining prison society either as a response to the deprivations of life in a "total institution" (one closed to the outside world) or as a result of the importation of criminal values and life styles into penal settings. A criminal career typically is a sequence of crimes, encounters with the police, outcomes of judicial proceedings, responses to the conditions of sentences, and decisions to discharge or release, followed by further encounters with police, courts, penal institutions, and parole agencies. With lengthy or repeated incarcerations, the features and habits of a criminal career interact with the prisoner's response to the conditions of confinement and measures of control exercised by the staff.

INTRODUCTION

1. Alistair Cooke, "Alcatraz: Summer 1959," *Letter from America* (Bath: BBC Audiobooks, 2003). This commentary on Alcatraz was selected by Cooke for a BBC collection of his radio broadcasts, 1946–1968. Cooke was incorrect in asserting that state prisoners were confined at Alcatraz and that an inmate, Gene Colson, was among the residents.

2. Harry Elmer Barnes and Negley K. Teeters, *New Horizons in Criminology* (New York: Prentice-Hall, 1945), 461.

3. Anthony M. Turano, "America's Torture Chamber," *American Mercury*, September 1938, 11–15.

4. Roy Gardner, *Hellcatraz: The Rock of Despair* (n.p., 1939).

5. Janet Maslin, "When Does Pain Make a Murderer a Victim?" *New York Times,* January 20, 1995.

6. Bernard Weintraub, "As Film Location, Alcatraz Lives Up to Its Dark Past," *New York Times,* March 3, 1994, 33.

7. For descriptions of more than a dozen movies made about Alcatraz, its inmates, or as a setting for fictionalized stories see Robert Lieber, *Alcatraz: The Ultimate Movie Book* (San Francisco: Golden Gate National Parks Conservancy, 2006); and Dashka Slater, *Lights, Camera, Alcatraz: Hollywood's View of an American Landmark* (San Francisco: Golden Gate National Parks Conservancy, 2005).

8. According to U.S. Senator John McCain, POWs who tried to escape or who "distinguished themselves as die-hard resisters" were confined in the Viet "Alcatraz." John McCain with Mark Salter, *Faith of My Fathers* (New York: Random House, 1999), 316–17.

9. Ian Fischer, "Missing Refugees Turn Up with Accounts of Abuse," *New York Times,* May 30, 1999, 7.

CHAPTER 1

1. David E. Ruth, *Inventing the Public Enemy: The Gangster in American Culture, 1918–1934* (Chicago: University of Chicago Press, 1996), 1–2.

2. John Kobler, *Capone: The Life and World of Al Capone* (New York: Collier Books, 1971), 181.

3. Ibid.

4. Ibid., 181–82, 186–87.

5. Sean Dennis Cashman, *Prohibition: The Lie of the Land* (New York: Free Press, 1981), 80.

6. Kobler, *Capone,* 190.

7. Ibid., 202, 204.

8. Ibid., 253; see 247–61 for an account of this event. A more recent book on the subject is William J. Helmer and Arthur J. Bilek, *The St. Valentine's Day Massacre* (Nashville, TN: Cumberland House, 2004).

9. Francis X. Busch, *Enemies of the State* (London: Arco Publications, 1957), 189.

10. Karl Sifakis, *The Encyclopedia of American Crime* (New York: Facts on File, 1982), 638.

11. Ibid., 637.

12. Kobler, *Capone,* 269–70.

13. Lawrence Bergreen, *Capone: The Man and the Era* (New York: Simon and Schuster, 1994), 322.

14. Ibid., 365–66.

15. Kobler, *Capone,* 277–78.

16. Frank Spiering, *The Man Who Got Capone* (Indianapolis: Bobbs-Merrill, 1976), 149.

17. Ibid., 192–93.

18. Ibid., 196–97.

19. "Capone Runs Underworld from Cell, U.S. Reveals: Al Living in Luxury," *Chicago Herald and Examiner,* December 18, 1932.

20. See Kobler, *Capone,* 351–54; and Melvin H. Purvis, Special-Agent-in-Charge, Bureau of Investigation, Chicago, Illinois, to Director, Bureau of Investigation, January 26, 1932.

21. On the way to Atlanta the U.S. marshal and his five deputies kept Capone in leg irons and handcuffed to a youth being transported to Florida for automobile theft. Capone was allowed out of the restraints while he put on his monogrammed sky blue silk pajamas but then the handcuffs were reattached. Through the night Capone was thus linked to the auto thief, requiring that they lie in the same berth; the young thief was said to have been so in awe of his traveling companion that he remained mute throughout the trip. Kobler, *Capone,* 355–56.

22. For a recent, exceptionally well-documented account of the exploits of key figures in the gangster era see Bryan Burrough, *Public Enemies: America's Greatest Crime Wave and the Birth of the FBI, 1933–1934* (New York: Penguin Press, 2004).

23. For a list of important robberies and ransom kidnappings from 1930–1937 see Jay Robert Nash, *Crime Chronology: A Worldwide Record, 1900–1983* (New York: Facts on File, 1984), 80–111.

24. See Burrough, *Public Enemies;* and Michael Wallis, *Pretty Boy Floyd: The Life and Times of Charles Arthur Floyd* (New York: St. Martins Press, 1992).

25. See Burrough, *Public Enemies;* and Steven Nickel and William J. Helmer, *Baby Face Nelson: Portrait of a Public Enemy* (Nashville, TN: Cumberland House, 2002).

26. Alvin Karpis, with Bill Trent, *The Alvin Karpis Story* (New York: Coward, McCann & Geoghegan, 1971), 118–19.

27. Ernest A. Alix, *Ransom Kidnapping in America, 1874–1974: The Creation of a Capital Crime* (Carbondale: Southern Illinois University Press, 1978), 51–55.

28. Alix's study of ransom kidnapping confirmed the wisdom of this decision, concluding that when businessmen were kidnap targets, there was much less societal approbation, successful prosecutions were rare, and when convictions were obtained, they were generally on lesser charges. Ibid.

29. Ibid., 61.

30. Other cases during the six months after federal legislation went into effect did not involve interstate transport of victims: "The 8-year-old son of a wealthy partner in the New York Stock Exchange, a wealthy Chicago couple, and an alleged New York City bootlegger." Ibid., 76.

31. For a more detailed account of this case see ibid., 79–80.

32. For five years until her death by suicide, McElroy was said to have been in despair over the prospect of never being united with her kidnapper. Ibid., 81, 82–84.

33. Ibid., 81.

34. For a kidnapper's account of this case, see Karpis, *Karpis Story,* 132–44.

35. Alix, *Ransom Kidnapping,* 85.

36. For descriptions of this case, see Burrough, *Public Enemies,* 68–75, 80–84, 87–94; and Federal Bureau of Investigation (FBI) reports by H. H. Colvin, August 5, 1933; and D. L. McCormick, August 7, 1933.

37. Dowd, FBI report, C-4, pp. 21–22.

38. This feature of criminal conduct has been identified or understood in few criminology studies except for Jack Katz, *Seductions of Crime: Moral and Sensual Attractions in Doing Evil* (New York: Basic Books, 1988).

39. For Bailey's description of his remarkable career as a bank robber and the Memorial Day break from the Kansas State Penitentiary at Lansing, see J. Evetts Haley, *Robbing Banks Was My Business: The Story of J. Harvey Bailey, America's Most Successful Bank Robber* (Canyon, TX: Palo Duro Press, 1973).

40. See the statements of Deputy Sheriff Charles W. Young to FBI agents, September 4, 1933, file 7–115–435, pp. 1–2; and Nick Tresp, September 5, 1933, file 7–115–418.

41. J. E. Hoover to Attorney General, September 5, 1933, file 7–115–405.

42. J. W. Hughs, memorandum to the Director, September 6, 1933, file 7–115–433.

43. Machine Gun Kelly is still famous in U.S. criminal history because his photograph is posted and his name is brought up every year to the 1.4 million tourists who visit Alcatraz and hear descriptions of the prison's most notorious convicts. For details about Kelly's criminal career see Burrough, *Public Enemies*. Kelly's life up to his arrest for the Urschel kidnapping has been described by his son, Bruce Barnes, in *Machine Gun Kelly: To Right a Wrong* (Perris, CA: Tipper Publications, 1991).

44. The Department of Justice, wishing to make the most of its apprehension of the Kellys, quickly turned to the matter of their transportation to Oklahoma City and the trial. Serious consideration was given to a suggestion that the defendants be locked up in a steel baggage car owned by the Rock Island Railway that could be fitted out with cots; however, since the press would watch every movement from the jail, it soon became clear that a train holding the Kellys would attract crowds at every station on the route west from Memphis. The decision was thus made to charter a plane to fly the Kellys to Oklahoma City; three and a half hours later, they were lodged in the same jail where their co-defendants were being held while they awaited sentencing. For an account of the apprehension of the Kellys see Burrough, *Public Enemies*, 116–25, 129–34.

45. For Bailey's description of these proceedings see Haley, *Robbing Banks*, 161–75.

46. Bryan Burrough was able to trace the origin of this famous statement to an account of the arrest of the Kellys by FBI agent William Rorer; given to "a *Chicago American* reporter hours after Kelly's capture, Rorer said it was Kathryn who uttered the historic word . . . at the moment she was arrested. 'Kelly's wife cried like a baby. She put her arms around [her husband] and said, Honey, I guess it's all up for us. The G-men won't ever give us a break.'" Burrough, *Public Enemies*, 133–34.

47. Basil Banghart Alcatraz file.

48. Roy Gardner and Joe Urbaytis, Alcatraz files.

49. U.S. Marshal J. B. Holahan to Attorney General Dougherty, September 29, 1921, Gardner Alcatraz file.

50. Holden and Keating, Alcatraz files.

51. For Nash's connection to the string of outlaw families descended from Quantrill's Raiders through the James, Younger, Dalton, Jennings, and Belle Starr

gangs, see Paul I. Wellman, *A Dynasty of Western Outlaws* (Lincoln: University of Nebraska Press, 1961), 296–300.

52. Earl Thayer was captured three days later, "delirious and half frozen . . . on the outskirts of Leavenworth carrying a 30.30 Winchester." FBI interesting case memorandum 62-26316-49, April 24, 1933. The FBI account of this escape was not at variance with Berta's except in stating that he was wounded in the shoulder during a "short skirmish"; Berta said that he was standing on the road with his hands up when a soldier shot him.

53. In addition to the author's two lengthy interviews with Charlie Berta (August 2, 1987; February 19, 1988), another source of information for this account of one of the most famous escapes in federal prison history is Jack Cope, U.S. Penitentiary [USP] commitment no. 72485, "1300 Metropolitan Avenue: A History of the United States Penitentiary at Leavenworth Kansas" (USP Leavenworth, n.d.), 69–70, written under the supervision of G. Cuthbertson, Supervisor of Education. See also Paul W. Keve, *Prisons and the American Conscience: A History of U.S. Federal Corrections* (Carbondale: Southern Illinois University Press, 1991), 109–10, where Keve comments on a policy the BOP developed after this escape, "that a warden, or any other staff person, taken hostage immediately loses all authority, no other staff is to accept any orders from him. . . . Such a policy was not in place in 1931."

54. James D. Calder, *The Origins and Development of Federal Crime Control Policy: Herbert Hoover's Initiatives* (Westport, CT: Praeger Publishers, 1993), 176.

55. FBI report, W. F. Trainor, January 7, 1935.

56. In his book about this event, *Missouri Waltz*, Maurice Milligan, the former U.S. attorney for the Western District of Missouri, claimed that the culprits were Pretty Boy Floyd, Verne Miller, and a Kansas City gangster, Adam Richetti. Maurice M. Milligan, *Missouri Waltz* (New York: Charles Scribner's Sons, 1948), 132–33. A more recent book by Robert Unger based on an analysis of 89 volumes of FBI files identified Verne Miller as one of the shooters, but the identity of a second man remains unknown. Unger's conclusion is that the shooting began when FBI agent Lackey accidentally discharged his shotgun, killing Nash and agent Caffrey. Robert Unger, *The Union Station Massacre: The Original Sin of J. Edgar Hoover's FBI* (Kansas City: Andrews McMeel, 1997), 230.

57. Director, FBI, to Director, BOP, October 13, 1933, file 7-115-791, pp. 1–2.

58. Homer Cummings, Attorney General, to Warden Robert Hudspeth, USP Annex, Fort Leavenworth, October 17, 1933, Albert Bates Alcatraz file. Hudspeth responded to this directive with a detailed description of the conditions of confinement for Bates and Bailey: "I issued instructions to the Deputy Warden to confine them in Seven Wing Basement . . . where the solitary confinement cells are located. . . . When the men are locked in their cells this leaves Bates and Bailey under double lock as the door leading into this hallway is also padlocked, having a heavy wire screening over the hall partition and leaving this door where it can be unlocked only by a guard from the outside. I selected three of the best guards I have in the institution who are personally in charge of these men at all times, with instructions from me to permit no one to come near this part of the

cellblock and to allow these men no privileges whatsoever except by written order by me." Warden Hudspeth to Director [Sanford] Bates, October 20, 1933.

59. E. E. Kirkpatrick, *Voices from Alcatraz* (San Antonio: Naylor, 1947), 119–20.

60. Director, BOP, to Warden [Fred G.] Zerbst, [USP Leavenworth,] October 17, 1933.

61. J. Edgar Hoover, memorandum to the Director, BOP, October 13, 1933.

62. Albert Bates thought he could last forty-two days without food or water and "beat Keenan at his own game." His resentment was directed toward the assistant attorney general, whom he held personally responsible for his placement in solitary confinement: along with his life sentence, it made the future appear completely hopeless. Warden Hudspeth advised him that if he revealed the location of his share of the ransom money, most of the restrictions might be removed; but Bates claimed it was too late for him to give information because the principal had died and if he did divulge information that led to the recovery of the money he would be "on the spot" with his underworld associates. Bates file.

63. Warden Hudspeth to Director, BOP, January 22, 1933. Even though he had no contact whatsoever with other prisoners, Harvey Bailey was disgusted with his placement in the Annex, which he regarded as a depository for Leavenworth's most degenerate offenders—drug addicts and homosexuals. For Bailey, who spurned a narcotic painkiller when his leg, broken during the escape from the Kansas State Penitentiary, was set, this was the ultimate indignity. The Annex was under BOP jurisdiction from 1929 to 1940, when it was returned to the army.

64. Paul W. Keve, *The McNeil Century: The Life and Times of an Island Prison* (Chicago: Nelson-Hall, 1984), 172, 167.

65. James V. Bennett to Sanford Bates, July 2, 1931.

66. Ibid.

67. Ibid.

68. John O'Donnell, "Rich U.S. Convicts Buy Vacations; Probe Bares New Scandal in Prisons," *New York Daily News,* July 10, 1931, 2, 4.

69. Spiering, *Man Who Got,* 162.

70. Kobler, *Capone,* 313.

71. Ibid., 313–14.

72. Controversy surrounded this film as Hollywood wrestled with the question of whether the spate of crime movies produced in late 1920s and early 1930s were glorifying gangsters or conveying the message that crime did not pay. Naturally a film about Public Enemy no. 1, a man described as "one of America's icons" and said to receive more media coverage than the president of the United States, attracted attention. After much editing, with all references to the city of Chicago deleted, and with a compromise title, *Scarface, Shame of the Nation* was finally released in May 1932—the same month that Capone arrived at the Atlanta Penitentiary.

73. A. C. Aderhold, [Warden, USP Atlanta,] to Director, BOP, July 5, 1932. In regard to visits, however, his Atlanta prison file indicates that Capone's family was allowed to visit him as regularly as a family living in the immediate area might—his wife made 27 trips during the 27 months he was imprisoned in At-

lanta; she was allowed 73 visiting periods, his mother made 54 visits on 20 trips, Al's son made 55 visits on 21 trips, his brother Earl saw him for 76 visits on 27 trips, his brother Albert came 12 times for 31 visits and his brother Matthew 4 times for 11 visits. Al's brother Ralph, who had recently been released from Mc-Neil Island Penitentiary, was denied a visit by Director Bates, although Warden Aderhold had said that he was prepared to make an exception to the rule that ex-prisoners could not visit inmates.

74. "Capone Becomes Fine Tennis Player," *Washington D.C. Times,* October 17, 1933, FBI file 69–180.

75. *New York Herald Tribune,* August 28, 1932.

76. Austin MacCormick, former assistant director, BOP, interview with the author, New York City, September 24, 1979.

77. Capone Atlanta file.

78. Sanford Bates to A. C. Aderhold, January 1934, ibid.

CHAPTER 2

1. Richard Gid Powers, *G-Men: Hoover's FBI in America's Popular Culture* (Carbondale: Southern Illinois University Press, 1983), 44–45; this is a well-researched account of how elements in popular culture and the media combined to create powerful, positive images of federal government forces, particularly the FBI and Alcatraz, arrayed to save the republic from the public enemies. On October 13, 1933, the secretary of war approved a permit for the Department of Justice "to occupy Alcatraz Island as a maximum security institution for hardened offenders, including racketeers and incorrigible recidivists." Sanford Bates, Director, memorandum to the Attorney General, October 17, 1933, Department of Justice [DOJ] file 4–49–3-2.

2. James D. Calder, *The Origins and Development of Federal Crime Control Policy* (Westport, CT: Praeger, 1993), 11.

3. Ibid., 2.

4. Ibid., 15.

5. Ibid., 13.

6. Paul W. Keve, *Prisons and the American Conscience* (Carbondale: Southern Illinois University Press, 1991), 95–96.

7. Calder, *Origins and Development,* 34.

8. Ibid., 159.

9. Powers, *G-Men,* 3.

10. Ibid., 42, 44.

11. *Real Detective,* January 1934, 26, as cited in Powers, *G-Men,* 298.

12. Powers, *G-Men,* 44.

13. Ibid.

14. This statement, from "Smash Racket Rule by Exiling Our Gangsters to a Devil's Island," *Cleveland Plain Dealer,* October, 8 1933, reprinted in William Helmer and Rick Mattix, *Public Enemies: America's Criminal Past, 1919–1940* (New York: Checkmark Books, 1998), 277, was accompanied by a drawing of Al Capone pulling a wagonload of firewood with a watchful Uncle Sam behind him.

15. *Real Detective,* as cited in Powers, *G-Men,* 298.

16. Ibid., 44.

17. The most detailed description of Alcatraz Island, particularly during its years as a fort and as a military prison, is Erwin N. Thompson's *The Rock: A History of Alcatraz Island, 1847–1972,* Historic Resource Study, National Park Service, U.S. Dept. of the Interior, Denver, May 1979.

18. DOJ file 4–49–3, sub 2.

19. Powers, *G-Men,* 44–45.

20. Blair Niles, *Condemned to Devil's Island* (New York: Harcourt, Brace, 1928). The convict who sold part of his story to Niles subsequently escaped, made his way to New York, and in 1938 published a more complete account of his penal servitude: *Dry Guillotine: Fifteen Years Among the Living Dead.* In 1940 another Hollywood movie, *Devil's Island,* featured Boris Karloff as a surgeon sent to Guiana for treason who leads a rebellion against the brutal regime. Several other films, *Strange Cargo* starring Clark Gable in 1940, and *Passage to Marseilles* with Humphrey Bogart in 1944, helped to further the strong negative image of the penal colony.

21. Before the first prisoners arrived, an article in the *Literary Digest* questioned the "wisdom of concentrating desperate criminals" on Alcatraz Island given the experience of island prisons established by France, Italy, Spain, and England. The writer did note that, unlike Devil's Island, Alcatraz would be "thoroughly modern, with steam heat, running water, and recreation facilities." The article concluded that despite the stories of disease, hunger, and brutal conditions at Devil's Island: "in France, a large section of public opinion is not inclined to sympathize with the hardships of men sent to Devil's Island." "America's Devil's Island—and Some Others," *Literary Digest,* October 28, 1933, 34.

22. *San Francisco News,* October 17, 1933.

23 Chief Quinn's objections were reported in a memorandum from Joseph B. Keenan, Assistant Attorney General, to the Attorney General, October 25, 1933, file 4–49–0.

24. Thompson, *The Rock,* 351.

25. Sanford Bates, memo re Alcatraz to Attorney General, October 26, 1933, file 4–49–0.

26. Notes on Alcatraz, BOP document, n.a., n.d.

27. Editorial, *Saturday Evening Post,* December 2, 1933.

28. John Bender, *Imagining the Penitentiary: Fiction and the Architecture of Mind in Eighteenth-Century England* (Chicago: University of Chicago Press, 1987), 220, 223.

29. For a description of the invention of the penitentiary in its classic forms at Eastern Penitentiary in Pennsylvania and at Auburn, New York, see David J. Rothman, *The Discovery of the Asylum: Social Order and Disorder in the New Republic* (Boston: Little, Brown, 1971), 79–108; and his *Conscience and Convenience: The Asylum and Its Alternatives in Progressive America* (Boston: Little, Brown, 1980).

30. Rothman, *Discovery of the Asylum,* 82–83.

31. Rothman, *Conscience and Convenience,* 117–58 in particular.

32. Sanford Bates to Attorney General, January 8, 1933.

33. Bates, memo to Attorney General, October 23, 1933.

34. Sanford Bates, *Prisons and Beyond* (New York: Macmillan, 1937), 142–43.

35. Paul W. Garrett and Austin H. MacCormick, eds., *Handbook of American Prisons and Reformatories* (New York: National Society on Penal Information, 1929), 30. Some of the "barbarous" means of punishment in American prisons were described more than a decade later by two prominent university criminologists, who cited the attorney general's survey of release procedures for 1944, which reported that twenty-six states used corporal punishment by means of a strap or a lash, with the number of strokes administered varying from one to twenty-five. Other types of punishment included the use of the ball and chain and cold baths at the Colorado State Prison in Canon City, the "sweat box" at Raiford Prison in Florida, and confining prisoners so tightly in a standing position that they could not move at the Jackson, Michigan, and Mansfield, Ohio, prisons. Many prisons, including those in Montana, West Virginia, and Wisconsin, handcuffed inmates to cell doors; at Moundsville in West Virginia troublemakers were subject to cold baths; and at Waupun in Wisconsin gagging was permitted. Harry Elmer Barnes and Negley K. Teeters, *New Horizons in Criminology* (New York: Prentice-Hall, 1945), 589–90.

36. Kenneth Lamott, *Chronicles of San Quentin: The Biography of a Prison* (London: John Long, 1963), 158–59.

37. National Commission on Law Observance and Enforcement, *Report on Penal Institutions, Probation and Parole* (Washington, DC: U.S. Government Printing Office, 1931).

38. For the definitive description of how penal policy moved from punishment of the body to punishment of the mind, see Michel Foucault, *Discipline and Punish: The Birth of the Prison* (New York: Pantheon Books, 1977).

39. After Alcatraz opened, Warden Johnston established an office in San Francisco where he occasionally answered questions from newspaper reporters and where business could be conducted with contractors and purveyors of equipment and various products used on the island.

40. As work continued, by early 1936 a new guard tower was built on the roof of the Model Shop; three detention rooms for handling mental health cases were constructed in the hospital; glass in the guard towers was replaced by shatterproof glass; to improve air circulation in the cell blocks, vents were installed in skylights, and the dirt-covered recreation yard was paved over. James A. Johnston [Warden, USP Alcatraz], to Director BOP, April 2, 1936, Dept. of Justice file 4–49–3, sub 2.

41. Johnston to Director Bates, July 19, 1934, file 4–49–0.

CHAPTER 3

1. [Sanford Bates,] Director, to Warden Zerbst, Leavenworth, October 17, 1933, file 4–49–3-46.

2. Henry Hill, Warden, USP Lewisburg, to Director, July 6, 1934, ibid.

3. Director to Warden Zerbst, Leavenworth, October 17, 1933, ibid.

4. [Edwin Swope,] Warden, USP McNeil Island, to Director, BOP, July 12, 1934, ibid.

5. Ibid.

6. Warden, Atlanta, to Director, BOP, July 12, 1934.

7. Warden, Leavenworth, to Director, BOP, July 14, 1934.

8. Assistant Director Hammack to Director Bates, July 12, 1934, file 4–49–3-46. Hammack reported that the warden at Leavenworth was of the opinion that too much concern was being expressed about the transfer and was of the opinion that five or six guards could accomplish the task without any difficulty but, "of course, that was only boloney [sic], and he would probably want the U.S. Army to help him if he were responsible for it."

9. Ibid.

10. Confidential instructions concerning prisoner movement, Sanford Bates, Director, August 1934, ibid.

11. Warden Zerbst to Director, August 5, 1934, ibid.

12. Warden Zerbst to Director, August 7, 1934, ibid.

13. Ruey Eaton [AZ-61], In Prison . . . and Out (n.p., n.d.), 65–66.

14. James A. Johnston to Sanford Bates, August 22, 1934, file 4–49–3-46.

15. "Bringing Sinister Cargo Here: Prison Train at Devil's Island," San Francisco Examiner, and "Rush Capone and Enemy to Alcatraz 'Devil's Isle,'" San Francisco Call-Bulletin, August 22, 1934.

16. Johnston press release, August 23,1934.

17. "Ex-Mogul of Underworld Cracks at Island Bastille," San Francisco Chronicle, August 23, 1934.

18. Eaton, In Prison.

19. Robert Baker, interview with the author, September 3, 1980. Baker was sent to McNeil Island penitentiary for training, including the use of weapons and judo. He returned to Alcatraz on May 1 to be briefed by army personnel about all " the nooks and crannies, all the hiding places, on the island."

20. The lesser stature of prisoners in this group was indicated by their transfer by regular coach from Washington, D.C., to Ogden, Utah, at which point they were placed in one of the Southern Pacific Railway prison cars; this car was detached at the passenger depot in Oakland and shunted over on a side track to a pier where the prison launch from Alcatraz picked up the prisoners and transported them to the island.

21. Conditions on the Leavenworth prison train turned out to be particularly uncomfortable, as described by Warden Johnston himself: "When they left Leavenworth the weather was broiling hot and it was hot all the way across the country. The car doors were closed; the windows were closed tight; the men could not move freely; they were anything but comfortable . . . as I received them. . . . They were hot, dirty, weary, unshaved, depressed, desperate, showing plainly that they felt they were at the end of the trail." James A. Johnston, Alcatraz Island Prison, and the Men Who Live There (New York: Charles Scribner's Sons, 1949), 24.

22. Upon his release from Leavenworth in June 1943, this former Alcatraz inmate sought to enlist in the army. His parole officer wrote to the parole executive supporting this request, arguing, "this man tells us that he has been convicted for shooting a Jap. Perhaps, if you allow him to be inducted, this time we can give him a medal."

23. Inmate no. 8, letter to the president, June 29, 1935. Five months later this man was transferred to McNeil Island.

24. These transfers came only after Director Bates—one year after the arrival of the convicts from Leavenworth and Atlanta—advised Warden Johnston to start sending out the military prisoners and "to rectify any [other] mistakes in classification." Bates to Johnston, September 16, 1935.

25. Warden Robert Hudspeth, Annex, Ft. Leavenworth, to James A. Johnston, September 19, 1934, file 4–49–3–46.

26. Warden Hudspeth to BOP, July 14, 1934.

27. John Carroll Alcatraz file.

28. Ibid.

29. Ibid.

30. Post Office Inspectors R. G. Rowan and W. O. Baumgartner to Post Inspector in Charge, Chicago, Illinois, September 24, 1928.

31. Charles Cleaver Alcatraz file December 6, 1935.

32. Joseph Urbaytis Alcatraz file, September 23, 1930.

33. C. R. F. Beall, MD, Atlanta, April 1931, Urbaytis file.

34. Urbaytis file. Another escape attempt came to light with the discovery on August 16, 1934, that Urbaytis had cut the bars to his cell and stuck them back in position with laundry soap. He had planned to escape with two others through the roof of the cell house.

35. Special summary at Atlanta, October 10, 1934, Urbaytis file.

36. John Paul Chase, admission summary, Alcatraz.

37. See Clifford James Walker, *One Eye Closed, The Other Red: The California Bootlegging Days* (Barstow, CA: Backdoor Publishing, 1991), 340–72.

38. This account is based on an FBI report by V. W. Peterson, Chicago, Illinois, March 29, 1935, file 26–5685, pp. 2–4. For a more detailed description of this event, see Bryan Burrough, *Public Enemies* (New York: Penguin Press, 2004), 474–83. On the Nelson and Chase relationship and their activities see Steven Nickel and William J. Helmer, *Baby Face Nelson: Portrait of a Public Enemy* (Nashville: Cumberland House, 2002).

39. This account is adapted from a history of the case by J. L. Fallon, FBI, July 4, 1935, file 7–39, pp. 1–4. Waley described these events in detail to the author during a daylong interview at his home on September 23, 1980.

40. Harmon Waley Alcatraz file.

41. Warden's notebook no. 477. These notebooks maintained by the four wardens of Alcatraz listed basic information about every inmate.

42. J. A. Johnston to W. F. Dorrington re report in case of Arthur Barker no. 268-AZ, n.d., Barker Alcatraz file.

43. See Burrough, *Public Enemies,* for a detailed description of Barker, his notorious family, and his criminal career.

44. Volney Davis, admission summary, Leavenworth, Kansas, July 10, 1935, p. 3.

45. E. A. Tamm, memorandum to the Director, FBI, February 8, 1935, file 7–576–4598.

46. F. G. Zerbst, Warden, Leavenworth, to Director, BOP, April 20, 1935.

47. Alvin Karpis was born Alvin Karpowicz, but he was always identified in Alcatraz records as "Karpavicz." Much of what has been written about Karpis and the Karpis-Barker mob overdramatizes Karpis's exploits, as authorized by

J. Edgar Hoover. Karpis's own book about his criminal career offers an alternative perspective. See Alvin Karpis, with Bill Trent, *The Alvin Karpis Story* (New York: Coward, McCann & Geoghegan, 1971) and Burrough's *Public Enemies*.

48. Ibid., 256.

49. Warden's notebook no. 325.

50. W. F. Whitely, report on Huron Ted Walters, January 7, 1939, FBI file 91–136.

51. Admission special progress report, Leavenworth, Kansas, January 24, 1940, Walters Alcatraz file.

CHAPTER 4

1. This statement was formalized in the institution's first rule book, which was not issued to inmates until 1956, "Rules and Regulations, USP Alcatraz." During the gangster era inmates were provided a copy of "Rules and Regulations for the Government and Discipline of the United States Penal and Correctional Institutions," May 1, 1930, and two mimeographed sheets listing the "daily routine of work and counts . . . regulations concerning mail and a list of approved magazines . . . additional information was provided verbally to new arrivals by the officer in charge of the cellhouse." J. A. Johnston to Director, December 14, 1937, file 4–49-3-14.

2. Robert Baker's comments for this chapter are taken from his lengthy interview with the author in 1980.

3. Letter to Assistant Director Hammack from James A. Johnston, July 9, 1934.

4. Ibid.

5. Johnston described this and other routines for Bureau headquarters. In regard to food he wrote, "What they take we require them to eat. We do not permit any waste of food. We do not allow prisoners to crumble and destroy food, spread it on the tables, or leave it on their trays. . . . Prisoners who attempt to waste food in any manner are reported." James A. Johnston to Director, August 21, 1935, file 4–49-3-57, p. 4.

6. Floyd Harrell, description and commentary tape recorded for the author July 10, 1983. All subsequent quotes attributed to Harrell in this chapter are from this source.

7. Hot running water in the cells was not introduced until the 1950s.

8. Harrell provided an interesting side note about movies: "Occasionally these shows would provide a nickname for a guard. One, *Blue Boy,* was about an oversized hog, which provided us with a nickname for one of the least-liked guards who was on the heavy side."

9. Sanford Bates, memorandum to Attorney General, March 20, 1934, file 4–49-3-14.

10. Educational and religious reports from Wayne L. Hunter, chaplain to J. A. Johnston, Warden, October 3 and 31, November 1, December 2, 1936, and March 3, April 2 and 7, 1937.

11. "Rules and Regulations, Alcatraz." Painting materials were also allowed.

12. In the mid-1950s, inmates were issued headsets so that they could listen

to one of two radio stations; guards monitoring the programs quickly changed stations if crime stories or any content they regarded as inappropriate came across the airwaves.

13. An earlier draft of rules from Bates to the attorney general called for lawyers to obtain approval from the attorney general to be allowed to visit their clients at Alcatraz. Sanford Bates, memorandum to the Attorney General, December 21, 1933, file 4–49–0.

14. Maurice E. Ordway, Prison Service Study Course lesson 9, September 1936.

15. Bates, memorandum for the Attorney General, December 1, 1936, file 4–49–3-14.

16. Ordway, Study Course lesson 3, October 1937.

17. Johnston to Director, August 21, 1935, pp. 6–7.

18. Ordway, Study Course lesson 9. In his July 18, 1977, interview with the author, Maurice Ordway, who spent his entire career at Alcatraz, first as an officer and then as a lieutenant, described the management challenge that prisoners presented to the staff:

> Alcatraz has been designated as a maximum-security institution for the housing of "incorrigible" prisoners . . . prisoners confined in this institution present as a whole a somewhat different disciplinary problem than do the prisoners of other institutions. Every individual confined in Alcatraz is classed as a disciplinary problem. If this were not true, they would not be in Alcatraz, for the population here is composed of the disciplinary problems of other institutions. For instance, we have here men who will not respond to either kind or harsh treatment, for they have reached a state of mind where nothing matters to them. These sort of inmates present one of the greatest problems here, for to keep them in line and keep them from influencing the would-be "good inmate" . . . is more than a problem.

19. Erwin N. Thompson, *The Rock: A History of Alcatraz Island, 1847–1942*, Historic Resource Study, National Park Service, U.S. Dept. of the Interior, Denver, May 1979, 278–79. A 1905 report by the Judge Advocate General, George B. Davis, noted that the dungeons had been abandoned in favor of an iron cage in a room on the second floor of the [lower] prison; 324. A 1909 report listing punishments for prisoners included "solitary confinement on restricted diet and handcuffed to door." Thompson's resource study provides the definitive description of Alcatraz during its years as a fort and as a military prison. Due to changes in construction, the "dungeons" cited in the 1893 report are not consistent with the much larger dungeon cells used by the Bureau of Prisons during the 1930s. Despite Alcatraz's becoming a disciplinary barracks and the army's limited efforts to rehabilitate the prisoners, the legends surrounding it continued to grow. Newspapers enjoyed playing up the story of tunnels and dungeons. Perhaps the ultimate development of this theme appeared in the *San Francisco Chronicle* in 1933, when the old kitchen basement of the citadel, then used as "dark and dreary cells under the prison building," was described as being a relic of a prison built by the Spaniards; 334.

20. Loring O. Mills, interview with Anthony Calabrese, May 21, 1980.

21. Baker interview.

22. Alcatraz was not the only federal prison with a disciplinary segregation

area called the "dungeon." Jesse Watkins, no. 229, escaped from the McNeil Island Penitentiary, was captured the next day, returned to the prison, and placed in a "dark cell on restricted diet for having wire concealed in the dungeon, hands cuffed to the wall," as detailed in Watkins's Leavenworth file:

UP (cuffed standing)	DOWN (uncuffed)
7:30 AM	11:30 AM
12:45 PM	3:20 PM

23. McIntosh was transferred to Leavenworth in March 1937 and then on to Atlanta to facilitate turning him over to state of Georgia authorities. In July 1937 he was conditionally released from Atlanta and taken into custody by the sheriff of Fulton County, where he subsequently received a sentence of sixty years for robbery. While awaiting transportation to the chain gang, McIntosh escaped from jail and remained free for four months. He was arrested in December 1937 after a gun battle with police in North Carolina during which he was shot and hospitalized for ten days and then returned to the Atlanta penitentiary as a conditional release violator. McIntosh's record is uneventful after this time, although he did write to Director Bennett in August 1938 requesting a transfer back to Alcatraz, where he preferred to serve his sentence.

24. Berta interviews in 1987 and 1988. An account of the use of dungeon cells with details somewhat at variance from those reported by Berta is contained in a book of reflections by E. F. Chandler, who was a guard at Alcatraz from 1934 through 1941. *Alcatraz: The Hard Years Remembered*, by Roy F. Chandler and E. F. Chandler (Orwigsburg, PA: Baker and Freeman, 1989); see 79 for a "charge out sheet" that identifies the cell location of all 258 prisoners on January 29, 1936. Listed under the heading "lower solitary" are the numbers of eight prisoners.

25. Ordway interview.

26. George Boatman, interview by the author, September 4, 1980. "There were no rats down there—the only time rats were on the island was during the war. We killed them off after the war. We went over to the army base and got some [rat poison] and spread it on fish heads and that was the end of the rats—there were field mice on the island all the time, but no rats."

27. James D. Calder, *The Origins and Development of Federal Crime Control Policy* (Westport, CT: Praeger, 1993), 164.

28. Director Bates to Warden Johnston, February 28, 1935, file 4-49-3-49.

29. James A. Johnston to Bates, March 9, 1935, ibid.

30. Director to Warden, March 27, 1935, ibid.

31. Bates to Johnston, April 12, 1935, ibid.

32. As it turned out, using the dungeons for purposes of internal control was a major factor contributing to the prison's image in the outside world becoming *too* harsh. For more on this dynamic, see the discussion in chapter 7.

33. John Bender, *Imagining the Penitentiary* (Chicago: University of Chicago Press, 1987), 55.

CHAPTER 5

1. James A. Johnston to Director, BOP, October 2, 1934, file 4-49-4-0.

2. Charles Berta Alcatraz file.

3. Harmon Waley Alcatraz file.

4. Waley interview in 1980.

5. J. A. Johnston, Warden, to J. V. Bennett, Director, "Recent Visitors to the Island," September 11, 1937, DOJ file 4–49–3-29.

6. George Sink Alcatraz file.

7. Johnston to Bennett, June 1938.

8. In the book Johnston wrote after his retirement he claimed, "strictly speaking we did not have any dungeons. When we took over the Island in 1934 we did not like the disciplinary cells that we inherited with the building. The army had solitary cells on one of the top tiers and dungeon cells in the basement. The basement was dry and the Army had established a mechanic's shop in the cross-corridor, but the floor was rough and the cells were in the corners close to the water cisterns, the brick walls of which were often damp. The building was erected by the War Dept. on top of the foundations of the fortified citadel erected in the 1850s. Despite corrections and explanations people persisted in the belief that the island had been occupied and the fortifications built by Spain. And we were sometimes accused of punishing prisoners by keeping them in the old Spanish dungeons. They were dungeons, but they were not Spanish though they were bad enough and I did not like them. They were badly located, poorly constructed and unsafe because they were easy to dig out of and in the few instances when we did use them we had to chain the men to keep them from breaking out and running amuck. We used them when we had strikes in 1936 and 1937 because at that time we had no other facilities for separating the noisy disturbers from those who wanted to work. I did not like these cells, in fact I was ashamed of them and used them only under necessity. When we got a P.W.A. *[sic]* appropriation in 1940 we tore out the dungeons, converted the basement into storage space, and built a new disciplinary unit now referred to as 'D' Block." James A. Johnston, *Alcatraz Island Prison, and the Men Who Live There* (New York: Charles Scribner's Sons, 1949), 252–53.

9. James V. Bennett, interview by the author, August 17, 1978.

10. James V. Bennett to Justice Harlan, February. 13, 1964.

11. Ordway interview in 1977.

12. Allen's Alcatraz file does not provide clear evidence that he had TB, although he always claimed that he had the disease and that his mother and sister died from tuberculosis.

13. J. Jacobsen, MD, to Dr. G. Hess, Chief Medical Officer, January 21, 1936.

14. C. J. Shuttleworth, Deputy Warden, to James A. Johnston, Warden, March 8, 1936, file 4–49–3-57.

15. "Fox Headed 3 Days of Madness in Western Crime Fortress" and "Capone Now Cowers in Cell Fearing Death from Mutineers," *Washington Herald,* February 9 and 10, 1936.

16. "Note Says 3 Driven Insane at Alcatraz: Brutality and Torture Charged in Letter Smuggled From 'Devil's Isle.' Ridiculous says Warden. Prisoner Declares Inmates Beaten, Shot with Gas Guns, Starved," *San Francisco News,* September 20, 1935.

17. Ibid.

18. BOP Assistant Director W. T. Hammack to Attorney General Cummings, August 23, 1935.

19. "Just a Life of Hell—That's Felon's Alcatraz Story—Monotony Breaks Spirit," *San Francisco Chronicle,* February 5, 1936.

20. While managing the Leavenworth Cardinals baseball team from a losing to a winning record, Johnson penned a short essay, "The Umpire, Baseball's Greatest Alibi," in which he noted that the decisions of umpires provided excuses for misplays and failures on the part of players. Harry Johnson Alcatraz file.

21. "Terrors and Tortures as the Background of the Riots on Uncle Sam's 'Devil's Island,'" *Toledo (OH) Mirror,* March 15, 1936.

22. Dr. [Edward M.] Twitchell, memo to Warden Johnston, February 22, 1935.

23. E. F. Chandler, report to Warden Johnston, April 27, 1936.

24. A. R. Archer to C. J. Shuttleworth, Deputy Warden, April 27, 1936.

25. As a result of this escape, Director Bates sent the following memo to the attorney general's office: "If it is advisable for us to surround Alcatraz prisoners with restrictions *while in the institution,* should there not be some very definite rules laid down by the Attorney General for the conduct of Marshals in custody of such prisoners *while out of the institution* upon a writ or pursuant to some legal process? It seems somewhat futile for the Prison Bureau to surround the prisoners with restrictive measures and then have the Dept. handle him in a routine manner as soon as he passes to the custody of the Marshal." Director, BOP, to Mr. Stanley, Attorney General's office, December 12, 1934, p. 2.

26. John Stadig Alcatraz file; Hammock memo, February 11, 1936, ibid.

27. Dr. Hess to Warden Johnston, June 26, 1935, ibid.

28. Dr. Twitchell to Warden Johnston, August 24, 1936, ibid.

29. M. R. King, Surgeon, to Director, BOP, August 31, 1936. Dr. King's letter concluded with the following comment on his tour of Alcatraz: "I was favorably impressed by the routine, sanitary conditions, morale and upkeep of grounds and buildings. I observed the manner in which the noon meal was served. The food was very well prepared and without waste. I like the one piece of outside clothing worn by the inmates. In other institutions, including the Medical Center, so many inmates appear slouchy and untidy with trousers suspended by the belts, with the shirt tail occasionally hanging out. It seems to me that the one piece suit adds to the neatness of a large group of inmates." Dr. Hess to Surgeon General, September 2, 1936, ibid.

30. The BOP's September 25, 1936, news release on Stadig's death reported that the patient had been placed in a room "where he could be under the observation of medical officers of the U.S. Public Health Service." But on the same day Warden Zerbst of Leavenworth wrote to Director Bates to complain: "These mental patients should not be left to the supervision of penitentiary inmates, which is the practice of our medical service at present. I wish, at this time, to repeat my previous suggestion that if the Public Health Service does not have the funds to employ more guard attendants, that the services of the female nurses be dispensed with and that guard attendants be employed instead. The female nurses are used largely to have charge of hospital linens." Fred G. Zerbst, Warden, to Director, BOP, September 25, 1936.

31. Word of Persful's self-mutilation took more than a month to reach the San Francisco newspapers. The Associated Press (AP) inaccurately reported that

"an inmate named 'Percival' secretly obtained an ax . . . filed the edge to razor sharpness and chopped off the left hand. He is said to have handed the ax to another prisoner with the plea 'cut off my right.' Warden Johnston would not deny or confirm the story." AP release, July 29, 1937, Persful Alcatraz file.

32. FBI report by N. E. Marshall, Little Rock, Arkansas, March 25, 1935, file 7–14, ibid.

33. On October 12, 1934, a few months after his release from the Arkansas prison Persful was arrested and subsequently convicted on federal charges of kidnapping and violating the National Motor Vehicle Theft Act. In one of these cases Persful and two associates at gunpoint took the night watchman at a store to the home of the store manager. While one of the men stood guard over the family, Persful and the second man forced the manager to return to the store and open the safe. The robbers took $1,000 in currency and some checks and left with the night watchman and manager, who were driven from Arkansas to Missouri, where they were left bound and gagged in a wooded area. Two nights earlier Persful and his partners had robbed a gas station and then forced the owner, his wife, and his sister to accompany them. The group drove to Oklahoma, where the victims were put out of the car and left on a highway.

Before Persful and his partners were apprehended in the kidnapping cases, the trio was involved in another crime that provided additional evidence of Persful's attitude toward his associates. Persful, Dewey, Kent, and Riley Gunn attempted to hold up a gas station in Oklahoma but the proprietor had been prepared for such a possibility and kept a gun in his pocket. When told to "stick them up," he pulled the pistol and fired at the robbers, hitting Kent. Persful and Gunn pulled the wounded Kent into the stolen car they were driving and sped away. Kent succumbed within minutes, and Persful, according to Gunn, "drove to Kent's home. . . . Carried Kent in the house and placed him on the bed. . . . Mrs. Kent begged them to get a doctor. [But] Persful told her, 'Lady, you don't need a doctor; what you need is a burying squad.'" Ibid.

For this series of crimes Persful received what would appear to be a modest federal sentence of twenty years, given his prior record of convictions and penitentiary time.

34. Persful BOP central office report, September 14, 1936.

35. Persful to Warren Squier, June 29, 1943, Persful file.

36. Hess, Chief Medical Officer, Twitchell, Psychiatrist, and Wolfson, Psychiatrist, memorandum of examination, April 9, 1937, Alcatraz, California.

37. Hayes Van Gorder federal prison file.

38. This letter from Johnston to Bennett provides further evidence that Bureau headquarters was aware that the warden was still placing inmates in the dungeon.

39. Burton Phillips Alcatraz file.

40. R. O. Culver, Day Watch Lieutenant, to E. J. Miller, Deputy Warden, Alcatraz, October 4, 1937.

41. Alvin Karpis, as told to Robert Livesey, *On the Rock: Twenty-Five Years in Alcatraz* (New York: Beaufort Books, 1980), 88.

42. Waley interview. Alvin Karpis made a similar observation in his book.

43. International News Service release, San Francisco, September 24, 1937.

44. Johnston to J. V. Bennett, October 11, 1937; Johnston to Director, BOP, November 6, 1937.

45. "The Rebellion in Alcatraz Prison," *Dallas (TX) Times-Herald,* September 29, 1937.

46. "No Pity for Convicts," *Rapid City (SD) Journal,* October 1, 1937.

47. "Prisons Should Be Grim," *Spokane (WA) Spokesman-Review,* October 2, 1937.

48. "What Happened at Alcatraz," *Kansas City (MO) Star,* September 27, 1937.

CHAPTER 6

1. Conduct report, January 20, 1936, Ted Cole Alcatraz file.

2. *San Francisco Examiner,* December 17, 1937.

3. N. J. L. Pieper, Special-Agent-in-Charge, San Francisco FBI office, to Director FBI, January 3, 1938. This poem was found in the prison laundry.

4. J. E. Hoover, memo to E. A. Tamm, December 20, 1937.

5. M. B. Myerson, FBI report, January 7, 1938, file 76–390.

6. Ibid., p. 32.

7. A captain at Atlanta who had been a guard at Alcatraz, and in whose office one of the interviews with an inmate was conducted, told the agents that it was a complete waste of time for them to try to get information from the ex-Alcatraz inmate they had just questioned, giving an example of the man's stoicism in the face of punishment that the captain had observed when both were at Alcatraz. FBI report by A. J. Lemaire, March 18, 1938, file 6–96.

> ____ had committed an infraction of the rules at Alcatraz and it was the custom of the warden there to require the prisoner to say that he was sorry. ___, because of his peculiar personality and his stubborn nature flatly refused to apologize, and as a disciplinary measure, he was put in the dungeon in chains. It was believed that such action would cause him to come about . . . he remained twenty-three days in the hole before he could be prevailed upon to say he was sorry and then it was only utter exhaustion that caused him to break.

8. *San Francisco Chronicle,* April 29, 1941.

9. Thomas Limerick Alcatraz file.

10. James Lucas Alcatraz file.

11. Several years later, in a letter to the parole board, which must be considered self-serving since he claimed that he was an unwilling participant, Lucas provided the following account of the escape attempt:

> Limerick and Franklin picked a little after one o'clock as the time the officer in charge of the shop went into the office to check his count sheet. At Alcatraz, each officer must check his men on the count sheet every thirty minutes. He also looked over the orders and stayed in the office about fifteen minutes. This routine never varied just as the officers changed places every thirty minutes on the roof and never varied. The day of the break came, Limerick said I was to work with him. At one, Mr. Cline went into his office as usual. Limerick got out a wedge he had built to hold the window open and level when he stood on it. He put it on and waited. Franklin went into the file room. He was to watch the officer patrol the back side and when he started back to the far end of the building and his back was to the win-

dow he was to walk out of the File Room. That would be the signal to go up on the roof. So that was the reason Franklin was in the file room. We stood on the floor near the window watching for Franklin to come out of the File Room. Then as we stood on the far side of the shop under the window, Mr. Cline came out of the office and walked slowly into the File Room. I don't know why he came out of his office so soon, he never had before. He never looked around, just walked slowly into the File Room. Maybe he went there to check on an order for supplies. I just don't know. I told Limerick let's put it off. His eyes were cold as ice, he shook his head. He said he didn't notice anything meaning Mr. Cline. We waited what seemed like a million years, but was only a minute or so according to time verified at the trial. Then Franklin walked out of the File Room with a hammer in his hand. Limerick grabbed my arm. Let's go he said, and crawled . . . out the window and stood up on the steel sash of the window. I crawled out the other side and stood on the steel sash also. I looked up and could see the officer in the tower, his back toward us, looking over the work area. The door to the glass tower stood open. He was totally unaware to what was creeping up behind him. I was supposed to help Limerick cut the barb wire. Franklin was below us now waiting to crawl out the window as soon as one of us went up. Before I could put up my hand and pretend to cut the wire, Limerick cut through two strands. I had to act fast as the officer was still sitting unaware of anything. As Limerick cut the third strand, I lifted my foot and kicked out one of the windows. I looked up at the officer, he never moved, my heart fell. Below Franklin jerked my pants leg. As he held one pant leg, I rested that foot on the steel sash of the window and kicked another pane of glass out. The window was only 3 panes wide. I looked up. The officer heard that one break. He slowly turned around and looked back. Limerick was crawling up on the roof. He stood up and charged the tower throwing everything he could at the tower. The officer kicked the door shut and he barely had time to bring his gun into action. At that time, the other officer was on the far side of the building getting ready to move a scaffold for workers putting in new steel. I got up on the roof and Mr. Stites was firing at everything and everybody. I was barely able to save my life by crawling under the tower. Limerick was killed at the door. Franklin came flying into action and charged the door and struck several times against the glass with a blood stained hammer. He was shot down and he struck again and again with the hammer. After everything was over, they dragged me out from under the tower. . . . I thought all there would be was an attempt to escape against me. But I wound up being tried for murder. The very thing I sacrificed myself to avoid. There was no plan to kill Mr. Cline, he just walked out into the room where there was a man who already had a life sentence in Alabama for murder. At the trial, I asked Franklin why he killed Mr. Cline and he said when Mr. Cline came into the room, he tried to tie him, but was resisted. He said Mr. Cline reached for his sap. Franklin said he hit him several times with his hammer before he fell.

12. *San Francisco News,* November 1, 1938.

13. *San Francisco Examiner,* November 7, 1938.

14. *San Francisco Examiner,* November 1, 1938.

15. "Alcatraz Killer Held Sane," *San Francisco Examiner,* October 29, 1938.

16. Cline's unpopularity with the inmates was noted by Alvin Karpis. Karpis, as told to Robert Livesey, *On the Rock: Twenty-Five Years in Alcatraz* (New York: Beaufort Books, 1980), 102:

Screw Cline stands six feet, four inches tall and brags openly of the "wetbacks" he had killed on the Texas Border Patrol. Every time a fight breaks out in the yard, he charges into the midst of the squabbling cons laying them out left and right with his "billy." His brutal actions inevitably initiate a chorus of boos from onlooking cons; he is hated for his sadistic streak.

Harmon Waley, in a note written to the author on April 12, 1982, regarding this escape attempt, commented, "Cline said to the inmates in the yard one day that he'd be glad to shoot all the men in Alcatraz if someone would pay for the shells; he wouldn't pay for it because they weren't worth that much—even dead. He used to take his sap [blackjack] out and pat it on his hand—Limerick patted him on the head with a hammer!"

17. *San Francisco Examiner,* November 5, 1938.

18. *San Francisco Examiner,* November 15, 1938.

19. AP release, November 26, 1938.

20. Dale Stamphill's account and all of his comments are taken from day-long interviews with the author, April 23, 1981, and October 15, 1995.

21. Henry Young, as told to George Dillon in "One Hour Pass from Hell," *Cavalier Magazine,* February 4, 1962, 72. Young said of Dock Barker, "He was one of America's most dangerous men. I knew, however, that he was determined and ruthless and that once he started on anything, nothing could stop him but death. I couldn't think of anyone I'd rather have with me on a break from Alcatraz."

22. The escapees hid some of the tools within toilet drains. The tools were attached to long strings and then lowered into the drain until they came to rest in the necks of turns in the pipes. The strings floated upward within arm's reach, but out of the sight of any guard who looked into toilet bowls during shake-downs. It was important for the inmates to dispose of their tools, not so much to avoid detection, but to keep the staff from uncovering evidence that an escape attempt was in progress and thus launching a search that would likely discover bars that had been cut and replaced.

23. N.J.L. Pieper, Special-Agent-in-Charge, San Francisco. FBI investigation file, January 14, 1939, pp. 36–37.

24. Ibid., pp. 8–9.

25. Ibid., pp. 20–21.

26. Warden Johnston notified the surviving member of Barker's family, his father, of the violent death of another son. Johnston was advised by George Barker—"Bury Arthur Barker there. Please send me location of grave to be moved later." On January 17, 1939, Barker was buried in Mount Olive Cemetery in San Francisco. A memo from Chaplain Hunter to Johnston reported that, with the business manager and several funeral home and cemetery employees present, "I read a brief service which consisted of some verses of scripture and a prayer. . . . I feel that we gave Barker a decent and respectable burial."

27. Pieper FBI investigation file, p. 35.

28. James V. Bennett to James A. Johnston, January 18, 1939, "Alcatraz: Escape Procedure," PR-G.

29. Memo to Attorney General, January 14, 1939; FBI investigation file, pp. 5–6. The agents incorrectly blamed the metal detection system for allowing the escapees' tools into the cell house, since the paraphernalia was hidden in a razor-sharpening machine and brought to the cell house by an unknowing guard.

30. Special-Agent-in-Charge Pieper to J. Edgar Hoover, January 16, 1939, p. 1.

31. Ibid., pp. 7–8.

32. The search of the industries area, described as "an unlimited source of materials for escape tools," produced a miter box saw (a rectangular saw with a handle high on the blades placed in a wooden frame in order to cut wood evenly at a 45-degree angle), a putty knife sharpened on one side to a knife-blade edge with the other edge converted into a saw, a thin steel bar that had been made into a saw edge on one side, and two pieces of heavy wire some thirty inches in length with the ends curved, devices that could be used to push or pull objects from any area or from one cell to another. The shakedown also turned up two hacksaw blades; and another handscrew jack or bar spreader was found on the top of D block.

33. Pieper to J. Edgar Hoover, p. 14.

34. J. Edgar Hoover to James V. Bennett, January 24, 1939.

35. E. A. Tamm, memo to Director [Hoover], March 29, 1939. According to the coroner as quoted on January 26, 1939, in the *San Francisco News*, "the inquest . . . shows that Alcatraz is not 'impregnable' against the super-cunning of the men caged there, the Rock is dynamite in our Bay!"

36. Henry Young Alcatraz file.

37. James V. Bennett to J. A. Johnston, January 4, 1940.

38. James A. Johnston to Director, BOP, January 29, 1940. Johnston wrote in the genteel style typical of communications between the director and the warden during this period when Bureau headquarters increasingly sought to exercise more and more influence over an administrator accustomed to running his own show, but about whose administrative abilities Bureau officials were becoming increasingly concerned.

CHAPTER 7

1. "Alcatraz Horrors Doom Men, Ex-Convict Says"; "Alcatraz Silence 'Breaks' Toughest Gangsters: Machine Gun Kelly Through Bragging; Karpis Is Cracking, Human Beings Can't Endure 'the Rock'"; "Riots and Bloodshed Are Forecast at Alcatraz; Convicts Can't Win But Silence Is Worse than Machine Guns; The Rock a Barrel of Dynamite with Tough Warden Sitting on Lid," *Philadelphia Inquirer,* November 29, 30, December 1, 1937. Because no news organization had been allowed to take photographs after federal prisoners arrived, the *Inquirer* illustrated its series with a photo from the Warner Brothers movie *Alcatraz Island.*

2. Alexander Kendrick, editorial, *Philadelphia Inquirer,* December 4, 1937.

3. Roy Gardner to J. V. Bennett, June 7, 1938, Gardner Alcatraz file.

4. "Roy Gardner Quits Prison," *San Francisco Call-Bulletin,* June 17, 1938.

5. First draft of *Hellcatraz,* 1–2, Gardner file. His book's full title is *Hellcatraz: The Rock of Despair, The Tomb of the Living Dead* (n.p., 1939). For an expanded description of Gardner's life and federal prison experience see Roy Gardner, *My Life Story, Hellcatraz,* ed. Tom Ryan (n.p.: Douglas/Ryan Communication, 2000).

6. "Gardner Quits Prison."

7. E. J. Miller, Acting Warden, to Director, BOP, February 28, 1939.

8. J. A. Johnston to Director, BOP, July 19, 1940.

9. Ibid. The variety of food given to Alcatraz convicts underscores the ad-

ministration's determination not to allow that feature of the regime to become a source of protest. It should also be noted that during the 1930s and 1940s employees were served the same food. No staff member or inmate interviewed for this project registered a complaint about the quantity or the quality of food.

10. Ibid., p. 2.

11. In March 1941 guards discovered that an inmate had managed to manufacture a couple of "crude" guns and have them smuggled past the metal detectors into the cell house. For obvious reasons, no contraband found on the island attracted as much staff attention as a gun, or the parts of a gun. A March 1941 statement by inmate William Dainard, the rap partner of Harmon Waley in the Weyerhaeuser kidnapping, that he knew where two guns were hidden produced an immediate response from Deputy Warden E. J. Miller. Dainard was upset over the length of his sentence, which was twenty years longer than Waley's. He became severely depressed, and two months after he arrived at McNeil Island he tried to commit suicide three times within a week. He was transferred to Leavenworth, where he was certified as having "an unsound mind" and sent on to the Springfield Medical Center, where he remained for two and a half years. Dainard was returned to Leavenworth, but in July he was shipped off to Alcatraz, due to his lengthy sentence, the nature of his offense, the detainers held against him, and the view that he was a "dangerous, hardened criminal and a potential escape risk."

Dainard's note to Deputy Warden Miller stated that he knew where two guns were hidden and would provide information as to their whereabouts if Miller would promise to get him a pardon. The subsequent investigation revealed that Dainard "had manufactured two firearms, hidden them in his cell, and concocted the story to bargain for a sentence reduction." For this ruse, Dainard was sent to disciplinary segregation, where he remained for seven years and four months. (This period included Dainard's loss of 1,300 days of good time for destroying property in D block. In December 1946 Dainard was charged with conspiring with guard Oscar Eastin to have Eastin smuggle some contraband in to him, Copenhagen snuff.)

The discovery of these guns, described by Warden Johnston as "very crude, of doubtful practicability, nevertheless fashioned with devilish ingenuity," was a matter of concern because Dainard had never been out of the cell house; the gun barrels therefore had to have been molded in the industries and workshop area and smuggled into the cell house by another inmate, revealing, once again, that the metal detectors had been foiled by the use of brass, a feature of which the inmates were clearly aware. Warden Johnston swore the senior staff to secrecy about the discovery of the guns to keep the information from reaching the San Francisco newspapers. Dainard Alcatraz file.

12. James V. Bennett, to Attorney General, June 14, 1939. Bennett claimed that using Alcatraz as a facility for "the lame, the halt, and the blind" would be consistent with the island's earlier use "as a health resort and sanitarium for enlisted men and officers returning from the Orient." Apparently, the director had missed the sight of his own guards, as well as the inmates, bundled up in heavy overcoats and huddled in the less windy corners of the prison yard seeking relief from the persistent cold winds and frequent dense fogs of San Francisco Bay.

13. Ibid., pp. 1–2.

14. Gardner file.

15. United Press International (UPI) release, San Francisco, January 11, 1940, ibid.

16. Ibid.

17. R. W. Gaynor, attempted interview with McCain, E. J. Miller, 10:45 A.M., December 3, 1940, Young Alcatraz file.

18. *San Francisco Chronicle,* February 12, 1941.

19. Warden Johnston wrote to Director Bennett describing the defense strategy: "They plan a defense based on psychological reasoning; theorizing that a man imprisoned for a long term and restricted in privileges and confined either in solitary or in isolation over a long period undergoes a mental and emotional strain so that when taunted or abused or threatened as they will indicate he was by McCain, he was seized with a sudden or irresistible impulse over which he had no control and that at the moment of the crime he was psychologically unconscious." April 16, 1941.

20. *San Francisco Chronicle,* April 17, 1941.

21. Edited transcript of the Henry Young trial prepared for Bureau headquarters by A. H. Connor, Commissioner of Prisoner Industries, pp. 8–9.

22. "Hard Rock Criminals to Attend Trial," *San Francisco Chronicle,* April 16, 1941.

23. Waley interview in 1980.

24. *San Francisco Examiner,* April 24, 1941. Waley told the author that denial of aspirin was not the issue in the incident he described in the trial: "Coming out of the dungeon I refused to go for no books, letters, one meal a day, and no tobacco in D block. I told them to take my clothes, cut off my water and food, and go to hell. They force-fed me. Lt. Culver had a guard hold each arm while he tried to hit me with his fist. I ducked my head so he'd hit my forehead and I think he broke his thumb on it. They took me to the hospital and put me in a straight sheet in bed." Written commentary by Harmon Waley on a copy of the edited transcript of Young trial.

25. *San Francisco Chronicle,* April 23, 1941.

26. *San Francisco News,* April 23, 1941.

27. Unidentified and undated San Francisco newspaper article by John U. Terrell, in Young file.

28. Ibid.

29. Several prisoners provided testimony that staff members carried, and used on prisoners, blackjacks or "saps," hunks of lead sewn up in pieces of leather, which contributed to the impression that harsh means of punishment were used on the island.

30. An example of callous treatment directed toward a seriously mentally disturbed prisoner is the death of Vito Giacalone after he left Alcatraz for the Federal Medical Center at Springfield, Missouri. An Italian immigrant who could not read, write, or speak intelligible English, and a first offender serving a ten-year sentence for counterfeiting, Giacalone was one of a number of puzzling choices for a prison intended for "public enemies." He was initially committed to Leavenworth, where he had a fight with another inmate but, because he was

regarded as "strange" and physically powerful, he was transferred to Alcatraz. Within two months of his arrival in March 1937 Giacalone was experiencing mental health problems. In various incidents he fought with other inmates, engaged in frenzies and tore up everything in his cell, and on one occasion made growling sounds as he pulled out his hair. He repeatedly took his clothes off and pounded the walls of his cell with his hands and his head. He spent "much time playing in the water [washbowl]" in his cell. He was confined to an isolation cell in A block but one day when a guard opened his cell door to recover a food tray, Giacalone kicked the officer in the stomach, knocking him to the floor. Another guard subdued him by a blow to the head with a gas billy club. His transfer to Springfield was "urgently recommended" by a neuropsychiatric board in February 1939.

The following July Giacalone, along with four other prisoners and accompanied by Alcatraz and Leavenworth guards, was placed in a barred prison car operated by the Santa Fe Railroad. As the train passed through Needles, California, on its way to Leavenworth and Springfield he was observed lunging forward and backward in his seat. Alcatraz Chief Medical Officer Emanuel Horwitz, sitting in an air-conditioned parlor car, was called back to the prisoners' car to treat Giacalone, who had a temperature of 107°. Ice packs and medications were applied, but Giacalone never regained consciousness; he died at 7:30 A.M. from heat prostration. The train did not stop from the time he became unconscious at 5 P.M. until the next day when his body was removed from the prison car at Willard, New Mexico, to be shipped by a local undertaker to Leavenworth. When his only relative, a cousin, declined to claim his body, he was buried in a cemetery for prisoners.

In the inquiry that followed, Alcatraz Lt. J. M. Concannon reported that the temperature in the steel prison car—the only coach without insulation or air conditioning—was estimated to have been 120° or higher. This incident prompted strong complaints from the accompanying officers who, like the prisoners, were confined to the prison car. Bureau officials, always sensitive to allegations that Alcatraz produced mental health problems, asked Warden Johnston for a report on Giacalone. According to Dr. Ritchey, the prisoner's "mental condition seems to have been present for some time before his admission to Alcatraz and was noted soon after arrival. There was nothing to indicate that his residence here had affected him adversely any more than confinement in any prison would bring about." If at a later date the inmate's family had cared enough to protest, Giacalone's death would likely have resulted in a civil suit challenging his death as a result of cruel and unusual conditions on a prison train. Giacalone Alcatraz file.

31. In regard to allegations of reprisals for testifying in the trial, Waley told the author, "Outside of dirty looks no [guard] said a word to me on the way to court and back."

32. *San Francisco Call-Bulletin,* April 24, 1941.

33. *San Francisco Chronicle,* April 26, 1941.

34. *San Francisco Examiner,* April 26, 1941. The balance of quoted material for Young's trial comes from this source.

35. This was the same Frank Murphy who served as attorney general in 1939, and to whom Bureau of Prisons director Bennett had sent his proposal to close

Alcatraz. President Roosevelt had appointed Murphy an associate justice of the Supreme Court on January 4, 1940.

36. Young Alcatraz file.

37. *San Francisco Chronicle,* May 3, 1941.

38. Statement of James V. Bennett, May 2, 1941.

39. James V. Bennett to Attorney General McGuire, May 29, 1941.

40. A. H. Connor to James V. Bennett, August 5, 1941.

41. James A. Johnston to Director, May 29, 1941. These reports were not for use in any federal court or congressional hearing but were prepared for Bureau of Prisons headquarters. The question of whether subordinates in a paramilitary organization can be expected to report improper behavior on the part of their superiors was of secondary concern to Bureau administrators, whose intention was to communicate to personnel in the field that they would be held accountable for actions that might bring discredit or embarrassment to the agency as a whole. Internal investigations were intended to influence the behavior of the custodial force because being instructed to answer these charges and to explain their own actions communicated clearly the message that Washington, D.C., not Warden James A. Johnston, was ultimately responsible for operations at Alcatraz.

42. Ibid., pp. 9–10. Johnston went on describe the policy regarding meals for men in solitary:

> Now as to solitary: we have followed the instructions . . . to increase the amount of food given to men confined to solitary on restricted diet. . . . If a prisoner is placed in solitary in the morning after he has had his breakfast, he is furnished bread at the noon-day meal and salads and one-fourth of the evening meal from the regular main-line menu. If he is placed in solitary in the afternoon, that is after he has had his full noon-day meal, then he gets only bread for the evening meal.
>
> In all cases the second day menu consists of a breakfast of cereal, milk and coffee; the noon-day meal, bread and soup; the evening meal is one-fourth of the allowance from the regular main-line menu leaving out the soup but feeding the salad and greens and bread and the hot drink, whether it happens to be tea or coffee.
>
> On the third day a man in solitary receives the full dinner meal at noon, also the one-quarter quantity, that is the light breakfast of cereal and milk and coffee and the light supper consisting of the salad and greens and bread and hot beverage, tea or coffee.

43. Ibid.

44. Ibid., p. 15. In a subsequent letter, Johnston gave his own analysis of the mortality rate at Alcatraz. To the deaths of three inmates by natural causes, he added the deaths by violence of three escapees (Joe Bowers, Thomas Limerick, and Arthur Barker) to that of Rufe McCain, who died at the hand of Henry Young, Edward Wutke's suicide, and the death on the prison train of Giacalone for a total of nine deaths in seven years of prison operation. Johnston argued that since the death rate for the general population in the Bay Area was nine per thousand for one year, the record of deaths at Alcatraz should be regarded as exemplary. James A. Johnston to Director, June 9, 1941.

45. Howard B. Gill to James V. Bennett, May 12, 1941.

46. Gill to Bennett, May 24, 1941.

47. The trial of Henry Young and Alcatraz did not fade into a footnote in the Bureau's files, as Commissioner Connor suggested. Young, the dungeons, and the

treatment of the prisoners returned as issues forty-five years later in the 1995 Hollywood movie *Murder in the First: The Trial That Brought Down Alcatraz.* Bureau of Prisons officials who had had nothing to do with the management of Alcatraz found themselves defending the policies and actions of their predecessors.

CHAPTER 8

1. Arnold Kyle, interview with the author, September 24, 1980. Kyle was gravely ill when I called to request an interview. His wife said she thought he was too ill, "but he wants to talk with you." I tape-recorded my interview in their home, and when I heard a loud click from behind the sofa it became apparent that Mr. Kyle was making his own recording of our meeting. He passed away several months later.

2. Lloyd Barkdoll began his long stay in the federal prison system at McNeil Island Penitentiary. The classification committee at McNeil Island described Barkdoll as hopeless and resentful about having received a life sentence for bank robbery, and he was considered "a serious custodial problem in that he is an organizer." Barkdoll was soon transferred to Alcatraz, where several months after his arrival he was locked up in isolation for "trying to agitate other inmates to strike." Lloyd Barkdoll Alcatraz file.

3. These elements of the escape plan have not been included in any previous accounts, including Warden Johnston's account in his book, *Alcatraz Island Prison.* Kyle described them in an interview, as did Floyd Hamilton. Hamilton also described this escape attempt in his book, *Public Enemy Number 1*, Acclaimed Books (Dallas, TX: International Prison Ministry, 1978), 138–42.

4. Kyle interview.

5. This is one of many examples at Alcatraz in which the prohibition in the convict code against snitching worked: no inmate in the Model Shop tried to barter to the staff the information he had about Hamilton's role for some gain for himself.

6. *San Francisco Call-Bulletin,* May 22, 1941.

7. James V. Bennett, Director, BOP, to the Attorney General, May 22, 1941.

8. N. J. L Pieper, Special-Agent-in-Charge, to the Director, FBI, May 22, 1941, file 91–626–42.

9. Ibid.

10. William T. Hammack to J. V. Bennett, June 12, 1941, "Alcatraz: Escape Procedure," PR-G.

11. Ibid.

12. James A. Johnston, Warden, to James V. Bennett, Director, September 20, 1941, John Bayless Alcatraz file. Johnston informed Bennett that the junior officer who had lost track of Bayless had been given a five-day suspension. Despite this experience, Bayless was not finished with escape attempts. In federal district court in San Francisco on December 21, 1942, for a hearing on a writ of habeas corpus related to his twenty-five-year sentence, Bayless leaped over the railing of the jury box and ran toward a courtroom door but was caught by a deputy U.S. marshal. Eventually, Bayless had his original sentence for bank robbery reduced from twenty-five to ten years and regained the days of good time

he had lost for his attempt to swim away from Alcatraz. Facing a much shorter sentence, he settled down to do easier time.

13. James A. Johnston to James V. Bennett, January 28, 1942.

14. U.S. Bureau of Prisons, *Gearing Federal Prisons to the War Effort* (USP Atlanta, 1942), 49–51, 89. See also John A. Martini, *Alcatraz at War* (San Francisco: Golden Gate National Parks Association, 2002), 59–71.

15. That Franklin was allowed out of his cell without supervision is surprising given the characterization by the officer in charge of D block that he was "a defiant agitator . . . a sneaking, treacherous man and should be watched closely at all times." Rufus Franklin Alcatraz file.

16. Fred Hunter Alcatraz file.

17. Brest had demanded a retrial on the kidnapping charge on the grounds that he was tried without competent counsel. A federal judge agreed with Brest, and he was returned to Pittsburgh, where he was provided new counsel. But in the second trial he was convicted again, again sentenced to life, and returned to Alcatraz.

18. L. E. Cranor, U.S. Marshal, to Attorney General, May 13, 1941, James Boarman Alcatraz file.

19. Floyd Hamilton, interview with the author, April 27, 1981, Dallas, Texas. All subsequent quotes attributed to Hamilton in this chapter are taken from the same interview.

20. Special-Agent-in-Charge Pieper to the Director, FBI, May 13, 1943, file 76–9499–11.

21. Ibid.

22. Ibid., pp. 27–28.

23. Ibid., pp. 29–30.

24. Hamilton's Alcatraz file, when examined by FBI agents, contained the following entry: "This inmate, while attempting to escape was drowned, the body was seen to sink by Warden Johnston and Chief Medical Officer Ritchey."

25. A. Rosen, memorandum to Director, FBI, Washington, D.C., April 16, 1943, file 76–9549–9X.

26. J. E. Hoover, Director, FBI, to J. V. Bennett, Director, BOP, June 16, 1943, file 76–9549–11.

27. James A. Johnston to James V. Bennett, August 8, 1943.

28. James V. Bennett, Director, to A. H. Connor, McNeil Island Penitentiary, August 12, 1943.

29. A. H. Connor, Associate Commissioner, to James V. Bennett, Director, August 25, 1943.

30. William T. Hammack, Assistant Director, to Warden Johnston, August 27, 1943.

31. Deputy Warden E. J. Miller, memorandum to Warden Johnston, May 23, 1944, "Findings in D Block."

32. John K. Giles Alcatraz file.

33. "10 Years of Planning—Brief Moment of Freedom" and "Alcatraz Guest Nonchalantly Sails Away," *San Francisco Chronicle*, August 1, 1945.

34. Other items found on Giles when he was searched on Angel Island included several pouches, a comb, two flashlight bulbs, small change, a memo book,

a flashlight, a box of blank furlough forms, a Colgate toothpaste tube containing glue, a medicine bottle containing ink, a razor, five safety pins, three matches
(each wrapped with a small needle and thread), and a small bar of green soap.
Details of the escape are taken from the FBI report compiled by William H. Hart-
ley, August 6, 1945, file 76–806.

35. James A. Johnston, Warden, to Captain A. H. Connor, Acting Director,
BOP, July 31, 1945.

36. Connor to Johnston, August 9, 1945.

37. *San Francisco News,* October 1, 1945. Giles promptly filed an appeal,
arguing that he had not "escaped from custody" because at the time of his escape no guards were supervising him and thus he was not in "custody." Two
judges agreed with the government that Giles was in custody even though not
under physical restraint at the time of the escape, the third judge agreed with
Giles. *J. K. Giles v. United States of America,* U.S. Circuit Court of Appeals for
the Ninth Circuit, Denman dissenting, no. 11,187, October 14, 1946.

38. The account of this escape plot is based on interviews conducted by Anthony Calabrese with James Quillen (September 26, 1981) and fictitious no. AZ-
1700 (June 18, 1980). Official reports of this escape attempt never identified 1700
as a participant, but his role was verified by Quillen, who described the events
in his book, *Alcatraz from Inside: The Hard Years, 1942–1952,* ed. Lynn Cullivan (San Francisco: Golden Gate National Parks Association, 1991), 67–80.

39. Number 1700 explained that the tunnel plot was exposed after a steam
pipe broke and employees who went into the tunnel to repair the damage found
the tools and saw evidence of the digging. According to 1700, the men had succeeded "in getting sixteen or eighteen feet" into the tunnel and "were underneath
the foundation of the building."

40. If an informant had revealed the escape plot and named Quillen and Pepper, it is likely that the staff would have pressured him to identify the men who
had secured the tools and transported them from the industries area to the kitchen.
The lack of follow-up in this case by the deputy warden, the warden, and BOP
headquarters is difficult to understand.

41. Quillen interview.

CHAPTER 9

1. This account is based on interviews with prisoners and custodial personnel who were present on the island during the attempted escape and ensuing
events, FBI files, and BOP reports and correspondence. Quotations and information on the backgrounds of the central inmate participants were obtained from
their Leavenworth, Atlanta, and Alcatraz files. The author interviewed the inmates Charles Berta (August 2, 1987; February 19, 1988), Floyd Hamilton
(April 27, 1981), Floyd Harrell (July 10, 1983), Arnold Kyle (September 24,
1980), William Radkay (April 24, 1981), Morton Sobell (January 11, 1980), Dale
Stamphill (April 23, 1981; October 15, 1995), and Harmon Waley (September
23, 1980); the author and Anthony Calabrese each interviewed James Quillen
(respectively, August 18, 1980, and September 26, 1981); Anthony Calabrese also
interviewed AZ-1700 (June 18, 1980). The author interviewed staff members

Robert Baker (September 3, 1980), Philip Bergen (April 29, 1983), George Boatman (September 4, 1980), Lawrence Delmore, Jr. (September 22, 1980), Don Martin (August 28, 1978), Maurice E. Ordway (July 18, 1977), Edward Stucker (July 28, 1981), senior officer X (January 16, 1980), and senior officer Y (April 30, 1981); Anthony Calabrese interviewed Loring O. Mills (May 21, 1980).

2. Coy's adjustment to life on the Rock seemed to be quite positive, as evidenced in a letter sent to his brother, who was locked up at the Atlanta Penitentiary:

> Contrary to general belief, we have an ideal home here at Alcatraz . . . [prior] to my arrival here on the island, I failed to determine heads from tails. I think I have it now however. The idea here in Alcatraz appears to be one of protection—not persecution. No place on earth have I been better provided for, nor more humanely treated. No one ever gets in our whiskers. And we go to great ends to reciprocate in consideration. Our food is remarkable, Dick. I shan't go into a detailed explanation, but how do you like chop suey, creamed ham on toast, and candied yams, creamed sweet peas, breaded steak, hot griddle cakes, and butter, and biscuits, and coffee with cream and sugar, whole wheat bread, or rye, or white, or raisins? And how do your teeth react to cream pies, spice layer cakes, cream puffs, apple turnovers, and chocolate eclairs? This is some of it. Our menu runs American one week and Spanish the next. And we do not know today what will be for tomorrow's dinner, not to mention what will repeat itself at dinner tomorrow ten years from now. I am doing my work in the bakery, and I know that what I eat the main line eats also. There is no big-shot tables here. They're all for cap-pistol guys in Alcatraz.
>
> —Your Brother Bernard Paul Coy no. 415

3. Hubbard's criminal career began when he spent thirty days on a Mississippi chain gang, followed by a three-year term for grand larceny in the Alabama state prison, from which he escaped and was returned. In 1943 he stole a car and was charged with a federal crime for taking the vehicle across state lines. He soon escaped from jail with two other prisoners by grabbing the night guard, taking his keys, and calling for a taxi to take them out of town; they forced the driver out of the vehicle and the three men drove to Tennessee. Several days later, a traffic cop noticed that the cab had an out-of-state license plate and signaled them to stop. When the officer approached their vehicle, he found himself facing a submachine gun and other weapons taken in the jail break. He was tied up and dumped in the back seat, and Hubbard and his associates drove south to Georgia, where they stopped at a barn and left their kidnap victim tied up. The officer was able to get loose and call from the farmhouse for assistance from local police. A road block was erected and after a gun battle in which one of his fellow escapees was shot and killed, Hubbard was taken into custody and transported to jail in Knoxville, Tennessee. An investigation by the United States marshal at the county jail indicated that after Hubbard and the other escapee were captured, they were beaten by law enforcement officers who had been alerted to the kidnapping of the traffic officer.

4. The federal offense that brought Thompson to Alcatraz occurred while he was on escape status from the Alabama state prison but was in custody in the county jail in Paris, Texas. Thompson and four other inmates escaped and immediately went to a residence, where they forced the occupant to accompany them in his automobile to Clarksville, Texas, and then forced him out of the car;

subsequently, the escapees stole cars in Texas, Oklahoma, and Nebraska. On March 12, 1945, Thompson and one of his confederates, named Day, were taken into custody at Amarillo, Texas, by police officer Lem Savage as "suspicious characters." On the way to city hall in the police car for questioning, Thompson drew a gun that he had concealed and shot Savage, fatally wounding him. The officer was then shoved out of the vehicle and Thompson drove out of town. On a road outside of Amarillo, by sounding the siren, Thompson and Day were able to stop a passenger car being driven by a woman accompanied by two employees from her ranch in New Mexico. Thompson brandished a gun, forced the woman out of the driver's seat and into the back seat, and then he and Day drove the three hostages across the state line into New Mexico. Near San Juan, however, their vehicle was stopped by police and Thompson and Day were apprehended.

5. State prison officials described Carnes as "bitter" over receiving such a long sentence when his age should have been taken into consideration. One foggy morning in February 1945, Carnes and two other prisoners on the rock-breaking crew escaped from the quarry on the grounds of the Oklahoma reformatory; they ran to a nearby farmhouse where Carnes forced the farmer, at knife point, to get in his car, and the four drove away. Subsequently Carnes and his compatriots stopped another car in order to get gas, and that driver and the farmer were tied up and left in the farmer's vehicle. A few hours later, Carnes separated from the other two escapees and began looking for another vehicle to steal, which involved kidnapping the driver. He was apprehended while still in Oklahoma and joined the other two escapees in the Oklahoma County Jail, where they immediately went to work on a plan to overpower the jailer when he opened the door to their cell to hand over their food trays. In the scuffle that followed, Carnes hit the man with a shower head and toilet plunger until he was knocked unconscious. Carnes and the others tore mattress covers into strips, which they tied together in order to lower themselves through a window to the floor below. The three then broke through the windows of several doors and ran out of the jail. But the alarm had been sounded and Carnes, after shots were fired at him by pursuing police officers, surrendered several blocks away.

6. William Radkay, interview with the author, April 24, 1981.

7. "Alcatraz Siege Ended; All Felons in Custody," *Baltimore Sun,* May 5, 1946.

8. AP release, May 4, 1946.

9. *San Francisco Examiner,* May 4, 1946; *Washington D.C. Times-Herald,* May 4, 1946.

10. Lawrence E. Davies, "Marines Land on Alcatraz to Battle Armed Convicts in Attempted Prison Break," *New York Times,* May 3, 1946.

11. George Draper, "Weapons Being Used on Alcatraz—Everything up to Heavy Machine Guns," *San Francisco Chronicle,* May 4, 1946.

12. Draper, "Weapons." "Toughest Killers and Gangsters Sent to 'Rock,'" *Times-Herald,* May 3, 1946, a UPI release, listed Al Capone (transferred), Machine Gun Kelly, Harvey Bailey, Albert Bates, John Paul Chase, Norman Whitaker, Alvin Karpis, Dock Barker (dead), Volney Davis, Harmon Waley, Tom Holden, and several convicts who had tried to escape—Joe Bowers (dead), John Giles, and Floyd Hamilton.

13. George Draper, *San Francisco Chronicle,* May 3, 1946.

14. According to Stucker, all twenty-one inmates were transferred to other prisons when Director Bennett learned of their exemplary behavior during the battle.

15. Al Ostrow, "Johnston of Alcatraz," *San Francisco News,* May 31, 1946.

16. *San Francisco News,* May 6, 1946.

17. *San Francisco Chronicle,* May 12, 1946.

18. W. H. Nichols, FBI, to D. M. Ladd, FBI, May 5, 1946.

19. Handwritten note by H (J. Edgar Hoover) added to Nichols's letter; original emphasis.

20. From E. A. Tamm to the Director, May 3, 1946, file 70–12090–25. On the bottom of this memo Hoover added a note, complaining, "Only wish our representatives [in the Dept. of Justice] were more alert in championing FBI interests and less 'Munich minded' in appeasement of the Prison Bureau . . . in every situation in which the Bureau becomes involved with the Bureau of Prisons, we end up behind the eight ball and we never get full cooperation from any federal prison."

21. E. A. Tamm to the Director, May 3, 1946, file 70–12090–441. In a subsequent telephone conversation, Tamm told Hoover that he warned Bennett that the FBI would not undertake any investigation unless it could be conducted "without interference, opposition, or any of the other unpleasantness which always arose from our dealings with the Bureau of Prisons. Mr. Bennett made a whinny *[sic]* protest and I told him that I thought it was a mistake to be hypocritical . . . [because] in every case where we tried to do something for the Bureau of Prisons, we end up behind the eight ball." Tamm went on to claim that all of the wardens "were hostile to us. . . . Bennett protested that he didn't know of any situations where we had trouble with wardens and I told him that this was silly because in my sixteen years in the Bureau, I have prepared for you [JEH] many memoranda relating to refusal of the wardens to permit us to interview prisoners, to afford proper facilities, to try to review copies of statements which we take from prisoners, etc., etc. Bennett whined about this. . . . I told [him] that at such time as he obtained additional facts and desired to discuss the conditions of the investigations, I would be glad to talk to him about it."

22. James V. Bennett to J. Edgar Hoover, May 6, 1946, file 70–12090.

23. E. A. Tamm to the Director, May 6, 1946, file 70–17090–14.

24. Tamm to A. Rosen, May 7, 1946, file 70–12090.

25. Tamm to the Director, ibid.

26. "Attorneys Plan Probe of Alcatraz Brutality" and "Defense Counsel for Riot Trio Slate Exposure of Penal Treatment," *San Francisco Examiner,* October 28, 1946.

27. Handwritten note on memo from Rosen to Tamm, December 11, 1946, file 70–12090.

28. Johnston to Bennett, November 22, 1946.

29. *San Francisco Examiner,* December 5, 1946.

30. *San Francisco News,* December 6, 1946.

31. Johnston to Bennett, December 12, 1946; *San Francisco Chronicle,* December 12, 1946.

32. *San Francisco News,* December 11, 1946.

33. *San Francisco News,* December 13, 1946.

34. "Lawyers Wind Up Cases in Rock Mutiny Murder Trial," [newspaper's name illegible], December 18, 1946, FBI file 70–12090.

35. *San Francisco Call-Bulletin,* December 18, 1946.

36. *San Francisco Examiner,* December 22 and 24, 1946.

37. D. G. Schmidt, MD, to Warden Clinton T. Duffy [San Quentin], January 28, 1946. Because the West Coast had no federal prison in which executions could be held, the Alcatraz prisoners were housed and executed at this California state prison.

38. L. B. Pilsburg, Chief Psychiatrist, Henry W. Rogers, Chief Psychiatrist Guidance Center, D. G. Schmidt, Acting Chief Medical Officer, to Warden Clinton T. Duffy, March 24, 1947.

39. Frank J. Hennessy to Theron L. Caudle, Assistant Attorney General, Dept. of Justice, Washington, D.C., May 23, 1947.

40. On July 8, 1947, Dr. Johnson submitted the results of this examination to Director Bennett, stating that he regarded Shockley as sane and found no indication that he had been insane in the past; George S. Johnson, MD, to Director, BOP. David G. Schmidt, MD, Robert G. Houlihan, MD, Henry W. Rogers, MD, San Quentin, July 22, 1948.

41. James V. Bennett to Daniel M. Lyons, Pardon Attorney, November 18, 1948.

42. Captain Ralph Tahash to Warden [Edwin] Swope re execution Shockley and Thompson, Dec 6, 1948.

43. "Alcatraz," *Newark News,* May 4, 1946.

44. William F. McDermott, "The Barbarism of Alcatraz," *Cleveland Plain Dealer,* BOP 1946 riot file.

45. Dillard Stokes, "The Rock, a Monument to Society's Failure," *Washington Post,* May 12, 1946.

46. Don Fairbairn, "What About Alcatraz? Is It America's Shameful Devil's Island?" *Philadelphia Bulletin,* May 11, 1946.

47. Leslie Cross, "Is Alcatraz a Relic of Medievalism?" *Milwaukee Journal,* May 10, 1946.

48. *Reno Gazette,* May 10, 1946; *Grand Rapids (MI) Press,* May 7, 1946.

49. *Manchester Union,* May 6, 1946; *Portland Press Herald,* May 4, 1946; *Detroit Free Press,* May 4, 1946.

50. Josh Eppinger, city editor, *San Francisco Examiner,* to William F. Knowland, United States Senate, May 27, 1946.

51. *San Francisco Examiner,* May 9, 1946. Yet another proposal, sent to California senators and congressional representatives, urged that the prison "be moved to an island in the Pacific hundreds of miles out from the nearest shore to discourage escape, although the location should be in a warm climate to relieve the prisoners' feelings of desperation." Gilbert Wales, Station KSAN, San Francisco, May 15, 1946. Former attorney general Frank Murphy visited Alcatraz "and came away declaring that the effect of the institution on the prisoners was sinister and vicious." In his opinion, it was unjust to the city of San Francisco to have "that place of horror at its doorstep." "Alcatraz Riot," *Washington Post,* May 5, 1946.

52. "California Wants Alcatraz Removed," UPI release, May 23, 1946.

53. In the book written after he retired from federal service, Johnston gave a view of the escape that differed little from the view he had held during and immediately after the event. He denied that Officer Stites had been killed by friendly fire, instead claiming that Cretzer "stood outside the floor door between C and D blocks and fired revolver shots," killing Stites and wounding three other officers. The warden described himself as calm and in complete charge at all times during the three-day battle; no fault was found with the staff, with the prison's riot and escape plans, or with the security arrangements in place when the trouble began. See James A. Johnston, "The Battle of Alcatraz," in *Alcatraz Island Prison, and the Men Who Live There* (New York: Charles Scribner's Sons, 1949), 221–37.

54. Bennett to Johnston, May 7, 1947.

55. C. J. Shuttleworth, Warden, Federal Correctional Institution, Milan, Michigan, to the Director, May 12, 1947.

56. Deputy Warden Edward Miller retired less than one year after the "mutiny"; Captain Henry Weinhold and Lt. Joseph Simpson, who had been injured, left federal service on disability retirements; Ernest Lageson, perhaps feeling he had his one piece of luck when Cretzer did not shoot to kill him, resigned from the federal prison system. The widows of Officers William Miller and Harold Stites received compensation from the federal government in the amount of $61.25 each monthly; at the time of their deaths each man had an annual salary of $2,600. Each of the officers' five children were authorized to received $17.50 each month until the age of eighteen. Employees throughout the BOP collected $6,900 to cover funeral costs and to assist the officers' families.

57. Willard Edwards, "Alcatraz Steel Curtain Lifted for First Time," *Chicago Daily Tribune*, August 13, 1947.

58. Albert Deutsch, "A Visit to Alcatraz, the Dreaded Isle of Dead-Enders in Crime," *Colliers Magazine*, June 8, 1948. Albert Deutsch was not, however, satisfied with a one-day visit and when Warden Johnston's book was published, he wrote to James Bennett saying that he was "shocked and really angry" that he had been denied information about individual prisoners when Johnston had freely described inmates, including those with mental health problems. Deutsch told Bennett, "I don't think you have the right to deny first-hand access . . . by a reputable journalist writing for a reputable periodical." Albert Deutsch to James V. Bennett, October 21, 1948. Bennett replied that Johnston's book had been written after he had retired from the Bureau and if Deutsch was allowed "exclusive" access to information, all of the San Francisco newspaper reporters and other journalists who had requested permission over the years to do stories on Alcatraz would be outraged.

CHAPTER 10

1. James A. Johnston, *Alcatraz Island Prison, and the Men Who Live There* (New York: Charles Scribner's Sons, 1949), 24.

2. Ibid.

3. There were several inmates who violated the prohibition against inform-

ing on rap partners. Isaac Costner turned state's evidence against his partner, a member of the Touhy gang, and spent his entire time at Alcatraz in constant fear of being killed by other gang members. Gordon Alcorn cooperated with federal prosecutors and testified against co-conspirators in the Boettcher kidnapping; at Alcatraz so many threats were made against Alcorn that he spent only fifty-six days on the island before the staff shipped him back to Leavenworth.

4. The convict code in American prisons was the subject of dozens of sociological studies beginning in the 1940s. The best known of these include Donald Clemmer's *The Prison Community* (New York: Holt, Rinehart and Winston, 1958); and Gresham Sykes, *The Society of Captives: A Study of a Maximum Security Prison* (Princeton: Princeton University Press, 1958). Since the early 1970s, what researchers called "the prison community" has been fragmented into warring factions divided along the lines of race and ethnicity, with a corresponding reduction in the importance of the convict code.

5. E. E. Kirkpatrick, *Voices from Alcatraz* (San Antonio: Naylor, 1947), 143. See chapter 11 for an expanded account of Kelly's reaction to doing time at Alcatraz.

6. Gresham M. Sykes and Sheldon L. Messinger, "The Inmate Social System," in *Theoretical Studies in Social Organization of the Prison* (New York: Social Science Research Council, 1960), 6–9.

7. In 1936 a hospital attendant was fired for smuggling out uncensored mail for several inmates, including Albert Bates. In 1937 Officer Eastin was indicted by a federal grand jury for taking out contraband letters and bringing in penicillin tablets, medicine bottles containing liquor, Benzedrine, and half pints of whiskey given to James Grove on Christmas Eve and New Year's Eve, even a box of snuff for William Dainard; Eastin was convicted and sentenced to six months in prison.

8. For example, see Ben M. Crouch and James W. Marquart, *An Appeal to Justice: Litigated Reform in Texas Prisons* (Austin: University of Texas Press, 1989); Thomas Murton and Joseph Hyams, *Accomplices to the Crime: The Arkansas Prison Scandal* (New York: Grove Press, 1969); and David M. Oshinsky, *Worse than Slavery: Parchman Farm and the Ordeal of Jim Crow Justice* (New York: Free Press, 1996).

9. Michel Foucault, *Discipline and Punish* (New York: Pantheon Books, 1977); Erving Goffman, *Asylums* (Garden City, NJ: Anchor Books, 1961).

10. See Lynn Goodstein, Doris Layton MacKenzie, and R. Lance Shotland, "Personal Control and Inmate Adjustment to Prison," *Criminology* 22, no. 2 (August 1984): 343–69.

11. Examinations of inmates' reactions, adaptations, and mechanisms to cope with imprisonment include Maurice L. Farber, "Suffering and Time Perspective of the Prisoner," *Iowa University Studies in Child Welfare* 20 (1943–44): 155–227; Edward Zamble and Frank J. Porporino, *Coping, Behavior, and Adaptation in Prison Inmates* (New York: Springer-Verlag, 1988); Robert Johnson and Hans Toch, eds., *The Pains of Imprisonment* (Beverly Hills: Sage Publications, 1982); Roger Sapsford, *Life Sentence Prisoners: Reaction, Response and Change* (Thetford, UK: Open University Press, 1983); Stanley Cohen and Laurie Taylor, *Psychological Survival: The Experience of Long Term Impris-*

onment (Baltimore: Penguin Books, 1982); and Hans Toch, Kenneth Adams, and J. Douglas Grant, *Coping: Maladaptation in Prison* (New Brunswick: Transaction, 1989).

12. John K. Irwin, "Sociological Studies of the Impact of Long-Term Confinement," in *Confinement in Maximum Custody,* ed. David A. Ward and Kenneth F. Schoen (Lexington, MA: Lexington Books/D. C. Heath, 1981), 49–52. Also see Irwin's description of "The Convict World," in *The Felon* (Englewood Cliffs, NJ: Prentice-Hall, 1970), 61–85.

13. Altercations between prisoners recorded as assaults were not those that involved simply pushing, shoving, wrestling around, or even throwing punches but those that involved the use of weapons or resulted in serious injury. Given the physical confines of the prison, the limited time and opportunities for movement outside their cells, and the large number of staff to observe inmates' activity and evidence of injuries, these figures represent a fair approximation of the actual number of assaults and homicides. It should be noted that none of the voluminous files compiled by the staff recorded what prisoners would characterize as assaults on them by prison personnel. These incidents would be defined by staff as "using necessary force" to subdue a resisting prisoner. Some serious inmate-on-inmate assaults might have ended up as homicides in free-world settings where prompt, proximate, experienced medical care was not so readily available.

14. Unhappy at Leavenworth, Herring had appealed to the attorney general for a transfer to Alcatraz, "where they treat you like a man." Maurice Herring Alcatraz file.

15. Cecil Snow Alcatraz file.

16. E. J. Miller, Acting Warden, to the Director, November 17, 1945.

17. Ralph Greene Alcatraz file.

18. Quillen interview in 1980.

19. Greene file. Ralph Greene's lengthy sojourn in D block is to be explained only in part by the administration of Alcatraz justice: he accumulated numerous misconduct reports for destroying government property (mainly his toilet bowl), creating disturbances, fighting with other prisoners (once for reaching through the cell bars trying to stab the orderly, and another when he was released for a shower and attacked another orderly, and twice for fighting in the yard with other D block prisoners until a tower guard fired warning shots). He also threatened an officer telling him, "I'll fuck you, you son of a bitch," and on numerous occasions was insolent and refused to obey orders. By the time he was released from D block he had forfeited 1,461 days of good time. Greene, like other convicts, filed writs and petitions including a claim that "refusal of prison authorities to permit him to purchase underwear heavier than prison issue constitutes cruel and unusual punishment." His writ of habeas corpus contended, "he had been thrown into a dungeon and beaten with a black jack by a guard he admitted to have struck during an altercation." Greene also wrote to NAACP president Thurgood Marshall complaining of beatings by guards and attempts to poison his food. This letter was not forwarded to Marshall because it did not "stick to the facts" and was intended to "create trouble."

20. James Grove Alcatraz file.

21. James Walsh Alcatraz file.

22. E. J. Miller, Acting Warden, to Director, March 6, 1939.

CHAPTER 11

1. Bob Gaucher, ed., *Writing as Resistance: The Journal of Prisoners on Prisons, 1998–2002* (Toronto: Canadian Scholars' Press, 2002).

2. Walter B. Martin, Acting Assistant Surgeon/Psychiatrist, Leavenworth, Kansas, August 26, 1931.

3. Director to James A. Johnston, October 1, 1935.

4. Edward W. Twitchell, MD, Psychiatrist, report to the Surgeon General re James Grove, October 16, 1935.

5. George Hess, Surgeon, Chief Medical Officer, James Grove Alcatraz file. All quotes and reports on Grove not otherwise cited come from this source.

6. M. R. King, Surgeon, U.S. Public Health Service (USPHS), Warden and Chief Medical Officer [Springfield], to Director, BOP, January 8, 1938.

7. Frank Loveland, memorandum to Mr. Bennett re James Grove, March 4, 1939.

8. Romney M. Ritchey, Surgeon, Chief Medical Officer, memorandum to the Warden, July 3, 1943.

9. James Grove to NAACP, July 31, 1946. These complaints prompted a review of his treatment by Warden Johnston, who forwarded Grove's letter to Bureau headquarters with a recommendation that it be sent on to the NAACP.

10. To Honorable Robert B. Patterson, Secretary of War, October 23, 1946.

11. [James Grove] Special progress report, February 8, 1952.

12. Ibid., p. 2.

13. Robert Baker, who worked at Alcatraz from 1934 to 1957, told the author that on one occasion in the early 1950s James Grove saved his life: "They had a bad habit up in the hospital of passing out pills, dope them up, cool them down. [Prisoners] came through the main gate and about twenty to twenty-five blacks were going up the stairs to the movies. Two of them were drunker than a skunk but not on liquor. There was nothing on their breath but they were all doped up. As I grabbed one of them, Jimmy Grove says, 'Mr. Baker, don't do that.' I said, 'Well that slob is drunk as a skunk on dope.' He says, 'I know, I know, I'll take care of him.' So I turned him loose and I looked around and there was about ten of them ready to pounce on me before I could have made any alarm or hit one of them with my foot. They'd have had me down with a shiv in my back." Baker interview in 1980.

14. James Grove to Hon. Chairman, NAACP, June 18, 1953, New York City.

15. James Grove, special progress report, November 26, 1954.

16. Grove, special progress report, March 27, 1959.

17. Waley interview in 1980. All subsequent quotes in this chapter attributed to Waley are from this interview.

18. Philip Bergen, interview with the author, April 29, 1983.

19. Milton Daniel Beacher, *Alcatraz Island: Memoirs of a Rock Doc*, ed. Dianne Beacher Perfit (Lebanon, NJ: Pelican Island Publishing, 2001). Perfit is his daughter.

20. James A. Johnston, Warden, to Director, August 31, 1936. See chapter 6 for a description of the dungeons.

21. Waley said he knew that Culver lived in Orlando, Florida, after he retired: "I was going to go down and kill him when I got out, but I decided why should I do that."

22. Beacher, *Memoirs*.

23. Ibid.

24. James A. Johnston to Director, December 3, 1937.

25. Letter to his mother, September 27, 1938, Harmon Waley Alcatraz file.

26. Walter Hansen, Jr. Officer, disciplinary report, Waley file.

27. Waley to James V. Bennett, November 28, 1940. "Of course [Miller] told you that he and your little Lt. Simpson were forced to knock me out with their fists, and by pounding my head against the cement wall, during the hunger strike. He told Dr. Ritchey that I attacked him with a bottle. As I explained to Dr. Ritchey, had I attacked him with a bottle I would have cut him but he never had a scratch. . . . As for me working in your institution that is out."

28. J. P. Simpson, Lt., to Deputy Warden, May 1941. This report was written months after the episode when Waley claimed he had been "beaten up" by Miller.

29. Report of writ of habeas corpus, April 14, 1939, Waley file.

30. Bert E. Haney, U.S. Circuit Judge, to James A. Johnston, January 7, 1942. Johnston met with Haney to inform the judge that the prison staff had read all legal mail but had to be "careful not to delay or impede them." The judge warned the warden to "be on guard against threats of dangerous men." James A. Johnston to James V. Bennett, January 11, 1942.

31. *San Francisco News*, April 23, 1941.

32. *San Francisco Examiner*, April 24, 1941.

33. Ibid.

34. Johnston memorandum, December 20, 1941, Waley file.

35. Waley letter, December 22, 1941, ibid.

36. Waley letter, March 1, 1944, ibid.

37. Ibid.

38. Report of disciplinary board, June 5, 1944, ibid.

39. Letter to his mother, October 3, 1940, Waley file.

40. Letters to Secretary of War, October 6, and October 9, 1940, ibid.

41. Director to James A. Johnston, January 10, 1941.

42. [Harmon Waley] Special progress report, June 3, 1948.

43. Special progress report, 1949.

44. Leon J. Whitsell, MD, Psychiatrist, to Warden, January 17, 1951, Waley file.

45. Special progress report, February 8, 1952.

46. Special progress report, October 28, 1955.

47. Autobiographical statement, p. 12, Richard Neumer Alcatraz file. Neumer also spelled his name N-U-M-E-R but no explanation for the name change was recorded in prison or FBI records.

48. Ibid., pp. 12–13.

49. Neumer file.

50. Special progress report, August 23, 1945, ibid.

51. Edward W. Twitchell, Psychiatrist, hospital report, July 3, 1945, ibid.

52. English A866, lesson no. 1, University of California Extension Division, December 27, 1946, ibid.

53. "The question raised by your action is whether a prisoner should be denied the opportunity to do something constructive and good because his motives are bad. . . . It had been intimated that Mr. Numer [sic] is already a good writer and that he should not be permitted to improve his skills in order to libel the prison administration. Of course, it will be a long time before Mr. Numer is released and I venture to say that the reputation of Alcatraz Prison will not depend upon what Mr. Numer says about it. I think the idea of a convict wanting to improve his writing abilities to lambaste the prison administration is extremely funny, and it provides one more story for your collection. Once the court denies the petition, I trust you will reconsider the matter and grant Mr. Numer an opportunity to take the course." Ernest Besig, Director, ACLU of Northern California, to James A. Johnston, January 18, 1947, ibid.

54. Richard A. Neumer no. 286 to Hon. Alexander Wiley, Senate Building, Washington, D.C., January 25, 1947, ibid.

55. James A. Johnston to Director, January 28, 1947, ibid.

56. Richard S. Yocum, Surgeon, memorandum to the Warden, February 10, 1948, ibid.

57. Ibid.

58. P. J. Madigan, memorandum re no. 268 Neumer, September 7, 1950, ibid.

59. J. V. Bennett on memo from R. J. Heaney re Richard Neumer, January 18, 1951, ibid.

60. According to Thomas Gaddis, Neumer spent "a day or two as a 'technical consultant' on the set watching Burt Lancaster play the role of Robert Stroud in the movie *The Birdman of Alcatraz*." Thomas E. Gaddis, *Unknown Men of Alcatraz* (Portland, OR: NewGate, 1977), 32.

61. E. J. Miller, Deputy Warden, to J. A. Johnston, November 15, 1937, Burton Phillips Alcatraz file.

62. Burton Phillips to James Bennett, October 29, 1940, ibid., pp. 3, 18, 49.

63. James Bennett to James Johnston, September 25, 1939, ibid.

64. Romney M. Ritchey, Surgeon, memorandum to the Warden, August 19, 1940.

65. Special progress report, September 12, 1945, Phillips parole file.

66. Phillips to Mrs. Ella Phillips, August 17, 1944.

67. Special progress report, October 24, 1949.

68. William C. Robinson, Chief U.S. Probation Officer, District of Kansas, to Joseph N. Shore, Parole Executive, Washington, D.C., July 6, 1965.

69. James V. Bennett to William Robinson, February 7, 1963, Phillips parole file.

70. William Robinson to Joseph Shore, July 6, 1965, ibid.

71. Urbaytis Alcatraz file.

72. Ibid.

73. Special progress report, August 19, 1935, Jack Hensley Atlanta file.

74. C. R. Beall, MD, Psychiatrist, USPHS, Atlanta, Georgia, August 24, 1935.

75. Special progress report, September 12, 1945, Hensley Alcatraz file.

76. Hensley Alcatraz file. See Thomas Murton and Joseph Hyams, *Accomplices to the Crime* (New York: Grove Press, 1969), for descriptions of prisons in Georgia before the intervention of the federal courts.

77. Romney M. Ritchey, Surgeon, Psychiatrist, neuro-psychiatric examination, November 7, 1938.

78. Romney Ritchey, Surgeon, Chief Medical Officer, memoranda to the Warden, August 5 and August 19, 1940.

79. While in prison in Arkansas, Hensley wrote to the governor, Sid McMath, who was looking to reform the state's prison system. The governor, on a trip to the prison, met Hensley, who advised McMath on needed areas of reform. In return McMath wrote a letter of support for Hensley, as did James Bennett, and Hensley's Arkansas sentence was commuted; ten days after his visit with the governor, he was released.

80. Jack Hensley to James V. Bennett, January 20, 1959. Hensley expressed his appreciation to Bennett for writing on his behalf to Arkansas prison authorities.

81. Howard Butler Alcatraz file.

82. In 1949 Butler appeared for routine classification before the committee: "He seemed in very good spirits and talked for some length about the colored population. He said, that with the exception of one or two negro prisoners, he had nothing in common with them and would appreciate it if he did not have to even see them. During the interview he suggested that the negro prisoners celling across from the second tier in B block be moved somewhere else, as he hated to look at them. He said that they were talking filthy and loudly, and stupidly caused much confusion and disturbance in the cell house. He said the last negro prisoners received, especially the Army inmates, were very low in intelligence and were a very bad bunch. He stated he wants nothing to do with the other colored inmates and his best friends were among the white population. He likes all the officers and officials and never had any 'beefs' where they were concerned. Butler said he appreciated consideration for restored good time and recently obtained 364 days restoration." Special progress report, December 16, 1959, Butler file. This statement may have been an attempt by a savvy convict to curry favor with staff by presenting himself as different from most black prisoners. That his statement was recorded as part of an official record suggests that Butler's remarks were a welcome reinforcement of negative racial stereotypes.

83. Butler file.

84. It is unclear whether Joe Urbaytis was a success or a failure; he lived outside of prison for three years before he was shot to death. In prison recidivism statistics he would be recorded as a "success" since he did not return to prison. If James Grove had not taken his own life (the ultimate form of resistance) before his release, he might have succeeded in staying out of prison as well.

CHAPTER 12

1. Dock Barker—another Public Enemy with a reputation at least as large as Karpis's—might have been in this category had he not died during an escape attempt early in his sentence. See chapter 5.

2. See the chapters on Alvin Karpis in J. Edgar Hoover, *Persons in Hiding* (Boston: Little, Brown, 1938); and in Courtney Ryley Cooper, *Ten Thousand Public Enemies* (Boston: Little, Brown, 1935). Arthur Barker and George and Kathryn Kelly are also featured in these books. See also the chapters on the Urschel kidnapping and the Barkers and Alvin Karpis in Irving Crump and John W. Newton, *Our G-Men* (New York: Dodd, Mead, 1937).

3. Alvin Karpis, as told to Robert Livesey, *On the Rock: Twenty-Five Years in Alcatraz* (New York: Beaufort Books, 1980), 60.

4. San Francisco FBI field office, February 27, 1935, file 62–1238.

5. In June 1935 a former inmate of Atlanta sent a 243-page manuscript titled "The Biography of Al Capone's Life in the Atlanta Penitentiary" to the office of *Real Detective Magazine* in New York. Its focus was the usual allegations of preferential treatment and Capone's ability to corrupt prison employees. The author reported that he had been employed as a secretary in the prison records office and therefore had access to all correspondence and records, including confidential correspondence between Atlanta officials and BOP headquarters. The FBI reviewed the incidents described in the manuscript and concluded that, with the exception of the case of a guard who was dismissed for carrying a letter from Capone out of the prison, the allegations were not based on fact. Al Capone, Alcatraz and Terminal Island files. All quotes and references to letters and reports on Capone are taken from this source.

6. Parole board members stopped by Alcatraz only to review cases of inmates whose time remaining on their sentences was becoming short, those who might be released directly to the West Coast, or, in Capone's case, to avoid being accused of denying a high-profile offender his legal right to a hearing.

7. Report of E. Twitchell, Psychiatrist, and G. Hess, Chief Medical Officer, Alcatraz, February 6, 1938.

8. E. J. Miller, to James A. Johnston, February 11, 1938.

9. *Time Magazine*, February 21, 1938.

10. R. Ritchey, MD, August 17, 1938.

11. James V. Bennett to Attorney General, December 14, 1938.

12. *San Francisco News*, September 9, 1939. When the island was opened to tourists by the National Park Service in 1975, the commercialization of Alcatraz began with shops selling pseudo Al Capone cigars, the Big Boy's picture on posters, and the claims of ex-guards and inmates that they had been "best friends" with Public Enemy no. 1.

13. G. Hess, MD, to Medical Director, BOP, January 16, 1939.

14. H. R. Lipton, MD, to Chief Medical Officer, psychiatric examination of Al Capone, September 9, 1939, p. 3.

15. R. B. Hood, Special-Agent-in-Charge, to Director, FBI, October 26, 1939, file 62–39128–101.

16. The specialist who agreed to treat Capone informed the Bureau that the patient's admission to the Johns Hopkins Hospital was contingent on several factors: that he be admitted under an assumed name and that the Capone family make every effort to avoid publicity; that visitors were to be limited to family members; that Capone's condition justify his management on the medical service rather than in the psychiatric ward; and that Capone's physical and mental

condition be sufficiently satisfactory to permit his management on the medical service but also offer some hope of improvement.

17. Harry H. Lipton, abstract of neuropsychiatric record, October 24, 1939, p. 29.

18. Special-Agent-in-Charge, Miami, to Director, FBI, April 15, 1945, file 62–39128–147.

19. John Kobler, *Capone: The Life and World of Al Capone* (New York: Collier Books, 1971), 38.

20. George Kelly, Alcatraz file. All quotes and references to letters and reports on Kelly come from this source.

21. George Kelly to Charles F. Urschel, April 11, 1940. This letter was forwarded to BOP headquarters and to Director Hoover. The sophisticated description of prison life in this letter may reflect Kelly's three years' attendance at the University of Mississippi as well as his reading habits at Alcatraz. Willie Radkay, a friend of his on the island, told the author that Kelly had the ability to use such language.

22. E. Swope to J. Bennett, 1948.

23. Radkay interview in 1981.

24. J. V. Bennett memo re Kelly transfer request, May 3, 1950.

25. Report, September 3, 1949.

26. A memorandum to J. Edgar Hoover from the FBI office in Oklahoma City regarding these charges contained this handwritten note from the director, "Be certain we watch closely and take steps to see Kelly does not get a parole. We can expect anything from Bennett's outfit." October 2, 1953, file 7–115–2788.

27. Director, FBI, to the Attorney General, November 1, 1949. A handwritten note on this memo from an FBI official stated, "I have been in touch with the Chairman of the Parole Board for the past several weeks re this matter and feel they will take no action on application. . . . Have made clear what our position is on this application." November 17, 1949, file SE 21 7–115–2200.

28. Director's note on memorandum from F. H. Schmidt to Mr. Rosen, subject: Chaplain Joseph M. Clark, October 31, 1949, file 62–29777–7119.

29. An article from an AP release on July 17, 1954, noted that the Kellys, Bates, Bailey, and Shannons were the first convictions under the Lindbergh kidnapping law, and that Kelly earned his nickname "because he could write his name with tommy gun bullets." It also mentioned that when Kelly was apprehended, he had, according to an FBI spokesman, "reached up his hands toward the ceiling, trembled, and said, 'Don't shoot, G-Men. Don't shoot.'" (The article's title and newspaper's name had been removed.) Kathryn Kelly and her mother, Ora Shannon, were released from prison in 1958, returned to Texas, and changed their names to Brooks.

30. Albert Bates Alcatraz file. All quotes and references to letters and reports on Bates are taken from this source.

31. Romney M. Ritchey, Surgeon/Psychiatrist, neuro-psychiatric examination of no. 137, December 9, 1938.

32. E. Swope, warden's bi-weekly report, July 16, 1948. "Urschel Kidnapper Takes Ransom Secret to Grave," International News Service, name of newspaper and date not attached to articles.

33. Admission summary, Leavenworth, Kansas, August 5, 1936. Sanford Bates to Warden, Leavenworth, July 30, 1936. Alvin Karpis Alcatraz file. All quotes and references to letters and reports on Karpis are taken from this source.

34. Richard Gid Powers, *G-Men: Hoover's FBI in America's Popular Culture* (Carbondale: Southern Illinois University Press, 1983), 178.

35. Karpis, *On the Rock*, 53.

36. Lester Davis, sheriff of Howell County, Missouri, informed Alcatraz officials that the widow of his predecessor, knowing that a trial would be unlikely given the passage of time and the death of witnesses, filed the murder charge to prevent Karpis from receiving a federal parole. According to Davis, "both Barker and Karpis were in the car which drove into a local garage and when the sheriff appeared on the scene looking for them four shots were fired into his body and he died instantly." Lester Davis to E. B. Swope, Warden, Alcatraz, May 23, 1951.

37. Lawrence Delmore, Jr., Associate Warden, to Warden, May 19, 1953.

38. Lt. Alden Severson, interview with the author, July 20, 1977.

39. Karpis, *On the Rock,* 235–36.

40. Morton Sobell, interview with the author, January 11, 1980. Sobell was convicted of conspiracy in the cases in which Julius and Ethel Rosenberg were sentenced to death. He arrived at Alcatraz in 1952.

41. Johan O. Pacillas, [D block] Treatment Unit Evening Watch, to Captain Bergen re "Proposed Hunger Strike in Treatment Unit," March 3, 1954. Conversations as inmates called out from one cell to another were routinely recorded by segregation-unit officers, who censored inmates' language as they saw fit. Karpavicz, special progress report, March 5, 1954.

42. Teletype, September 19, 1958, to Frank Loveland, Assistant Director, BOP. C. H. Looney, Warden [Leavenworth], to James V. Bennett, September 15, 1952. Two days later Karpis was on his way back to Alcatraz.

43. P. J. Madigan to Director, BOP, October 21, 1958.

44. U.S. Board of Parole, transcript of minutes, by Richard A. Chappell, Chairman, June 24, 1961.

45. "Ex-Mob King Seeks Parole," *San Francisco Chronicle,* January 26, 1962. "Widow to Fight Karpis' Release From Alcatraz," *Springfield (MO) Leader-Press,* February 6, 1962. "'Hood' Karpis Eyes Parole," *Chicago Sunday American,* February 11, 1962.

46. Comment on copy of *Chicago Sunday American* article, March 14, 1962, FBI file 7–576–15474. Director, FBI, to Attorney General, February 14, 1962.

47. "No Reason for Leniency," *Washington Star,* April 1, 1962.

48. "He and Ma Barker's Boy: Ex-Public Enemy No. 1 Now a Model Prisoner," *Tacoma News Tribune,* July 5, 1966. U.S. Board of Parole, transcript of minutes, case of Alvin Karpavicz, McNeil Camp, WA, September 29, 1966.

49. James M. Carty, Attorney, Woodland, WA, to Alvin Karpavicz, December 20, 1967.

50. Paul Madigan to Joseph N. Shore, Executive Parole Secretary, January 5, 1968.

51. Raymond W. May to Joseph Shore, December 30, 1966. This was written on the date of May's retirement after thirty years with the BOP.

52. ˙[Parole board chairman] Walter Dunbar, interview with Karpis, April 16, 1968.

53. "Kidnapper, 60, Seeks New Life," *Washington Star,* January 1, 1969.

54. Alvin Karpis, as told to Bill Trent, "A New Life for Public Enemy #1," *St Paul Pioneer Press,* March 1, 1970.

55. Alvin Karpis, with Bill Trent, *The Alvin Karpis Story* (New York: Coward, McCann and Geoghegan, 1971), 230–33, 255–56.

56. T. E. Bishop to Mr. Mohr, Subject: Alvin Karpis Appearance on NBC Television Network Show Entitled "Comment," February 28, 1971, February 25, 1971; FBI file 7–576–15563; M. A. Jones to Mr. Bishop, Subject: Karpis Appearance on NBC, March 1, 1971, FBI file 7–576–15563, p. 4; Jones to Bishop, Subject: Alvin Karpis Apprehension, March 1, 1971, FBI file 7–576–15561; Jones to Bishop, Subject: Review of Book, *The Alvin Karpis Story;* March 5, 1971, FBI file 7–576–15562.

57. Richard Hack in a recent biography reviewed the different versions of this famous incident as expressed by Karpis and by Hoover in newspaper interviews, in Hoover's ghostwritten book, *Persons in Hiding,* and in another book, *The FBI Story,* by Don Whitehead written "with Hoover's endorsement." Hack also did extensive analysis of FBI files. He concluded, "Whichever is the authentic story . . . there is no denying that Hoover altered his version with each retelling, seemingly determined to sacrifice veracity for drama. His lies, or at least exaggerations, were more of proportion than substance." Richard Hack, *Puppetmaster: The Secret Life of J. Edgar Hoover* (Beverly Hills: New Millennium Press, 2004), 176–77. Other books give a variety of different verdicts. One book, by ex-FBI employees, accepts Hoover's version of the story. Neil J. Welch and David W. Marston, *Inside Hoover's FBI: The Top Field Chief Reports* (Garden City, NY: Doubleday, 1984), 134. Another book, written by the number three man in the FBI hierarchy, disputed Hoover's claims, noting that pistols said to have been taken from Karpis were on display in a glass case in the director's outer office and that "these pistols were the closest Hoover ever came to a real gun since he didn't know how to use one. He was with the FBI for forty-eight years, but he never made an arrest or conducted an investigation." William C. Sullivan with Bill Brown, *The Bureau: My Thirty Years in Hoover's FBI* (New York: W. W. Norton, 1970), 101. Another biography of Hoover offers accounts of the arrest by both Hoover and Karpis: "Although those special agents who participated in the capture of Alvin Karpis were well aware that the director's version wasn't exactly the way it happened, none ever *publicly* disputed the official account." Curt Gentry, *J. Edgar Hoover: The Man and the Secrets* (New York: W. W. Norton, 1991), 194; original emphasis.

58. Gentry, *The Man,* 195.

59. Karpis left a detailed account of his experiences at Alcatraz that was published after his death—Alvin Karpis, as told to Robert Livesey, *On the Rock: Twenty-Five Years in Alcatraz* (New York: Beaufort Books, 1980). Harmon Waley provided the author with a detailed written commentary on the pages of *On the Rock.* Among Waley's observations, "There is too much foul language in this book. I am positive Karpis did not use so much of it. He was not foul mouthed, neither were most of the inmates, guards—federal prisoners, in the main, have

higher IQs than state prisoners and are better educated. Livesey got carried away in his idea of how men in Alcatraz, the guards et. al. speak—'Go to Hell,' 'Screw You,' 'Kiss my butt,' etc. is about as strong as he should have gone. The officials seldom, if ever, used foul language. 'I'll see you rot in the hole, we'll keep you here til you rot' etc. was official talk. I think this book is fairly accurate save as noted but . . . I didn't know some that he named were homos beyond Jimmy Groves." Note: several of the men interviewed for this project were of the opinion that Karpis was too free, and often wrong, in identifying inmates he claimed were involved in homosexual conduct.

CHAPTER 13

1. Over the twenty-five years of Alcatraz history during which he served as director, James Bennett made many visits to the island and met with prisoners in his "office," a cell in A block. He established cordial relationships with a number of men—relationships that continued after their release from prison. Bennett tried to find employment for Roy Gardner after his release; assisted Jack Hensley to obtain a release from his state prison sentence; and corresponded with Charlie Berta and other releasees.

2. Willie Radkay, a friend of Chase's at Alcatraz and afterward, provided the author with a copy of this letter.

3. Radkay interview in 1981.

4. Quillen interview in 1981.

5. Success rates for the latter cohorts may have been slightly suppressed relative to the first cohort because the parole system became more extensive and professionalized during the 1950s and 1960s and may have increased the chances of a parolee being returned to prison for violations of parole conditions. However, this effect may have been cancelled out by the extra attention given to men released during the 1930s and 1940s because of their reputations as gangsters and "public enemies."

6. At the beginning of this project, we anticipated that the question would be raised as to whether the postrelease success or failure rates of the Alcatraz inmates corresponded to rates for a standard maximum-security penitentiary population. The Bureau of Prisons made it possible for us to answer this question by instructing the records office staff at Leavenworth to randomly select a sample of their inmates from the same years that Alcatraz operated, 1934–1963. We received the files of 414 Leavenworth prisoners but were able to find postrelease arrest and conviction records for only 257 of these men. This latter sample is the basis of our comparisons to the Alcatraz population. This analysis showed that 63.4 percent of Leavenworth inmates succeeded in avoiding a return to prison.

7. For examples see Daniel Glaser, *The Effectiveness of a Prison and Parole System* (Indianapolis: Bobbs-Merrill, 1964); and Gene Kassebaum, David A. Ward, and Daniel M. Wilner, *Prison Treatment and Parole Survival: An Empirical Assessment* (New York: John Wiley and Sons, 1971).

8. E. E. Kirkpatrick to Warden C. H. Looney, Leavenworth, April 2, 1953.

9. Conduct report, September 27, 1937, Harvey Bailey Alcatraz file.

10. James V. Bennett to C. H. Looney, May 2, 1958, Bailey Leavenworth file.

11. Affidavit of Harvey Bailey to U.S. District Court for the Western District of Oklahoma, July 3, 1958.

12. E. E. Kirkpatrick to U.S. Board of Parole, Washington, D.C., July 18, 1958.

13. Bailey to U.S. Board of Parole, September 30, 1958.

14. Special progress report, Leavenworth, September 1958.

15. H. J. Bailey to John C. Taylor, Warden, Leavenworth, July 9, 1960, Bailey Seagoville file.

16. [Seagoville] Warden L. P. Gollaher to Board of Parole, March 2, 1962, ibid.

17. Lawrence E. Miggins, Chief U.S. Probation Officer, to L. J. Gengler, Chief, Classification and Parole, Seagoville, March 21, 1962, ibid.

18. Warden L. P. Gollaher to Joseph Shore, Parole Executive, U.S. Board of Parole, June 13, 1962, ibid. J. Edgar Hoover had written to Scovel Richardson, Chairman, U.S. Board of Parole, on December 23, 1955, arguing "that the offense for which Bailey was found guilty was one of the most heinous against society and any effort on his part to obtain parole should be opposed." In July 1958 Warden Looney notified Director Bennett that the FBI office in Kansas City "asked that I keep them informed of any effort which Bailey makes toward obtaining release."

19. Wilbur Leonard, Chair, Board of Probation and Parole, to Warden Gollaher, Seagoville, October 5, 1962, ibid.

20. J. Evetts Haley, *Robbing Banks Was My Business* (Canyon, TX: Palo Duro Press, 1973), 182–83.

21. Special progress report, February 19, 1954. John Paul Chase accumulated a dozen misconduct reports during his nineteen years at Alcatraz, all but one related to violations of minor rules for which the punishment was "warn and reprimand" or a brief loss of privileges.

22. Thomas McDade to Fr. Joseph Clark, Alcatraz, October 23, 1952.

23. Petition for executive clemency, Leavenworth, July 18, 1961.

24. Special progress report, March 16, 1966.

25. Thormod H. Hanson, U.S. Probation Officer, evaluation of parolee progress, April 24, 1968. Hanson reported that Chase's status as a parolee was known to "only a very select few . . . he does not particularly wish to associate with other individuals," some of whom were parolees from California state prisons.

26. Chase from Douglas G. Dilfer, U.S. Probation Officer, October 12, 1971.

27. Frank Sawyer to Robert Coffey, U.S. Probation Officer, October 16, 1973.

28. Thormod H. Hanson, Supervisory U.S. Probation Officer, to Steve D. Johnston, Parole Executive, U.S. Board of Parole, November 5, 1973.

29. Special progress report, May 11, 1956.

30. F. Loveland to Mr. Bennett, May 24, 1956.

31. Special progress report, McNeil Island, March, 1963.

32. "Waley, Weyerhaeuser Kidnapper, Goes Free," June 5, 1963, Waley prison file. The newspaper's name was not identified.

33. Harmon M. Waley to George H. Weyerhaeuser, March 2, 1960.

34. Waley interview in 1980.

35. Ibid.

36. Palmer G. Lee, U.S. Probation Officer, District of Oregon to Reed Cozart, Pardon Attorney, U.S. Dept. of Justice, October 30, 1967.

37. George H. Weyerhaeuser to Arthur R. Lehwalder, U.S. Parole Office, Seattle, May 14, 1975.

38. In addition to a daylong interview in his home, Harmon Waley and I had numerous telephone conversations for several years thereafter, and he produced a large amount of correspondence on various topics from Alcatraz to penal policy; he also provided line by line, handwritten critiques of a transcript of the Henry Young trial prepared for BOP officials, *On the Rock*, the book written by Alvin Karpis, the only man who had put in more time on the island, and of Clark Howard's account of the 1946 escape attempt by Cretzer, Coy, and assorted others, *Six Against the Rock*. The latter he described as "the largest crock of crap that I have ever encountered."

39. R. S. Yocum, Senior Surgeon and Chief Medical Officer, release progress report, August 9, 1949.

40. Berta interview in 1987. When Berta left the island forty-three cartons of books and magazines on welding, blacksmithing, and forging were shipped to him in care of Father Clark's residence in San Francisco.

41. Charles Berta to James V. Bennett, February 26, 1953. Bennett replied to Berta, acknowledging his success in finding work, and noted that Berta's mother "would be proud to know that you have been successful since you were released. I am always pleased to hear from men who are doing their best to live useful, law-abiding lives. I am particularly interested when I hear from men who had been in a lot of really serious trouble earlier in their lives, but who have overcome their past and have really turned over a new leaf. Let me hear from you again from time to time, and I'll look you up if and when I get to Frisco again." J. V. Bennett to Charles Berta, March 11, 1953.

42. *San Francisco Examiner* article, May 14, 1954.

43. Berta interview in 1988.

44. [James Quillen] Misconduct report, January 9, 1945.

45. James Quillen, *Alcatraz from Inside* (San Francisco: Golden Gate National Parks Association, 1991), 129; see 147–53 for details of Quillen's ups and downs after his release from prison.

46. Special progress report, March 21, 1952.

47. James V. Bennett to Acting Warden, McNeil Island, re James Quillen, November 2, 1954. On this note Bennett added a handwritten comment suggesting that Quillen be transferred to California to make him eligible for parole.

48. John F. Douville, Chief U.S. Probation Officer, to William A. Barrett, U.S. Probation Officer, U.S. District Court, Eastern District Court of California, November 17, 1976.

49. Hamilton interview in 1981.

50. Hamilton's file included a letter in which he denied the claim by another inmate that he was a homosexual. No reference to this activity was recorded in his federal prison record; Texas prison officials determined that the prisoner that made this accusation was wrong and Hamilton was released from the solitary confinement.

51. Harry McCormick had been kidnapped by Floyd's brother Raymond. In their book *Public Enemies: America's Criminal Past, 1919–1940* (New York: Checkmark Books, 1998), 228, authors William Helmer and Rich Mattix report that this "kidnapping" was a ruse to allow McCormick to get a story: "March 19, 1935. Raymond Hamilton allegedly kidnaps Houston newspaper man Harry McCormick, dictates his version of his criminal career for publication, then releases him. Years later, the newspaper man will write that he contacted Hamilton and arranged the interview, then concocted the kidnapping story to avoid a harboring charge."

52. When Hamilton was on his way from Leavenworth to the state prison in Texas, Hinton told Hamilton: "Back in the 1930s I was trying to either kill you or put you in prison, but now I am up here to help you get out."

53. *The True Story of Floyd Hamilton, Public Enemy #1, as Told to Chaplain Ray* (Dallas, TX: International Prison Ministry, n.d.), 29. Hamilton's life story was also featured in another International Prison Ministry publication, "Last of the Bonnie and Clyde Gang: The True Story of Floyd Hamilton Public Enemy #1 as Told to Chaplain Ray." Both booklets featured photos of Hamilton and Chaplain Ray standing in front of cell number 13 in D-block—the site of Hamilton's conversion, as he put it, "from crime to Christ." He also recounted his life story in *Public Enemy #1*, Acclaimed Books (Dallas, TX: International Prison Ministry, 1978).

54. AP release, July 28, 1984.

55. [Volney Davis] Misconduct report, January 20, 1936.

56. Misconduct report, April 10, 1939.

57. Misconduct report, January 29, 1942.

58. Volney Davis refused further interviews with agents at Alcatraz, he said, because such interviews might "have caused me to lose my life out there . . . [refusing to be interviewed] is the only reason I am here to write this letter." He went on to describe a serious assault by two inmates that could have cost him his life if a civilian employee had not entered the area; he was taken to the hospital for stitches in his jaw, but this incident was noted in Alcatraz records as an "accident." Volney Davis Alcatraz file.

59. J. Edgar Hoover note on memo from A. Rosen regarding the Bremer kidnapping, July 28, 1959.

60. Volney Davis to Edward G. Bremer, July 26, 1956.

61. George E. MacKinnon, U.S. Attorney, to Scovel Richardson, Chairman, Board of Parole, July 27, 1956; July 31, 1956.

62. James V. Bennett to Volney Davis, July 21, 1964.

63. Albert Wahl to Reed Cozart, Pardon Attorney, U.S. Dept. of Justice, September 16, 1964. Other federal probation officers who had supervised Davis were William Meyer and William Adams.

64. This was one of two interviews of former Alcatraz prisoners not conducted by the author or another member of the project staff. Number 1600 responded to our list of questions by speaking into a tape recorder and sending the tapes to the author, August 14, 1983. The other involved the assistance of Federal probation officer Richard G. Sullivan, who read our questions, without comment, to the interviewee, speaking into a tape recorder in Birmingham, Alabama, June 3, 1981.

65. He also wrote to U.S. Senator William Langer stating, "I am being tortured mentally and most certainly abused physically and I cannot take this any longer without a crack-up somewhere." Letters to sister and Senator Langer, 1947.

66. This passage was taken from a letter no.1600 sent to family members who were interested in the life he had lived and years later offered it to the author.

67. Special progress report, Springfield Medical Center, March 9, 1948.

68. Robert B. Neu, Senior Assistant Surgeon, addendum to the psychiatric report, January 18, 1949.

69. Special progress report, November 22, 1949.

70. Admission summary, Reception and Guidance Unit, Washington State Penitentiary (Walla Walla), April 21, 1955.

71. Progress report, Walla Walla, December 1966.

72. Progress report, Walla Walla, November 25, 1968.

73. G. W. Stouder, Food Administrator, Leavenworth, to Warden David M. Heritage, Atlanta, May 18, 1961, Parole Board file.

74. Rufus Franklin, Parole Board, Special Review, Atlanta Penitentiary, April 29, 1974.

75. Rufus Franklin, no. 48531, Atlanta, to the U.S. Board of Parole, Washington, D.C., April 12, 1960, Parole Board file.

76. William T. Peek, U.S. Probation Officer, pre-sentence report, U.S. District Court, Western District of Washington at Seattle, September 11, 1974, pp. 3–4.

77. Philip M. Spears, Senior Case Manager, Federal Correctional Institution, Lexington, Kentucky, March 1, 1979.

78. James Audett, *Rap Sheet: My Life Story* (New York: William Sloane Associates, 1954); James Audett, "My Forty Years Outside the Law," *True: The Man's Magazine* 35, no. 218 (July 1955); Jay Robert Nash wrote *Crime Chronology: A World Wide Report 1900–1983* (1984), and *Almanac of World Crime* (1981). In his interview for this project, conducted by Philip Bush at McNeil Island, August 29, 1977, Audett noted that *some* of the events he described in *Rap Sheet* were true and claimed that he had written another book, *I Dodged 10,000 Bullets*, which we were not able to locate.

79. Audett, "My Forty Years," 103.

80. Admission summary, Atlanta, April 17, 1940, Gerard Peabody Atlanta file.

81. Special progress report, October 25, 1944, ibid.

82. Special progress report, March 23, 1961, Peabody Alcatraz file.

83. Special progress report, July 2, 1965, Peabody McNeil Island file.

84. Special progress reports, March 1968 and April 1971, ibid. His rap partner in the 1956 bank robbery was paroled from Leavenworth in 1970.

85. Special progress report, May 2, 1979, Springfield Medical Center file. Thomas E. Gaddis, *Unknown Men of Alcatraz* (Portland, OR: NewGate, 1977) included a chapter on Audett and Peabody that asked why at their advanced ages they resorted one last time to robbing banks.

> Outside [prison] they were one jump from hated welfare, charity handouts or a county nursing home. They carried a heavy identity—because once, for better or worse, they had mattered! So they took the gamble they knew best, the one that spreads the cost by taking from insured institutions. It was a great risk to the rob-

ber; but the money was there in one place. Their old man options were these: if they shoot you, you've lived too long anyhow. If you make it, you live high awhile, like in the old days. If you're nailed, you get a hard roof overhead, three squares, medical attention, and you're back in the news.

And no deals, no copouts. You're not guilty. Make 'em prove it. Jury trial. You've been thieves for longer than most men live, and never killed anybody. . . . *But if you're caught and sentenced, then you're back in as members of the only club you ever knew. In prison, you're esteemed elders, telling cons and guards How It Was.* (*Unknown Men*, 121; original emphasis)

86. James A. Johnston to James V. Bennett, January 13, 1942, Ted Walters Alcatraz file.

87. Chaplain Ray with Walter Wagner, *God's Prison Gang* (Old Tappan, NJ: Fleming H. Revell, 1977), 77–78.

88. Leavenworth recommendation for transfer to Alcatraz noted in special progress report, Alcatraz, December 12, 1941.

89. Special progress report, Leavenworth, November 19, 1945.

90. As cited in Michael and Judy Ann Newton, *The FBI Most Wanted: An Encyclopedia* (New York: Garland Publishing, 1989), 2.

91. Stamphill was involved in an escape from an Oklahoma reformatory during which a guard was killed; while at large he was arrested for kidnapping, received a life sentence, and was sent to Leavenworth. He was transferred to Alcatraz in January 1938 because he showed no remorse over the guard's death and was considered "a detriment." Frank Loveland, Supervisor of Classification, memorandum to J. V. Bennett, January 3, 1938.

92. Stamphill federal probation file.

93. Statement to U.S. Probation Officers Richard H. Johnson and Edward B. Murray, ibid.

94. Stamphill's probation officer's closing memo described the parolee he had come to know: "The subject has been one of the most pleasant people to supervise that the writer has ever known. This was [my] third request to have his supervision terminated. The reason that the parole commission showed any reluctance . . . was the grave seriousness of his offenses that occurred over 30 years ago. The writer is confident that [Stamphill] will never violate the law again." January 1980, ibid.

CHAPTER 14

1. It should be noted that the rule violation rate for the three phases of imprisonment can reflect the lesser amount of time at prisons before and after Alcatraz. The low rate of misconduct after Alcatraz can reasonably be explained by the proximity to parole, and the rate before Alcatraz may reflect the limited tolerance for troublemaking at transferring prisons, especially if that misconduct involved escape plots or threats to staff or prison order. Leavenworth, Atlanta, and McNeil Island wardens had the convenient option of shipping their "management problems" off to Alcatraz.

2. Although these differences were not statistically significant, the direction of this finding is a departure from the expectations of both staff and inmates them-

selves. A statistical analysis exploring the relation between six factors identified age at release and number of months served (meaning more prison experience) as most significantly related to postrelease success; these and other results for the entire inmate population will be included in a second book, *The End of the Rock: Alcatraz, 1949–1963.*

3. See Lynne Goodstein, Doris Layton MacKenzie, and R. Lance Shotland, "Personal Control and Inmate Adjustment to Prison," *Criminology* 22, no. 2 (August 1984): 343–69.

4. Some instances of misconduct may have been calculated. A number of interviewees commented that a record of no misconduct did not provide evidence of positive behavior change to a parole board. This was particularly important for men serving time in a prison where no psychologically based treatment programs, vocational training, or formal educational activities were available for them to participate in as indicators that they had decided to go along with the program. Experienced convicts considered it wise to commit a series of rule violations that did not involve actual assaults on staff members, rioting, or attempting to escape and then, when their misconduct reports dropped off, let prison staff and parole board members notice the men's improved "attitude." One of the great guessing games in all prisons involves staff trying to determine whether any change for the better in an inmate's behavior is genuine or the result of the prisoner's "gaming" staff.

5. Other studies, based on standard prison populations, have reached the same conclusion—they show that there is either no relation or a negative relation between prison misconduct and parole performance. See for example, V. O'Leary and D. Glaser, "The Assessment of Risk in Parole Decision Making," in *The Future of Parole,* ed. D. West (New York: International Publications Service, 1972); Carroll et al., "Evaluation, Diagnosis, and Prediction in Parole Decision Making," *Law and Society Review* 17 (1982): 199–228; and James Scott, "The Use of Discretion in Determining the Severity of Punishment for Incarcerated Offenders," *Journal of Criminal Law and Criminology* 65 (1974): 214–24.

6. "Note Says 3 Driven Insane at Alcatraz: Brutality and Torture Charged in Letter Smuggled From 'Devil's Isle.' Ridiculous says Warden. Prisoner Declares Inmates Beaten, Shot with Gas Guns, Starved," *San Francisco News,* September 20, 1935.

7. Doris Layton MacKenzie and Lynne Goodstein, "Long-Term Incarceration Impacts and Characteristics of Long-Term Offenders," in *Long-Term Imprisonment: Policy, Science and Correctional Practice,* ed. Timothy J. Flanagan (Thousand Oaks, CA: Sage Publications, 1995), 66.

8. Number 1800, Alcatraz file. Except for a letter in his Springfield file— Frank L. Loveland to Mr. Bay, August 17, 1948—subsequent quotes and references to reports on AZ-1800 are taken from this source.

9. See K. J. Heskin, N. Bottom, F. V. Smith, and P. A. Banister, "Psychological Correlates of Long-Term Imprisonment: III, Attitudinal Variables," *British Journal of Criminology* 14 (1974):150–57; H. Toch, *Men in Crisis: Human Breakdowns in Prison* (Chicago: Aldine Publishing, 1975); and W. Sluga, "Treatment of Long-Term Prisoners Considered from the Medical and Psychiatric Points of View," in *Treatment of Long-Term Prisoners* (Strasbourg: Council of Europe,

1977), 35–42. Few studies of the mental health of inmates in high-security prisons in this country have been reported following the dramatic increase in prison violence that began in the mid-1960s and continues to this day.

10. MacKenzie and Goodstein, "Long-Term," 64.

11. John K. Irwin, "Sociological Studies of the Impact of Long-Term Confinement," in *Confinement in Maximum Custody,* ed. David A. Ward and Kenneth F. Schoen (Lexington, MA: Lexington Books/D. C. Heath, 1981), 49. See also Stanley Cohen and Laurie Taylor, *Psychological Survival: The Experience of Long-Term Imprisonment* (Baltimore: Penguin Books, 1982).

12. Donald R. Cressey, "Adult Felons in Prison," in *Prisoners in America,* ed. Lloyd E. Ohlin (Englewood Cliffs, NJ: Prentice-Hall, 1973), 117–18.

13. For an effort to determine the extent of serious mental health problems among inmates at the federal government's high-security penitentiaries at Marion, Illinois, and Florence, Colorado, see David A. Ward and Thomas G. Werlich, "Alcatraz and Marion: Evaluating Super-Maximum Custody," *Punishment and Society* 5 (2003): 53–75.

EPILOGUE

1. BOP to E. B. Swope [Warden, Alcatraz], re monthly classification reports, November 4, 1948.

2. To Director [James V. Bennett], monthly report of parole classification activities, Frank G. Austin, Jr., Correctional Office, (Acting) Parole-Classification Officer, July 1951.

3. Director, memorandum for Mr. Loveland, May 3, 1950.

4. In October 1984, before the Alcatraz project was completed, the murder of two officers in a single day at the federal penitentiary in Marion, Illinois, resulted in a decision to terminate all programs and congregate activities. Establishing an "indefinite administrative segregation" regime produced controversy, which led the Judiciary Committee in the United States House of Representatives to authorize an investigation of what was called the lockdown. I was asked to conduct this investigation with Allen Breed of the National Council on Crime and Delinquency. This assignment, which involved gathering data and interviewing prisoners and staff at the Rock's successor evolved into an opportunity for me to expand the study of the effects of long-term confinement under conditions of supermaximum custody—in other words, a chance to replicate several key findings of the Alcatraz study for its successor. For a report of basic findings from this investigation, see David A. Ward and Thomas G. Werlich, "Alcatraz and Marion: Evaluating Super-Maximum Custody," *Punishment and Society* 5 (2003): 53–75.

After operations ceased at Alcatraz in March 1963, two books were published that provided descriptions of notable prisoners and events during the prison's three decades as a federal penitentiary. The authors, both journalists, were at a severe disadvantage in that they did not have access to inmates, staff, or records from Alcatraz or the Bureau of Prisons. As a result these books contain numerous inaccuracies. The dust jacket of John Godwin's *Alcatraz: 1868–1963* (Garden City, NY: Doubleday, 1963) claimed, for example, that "the average con spent a great deal of his time hunting for homosexual companionship." Interviews with any of the men who worked, or served time, on the island, particularly from 1934–1948, would have corrected that contention. J. Campbell Bruce wrote *Escape from Alcatraz: A Farewell to the Rock* (London: Hammond, Hammond, 1963) without the assistance of the Bureau of Prisons. In a meeting with James V. Bennett, he said the director told him, "I can't let you talk with guards and take up their time and waste taxpayers' money." Bruce was also unsuccessful in obtaining any information from the warden or from the U.S. attorney in San Francisco; he concluded that "the veil of secrecy [around Alcatraz] hid nothing mysterious, only incompetence" (see 243–45).

In more recent years, dozens of books have been written about Alcatraz, and a number of them have particular strengths that make them worthwhile reading. Many are based on the records salvaged and assembled for this study after they were returned to the Federal Bureau of Prisons, which then deposited them in the Western Regional Office of the National Archives, in San Bruno, California.

Surviving prisoners, employees, and their relatives, having become aware that each year more than a million visitors pass through the bookstores and souvenir shops on the island, have written personal accounts about their experiences on Alcatraz. These books do not attempt to cover the thirty-year history of the prison nor do they include information about the larger population of prisoners, but many of these authors claim to have had personal relationships with Al Capone, Machine Gun Kelly, Robert Stroud, and other high-profile prisoners, and to have special knowledge of incidents and escape attempts. That their experiences at Alcatraz induced so many of its former prisoners and employees to publish memoirs is one more indicator of the exceptional nature of this prison.

Several books provide valuable and reliable information related to the gangster era and should be of interest to historians, criminologists, legal scholars, and readers of this book. In *Public Enemies: America's Greatest Crime Wave and the Birth of the FBI, 1933–1934* (New York: Penguin Press, 2004), Bryan Burrough provides detailed, well-documented descriptions of not only the criminal careers of gangsters such as John Dillinger, Baby Face Nelson, Bonnie Parker, and Clyde Barrow, who were killed in altercations with federal agents, but also the criminal activities of those who survived these shootouts and lived to be confined on Alcatraz. Of particular relevance are the bank robberies and ransom kidnappings engineered by George Kelly, Albert Bates, Harvey Bailey, Alvin Karpis, Arthur Barker, and John Paul Chase. The stories and the publicity surrounding the lives of these men continue in Richard Gid Powers, *G-Men: Hoover's FBI in American Popular Culture* (Carbondale: Southern Illinois University Press, 1983). Powers places Alcatraz and the campaign by the FBI to subdue public enemies in the context of popular culture and the style of the mainstream media during the 1920s and 1930s. Also recommended is David E. Ruth, *Inventing the Public Enemy: The Gangster in American Culture, 1918–1934* (Chicago: University of Chicago Press, 1996). Ruth explains how gangsters became important cultural figures during the first part of the twentieth century.

The authoritative source for detailed information on the history of Alcatraz as a fort, as a military prison, and after its conversion to a federal penitentiary is Erwin N. Thompson, *The Rock: A History of Alcatraz Island, 1847–1972*, Historic Resource Study, National Park Service, U.S. Dept. of the Interior, Denver, May 1979. Alcatraz Island historian John A. Martini has also written two valuable books about its years as a fort: *Fortress Alcatraz: Guardian of the Golden Gate* (Kailua, HI: Pacific Monograph, 1990) and *Alcatraz at War* (San Francisco: Golden Gate National Parks Association, 2002).

Several books by prisoners who were on the island during the gangster era offer excellent first-person accounts. James Quillen's thoughtful description of his ten years, *Alcatraz from Inside: The Hard Years, 1942–1952*, ed. Lynn Cullivan (San Francisco: Golden Gate National Parks Association, 1991), is one of the best. During two lengthy interviews, Jim also gave important information for this book. *On the Rock: Twenty-Five Years in Alcatraz* by Alvin Karpis, as told to Robert Livesey (New York: Beaufort Books, 1980) covers most of the prison's history. A book that combines descriptions of both criminal and prison life is Floyd Hamilton, *Public Enemy #1*, Acclaimed Books (Dallas, TX: International Prison Ministry, 1978). William Radkay's recollections of his years as lawbreaker and prisoner on the Rock from 1944 to 1952 are the basis for a book by his niece Patty Terry, *A Devil Incarnate: From Altar Boy to Alcatraz* (Leawood, KS: Leathers Publishing, 2005). Willie provided valuable information to me not only about living conditions in other state and federal prisons where he did time and his life at Alcatraz, but also his relationships with his celebrity convict friends, particularly George Kelly, Harvey Bailey, and John Chase. His ability to recall past events with clarity and detail during our five interviews was remarkable.

At least five books by former employees are notable as well. Of particular relevance for the gangster era are several books by men who worked on the island during the 1930s and 1940s. Milton Daniel Beacher, MD, a U.S. Public Health Service physician (not a BOP employee) assigned to Alcatraz for about one year beginning in April 1937, wrote *Alcatraz Island: Memoirs of a Rock Doc*, ed. Dianne Beacher Perfit (Lebanon, NJ: Pelican Island Publishing, 2001). This memoir (edited by his daughter) includes interesting observations about Al Capone, Harmon Waley, Thomas Robinson, and Rufe Persful, as well as descriptions of strikes, discipline, and daily life on the island. Another noteworthy book that focuses on the prison's early years is Erville F. Chandler, *Alcatraz: The Hard Years* (Orwigsburg, PA: Bacon and Freeman, 1989). This book is based on former correctional officer Chandler's conversations with his son, Roy F. Chandler, and includes reproductions of rare photographs and documents, such as charge out sheets from 1936 and 1937 that identify the location and job assignments of all inmates, and lists of the first thirty-six guards and the first four hundred convicts.

Many books sold on the island feature the May 1946 breakout attempt by six convicts and the battle that followed. Former captain Philip Bergen, a central participant in this epic prison drama, co-wrote with Don DeNevi (and provided many of the photographs for) *Alcatraz '46: The Anatomy of a Classic Prison Tragedy* (San Rafael, CA: Lesswing Press, 1974). In a note to the author, Bergen commented, "*Alcatraz '46*, although it is insufficiently definite in some respects, is the best available USP Alcatraz saga. I wish that I could rewrite it!" Since Mr. Bergen gave two extended interviews for this volume, perhaps these flaws have now been corrected. A carefully researched and interesting account of the trial of the three inmates who did not die during the battle is Ernest B. Lageson, *Alcatraz Justice: The Rock's Most Famous Murder Trial* (Berkeley: Creative Arts Book, 2002). Lageson, a trial attorney, had the advantage of utilizing the firsthand knowledge of his father, correctional officer Ernest Lageson, who was one of the prisoners' hostages and appeared as a witness in the subsequent trial of the three inmate survivors.

Finally, any commentary on the books written about Alcatraz cannot fail to mention Warden James A. Johnston, *Alcatraz Island Prison, and the Men Who Live There* (New York: Charles Scribner's Sons, 1949). Johnston was the central figure at Alcatraz from its beginning as a federal penitentiary to his departure in 1948. He had access to all records for prisoners, employees, and the prison; he himself produced many of them. He found little to fault in his administration of the prison. Former officer Chandler commented on Johnston's effort in his book (*The Hard Years*, 99; original emphasis): "A weakness lies in that 'the general knows mostly what he is told' and 'the troops tend to tell it one way while handling it another' . . . guards saw most things more 'closely' than did their warden." According to Chandler, "there is no complete book about Alcatraz. Many are inaccurate and fleshed out with fanciful tales. Others are boring or too incomplete. The *great* Alcatraz book is still to be written. . . . Those who really know are gone. Most of what is left is second or third hand . . . but those involved would prefer having the prison's history more correctly recorded." With the benefit of extensive interviews with one hundred former prisoners and employees and access to records for all of these prisoners and the prison, *Alcatraz: The Gangster Years* tries to achieve this goal.

David A. Ward is Professor Emeritus of Sociology, University of Minnesota. He co-authored with Gene G. Kassebaum two books about California prisons: *Women's Prison: Sex and Social Structure* (1965), and *Prison Treatment and Parole Survival* (also with Daniel M. Wilner; 1971), an evaluation of psychologically based treatment programs. He co-edited with Kenneth F. Schoen, *Confinement in Maximum Custody: New Last-Resort Prisons in the United States and Western Europe* (1981). He was a Fellow in Law and Sociology at Harvard Law School and as a Fulbright Scholar studied prisons and penal policy in Sweden and Denmark. He served as consultant to the Subcommittee on Courts, Civil Liberties, and the Administration of Justice of the Committee on the Judiciary, U.S. House of Representatives for an investigation of the permanent lockdown regime at the Federal Penitentiary, Marion, Illinois, Alcatraz's successor. He lives in the San Francisco Bay Area.

Gene G. Kassebaum is Professor Emeritus of Sociology, University of Hawaii. In addition to co-authoring the books cited above, he co-edited *Narcotics* with Daniel M. Wilner (1965) and wrote *Delinquency and Social Policy* (1974). In Hawaii he served as a member of the Governor's Commission for the Revision of the Hawaii Penal Code and conducted contract research for state justice, parole, probation, and corrections agencies. Earlier in his career he was on the faculty at the American University in Cairo, Egypt, and was awarded two Fulbright scholarships to India. He now divides his time between Bangalore, Honolulu, and San Francisco.

INDEX

Abdul-Rahman, Omar, 466
Abrams, Sol: post-trial comments of,
201; as Young's attorney, 190, 192–
93, 194–97, 199–200
ACLU (American Civil Liberties Union),
117, 325, 505n53
adaptation, 283, 353–54. *See also* coping
mechanisms; daily routines; inmates;
psychological issues; resistance
Aderhold, A. C., 46, 47–48, 76, 341
Administrative Max (ADX, Florence,
CO), 9, 59, 284, 466
Administrative Office of U.S. Courts,
xiv, xv
Alabama: Franklin returned to, 428;
robbery and murder in, 160; state
prison in, 160, 239, 496–97n5,
496n3.
Alcatraz: basic goal of, 2–3, 292, 464–
65; budget of, 279; call for removal
of, 275–76, 499n51; cave on, 219,
221–23; closure of, xi, 6, 152, 386,
435, 463–64; conundrum of, 201;
decision to establish, 48, 49, 53–55;
facility modifications of, 68, 476n40;
functional shift in, 462; government
permit for, 474n1; internal control vs.
external image of, 117–19; isolation
of, 105, 107; lessons of, 455–60; location choice for, 55–58; maintenance
tasks at, 80–81; as maximum-security,
minimum-privilege, 65–67; misconduct
patterns at, 446–49; mortality rate at,
492n44; name of, 1; new industries
building of, 206, 215, 227–28; number
of cells, 70; opening of, 2; periods
of, xx; proposed conversion of, 187,
489n12, 491–92n35; rationale for,
58–65; realities of, 7–9; reputation
of, ix–x, xii, 283–84, 459; sounds of,
103–4. *See also* cafeteria and meals;
convict code and culture; daily routines; disciplinary measures; employees

and staff; inmates; escape attempts
and escapes; mythology of Alcatraz;
protests and strikes; rules and regulations; secrecy; security; transfers to
Alcatraz; wardens
Alcatraz Alumni Association, xvi
Alcatraz Island, Golden Gate National
Recreation Area: army's departure
from, 68; commercialization of,
507n12; interpretive program of,
xi, xii, 467n3; photography exhibit
at, 471n43; pre-prison uses of, 55–56,
58, 475n17; tours of, 5, 184; visitors'
views of, 97, 459
Alcatraz Island (film), 488n1
Alcoholics Anonymous, 419, 426, 427,
441
alcoholism, 441–42, 458
Alcorn, Gordon, 24–25, 81, 500–501n3
Alderson (WV) Federal Women's Prison,
83, 467n5. *See also* Kelly, Kathryn
Alix, Ernest A., 470nn27–28
Allen, Jack, 128–30, 164
The Alvin Karpis Story (film), 338
Amende, Milton, 302
American Civil Liberties Union (ACLU),
117, 325, 505n53
American Society of Radiological Techni-
cians, 412
Angel Island: searched for escapees, 154–
55; U.S. Army ferry to, 231–33
Anglin brothers, xi, 463
anticrime crusade: beginning of, 49–
50; commission's findings and, 63–
64; prison reform in, 50–52; victories
in, 54
Archer, Finch, 42
Arizona: kidnappings in, 23
Arkansas: crimes in, 95, 140, 153,
484n33; prison farm in, 140, 141,
333, 334, 464; state penitentiary of,
140, 152
Arnold, Tom, 438

Hubert H. Humphrey Institute of Public
Affairs, xvii
Hudspeth, Robert, 39–40, 472–73n58,
473n62
Hughes, Howard, 45
hunger strikes: force-feeding to end, 202,
315–16, 427; as individual resistance,
315–16; Karpis's refusal to join, 374;
in Leavenworth, 41, 473n62; media's
response to, 184, 186; mental illness
and, 179; murder in context of, 195;
participants in, 129–30; transfer to
Alcatraz for, 78
Hunter, Fred: arrest of, 379–80; associates of, 94; escape attempts of, 215–
22, 226–27; illness of, 215–16
Hunter, Wayne, 102–3
Huxley, Aldous, 328

Idaho State Penitentiary, 90
Illinois: crimes in, 23, 26, 84–85, 91–92;
FBI-gangster shootout in, 89; state
prison in (Joliet), 33, 82, 88, 439;
supermax prisons in, 464. See also
Chicago; Marion (IL) federal supermax
penitentiary
Immigration and Naturalization Service,
133
Indiana: crimes in, 22, 23, 89, 95; federal penitentiary in, ix; state prison
of (Michigan City), 33
industrial good time: use of term, 101.
See also good time forfeiture
industries building (new), 206, 215, 227–
28. See also laundry
inmate-on-inmate violence: convict code
on, 287, 289; as coping mechanism,
298; murders in, 6–7, 152–53, 189–
90, 298–303, 423, 492n44; other
inmates' interest in, 109; past acts as
reason for, 140–41, 142–43; rarity of,
8, 302–3; types of, 502n13
inmates: arrival of, 72–82, 97, 120; on
Bowers incident, 134, 136–37; catego-
rization of, 391; celebrity type of, 338–
39; cell location chosen by, 176; characteristics of, 62, 127–28, 272, 285,
362, 445, 457, 465–66; counts of, 99–
100; of federal vs. state prisons, 457–
59; first death, 129; "habitual and
incorrigible," 59–65, 95, 153, 160,
431, 445, 459; heroes of, 288–89; for
institutional maintenance tasks, 80–
81; island terrain known by, 212; lax
attitudes toward, 276–78; as "living
dead," 183–84; management challenges of, 480n18; misconduct patterns

among, 446–49; as movie protagonists, 6–7; "nerves" of, 151; overview
of, 79–82, 283–84; patriotic acts of,
214; personal items allowed to, 104–5;
preparation for first, 67–69; prisonization of, 450; prison records of, xiii–
xiv, xv–xvi, xvii–xviii; psychological
support for, 456–57; realities of, 7–9;
relationships among, 130, 141, 286;
selected for Alcatraz, 70–72; spies as,
289; status reviews of, 461–62; talks
for, 416–17; testimony on Alcatraz
conditions by, 190–93; WWII fears of,
213. See also convict code and culture;
daily routines; inmate-on-inmate violence; inmates, post-Alcatraz; interviews (by author); letters and letter
writing; military prisoners in Alcatraz;
psychological issues; resistance; sentence length
inmates, post-Alcatraz: age of, 390, 446,
456; cohort differences among, 391–
92, 511n5; conditions sensationalized
by, 132–34; effect of experience on,
x; expectations concerning, xix, 8–9,
385–94; factors in success/failure of,
442–44, 445–49; locations of, xiv–xv;
media interviews of, 5, 182–83; progress
reports on, 389–90; statistics on, xiv,
386, 390–91, 391; study of, xii–xiii.
See also interviews (by author)
inmates, post-Alcatraz failures: Audett,
431–34; Holden, 438–39; Peabody,
434–36; Stamphill, 439–42; Walters,
436–38
inmates, post-Alcatraz successes: Bailey,
394–400; Berta, 407–9; Butler, 337;
Capone, 394; Chase, 400–403; Davis,
417–20; Franklin, 427–31; Gardner,
394; Hamilton, 413–17; Hensley, 335,
337; Neumer, 326, 337; Number 1600,
420–23; Phillips, 331, 337; Quillen,
409–13; Urbaytis, 394; Waley, 322,
337, 403–7; Young, 423–27
inmate-staff relationship: convict code
on, 291; fraternization in, 108–9;
inmates' assaults and, 93, 126, 145–
47, 184, 298, 301–2, 309–10; personal
attention in, 327–30, 458, 465; restrictions on communications in, 158. See
also silent system
Internal Revenue Service, 19–21
International Prison Ministry, 416–17,
514n53
interviews (by author): anonymity offered
in, 468n10; approach to, xvi–xvii, xix,
8, 97; honorariums for, xvii; initial

Text:	Sabon
Display:	Franklin Gothic
Compositor:	Integrated Composition Systems
Indexer:	Margie Towery
Printer and binder:	Thomson-Shore, Inc.